Solutions Manual

MATHEMATICS

Applications and Connections

COURSE 3

GLENCOE

Macmillan/McGraw-Hill

Lake Forest, Illinois   Columbus, Ohio   Mission Hills, California   Peoria, Illinois

The copy in this text was word processed using ChiWriter Software from Horstmann
Software, P.O. Box 5039, San Jose, California 95192

Send all inquiries to:
GLENCOE DIVISION
Macmillan/McGraw-Hill
936 Eastwind Drive
Westerville, OH 43081

ISBN 0-02-824070-7

Printed in the United States of America

2 3 4 5 6 7 8 9 10 POH 01 00 99 98 97 96 95 94 93 92

Contents

Chapter 1   Tools for Problem Solving

PAGE 6   CHECKING FOR UNDERSTANDING

1. Explore: Determine what information is given and what you need to find.

   Plan: Estimate the answer and then select a strategy for solving.

   Solve: Carry out the plan and solve.

   Examine: Compare answer to estimate and determine if it is reasonable. If not, make a new plan.

2. Make a new plan.

3. See students' work.

4.

Event	How long does it take?	When is it over?
2nd showing	2 hr 10 min	7:45 + 2:10 = 9:55
Intermission	15 min	9:55 + 0:15 = 10:10
Previews	10 min	10:10 + 0:10 = 10:20
3rd showing	2 hr 10 min	10:20 + 2:10 = 12:30

   The third showing is over at 12:30 A.M.

5. a. beaker + sodium chloride = 84.8 grams; beaker = 63.3 grams

   b. Subtract the two masses.

   c. 84.8 g - 63.3 g = 21.5 g

   d. yes

PAGE 7   EXERCISES

6. The shorter side will increase from 15 cm to 30 cm or will double in length. Therefore, the longer side will also double in length.

   25 cm x 2 = 50 cm

   The longer side will be 50 cm after the enlargement.

7. The total temperature increase is 90°C.

   $$\frac{90°C}{9°C} = 10$$

   10 × 300 ft = 3,000 ft

   You would have to dig 2,700 ft.

8. 342 - 36 = 306

   There are 306 passengers in coach class.

   36 × $750 = $27,000   306 × $450 = $137,700

   Ticket sales = $27,000 + $137,700 = $164,700

9.

Amount Donated	Number of Coins Donated by Each Person		
	Maya	Kim	Kareem
25¢	5	X	1
30¢	6	3	X
35¢	7	X	X
40¢	8	4	X
45¢	9	X	X
50¢	10	5	2

   50¢ is the least each could donate.

10. 2 × 23¢ = 46¢

    46¢ + 28¢ = 74¢

    2 tablets and 1 pen

11. 1,200 ft + 1,500 ft = 2,700 ft

    4,700 ft - 2,700 ft = 2,000 ft

12. The area used was $\frac{1}{100}$th of the area of the entire ceiling. Therefore, multiply 28 by 100.

13. V = length × width × height, where length = width = height

    4 × 4 × 4 = 64   5 × 5 × 5 = 125

    So 4 × 4 × 4 is the largest cube.

14. See students' work.

PAGE 9-10   CHECKING FOR UNDERSTANDING

1. Add $0.02 to $1.98 and subtract $0.02 from $3.98.

2. 25 + 75 + 80

3. Answers will vary.

4. 15 + 15 + 37 = 30 + 37   5. 45 + 100 = 145
   = 67

6. 699 - 22 = 677

7. (20 + 20) · 8 = 20 · 8 + 20 · 8
   = 160 + 160
   = 320

8. 80 + 20 + 48 = 100 + 48
   = 148

9. 20 · 50 · 93 = 1,000 · 93
   = 93,000

10. 7 · (30 + 5) = 7 · 30 + 7 · 5
    = 210 + 35
    = 245

11. 2 · 50 · 43 = 100 · 43
    = 4,300

12. 60 + 40 + 69 = 100 + 69
    = 169

1

13. $70 + 10 + 73 = 80 + 73$
$= 153$

14. $13 \cdot (4 \cdot 25) = 13 \cdot 100$
$= 1,300$

15. $9 \cdot (10 + 5) = 9 \cdot 10 + 9 \cdot 5$
$= 90 + 45$
$= 135$

16. $599 - 242 = 357$ 17. $53 \cdot 100 = 5,300$

18. $37 + 3 + 29 = 40 + 29$ 19. $500 + 327 = 827$
$= 69$

20. $740 + 60 + 987 = 800 + 987$
$= 1,787$

21. $5(10 + 10) = 5 \cdot 10 + 5 \cdot 10$
$= 50 + 50$
$= 100$

22. $21 \times (2 \times 50) = 21 \times 100$
$= 2,100$

23. $25 \cdot 4 \cdot 14 \cdot = 100 \cdot 14$
$= 1,400$

24. $70 + 30 + 93 = 100 + 93$
$= 193$

25. $43 + 7 + 29 = 50 + 29$ 26. $699 - 595 = 104$
$= 79$

27. $623 + (420 + 80) = 623 + 500$
$= 1,123$

28. $423 \times (50 \times 2) = 423 \times 100$
$= 42,300$

29. $(10 + 2) \cdot 25 = 25 \cdot 10 + 25 \cdot 2$
$= 250 + 50$
$= 300$

30. $a = 14 \times (10 + 10 + 10)$
$a = 14 \times 10 + 14 \times 10 + 14 \times 10$
$a = 140 + 140 + 140$
$a = 420$

31. $30 \text{ min} - 5 \text{ min} = 25 \text{ min}$
$25 \text{ min} \times 10¢ = \$2.50$
$\$2.50 + \$0.15 = \$2.65 \text{ for 30 min}$

32. $\frac{45}{15} = 3$ hours

33. $20 - 16 = 4$
Every week Romo's collection increases by
four cards.
$7 \times 4 = 28$
After 7 weeks he will have 28 cards.

34. $200 - 51 - 49 - 38 = 200 - 50 - 50 - 38$
$= 200 - 100 - 38$
$= 100 - 38$
$= 99 - 37$
$= 62 \text{ in.}$

35.

	Breakfast	Lunch	Dinner	Total Pills Taken
Monday	2	2	2	6
Tuesday	2	2	2	12
Wednesday	1	1	1	15
Thursday	1	1	1	18
Friday	1	1	1	21
Saturday	1	1	1	24
Sunday	1	1	1	27
Monday	1	1	1	30

The last capsule will be taken the following
Monday at dinner.

36. Compensate is to make up for or offset.
In the compensation strategy, altering is
done to the problem and then that altering
needs to be offset.

1-3 Estimation Strategies

1. to use as a quick check and to approximate

2. Depending on the numbers, rounding or front-end
estimation would be good to use.

3. In rounding, you round to the largest place-
value. In front-end estimation, you add the
two largest place values.

4. 5,000   5. 700   6. 0.09

7. front-end estimation

$$
\begin{array}{r} 6\,|28 \\ 5\,|47 \\ +\ 4\,|32 \\ \hline 15\,|00 \end{array}
\rightarrow
\begin{array}{r} 6\,|2|8 \\ 5\,|4|7 \\ +\ 4\,|3|2 \\ \hline 9|0 \end{array}
+ \quad = 1,590
$$

8. rounding
$4,400 - 3,000 = 1,400$

9. rounding
$5,200 - 4,100 = 1,100$

10. rounding
$\$13.00 - \$4.00 = \$9.00$

11. rounding
$6.000 \div 1.000 = 6$

12. clustering
$2.5 + 2.5 + 2.5 + 2.5 = 10$

13. rounding
$5,000 + 4,000 = 9,000$

front-end estimation

$$
\begin{array}{r} 5\,|,293 \\ +\ 3\,|,733 \\ \hline 8\,|,000 \end{array}
\rightarrow
\begin{array}{r} 5,\,|2|93 \\ +\ 3,\,|7|33 \\ \hline 9|00 \end{array}
+ \quad = 8,900
$$

14. rounding

$7 + 5 + 2 = 14$

front-end estimation

$$
\begin{array}{r}
6.59 \\
4.65 \\
+\ 2.28 \\
\hline
12.00
\end{array}
\rightarrow
\begin{array}{r}
6\ 5\ 9 \\
4.\ 6\ 5 \\
+\ 2.\ 2\ 8 \\
\hline
1.\ 3\ 0
\end{array}
= 13.3
$$

15. rounding

$1.0 - 1.0 = 0$

front-end estimation

$$
\begin{array}{r}
0.7829 \\
-\ 0.5392 \\
\hline
0.2000
\end{array}
\rightarrow
\begin{array}{r}
0.7\ 8\ 29 \\
-\ 0.5\ 3\ 92 \\
\hline
0.0\ 5\ 00
\end{array}
= 0.25
$$

16. rounding

$8,000 - 5,000 = 3,000$

front-end estimation

$$
\begin{array}{r}
7,623 \\
-\ 5,450 \\
\hline
2,000
\end{array}
\rightarrow
\begin{array}{r}
7,\ 6\ 23 \\
-\ 5,\ 4\ 50 \\
\hline
2\ 00
\end{array}
= 2,200
$$

17. $3,600 \div 60 = 60$ 18. $7.2 \div 0.8 = 9$

19. $5,000 + 5,000 + 5,000 + 5,000 = 20,000$

20. $\$2.00 + \$2.00 + \$2.00 + \$2.00 + \$2.00 = \$10.00$

21. rounding   22. rounding

$600 - 400 = 200$ $5 - 3 = 2$

23. compatible numbers

$3,600 \div 60 = 60$

24. front-end estimation

$$
\begin{array}{r}
527 \\
915 \\
+\ 467 \\
\hline
1800
\end{array}
\rightarrow
\begin{array}{r}
5\ 27 \\
9\ 15 \\
+\ 4\ 67 \\
\hline
9\ 0
\end{array}
= 1,890
$$

25. front-end estimation

$$
\begin{array}{r}
82.43 \\
79.28 \\
+\ 37.41 \\
\hline
180.00
\end{array}
\rightarrow
\begin{array}{r}
8\ 2.43 \\
7\ 9.28 \\
+\ 3\ 7.41 \\
\hline
1\ 8.00
\end{array}
= 198
$$

26. rounding

$\$6.00 + \$7.00 + \$7.00 = \$20.00$

27. 240 cups $\div$ 40 cups/lb = 6 lb each day

For 1 week or 7 days:

6 lb $\times$ 7 = 42 lb

28. 215 lb - 119 lb = 96 lb

Tisha weights 96 pounds.

29. $21(10 + 5) = 21 \cdot 10 + 21 \cdot 5$

$= 210 + 105$

$= 315$

30. $522 + 100 = 622$

31. 423×500 or by rounding $400 \times 500 = 200,000$ sheets of paper left.

32. a. Use compensation to make the problem
8,339 - 5,000.

b. Use compensation to make the problem workable and then complete the front-end estimation.

c. 5,646 - 3,000

$$
\begin{array}{r}
5,646 \\
-\ 3,000 \\
\hline
2,000
\end{array}
\rightarrow
\begin{array}{r}
5,\ 6\ 46 \\
-\ 3,\ 0\ 00 \\
\hline
6\ 00
\end{array}
= 2,600
$$

33. a. clustering

500 ft + 500 ft + 500 ft + 500 ft + 500 ft

= 2,500 ft

b. Answers will vary.

34. Round each price to the nearest 50¢.

1–4 Determine Reasonable Answers

1. $5.55 is about $5.50; $0.44 is about $0.50. The total is about $6.00. So the change is about $4.00. This does not affect the answer to the problem.

2. This ensures that there will be more than enough paint.

3. No. $45,000 \div 1,500$ is 30, not 300.

4. Estimate total pounds.

$1,300 + 900 + 600 = 2,800$ lb

$2,800 \div 14 = 200$ crates

5. $3 \cdot \$0.50 + 5 \cdot \$1.00 + \$0.75$

$= \$1.50 + \$5.00 + \$0.75$

$= \$7.25$

You need to take $10.00 with you.

6. $65,000 \div 2,500 = 26$ cars

7.

Age	Twice Age	or $32
14	$28	$32
15	$30	$32
16	$32	$32
17	$34	$32
18	$36	$32
Total	$160	$160

They are the same

8. $6000,000 \div 8 = 75,000$ people

9. $5 + 5 + 5 + 5 + 5 + 5 + 5 + 5 + 5 + 5$

= 50 sit-ups

10. $60,099 - 60,095 = 4$ mi

11. $\$0.30 + \$0.25 + \$0.25 + \$0.25 + \$0.25 + \$0.25 + \$0.25 = \$1.80$

Less than $1.80 since everything was rounded up.

3

1-5 Eliminate Possibilities

1. Estimate what the answer should be, then eliminate the choices that are not close to your estimate.

2. distance from home, conflict of time, so on

3. b; 18,000 − 17,000 = 1,000

4. c; 700,000 ÷ 100 = 7,000

5. b; 20,000 × $10.00 = $200,000

PAGES 18-19   PROBLEM SOLVING

6. a; 18,000 mi/h × 900 mi/h = 20

7. Sample answers: 1101, 3981

8. b; 3.5 + 2.5 + 3 = 9 m; 9 m ÷ 0.25 m = 36

9. Suppose the five colors are red, yellow, blue, pink, and orange. There are ten possible combinations.

   red-yellow-blue   yellow-blue-pink
   red-yellow-pink   yellow-blue-orange
   red-yellow-orange   yellow-pink-orange
   red-blue-pink   blue-pink-orange
   red-blue-orange   red-pink-orange

10. 300 + 100 + 100 + 900 + 0 + 100 = 1,500
    1,500 ÷ 6 = 250

11. a; 100 × 50 × 25 × 350 = 43,750,000

Mid-Chapter Review

PAGE 19

1. 38 · $1.39 + 2 · $1.10 = $52.82 + $2.20
                              = $55.02

2. 10 + 20 + 35 = 65   3. $3.00 + $4.97 = $7.97

4. 6(10 + 20) = 6 · 10 + 6 · 20
              = 60 + 120
              = 180

5. clustering   6. compatible numbers
   7 + 7 + 7 + 7 = 28   6,400 ÷ 80 = 80

7. rounding   8. rounding
   8,000 − 7,000 = 1,000   9 × 11 = 99

9. 300,000,000 ÷ 7,500,000 = 40; 37 people per square mile

10. c; 1,200 ÷ 200 = 600
       600 × $0.05 = $30.00

Decision Making

PAGES 20-21

1. yes

2. probably not; Most expensive computer with color monitor is $1,829.88. Shipping should not cost more than $252.12.

3. Prices range from $24.98 to $199.98 for one year and from $39.98 to $269.98 for two years.

4. See students' work.

5. See students' work.

6. See students' work.

7. See students' work.

8. See students' work.

1-6A Mathematics Lab: Using Nonstandard Units

PAGE 22   WHAT DO YOU THINK?

1. no

2. If your partner's wrist is larger, the measurements will be less.

3. the student with the smaller wrist; the larger wrist; yes, The smaller wrist gives the smaller amount while the larger wrist gives the greater amount.

1-6 The Metric System

PAGES 24-25   CHECKING FOR UNDERSTANDING

1. A kilogram is a larger unit than a gram.

2. When multiplying by 100, the decimal point is moved two places to the left.

3. A kilometer is 100,000 times longer than a centimeter.

4. centimeter   5. milliliter   6. kilogram

7. kilometer   8. kiloliter   9. millimeter

10. multiply by 1,000; 10,000 mm

11. multiply by 1,000; 1,000,000 m

12. divide by 1,000; 0.00439 L

13. divide by 1,000; 0.0015 L

14. divide by 1,000; 0.00593 kg

15. divide by 1,000; 0.00789 km

PAGE 25 EXERCISES

16. 3.54 m × 1,000 = 3,540 mm

17. 525 g ÷ 1,000 = 0.525 kg

18. 4.23 L × 1,000 = 4,230 mL

19. 1.37 km × 1,000 = 1,370 m

20. $5.23 \text{ g} \times 1{,}000 = 5{,}230 \text{ mg}$

21. $9.24 \text{ kL} \times 1{,}000 = 9{,}240 \text{ L}$

22. $2{,}354 \text{ mL} \div 1{,}000 - 2.354 \text{ L}$

23. $0.924 \text{ m} \times 100 = 92.4 \text{ cm}$

24. $427 \text{ m} \div 1{,}000 = 0.427 \text{ km}$

25. $0.00723 \text{ cm} \times 10 = 0.0723 \text{ mm}$

26. $0.875 \text{ kg} \times 1{,}000 = 875 \text{ g}$

27. $0.947 \text{ L} \times 1{,}000 = 947 \text{ mL}$

28.

Number of Fish	Total Amount
1	$0.59
2	$1.18
3	$1.77
4	$2.36
5	$2.95

Lora can buy 4 goldfish.

29. distributive property

$9 \cdot (40 + 2) = 9 \cdot 40 + 9 \cdot 2 = 360 + 18 = 378$

30. $7{,}000 - 3{,}000 = 4{,}000$

31. $2.4 \div 0.4 = 6$

32. yes;

The dimensions of the box are 38 mm by 200 mm.

33. a. 260 mL

b. 260 cm^3

c. $520 \text{g} \div 260 \text{ cm}^3 = 2 \text{ g/cm}^3$

d. See students' work.

1-7   The Customary System

PAGE 27   CHECKING FOR UNDERSTANDING

1. It is easier to change from one unit to another.

2. 6 cups = 3 pints; 3 pints = 1.5 quarts;
   1.5 quarts = 0.375 gallons

3. Answers will vary.

4. multiply by 16; $3 \text{ lb} \times 16 = 48 \text{ oz}$

5. divide by 2,000; $6{,}000 \text{ lb} \div 2{,}000 = 3 \text{ T}$

6. divide by 4; $24 \text{ c} \div 4 = 6 \text{ qt}$

7. multiply by 36; $2\frac{1}{2} \text{ yd} \times 36 = 90 \text{ in.}$

8. divide by 5,280; $8{,}000 \text{ ft} \div 5{,}280 = 1.\overline{51} \text{ mi}$

9. multiply by 8; $10 \text{ gal} \times 8 = 80 \text{ pt}$

PAGE 28   EXERCISES

10. $12 \text{ ft} \div 3 = 4 \text{ yd}$

11. $5 \text{ mi} \times 5{,}280 = 26{,}400 \text{ ft}$

12. $2.5 \text{ gal} \times 4 = 10 \text{ qt}$

13. $3.5 \text{ lb} \times 16 = 56 \text{ oz}$

14. $2 \text{ T} \times 2{,}000 = 4{,}000 \text{ lb}$ 15. $7 \text{ c} \div 2 = 3.5 \text{ pt}$

16. $20 \text{ qt} \div 4 = 5 \text{ gal}$ 17. $3\frac{1}{2} \text{ ft} \times 12 = 42 \text{ in.}$

18. $2 \text{ gal} \times 128 = 256 \text{ oz}$ 19. $32 \text{ oz} \div 128 = \frac{1}{4} \text{ gal}$

20. $15 \text{ in.} \div 12 = 1\frac{1}{4} \text{ ft}$ 21. $4 \text{ yd} \times 36 = 144 \text{ in.}$

22. $7\frac{1}{2} \text{ yd} \times 3 = 22\frac{1}{2} \text{ ft}$

23. Subtract 5 from both numbers and subtract the new numbers; $399 - 148 = 251$

24.
$$\begin{array}{r} \boxed{4}{,}521 \\ - \boxed{3}{,}158 \\ \hline \boxed{1}{,}000 \end{array} \rightarrow \begin{array}{r} 4{,}\boxed{5}21 \\ - 3{,}\boxed{1}58 \\ \hline + \boxed{4}00 \end{array} = 1{,}400$$

25. $2.79 \text{ m} \times 100 = 279 \text{ cm}$

26. $12 \text{ L} \times 1{,}000 = 12{,}000 \text{ mL}$

$12{,}000 \text{ mL} \div 375 \text{ mL} = 32 \text{ coffee mugs}$

27. No, weight and capacity are not the same.

28. $8{,}000 \text{ lb} \div 2000 = 4 \text{ T}$

$4 \text{ T} \times 17 = 68 \text{ trees}$

29. $3\frac{1}{2} \text{ yd} \times 3 = 10\frac{1}{2} \text{ ft}$

$10\frac{1}{2} \text{ ft} \times 10 = 105 \text{ ft}$

30. rod $= 16\frac{1}{2} \text{ ft}$

chain = 66 ft (surveyor's chain)

chain = 100 ft (engineer's chain)

31. $16 \text{ ft} + 18 \text{ ft} + 11 \text{ ft} = 45 \text{ ft}$

32. $150 \text{ lb} \times 600 = 90{,}000 \text{ lb}$

$90{,}000 \text{ lb} \rightarrow 2{,}000 = 45 \text{ T}$

33. $2{:}05.96 - 1{:}56.24 = 2{:}06 - 1{:}56.28$

$= 9.72 \text{ sec faster}$

1-7B   Mathematics Lab: Customary Measures

PAGE 29   WHAT DO YOU THINK?

1. See students' work.

2. See students' work.

3. See students' work.

PAGE 29   EXTENSION

4. See students' work.

1-8A   Mathematics Lab: Spreadsheets

PAGE 30   WHAT DO YOU THINK?

1. E3 contains the expenses incurred in April.

2. labels

3. yes, yes

PAGE 31   WHAT DO YOU THINK?

4. B2 * C2, B3 * C3, B4 * C4

5. B2 + B3 + B4

6. D2 + D3 + D4

7. D3 = $4,200, D4 = $4,500, D6 = $12,450

8. B6 = B2 + B3 + B4 + B5, D6 = D2 + D3 + D4 + D5

9. Answers may include: budgets, tax information

10. See students' work.

1-8   Guess and Check

PAGE 34   CHECKING FOR UNDERSTANDING

1. By using estimation you would come closer to a correct guess.

2. Put your guess back into the problem to see if it checks.

3. See students' work.

4. 7; $7 + 2 \cdot 7 = 7 + 14 = 21$

5. 14; $14 \cdot 14 = 196$

6. 100; $100 + 100 = 200$

7. all but 0; $5 \div 5 = 1$, $3 \div 3 = 1$, etc.

8. 3; $3 \cdot 4 \cdot 5 = 3 \cdot 20 = 60$

PAGE 34   PROBLEM SOLVING

9.

José Now	Mother Now	José in 5 Years	Mother in 5 Years
4	20	9	25
5	25	10	30

José is five years old.

10. $6 \times \$0.19 + 5 \times \$0.29 = \$2.59$

She sent 6 postcards and 5 letters.

11. 42 in. $\div 12 = 3\frac{1}{2}$ ft

$3\frac{1}{2}$ ft $\times \$5.80/\text{ft} = \$20.30$

12. a. $10.3 + 12.5 = 22.8$ million, Dallas/Fort Worth

b. $\frac{22.6}{2} = 11.3$ million, Denver

c. east: $25.6 + 22.6 + 10.5 + 9.8 + 9.8 = 78.3$ million

west: $22.8 + 18.1 + 13.3 + 11.9 + 10.3 = 76.4$ million

east side

1-9   Powers and Exponents

PAGE 36   CHECKING FOR UNDERSTANDING

1. base: 10; exponent: 5

2. 5^4

3. $4^3 = 4 \cdot 4 \cdot 4 = 64$; $3^5 = 3 \cdot 3 \cdot 3 \cdot 3 \cdot 3 = 243$

4. $3^2 = 3 \cdot 3 = 9$; $2^3 = 2 \cdot 2 \cdot 2 = 8$; $9 \neq 8$

5. 5^3 6. 10^4 7. 8^5

8. $5 \cdot 5 \cdot 5 = 125$ 9. $7 \cdot 7 = 49$

10. $3 \cdot 3 \cdot 4 \cdot 4 = 9 \cdot 16 = 144$

11. $5 \cdot 6 \cdot 6 \cdot 6 \cdot 10 \cdot 10 \cdot 10 = 5 \cdot 216 \cdot 1{,}000$

   $= 1{,}080{,}000$

PAGES 36-37   EXERCISES

12. $3^2 \cdot 5^3$ 13. $6^3 \cdot 7^2$ 14. $2^2 \cdot 3^2 \cdot 5$

15. $5 \cdot 5 \cdot 5 \cdot 5 = 625$

16. $4 \cdot 4 \cdot 4 = 64$ 17. $2 \cdot 2 \cdot 2 \cdot 2 \cdot 2 = 32$

18. $1^{40} = 1$

19. $2 \cdot 2 \cdot 7 \cdot 7 = 4 \cdot 49 = 196$

20. $5 \cdot 5 \cdot 8 \cdot 8 \cdot 3 \cdot 3 \cdot 3 = 25 \cdot 64 \cdot 27$

   $= 43{,}200$

21. $100 \cdot 100 \cdot 100 = 1{,}000{,}000$

22. $56 \cdot 56 \cdot 56 \cdot 56 = 9{,}834{,}496$

23. $36 - 4 = 32$ 24. $16 \cdot 9 = 144$

25. $2 \cdot 9 + 9 \cdot 36 = 18 + 324$

   $= 342$

26. $\$10.00 + \$10.00 + \$10.00 + \$10.00 = \$40.00$

27. $5{,}734 \text{ g} \div 1{,}000 = 5.734 \text{ kg}$

28. $6 \text{ c} \div 2 = 3 \text{ pt}$

29. $2.5 \text{ lb} \times 16 = 40 \text{ oz}$

   2.5 pounds for $2.70 is the better purchase price.

30. a. $30 \cdot 30 \cdot 30 = 30^3$

   b. $30^3 = 27{,}000 \text{cm}^3$

31. a. 3   b. 6   c. 4; 2

32. $36 \cdot 4 \div 2.5 = 144 \div 2.5 = 57.6$

   To the nearest 10 the horsepower would by 60.

33. $2^{11} = 1{,}024 \cdot 2 = 2048$

34. 3; See students' work.

35. a. 2,870,000,000km   b. 10^7 and 10^8

Chapter 1 Study Guide and Review

PAGE 38   COMMUNICATING MATHEMATICS

1. liter   2. ounce   3. commutative

4. exponent   5. rounding   6. based on 10

PAGES 38-39   SKILLS AND CONCEPTS

7. The distance to Bill's house is 90 ft or $9 \cdot 10$ ft. It will take John $9 \cdot 3$ sec or 27 sec.

8. $47 \text{ ft} \cdot 50 \text{ ft} \cdot 2 \text{ ft} = 4{,}700 \text{ ft}^3$

9. $55 + 90 = 145$ 10. $599 - 460 = 139$

11. $400 + 117 = 517$ 12. $399 - 234 = 165$

13. $\$3.00 + \$4.56 = \$7.56$

14. $899 - 580 = 319$

15. $7 \cdot 2 + 7 \cdot 10 = 14 + 70$

                 $= 84$

16. $80 + 320 = 400$

17. $34 + 66 + 49 = 100 + 49$

                 $= 149$

18. $(4 \cdot 25) \cdot 19 = 100 \cdot 19$

                 $= 1,900$

19. $5 \cdot 20 \cdot 34 = 100 \cdot 34$

                 $= 3,400$

20. $18 \cdot 100 = 1,800$

21. compatible numbers   22. rounding

    $2,800 \div 70 = 40$ $600 + 500 + 800 = 1,900$

23. clustering

    $5,000 + 5,000 + 5,000 + 5,000 = 20,000$

24. front-end estimation

$$
\begin{array}{ccc}
\boxed{9}.872 & & 9.\boxed{8}72 \\
-\ \boxed{5}.344 & \rightarrow & -\ 5.\boxed{3}44 \\
\hline
\boxed{4}.000 & + & .\boxed{5}00
\end{array}
\quad = 4.500
$$

25. $3.4 \text{ m} \div 1,000 = 0.0034 \text{ km}$

26. $2.71 \text{ L} \times 1,000 = 2,710 \text{ mL}$

27. $620 \text{ g} \div 1,000 = 0.620 \text{ kg}$

28. $0.748 \text{ m} \times 100 = 74.8 \text{ cm}$

29. $8.62 \text{ mL} \rightarrow 1,000 = 0.00862 \text{ L}$

30. $4.25 \text{ g} \times 1,000 = 4,250 \text{ mg}$

31. $54 \text{ in.} \div 12 = 4.5 \text{ ft}$

32. $2.5 \text{ T} \times 2,000 = 5,000 \text{ lb}$

33. $15 \text{ ft} \div 3 = 5 \text{ yd}$

34. $6 \text{ pt} \times 2 = 12 \text{ c}$

35. $4 \text{ lb} \times 16 = 64 \text{ oz}$

36. $22 \text{ gal} \times 4 = 88 \text{ qt}$

37. $3^2 \cdot 8^3$ 38. $4^3 \cdot 6^2 \cdot 7$

39. $2 \cdot 2 \cdot 2 \cdot 2 = 16$

40. $3 \cdot 3 \cdot 4 \cdot 4 \cdot 4 = 9 \cdot 64$

                     $= 576$

41. $5 \cdot 5 \cdot 5 \cdot 100 \cdot 100 = 125 \cdot 10,000$

                              $= 1,250,000$

PAGE 40   APPLICATIONS AND PROBLEM SOLVING

42. $2 \cdot \$8.95 + 2 \cdot \$2.25 + 2 \cdot \$2.75 + 2 \cdot \$1.59$

    $= \$31.08$

    more than \$30

43. $25,000,000 \div 186,272 = 134$ seconds or about

    2 min.; 2.25 minutes

44. $10 \cdot \$0.25 + 5 \cdot \$0.10 = \$2.50 + \$0.50$

                           $= \$3.00$

45. $10 \text{ yd} + 20 \text{ yd} + 20 \text{ yd} + 30 \text{ yd} = 80 \text{ yd}$

46. $198,000 \text{ mg} \div 1,000 = 198 \text{ g}$

    $0.221 \text{ kg} \times 1,000 = 221 \text{ g}$

    $198 \text{ g} + 221 \text{ g} + 186 \text{ g} = 605 \text{ g}$

Chapter 1 Test

PAGE 41

1. front-end estimation

$$
\begin{array}{ccc}
\boxed{8}.25 & & 8.\boxed{2}5 \\
3.59 & \rightarrow & 3.\boxed{5}9 \\
+\ 5.76 & & +\ 5.\boxed{7}6 \\
\hline
\boxed{16}.00 & + & \boxed{1.4}0
\end{array}
\quad = 17.4
$$

2. compatible numbers

    $3,000 \div 50 = 60$

3. front-end estimation

$$
\begin{array}{ccc}
\boxed{7},548 & & 7,\boxed{5}48 \\
-\ \boxed{4},139 & \rightarrow & -\ 4,\boxed{1}39 \\
\hline
\boxed{3},000 & + & \boxed{4}00
\end{array}
\quad = 3,400
$$

4. front-end estimation

$$
\begin{array}{ccc}
\boxed{5},842 & & 5,\boxed{8}42 \\
+\ \boxed{3},112 & \rightarrow & +\ 3,\boxed{1}12 \\
\hline
\boxed{8},000 & + & \boxed{9}00
\end{array}
\quad = 8,900
$$

5. clustering   6. $500 \cdot 20 = 10,000$

    $2 + 2 + 2 + 2 = 8$

7. $(650 + 50) + 793 = 700 + 793 = 1,493$;

    associative property

8. Use compensation to change the problem to

    $499 - 231 = 268$

9. $5 \text{ yd} \times 3 = 15 \text{ ft}$

10. $735 \text{ g} \div 1,000 = 0.735 \text{ kg}$

11. $8.2 \text{ L} \times 1,000 = 8,200 \text{ mL}$

12. $3.5 \text{ lb} \times 16 = 56 \text{ oz}$ 13. $0.52 \text{ m} \times 100 = 52 \text{ cm}$

14. $4.21 \text{ km} \times 1,000 = 4,210 \text{ m}$

15. $9 \text{ c} \div 2 = 4.5 \text{ pt}$ 16. $6 \text{ gal} \times 4 = 24 \text{ qt}$

17. $6^3 \cdot 7^2$ 18. $3^2 \cdot 4^3 \cdot 8$

19. $2 \cdot 2 \cdot 2 \cdot 4 \cdot 4 = 8 \cdot 16$

                   $= 128$

20. $2 \cdot 2 \cdot 5 \cdot 5 \cdot 4 \cdot 4 \cdot 4 = 4 \cdot 25 \cdot 64$

                         $= 100 \cdot 64$

                         $= 6,400$

21. $51 + 51 + 46 + 46 + 46 = 240$ min or 4 h

22. They must shovel a total of 16 driveways.

    In two hours Emilio can shovel 10 driveways

    and Maria can shovel 6 driveways for a total

    of 16 driveways.; 2h

23. $3 \cdot \$50,000 = \$150,000$

    \$145,600

24. b; $\$130 + \$170 + \$2,150 - \$30 - \$150 = \$2,270$

25. $\$2 \div 4 = \$0.50$ for a pear

    $\$3 \div 3 = \$1$ for apple juice

    about \$1.50

PAGE 41   BONUS

$4 \cdot 4 \cdot 4 = 4 \cdot 16 = 64$

$x = 4$

Chapter 2   An Introduction to Algebra

PAGE 46   CHECKING FOR UNDERSTANDING

1. $6 \cdot x$, $6(x)$, $6x$

2. Numerical expressions contain only numbers and algebraic expressions contain numbers and variables.

3. $7^2 - 30 = 49 - 30$
   $= 19$

4. The parentheses change the order of operations.

5. multiplication
   $21 + 18 = 39$

6. multiplication
   $15 + 2 = 17$

7. division
   $6 - 5 = 1$

8. addition
   $10 \div 2 = 5$

9. square 3
   $5 \cdot (6 + 9) = 5 \cdot 15$
   $= 75$

10. subtraction
    $2^3 - \dfrac{12}{3 \cdot 2} = 8 - \dfrac{12}{6}$
    $= 8 - 2$
    $= 6$

11. $3 \cdot 7 + 4 \cdot 6 - 2 \cdot 3 = 21 + 24 - 6$
    $= 39$

12. $7 \cdot 6 \cdot 4 \div 21 = 42 \cdot 4 \div 21$
    $= 168 \div 21$
    $= 8$

13. $(3 \cdot 6 + 2 \cdot 4) \cdot 3 = (18 + 8) \cdot 3$
    $= 26 \cdot 3$
    $= 78$

14. $3 \cdot 6 + (2 \cdot 4 \cdot 3) = 18 + (8 \cdot 3)$
    $= 18 + 24$
    $= 42$

15. $4 \cdot 3^2 = 4 \cdot 9$
    $= 36$

16. $(4 \cdot 3)^2 = 12^2$
    $= 144$

PAGES 46-47   EXERCISES

17. $3 \cdot 15 + \dfrac{23 - 7}{2} = 45 + \dfrac{16}{2}$
    $= 45 + 8$
    $= 53$

18. $16 - 12 + 0 = 4$

19. $(49 + 1) \div 5 = 50 \div 5$
    $= 10$

20. $\dfrac{21}{3^2 - 2} = \dfrac{21}{9 - 2}$
    $= \dfrac{21}{7}$
    $= 3$

21. $(4 + 4^2) + 2 = (4 + 16) + 2$
    $= 20 + 2$
    $= 22$

22. $(7 - 2^2) - 1 = (7 - 4) - 1$
    $= 3 - 1$
    $= 2$

23. $(7 \cdot 2) \div 7 = 14 \div 7$
    $= 2$

24. $17 - 2(8 - 3) = 17 - 2 \cdot 5$
    $= 17 - 10$
    $= 7$

25. $7 \cdot 12 - 3 + 2 \cdot 10 = 84 - 3 + 20$
    $= 81 + 20$
    $= 101$

26. $10^2 + 5^2 - 4^3 = 100 + 25 - 64$
    $= 125 - 64$
    $= 61$

27. $\dfrac{25 \cdot 36}{20} - (25 + 20) = \dfrac{900}{20} - 45$
    $= 45 - 45$
    $= 0$

28. don't need any

29. $72 \div (6 + 3) = 8$

30. don't need any

31. $7 + 4^2 \div (2 + 6) = 9$

32. $3[8 - (5 + 1)] = 6$

33. $4 + 8 - (7 - 5) = 10$

34.

# of dimes	# of nickels	$
1	1	$0.15
2	2	$0.30
3	3	$0.45

3 dimes and 3 nickels

35. rounding
    $300 + 700 + 500 = 1{,}500$

36. $1.725 \cdot 1{,}000 = 1{,}725 \rightarrow 1.725 \text{ km} = 1{,}725 \text{ m}$

37. $2 \cdot 2{,}000 = 4{,}000 \rightarrow 2 \text{ T} = 4{,}000 \text{ lb}$

38. $8 \cdot 36 = 288$

39. $\dfrac{2{,}176}{8 \cdot 4} = \dfrac{2{,}176}{32}$
    $= 68 \text{ grams of protein}$

40. $48 \div (4 \cdot 6) = 2$
    $48 \div 24 = 2$
    $2 = 2$
    $M = 48$, $A = 4$, $T = 6$, $H = 2$

41. Answers will vary.
    An example would be:
    $[(7 + 3) + (4 + 6)] \cdot (2 - 1) \cdot 5$

42. a. $A = 5 \cdot 4 = 20$
    b. $A = 2 \cdot 12 = 24$
    c. $A = \dfrac{4}{2} = 2$
    d. $A = \dfrac{12}{3} = 4$
    e. $A = \dfrac{12}{4} = 3$
    f. $A = 4 \cdot 12 = 48$

2-2 Equations

1. =

2. Multiply 15 and 6.

3. A replacement set is the given set of numbers from which to choose the correct value of the variable. The solution is a part of this set.

4. $52 \stackrel{?}{=} 14 + 38$
   $52 = 52$

5. $\$1.30 - \$0.80 \stackrel{?}{=} \$0.50$
   $\$0.50 = \$0.50$

6. $3 \cdot 16 \stackrel{?}{=} 48$
   $48 = 48$

7. $\frac{792}{99} \stackrel{?}{=} 8$
   $8 = 8$

8. $5 \cdot 20 \stackrel{?}{=} 100$
   $100 = 100$
   20 is a solution.

9. $34 + 16 \stackrel{?}{=} 50$
   $50 = 50$
   50 is a solution.

10. $\$2.99 - \$1.25 \stackrel{?}{=} \$1.74$
    $\$1.74 = \$1.74$
    $\$1.74$ is a solution.

11. $15 + 45 \stackrel{?}{=} 60$
    $60 = 60$
    15 is a solution.

12. $4 \cdot 31 \stackrel{?}{=} 124$
    $124 = 124$
    31 is a solution.

13. $\$2.67 \stackrel{?}{=} \$5 - \$2.33$
    $\$2.67 = \$2.67$
    $\$2.67$ is a solution.

14. $\frac{456}{6} \stackrel{?}{=} 76$
    $76 = 76$
    6 is a solution.

15. $\$4.50 + \$1.56 \stackrel{?}{=} \$6.06$
    $\$6.06 = \$6.06$
    $\$6.06$ is a solution.

16. $6 \cdot 34 \stackrel{?}{=} 204$
    $204 = 204$
    204 is a solution.

17. $\frac{98}{14} \stackrel{?}{=} 7$
    $7 = 7$
    7 is a solution.

18. $10 + 8 \stackrel{?}{=} 18$
    $18 = 18$
    10 is a solution.

19. $31 - 7 = 24$
    $24 = 24$
    31 is a solution.

20. $2 \cdot 12 \stackrel{?}{=} 24$
    $24 = 24$
    12 is a solution.

21. $42 \stackrel{?}{=} 6 \cdot 7$
    $42 = 42$
    7 is a solution.

22. $\frac{42}{6} \stackrel{?}{=} 4 + 3$
    $7 = 7$
    6 is a solution.

23. $(2 \cdot 50) \cdot 78 = 100 \cdot 78$
    $= 7,800$

24. front-end estimation

    $\boxed{9},728 \qquad 9,\boxed{7}28$
    $-\boxed{6},284 \rightarrow -6,\boxed{2}84$
    $\boxed{3},000 \qquad + \boxed{5}00 = 3,500$

25. $5^2 \cdot 8^3$

26. $\frac{36}{9 + 3} = \frac{36}{12}$
    $= 3$

27. $A = 120 \cdot 90$
    $A = 10,800 \text{ ft}^2$

28. a. $\{0, 1, 2, 3, 4, 5, 6, 7, 8, 9\}$
    b. $3 \cdot 3 + 5 \stackrel{?}{=} 14$
       $9 + 5 \stackrel{?}{=} 14$
       $14 = 14$
       3 is a solution.

29. $\$5.50 \cdot (6.5 + 5 + 3.5 + 3) = \$5.50 \cdot 18$
    $= \$99.00$

30. $C = \frac{5(32 - 32)}{9}$
    $C = \frac{5(0)}{9}$
    $C = \frac{0}{9}$
    $C = 0$

31. $150 - 1.5 + 0.3 = 148.8$
    Less than 150 pounds.

2-3 Solving Subtraction and Addition Equations

1. They "undo" each other.

2. These properties help to isolate the variable and keep the equation equal.

3. $280,000 + f = 370,000$
   $280,000 - 280,000 + f = 370,000 - 280,000$
   $f = 90,000$

4. Let a cup represent x. Put a cup and one counter on one side of the mat and six counters on the other side. These two quantities are equal. Take one counter away from each side. What you have left is the value of the cup, which is also the value of x. So $x = 5$.

5. $15 + x = 21$
   $15 - 15 + x = 21 - 15$
   $x = 6$

6. $40 + n = 70$
   $40 - 40 + n = 70 - 40$
   $n = 30$

7. $p - 82 = 142$
   $p - 82 + 82 = 142 + 82$
   $p = 224$

8. $y = 34 + 89$
   $y = 123$

9. $r - 14 = 19$
   $r - 14 + 14 = 19 + 14$
   $r = 33$

10. $81 - 56 = z$
    $25 = z$

11. $24 = x - 5$
    $24 + 5 = x - 5 + 5$
    $29 = x$

12. $m + 1.2 = 1.5$
    $m + 1.2 - 1.2 = 1.5 - 1.2$
    $m = 0.3$

13.

$$19 = 13 + s$$
$$19 - 13 = 13 - 13 + s$$
$$6 = s$$

14.
$$m + 30 = 110$$
$$m + 30 - 30 = 110 - 30$$
$$m = 80$$

15.
$$173 = x + 83$$
$$173 - 83 = x + 83 - 83$$
$$90 = x$$

16.
$$2.34 + 1.22 = p$$
$$3.56 = p$$

17.
$$s - 5.8 = 14.3$$
$$s - 5.8 + 5.8 = 14.3 + 5.8$$
$$s = 20.1$$

18.
$$14 + r = 23$$
$$14 - 14 + r = 23 - 14$$
$$r = 9$$

19.
$$p - 72 = 182$$
$$p - 72 + 72 = 182 + 72$$
$$p = 254$$

20. $125 - 52 = q$
$$73 = q$$

21.
$$0.5 + x = 2.72$$
$$0.5 - 0.5 + x = 2.72 - 0.5$$
$$x = 2.22$$

22.
$$24 = r - 18$$
$$24 + 18 = r - 18 + 18$$
$$42 = r$$

23.
$$x + 1.4 = 11.2$$
$$x + 1.4 - 1.4 = 11.2 - 1.4$$
$$x = 9.8$$

24. $w = 312 + 120$
$w = 432$

25. $6.01 - 3.12 = t$
$2.89 = t$

26.
$$800 - 1 \longrightarrow 799$$
$$\underline{-\ 356 - 1 \longrightarrow -\ 355}$$
$$444$$

27. $4.280 \longrightarrow 4,280$
4.28 g $\longrightarrow 4,280$ mg

28. $10 \div 4 = 2\frac{1}{2} \longrightarrow 10$ qt $= 2\frac{1}{2}$ gal

29. $52 - 32 \overset{?}{=} 20$
$20 = 20$
20 is a solution.

30. all real numbers;
See student's work.

31.
$$a + b = 90°$$
$$30° + b = 90°$$
$$30° - 30° + b = 90° - 30°$$
$$b = 60°$$

2-4

Solving Division and Multiplication Equations

1. The goal is to solve the equation by "undoing" the operations and keeping the equation equal.

2. Use a calculator to divide 31 by 13. The answer rounded to the nearest tenth is 2.4.

3. $4x = 12$
$$\frac{4x}{4} = \frac{12}{4}$$
$$x = 3$$

4. $16x = 48$
$$\frac{16x}{16} = \frac{48}{16}$$
$$x = 3$$

5. $24 = 6p$
$$\frac{24}{6} = \frac{6p}{6}$$
$$4 = p$$

6. $q = \frac{240}{30}$
$$q = 8$$

7. $\frac{s}{7} = 18$
$$7 \cdot \frac{s}{7} = 18 \cdot 7$$
$$s = 126$$

8. $23 \cdot 4 = w$
$$92 = w$$

9. $9 = \frac{c}{60}$
$$9 \cdot 60 = \frac{c}{60} \cdot 60$$
$$540 = c$$

10. $18.4 = 0.2q$
$$\frac{18.4}{0.2} = \frac{0.2q}{0.2}$$
$$92 = q$$

11. $\frac{p}{0.6} = 3.6$
$$0.6 \cdot \frac{p}{0.6} = 3.6 \cdot 0.6$$
$$p = 2.16$$

12. $243 \div 6 = t$
$$40.5 = t$$

13. $3m = 183$
$$\frac{3m}{3} = \frac{183}{3}$$
$$m = 61$$

14. $\frac{f}{7} = 56$
$$7 \cdot \frac{f}{7} = 56 \cdot 7$$
$$f = 392$$

15. $14 \cdot 25 = w$
$$350 = w$$

16. $102 = 17p$
$$\frac{102}{17} = \frac{17p}{17}$$
$$6 = p$$

17. $1.4t = 3.22$
$$\frac{1.4t}{1.4} = \frac{3.22}{1.4}$$
$$t = 2.3$$

18. $2.45 \div 5 = q$
$$0.49 = q$$

19. $8 = \frac{s}{25}$
$$8 \cdot 25 = \frac{s}{25} \cdot 25$$
$$200 = s$$

20. $\frac{d}{0.11} = 5$
$$0.11 \cdot \frac{d}{0.11} = 5 \cdot 0.11$$
$$d = 0.55$$

21. $\$5.44 = \$0.34b$
$$\frac{\$5.44}{\$0.34} = \frac{\$0.34b}{\$0.34}$$
$$\$16 = b$$

22. $8r = 480$
$$\frac{8r}{8} = \frac{480}{8}$$
$$r = 60$$

23. $5{,}412 \div 58 \longrightarrow 5{,}400 \div 60 = 90$

$5{,}412 \div 58$ is about 90.

24. $(17 - 8) \div 3 + 5^2 = 9 \div 3 + 25$

$\qquad\qquad\qquad\quad = 3 + 25$

$\qquad\qquad\qquad\quad = 28$

25. $\qquad y + 28 = 65$

$\qquad y - 28 + 28 = 65 + 28$

$\qquad\qquad\qquad y = 93$

26. $\dfrac{1}{n} < \dfrac{n}{1}; \dfrac{1}{3} < \dfrac{3}{1}; \dfrac{1}{-15} < \dfrac{-15}{1}$

27. $\qquad 0.05j = w$

$\qquad 0.05 \cdot 7{,}000 = w$

$\qquad\qquad\quad 350 = w$

28. $\qquad m = rg$

$\qquad 2{,}450 = r \cdot 112$

$\qquad \dfrac{2{,}450}{112} = \dfrac{112r}{112}$

$\qquad\qquad r = 21.875$ mi/gal

29. Answers will vary.

2-5 Work Backward

PAGE 58   CHECKING FOR UNDERSTANDING

1. You begin with the answer.

2. Reverse the order.

3. halve, subtract 14, multiply by 10, divide by 4

4. $2 + 10 - 11 = 12 - 11$

$\qquad\qquad\qquad = 1$

5. $(9 \div 3 \cdot 13 - 34) \cdot 20 = (3 \cdot 13 - 34) \cdot 20$

$\qquad\qquad\qquad\qquad\qquad = (39 - 34) \cdot 20$

$\qquad\qquad\qquad\qquad\qquad = 5 \cdot 20$

$\qquad\qquad\qquad\qquad\qquad = 100$

6. $2\sqrt{9801} = 2 \cdot 99$

$\qquad\qquad\quad = 198$

PAGE 59   PROBLEM SOLVING

7. $\$45.50 \cdot 3 = \$136.50$

8. $13 \cdot 10 \cdot 3 \cdot 11 = 4{,}290$

9. $\$1.20 \cdot 44 = \$52.80$

10. $\$127.68 \div 19 = \$6.72$

11. $5 \cdot 12 \cdot \$400 - \$15{,}900 = 60 \cdot \$400 - \$15{,}900$

$\qquad\qquad\qquad\qquad\qquad\quad = \$24{,}000 - \$15{,}900$

$\qquad\qquad\qquad\qquad\qquad\quad = \$8{,}100$

Mid-Chapter Review

PAGE 59

1. $2 + 15 + 27 - 4 = 44 - 4$

$\qquad\qquad\qquad\qquad = 40$

---

2. $6 \cdot 7 \div (12 - 8) = 42 \div 4$

$\qquad\qquad\qquad\qquad = 10.5$

3. $2 \cdot 2 + 3^2 - 5 \cdot 0 + 2 \cdot 3 \cdot 1 = 4 + 9 - 0 + 6$

$\qquad\qquad\qquad\qquad\qquad\qquad\quad = 19$

4. $142 - 51 \overset{?}{=} 91$

$\qquad 91 = 91$

142 is a solution.

5. $38 - (7 + 9 + 8 + 5) = 38 - 29$

$\qquad\qquad\qquad\qquad\qquad = 9 \ m$

6. $\qquad 45 + x = 140$

$\qquad 45 - 45 + x = 140 - 45$

$\qquad\qquad\qquad\quad x = 95$

7. $\qquad y - 8.9 = 10.2$

$\qquad y - 8.9 + 8.9 = 10.2 + 8.9$

$\qquad\qquad\qquad\qquad y = 19.1$

8. $3w = 45.6$ $\qquad\qquad$ **9.** $\qquad 50 = \dfrac{p}{3}$

$\dfrac{3w}{3} = \dfrac{45.6}{3}$ $\qquad\qquad\qquad\quad 3 \cdot 50 = \dfrac{p}{3} \cdot 3$

$w = 15.2$ $\qquad\qquad\qquad\qquad 150 = p$

10. $140 \div 2 \cdot 3 - 30 = 70 \cdot 3 - 30$

$\qquad\qquad\qquad\qquad = 210 - 30$

$\qquad\qquad\qquad\qquad = 180$ cm

2-6A Mathematics Lab: Writing Expressions and Equations

PAGE 61   WHAT DO YOU THINK?

1. 4 coins

2. The total number of cans is written on each bag.

3. Look for clues that give definite amounts.

PAGE 61   EXTENSION

4. See students' work.

5. Bag A: $V = 6$, $S + V + F = 14$, $F = V - 1$

Bag B: $S + V + F = 8$, $F = 2$, $S = 2 + F$

Bag C: $V = 2$, $F = 3V$, $S + V + F = 10$

Bag D: $S + V + F = 19$, $F = 3$, $4F = S$

2-6 Writing Expressions and Equations

PAGE 63   CHECKING FOR UNDERSTANDING

1. 7 more than y; y increased by 7

2. 5 time units until blastoff

3. is $\qquad\qquad$ **4.** $p + 17$ $\qquad\qquad$ **5.** $\dfrac{x}{3}$

6. $6r$ $\qquad\qquad$ **7.** $m - 4$ $\qquad\qquad$ **8.** $2t + 3$

9. $6 - m = 25$ $\quad$ **10.** $8 - \dfrac{4}{a} = 19$ $\quad$ **11.** $5x + 2 = 37$

12. $p + 4$ **13.** $18 - n$ **14.** $5y + 9$

15. $24 - 2x$ **16.** $d + \$5$ **17.** $s + \$200$

18. $3h$ **19.** $\frac{24}{x} - 2 = 2$ **20.** $5x - (5 + x)$

21. $2p + 6$ **22.** $5x = 45$ **23.** $3c - 14 = 46$

24. $\frac{x}{3} - 6 = 47$ **25.** $64 + 28 + 6 = 64 + 6 + 28$
$$= 70 + 28$$
$$= 98$$

26. $34.7 \div 1{,}000 = 0.0347 \rightarrow 34.7 \text{ mL} = 0.0347 \text{ L}$

27. $3\frac{1}{2} \cdot 16 = 56 \rightarrow 3\frac{1}{2} \text{ lb} = 56 \text{ oz}$

28. $t - 9 = 23$ **29.** $35 = 5m$
$$t - 9 + 9 = 23 + 9 \qquad \frac{35}{5} = \frac{5m}{5}$$
$$t = 32 \qquad\qquad\quad 7 = m$$

30. **a.** $s - 9 = 70 - 9 = 61$ mph, pronghorn antelope

   b. wildebeest and Thompson's gazelle

   c. $w + 11$

31. $5(2x + 4) - 5 = 15 + 2$

32. Bob scored 12 points higher on the test than Paulo.

2-7A   Mathematics Lab: Function Input and Output

PAGE 65   WHAT DO YOU THINK?

1. Multiply 3 by 4. Add 2 to the product.

2. $4x + 2$ 3. by working backward

PAGE 66   WHAT DO YOU THINK?

4. The process used the opposite operation and worked on the output first.

5. **a.** $\frac{x}{3} - 3 = 24$

   b. $\frac{81}{3} - 3 \overset{?}{=} 24$
   $$27 - 3 \overset{?}{=} 24$$
   $$24 = 24$$
   81 is the solution.

2-7   Solving Two-Step Equations

PAGE 68   CHECKING FOR UNDERSTANDING

1. Add 5 to both sides.

2. You "undo" addition/subtraction first and then you "undo" multiplication/division.

---

3. Take 5 counters from each mat. Separate the remaining counters into 3 groups to correspond to the 3 cups.

4. subtract 3   5. subtract 8
$$7c + 3 = 17 \qquad\qquad 8 + 3d = 17$$
$$7c + 3 - 3 = 17 - 3 \qquad 8 - 8 + 3d = 17 - 8$$
$$7c = 14 \qquad\qquad\qquad 3d = 9$$
$$\frac{7c}{7} = \frac{14}{7} \qquad\qquad\quad \frac{3d}{3} = \frac{9}{3}$$
$$c = 2 \qquad\qquad\qquad\quad d = 3$$

6. add 5.3
$$11e - 5.3 = 5.7$$
$$11e - 5.3 + 5.3 = 5.7 + 5.3$$
$$11e = 11$$
$$\frac{11e}{11} = \frac{11}{11}$$
$$e = 1$$

7. subtract 0.8
$$\frac{b}{9} + 0.8 = 1.3$$
$$\frac{b}{9} + 0.8 - 0.8 = 1.3 - 0.8$$
$$\frac{b}{9} = 0.5$$
$$9 \cdot \frac{b}{9} = 0.5 \cdot 9$$
$$b = 4.5$$

8. add 3   9. subtract 7
$$\frac{f}{4} - 3 = 4 \qquad\qquad 7 + \frac{g}{2} = 8$$
$$\frac{f}{4} - 3 + 3 = 4 + 3 \qquad 7 - 7 + \frac{g}{2} = 8 - 7$$
$$\frac{f}{4} = 7 \qquad\qquad\qquad \frac{g}{2} = 1$$
$$4 \cdot \frac{f}{4} = 7 \cdot 4 \qquad\qquad 2 \cdot \frac{g}{2} = 1 \cdot 2$$
$$f = 28 \qquad\qquad\qquad g = 2$$

PAGE 69   EXERCISES

10. $3x + 4 = 7$ 11. $4r - 9 = 7$
$$3x + 4 - 4 = 7 - 4 \qquad 4r - 9 + 9 = 7 + 9$$
$$3x = 3 \qquad\qquad\qquad 4r = 16$$
$$\frac{3x}{3} = \frac{3}{3} \qquad\qquad\quad \frac{4r}{4} = \frac{16}{4}$$
$$x = 1 \qquad\qquad\qquad r = 4$$

12. $1.2 + 6t = 3.6$
$$1.2 - 1.2 + 6t = 3.6 - 1.2$$
$$6t = 2.4$$
$$\frac{6t}{6} = \frac{2.4}{6}$$
$$t = 0.4$$

13.
$$5 + 14s = 33$$
$$5 - 5 + 14s = 33 - 5$$
$$14s = 28$$
$$\frac{14s}{14} = \frac{28}{14}$$
$$s = 2$$

14.
$$\frac{p}{5} - 1 = 13$$
$$\frac{p}{5} - 1 + 1 = 13 + 1$$
$$\frac{p}{5} = 14$$
$$5 \cdot \frac{p}{5} = 14 \cdot 5$$
$$p = 70$$

15.
$$\frac{f}{8} + 3 = 27$$
$$\frac{f}{8} + 3 - 3 = 27 - 3$$
$$\frac{f}{8} = 24$$
$$8 \cdot \frac{f}{8} = 24 \cdot 8$$
$$f = 192$$

16.
$$\frac{d}{12} - 4 = 8$$
$$\frac{d}{12} - 4 + 4 = 8 + 4$$
$$\frac{d}{12} = 12$$
$$12 \cdot \frac{d}{12} = 12 \cdot 12$$
$$d = 144$$

17.
$$2e + 5.0 = 6.0$$
$$2e + 5.0 - 5.0 = 6.0 - 5.0$$
$$2e = 1.0$$
$$\frac{2e}{2} = \frac{1.0}{2}$$
$$e = 0.5$$

18.
$$3f - 15 = 6$$
$$3f - 15 + 15 = 6 + 15$$
$$3f = 21$$
$$\frac{3f}{3} = \frac{21}{3}$$
$$f = 7$$

19.
$$4g + 1.7 = 2.3$$
$$4g + 1.7 - 1.7 = 2.3 - 1.7$$
$$4g = 0.6$$
$$\frac{4g}{4} = \frac{0.6}{4}$$
$$g = 0.15$$

20.
$$35 = 18h - 1$$
$$35 + 1 = 18h - 1 + 1$$
$$36 = 18h$$
$$\frac{36}{18} = \frac{18h}{18}$$
$$2 = h$$

21.
$$0.42 = 0.17 + 0.5k$$
$$0.42 - 0.17 = 0.17 - 0.17 + 0.5k$$
$$0.25 = 0.5k$$
$$\frac{0.25}{0.5} = \frac{0.5k}{0.5}$$
$$0.5 = k$$

22.
$$2x - 5 = 46$$
$$2x - 5 + 5 = 46 + 5$$
$$2x = 51$$
$$\frac{2x}{2} = \frac{51}{2}$$
$$x = 25.5$$

23.
$$\frac{x}{6} - 7 = 12$$
$$\frac{x}{6} - 7 + 7 = 12 + 7$$
$$\frac{x}{6} = 19$$
$$6 \cdot \frac{x}{6} = 19 \cdot 6$$
$$x = 114$$

24.
$$\frac{1}{2}T + \$3 = \$5$$
$$\frac{1}{2}T + \$3 - \$3 = \$5 - \$3$$
$$\frac{1}{2}T = \$2$$
$$2 \cdot \frac{1}{2}T = \$2 \cdot 2$$
$$T = \$4$$

25. $3.21 + 2.95 + 3.12 + 2.89 \rightarrow 3 + 3 + 3 + 3 = 12$
$3.21 + 2.95 + 3.12 + 2.89$ is about 12.

26. $3^3 \cdot 4^2 \cdot 1^5 = 27 \cdot 16 \cdot 1$
$$= 432$$

27.
$$p + 84 = 196$$
$$p + 84 - 84 = 196 - 84$$
$$p = 112$$

28. $4x - 8$

29. a. $\frac{x}{625} = 24$

b.
$$\frac{x}{625} = 24$$
$$625 \cdot \frac{x}{625} = 24 \cdot 625$$
$$x = 15,000 \text{ cans}$$

30.
$$\frac{(t + 3)}{6} + 5 = 7$$
$$\frac{(t + 3)}{6} + 5 - 5 = 7 - 5$$
$$\frac{(t + 3)}{6} = 2$$
$$6 \cdot \frac{(t + 3)}{6} = 2 \cdot 6$$
$$t + 3 = 12$$
$$t + 3 - 3 = 12 - 3$$
$$t = 9$$

Substitute 9 into the equation for t.

31.
$$10 + 6x = 40$$
$$10 - 10 + 6x = 40 - 10$$
$$6x = 30$$
$$\frac{6x}{6} = \frac{30}{6}$$
$$x = 5 \text{ words/week}$$

32.
$$3d + 6 = 21$$
$$3d + 6 - 6 = 21 - 6$$
$$3d = 15$$
$$\frac{3d}{3} = \frac{15}{3}$$
$$d = 5 \text{ more days}$$

33. See students' work. Sample answer: Three more than twice a number is 15. What is the number?

2-8 Use an Equation

PAGE 71   CHECKING FOR UNDERSTANDING

1. Represent it with a variable expression.

2. money earned - money paid back = money he has

   $\$2 \cdot 4f \quad - \quad \$2 \cdot f \quad = \quad \$5$

   $8f - 2f = 5$

3. Let f = the number of tests passed.

   Then $4f$ = the number of tests failed.

   $\$2 \cdot f - \$2 \cdot 4f = \$5$.

4. Let c = the amount of change.

   $c = \$125 - 2 \cdot \$52.22 - 2 \cdot \$9.94$

   $c = \$125 - \$104.44 - \$19.88$

   $c = \$0.68$

5. Let x = the number.

   $3x - 2x + 1 = 6$

   $x + 1 = 6$

   $x + 1 - 1 = 6 - 1$

   $x = 5$

6. Let n = the number of adults that attended.

   Then $2n$ = the number of students that attended.

   $\$5.50 \cdot n + \$5.00 \cdot 2n = \$1,953$

   $\$5.50n + \$10.00n = \$1,953$

   $\$15.50n = \$1,953$

   $\dfrac{\$15.50n}{\$15.50} = \dfrac{\$1,953}{\$15.50}$

   $n = 126$

   126 adult, 252 student

PAGE 71-72   PROBLEM SOLVING

7. Let d = the number of days.

   $8 \cdot 60 \cdot d = 15,000$

   $480d = 15,000$

   $\dfrac{480d}{480} = \dfrac{15,000}{480}$

   $d = 31.25$ days

8. Let m = the number of miles.

   $\dfrac{m}{17} = 29.5$

   $17 \cdot \dfrac{m}{17} = 29.5 \cdot 17$

   $m = 501.5$ mi

9. Let y = the number.

   $17y + 55 = 51 \cdot 5 + 4$

   $17y + 55 = 255 + 4$

   $17y + 55 = 259$

   $17y + 55 - 55 = 259 - 55$

   $17y = 204$

   $\dfrac{17y}{17} = \dfrac{204}{17}$

   $y = 12$

10. Let a = the amount she earned.

    $a = \$6.25 \cdot 35 + 2 \cdot \$6.25 \cdot 3$

    $a = \$218.75 + \$37.50$

    $a = \$256.25$

11. $127 \div 60$ is about $120 \div 60 = 2$.

    There are about 2 resorts per mile of beach.

12. Let r = the amount Ray earned.

    Let ℓ = the amount Lyla earned.

    $\ell - r = \$5.50 \cdot 610 - \$3.90 \cdot 610$

    $\ell - r = \$3,355 - \$2,379$

    $\ell - r = \$976$

13. Let p = the difference between the average price per can.

    $p = \dfrac{\$2.60}{6} - \dfrac{\$2.00}{6}$

    $p = \$0.43\frac{1}{3} - 0.33\frac{1}{3}$

    $p = \$0.10$

14. Let d = the number.

    $\dfrac{3d}{3} - 2 = 10$

    $\dfrac{3d}{3} - 2 + 2 = 10 + 2$

    $\dfrac{3d}{3} = 12$

    $3 \cdot \dfrac{3d}{3} = 12 \cdot 3$

    $3d = 36$

    $\dfrac{3d}{3} = \dfrac{36}{3}$

    $d = 12$

15. a. Let x = the amount of gold needed to balance the scale.

    $x + 5.2 = 45$

    $x + 5.2 - 5.2 = 45 - 5.2$

    $x = 39.8$ g

    b. $\frac{2}{3}$ gold $\cdot$ 24 karats = 16-karat gold

2-9 Perimeter and Area

PAGE 75   CHECKING FOR UNDERSTANDING

1. See students' work.

2. $P = 2\ell + 2w$

   $P = 2\left(2\frac{1}{2}\right) + 2(1)$

3. Perimeter is the distance around, while area is the space inside (two-dimensional).

4. $P = 4s$ $A = s^2$

   $P = 4 \cdot 6.5$ $A = (6.5)^2$

   $P = 26$ m $A = 42.25$ m^2

14

5. $P = 2l + 2w$ $A = lw$

$P = 2 \cdot 6 + 2 \cdot 5$ $A = 6 \cdot 5$

$P = 12 + 10$ $A = 30 \text{ yd}^2$

$P = 22 \text{ yd}$

6. $P = 2a + 2b$ $A = bh$

$P = 2 \cdot 7 + 2 \cdot 11$ $A = 11 \cdot 6$

$P = 14 + 22$ $A = 66 \text{ ft}^2$

$P = 36 \text{ ft}$

PAGES 75-76   EXERCISES

7. $P = 2l + 2w$ $A = lw$

$P = 2 \cdot 6.2 + 2 \cdot 3$ $A = 6.2 \cdot 3$

$P = 12.4 + 6$ $A = 18.6 \text{ in.}^2$

$P = 18.4 \text{ in.}$

8. $P = 2a + 2b$ $A = bh$

$P = 2 \cdot 3 + 2 \cdot 4$ $A = 4 \cdot 2$

$P = 6 + 8$ $A = 8 \text{ m}^2$

$P = 14 \text{ m}$

9. $P = 2l + 2w$ $A = lw$

$P = 2 \cdot 6 + 2 \cdot 4$ $A = 6 \cdot 4$

$P = 12 + 8$ $A = 24 \text{ units}^2$

$P = 20 \text{ units}$

10. $P = 4s$ $A = s^2$

$P = 4 \cdot 3$ $A = 3^2$

$P = 12 \text{ yd}$ $A = 9 \text{ yd}^2$

11. $P = 2a + 2b$ $A = bh$

$P = 2 \cdot 4 + 2 \cdot 4$ $A = 4 \cdot 3.1$

$P = 8 + 8$ $A = 12.4 \text{ m}^2$

$P = 16 \text{ m}$

12. $P = 2 + 2 + 1 + 2 + 4 + 2 + 1 + 2 = 16 \text{ units}$,

$A = 12 \text{ units}^2$

13. $P = 2l + 2w$ **14.** $A = bh$

$P = 2 \cdot 2w + 2w$ $7b = 91$

$P = 2 \cdot 2 \cdot 8 + 2 \cdot 8$ $\dfrac{7b}{7} = \dfrac{91}{7}$

$P = 32 + 16$ $b = 13 \text{ yd}$

$P = 48 \text{ cm}$

15. $6.5 \cdot 2{,}000 = 13{,}000 \rightarrow 6.5 \text{ T} = 13{,}000 \text{ lb}$

16. $\dfrac{r}{5} = 20$ **17.** $12 + 5d = 72$

$5 \cdot \dfrac{r}{5} = 20 \cdot 5$ $12 - 12 + 5d = 72 - 12$

$r = 100$ $5d = 60$

$\dfrac{5d}{5} = \dfrac{60}{5}$

$d = 12$

18. Let $c =$ the cost.

$c = \$0.79 \cdot A$

$c = \$0.79 \cdot lw$

$c = \$0.79 \cdot 20 \cdot 15$

$c = \$237$

19. $A = lw$ $A = bh$

$A = (8 - 2)(12 - 6)$ $A = (10 - 2)(8 - 5)$

$A = 6 \cdot 6$ $A = 8 \cdot 3$

$A = 36 \text{ in.}^2$ $A = 24 \text{ m}^2$

20. $P = 2l + 2w$

$P = 2 \cdot 12 + 2 \cdot 8$

$P = 24 + 16$

$P = 40 \text{ in.}$

21. a.

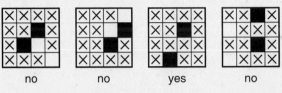

no   no   yes   no

b. when the darkened squares are not squares of the color on a checkerboard

22. See students' work. Sample answers:

perimeter: putting up a wallpaper border; putting on base molding

area: laying carpet; painting a ceiling

2-10 Solving Inequalities

PAGE 78   CHECKING FOR UNDERSTANDING

1. $\{6, 7, 8, \ldots\}$ **2.** Sample answers: 8, 5, 1

3. In both, the goal is to isolate the variable by "undoing" operations.

4. [number line with open circle at 8, marks at 2 4 6 8 10]

5. $6 + t > 11$ **6.** $a - 4 > 3$

$6 - 6 + t > 11 - 6$ $a - 4 + 4 > 3 + 4$

$t > 5$ $a > 7$

[number line with open circle at 5, marks 0 2 4 6 8]   [number line with open circle at 7, marks 2 4 6 8 10]

7. $12 + d < 21$ **8.** $3y < 15$

$12 - 12 + d < 21 - 12$ $\dfrac{3y}{3} < \dfrac{15}{3}$

$d < 9$ $y < 5$

[number line with open circle at 9, marks 4 6 8 10 12]   [number line with open circle at 5, marks 0 2 4 6 8]

9. $2m - 3 > 7$

$2m - 3 + 3 > 7 + 3$

$2m > 10$

$\dfrac{2m}{2} > \dfrac{10}{2}$

$m > 5$

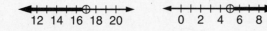

10. $\dfrac{p}{3} + 8 < 11$

$\dfrac{p}{3} + 8 - 8 < 11 - 8$

$\dfrac{p}{3} < 3$

$\dfrac{p}{3} \cdot 3 < 3 \cdot 3$

$p < 9$

PAGES 78-79   EXERCISES

11. $x - 3 < 14$

$x - 3 + 3 < 14 + 3$

$x < 17$

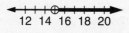

12. $y + 4 > 9$

$y + 4 - 4 > 9 - 4$

$y > 5$

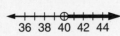

13. $b - 9 > 6$

$b - 9 + 9 > 6 + 9$

$b > 15$

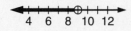

14. $2e < 16$

$\dfrac{2e}{2} < \dfrac{16}{2}$

$e < 8$

15. $3g < 27$

$\dfrac{3g}{3} < \dfrac{27}{3}$

$g < 9$

16. $\dfrac{s}{8} > 5$

$8 \cdot \dfrac{s}{8} > 5 \cdot 8$

$s > 40$

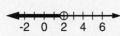

17. $2a - 5 > 9$

$2a - 5 + 5 > 9 + 5$

$2a > 14$

$\dfrac{2a}{2} > \dfrac{14}{2}$

$a > 7$

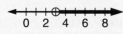

18. $5 + 3b < 11$

$5 - 5 + 3b < 11 - 5$

$3b < 6$

$\dfrac{3b}{3} < \dfrac{6}{3}$

$b < 2$

19. $5c - 8 > 7$

$5c - 8 + 8 > 7 + 8$

$5c > 15$

$\dfrac{5c}{5} > \dfrac{15}{5}$

$c > 3$

20. $9d + 4 < 22$

$9d + 4 - 4 < 22 - 4$

$9d < 18$

$\dfrac{9d}{9} < \dfrac{18}{9}$

$d < 2$

21. $\dfrac{a}{4} + 5 > 6$

$\dfrac{a}{4} + 5 - 5 > 6 - 5$

$\dfrac{a}{4} > 1$

$4 \cdot \dfrac{a}{4} > 1 \cdot 4$

$a > 4$

22. $\dfrac{c}{5} - 8 < 2$

$\dfrac{c}{5} - 8 + 8 < 2 + 8$

$\dfrac{c}{5} < 10$

$5 \cdot \dfrac{c}{5} < 10 \cdot 5$

$c < 50$

23. $5x > 60$

$\dfrac{5x}{5} > \dfrac{60}{5}$

$x > 12$

24. $x - 3 < 14$

$x - 3 + 3 < 14 + 3$

$x < 17$

25. $4x + 5 > 13$

$4x + 5 - 5 > 13 - 5$

$4x > 8$

$\dfrac{4x}{4} > \dfrac{8}{4}$

$x > 2$

26. $698 + 2 \rightarrow 700$

$\underline{+ 471 - 2 \rightarrow + 469}$

$ 1{,}169$

27. $\dfrac{x}{3} + 20 = 25$

28. $\dfrac{n}{2} + 31 = 45$

$\dfrac{n}{2} + 31 - 31 = 45 - 31$

$\dfrac{n}{2} = 14$

$2 \cdot \dfrac{n}{2} = 14 \cdot 2$

$n = 28$

29. $P = 2\ell + 2w$ $\qquad$ $A = \ell w$

$P = 2 \cdot 5 + 2 \cdot 2$ $\qquad$ $A = 5 \cdot 2$

$P = 10 + 4$

$P = 14$ cm $\qquad$ $A = 10$ cm^2

30. $3 \cdot 5 - 5 \overset{?}{>} 12$ $\quad$ $3 \cdot 6 - 5 \overset{?}{>} 12$ $\quad$ 6 is the answer.

$15 - 5 \overset{?}{>} 12$ $\qquad$ $18 - 5 \overset{?}{>} 12$

$10 < 12$ $\qquad\qquad$ $13 > 12$

31. $425 + x \le 800$

32. a.

n	$4n$	4^n	n^4
0	0	1	0
1	4	4	1
2	8	16	16
3	12	64	81
4	16	256	256

b. $n = 2$ and $n = 4$;

$n = 3$

33. a.

n	$4n$	4^n	n^4
0	0	1	0
1	4	4	1
2	8	16	16
3	12	64	81
4	16	256	256

b. $n = 2, 4$

$n = 3$

$n = 0, 1$

34. a. Answers will vary.

b. Answers will vary.

Chapter 2 Study Guide and Review

1. false; numerical
2. false, inequality
3. true
4. false; second
5. true
6. true
7. An equation contains an algebraic expression and an equal sign.

8. $cd^2 + (4b - 3) = 5 \cdot 2^2 + (4 \cdot 8 - 3)$

$\qquad = 5 \cdot 2^2 + (32 - 3)$

$\qquad = 5 \cdot 2^2 + 29$

$\qquad = 5 \cdot 4 + 29$

$\qquad = 20 + 29$

$\qquad = 49$

9. $abd - 6a = 3 \cdot 8 \cdot 2 - 6 \cdot 3$

$\qquad = 24 \cdot 2 - 18$

$\qquad = 48 - 18$

$\qquad = 30$

10. $(2c + b) \div ad = (2 \cdot 5 + 8) \div 3 \cdot 2$

$\qquad = (10 + 8) \div 6$

$\qquad = 18 \div 6$

$\qquad = 3$

11. $4a + 2c - d = 4 \cdot 3 + 2 \cdot 5 - 2$

$\qquad = 12 + 10 - 2$

$\qquad = 22 - 2$

$\qquad = 20$

12. $4 \cdot 130 \stackrel{?}{=} 520$

$520 = 520$

30 is the solution.

13. $56 + 12 \stackrel{?}{=} 68$

$68 = 68$

56 is the solution.

14. $84 - 37 \stackrel{?}{=} 47$

$47 = 47$

37 is the solution.

15. $n + 50 = 80$

$n + 50 - 50 = 80 - 50$

$n = 30$

16. $s - 12 = 61$

$s - 12 + 12 = 61 + 12$

$s = 73$

17. $145 = a + 32$

$145 - 32 = a + 32 - 32$

$113 = a$

18. $7.2 = 3.6 + t$

$7.2 - 3.6 = 3.6 - 3.6 + t$

$3.6 = t$

19. $r - 13 = 29$

$r - 13 + 13 = 29 + 13$

$r = 42$

20. $1.2 = p - 2.7$

$1.2 + 2.7 = p - 2.7 + 2.7$

$3.9 = p$

21. $2.3m = 11.5$

$\dfrac{2.3m}{2.3} = \dfrac{11.5}{2.3}$

$m = 5$

22. $\dfrac{s}{6} = 45$

$6 \cdot \dfrac{s}{6} = 45 \cdot 6$

$s = 270$

23. $\dfrac{r}{0.4} = 6.2$

$0.4 \cdot \dfrac{r}{0.4} = 6.2 \cdot 0.4$

$r = 2.48$

24. $4 = \dfrac{d}{26}$

$4 \cdot 26 = \dfrac{d}{26} \cdot 26$

$104 = d$

25. $72 = 12i$

$\dfrac{72}{12} = \dfrac{12i}{12}$

$6 = i$

26. $8.68 = 0.62j$

$\dfrac{8.68}{0.62} = \dfrac{0.62j}{0.62}$

$14 = j$

27. $y - 8 = 31$

28. $7x$

29. $8 + 6u$

30. $6f - 17 = 37$

$6f - 17 + 17 = 37 + 17$

$6f = 54$

$\dfrac{6f}{6} = \dfrac{54}{6}$

$f = 9$

31. $\dfrac{h}{5} + 20 = 31$

$\dfrac{h}{5} + 20 - 20 = 31 - 20$

$\dfrac{h}{5} = 11$

$5 \cdot \dfrac{h}{5} = 11 \cdot 5$

$h = 55$

32. $18 = \dfrac{t}{2} - 6$

$18 + 6 = \dfrac{t}{2} - 6 + 6$

$24 = \dfrac{t}{2}$

$2 \cdot 24 = \dfrac{t}{2} \cdot 2$

$48 = t$

33. $\dfrac{m}{8} + 12 = 14$

$\dfrac{m}{8} - 12 + 12 = 14 + 12$

$\dfrac{m}{8} = 26$

$8 \cdot \dfrac{m}{8} = 26 \cdot 8$

$m = 208$

34. $2k + 15 = 83$

$2k + 15 - 15 = 83 - 15$

$2k = 68$

$\dfrac{2k}{2} = \dfrac{68}{2}$

$k = 34$

35. $30 = 9 + 3c$

$30 - 9 = 9 - 9 + 3c$

$21 = 3c$

$\dfrac{21}{3} = \dfrac{3c}{3}$

$7 = c$

36. $P = 2\ell + 2w$ $A = \ell w$

$P = 2 \cdot 10 + 2 \cdot 6$ $A = 10 \cdot 6$

$P = 20 + 12$ $A = 60 \text{ ft}^2$

$P = 32 \text{ ft}$

37. $P = 2a + 2b$ $A = bh$

$P = 2 \cdot 7 + 2 \cdot 5$ $A = 7 \cdot 4$

$P = 14 + 10$ $A = 28 \text{ m}^2$

$P = 24 \text{ m}$

38.

$$2r - 4 < 10$$
$$2r - 4 + 4 < 10 + 4$$
$$2r < 14$$
$$\frac{2r}{2} < \frac{14}{2}$$
$$r < 7$$

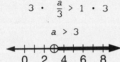

39. $4g > 24$

$$\frac{4g}{4} > \frac{24}{4}$$
$$g > 6$$

40.

$$6w + 5 < 29$$
$$6w + 5 - 5 < 29 - 5$$
$$6w < 24$$
$$\frac{6w}{6} < \frac{24}{6}$$
$$w < 4$$

41.

$$\frac{a}{3} + 7 > 8$$
$$\frac{a}{3} + 7 - 7 > 8 - 7$$
$$\frac{a}{3} > 1$$
$$3 \cdot \frac{a}{3} > 1 \cdot 3$$
$$a > 3$$

PAGE 82   APPLICATIONS AND PROBLEM SOLVING

42.

$$C + 2S + 3B = \$38 \qquad 2B = S + 3C$$
$$C + 2 \cdot \$3 + 3B = \$38 \qquad 2B = \$3 + 3C$$
$$C + \$6 + 3B = \$38 \qquad 2B = \$3 + 3(\$32 - 3B)$$
$$C + 3B = \$32 \qquad 2B = \$3 + \$96 - 9B$$
$$C = \$32 - 3B \qquad 11B = \$99$$
$$B = \$9$$

$$2B = S + 3C$$
$$\$18 = \$3 + 3C$$
$$\$15 = 3C$$
$$\$5 = C \qquad \text{cup, \$5; saucer, \$3; bowl, \$9}$$

43. Let A = regular rate. Let B = overtime rate.

Then $B = \frac{3}{2}A$.

$$8A + 2B = \$88$$
$$8A + 2 \cdot \frac{3}{2}A = \$88$$
$$8A + 3A = \$88$$
$$11A = \$88$$
$$\frac{11A}{11} = \frac{\$88}{11}$$

$$A = 8; \; B = \frac{3}{2}A = \frac{3}{2} \cdot \$8 = \$12$$

44.

$$\$1.99p = \$5.97$$
$$\frac{\$1.99p}{\$1.99} = \frac{\$5.97}{\$1.99}$$
$$p = 3 \text{ pounds}$$

45.

$$2n - 4 = 6$$
$$2n - 4 + 4 = 6 + 4$$
$$2n = 10$$
$$\frac{2n}{2} = \frac{10}{2}$$
$$n = 5 \text{ necklaces}$$

46.

$$P = 4s$$
$$P = 4 \cdot 500$$
$$P = 2,000 \text{ ft}$$
$$4P = 8,000 \text{ ft}$$

Chapter 2 Test

PAGE 83

1. $8 \cdot 14 \overset{?}{=} 112$

$112 = 112$

14 is the solution.

2. $3(6 - 4)^2 + 13 \cdot 5 = 3(2)^2 + 13 \cdot 5$
$$= 3 \cdot 4 + 13 \cdot 5$$
$$= 12 + 65$$
$$= 77$$

3. $[6^2 - (24 \div 8)] - 20 = [6^2 - 3] - 20$
$$= [36 - 3] - 20$$
$$= 33 - 20$$
$$= 13$$

4. $\dfrac{47 + 3}{5} + 48 \div 6 = \dfrac{50}{5} + 48 \div 6$
$$= 10 + 8$$
$$= 18$$

5.

$$k - 20 = 55$$
$$k - 20 + 20 = 55 + 20$$
$$k = 75$$

6. $0.4m = 9.6$

$$\frac{0.4m}{0.4} = \frac{9.6}{0.4}$$
$$m = 24$$

7.

$$\frac{x}{2} + 39 = 49$$
$$\frac{x}{2} + 39 - 39 = 49 - 39$$
$$\frac{x}{2} = 10$$
$$2 \cdot \frac{x}{2} = 10 \cdot 2$$
$$x = 20$$

8.

$$\$3.50 = \$1.90 + b$$
$$\$3.50 - \$1.90 = \$1.90 - \$1.90 + b$$
$$\$1.60 = b$$

9.

$$\frac{n}{1.5} = 6$$
$$1.5 \cdot \frac{n}{1.5} = 6 \cdot 1.5$$
$$n = 9$$

10.

$$11 = \frac{a}{4} - 9$$
$$11 + 9 = \frac{a}{4} - 9 + 9$$
$$20 = \frac{a}{4}$$
$$4 \cdot 20 = \frac{a}{4} \cdot 4$$
$$80 = a$$

11. $d = 6.34 - 2.96$
$$d = 3.38$$

12.

$$30 + g = 61$$
$$30 - 30 + g = 61 - 30$$
$$g = 31$$

13. $P = 2\ell + 2w$
$$P = 2 \cdot 7 + 2 \cdot 14$$
$$P = 14 + 28$$
$$P = 42 \text{ m}$$

14. $\dfrac{6}{y} - 12$

15. $8 + 5c = 48$

16. $\dfrac{xy}{z} + x^2z = \dfrac{3 \cdot 6}{9} + 3^2 \cdot 9$
$$= \frac{18}{9} + 9 \cdot 9$$
$$= 2 + 81$$
$$= 83$$

18

17. $P = 2\ell + 2w$ $\qquad$ $A = \ell w$

$\quad$ $P = 2 \cdot 7.5 + 2 \cdot 4.5$ $\qquad$ $A = 7.5 \cdot 4.5$

$\quad$ $P = 15 + 9$ $\qquad\qquad$ $A = 33.75$ cm^2

$\quad$ $P = 24$ cm

18. $P = 2a + 2b$ $\qquad$ $A = bh$

$\quad$ $P = 2 \cdot 5 + 2 \cdot 10$ $\qquad$ $A = 10 \cdot 4$

$\quad$ $P = 10 + 20$ $\qquad\qquad$ $A = 40$ in.^{2}

$\quad$ $P = 30$ in.

19. $\qquad$ $3h - 5 = 31$

$\quad$ $3h - 5 + 5 = 31 + 5$

$\qquad\qquad$ $3h = 36$

$\qquad\qquad$ $\dfrac{3h}{3} = \dfrac{36}{3}$

$\qquad$ $h = 12$ hamburgers

20. $\qquad$ $x + 4 > 16$ $\qquad$ 21. $\qquad$ $4c - 5 < 7$

$\quad$ $x + 4 - 4 > 16 - 4$ $\qquad$ $4c - 5 + 5 < 7 + 5$

$\qquad\qquad$ $x > 12$ $\qquad\qquad\qquad$ $4c < 12$

$\qquad\qquad\qquad\qquad\qquad\qquad\qquad$ $\dfrac{4c}{4} < \dfrac{12}{4}$

$\qquad\qquad\qquad\qquad\qquad\qquad\qquad\qquad$ $c < 3$

22. $\qquad$ $\dfrac{z}{3} + 8 < 10$ $\qquad$ 23. $3f > 45$

$\quad$ $\dfrac{z}{3} + 8 - 8 < 10 - 8$ $\qquad\qquad$ $\dfrac{3f}{3} > \dfrac{45}{3}$

$\qquad\qquad$ $\dfrac{z}{3} < 2$ $\qquad\qquad\qquad\qquad$ $f > 15$

$\qquad\quad$ $3 \cdot \dfrac{z}{3} < 2 \cdot 3$

$\qquad\qquad\quad$ $z < 6$

24. $x = \$3{,}193 + \$75$ $\qquad$ 25. $p - \dfrac{1}{3}p = \$9.90$

$\quad$ $x = \$3{,}268$

$\qquad\qquad\qquad\qquad\qquad\qquad$ $\dfrac{2}{3}p = \$9.90$

$\qquad\qquad\qquad\qquad\quad$ $\dfrac{3}{2}\left(\dfrac{2}{3}p\right) = \$9.90 \cdot \dfrac{3}{2}$

$\qquad\qquad\qquad\qquad\qquad\qquad\qquad$ $p = \$14.85$

PAGE 83 $\qquad$ **BONUS**

$\quad$ $4[(7 - 3) + 3x] = \dfrac{156}{3}$

$\qquad\qquad$ $4[4 + 3x] = 52$

$\qquad\qquad$ $16 + 12x = 52$

$\quad$ $16 - 16 + 12x = 52 - 16$

$\qquad\qquad\qquad$ $12x = 36$

$\qquad\qquad\qquad$ $\dfrac{12x}{12} = \dfrac{36}{12}$

$\qquad\qquad\qquad\quad$ $x = 3$

19

Chapter 3   Integers

3-1   Integers and Absolute Value

PAGES 87-88   CHECKING FOR UNDERSTANDING

1. Sample answer : temperature

2. Draw a number line. Locate -12. Draw a dot there.

3. $|-4| = 4$

4.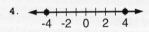
   -4 -2 0 2 4

5. A : -6, B : -1, C : 2, D : 5

6. $|4| = 4$

7. $|-3| = 3$

8. $|-23| = 23$

9. $|124 + 5| = |129|$
   $= 129$

10. $|0| = 0$

11.
   -6 -4 -2 0 2

12.
   0 2 4 6 8

13.
   -4 -2 0 2 4

PAGE 88   EXERCISES

14.
   -8 -6 -4 -2 0 2 4 6 8 10 12

15.
   -12 -10 -8 -6 -4

16.
   -4 -2 0 2 4

17. $|34| = 34$

18. $|-93| = 93$

19. $|-87| = 87$

20. $|132 - 20| = |112|$
    $= 112$

21. $b + |a - c| = 2 + |1 - 0|$
    $= 2 + |1|$
    $= 2 + 1$
    $= 3$

22. $xy - |-30| = 10 \cdot 4 - |-30|$
    $= 40 - |-30|$
    $= 40 - 30$
    $= 10$

23. $297 + 3 \rightarrow 300$
    $\underline{+ 478 - 3 \rightarrow + 475}$
    $ 775$

24. $q + 6.8 = 15.2$
    $q + 6.8 - 6.8 = 15.2 - 6.8$
    $q = 8.4$

25. $\dfrac{b}{2} - 1 > 2$

   $\dfrac{b}{2} - 1 + 1 > 2 + 1$

   $\dfrac{b}{2} > 3$

   $2\left(\dfrac{b}{2}\right) > 3 \cdot 2$

   $b > 6$

   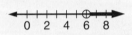
   0 2 4 6 8

26. a. greater than
    b. They are less than that coordinate.

27.
   After After After After After After After
   Day 1 Day 2 Day 3 Day 4 Day 5 Day 6 Day 7   Day 8
   0 1 2 3 4 5 6 7 8 9 10 feet

28.

Situation	Negative	Positive	Neither Positive nor Negative
altitude of a city	below sea level	above sea level	sea level
football	5 yard loss	10 yard gain	no gain
time	yesterday	tomorrow	today
money	loss	profit	break even

3-2   Comparing and Ordering

PAGE 90   CHECKING FOR UNDERSTANDING

1. $-245 < 612$, $612 > -245$

2. always points to lesser number

3.
   -6 -4 -2 0 2

   -2 0 2 4 6

   $-3 > -6$
   $|-3| = 3$, $|-6| = 6$
   $|-3| < |-6|$

4. $-19 > -22$

5. $0 > -7$

6. $4 < 87$

7. $-56 < 0$

8. $|-9| = 9$, $|-3| = 3$
   $|-9| > |-3|$

9. $-459 < -23$

10. $\{-99, -7, -1, 0, 8, 34, 123\}$

11. $\{129, 78, 65, 34, 1, -6, -99, -665\}$

PAGE 90   EXERCISES

12. $-14 < 0$

13. $-23 < 9$

14. $-99 > -789$

15. $|-7| = 7$
    $0 < |-7|$

16. $90 > 21$

17. $|-34| = 34$, $|-9| = 9$
    $|-34| > |-9|$

18. $-632 < -347$

19. $-56 < 56$

20

20. $|214| = 214$, $|-214| = 214$
    $|214| = |-214|$

21. $\{-56, -33, -9, -7, 0, 34, 99\}$

22. $\{93, 40, 12, 8, 0, -50, -66, -999\}$

23. $(13 - 9)^2 + \dfrac{15}{21 \div 7} = 4^2 + \dfrac{15}{21 \div 7}$

$$= 16 + \dfrac{15}{21 \div 7}$$

$$= 16 + \dfrac{15}{3}$$

$$= 16 + 5$$

$$= 21$$

24. $\quad 4m - 28 = 68$

$4m - 28 + 28 = 68 + 28$

$\qquad\qquad 4m = 96$

$\qquad\qquad \dfrac{4m}{4} = \dfrac{96}{4}$

$\qquad\qquad m = 24$

25. $|4^2| = |16|$

$\qquad\qquad = 16$

26. a. 3rd quarter: \$68.2 million

4th quarter: -\$215.1 million

1st quarter: -\$195.6 million

2nd quarter: \$10.3 million

b. $-\$215.1 - \$68.2 = -\$215.1 + (-\$68.2)$

$$= -\$283.3 \text{ million}$$

$-\$195.6 - (-\$215.1) = -\$195.6 + \$215.1$

$$= \$19.5 \text{ million}$$

$\$10.3 - (-\$195.6) = \$10.3 + \$195.6$

$$= \$205.9 \text{ million}$$

27.

-6 -4 -2 0 2 4 6

28. $-6 < -5.35$

$INT(-5.35) = -6$

3-3 Adding Integers

1. I : $x = -15 + 23$

$\quad |23| > |15|$

$\quad 23 - 15 = 8$

$\qquad\quad x = 8$

II : $x = 15 + 23$

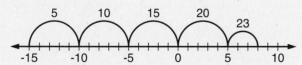

5   10   15   20   23

-15   -10   -5   0   5   10

2. Use the sign of the integer with the greatest absolute value.

3. If the signs are the same, add. If they are different, subtract. See students' work for examples.

4. a. $-6 + 3 = -3$

b. $-5 + 5 = 0$

c. $-12 + 24 = 12$

5. negative

6. $|-9| > |3|$
   negative

7. positive

8. $|-32| < |40|$
   positive

9. 0

10. $|34| < |-60|$
    negative

11. $29 + (-9) = e$
    $|29| > |-9|$
    $29 - 9 = 20$
    $e = 20$

12. $5 + (-12) = p$
    $|5| < |-12|$
    $12 - 5 = 7$
    $p = -7$

13. $z = -34 + 75$
    $|-34| < |75|$
    $75 - 34 = 41$
    $z = 41$

14. $-41 + (-18) = w$
    $41 + 18 = 59$
    $w = -59$

15. $-42 + 42 = q$
    $0 = q$

16. $f = 63 + 45$
    $f = 108$

17. $-54 + 21 = y$
    $|-54| > |21|$
    $54 - 21 = 33$
    $y = -33$

18. $-456 + (-23) = j$
    $456 + 23 = 479$
    $j = -479$

19. $z = 60 + 12$
    $z = 72$

20. $35 + (-32) = m$
    $|35| > |-32|$
    $35 - 32 = 3$
    $m = 3$

21. $n = -98 + (-32)$
    $98 + 32 = 130$
    $n = -130$

22. $s = -34 + 56$
    $|-34| < |56|$
    $56 - 34 = 22$
    $s = 22$

23. $r = -19 + (-37)$
    $19 + 37 = 56$
    $r = -56$

24. $r = -319 + (-100)$
    $319 + 100 = 419$
    $r = -419$

25. $56 + (-2) = b$
    $|56| > |-2|$
    $56 - 2 = 54$
    $b = 54$

26. $-60 + 30 = v$
    $|-60| > |30|$
    $60 - 30 = 30$
    $v = -30$

27. $409 + 309 = a$
    $718 = a$

28. $c = 76 + (-45)$
    $|76| > |-45|$
    $76 - 45 = 31$
    $c = 31$

29. $r + 45 = 5 + 45$
    $\quad = 50$

30. $w + (-7) = -3 + (-7)$
    $\qquad = -10$

31. $t + w = -5 + (-3)$
    $\quad = -8$

32. $-9 + t = -9 + (-5)$
    $\qquad = -14$

33. $-2 + w = -2 + (-3)$
    $\qquad = -5$

34. $(r + t) + w = (5 + (-5)) + (-3)$
    $\qquad\qquad = 0 + (-3)$
    $\qquad\qquad = -3$

35. $4 + \frac{1}{2}(4) = 4 + 2$
$= 6$ lb

36. $4 \cdot 4 \cdot 6 \cdot 6 \cdot 6 = 4^2 \cdot 6^3$

37. $6x = 42$ 38. $4x$ 39. $-114 < -97$
$\frac{6x}{6} = \frac{42}{6}$
$x = 7$

40. a.

b. $x = 4 + (-6)$

c. 2 blocks west

41. $\$38.98 + \$25.00 = \$63.98$
$\frac{1}{2} \cdot \$63.98 = \$31.99$
$\$38.98 - \$31.99 = \$6.99$
$\$6.99$ loss
The selling price is less than the
wholesale price.

42. She added all the positive numbers and then all the negative numbers. Then she subtracted when adding the two sums.

43. a. about 1,200
b. No one could afford telephone service during the depression.

3-4 **More About Adding Integers**

PAGE 96   CHECKING FOR UNDERSTANDING

1. Use the commutative property to change order then use the associative property to group the first two addends.

2. Look for groupings that make the sum easier to find.

3. $x = -4 + 8 + 12 + (-6) + (-3) + 13$
I: $x = [-4 + (-6)] + [8 + 12] + [-3 + 13]$
$= -10 + 20 + 10 = 20$
II: $x = [-4 + 8] + [12 + (-6)] + [-3 + 13]$
$= 4 + 6 + 10 = 20$
III: $x = [-4 + (-6) + (-3)] + [8 + 12 + 13]$
$= -13 + 33 = 20$

4. $y = 21 + 3 + (-6)$ 5. $(-3) + 8 + 9 = c$
$y = 24 + (-6)$ $(-3) + 17 = c$
$y = 18$ $14 = c$

6. $(-2) + 3 + (-10) + 6 = f$
$[(-2) + (-10)] + [3 + 6] = f$
$-12 + 9 = f$
$-3 = f$

7. $d = 7 + 20 + (-5)$
$d = 27 + (-5)$
$d = 22$

8. $w = (-4) + (-3) + 4 + 3$
$w = -7 + 7$
$w = 0$

9. $(-8) + 4 + 12 + (-11) = r$
$[(-8) + (-11)] + [4 + 12] = r$
$-19 + 16 = r$
$-3 = r$

10. $s = 9 + 10 + (-6) + 6$ 11. $21 + 3 + (-9) = g$
$s = 19 + 0$ $24 + (-9) = g$
$s = 19$ $15 = g$

12. $(-7) + 12 + 9 = q$
$(-7) + 21 = q$
$14 = q$

13. $p = (-6) + 12 + (-11) + 1$
$p = [(-6) + (-11)] + [12 + 1]$
$p = -17 + 13$
$p = -4$

PAGES 96-97   EXERCISES

14. $a = 6 + 9 + (-11)$ 15. $c = (-8) + 4 + 21$
$a = 15 + (-11)$ $c = (-8) + 25$
$a = 4$ $c = 17$

16. $19 + 23 + (-8) + 12 = f$
$19 + 23 + 12 + (-8) = f$
$54 + (-8) = f$
$46 = f$

17. $(-4) + 5 + 7 + 12 = g$
$(-4) + 24 = g$
$20 = g$

18. $w = -32 + 32 + 70$
$w = 0 + 70$
$w = 70$

19. $x = 5 + (-12) + 7 + 3$
$x = (-12) + 5 + 7 + 3$
$x = (-12) + 15$
$x = 3$

20. $j = -8 + 6 + (-20)$
$j = 6 + [(-8) + (-20)]$
$j = 6 + (-28)$
$j = -22$

21. $m = (-50) + 9 + 3 + 50$
$m = [(-50) + 50] + [9 + 3]$
$m = 0 + 12$
$m = 12$

22. $p = -13 + (-5) + 7 + (-20)$
$p = [-13 + (-5) + (-20)] + 7$
$p = -38 + 7$
$p = -31$

23. $8 + 30 + 21 + (-5) = r$

$59 + (-5) = r$

$54 = r$

24. $14 + 7 + (-23) + 10 = t$

$14 + 7 + 10 + (-23) = t$

$31 + (-23) = t$

$8 = t$

25. $v = (-30) + 5 + 12 + (-23)$

$v = [(-30) + (-23)] + [5 + 12]$

$v = -53 + 17$

$v = -36$

26. $r = 4 + (-10) + 6$

$r = (-10) + 4 + 6$

$r = (-10) + 10$

$r = 0$

27. $-21 + 17 + 10 + (-17) = z$

$[-21 + 10] + [17 + (-17)] = z$

$-11 + 0 = z$

$-11 = z$

28. $c + 3 + 4 + (-8) = 5 + 3 + 4 + (-8)$

$= 12 + (-8)$

$= 4$

29. $(-6) + x + 2 + 10 = (-6) + (-4) + 2 + 10$

$= -10 + 12$

$= 2$

30. $(-5) + h + 1 = (-5) + 6 + 1$

$= (-5) + 7$

$= 2$

31. $(-5) + 16 + c + h = (-5) + 16 + 5 + 6$

$= (-5) + 27$

$= 22$

32. $2.25 \cdot 16 = 36 \rightarrow 2.25$ lb $= 36$ oz

33. $\dfrac{448}{32} \overset{?}{=} 14$

$14 = 14$

32 is a solution.

34. $4s < 36$

$\dfrac{4s}{4} < \dfrac{36}{4}$

$s < 9$

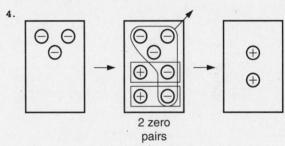

35. $p = 85 + (-47)$

$|85| > |-47|$

$85 - 47 = 38$

$p = 38$

36. $n = -1{,}800 + (-1{,}400)$

$n = -3{,}200$ miles

37. Answers will vary.

(1) Round:

$300 + (-100) + 200 + (-300) + (-200) = -100$

(2) Reorder:

$[326 + (-330)] + (-76) + [210 + (-215)] =$

about $0 + (-76) +$ about $0 = -76$

38.

Time	Elevation
1 hour	910 feet below sea level
2 hours	510 feet below sea level
3 hours	110 feet below sea level
4 hours	290 feet above sea level

A little more than 3 hours.

39. a. $-5 + 8 = 3$

3 yards gained

b. $15 + (-23) = -8$

8 yards lost

3-5 Subtracting Integers

PAGE 100 CHECKING FOR UNDERSTANDING

1. Sample answers: $1, -1$; $-5, 5$; $49, -49$

2. $d = 29{,}028 - (-35{,}840)$

$d = 29{,}028 + 35{,}840$

$d = 64{,}868$ ft

3. yes; 0

4.

2 zero pairs

5. $10 + (-10) = 0$; -10

6. $-9 + 9 = 0$; 9

7. $30 + (-30) = 0$; -30

8. $-29 + 29 = 0$; 29

9. $4 - (-7) = y$

$4 + 7 = y$

$11 = y$

10. $n = -43 - 99$

$n = -43 + (-99)$

$n = -142$

11. $p = -23 - (-2)$

$p = -23 + 2$

$p = -21$

12. $53 - 78 = z$

$53 + (-78) = z$

$-25 = z$

13. $y = 14 - 14$

$y = 14 + (-14)$

$y = 0$

14. $11 - (-19) = p$

$11 + 19 = p$

$30 = p$

15. $x = 17 - (-26)$

$x = 17 + 26$

$x = 43$

16. $123 - (-33) = n$

$123 + 33 = n$

$156 = n$

17. $b = -345 - 67$

$b = -345 + (-67)$

$b = -412$

PAGES 100-101 EXERCISES

18. $j = 44 - (-11)$

$j = 44 + 11$

$j = 55$

19. $4 - (-89) = u$

$4 + 89 = u$

$93 = u$

20. $56 - (-78) = p$

$56 + 78 = p$

$134 = p$

21. $435 - (-878) = u$

$435 + 878 = u$

$1{,}313 = u$

22. $k = -99 - 4$
$k = -99 + (-4)$
$k = -103$

23. $w = -43 - 88$
$w = -43 + (-88)$
$w = -131$

24. $x = -78 - (-98)$
$x = -78 + 98$
$x = 20$

25. $\quad -5 - 3 = k$
$-5 + (-3) = k$
$\quad\quad -8 = k$

26. $\quad 63 - 92 = q$
$63 + (-92) = q$
$\quad\quad -29 = q$

27. $m = 56 - (-22)$
$m = 56 + 22$
$m = 78$

28. $r = -9 - (-4)$
$r = -9 + 4$
$r = -5$

29. $-789 - (-54) = s$
$\quad -789 + 54 = s$
$\quad\quad\quad -735 = s$

30. $x = -351 - 245$
$x = -351 + (-245)$
$x = -596$

31. $v = 89 - (-54)$
$v = 89 + 54$
$v = 143$

32. $-109 - (-34) = g$
$\quad -109 + 34 = g$
$\quad\quad\quad -75 = g$

33. $45 - y = 45 - (-7)$
$\quad\quad\quad = 45 + 7$
$\quad\quad\quad = 52$

34. $67 - p = 67 - 9$
$\quad\quad\quad = 58$

35. $x - (-23) = -10 - (-23)$
$\quad\quad\quad\quad = -10 + 23$
$\quad\quad\quad\quad = 13$

36. $y - x = -7 - (-10)$
$\quad\quad\quad = -7 + 10$
$\quad\quad\quad = 3$

37. $x - y = -10 - (-7)$
$\quad\quad\quad = -10 + 7$
$\quad\quad\quad = -3$

38. $-240 - x = -240 - (-10)$
$\quad\quad\quad\quad = -240 + 10$
$\quad\quad\quad\quad = -230$

39. $y - p - x = -7 - 9 - (-10)$
$\quad\quad\quad\quad = -7 + (-9) + 10$
$\quad\quad\quad\quad = -7 + 1$
$\quad\quad\quad\quad = -6$

40. $x - y - p = -10 - (-7) - 9$
$\quad\quad\quad\quad = -10 + 7 + (-9)$
$\quad\quad\quad\quad = -10 + (-2)$
$\quad\quad\quad\quad = -12$

41. $5^3 = 5 \cdot 5 \cdot 5$
$\quad = 5 \cdot 25$
$\quad = 125$

42. $8x - 2y = 8 \cdot 6 - 2 \cdot 14$
$\quad\quad\quad = 48 - 28$
$\quad\quad\quad = 20$

43. $A = s^2$
$A = 8^2$
$A = 64 \text{ cm}^2$

44. $\{128, 52, 15, 4, 0, -3, -22, -78\}$

45. $44 + 8 + (-20) + 15 = s$
$44 + 8 + 15 + (-20) = s$
$\quad\quad 67 + (-20) = s$
$\quad\quad\quad\quad 47 = s$

46. Asia: about 9,400 m
South America: about 7,100 m
North America: about 6,200 m
Europe: about 5,100 m
Africa: about 6,200 m

47. a. Asia: $8,848 - (-399) = 8,848 + 399 = 9,247$ m
South America: $6,959 - (-40) = 6,959 + 40$
$\quad\quad\quad\quad\quad = 6,999$ m
North America: $6,194 - (-86) = 6,194 + 86$
$\quad\quad\quad\quad\quad = 6,280$ m
Europe: $5,633 - (-28) = 5,633 + 28$
$\quad\quad\quad\quad\quad = 5,661$ m
Africa: $5,895 - (-155) = 5,895 + 155$
$\quad\quad\quad\quad\quad = 6,050$ m

b. $-155 - (-40) = -155 + 40 = -115$ m

48. no; $-53 - (23 - 37) \stackrel{?}{=} (-53 - 23) - 37$
$\quad\quad -53 - (-14) \stackrel{?}{=} -76 - 37$
$\quad\quad\quad -53 + 14 \stackrel{?}{=} -76 - 37$
$\quad\quad\quad\quad\quad -39 \neq -113$

49. a. $P = I - E$
$P = \$18,345 - \$25,000$
$P = \$18,345 + (-\$25,000)$
$P = -\$6,655$

b. This is a loss.

Mid-Chapter Review

PAGE 101

1. $|64| = 64$
2. $|-31| = 31$
3. $|-4| = 4$

4.

5. $\{-7, -3, -2, 0, 5, 6, 8\}$

6. $x = 3 + (-5)$
$|3| < |-5|$
$5 - 3 = 2$
$\quad x = -2$

7. $y = 2 + (-4) + (-6) + 8$
$y = [2 + 8] + [(-4) + (-6)]$
$y = 10 + (-10)$
$y = 0$

8. $\quad 514 - 600 = r$
$514 + (-600) = r$
$\quad\quad -86 = r$

9. $90 + (-90) = p$
$\quad\quad 0 = p$

10. $w = 67 - (-32)$
$w = 67 + 32$
$w = 99$

11. $m = -89 - 25$
$m = -89 + (-25)$
$m = -114$

3-6 Multiplying Integers

PAGE 104 CHECKING FOR UNDERSTANDING

1. Multiplication is commutative.

2. $y = (7)(-9)(6)$
$y = (7)(6)(-9)$
$y = (42)(-9)$
$y = -378$

3. 6 $\boxed{+/-}$ $\boxed{x^2}$ 36

24

4.

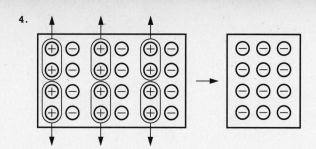

5. y is always positive.

6. negative   7. negative   8. positive   9. zero

10. $t = 9(-3)$ 11. $g = 5(-30)$ 12. $q = 9(-11)$
    $t = -27$ $g = -150$ $q = -99$

13. $-3(-7) = k$ 14. $g = -8(-3)$ 15. $-12(-8) = p$
        $21 = k$ $g = 24$ $96 = p$

16. $b = -9(12)$ 17. $w = 4(30)$ 18. $d = 6(-3)$
    $b = -108$ $w = 120$ $d = -18$

19. $(-8)^2 = y$ 20. $-5(-14) = f$ 21. $y = 7(5)$
    $(-8)(-8) = y$ $70 = f$ $y = 35$
        $64 = y$

PAGES 104-105   EXERCISES

22. $p = 6(8)$ 23. $w = -9(7)$ 24. $7(-14) = y$
    $p = 48$ $w = -63$ $-98 = y$

25. $9(-9) = k$ 26. $r = 55(-11)$ 27. $w = -6(-13)$
    $-81 = k$ $r = -605$ $w = 78$

28. $-5(80)(-2) = m$ 29. $(-6)(7)(-12) = p$
    $-400(-2) = m$ $-42(-12) = p$
        $800 = m$ $504 = p$

30. $u = 9(-10)(3)$ 31. $q = 7(23)(5)$
    $u = -90(3)$ $q = 7(115)$
    $u = -270$ $q = 805$

32. $-4(-50)(-1) = j$ 33. $(-21)^2 = t$
    $200(-1) = j$ $(-21)(-21) = t$
        $-200 = j$ $441 = t$

34. $(-8)(9)(6)^2 = k$ 35. $(3)(12)(-2) = k$
    $(-8)(9)(36) = k$ $(3)(-24) = k$
    $(-8)(324) = k$ $-72 = k$
    $-2{,}592 = k$

36. $m = (6)^2 \cdot (-3)^2$ 37. $3ab = 3(-3)(-6)$
    $m = 36 \cdot 9$ $= -9(-6)$
    $m = 324$ $= 54$

38. $-10ac = -10(-3)(10)$ 39. $ab^2 = (-3)(-6)^2$
        $= 30(10)$ $= (-3)(36)$
        $= 300$ $= -108$

40. $12abc = 12(-3)(-6)(10)$
        $= -36(-6)(10)$
        $= 216(10)$
        $= 2{,}160$

41. $c = \$20 \cdot 2 + \$0.15 \cdot 100$
    $c = \$40 + \$15$
    $c = \$55$

42. $39.4 \div 1{,}000 = 0.0394 \rightarrow 39.4$ m $= 0.0394$ km

43. $8.2 \div 0.2 = t$
        $41 = t$

44.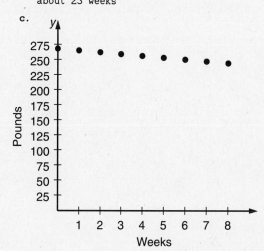

45. $57 - (-26) = d$
    $57 + 26 = d$
        $83 = d$

46. a. 3 pounds/week $\cdot$ 11 weeks = 33 pounds lost
       $268 - 33 = 235$ pounds

    b. $235 - 168 = 67$ more pounds to lose
       67 pounds $\div$ 3 pounds/week $= 22\frac{1}{3}$ weeks
       about 23 weeks

    c.

(graph: Pounds vs. Weeks, y-axis labeled in increments of 25 from 25 to 275, x-axis labeled 1–8, points descending from about 268 down near 245)

47. $b = \$25 + 3 \cdot \$21.19$
    $b = \$25 + \$63.57$
    $b = \$88.57$

48. a. $(-1)^2 = (-1)(-1)$ b. $(-1)^3 = (-1)(-1)(-1)$
           $= 1$ $= (-1)(1)$
                                      $= 1$

    c. $(-1)^4 = (-1)(-1)(-1)(-1)$
           $= [(-1)(-1)][(-1)(-1)]$
           $= (1)(1)$
           $= 1$

    d. $(-1)^5 = (-1)(-1)(-1)(-1)(-1)$
           $= (-1)[(-1)(-1)][(-1)(-1)]$
           $= (-1)(1)(1)$
           $= (-1)(1)$
           $= -1$

    e. $(1)^{5{,}280} = 1$

    f. If n is odd, then $(-1)^n = -1$. If n is even,
       then $(-1)^n = 1$.

49. p will be positive since there are 8 negative
    factors. If the number of negative factors is
    even, the product is positive. If the number of
    negative factors is odd, the product is negative.

3-7   Dividing Integers

1. $45 \div (-9) = t$; $\frac{45}{-9} = t$

2. $-8p = 320$

3. If $\frac{a}{b} = c$, check by seeing if $b \cdot c = a$.

4. negative

5. negative

6. positive

7. negative

8. $240 \div (-60) = y$
$$-4 = y$$

9. $365 \div (-5) = r$
$$-73 = r$$

10. $-12 \div (-4) = h$
$$3 = h$$

11. $f = \frac{245}{-5}$
$$f = -49$$

12. $d = \frac{224}{-32}$
$$d = -7$$

13. $\frac{-88}{44} = t$
$$-2 = t$$

14. $\frac{90}{10} = z$
$$9 = z$$

15. $-56 \div (-2) = p$
$$28 = p$$

16. $w = 49 \div 7$
$$w = 7$$

17. $\frac{62}{-2} = n$
$$-31 = n$$

18. $\frac{700}{-100} = k$
$$-7 = k$$

19. $m = 564 \div (-3)$
$$m = -188$$

20. $-26 \div (-13) = b$
$$2 = b$$

21. $295 \div 5 = y$
$$59 = y$$

22. $t = -930 \div (-30)$
$$t = 31$$

23. $\frac{588}{-6} = g$
$$-98 = g$$

24. $k = \frac{-195}{65}$
$$k = -3$$

25. $\frac{99}{r} = \frac{99}{3}$
$$= 33$$

26. $-\frac{99}{c} = -\frac{99}{(-9)}$
$$= -(-11)$$
$$= 11$$

27. $\frac{800}{t} = \frac{800}{-10}$
$$= -80$$

28. $\frac{c}{-3} = \frac{-9}{-3}$
$$= 3$$

29. $t \div (-2) = -10 \div (-2)$
$$= 5$$

30. $50 \div t = 50 \div (-10)$
$$= -5$$

31. $342 \div c = 342 \div (-9)$
$$= -38$$

32. $-342 \div r = -342 \div 3$
$$= -114$$

33. $cr - 4 = (-9)(3) - 4$
$$= -27 - 4$$
$$= -31$$

34. $rt \div (-5) = 3(-10) \div (-5)$
$$= -30 \div (-5)$$
$$= 6$$

35. $5ct \div r = 5(-9)(-10) \div 3$
$$= -45\,(-10) \div 3$$
$$= 450 \div 3$$
$$= 150$$

36. $(crt)^2 \div t = [(-9)(3)(-10)]^2 \div (-10)$
$$= [-27(-10)]^2 \div (-10)$$
$$= [270]^2 \div (-10)$$
$$= 72{,}900 \div (-10)$$
$$= -7{,}290$$

37. $42 + 86 + 58 = 42 + 58 + 86$
$$= 100 + 86$$
$$= 186$$

38. $c + 9 = 27$
$$18 + 9 \stackrel{?}{=} 27$$
$$27 = 27$$
$c = 18$ is a solution.

39. $P = 2\ell + 2w$
$$P = 2 \cdot (3 \cdot 4) + 2 \cdot 4$$
$$P = 2 \cdot 12 + 8$$
$$P = 24 + 8$$
$$P = 32 \text{ inches}$$

40. $z = -5 + 24 + (-8)$
$$z = -5 + 16$$
$$z = 11$$

41. $u = -8(10)(-12)$
$$u = -8(-120)$$
$$u = 960$$

42. Sample answer: $a = -156$, $b = 13$, $c = -12$

(1) $13 > -156$, $-12 < 13$, and $-156 < 0$.

(2) -156 has three digits.

(3) 13 and -12 each have two digits.

(4) -12 is divisible by 2 and 3.

(5) 13 can only be divided by 1 and itself.

(6) $-156 \div 13 = -12$.

43. $\$36{,}050 \div 7 = \$5{,}150$

about $\$5{,}150$

44. $-\$345.15 \div (-\$38.35) = 9$ teens

45. a. $-12 \div 3$ means to separate -12 into 3 equal groups.

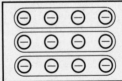

There are -4 counters in each group, so $-12 \div 3 = -4$.

b. $8 \div (-2)$ means to separate 8 into groups of -2 or to take out 2 groups so that 8 positive counters remain. Start with 8 zero pairs.

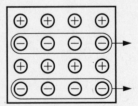

You can take out 2 groups of -4, so $8 \div (-2) = -4$.

c. $-6 \div (-3)$ means to separate -6 into groups of -3.

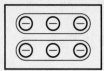

There are 2 groups of -3, so $-6 \div (-3) = 2$.

3-8 Classify Information

1. Answers will vary.   2. See students' work.

3. not enough information

4. $r = 120 - (-23)$

   $r = 120 + 23$

   $r = 143$

   $143°F$, too much information

5. $h = 5,283 - 2,838$

   $h = 2,445$

   about 2,500 feet, too much information

6. $w = 0.014 \cdot 50 = 0.7$ grams

7. not enough information

8. $6n = -36$

   $\dfrac{6n}{6} = \dfrac{-36}{6}$

   $n = -6$

9. $2s - 82 = 168$

   $2s - 82 + 82 = 168 + 82$

   $2s = 250$

   $\dfrac{2s}{2} = \dfrac{250}{2}$

   $s = 125$

10. not enough information

11. $x = 2 \cdot \$35 \cdot 8$

    $x = \$70 \cdot 8$

    $x = \$560$

3-9A Mathematics Lab: Solving Equations

1. $x = 13$

2. the opposite of what is already there

3. The right side of the mat contains 3 groups of 3 counters. So 3 counters correspond to each cup.

4. $x = 3$

5. $2x - 3 = 4$ 6. $-11 = 4x - 3$

7. $x = 6$ 8. $x = 8$ 9. $x = 10$

10. $x = -8$ 11. $x = 2$ 12. $x = -7$

13. $x = -5$ 14. $x = 7$ 15. $x = 3$

16. $x = 6$ 17. $x = -4$ 18. $x = 0$

3-9 Solving Equations

1. Subtract 5 from each side.

2.

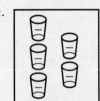 =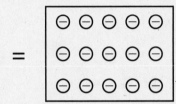

 =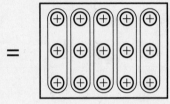

3. To make sure the solution is correct.

4. $2y = -90$

   $\dfrac{y}{2} = \dfrac{-90}{2}$

   $y = -45$

5. $c + 16 = -64$

   $c + 16 - 16 = -64 - 16$

   $c = -80$

6. $\dfrac{m}{-14} = 32$

   $(-14)\left(\dfrac{m}{-14}\right) = 32 \cdot (-14)$

   $m = -448$

7. $x - (-35) = -240$

   $x + 35 = -240$

   $x + 35 - 35 = -240 - 35$

   $x = -275$

8. $36 = -12 + 8m$

   $36 + 12 = -12 + 12 + 8m$

   $48 = 8m$

   $\dfrac{48}{8} = \dfrac{8m}{8}$

   $6 = m$

9. $-3y + 15 = 75$

   $-3y + 15 - 15 = 75 - 15$

   $-3y = 60$

   $\dfrac{-3y}{-3} = \dfrac{60}{-3}$

   $y = -20$

10. $\dfrac{t}{6} - 5 = -13$

$\dfrac{t}{6} - 5 + 5 = -13 + 5$

$\dfrac{t}{6} = -8$

$6\left(\dfrac{t}{6}\right) = -8 \cdot 6$

$t = -48$

11. $2x - (-34) = 16$

$2x + 34 = 16$

$2x + 34 - 34 = 16 - 34$

$2x = -18$

$\dfrac{2x}{2} = \dfrac{-18}{2}$

$x = -9$

PAGES 115-116 EXERCISES

12. $2t = -98$

$\dfrac{2t}{2} = \dfrac{-98}{2}$

$t = -49$

13. $s - (-350) = 32$

$s + 350 = 32$

$s + 350 - 350 = 32 - 350$

$s = -318$

14. $\dfrac{y}{15} = 22$

$15\left(\dfrac{y}{15}\right) = 22 \cdot 15$

$y = 330$

15. $2w + 35 = 105$

$2w + 35 - 35 = 105 - 35$

$2w = 70$

$\dfrac{2w}{2} = \dfrac{70}{2}$

$w = 35$

16. $45 = y - 13$

$45 + 13 = y - 13 + 13$

$58 = y$

17. $-200 = \dfrac{z}{3}$

$3 \cdot (-200) = \left(\dfrac{z}{3}\right) 3$

$-600 = z$

18. $4p - 15 = -75$

$4p - 15 + 15 = -75 + 15$

$4p = -60$

$\dfrac{4p}{4} = \dfrac{-60}{4}$

$p = -15$

19. $-69t = -4,968$

$\dfrac{-69t}{-69} = \dfrac{-4,968}{-69}$

$t = 72$

20. $q + (-367) = 250$

$q + (-367) + 367 = 250 + 367$

$q = 617$

21. $-30 = 42 + c$

$-30 - 42 = 42 - 42 + c$

$-72 = c$

22. $5d + 120 = 300$

$5d + 120 - 120 = 300 - 120$

$5d = 180$

$\dfrac{5d}{5} = \dfrac{180}{5}$

$d = 36$

23. $4m - 15 = 45$

$4m - 15 + 15 = 45 + 15$

$4m = 60$

$\dfrac{4m}{4} = \dfrac{60}{4}$

$m = 15$

24. $x + (-13) = -24$

$x + (-13) + 13 = -24 + 13$

$x = -11$

25. $-7x = 35$

$\dfrac{-7x}{-7} = \dfrac{35}{-7}$

$x = -5$

26. $2x + 7 = -21$

$2x + 7 - 7 = -21 - 7$

$2x = -28$

$\dfrac{2x}{2} = \dfrac{-28}{2}$

$x = -14$

27. $4,286 + 3,716 \rightarrow 4,300 + 3,700 = 8,000$

28. $30 = k - 141$

$30 + 141 = k - 141 + 141$

$171 = k$

29. $9 = \dfrac{h}{4} - 6$

$9 + 6 = \dfrac{h}{4} - 6 + 6$

$15 = \dfrac{h}{4}$

$4 \cdot 15 = \left(\dfrac{h}{4}\right) 4$

$60 = h$

30. $g = -56 - 77$

$g = -56 + (-77)$

$g = -133$

31. $f = 320 \div (-40)$

$f = -8$

32. $2x = -2$ $\qquad$ $3x = -6$ $\qquad$ $4x = -16$ $\qquad$ $5x = -40$

$\dfrac{2x}{2} = \dfrac{-2}{2}$ $\qquad$ $\dfrac{3x}{3} = \dfrac{-6}{3}$ $\qquad$ $\dfrac{4x}{4} = \dfrac{-16}{4}$ $\qquad$ $\dfrac{5x}{5} = \dfrac{-40}{5}$

$x = -1$ $\qquad$ $x = -2$ $\qquad$ $x = -4$ $\qquad$ $x = -8$

$6x = -96$

$\dfrac{6x}{x} = \dfrac{-96}{6}$

$x = -16$

a. Each increases by $1x$.

b. Each is twice the previous one.

c. $7x = -224$

$8x = -512$

$9x = -1,152$

$10x = -2,560$

$11x = -5,632$

33. $70 \div 14 = 5$, averaged 5 yard loss on each play

34. a. $3.1 + (-2.1) = x$

$1 = x$

b. $4.5 - (4.5) = z$

$0 = z$

c. $5(-2.50) = w$

$-12.5 = w$

d. $\dfrac{-8.758}{2} = m$

$-4.379 = m$

e. $(-3.470)(-2.11) = r$

$7.3217 = r$

f. $\dfrac{-5.5555}{-1.1111} = f$

$5 = p$

g. They are solved in the same manner.

35. a. $35n - 150 = P$

$35(4) - 150 = P$

$140 - 150 = P$

$-\$10 = P$

b. There was a loss.

36. See students' work.

3-10 Coordinate System

PAGE 118 CHECKING FOR UNDERSTANDING

1. See students' work. 2. $(0, 0)$

3. From $(0, 0)$, go 5 units right, then 7 units down.

4. Point E has the corrdinates $(6, 10)$.

5. $(-3, 5)$ 6. $(3, 4)$ 7. $(5, 0)$

8. $(3, -4)$ 9. $(-3, -3)$ 10. $(-5, 2)$

11-16.

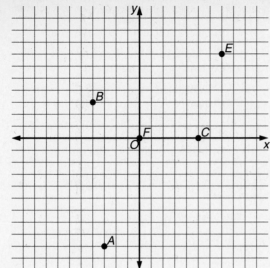

PAGE 119   EXERCISES

17. (-2, 3)   **18.** (-4, 3)   **19.** (-3, -1)

20. (-1, 0)   **21.** (-3, -3)   **22.** (1, -3)

23. (3, -2)   **24.** (1, 1)   **25.** (3, 3)

26-33.

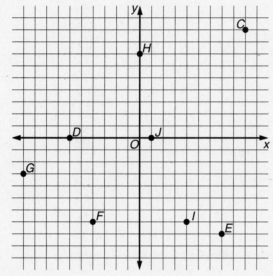

34. $9r = 54$

$\frac{9r}{9} = \frac{54}{9}$

$r = 6$

35. $4x < 20$

$\frac{4x}{4} < \frac{20}{4}$

$x < 5$

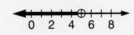

36. $-7 (-31) = w$

$217 = w$

37. $\frac{-108}{12} = a$

$-9 = a$

38. $-2y + 15 = 55$

$-2y + 15 - 15 = 55 - 15$

$-2y = 40$

$\frac{-2y}{-2} = \frac{40}{-2}$

$y = -20$

39. a. I   **b.** III   **c.** II

d. IV   **e.** III   **f.** I

40.

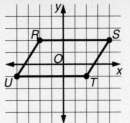

parallelogram

41.

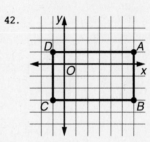

(1, 5)

42.

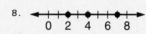

$A = \ell \cdot w$

$A = 7 \cdot 4$

$A = 28$ units^2

43. See students' work.

Chapter 3 Study Guide and Review

PAGE 120   COMMUNICATING MATHEMATICS

1. e   **2.** f   **3.** a   **4.** b   **5.** g   **6.** c

7. The only number you can add to 0 to get 0 is 0.

PAGES 120-121   SKILLS AND CONCEPTS

8. ◄──┼──●─┼─●─┼─●──┼──►
         0   2   4   6   8

9. ◄──┼──┼──●──●─●──┼──►
         -6 -4 -2   0   2

10. ◄──●──┼──●──┼──●──┼──►
          -6 -4 -2   0   2   4

11. ◄──┼──●──┼──●──●──┼──►
          -6 -4 -2   0   2   4

12. $-29 > -345$

13. $|-481| = 481$

14. $-15 < 1$

15. $-8 < |-8|$

16. $128 + (-75) = z$

$|128| > |-75|$

$128 - 75 = 53$

$z = 53$

17. $-64 + (-218) = j$

$64 + 218 = 282$

$j = -282$

18. $m = -47 + 29$

$|-47| > |29|$

$47 - 29 = 18$

$m = -18$

19. $21 + 15 + (-7) + 3 = k$

$21 + 15 + 3 + (-7) = k$

$39 + (-7) = k$

$32 = k$

20.
$$-16 + 38 + (-25) + 1 = x$$
$$[-16 + (-25)] + [38 + 1] = x$$
$$-41 + 39 = x$$
$$-2 = x$$

21. $v = -54 + 81 + 54$
$v = [-54 + 54] + 81$
$v = 0 + 81$
$v = 81$

22.
$$29 + (-60) + 11 + (-5) = p$$
$$[29 + 11] + [(-60) + (-5)] = p$$
$$40 + (-65) = p$$
$$-25 = p$$

23. $46 - (-62) = b$
$46 + 62 = b$
$108 = b$

24. $y = -59 - 33$
$y = -59 + (-33)$
$y = -92$

25. $j = -86 - (-96)$
$j = -86 + 96$
$j = 10$

.26. $-17 - 28 = n$
$-17 + (-28) = n$
$-45 = n$

27. $u = -8(12)$
$u = -96$

28. $w = -5(-20)$
$w = 100$

29. $(-10)(-2)(4) = q$
$(20)(4) = q$
$80 = q$

30. $(25)(-3)(1) = g$
$(-75)(1) = g$
$-75 = g$

31. $\frac{-66}{6} = c$
$-11 = c$

32. $\frac{-280}{-7} = h$
$40 = h$

33. $z = \frac{160}{5}$
$z = 32$

34. $b = \frac{360}{-24}$
$b = -15$

35. $-3s = -54$
$s = \frac{-54}{-3}$
$s = 18$

36. $3p - (-18) = 63$
$3p + 18 = 63$
$3p + 18 - 18 = 63 - 18$
$3p = 45$
$\frac{3p}{3} = \frac{45}{3}$
$p = 15$

37. $28 + m = -94$
$28 - 28 + m = -94 - 28$
$m = -122$

38. $\frac{r}{4} - 13 = -15$
$\frac{r}{4} - 13 + 13 = -15 + 13$
$\frac{r}{4} = -2$
$4\left(\frac{r}{4}\right) = -2 \cdot 4$
$r = -8$

39-42.

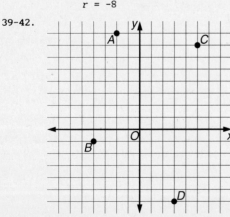

43. a. Niko: $6(1) + 0(-1) = 6 + 0 = 6$
Chuck: $2(1) + 4(-1) = 2 + (-4) = -2$
Rachel: $1(1) + 5(-1) = 1 + (-5) = -4$
Trenna: $4(1) + 2(-1) = 4 + (-2) = 2$
Amanda: $3(1) + 3(-1) = 3 + (-3) = 0$

b.

R C A T N
-4 -2 0 2 4 6

44. $2 + (-6) + 8 = (-4) + 8 = 4$ spaces forward

45. $5(-3) = -15$
She lost 15 points.

46. not enough information

47. $\frac{-4[n + 5 - (-10)]}{6} = 12$

$$\frac{-4[n + 5 + 10]}{6} = 12$$

$$\frac{-4[n + 15]}{6} = 12$$

$$6\left(\frac{-4[n + 15]}{6}\right) = 12 \cdot 6$$

$$-4[n + 15] = 72$$
$$-4n - 60 = 72$$
$$-4n - 60 + 60 = 72 + 60$$
$$-4n = 132$$
$$\frac{-4n}{-4} = \frac{132}{-4}$$
$$n = -33$$

Chapter 3 Test

1. $|-9| = 9$

2. $3 > -20$

3. $|-44| = 44$

4. $-837 < -164$

5. $|-51| = 51, \ |-14| = 14$
$|-51| > |-14|$

6. $\{-348, -179, -67, -6, 5, 20, 134\}$

7. $r = -582 + 68$
$r = -514$

8. $p = -4(-16)$
$p = 64$

9. $m = -112 \div 16$
$m = -7$

10. $-231 - 128 = d$
$-231 + (-128) = d$
$-359 = d$

11. $(8)(-10)(3) = h$
$(-80)(3) = h$
$-240 = h$

12. $3g - 14 = -50$
$3g - 14 + 14 = -50 + 14$
$3g = -36$
$\frac{3g}{3} = \frac{-36}{3}$
$g = -12$

13. $3t = 48 - (-72)$
$3t = 48 + 72$
$3t = 120$
$\frac{3t}{3} = \frac{120}{3}$
$t = 40$

14.
$$-8 + 21 + (-12) + 15 = s$$
$$[-8 + (-12)] + [21 + 15] = s$$
$$-20 + 36 = s$$
$$16 = s$$

15.

$$-4 \quad -2 \quad 0 \quad 2 \quad 4 \quad 6$$

16. The product will be negative, since there are an odd number of factors.

17.
$$3mc^2 = 3(5)(-4)^2$$
$$= 3(5)(16)$$
$$= 15(16)$$
$$= 240$$

18.
$$2ct \div m = 2(-4)(-10) \div 5$$
$$= -8(-10) \div 5$$
$$= 80 \div 5$$
$$= 16$$

19.
$$-6c - 60 = -6(-4) - 60$$
$$= 24 - 60$$
$$= -36$$

20.
$$\frac{n}{-4} + 20 = 26$$
$$\frac{n}{-4} + 20 - 20 = 26 - 20$$
$$\frac{n}{-4} = 6$$
$$(-4)\left(\frac{n}{-4}\right) = 6 \cdot (-4)$$
$$n = -24$$

21. (3, 4)

22. (-2, -3)

23. (2, -2)

24. (-1, 3)

25. $24 \div 4 = 6$ degrees

PAGE 123   BONUS

$x = 6, \ y = -2$

$6 > -2$

$6(-2) = -12$

$6 \div (-2) = -3$

Academic Skills Test

PAGES 124-125

1. C; $\$108 \div 3 = \$36$

2. C; $(3 \times 8) + (17 \times 8) = (3 + 17) \times 8$
$$= 20 \times 8$$

3. C; $\$540 \div 12 = \$45$

4. C; $3 \cdot 365 \cdot 10 = 10{,}950$

5. A; $14.5 \div 100 = 0.145 \rightarrow 14.5$ cm $= 0.145 \ m$

6. A; $x^2 = 576$
$$x = 24$$

7. B; $4 \cdot 4 \cdot 4 = 4^3$

8. C; $ab = 6 \cdot 3$
$$= 18$$

9. B; $x + 5 = 12$
$$x + 5 - 5 = 12 - 5$$

10. D; $\frac{n}{4} - 5 = 25$
$$\frac{n}{4} - 5 + 5 = 25 + 5$$
$$\frac{n}{4} = 30$$
$$4\left(\frac{n}{4}\right) = 30 \cdot 4$$
$$n = 120$$

11. A; $12 > t + 8$
$$12 - 8 > t + 8 - 8$$
$$4 > t$$

12. A; $2x + 3 = 14$

13. C; $P = 2\ell + 2w$
$$P = 2(14.5) + 2(10)$$
$$P = 29 + 20$$
$$P = 49 \text{ cm}$$

14. C; $\{-5, -2, 0, 1\}$

15. A; $|-5.2| = 5.2$
$$-4.5 < |-5.2|$$

16. C; $56 + (-32) = 24$

17. A; $20 \cdot (-9) = -180$

18. B; $-64 \div 8 = -8$

19. A; $\frac{c}{-3} = 6$
$$(-3)\left(\frac{c}{-3}\right) = 6 \cdot (-3)$$
$$c = -18$$

20. C; M

31

Chapter 4   Statistics and Data Analysis

4-1A   Mathematics Lab: Data Base

PAGE 128   WHAT DO YOU THINK?

1. B & G International

2. a. Ask the computer to retrieve all records from specific states.

   b. The customers in states where it snows would be interested.

PAGE 129   WHAT DO YOU THINK?

3. 1.10

4. REPLACE ALL BONUS WITH BONUS *1.15.

5. REPLACE ALL BONUS WITH BONUS + 200.

PAGE 129   EXTENSION

6. a. REPLACE ALL BONUS WITH BONUS * 1.20 FOR SALES AMOUNT > 3000.

   b. Record 5 would receive the 20% raise.

   c. New Bonuses

   50.00

   8.99

   105.00

   92.50

   961.20

   300.00

   250.00

   175.00

7. a. REPLACE ALL BONUS WITH BONUS * 1.05 FOR SALES AMOUNT < 1000.

   b. Records 1, 2, and 4 would receive the bonus.

   c. New Bonuses

   52.50

   9.44

   105.00

   97.13

   801.00

   300.00

   250.00

   175.00

4-1   Make a Table

PAGES 131-132   CHECKING FOR UNDERSTANDING

1. The intervals overlap.

2. Sample answer: Folk music is least popular and rock music is most popular.

3.

Talking on Phone Time (hrs)	Tally	Frequency
0-1	ℍℍ I	6
2-3	ℍℍ IIII	9
4-5	IIII	4
6-7	I	1

4.

Number of Pins	Tally	Frequency
86-105	I	1
106-125	III	3
126-145	ℍℍ II	7
146-165	I	1
166-185	IIII	4
186-205	IIII	4

PAGE 132   PROBLEM SOLVING

5.

Video Game Prices ($)	Tally	Frequency
0-9.99		0
10-19.99	IIII	4
20-29.99	III	3
30-39.99	ℍℍ	5
40-49.99	IIII	4
50-59.99	II	2

   a. 18 games

   b. $40

6. $(0.97)(1433) = 1390.01$

   $1433 - 1390.01 = 42.99$

   About 43 employees use public transportation.

7.

Magazine Subscriptions Sold	Tally	Frequency
0-19	II	2
20-39	ℍℍ	5
40-59	ℍℍ	5
60-79	ℍℍ II	7
80-99	I	1

8. $x \div 0.4 = 20$

   $0.4\left(\dfrac{x}{0.4}\right) = 0.4(20)$

   $x = 8$

9.

Points Scored	Tally	Frequency
51-70	III	3
71-90	ℍℍ I	6
91-110	ℍℍ IIII	8
111-130	III	3

10. Let x = packages of vegetables

$$9 + x + 2x = 15$$
$$9 + 3x = 15$$
$$9 - 9 + 3x = 15 - 9$$
$$3x = 6$$
$$\frac{3x}{3} = \frac{6}{3}$$
$$x = 2$$

9 muffins, 4 frozen dinners, 2 vegetables

4-2   Histograms

PAGE 134   CHECKING FOR UNDERSTANDING

1. Both are bar graphs, but a histogram displays the data in equal intervals.

2. Sample answer: Data can be grouped into intervals so fewer bars are used.

3. It is more visual; See students' work.

4. Because intervals include all possible values.

5. Sample answer: the frequency of twenty science test scores ranging from 41-100

6. 10 scores

7. intervals 61-70 and 81-90

8. Intervals from 1-40 have been omitted.

9.

Science Test Scores	
Scores	Frequency
41-50	1
51-60	2
61-70	5
71-80	4
81-90	5
91-100	3

PAGE 135   EXERCISES

10.

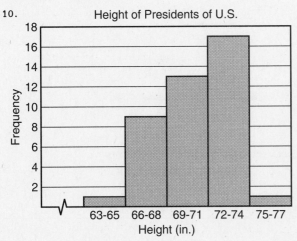

Height of Presidents of U.S.

a. $1 + 9 + 13 + 17 + 1 = 41$

b. range 72-74

c. $6 \times 12 = 72$

Use ranges 72-74 and 75-77.

$17 + 1 = 18$

So $\frac{18}{41}$ presidents have been 6 feet or taller.

11.

Amount of Change		
Cents	Tally	Frequency
61-70	||||	4
71-80	⊮ |||	8
81-90	⊮ |	6
91-100	||	2

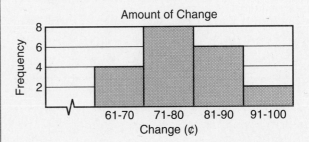

Amount of Change

12.

$$7 = \frac{r}{15}$$
$$15(7) = 15\left(\frac{r}{15}\right)$$
$$105 = r$$

Check: $7 \overset{?}{=} \frac{105}{15}$

$7 = 7$ ✓

13.

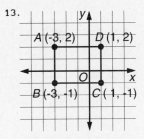

$$P = 4 + 3 + 4$$
$$= 14 \text{ units}$$

14. a.

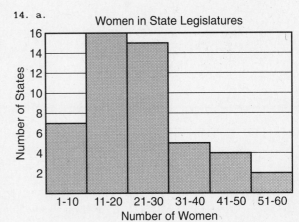

Women in State Legislatures

b. The two tallest bars represent 31 of 49 women.

c. It has more than twice the number of women in State Legislatures.

15. a. You cannot tell, individual data is not shown.

b. Answers may vary. Sample answer: Leadership is associated with tallness.

16. The West

33

4-3 Line Plots

1. They both show how many times each piece of data occurs.

2. See students' work.

3. Most players are 64 or 65 inches tall.

4.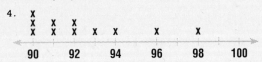

5. a.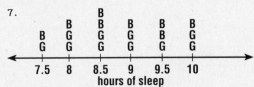

   b. Answers may vary. Sample answer: Most weigh 72 pounds.

PAGE 138   EXERCISES

6. a.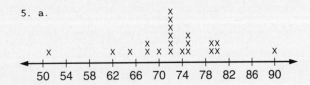

   b. 50 was highest; 31 was lowest.

   c. 41, 42, and 45

   d. 17

7.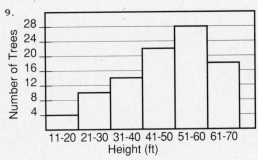

   Girls get less sleep than boys.

8. $n = -241$

9.

10. a.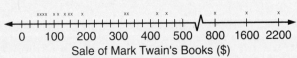

    b. 10 books

11. a.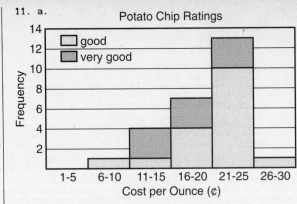

    b. Answers may vary. Sample answer: Heights of bars and stacked letters are similar.

12. See students' work.

4-3B Mathematics Lab: Maps and Statistics

PAGE 140   WHAT DO YOU THINK?

1. Answers may vary. Sample answer: There are more pieces of data in the smaller ranges and less pieces of data in the wider ranges.

2. There are only 6 primary and secondary colors: red, orange, yellow, green, blue, violet.

3. CA, NM, TX; They are close to Mexico.

4. A map is more visual.

PAGE 140   EXTENSION

5. Color states with a small Hispanic population dark and states with a large Hispanic population light.

6. More states are in the 0-3 range. This color is more dominant.

PAGE 140   APPLICATION

7. a. See students' work.

   b. Make large range sizes for the large percents and color those ranges dark.

   c. Make large range sizes for the small percents and color those ranges dark.

4-4 Stem-and-Leaf Plots

PAGES 142-143   CHECKING FOR UNDERSTANDING

1. the greatest place value of the data

2. 809

3. Answers may vary. Sample answer: when you have a set of data with a lot of values concentrated in one area; See students' work.

4. 55 in.

5. 72 in.

6. **a.** 5 | G G G B
      6 | B B B B B G B G B G G G G
      7 | G B B

   b. You can compare the data from both groups.

   c. You lose individual values.

7. **a.** 0, 1, 2, 3, 4, 5, 6

   b. 0 | 789
      1 | 1234467889
      2 | 2245
      3 | 022345
      4 | 1356
      5 | 16
      6 | 1
      3 | 3 means 33 yrs. old

   c. 7 years old is youngest; 61 years old is oldest

   d. ages 10-19, or teens

PAGES 143-144   EXERCISES

8. 1, 2, 3, 4   1 | 7
            2 |
            3 | 245
            4 | 12
            3 | 4 means 34

9. 0, 1, 2, 3, 4, 5   0 | 9
              1 | 124
              2 | 4
              3 | 3
              4 |
              5 | 1
              3 | 3 means 33

10. 25, 26, 27, 28, 29   25 | 3
                26 | 7
                27 | 2
                28 | 0
                29 | 45
                29 | 5 means 295

11. 5, 6, 7, 8   5 | 49
           6 | 3
           7 | 15
           8 | 6
           6 | 3 means 6.3

12. **a.**

Mathematics		Science
6	5	7
950	6	34588
8533	7	023358
97753	8	137
743	9	8

   3 | 7 means 73   8 | 1 means 81

   b. 97

   c. tens

   d. 70's

   e. mathematics; There are fewer scores in the 50-79 range than in the 80-99 range.

13. **a.** Bender Company

   b. Answers may vary. Sample answer: health-care benefits expense

14. 20

15. $c = -16$

16.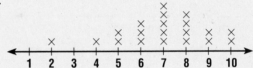

17. Each show the frequencies in regular intervals.

18. **a.** American League

   b. The lines would be too long otherwise and this way they group better.

19. **a.** See students' work.

   b. See students' work.

4-5 Measures of Central Tendency

PAGE 147   CHECKING FOR UNDERSTANDING

1. The number that has the most x's above it.

2. 3, 5, 7, 8, 9, 10, 12, 13, 15, 17
   $$\frac{9 + 10}{2} = \frac{19}{2} = 9.5$$

3. Answers may vary. Sample answer: If an odd-numbered set of data has a lot of high and low numbers and not many middle numbers, then the mean would be a middle number but the median would be a high or low number.

4. Median: 13
   Mean: $\frac{10 + 11 + 12 + 12 + 13 + 14 + 14 + 14 + 15}{9}$
   $= \frac{115}{9} \approx 12.8$
   Mode: 14
   Median, because the mode is close to an extreme and the mean is close to the median.

5.

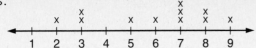

Mean: $\dfrac{2 + 3 + 3 + 5 + 6 + 7 + 7 + 7 + 8 + 8 + 9}{11}$

$= \dfrac{65}{11} \approx 5.9 \text{ or } 6$

Median: 7

Mode: 7

6.
```
2 | 24556
3 | 45
```
2 | 6 means 26

Mean: $\dfrac{22 + 24 + 25 + 25 + 26 + 34 + 35}{7}$

$= \dfrac{191}{7} \approx 27.3 \text{ or } 27$

Median: 25

Mode: 25

7.

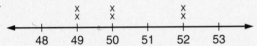

Mean: $\dfrac{48 + 48 + 50 + 50 + 52 + 52}{6} = \dfrac{300}{6} = \$50$

Median: $50

Mode: $49, $50, $52

8.

Values	Tally	Frequency
0–4.99	|	1
5–9.99	||||	4
10–14.99	|||	3
15–19.99	||	2

Mean: $\dfrac{3.5 + 5.5 + 7 + 8.8 + 9.6 + 10.74 + 12.9 +}{10}$

$\dfrac{13.1 + 15.6 + 17.2}{10} = \dfrac{103.94}{10} \approx 10.4$

Median: $\dfrac{9.6 + 10.74}{2} = \dfrac{20.34}{2} = 10.17$

Mode: none

PAGES 147–148   EXERCISES

9. 2, 4, 5, 5, 6, 6, 8, 13, 13

Mean: $\dfrac{2 + 4 + 5 + 5 + 6 + 6 + 8 + 13 + 13}{9} = \dfrac{62}{9}$

$= 6.9$

Median: 6

Mode: 5, 6, 13

10. 73, 75, 78, 79, 80, 81, 84, 84

Mean: $\dfrac{73 + 75 + 78 + 79 + 80 + 81 + 84 + 84}{8}$

$= \dfrac{634}{8} = 79.3$

Median: $\dfrac{79 + 80}{2} = \dfrac{159}{2} = 79.5$

Mode: 84

11. 130, 148, 155, 172, 184

Mean: $\dfrac{130 + 148 + 155 + 172 + 184}{5} = \dfrac{789}{5} = 157.8$

Median: 155

Mode: none

12. 18, 21, 21, 24

Mean: $\dfrac{18 + 21 + 21 + 24}{4} = \dfrac{84}{4} = 21$

Median: 21

Mode: 21

13. 1.8, 1.8, 2.3, 2.6, 3.1, 3.4

Mean: $\dfrac{1.8 + 1.8 + 2.3 + 2.6 + 3.1 + 3.4}{6} = \dfrac{15}{6}$

$= 2.5$

Median: $\dfrac{2.3 + 2.6}{2} = \dfrac{4.9}{2} = 2.45 \text{ or } 2.5$

Mode: 1.8

14. 25, 25.98, 30, 45.36, 45.36

Mean: $\dfrac{25 + 25.98 + 30 + 45.36 + 45.36}{5} = \dfrac{171.7}{5}$

$= 34.3$

Median: 30

Mode: 45.4

15. Mean: $\dfrac{42 + 50 + 55 + 61 + 62 + 68 + 70 +}{13}$

$\dfrac{73 + 75 + 75 + 81 + 87 + 88}{13}$

$= \dfrac{887}{13} = 68.2$

Median: 70

Mode: 75

16. Mean: $\dfrac{12 + 13 + 13 + 15 + 15 + 15 + 16 +}{14}$

$\dfrac{16 + 16 + 16 + 17 + 18 + 18 + 19}{14}$

$= \dfrac{219}{14} = 15.6$

Median: 16

Mode: 16

17. a. 3.6, 3.6, 3.7, 3.9, 4.8

Mean: $\dfrac{3.6 + 3.6 + 3.7 + 3.9 + 4.8}{5} = \dfrac{19.6}{5}$

$= 3.92 \text{ in.}$

Mode: 3.6 in.

Median: 3.7 in.

b. Only the mean would change. It would increase.

c. Mean: $\dfrac{3.6 + 3.6 + 3.9 + 4.8}{4} = \dfrac{16}{4} = 4 \text{ in.}$

Mode: 3.6 in.

Median: 3.75 in.

The mean increases slightly, the mode stays the same, and the median increases slightly.

18. $5.17 = \dfrac{k}{2} + 3.68$

$5.17 - 3.68 = \dfrac{k}{2} + 3.68 - 3.68$

$1.49 = \dfrac{k}{2}$

$2(1.49) = 2\left(\dfrac{k}{2}\right)$

$2.98 = k$

19. $b = 65 - (-87)$

$b = 65 + 87$

$b = 152$

20.

1	568
2	123469
3	24567
4	2358
5	26

4 | 3 means 43

21. $77 \times 4 = 308$

$$\frac{308 + x}{5} = 80$$

$$5\left(\frac{308 + x}{5}\right) = 5\ (80)$$

$$308 + x = 400$$

$$308 - 308 + x = 400 - 308$$

$$x = 92$$

Mikael must score a 92 on his last test.

22. a. Mean: $\dfrac{7 + 7 + 7 + 7 + 9 + 9 + 9 + 10 + 10 +}{12}$

$$\frac{10 + 10 + 10}{12} = \frac{105}{12} = 8.75$$

Median: 9

Mode: 10

b. median; The mode is an extreme and the mean is close to the median.

23. See students' work.

Mid-Chapter Review

PAGE 148

1.

Score	Frequency
11-13	2
14-16	6
17-19	6
20-22	4
23-25	6

2.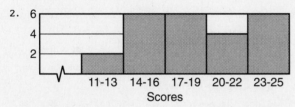

3. range 16-20

4.

1	12455666777799
2	0022334445

1 | 9 means 19

5. Mean: $\dfrac{448}{24} = 18.7$

Median: $\dfrac{17 + 19}{2} = \dfrac{36}{2} = 18$

Mode: 17

The mode is the best measure because it is most representative of the central values.

PAGE 150   WHAT DO YOU THINK?

1. The letter E because it occurs most often in the English language.

2. B = E, X = T, K = A, L = O, Q = N, F = R, E = I, P = S, A = H

3. I have wished a bird would fly away,
   And not sing by my house all day;

   Have clapped my hands at him from the door
   When it seemed as if I could bear no more.

   The fault must partly have been in me.
   The bird was not to blame for his key.

   And of course there must be something wrong
   In wanting to silence any song.

4. About $\dfrac{1}{3}$ are correct, others are close to the frequency.

5. The frequencies would not match the normal amounts.

4-6   **Measures of Variation**

PAGE 153   CHECKING FOR UNDERSTANDING

1. Answers may vary. Sample answer: Measures of variation describe the dispersal of data. Measures of central tendency describe the set as a whole.

2. See students' work.

3. Find the median of the entire set of data, then find the medians of the upper half and lower half of the data.

4. The interquartile range is the range of the middle half of the data.

5. $10 - 3 = 7$

6. 12, 16, 17, 18, 23
   $23 - 12 = 11$

7. 125, 135, 136, 145, 156, 170, 174, 180, 188
   $188 - 125 = 63$

8. Median: 7
   UQ: 8
   LQ: 4

9. Median: 17
   UQ: $\dfrac{18 + 23}{2} = \dfrac{41}{2} = 20.5$
   LQ: $\dfrac{12 + 16}{2} = \dfrac{28}{2} = 14$

10. Median: 156
    UQ: $\dfrac{174 + 180}{2} = \dfrac{354}{2} = 177$
    LQ: $\dfrac{135 + 136}{2} = \dfrac{271}{2} = 135.5$

11. $177 - 135.5 = 41.5$

12. $46 - 12 = 34$

13. 26

14. UQ: $\frac{30 + 31}{2} = \frac{61}{2} = 30.5$

LQ: 23

15. $30.5 - 23 = 7.5$

16.
```
2 | 4588999
3 | 0011222347889
4 | 244
5 | 7
```
5 | 7 means 57

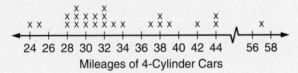

Mileages of 4-Cylinder Cars

17. 57   18. 24   19. $57 - 24 = 33$

20. 32   21. UQ: 38   22. $38 - 29 = 9$
                    LQ: 29

23. $9^2 - 2^3 = 81 - 8$ 24. $960 = f$
    $= 73$

25. 4, 6, 6, 7, 8, 9, 10, 11, 12, 12

Mean: $\frac{4 + 6 + 6 + 7 + 8 + 9 + 10 + 11 + 12 + 12}{10}$

$= \frac{85}{10} = 8.5$

Median: $\frac{8 + 9}{2} = \frac{17}{2} = 8.5$

Mode: 6, 12

26. a. Neither; both average $63°$ and the median and mode of both cities is $60°$.

b. Cincinnati: UQ: 73

LQ: 53

IQ Range: $73 - 53 = 20$

Baltimore: UQ: 77

LQ: 49

IQ Range: $77 - 49 = 28$

The company will choose Cincinnati because its interquartile range is less.

27. See students' work.

28. The data is clustered around the median.

4-7   Box-and-Whisker Plots

1. the middle half of the data

2. the lower extreme and the upper extreme

3. median, lower quartile, upper quartile, lower extreme, upper extreme, outliers

4. if it is more than 1.5 times the interquartile range from the nearest quartile value

5. They have the same median and the same least value.

6. Answers may vary. Sample answer: The top set of data is more widely dispersed than the lower one.

7. top plot; The box is longer.

8.
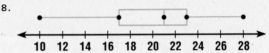

9. 21   10. 23   11. 17   12. 10

13. $23 - 17 = 6$

14. $1.5 \times 6 = 9$ 15. $1.5 \times 6 = 9$

$23 + 9 = 32$ $23 + 9 = 32$

$17 - 9 = 8$ $17 - 9 = 8$

$10 > 8$ 8 and 32

$28 < 32$ are limits.

no outliers

16. Answers may vary. Sample answer: Both are displayed using a number line and you can see where data are concentrated. Median is more visible on box-and-whisker plot but other measures of central tendency can be calculated from a line plot.

17. 63   18. $72 - 55 = 17$ 19. 67.5

20. 60   21. $67.5 - 60 = 7.5$ 22. 55 and 72

23. $7.5 \times 1.5 = 11.25$

$67.5 + 11.25 = 78.75$

$60 - 11.25 = 48.75$

The limits are 48.75 and 78.75.

Since $78.75 > 72$ and $48.75 < 55$, there are no outliers.

24. One-half, or 10 of the 20 students are represented by the box, and half of them, or 5, are represented by the area from the lower quartile to the median.

25. Since the median is 63, one-half, or 10, are less than 63 inches tall.

26. The mean falls between the median and the upper quartile.

27. Median: 65 $12 \times 1.5 = 18$

UQ: 74 $74 + 18 = 92$

LQ: 62 $62 - 18 = 44$

IQ Range: $74 - 62 = 12$ Outliers: none

Extremes: 52 and 89

28. $\frac{14}{4}$ = 3.5 gallons

29. 4^2 + 6(12 - 8) - 15 ÷ 3 = 16 + 6(4) - 15 ÷ 3

    = 16 + 24 - 5

    = 35

30. {120, 18, 3, -24, -52, -186, -219}

31. 160, 168, 176, 180, 184, 188, 192, 196, 200

    Median: 184

    UQ: $\frac{192 + 196}{2} = \frac{388}{2}$ = 194

    LQ: $\frac{168 + 176}{2} = \frac{344}{2}$ = 172

32. a. x: 11.4, 14, 14, 15, 15, 15.5, 16, 16.7,

    19, 24

    Median: $\frac{15 + 15.5}{2} = \frac{30.5}{2}$ = 15.25

    UQ: 16.7

    LQ: 14

    IQ Range: 16.7 - 14 = 3.7

    3.7 × 1.5 = 5.55

    16.7 + 5.55 = 22.25

    14 - 5.55 = 8.45

    Outliers: 24

    Extremes: 11.4 and 19.

    y: 9, 12, 13, 14, 15, 15.8, 16, 16, 18, 20

    Median: $\frac{15 + 15.8}{2} = \frac{30.8}{2}$ = 15.4

    UQ: 16

    LQ: 13

    IQ Range: 16 - 13 = 3

    3 × 1.5 = 4.5

    16 + 4.5 = 20.5

    13 - 4.5 = 8.5

    Outliers: none

    Extremes: 9 and 20

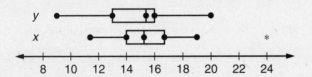

    b. Buy from manufacturer X; it has a better average life span.

33. Answers may vary. Sample answer: 1, 2, 3, 4, 5, 10, 10, 10, 10, 10.

34. Finding the median and quartile values is easier; finding the mean and mode is more difficult.

35. Before: 56, 64, 68, 70, 75, 78, 79, 79, 80, 83,

    84, 85, 86, 87, 89, 89, 90, 92, 95

    Median: 83

    UQ: 89

    LQ: 75

    IQ Range: 89 - 75 = 14

    14 × 1.5 = 21

    89 + 21 = 110

    75 - 21 = 54

    Outliers: none

    Extremes: 56 and 95

    After: 82, 87, 88, 88, 89, 89, 90, 90, 93, 93,

    93, 94, 95, 95, 96, 97, 99, 100, 100

    Median: 93

    UQ: 96

    LQ: 89

    IQ Range: 96 - 89 = 7

    7 × 1.5 = 10.5

    97 + 10.5 = 107.5

    89 - 10.5 = 78.5

    Outliers: none

    Extremes: 82 and 100

    The student scores did improve.

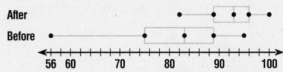

36. Answers may vary. Sample answer: All the numbers do not have to be displayed, but it does not show the frequency.

4-8 Scatter Plots

PAGE 160   CHECKING FOR UNDERSTANDING

1. Answers may vary. Sample answer: Collect two sets of data and form ordered pairs. Then graph the ordered pairs.

2. The line drawn where half the points are above it and half the points are below it would be slanted upward and to the right.

3. negative   4. positive

5. negative   6. positive

7. no relationship   8. positive

9. no relationship   10. negative

11. positive

PAGES 160-161   EXERCISES

12. positive   13. no relationship

14. no relationship   15. positive

16. negative   17. negative

39

18. a. the Chicago player who shot 24 times and made 14 field goals
    b. $C(2, 2)$
    c. No, both are positive.
    d. about 6
    e. 2
    f. There is a positive relationship for both teams.

19. $158 = s - 36$
    $158 + 36 = s - 36 + 36$
         $194 = s$

20. $5x + 32 < 42$
    $5x + 32 - 32 < 42 - 32$
              $5x < 10$
              $\frac{5x}{5} < \frac{10}{5}$
               $x < 2$

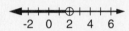
    -2 0 2 4 6

21. $h = -28 + 15 + 6 + (-30)$
      $= -13 + 6 + (-30)$
      $= -7 + (-30)$
      $= -37$

22. 11, 15, 20, 24, 26, 29, 32, 33, 36, 38, 42, 44, 47
    Median: 32
    UQ: $\frac{38 + 42}{2} = \frac{80}{2} = 40$
    LQ: $\frac{20 + 24}{2} = \frac{44}{2} = 22$
    IQ Range: $40 - 22 = 18$
    $18 \times 1.5 = 27$
    $40 + 27 = 67$
    $22 - 27 = -5$
    Outliers: none
    Extremes: 11 and 47

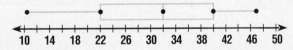
    10 14 18 22 26 30 34 38 42 46 50

23.
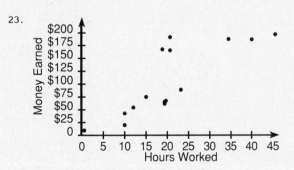
    a. (hours worked, money earned)
    b. yes, a positive relationship

24. a. Answers may vary. Sample answer: In warmer weather, students may study less and play outside more.
    b. no; Answers may vary. Sample answer: There may be another factor that relates to both factors.
    c. Answers may vary. Sample answer: study time, amount of sleep the night before a test
    d. $50 - 37 = 13$
    e. Answers may vary. Sample answer: The data might show no pattern exists on the plot or they may tend to form the same pattern.

25. Answers may vary. Sample answer: He could look for a positive slope if the scatter plot has amount of fertilizer on the horizontal axis and crop yield on the vertical axis.

Decision Making

PAGES 162-163
1. Wednesday and Thursday
2. yes
3. See students' work.
4. See students' work.
5. See students' work.
6. See students' work.

| 4-9 | Misleading Graphs and Statistics |

PAGES 165-166   CHECKING FOR UNDERSTANDING
1. Answers may vary. Sample answer: The graphs may use a different scale or a graph may only show part of the data.
2. Answers may vary. Sample answer: who was surveyed, how many people were surveyed, where was the survey taken
3. See students' work.
4. a. $8,000 - 6,000 = 2,000$
    The number of house sales increased by 2,000.
    b. The change in sale is relatively small, but the picture of the house grew wider and taller.
    c. yes; The change in the size of the houses indicates a larger change in sales than the actual change.

40

5. Mean: $\dfrac{88 + 86 + 85 + 78 + 88}{5} = \dfrac{425}{5} = 85$

Median: 86

Mode: 88

The students hope their teacher will use the mode because it is the highest.

PAGES 166-167   EXERCISES

6. **a.** Left graph is misleading.

   b. He would use the right graph, because it shows a smaller increase.

7. Mean: $\dfrac{45 + 60 + 63 + 75 + 75 + 90}{6} = \dfrac{408}{6} = 68$

   Median: $\dfrac{63 + 75}{2} = \dfrac{138}{2} = 69$

   Mode: 75

   The company would use the mean to promote low calorie count.

8. Yes, all interests and age groups can be represented.

9. No, most people at the concert would prefer that type of entertainment.

10. No, most apartment complexes do not allow pets.

11. No, not all age groups would be represented.

12. **a.**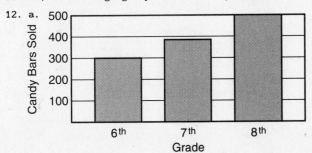

   b.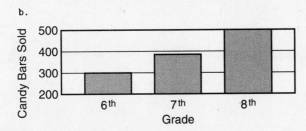

13. $15 \cdot 2 = 30$, $30 \cdot 6 = 180$

14.
$$-460 = -16a + 52$$
$$-460 - 52 = -16a + 52 - 52$$
$$-512 = -16a$$
$$\dfrac{-512}{-16} = \dfrac{-16a}{-16}$$
$$32 = a$$

15. no relationship; Fishing is mostly chance.

16. **a.** The fewer the number of doctors in the survey, the less reliable the results.

   b. No, it does not.

   c. Answers may vary. Sample answer: Multi-Zip may not be sold in Lincoln, Nebraska.

17. **a.**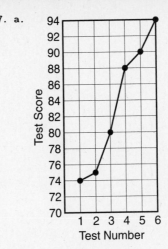

   b. Mean: $\dfrac{74 + 75 + 80 + 88 + 90 + 94}{6} = \dfrac{501}{6} = 83.5$

   Median: $\dfrac{80 + 88}{2} = \dfrac{168}{2} = 84$

   Mode: none

   Use the median because it is highest.

18. Answers may vary. Sample answer: Go to a soccer game and ask the people there.

19. **a.** No, the sample should contain cups from the beginning, middle, and end of production.

   b. Answers may vary. Sample answer: What is the past history of the product or is it a new product?

Chapter 4 Study Guide and Review

PAGE 168   COMMUNICATING MATHEMATICS

1. stem   2. scatter plot   3. histogram

4. range   5. ouliers   6. sample

7. mean

8. upper and lower quartile values, median, outliers, interquartile range

9. The mean is the average of the set and the median is the middle number.

PAGES 168-170   SKILLS AND CONCEPTS

10.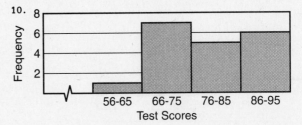

11.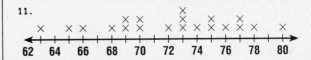

12.

4	58
5	136
6	02568
7	2379
8	24

7 | 3 means 73

13. 6.8, 7.1, 7.4, 8.2, 8.3, 8.5

Mean: $\dfrac{6.8 + 7.1 + 7.4 + 8.2 + 8.3 + 8.5}{6} = \dfrac{46.3}{6}$

  $= 7.7$

Median: $\dfrac{7.4 + 8.2}{2} = \dfrac{15.6}{2} = 7.8$

Mode: none

14. 20, 21, 26, 30, 35, 41, 41

Mean: $\dfrac{20 + 21 + 26 + 30 + 35 + 41 + 41}{7} = \dfrac{214}{7}$

  $= 30.6$

Median: 30

Mode: 41

15. 118, 132, 157, 173, 191

Mean: $\dfrac{118 + 132 + 157 + 173 + 191}{5} = \dfrac{771}{5} = 154.2$

Median: 157

Mode: none

16. 2, 3, 4, 4, 6, 8, 11, 12

Mean: $\dfrac{2 + 3 + 4 + 4 + 6 + 8 + 11 + 12}{8} = \dfrac{50}{8} = 6.3$

Median: $\dfrac{4 + 6}{2} = \dfrac{10}{2} = 5$

Mode: 4

17. 120, 126, 132, 137, 142, 144, 149, 151, 166

Range: 166 - 120 = 46

UQ: $\dfrac{149 + 151}{2} = \dfrac{300}{2} = 150$

LQ: $\dfrac{126 + 132}{2} = \dfrac{258}{2} = 129$

18. 1, 1, 1, 2, 2, 3, 3, 3, 4, 4, 5, 5, 6, 6, 6

Range: 6 - 1 = 5

UQ: 5

LQ: 2

19. 22, 24, 25, 28, 30

Range: 30 - 22 = 8

UQ: $\dfrac{28 + 30}{2} = \dfrac{58}{2} = 29$

LQ: $\dfrac{22 + 24}{2} = \dfrac{46}{2} = 23$

20. 12, 14, 15, 17, 18, 20

Median: $\dfrac{15 + 17}{2} = \dfrac{32}{2} = 16$ $4 \times 1.5 = 6$

UQ: 18 $18 + 6 = 24$

LQ: 14 $12 - 6 = 6$

IQ Range: 18 - 14 = 4   Outliers: none

Extremes: 12 and 20

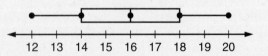

21. 20, 22, 23, 31, 35, 36, 37, 41, 42, 45, 49, 51, 54

Median: 37

UQ: $\dfrac{45 + 49}{2} = \dfrac{94}{2} = 47$

LQ: $\dfrac{23 + 31}{2} = \dfrac{54}{2} = 27$

IQ Range: 47 - 27 = 20

$20 \times 1.5 = 30$

$47 + 30 = 77$

$27 - 30 = -3$

Outliers: none

Extremes: 20 and 54

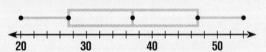

22. no relationship

23. negative

24. The right graph might be misleading because the scale is incorrect.

PAGE 170   APPLICATIONS AND PROBLEM SOLVING

25. a.

Denver to Newark Air Fares	
Cost($)	Frequency
201–400	9
401–600	2
601–800	5
801–1,000	2

b.

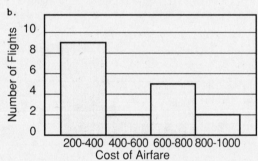

26. $\dfrac{78 + 85 + 83 + 76 + 80}{5} = \dfrac{402}{5} = 80.4$

Yes, Ling will receive a B.

27. 6, 7, 7, 8, 8, 8, 9, 10, 12, 12, 13, 14, 14, 15, 17

Median: 10 $6 \times 1.5 = 9$

UQ: 14 $14 + 9 = 23$

LQ: 8 $8 - 9 = -1$

IQ Range: 14 - 8 = 6   Outliers: none

Extremes: 6 and 17

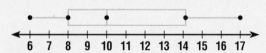

Chapter 4 Test

1. 6-8   **2.** 6   **3.** 8 + 6 + 9 + 5 + 2 = 30

4. 9 + 5 + 2 = 16

5.

Score	Tally	Frequency
31-35	||||	4
36-40		5
41-45		10
46-50		6

6.

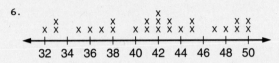

7.

```
3 | 23356788
4 | 011222334557899
5 | 00

4 | 2 means 42
```

8. 3   **9.** 2   **10.** 8

11. 31, 32, 33, 34

12. 12, 14, 14, 18, 19, 20, 23, 30

Mean: $\dfrac{12 + 14 + 14 + 18 + 19 + 20 + 23 + 30}{8}$

$= \dfrac{150}{8} = 18.75$

Median: $\dfrac{18 + 19}{2} = \dfrac{37}{2} = 18.5$

Mode: 14

13. 48 - 12 = 36

14. 12, 13, 15, 18, 20, 23, 25, 26, 29, 31, 34, 35, 38, 40, 41, 45, 48

Median: 29

15. UQ: $\dfrac{38 + 40}{2} = \dfrac{78}{2} = 39$

LQ: $\dfrac{18 + 20}{2} = \dfrac{38}{2} = 19$

16. 39 - 19 = 20

17. 20 × 1.5 = 30

Limits: 39 + 30 = 69

19 - 30 = -11

Outliers: none

18.

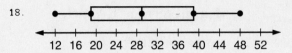

19.

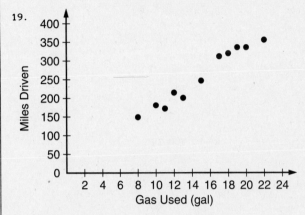

The data show a positive relationship.

20.

Points	Frequency
61-70	3
71-80	2
81-90	3
91-100	4
101-110	5
111-120	2
121-130	1

Answers may vary. Sample answer:

26, 37, 40, 40, 44, 53

Chapter 5   Investigations in Geometry

**5-1A   Mathematics Lab:
Measurement in Geometry**

PAGE 174   WHAT DO YOU THINK?

1. $\overline{AB}$, $\overline{JK}$; $\overline{CD}$, $\overline{LM}$; $\overline{HI}$, $\overline{RS}$

2. $\overline{AB} \cong \overline{JK}$; $\overline{CD} \cong \overline{LM}$; $\overline{HI} \cong \overline{RS}$

PAGE 174   EXTENSION

3. See students' work.

PAGE 175   WHAT DO YOU THINK?

4. Use the scale where $0°$ aligns with one side
   of the angle.

5. $\angle XYZ \cong \angle ABC$

PAGE 175   EXTENSION

6. See students' work.

5-1   Parallel Lines

PAGE 178   CHECKING FOR UNDERSTANDING

1. Parallel lines are the same distance apart and
   never meet.

2. Opposite pairs of sides are parallel.

3. Sample answers: opposite sides of tile lines;
   top and bottom of chalkboard

4.

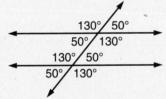

130° / 50°
50° / 130°
130° / 50°
50° / 130°

5. Two angles are supplementary if the sum of
   their angle measures is $180°$.

6. $\overline{PQ} \parallel \overline{SR}$, $\overline{PS} \parallel \overline{QR}$ 7. $\overline{WX} \parallel \overline{ZY}$, $\overline{WZ}$, $\overline{XY}$

8. $\overline{AB} \parallel \overline{ED}$, $\overline{BC} \parallel \overline{EF}$, $\overline{CD} \parallel \overline{FA}$

9. a. $m\angle a = m\angle h$ b. $m\angle b = 180° - m\angle a$
       $a = 60$ $= 180° - 60°$
                                    $= 120°$
                                 $b = 120$

   c. $m\angle c = m\angle b$ d. $m\angle d = m\angle a$
       $c = 120$ $d = 60$

e. $m\angle e = m\angle h$ f. $m\angle f = m\angle b$
   $e = 60$ $f = 120$

g. $m\angle g = m\angle f$
   $g = 120$

PAGE 179   EXERCISES

10. $\overline{AB} \parallel \overline{ED}$ 11. none

12. $\overline{ST} \parallel \overline{NM}$, $\overline{TO} \parallel \overline{NG}$, $\overline{OP} \parallel \overline{GI}$, $\overline{PM} \parallel \overline{IS}$

13. $m\angle 6 = m\angle 2$ 14. $m\angle 3 = m\angle 5$
    $m\angle 6 = 35°$ $m\angle 3 = 77°$

15. $m\angle 4 = m\angle 8$ 16. $m\angle 7 = m\angle 1$
    $m\angle 4 = 122°$ $m\angle 7 = 68°$

17. $9x = 36$ 18. $x + 30 = 68$
    $\dfrac{9x}{9} = \dfrac{36}{9}$ $x + 30 - 30 = 68 - 30$
                                     $x = 38$
    $x = 4$

19. $3x - 60 = 120$ 20. $\$5.00 - 1 \rightarrow \$4.99$
       $3x - 60 + 60 = 120 + 60$ $-\$2.49 - 1 \rightarrow \$2.48$
              $3x = 180$ $\$2.41$
       $\dfrac{3x}{3} = \dfrac{180}{3}$
              $x = 60$

21. $|10| = 10$

22. The mean would be used since the range is not
    great.

23. a. They are parallel.
    b. They are parallel.
    c. $90°$

24. 30; Alternate exterior angles are congruent.

25. Two lines parallel to the same line are parallel
    to each other.

**5-1B   Mathematics Lab:
Constructing Parallel Lines**

PAGE 180   WHAT DO YOU THINK?

1. corresponding lines

2. error in construction

5-2   Use a Venn Diagram

PAGE 182   CHECKING FOR UNDERSTANDING

1. It represents states that produce over 100
   million bushels of all three grains.

2. 11 states   3. a. 13 states
                               b. 0 states

4. wheat cereal   rice

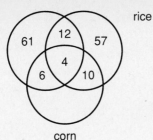

corn

PAGE 182   PROBLEM SOLVING

5. a. Cooking Club Preferences

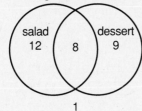

b. 12 people   **c.** 1 person

6. $500 + c = 625$

$500 - 500 + c = 625 - 500$

$c = 125 \text{ cm}^3$

7. $n + 29 = 2n - 6$

$n + 29 + 6 = 2n - 6 + 6$

$n + 35 = 2n$

$n - n + 35 = 2n - n$

$35 = n$

8. a. 4 + 1 = 5 students

b. 7 + 2 + 1 + 4 + 3 + 8 = 25 students

c. no; There are 7 + 2 + 1 + 4 or 14 students in the band and 6 + 2 + 1 + 3 or 12 students in the orchestra.

5-3   Classifying Triangles

PAGES 184-185   CHECKING FOR UNDERSTANDING

1. Equilateral triangles are isosceles triangles, but isosceles triangles are not equilateral triangles.

2. 180

3.

4. perpendicular to

5. Solve $100 + 50 + x = 180$

$150 + x = 180$

$150 - 150 + x = 180 - 150$

$x = 30$

6. scalene, right   **7.** scalene, acute

8. isoscles, acute   **9.** equilateral, acute

---

10. scalene, obtuse   **11.** isosceles, right

PAGES 185-186   EXERCISES

12. equilateral, acute   **13.** isosceles, right

14. isosceles, obtuse   **15.** scalene, right

16. isosceles, acute   **17.** equilateral, acute

18. true;

19. true;   8.25 m

6.25 m

20. false;

21. false;

22. true;

23. true;

24. $90 + 32 + x = 180$

$122 + x = 180$

$122 - 122 + x = 180 - 122$

$x = 58$

25. $2x + 64 + 36 = 180$

$2x + 100 = 180$

$2x + 100 - 100 = 180 - 100$

$2x = 80$

$\dfrac{2x}{2} = \dfrac{80}{2}$

$x = 40$

26. $b - 19 = 73$ **27.** $e = 8(-3)(-4)^2$

$b - 19 + 19 = 73 + 19$ $e = 8(-3)(16)$

$b = 92$ $e = -24(16)$

$e = -384$

45

28. $\frac{3}{4}$ of the days

29. $\overline{HI} \parallel \overline{KJ}$

30. 3, 1, equilateral

4, 0

5, 1, isosceles

6, 1, equilateral

7, 2, isosceles

9, 3, equilateral, isosceles, scalene

12, 3, equilateral, isosceles, scalene

a. yes; for 4 units

b. no; 5 + 2 is not greater than 7.

c. The sum of the lengths of two sides of a triangle must be greater than the length of the third side.

31. a. See students' work.

b. Triangles will not collapse as easily as other figures.

32.

33. scalene, acute; scalene, right; scalene, obtuse; isosceles, acute; isosceles, right; isosceles, obtuse; equilateral, acute

34. a.
$$x + 90 = 180$$
$$x + 90 - 90 = 180 - 90$$
$$x = 90$$

b.
$$A = \frac{1}{2}bh$$
$$A = \frac{1}{2}(7)(9)$$
$$A = \frac{1}{2}(63)$$
$$A = 31.5 \text{ cm}^2$$

5-4 Classifying Quadrilaterals

PAGES 188-189   CHECKING FOR UNDERSTANDING

1. 4 sides

2.

3. A parallelogram has two pairs of opposite sides that are parallel, while a trapezoid has only one pair of opposite sides that are parallel.

4. 360

5. Q, P, R, S, RH

6. Q, T

7. Q

8.
$$90 + 90 + 120 + d = 360$$
$$300 + d = 360$$
$$300 - 300 + d = 360 - 300$$
$$d = 60$$
$$m\angle D = 60°$$

PAGES 189-190   EXERCISES

9. Q, P

10. Q, P, R

11. Q, P, R, S, RH

12. Q, P, RH

13. Q

14. Q, T

15. rhombus, parallelogram, rectangle, square

16. rectangle, square

17. square, rhombus

18. true;

19. false;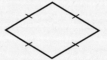

20. false;

21.
$$2a + 40 + 110 + 70 = 360$$
$$2a + 220 = 360$$
$$2a + 220 - 220 = 360 - 220$$
$$2a = 140$$
$$\frac{2a}{2} = \frac{140}{2}$$
$$a = 70$$

22.
$$60 + x + 60 + x = 360$$
$$2x + 120 = 360$$
$$2x + 120 - 120 = 360 - 120$$
$$2x = 240$$
$$\frac{2x}{2} = \frac{240}{2}$$
$$x = 120$$

23.
$$P = 2\ell + 2w$$
$$P = 2(3) + 2(5.5)$$
$$P = 6 + 11$$
$$P = 17 \text{ cm}$$

$$A = \ell w$$
$$A = 3 \cdot 5.5$$
$$A = 16.5 \text{ cm}^2$$

24. quadrant IV

25.
$$4x + 60 + 72 = 180$$
$$4x + 132 = 180$$
$$4x + 132 - 132 = 180 - 132$$
$$4x = 48$$
$$\frac{4x}{4} = \frac{48}{4}$$
$$x = 12$$

26.

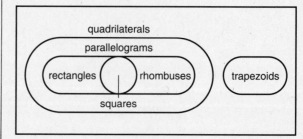

27. Sample answer:

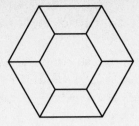

28. rectangle, square

29. a.

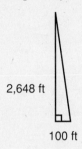

2,648 ft

100 ft

  b. Yes, the height would only be 176 feet
     instead of 2,648 feet.

Mid-Chapter Review

PAGE 190

1. $\overline{AB} \parallel \overline{CD}$

2. $x° = m\angle BCD$
   $x° = 64°$
   $x = 64$

3. scalene, acute

4.
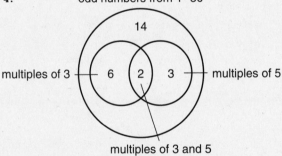

odd numbers from 1–50

14

multiples of 3 — 6   2   3 — multiples of 5

multiples of 3 and 5

5. See students' work. square

5-5A	**Mathematics Lab: Reflections**

PAGE 191   WHAT DO YOU THINK?

1. yes   2. trapezoid

3. See students' work.

4.
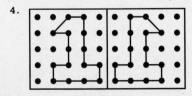

5.
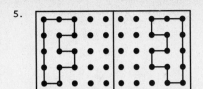

6.
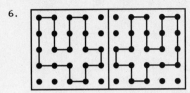

7.
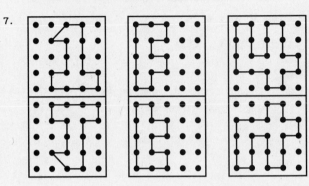

They are rotations of the first reflections.

5-5	**Symmetry**

PAGE 194   CHECKING FOR UNDERSTANDING

1. In line symmetry, the right half is a reflection
   of the left half.

2. Sample answer: 3. 360

4.   5.
        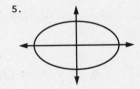

6.

7. all of them

47

8.

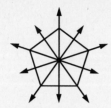

9. no line symmetry

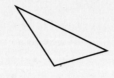

10.

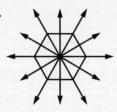

11. yes

12. yes   13. yes

14. rectangle, square, rhombus; See students' work.

15. rhombus, parallelogram, rectangle, square;
    See students' work.

16. yes

17. $-281 - (-52) = j$
    $-281 + 52 = j$
    $-229 = j$

18. positive relationship

19. $120 + 120 + 2x + 60 = 360$
    $300 + 2x = 360$
    $300 - 300 + 2x = 360 - 300$
    $2x = 60$
    $\frac{2x}{2} = \frac{60}{2}$
    $x = 30$

20. See students' work.

21. $A, B, C, D, E, H, I, K, M, O, T, U, V, W, X, Y$

22. a.   b.   c.

5-6A   Mathematics Lab: Dilations

1. The enlargement is 3 times taller.

2. a grid with squares that are smaller than the original

3. no; Enlarging or reducing does not distort the figure.

4. a. See students' work.
   b. It is $\frac{1}{3}$ smaller than the original.

5-6   Congruence and Similarity

1. They must have the same size and the same shape.

2. Two figures are similar if they have the same shape but differ in size.

3.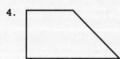

4.

5. They have the same shape, as well as being the same size.

6. similar; The triangles have the same shape but different sizes.

7. congruent; The triangles have the same size and shape.

8. neither; The parallelograms have different shapes.

9. similar; The triangles have the same shape but different sizes.

10. congruent; The trapezoids have the same size and shape.

11. congruent; The squares have the same size and shape.

12. neither; The figures do not have the same shape.

13. similar; The triangles have the same shape but different sizes.

14. $3x - 5 = 70$
    $3x - 5 + 5 = 70 + 5$
    $3x = 75$
    $\frac{3x}{3} = \frac{75}{3}$
    $x = 25$

15. $6x = 108$
    $\frac{6x}{6} = \frac{108}{6}$
    $x = 18$

16. rounding:

$$5,381 \rightarrow 5,000$$
$$+ 3,416 \rightarrow + 3,000$$
$$8,000$$

front-end estimation:

5	,381 $\rightarrow$	5,	3	81
+ 3	,416	+ 3,	4	16
8	,000	+	7	00 = 8,700

17. $5a^2 - (b + c) = 5 \cdot 3^2 - (8 + 10)$
$$= 5 \cdot 3^2 - 18$$
$$= 5 \cdot 9 - 18$$
$$= 45 - 18$$
$$= 27$$

18. yes

19. a. $\$114 \div 4 = \$28.50$

  b. family show

20. $x = 2 \cdot 4 \qquad y = \frac{1}{2} \cdot 10 \qquad z = 53$

  $x = 8 \qquad y = 5$

21. See students' work.

5-6B Mathematics Lab: Constructing Congruent Triangles

1. $\overline{AB} \cong \overline{GH}$; $\overline{BC} \cong \overline{HI}$; $\overline{CA} \cong \overline{IG}$

2. Corresponding angles are congruent.

3. $\triangle ABC \cong \triangle GHI$

5-7 Transformations and M. C. Escher

1. translation, rotation

2. A tessellation is a repetitive, interlocking pattern.

3.
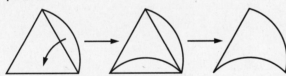

4.
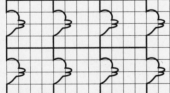

5.
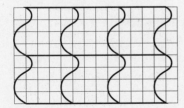

6.
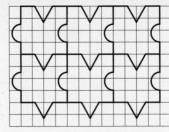

7. Exercise 4: translation; 5: rotation; 6: two translations.

8.
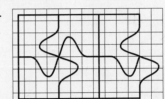

9.
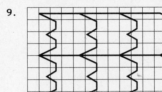

10.
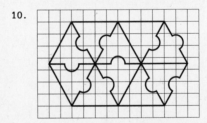

11.
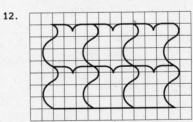

12.
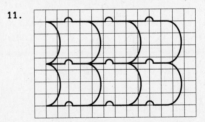

13.
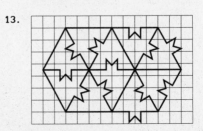

14.
$$\frac{a}{15} - 5 = 1$$
$$\frac{a}{15} - 5 + 5 = 1 + 5$$
$$\frac{a}{15} = 6$$
$$15\left(\frac{a}{15}\right) = 6 \cdot 15$$
$$a = 90$$

15.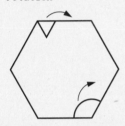

16. congruent

17. a. hexagon

    b. rotation

    c.

Rotate changes about the midpoint of the side.

18. a. See students' work.

    b. hexagon

    c. rotation

19. See students' work.

20. a.   **b.**

Chapter 5 Study Guide and Review

PAGE 206   COMMUNICATING MATHEMATICS

1. transversal   **2.** rotations

3. rhombus   **4.** line symmetry

5. obtuse   **6.** ||

7. ⊥   **8.** ~

9. If a figure can be turned less than 360° about its center and it looks like the original, then the figure has rotational symmetry.

10.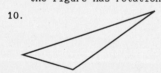

PAGES 206–207   SKILLS AND CONCEPTS

11. $\overline{WX}$ || $\overline{ZY}$, $\overline{ZW}$ || $\overline{YX}$ **12.** $\overline{DH}$ || $\overline{NM}$

13. scalene, right   **14.** isosceles, obtuse

15. Q, P, RH   **16.** Q, T

17.   **18.**

19. yes   **20.** no

21. similar   **22.** neither

23.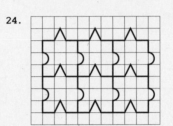

24.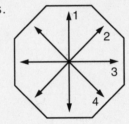

PAGE 208   APPLICATIONS AND PROBLEM SOLVING

25. 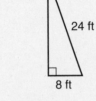   4 pairs

26. a.   **b.** scalene right triangle

24 ft

8 ft

27. Atlantic City: 9 + 3 + 5 + 8 = 25

Barnegat Bay: 8 + 3 + 5 + 6 = 22

Cape May: 10 + 8 + 5 + 6 = 29

Cape May had the most votes.

28. a.

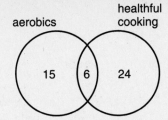

aerobics   healthful cooking

15   6   24

b. 15 + 6 + 24 = 45 members

Chapter 5 Test

1. $m\angle 1 = 180° - m\angle 4$
$m\angle 1 = 180° - 40°$
$m\angle 1 = 140°$

2. $m\angle 2 = m\angle 4$
$m\angle 2 = 40°$

3. $m\angle 3 = m\angle 1$
$m\angle 3 = 140°$

4. $m\angle 5 = m\angle 1$
$m\angle 5 = 140°$

5. yes;

6. equilateral, acute

7. scalene, acute

8. scalene, obtuse

9.

10. $66 + 114 + 66 + 2x = 360$
$246 + 2x = 360$
$246 - 246 + 2x = 360 - 246$
$2x = 114$
$\frac{2x}{2} = \frac{114}{2}$
$x = 57$

11. Q, P, R

12. Q, T

13. Q, P, R, S, RH

14.

15. yes;

16. yes

17. $2x - 4 = 28$
$2x - 4 + 4 = 28 + 4$
$2x = 32$
$\frac{2x}{2} = \frac{32}{2}$
$x = 16$

18. $3x - 15 = 60$
$3x - 15 + 15 = 60 + 15$
$3x = 75$
$\frac{3x}{3} = \frac{75}{3}$
$x = 25$

19. rotation

20.

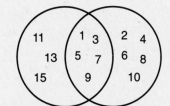

11   1   3   2   4
13   5   7   6   8
15   9   10

odd numbers from 1-15   counting numbers from 1-10

Sample answer:

Chapter 6   Patterns and Number Sense

6-1   ## Divisibility Patterns

1. When 42 is divided by 7, the remainder is zero.

2. Sample answers: 2, 39; 3, 26; 6, 13

3. If a number is divisible by 6, then it is also divisible by 2 and 2 is not a factor of an odd number.

4. Since 3 is a factor of 9, it is also a factor of all numbers divisible by 9.

5. 2: The ones digit is divisible by 2. So 58 is divisible by 2.

   3: The sum of the digits, 5 + 8 = 13, is not divisible by 3. So 58 is not divisible by 3.

   4: The number formed by the last 2 digits, 58, is not divisible by 4. So 58 is not divisible by 4.

   5: The ones digit is not 0 or 5. So 58 is not divisible by 5.

   6: The number 58 is divisible by 2 but not by 3. So 58 is not divisible by 6.

   8: The number formed by the last 3 digits 58, is not divisible by 8. So 58 is not divisible by 8.

   9: The sum of the digits, 5 + 8 = 13, is not divisible by 9. So 58 is not divisible by 9.

   10: The ones digit is not 0. So 58 is not divisible by 10.

6. 2: The ones digit is not divisible by 2. So 153 is not divisible by 2.

   3: The sum of the digits, 1 + 5 + 3 = 9, is divisible by 3. So 153 is divisible by 3.

   4: The number formed by the last 2 digits, 53, is not divisible by 4. So 153 is not divisible by 4.

   5: The ones digit is not 0 or 5. So 153 is not divisible by 5.

   6: The number 153 is divisible by 3 but not by 2. So 153 is not divisible by 6.

   8: The number formed by the last 3 digits, 153, is not divisible by 8. So 153 is not divisible by 8.

   9: The sum of the digits, 1 + 5 + 3 = 9, is divisible by 9. So 153 is divisible by 9.

   10: The ones digit is not 0. So 153 is not divisible by 10.

7. 2: The ones digit is divisible by 2. So -330 is divisible by 2.

   3: The sum of the digits, 3 + 3 + 0 = 6, is divisible by 3. So -330 is divisible by 3.

   4: The number formed by the last 2 digits, 30, is not divisible by 4. So -330 is not divisible by 4.

   5: The ones digit is 0. So -330 is divisible by 5.

   6: The number -330 is divisible by 2 and 3. So -330 is divisible by 6.

   8: The number formed by the last 3 digits, 330, is not divisible by 8. So -330 is not divisible by 8.

   9: The sum of the digits, 3 + 3 + 0 = 6, is not divisible by 9. So -330 is not divisible by 9.

   10: The ones digit is 0. So -330 is divisible by 10.

8. 2: The ones digit is not divisible by 2. So 881 is not divisible by 2.

   3: The sum of the digits, 8 + 8 + 1 = 17, is not divisible by 3. So 881 is not divisible by 3.

   4: The number formed by the last two digits, 81, is not divisible by 4. So 881 is not divisible by 4.

   5: The ones digit is not 0 or 5. So 881 is not divisible by 5.

   6: The number 881 is not divisible by 2 or 3. So 881 is not divisible by 6.

   8: The number formed by the last 3 digits, 881, is not divisible by 8. So 881 is not divisible by 8.

   9: The sum of the digits, 8 + 8 + 1 = 17, is not divisible by 9. So 881 is not divisible by 9.

   10: The ones digit is not 0, so 881 is not divisible by 10.

9. 2: The ones digit is not divisible by 2. So
       12,345 is not divisible by 2.

    3: The sum of the digits, 1 + 2 + 3 + 4 + 5 =
       15, is divisible by 3. So 12,345 is divisible
       by 3.

    4: The number formed by the last two digits, 45,
       is not divisible by 4. So 12,345 is not
       divisible by 4.

    5: The ones digit is 5. So 12,345 is divisible
       by 5.

    6: The number 12,345 is divisible by 3 but not
       by 2. So 12,345 is not divisible by 6.

    8: The number formed by the last 3 digits, 345,
       is not divisible by 8. So 12,345 is not
       divisible by 8.

    9: The sum of the digits, 1 + 2 + 3 + 4 + 5 =
       15, is not divisible by 9. So 12,345 is not
       divisible by 9.

   10: The ones digit is not 0. So 12,345 is not
       divisible by 10.

10. The ones digit of 228 is divisible by 2, so 2 is
    a factor of 228. The sum of the digits of 228,
    2 + 2 + 8 = 12, is divisible by 3. So 3 is a
    factor of 228. Therefore 6 is a factor of 228.

11. The ones digit of 523 is not 0 or 5. So 5 is not
    a factor of 523.

12. The sum of the digits of 231, 2 + 3 + 1 = 6, is
    not divisible by 9. So 231 is not divisible by 9.

13. The number formed by the last two digits of 432,
    32, is divisible by 4. So 432 is divisible by 4.

14. Sample answers: 2 × 63, 3 × 42, 6 × 21, 7 × 18,
    9 × 14

15. Sample answers: 6, 12, 18

PAGE 214   EXERCISES

16. Yes, the ones digit is divisible by 2.

17. Yes, the ones digit is 5.

18. No, the sum of the digits, 19, is not divisible
    by 3.

19. No, the sum of the digits, 11, is not divisible
    by 3.

20. Yes, the number formed by the last three digits,
    112, is divisible by 8.

21. Yes, the sum of the digits, 9, is divisible by
    9.

22. No, the number formed by the last two digits,
    42, is not divisible by 4.

23. No, the ones digit is not 0.

24. Sample answers: 2 × 492, 3 × 328, 4 × 246,
    6 × 164, 8 × 123

25. Sample answers: 2 × 21,605, 5 × 8,642,
    10 × 4,321

26. Sample answer: 36

27. Sample answer: 486

28. Sample answer: 3,996

29. Sample answer: 26,378

30. 9 · 10¢ + 9 · 11¢ = 90¢ + 99¢
                      = \$1.89

31. $p = -654 - 175$ 32. probably no
    $p = -654 + (-175)$ relationship
    $p = -829$

33.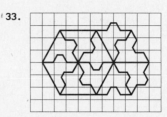

34. 1 × 144, 2 × 72, 3 × 48, 4 × 36, 6 × 24, 8 × 18,
    9 × 16, 12 × 12

35. 999,998; The number formed by the last two
    digits, 98, is not divisible by 4. The sum of
    the digits, 53, is not divisible by 9.

36. 96, 90, 84, 72, and 60 each have 12 factors.

6-2   Prime Factorization

PAGE 217   CHECKING FOR UNDERSTANDING

1. Prime numbers have exactly two factors while
   composite numbers have more than two factors.

2.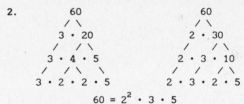

3. $2^3 \cdot 3^2 = 8 \cdot 9$
            $= 72$

4. composite; 52 = 2 × 26   5. prime

6. prime   7. composite; 51 = 3 × 17

8.   57   9.   36
      /\   /\
   3 · 19   3 · 12
   57 = 3 · 19   /   /\
                          3 · 2 · 6
                         /   / /\
                      3 · 2 · 2 · 3
                      $36 = 2^2 \cdot 3^2$

10.   90   11.   180
      /\   /\
   3 · 30   3 · 60
   / /\   / /\
 3 · 3 · 10   3 · 2 · 30
 / / /\   / / /\
3 · 3 · 2 · 5   3 · 2 · 2 · 15
$90 = 2 \cdot 3^2 \cdot 5$ / / / /\
                   3 · 2 · 2 · 3 · 5
                   $180 = 2^2 \cdot 3^2 \cdot 5$

12. prime

13. composite; $93 = 3 \cdot 31$

14. composite; $77 = 7 \times 11$

15. composite; $68 = 2 \cdot 34$

16. neither

17. composite; $453 = 3 \cdot 151$

18. composite; $4,300 = 4 \cdot 1,075$

19. prime   20. 2

21. $81 = 3 \cdot 27$ 22. $605 = 5 \cdot 121$
    $81 = 3 \cdot 3 \cdot 9$ $605 = 5 \cdot 11 \cdot 11$
    $81 = 3 \cdot 3 \cdot 3 \cdot 3$ $605 = 5 \cdot 11^2$
    $81 = 3^4$

23. $64 = 2 \cdot 32$ 24. $31 = 1 \cdot 31$
    $64 = 2 \cdot 2 \cdot 16$
    $64 = 2 \cdot 2 \cdot 2 \cdot 8$
    $64 = 2 \cdot 2 \cdot 2 \cdot 2 \cdot 4$
    $64 = 2 \cdot 2 \cdot 2 \cdot 2 \cdot 2 \cdot 2$
    $64 = 2^6$

25. $400 = 5 \cdot 80$
    $400 = 5 \cdot 5 \cdot 16$
    $400 = 5 \cdot 5 \cdot 2 \cdot 8$
    $400 = 5 \cdot 5 \cdot 2 \cdot 2 \cdot 4$
    $400 = 5 \cdot 5 \cdot 2 \cdot 2 \cdot 2 \cdot 2$
    $400 = 2^4 \cdot 5^2$

26. $-144 = -1 \cdot 3 \cdot 48$
    $-144 = -1 \cdot 3 \cdot 3 \cdot 16$
    $-144 = -1 \cdot 3 \cdot 3 \cdot 2 \cdot 8$
    $-144 = -1 \cdot 3 \cdot 3 \cdot 2 \cdot 2 \cdot 4$
    $-144 = -1 \cdot 3 \cdot 3 \cdot 2 \cdot 2 \cdot 2 \cdot 2$
    $-144 = -1 \cdot 2^4 \cdot 3^2$

27. $-2,700 = -1 \cdot 3 \cdot 900$
    $-2,700 = -1 \cdot 3 \cdot 3 \cdot 300$
    $-2,700 = -1 \cdot 3 \cdot 3 \cdot 3 \cdot 100$
    $-2,700 = -1 \cdot 3 \cdot 3 \cdot 3 \cdot 5 \cdot 20$
    $-2,700 = -1 \cdot 3 \cdot 3 \cdot 3 \cdot 5 \cdot 5 \cdot 4$
    $-2,700 = -1 \cdot 3 \cdot 3 \cdot 3 \cdot 5 \cdot 5 \cdot 2 \cdot 2$
    $-2,700 = -1 \cdot 2^2 \cdot 3^3 \cdot 5^2$

28. $20,310 = 5 \cdot 4,062$ 29. $4m < 24$
    $20,310 = 5 \cdot 2 \cdot 2,031$ $\dfrac{4m}{4} < \dfrac{24}{4}$
    $20,310 = 5 \cdot 2 \cdot 3 \cdot 677$ $m < 6$
    $20,310 = 2 \cdot 3 \cdot 5 \cdot 677$

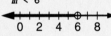

30.

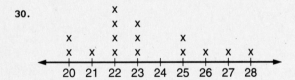

31. no symmetry

32. The sum of the digits, 15, is divisible by 3.
    So 672 is divisible by 3.

33. a. 3, 5; 5, 7; 11, 13; 17, 19; 29, 31; 41, 43;
       59, 61; 71, 73
    b. 6, 12, 18, 30; They are multiples of 6; yes;
       Because they are even and divisible by 3.

34. $9 = 3 \cdot 3$ $36 = 3 \cdot 12$
    $9 = 3^2$ $36 = 3 \cdot 3 \cdot 4$
                                 $36 = 3 \cdot 3 \cdot 2 \cdot 2$
                                 $36 = 2^2 \cdot 3^2$

    $100 = 5 \cdot 20$
    $100 = 5 \cdot 5 \cdot 4$
    $100 = 5 \cdot 5 \cdot 2 \cdot 2$
    $100 = 2^2 \cdot 5^2$

    a. All exponents are even.
    b. yes; They either have two prime factors or
       the two factors are also perfect squares.

35. $3a + 4b = 3 \cdot 5 + 4 \cdot 4$
            $= 15 + 16$
            $= 31$; prime

36. 2, 3   37. 41; $41^2 - 41 + 41 = 41^2$
                                        $= 1,681$

Mathematics Lab: Basketball Math

1. 1, 3, 7, 9
2. They are odd numbers and not factors of 10.
3. 1   4. The greatest common factor is 1.
5. The team got a water break when a number was
   relatively prime with 10.

6-3 ## Make a List

1. Square it.   2. 8 is not a double or triple
                        of a prime number.

3. 2 factors: 53; 3 factors: 121;
   4 factors: 51; 5 factors: 81
4. 6; 123, 132, 213, 231, 312, 321
5. 81, 625, 2,401; n^4, where n is prime

6. After Marty takes the first slice of pizza, there are 8 slices left. Eight slices of pizza can be evenly distributed among 4 or 8 people. Note that even though 8 is also divisible by 2, this does not satisfy the conditions of the problem.

7. $108 \div 9 = 12$ teams

8.
Number of Packages of 75	$350 - 75n$	Number from the Second Column Divisible by 4?
1	275	no
2	200	yes
3	125	no
4	50	no

2 packages

9. Let n = amount of water in the beaker.

$\frac{1}{2}\left(\frac{n}{2}\right) = 225$

$\frac{n}{4} = 225$

$4\left(\frac{n}{4}\right) = 225 \cdot 4$

$n = 900$ mL

10. Factor 14.

11. After Mary takes the first muffin there are 20 muffins left. Twenty muffins can be evenly distributed among 2, 4, 5, 10 or 20 people.

12. See students' work.

6-4 Greatest Common Factor

1. Find the product of the common prime factors.

2.
```
        120                    168
        /\                     /\
      5 · 24                 7 · 24
      /  /\                  /  /\
     5 · 3 · 8              7 · 3 · 8
     /  /  /\               /  /  /\
    5 · 3 · 2 · 4          7 · 3 · 2 · 4
    /  /  /  /\            /  /  /  /\
   5 ·(3)·(2)·(2)·(2)    7 ·(3)·(2)·(2)·(2)
```

3. $2 \cdot 2 \cdot 3 = 12$ 4. Sample answer: 30, 45

5. $2 \cdot 2 = 4$ 6. 5   7. $2 \cdot 7 = 14$

8. $60 = 2 \cdot 2 \cdot 3 \cdot 5$ 9. $9 = 3 \cdot 3$

$105 = 3 \cdot 5 \cdot 7$ $15 = 3 \cdot 5$

GCF $= 3 \cdot 5 = 15$ $24 = 2 \cdot 2 \cdot 2 \cdot 3$

GCF $= 3$

10. $15 = 3 \cdot 5$ 11. $18 = 2 \cdot 3 \cdot 3$

$45 = 3 \cdot 3 \cdot 5$ $27 = 3 \cdot 3 \cdot 3$

GCF $= 3 \cdot 5 = 15$ GCF $= 3 \cdot 3 = 9$

12. factors of 7: 1, 7

factors of 11: 1, 11

GCF $= 1$

13. $26 = 2 \cdot 13$

$34 = 2 \cdot 17$

$64 = 2 \cdot 2 \cdot 2 \cdot 2 \cdot 2 \cdot 2$

GCF $= 2$

14. $8 = 2 \cdot 2 \cdot 2$ 15. $16 = 2 \cdot 2 \cdot 2 \cdot 2$

$34 = 2 \cdot 17$ $24 = 2 \cdot 2 \cdot 2 \cdot 3$

GCF $= 2$ GCF $= 2 \cdot 2 \cdot 2 = 8$

16. $36 = 2 \cdot 2 \cdot 3 \cdot 3$ 17. $125 = 5 \cdot 5 \cdot 5$

$27 = 3 \cdot 3 \cdot 3$ $100 = 2 \cdot 2 \cdot 5 \cdot 5$

GCF $= 3 \cdot 3 = 9$ GCF $= 5 \cdot 5 = 25$

18. $28 = 2 \cdot 2 \cdot 7$

$56 = 2 \cdot 2 \cdot 2 \cdot 7$

GCF $= 2 \cdot 2 \cdot 7 = 28$

19. $96 = 2 \cdot 2 \cdot 2 \cdot 2 \cdot 2 \cdot 3$

$108 = 2 \cdot 2 \cdot 3 \cdot 3 \cdot 3$

GCF $= 2 \cdot 2 \cdot 3 = 12$

20. $12 = 2 \cdot 2 \cdot 3$ 21. $10 = 2 \cdot 5$

$18 = 2 \cdot 3 \cdot 3$ $15 = 3 \cdot 5$

$30 = 2 \cdot 3 \cdot 5$ $30 = 2 \cdot 3 \cdot 5$

GCF $= 2 \cdot 3 = 6$ GCF $= 5$

22. $45 = 3 \cdot 3 \cdot 5$ 23. $210 = 2 \cdot 3 \cdot 5 \cdot 7$

$105 = 3 \cdot 5 \cdot 7$ $330 = 2 \cdot 3 \cdot 5 \cdot 11$

$75 = 3 \cdot 5 \cdot 5$ $150 = 2 \cdot 3 \cdot 5 \cdot 5$

GCF $= 3 \cdot 5 = 15$ GCF $= 2 \cdot 3 \cdot 5 = 30$

24. $510 = 2 \cdot 3 \cdot 5 \cdot 17$ 25. If the units digits

$714 = 2 \cdot 3 \cdot 7 \cdot 17$ are 0 or 5.

$306 = 2 \cdot 3 \cdot 3 \cdot 17$

GCF $= 2 \cdot 3 \cdot 17 = 102$

26. $3 \cdot 5 = 15$

27. $864 \div 1,000 = 0.864 \rightarrow 864$ mL $= 0.864$ L

28. $|-21| = 21$ 29. scalene, obtuse

30. $56 = 7 \cdot 8$

$56 = 7 \cdot 2 \cdot 4$

$56 = 7 \cdot 2 \cdot 2 \cdot 2$

$56 = 2^3 \cdot 7$

31. a. $30 = 2 \cdot 3 \cdot 5$

   $24 = 2 \cdot 2 \cdot 2 \cdot 3$

   GCF $= 2 \cdot 3 = 6$

   6 in. × 6 in. tile

b.

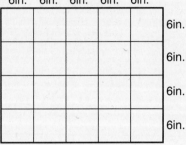

   20 tiles

32. $24 = 2 \cdot 2 \cdot 2 \cdot 3$ **33.** Sample answer:

   $18 = 2 \cdot 3 \cdot 3$ 7, 14, 21

   $12 = 2 \cdot 2 \cdot 3$

   GCF $= 2 \cdot 3 = 6$ times

34. a. $8p = 2 \cdot 2 \cdot 2 \cdot p$

   $16p = 2 \cdot 2 \cdot 2 \cdot 2 \cdot p$

   GCF $= 2 \cdot 2 \cdot 2 \cdot p = 8p$

b. $15p = 3 \cdot 5 \cdot p$

   $27p = 3 \cdot 3 \cdot 3 \cdot p$

   GCF $= 3p$

35. a. true; Their only common factor is 1.

b. false; 4 and 9 are relatively prime but neither is prime.

6-5 Rational Numbers

PAGES 225-226   CHECKING FOR UNDERSTANDING

1. if it can be expressed in the form $\frac{a}{b}$, where a and b are integers and $b \neq 0$

2. $\frac{3}{4}$ 3. If the GCF of the numerator and the denominator is 1.

4. Divide 20 and 25 by their GCF.

5. rational numbers   6. rational numbers

7. rational numbers

8. whole numbers, integers, rational numbers

9. $-\frac{42}{48} = -\frac{\overset{1}{\cancel{2}} \cdot \overset{1}{\cancel{3}} \cdot 7}{\cancel{2} \cdot 2 \cdot 2 \cdot 2 \cdot \cancel{3}} = -\frac{7}{8}$

10. simplest form

11. $\frac{8}{16} = \frac{\overset{1}{\cancel{2}} \cdot \overset{1}{\cancel{2}} \cdot \overset{1}{\cancel{2}}}{\cancel{2} \cdot \cancel{2} \cdot \cancel{2} \cdot 2} = \frac{1}{2}$ 12. $\frac{13}{52} = \frac{\overset{1}{\cancel{13}}}{4 \cdot \cancel{13}} = \frac{1}{4}$

13. simplest form

PAGE 226   EXERCISES

14. rational numbers   15. rational numbers

16. integers, rational numbers

17. whole numbers, integers, rational numbers

18. $-\frac{2}{8} = -\frac{\overset{1}{\cancel{2}}}{\underset{1}{\cancel{2}} \cdot 2 \cdot 2} = -\frac{1}{4}$

19. $-\frac{3}{12} = -\frac{\overset{1}{\cancel{3}}}{2 \cdot 2 \cdot \underset{1}{\cancel{3}}} = -\frac{1}{4}$

20. $\frac{6}{21} = \frac{2 \cdot \overset{1}{\cancel{3}}}{\underset{1}{\cancel{3}} \cdot 7} = \frac{2}{7}$ 21. $\frac{24}{54} = \frac{\overset{1}{\cancel{2}} \cdot 2 \cdot 2 \cdot \overset{1}{\cancel{3}}}{\underset{1}{\cancel{2}} \cdot \underset{1}{\cancel{3}} \cdot 3 \cdot 3} = \frac{4}{9}$

22. $-\frac{5}{8}$ 23. $\frac{3}{51} = \frac{\overset{1}{\cancel{3}}}{\underset{1}{\cancel{3}} \cdot 17} = \frac{1}{17}$

24. $-\frac{10}{16} = -\frac{\overset{1}{\cancel{2}} \cdot 5}{\cancel{2} \cdot 2 \cdot 2 \cdot 2} = -\frac{5}{8}$

25. $-\frac{45}{72} = -\frac{\overset{1}{\cancel{3}} \cdot \overset{1}{\cancel{3}} \cdot 5}{2 \cdot 2 \cdot 2 \cdot \underset{1}{\cancel{3}} \cdot \underset{1}{\cancel{3}}} = -\frac{5}{8}$

26. $\frac{81}{99} = \frac{\overset{1}{\cancel{3}} \cdot \overset{1}{\cancel{3}} \cdot 3 \cdot 3}{\underset{1}{\cancel{3}} \cdot \underset{1}{\cancel{3}} \cdot 11} = \frac{9}{11}$

27. $\frac{14}{66} = \frac{\overset{1}{\cancel{2}} \cdot 7}{\underset{1}{\cancel{2}} \cdot 3 \cdot 11} = \frac{7}{33}$ 28. $\frac{-10}{1}$ or $\frac{10}{-1}$

29. $3[14 - (8 - 5)^2] + 20 = 3[14 - (3)^2] + 20$

   $= 3[14 - 9] + 20$

   $= 3[5] + 20$

   $= 15 + 20$

   $= 35$

30. $s = -\frac{132}{11}$

   $s = -12$

31. 212, 216, 226, 232, 239, 243, 250

   LQ: 216

   UQ: 243

   Interquartile Range: $243 - 216 = 27$

32. $36 = 2 \cdot 2 \cdot 3 \cdot 3$ 33. yes; 2.5 or $2\frac{1}{2}$

   $108 = 2 \cdot 2 \cdot 3 \cdot 3 \cdot 3$

   $180 = 2 \cdot 2 \cdot 3 \cdot 3 \cdot 5$

   GCF $= 2 \cdot 2 \cdot 3 \cdot 3 = 36$

34. yes; It is not in simplest form. All even numbers can be divided by 2. Therefore the even numerator and the even denominator can still be divided by 2.

35. $\frac{16}{25}$

36. a. $\frac{6}{8}$ or $\frac{3}{4}$ as many in 1970 as in 1985

   b. 1970: $\frac{6}{6.5}$; 1980: $\frac{7}{5}$; 1985: $\frac{8}{5}$;

   1987: $\frac{8.25}{4.5}$; 1990: $\frac{8.75}{4.25}$

6-6 Rational Numbers and Decimals

PAGE 228   CHECKING FOR UNDERSTANDING

1. Divide the numerator by the denominator.

2. Sample answers: $\frac{1}{2}$, $\frac{3}{4}$ 3. $0.37 = \frac{37}{100}$

4. 0.016, $\frac{16}{1,000}$ 5. $\frac{2}{5} = 0.4$

6. $-\frac{7}{8} = -0.875$ 7. $\frac{13}{4} = 3.25$

8. $-\frac{7}{20} = -0.35$ 9. $3\frac{14}{25} = 3.56$

10. $-0.4 = -\frac{4}{10}$ 11. $0.75 = \frac{75}{100}$

   $= -\frac{2}{5}$ $= \frac{3}{4}$

12. $0.17 = \frac{17}{100}$ 13. $3.12 = 3\frac{12}{100}$

                                        $= 3\frac{3}{25}$

14. $-5.375 = -5\frac{375}{1,000}$

   $= -5\frac{3}{8}$

PAGES 228-229

15. $-\frac{4}{5} = -0.8$ 16. $\frac{9}{10} = 0.9$

17. $-\frac{7}{25} = -0.28$ 18. $\frac{11}{4} = 2.75$

19. $-5\frac{3}{8} = -5.375$ 20. $\frac{5}{16} = 0.3125$

21. $7\frac{1}{4} = 7.25$ 22. $-\frac{17}{20} = -0.85$

23. $-\frac{9}{32} = -0.28125$ 24. $\frac{71}{40} = 1.775$

25. $0.05 = \frac{5}{100}$ 26. $-1.3 = -1\frac{3}{10}$

   $= \frac{1}{20}$

27. $0.64 = \frac{64}{100}$ 28. $-8.52 = -8\frac{52}{100}$

   $= \frac{16}{25}$ $= -8\frac{13}{25}$

29. $3.85 = 3\frac{85}{100}$ 30. $4.105 = 4\frac{105}{1,000}$

   $= 3\frac{17}{20}$ $= 4\frac{21}{200}$

31. $-0.075 = -\frac{75}{1,000}$ 32. $-20.35 = -20\frac{35}{100}$

   $= -\frac{3}{40}$ $= -20\frac{7}{20}$

33. $\frac{131}{200} = 0.655$; terminating

34. 11 $\boxed{\div}$ 15 $\boxed{+}$ 9   35. $\frac{y}{3} - 15$

36. $10 > -10$ 37. 9, 10, 11, 12

38. integers, rational numbers

39. $\frac{1}{2}, \frac{1}{4}, \frac{1}{5}, \frac{1}{8}, \frac{1}{10}, \frac{1}{16}$ 40. $0.084 = \frac{84}{1,000}$

                                        $= \frac{21}{250}$

Mid-Chapter Review

1. yes; The ones digit is divisible by 2, so 582 is divisible by 2. The sum of the digits, 15, is divisible by 3, so 582 is divisible by 3. Therefore 582 is divisible by 6.

2. no; The number formed by the last two digits, 38, is not divisible by 4.

3. yes; The sum of the digits, 9, is divisible by 9.

4. yes; The ones digit is 0.

5. $36 = 3 \cdot 12$ 6. $-45 = -1 \cdot 5 \cdot 9$

   $36 = 3 \cdot 2 \cdot 6$ $-45 = -1 \cdot 5 \cdot 3 \cdot 3$

   $36 = 3 \cdot 2 \cdot 2 \cdot 3$ $-45 = -1 \cdot 3^2 \cdot 5$

   $36 = 2^2 \cdot 3^2$

7. $128 = 2 \cdot 64$

   $128 = 2 \cdot 2 \cdot 32$

   $128 = 2 \cdot 2 \cdot 2 \cdot 16$

   $128 = 2 \cdot 2 \cdot 2 \cdot 2 \cdot 8$

   $128 = 2 \cdot 2 \cdot 2 \cdot 2 \cdot 2 \cdot 4$

   $128 = 2 \cdot 2 \cdot 2 \cdot 2 \cdot 2 \cdot 2 \cdot 2$

   $128 = 2^7$

8. $200 = 5 \cdot 40$

   $200 = 5 \cdot 5 \cdot 8$

   $200 = 5 \cdot 5 \cdot 2 \cdot 4$

   $200 = 5 \cdot 5 \cdot 2 \cdot 2 \cdot 2$

   $200 = 2^3 \cdot 5^2$

9.

Temperature	Frequency
26°F	||
27°F	||
28°F	||
29°F	||
30°F	|||
31°F	||
32°F	|

The mode is 30°F.

10. $25 = 5 \cdot 5$

   $30 = 2 \cdot 3 \cdot 5$

   GCF $= 5$

11. $64 = 2 \cdot 2 \cdot 2 \cdot 2 \cdot 2 \cdot 2$

   $48 = 2 \cdot 2 \cdot 2 \cdot 2 \cdot 3$

   GCF $= 2 \cdot 2 \cdot 2 \cdot 2 = 16$

12. $12 = 2 \cdot 2 \cdot 3$

   $72 = 2 \cdot 2 \cdot 2 \cdot 3 \cdot 3$

   $24 = 2 \cdot 2 \cdot 2 \cdot 3$

   GCF $= 2 \cdot 2 \cdot 3 = 12$

13. $\frac{8}{32} = \frac{\overset{1}{\cancel{2}} \cdot \overset{1}{\cancel{2}} \cdot \overset{1}{\cancel{2}}}{\underset{1}{\cancel{2}} \cdot \underset{1}{\cancel{2}} \cdot \underset{1}{\cancel{2}} \cdot 2 \cdot 2} = \frac{1}{4}$

14. $-\frac{45}{60} = -\frac{\overset{1}{\cancel{3}} \cdot 3 \cdot \overset{1}{\cancel{5}}}{2 \cdot 2 \cdot \underset{1}{\cancel{3}} \cdot \underset{1}{\cancel{5}}} = -\frac{3}{4}$

15. $\frac{35}{175} = \frac{\overset{1}{\cancel{5}} \cdot \overset{1}{\cancel{7}}}{\underset{1}{\cancel{5}} \cdot 5 \cdot \underset{1}{\cancel{7}}} = \frac{1}{5}$

57

16. $\frac{27}{15} = \frac{\overset{1}{\cancel{3}} \cdot 3 \cdot 3}{\underset{1}{\cancel{3}} \cdot 5} = \frac{9}{5} = 1\frac{4}{5}$

17. $-0.8 = -\frac{8}{10}$

      $= -\frac{4}{5}$

18. $\frac{13}{25} = 0.52$

19. $-\frac{5}{8} = -0.625$

20. $4.85 = 4\frac{85}{100}$

               $= 4\frac{17}{20}$

6-7   Repeating Decimals

PAGE 231   CHECKING FOR UNDERSTANDING

1. $3 \div 11 + 2$

2. Sample answers: $\frac{1}{3}$, $\frac{1}{6}$

3. 100 because 2 digits repeat

4. So the repeating part can be eliminated.

5. 0.2642642642

6. 0. 9222222222

7. 0.5082508250

8. 0.5082082082

9. 0.2161616161

10. 100

11. 10

12. 10

13. 100

PAGES 231-232   EXERCISES

14. $0.1\overline{6}$

15. $29.\overline{27}$

16. $0.\overline{428571}$

17. $-2.\overline{45}$

18. $98.\overline{6}$

19. $-7.0\overline{74}$

20. 10^3 or $1,000$

21. 8.32

22. Let $N = 0.\overline{4}$. Then $10N = 4.\overline{4}$.

    $10N = 4.\overline{4}$

    $\underline{-\ N = 0.\overline{4}}$

    $9N = 4$

      $N = \frac{4}{9}$

    So, $0.\overline{4} = \frac{4}{9}$.

23. Let $N = -1.\overline{7}$. Then $10N = -17.\overline{7}$.

    $10N = -17.\overline{7}$

    $\underline{-\ N = -1.\overline{7}}$

    $9N = -16$

      $N = -\frac{16}{9} = -1\frac{7}{9}$

    So, $-1.\overline{7} = -1\frac{7}{9}$.

24. Let $N = 2.\overline{6}$. Then $10N = 26.\overline{6}$.

    $10N = 26.\overline{6}$

    $\underline{-\ N = 2.\overline{6}}$

    $9N = 24$

      $N = \frac{24}{9} = 2\frac{2}{3}$

    So, $2.\overline{6} = 2\frac{2}{3}$.

25. Let $N = 0.\overline{54}$. Then $100N = 54.\overline{54}$.

    $100N = 54.\overline{54}$

    $\underline{-\ N = 0.\overline{54}}$

    $99N = 54$

      $N = \frac{54}{99} = \frac{6}{11}$

So, $0.\overline{54} = \frac{6}{11}$.

26. Let $N = -4.\overline{01}$. Then $100N = -401.\overline{01}$.

    $100N = -401.\overline{01}$

    $\underline{-\ N = -4.\overline{01}}$

    $99N = -397$

      $N = -\frac{397}{99} = -4\frac{1}{99}$

So, $-4.\overline{01} = -4\frac{1}{99}$.

27. Let $N = 2.\overline{5}$. Then $10N = 25.\overline{5}$.

    $10N = 25.\overline{5}$

    $\underline{-\ N = 2.\overline{5}}$

    $9N = 23$

      $N = \frac{23}{9} = 2\frac{5}{9}$

So, $2.\overline{5} = 2\frac{5}{9}$.

28. Let $N = 0.6\overline{2}$. Then $10N = 6.\overline{2}$.

    $10N = 6.\overline{2}$

    $\underline{-\ N = 0.6\overline{2}}$

    $9N = 5.6$

      $N = \frac{5.6}{9} = \frac{28}{45}$

So, $0.6\overline{2} = \frac{28}{45}$.

29. Let $N = 0.\overline{24}$. Then $100N = 24.\overline{24}$.

    $100N = 24.\overline{24}$

    $\underline{-\ N = 0.\overline{24}}$

    $99N = 24$

      $N = \frac{24}{99} = \frac{8}{33}$

So, $0.\overline{24} = \frac{8}{33}$.

30. Let $N = 7.\overline{52}$. Then $100N = 752.\overline{52}$.

    $100N = 752.\overline{52}$

    $\underline{-\ N = 7.\overline{52}}$

    $99N = 745$

      $N = \frac{745}{99} = 7\frac{52}{99}$

So, $7.\overline{52} = 7\frac{52}{99}$.

31. Let $N = 0.\overline{345}$. Then $1,000N = 345.\overline{345}$.

    $1,000N = 345.\overline{345}$

    $\underline{-\ \ \ \ N = 0.\overline{345}}$

    $999N = 345$

      $N = \frac{345}{999} = \frac{115}{333}$

So, $0.\overline{345} = \frac{115}{333}$.

32. $4^3 \cdot 5^2$

33. $63.45 = 4.23g$

$$\frac{63.45}{4.23} = \frac{4.23g}{4.23}$$

$$15 = g$$

34. $x + 15 = 40$

$x + 15 - 15 = 40 - 15$

$x = 25$

35.

110 120 130 140 150 160 170 180 190 200

Extremes: 111, 194

36. $8.68 = 8\frac{68}{100}$ **37.** $\frac{17}{57} = 0.2982456$

$= 8\frac{17}{25}$

38. a. $0.\overline{3}$ **b.** 0.2727273 **c.** $0.\overline{272727}$

39. Sample answers: 3, 6, 7, 9, 11; 2, 4, 5, 8, 10; If the prime factors of the denominator are not 2 or 5, the fraction can be expressed as a repeating decimal.

40. Sample answer: 8.314.

41. See students' work.

6-8   Simple Events

PAGE 234   CHECKING FOR UNDERSTANDING

1. chance that an event will happen

2. That outcome is certain to happen.

3. Sample answer: When flipping a coin you will get a head or tail.

4. No number is divisible by 3.

5.

Sample answer: probability of spinning a 1

6. $\frac{1}{2}$ or 0.5

7. 0   **8.** $\frac{2}{6} = \frac{1}{3}$ or $0.\overline{3}$ **9.** $\frac{1}{7}$ or $0.\overline{142857}$

10. 1   **11.** 0   **12.** $\frac{6}{20} = \frac{3}{10}$ **13.** $\frac{7}{20}$

14. $\frac{16}{20} = \frac{4}{5}$ **15.** 1   **16.** $\frac{3 + 7 + 6}{20} = \frac{16}{20} = \frac{4}{5}$

PAGE 235   EXERCISES

17. $P(t) = \frac{2}{11}$ **18.** $P(vowel) = \frac{5}{11}$

19. $P(n) = \frac{1}{11}$ **20.** $P(not\ c) = \frac{10}{11}$

21. $P(m\ or\ v) = \frac{2 + 1}{11} = \frac{3}{11}$

22. $P(not\ m\ or\ t) = \frac{7}{11}$

---

23. $P(\text{an even number}) = \frac{24}{49}$

24. $P\ (\text{a two-digit number}) = \frac{40}{49}$

25. $P(\text{a positive number}) = \frac{49}{49} = 1$

26. $P(\text{a perfect square}) = \frac{7}{49} = \frac{1}{7}$

27. $P(\text{a number divisible by 10}) = \frac{4}{49}$

28. $P(\text{a negative number}) = \frac{0}{49} = 0$

29. $P(\text{a number that is the product of four different prime numbers}) = \frac{0}{49} = 0$

30. $P = 2a + 2b$ $A = bh$

$P = 2 \cdot 6 + 2 \cdot 12$ $A = 12 \cdot 5$

$P = 12 + 24$ $A = 60\ in.^2$

$P = 36\ in.$

31. $s = -72 + 59$ **32.** similar; They have

$s = -13$ the same shape but not the same size.

33. Let $N = 8.\overline{72}$. Then $100N = 872.\overline{72}$.

$100N = 872.\overline{72}$

$- \quad N = \quad\ 8.\overline{72}$

$99N = 864$

$N = \frac{864}{99} = 8\frac{72}{99} = 8\frac{8}{11}$

So, $8.\overline{72} = 8\frac{8}{11}$.

34. See students' work.

35. a. $\frac{n}{10,000} = 0.015$

$10,000\left(\frac{n}{10,000}\right) = 0.015 \cdot 10,000$

$n = 150$

b. $\frac{n}{10,000} = 0.2$

$10,000\left(\frac{n}{10,000}\right) = 0.2 \cdot 10,000$

$n = 2,000$

c. $\frac{n}{10,000} = 0.04$

$10,000\left(\frac{n}{10,000}\right) = 0.04 \cdot 10,000$

$n = 400$

d. $n = 10,000 - 150 - 2,000 - 400$

$n = 7,450$

36. no; The number of ways an event can occur cannot exceed the number of possible outcomes.

37. no; The number of ways an event can occur cannot be negative.

38.

Land on   Move to

Land on Square	Move to Square	Result
1	2	R
2	1	R
	3	W
	4	W
3	2	R
4	2	R
	5	R
5	4	W
	6	W
6	5	R

There are 6 ways out of 10 possibilities to end up on red.

6-9   Least Common Multiple

PAGES 237-238   **CHECKING FOR UNDERSTANDING**

1. Multiply that number by 0, 1, 2, 3, 4, and 5.
2. Write the prime factorization of each number. Determine the factors common to all the numbers in the set. Multiply all the factors using the common factors only once.
3. It is zero.
4. multiply   5. 0, 5, 10, 15, 20, 25
6. 0, 18, 36, 54, 72, 90   7. 0, 20, 40, 60, 80, 100
8. 0, n, $2n$, $3n$, $4n$, $5n$
9. multiples of 1: 0, 1, 2, 3, 4, 5, 6, 7, 8, 9, 10, 11, 12, 13, 14, 15,...
   multiples of 3: 0, 3, 6, 9, 12, 15, 18, 21,...
   multiples of 15: 0, 15, 30, 45, 60, 75, 90,...
   The LCM is 15.
10. multiples of 7: 0, 7, 14, 21, 28, 35, 42, 49, 56, 63, 70, 77, 84, 91, 98, 105, 112, 119,...
    multiples of 21: 0, 21, 42, 63, 84, 105, 126, 147, 168,...
    multiples of 5: 0, 5, 10, 15, 20, 25, 30, 35, 40, 45, 50, 55, 60, 65, 70, 75, 80, 85, 90, 95, 100, 105,...
    The LCM is 105.
11. multiples of 15: 0, 15, 30, 45, 60, 75, 90, 105, 120, 135, 150, 165, 180, 195, 210, 225,...
    multiples of 45: 0, 45, 90, 135, 180, 225, 270, 315,...
    multiples of 60: 0, 60, 120, 180, 240, 300, 360, 420,...
    The LCM is 180.

12. multiples of 8: 0, 8, 16, 24,..., 824, 832, 840, 848,...
    multiples of 28: 0, 28, 56,..., 812, 840,...
    multiples of 30: 0, 30, 60,..., 810, 840,...
    The LCM is 840.

13. $12 = 2 \cdot 2 \cdot 3$
    $16 = 2 \cdot 2 \cdot 2 \cdot 2$
    $LCM = 2^4 \cdot 3 = 48$

14. $10 = 2 \cdot 5$
    $15 = 3 \cdot 5$
    $20 = 2 \cdot 2 \cdot 5$
    $LCM = 2^2 \cdot 3 \cdot 5 = 60$

15. $35 = 5 \cdot 7$
    $25 = 5 \cdot 5$
    $49 = 7 \cdot 7$
    $LCM = 5^2 \cdot 7^2 = 1,225$

16. $18 = 2 \cdot 3 \cdot 3$
    $24 = 2 \cdot 2 \cdot 2 \cdot 3$
    $LCM = 2^3 \cdot 3^2 = 72$

PAGE 238   **EXERCISES**

17. $12 = 2 \cdot 2 \cdot 3$
    $15 = 3 \cdot 5$
    $LCM = 2^2 \cdot 3 \cdot 5 = 60$

18. $16 = 2 \cdot 2 \cdot 2 \cdot 2$
    $88 = 2 \cdot 2 \cdot 2 \cdot 11$
    $LCM = 2^4 \cdot 11 = 176$

19. $12 = 2 \cdot 2 \cdot 3$
    $35 = 5 \cdot 7$
    $LCM = 2^2 \cdot 3 \cdot 5 \cdot 7 = 420$

20. $16 = 2 \cdot 2 \cdot 2 \cdot 2$
    $24 = 2 \cdot 2 \cdot 2 \cdot 3$
    $LCM = 2^4 \cdot 3 = 48$

21. $20 = 2 \cdot 2 \cdot 5$
    $50 = 2 \cdot 5 \cdot 5$
    $LCM = 2^2 \cdot 5^2 = 100$

22. $7 = 7$
    $12 = 2 \cdot 2 \cdot 3$
    $LCM = 2^2 \cdot 3 \cdot 7 = 84$

23. $4 = 2 \cdot 2$
    $8 = 2 \cdot 2 \cdot 2$
    $12 = 2 \cdot 2 \cdot 3$
    $LCM = 2^3 \cdot 3 = 24$

24. $10 = 2 \cdot 5$
    $12 = 2 \cdot 2 \cdot 3$
    $14 = 2 \cdot 7$
    $LCM = 2^2 \cdot 3 \cdot 5 \cdot 7 = 420$

25. $24 = 2 \cdot 2 \cdot 2 \cdot 3$
    $12 = 2 \cdot 2 \cdot 3$
    $6 = 2 \cdot 3$
    $LCM = 2^3 \cdot 3 = 24$

26. $45 = 3 \cdot 3 \cdot 5$
    $10 = 2 \cdot 5$
    $6 = 2 \cdot 3$
    $LCM = 2 \cdot 3^2 \cdot 5 = 90$

27. $71 = 71$
    $17 = 17$
    $7 = 7$
    $LCM = 7 \cdot 17 \cdot 71 = 8,449$

28. $68 = 2 \cdot 2 \cdot 17$
    $170 = 2 \cdot 5 \cdot 17$
    $4 = 2 \cdot 2$
    $LCM = 2^2 \cdot 5 \cdot 17 = 340$

29. multiples of 6: 0, 6, 12, 18, 24, 30, 36, 42, 48, 54, 60, 66, 72, 78, 84, 90, 96, 102, 108, 114, 120,...
    no

30. $320 + 159 + 80 = 320 + 80 + 159$
$$= (320 + 80) + 159$$
$$= 400 + 159$$
$$= 559$$

31. $12 = \frac{a}{14} + 10$

$12 - 10 = \frac{a}{14} + 10 - 10$

$2 = \frac{a}{14}$

$14 \cdot 2 = \left(\frac{a}{14}\right)14$

$28 = a$

32. $r + (-125) = 483$

$r + (-125) + 125 = 483 + 125$
$r = 608$

33. no; Most of the people in a pet store would own a pet.

34. true; See students' work.

35. $\frac{3}{6} = \frac{1}{2}$

36. a. $9 = 3 \cdot 3$
$12 = 2 \cdot 2 \cdot 3$
$18 = 2 \cdot 3 \cdot 3$
$LCM = 2^2 \cdot 3^2 = 36$ cm

b. 9 cm long: $3 \times 4 \times 6 = 72$
12 cm long: $3 \times 3 \times 6 = 54$
18 cm long: $3 \times 2 \times 6 = 36$

37. when one number is a factor of the other number

38. when the GCF is 1

39. $3n = 3 \cdot n$
$6n^2 = 2 \cdot 3 \cdot n \cdot n$
$8 = 2 \cdot 2 \cdot 2$
$LCM = 2^3 \cdot 3 \cdot n^2$ or $24n^2$

40. Sample answer: 3, 5, 7 **41.** See students' work.

6-10A Mathematics Lab: Density Property

PAGE 239   WHAT DO YOU THINK?

1. The midpoint is the mean of the sum of the endpoints.

2. They are the same.

3. Add them together and divide by 2.

4. Add the two numbers together and divide by 2.

PAGE 240   WHAT DO YOU THINK?

5. The new number is between the original numbers.

6. Adding a digit creates a number that is between the original numbers with zeros annexed to them.

7. See students' work.

8. The new fraction is between the original fractions.

6-10 Comparing and Ordering Rational Numbers

PAGE 243   CHECKING FOR UNDERSTANDING

1. Express $\frac{1}{2}$ as a decimal and compare the decimals. Express 0.625 as a fraction and express both fractions as equivalent fractions with like denominators.

2.

The area representing 0.2 is larger than the area representing 0.09. So $0.2 > 0.09$.

3. The LCD is $\frac{1}{2}$ and $\frac{1}{3}$ is the LCM of 2 and 3, which is 6.

4. The LCD of $\frac{2}{5}$ and $\frac{3}{8}$ is the LCM of 5 and 8, which is 40.

5. The LCD of $\frac{5}{6}$ and $\frac{7}{9}$ is the LCM of 6 and 9, which is 18.

6. The LCD of $\frac{7}{25}$ and $-\frac{3}{4}$ is the LCM of 25 and 4, which is 100.

7. $3\frac{3}{7} = \frac{24}{7} = \frac{216}{63}$, $3\frac{4}{9} = \frac{31}{9} = \frac{217}{63}$
$3\frac{3}{7} < 3\frac{4}{9}$

8. $\frac{1}{6} = 0.1\overline{6}$

9. $-\frac{7}{2} = -\frac{14}{4}$
$-\frac{7}{2} < -\frac{3}{4}$

10. $1.4 < 1.403$

11. $-1.808 > -1.858$

12. $10\frac{2}{5} = 10.4$

13. $5.92 = 5\frac{23}{25}$

14. $-12, -5, -1, 2, 5$

15. $\frac{1}{2} = 0.5$, $\frac{4}{5} = 0.8$, $\frac{2}{5} = 0.4$
$0, \frac{2}{5}, \frac{1}{2}, \frac{4}{5}$

16. $\frac{3}{8} = 0.375$, $\frac{2}{5} = 0.4$
$0.367, \frac{3}{8}, 0.376, \frac{2}{5}$

17. $-4.6 < 4.58$

18. $1.5 > -1.52$

19. $0.88 < 0.\overline{8}$

20. $\frac{5}{7} = \frac{15}{21}$

$\frac{5}{7} > \frac{9}{21}$

21. $-9\frac{2}{3} < 8\frac{7}{8}$

22. $\frac{4}{5} = \frac{8}{10}$

23. $11\frac{1}{8} = 11.125$

24. $7.47 = 7\frac{47}{100}$

$11\frac{1}{8} < 11.26$

25. $-5.2 < 5\frac{1}{5}$

26.

-7.4 is to the left
of -7 on the number
line.

27. The LCD of $\frac{3}{8}$ and $\frac{13}{25}$ is the LCM of 8 and 25,

which is 200.

28. 0.056, 0.06, 0.5, 0.56

29. $\frac{1}{9} = 0.\overline{1}$, $\frac{1}{10} = 0.1$, $-\frac{1}{3} = -0.\overline{3}$, $-\frac{1}{4} = -0.25$

$-\frac{1}{3}$, $-\frac{1}{4}$, $\frac{1}{10}$, $\frac{1}{9}$

30. $\frac{17}{9} = 1.\overline{8}$, $\frac{18}{9} = 2$

1.07, 1.8, 1.$\overline{8}$, 2

31. $0.\overline{18}$, 0.182, $0.18\overline{2}$, $0.182\overline{5}$

32. $3\frac{1}{2} \cdot 4 = 14 \rightarrow 3\frac{1}{2}$ gal = 14 qt

33. $t = -62 + 47 + (-18) + 22$

$t = [-62 + (-18)] + [47 + 22]$

$t = -80 + 69$

$t = -11$

34. 2, 3, 3, 6, 7, 8, 9, 11, 14

Mean: $\dfrac{2 + 3 + 3 + 6 + 7 + 8 + 9 + 11 + 14}{9} = \dfrac{63}{9}$

$= 7$

Median: 7

Mode: 3

35. $8 = 2 \cdot 2 \cdot 2$

$15 = 3 \cdot 5$

$12 = 2 \cdot 2 \cdot 3$

LCM $= 2^3 \cdot 3 \cdot 5 = 120$

36. $\frac{5}{16} = 0.3125$, $\frac{21}{64} = 0.328125$

$\frac{5}{16} < \frac{21}{64}$; Bob

37. $\frac{4.69}{3} = \frac{18.76}{12}$

38. no; because $0.\overline{4} = \frac{4}{9}$

$\frac{4.69}{3} > \frac{14.50}{12}$; $14.50 a dozen

39. a. 0.3, 1.2, 1.5, 2.4, 2.7, 2.7, 2.8, 3.4, 3.8

Median: 2.7

b.

City	Median Precipitation
Asheville, NC	4.2
Burlington, VT	2.8
Columbus, OH	3.4
Honolulu, HI	1.5
Kansas City, MO	2.7
Los Angeles, CA	1.2
Phoenix, AR	0.3
Seattle, WA	2.4
San Antonio, TX	2.7

Asheville, NC

40. The electrical charge of 3 magneium and 1
phosphate ion is $3 \cdot (+2) + 1 \cdot (-3) = +6 + (-3)$
$= +3$. The electrical charge of 2 aluminum and
3 oxide ions is $2 \cdot (+3) + 3 \cdot (-2) = +6 + (-6)$
$= 0$. So 3 magnesium and 1 phosphate ion has a
greater electrical charge.

6-11 Scientific Notation

PAGE 247   CHECKING FOR UNDERSTANDING

1. 45.6 and 0.456 are not greater than or equal to
1 and less than 10.

2. Sample answer: 4.78×10^3

3. To lessen the chance of omitting a zero or
misplacing the decimal point.

4. $3.45 \times 10^7 = 3.45 \times 10,000,000$
$= 34,500,000$

5. $8.9 \times 10^{-5} = 8.9 \times 0.00001$
$= 0.000089$

6. $3.777 \times 10^4 = 3.777 \times 10,000$
$= 37,770$

7. 12,300,000
$12,300,000 = 1.23 \times 10^7$

8. 1,230,000
$1,230,000 = 1.23 \times 10^6$

9. 0.000123
$0.000123 = 1.23 \times 10^{-4}$

10. 12.3
$12.3 = 1.23 \times 10^1$

11. 0.0056789
$0.0056789 = 5.6789 \times 10^{-3}$

12. 829
$829 = 8.29 \times 10^2$

13. 0.000007
$0.000007 = 7.0 \times 10^{-6}$

14. $0.001^2 = 0.000001$
$0.001^2 = 1.0 \times 10^{-6}$

PAGE 247   EXERCISES

15. $-9.999 \times 10^{-8} = -9.999 \times 0.00000001$
$= -0.00000009999$

16. $4.2 \times 10^6 = 4.2 \times 1,000,000$

$= 4,200,000$

17. $4.2 \times 10^{-6} = 4.2 \times 0.000001$

$= 0.0000042$

18. $2.54 \times 10^3 = 2.54 \times 1,000$

$= 2,540$

19. $9.6 \times 10^{-2} = 9.6 \times 0.01$

$= 0.096$

20. $3.853 \times 10^4 = 3.853 \times 10,000$

$= 38,530$

21. $9.3 \times 10^7 = 9.3 \times 10,000,000$

$= 93,000,000 \text{ mi}$

22. $9,700,000$

$9,700,000 = 9.7 \times 10^6$

23. $85,420,000$

$85,420,000 = 8.542 \times 10^7$

24. 0.0000635

$0.0000635 = 6.35 \times 10^{-5}$

25. 0.000056

$0.000056 = 5.6 \times 10^{-5}$

26. $3,478$

$3,478 = 3.478 \times 10^3$

27. $0.0002^2 = 0.00000004$

$0.0002^2 = 4.0 \times 10^{-8}$

28. $7,000,000 \times 800 = 5,600,000,000$

$7,000,000 \times 800 = 5.6 \times 10^9$

29. $0.00008 \times 0.0009 = 0.000000072$

$0.00008 \times 0.0009 = 7.2 \times 10^{-8}$

30. $y - 8.3 = 20.9$

$y - 8.3 + 8.3 = 20.9 - 8.3$

$y = 12.6$

31. $\frac{c}{4} + 8 > 10$

$\frac{c}{4} + 8 - 8 > 10 - 8$

$\frac{c}{4} > 2$

$4\left(\frac{c}{4}\right) > 2 \cdot 4$

$c > 8$

```
  +--+--+--+--⊕--+--+--+--+
  4     6     8    10    12
```

32. $-319 - (-98) = w$

$-319 + 98 = w$

$-221 = w$

33. The LCD of $-\frac{5}{6}$ and $\frac{3}{8}$ is the LCM of 6 and 8, which is 24.

34. $65,000,000 \times (9.46 \times 10^{12})$

$= 65,000,000 \times 9,460,000,000,000$

$= 614,900,000,000,000,000,000$

$= 6.149 \times 10^{20}$

35. a. Jupiter

b. 4.83×10^8 mi

c. $(4.83 \times 10^8) - (9.29 \times 10^7)$

$= 483,000,000 - 92,900,000$

$= 390,100,000$

$= 3.901 \times 10^8 \text{ mi}$

Chapter 6 Study Guide and Review

PAGE 248   COMMUNICATING MATHEMATICS

1. factors   2. prime   3. simplest form

4. LCM   5. 1

6. Let N = the repeating decimal. Multiply by a power of ten so that when you subtract the two resulting decimals, the decimal fraction part is eliminated. Solve the remaining equation for N.

PAGES 248-250   SKILLS AND CONCEPTS

7. no; The sum of the digits, 10, is not divisible by 3.

8. yes; The ones digit is 5.

9. yes; The number formed by the last two digits, 28, is divisible by 4.

10. no; The number formed by the last three digits, 291, is not divisible by 8.

11. yes; 16,542 is divisible by 2 and 3.

12. no; the ones digit is not 0.

13. $48 = 3 \cdot 16$

$48 = 3 \cdot 2 \cdot 8$

$48 = 3 \cdot 2 \cdot 2 \cdot 4$

$48 = 3 \cdot 2 \cdot 2 \cdot 2 \cdot 2$

$48 = 2^4 \cdot 3$

14. $-56 = -1 \cdot 7 \cdot 8$

$-56 = -1 \cdot 7 \cdot 2 \cdot 4$

$-56 = -1 \cdot 7 \cdot 2 \cdot 2 \cdot 2$

$-56 = -1 \cdot 2^3 \cdot 7$

15. $175 = 5 \cdot 35$

$175 = 5 \cdot 5 \cdot 7$

$175 = 5^2 \cdot 7$

16. $-252 = -1 \cdot 7 \cdot 36$

$-252 = -1 \cdot 7 \cdot 3 \cdot 12$

$-252 = -1 \cdot 7 \cdot 3 \cdot 2 \cdot 6$

$-252 = -1 \cdot 7 \cdot 3 \cdot 2 \cdot 2 \cdot 3$

$-252 = -1 \cdot 2^2 \cdot 3^3 \cdot 7$

17. $33 = 3 \cdot 11$

18. $-27 = -1 \cdot 3 \cdot 9$

$-27 = -1 \cdot 3 \cdot 3 \cdot 3$

$-27 = -1 \cdot 3^3$

19. $18 = 2 \cdot 3 \cdot 3$

$54 = 2 \cdot 3 \cdot 3 \cdot 3$

GCF $= 2 \cdot 3 \cdot 3 = 18$

20. $15 = 3 \cdot 5$

$45 = 3 \cdot 3 \cdot 5$

GCF $= 3 \cdot 5 = 15$

21. $14 = 2 \cdot 7$

$28 = 2 \cdot 2 \cdot 7$

$49 = 7 \cdot 7$

GCF $= 7$

22. $36 = 2 \cdot 2 \cdot 3 \cdot 3$

$84 = 2 \cdot 2 \cdot 3 \cdot 7$

$108 = 2 \cdot 2 \cdot 3 \cdot 3 \cdot 3$

GCF $= 2 \cdot 2 \cdot 3 = 12$

23. $120 = 2 \cdot 2 \cdot 2 \cdot 3 \cdot 5$
$440 = 2 \cdot 2 \cdot 2 \cdot 5 \cdot 11$
$360 = 2 \cdot 2 \cdot 2 \cdot 3 \cdot 3 \cdot 5$
$GCF = 2 \cdot 2 \cdot 2 \cdot 5 = 40$

24. $-\dfrac{15}{18} = -\dfrac{\overset{1}{\cancel{3}} \cdot 5}{2 \cdot \underset{1}{\cancel{3}} \cdot 3} = -\dfrac{5}{6}$

25. $\dfrac{12}{16} = \dfrac{\overset{1}{\cancel{2}} \cdot \overset{1}{\cancel{2}} \cdot 3}{\underset{1}{\cancel{2}} \cdot \underset{1}{\cancel{2}} \cdot 2 \cdot 2} = \dfrac{3}{4}$

26. $\dfrac{63}{72} = \dfrac{\overset{1}{\cancel{3}} \cdot \overset{1}{\cancel{3}} \cdot 7}{2 \cdot 2 \cdot 2 \cdot \underset{1}{\cancel{3}} \cdot \underset{1}{\cancel{3}}} = \dfrac{7}{8}$

27. $-\dfrac{42}{63} = -\dfrac{2 \cdot \overset{1}{\cancel{3}} \cdot \overset{1}{\cancel{7}}}{\underset{1}{\cancel{3}} \cdot 3 \cdot \underset{1}{\cancel{7}}} = -\dfrac{2}{3}$

28. $\dfrac{3}{8} = 0.375$

29. $\dfrac{4}{22} = 0.1\overline{8}$ 30. $1\dfrac{2}{5} = 1.4$

31. $6\dfrac{8}{12} = 6.\overline{6}$ 32. $0.45 = \dfrac{45}{100}$
$= \dfrac{9}{20}$

33. $-0.028 = -\dfrac{28}{1,000}$ 34. $-11.375 = -11\dfrac{375}{1,000}$
$= -\dfrac{7}{250}$ $= -11\dfrac{3}{8}$

35. $4.8125 = 4\dfrac{8,125}{10,000}$
$= 4\dfrac{13}{16}$

36. Let $N = 0.\overline{7}$. Then $10N = 7.\overline{7}$.
$10N = 7.\overline{7}$
$\underline{-\ \ N = 0.\overline{7}}$
$9N = 7$
$N = \dfrac{7}{9}$

So, $0.\overline{7} = \dfrac{7}{9}$.

37. Let $N = -5.\overline{28}$. Then $100N = -528.\overline{28}$.
$100N = -528.\overline{28}$
$\underline{-\ \ N = \quad -5.\overline{28}}$
$99N = -523$
$N = -\dfrac{523}{99} = -5\dfrac{28}{99}$

So, $-5.\overline{28} = -5\dfrac{28}{99}$.

38. Let $N = -0.3\overline{18}$. Then $100N = -31.\overline{81}$.
$100N = -31.\overline{81}$
$\underline{-\ \ N = -0.3\overline{18}}$
$99N = -31.5$
$N = -\dfrac{31.5}{99} = -\dfrac{63}{198} = -\dfrac{7}{22}$

So, $-0.3\overline{18} = -\dfrac{7}{22}$.

39. Let $N = 6.\overline{630}$. Then $1,000N = 6,630.\overline{630}$.
$1,000N = 6,630.\overline{630}$
$\underline{-\ \ \ \ N = \qquad\ 6.\overline{630}}$
$999N = 6,624$
$N = \dfrac{6,624}{999} = 6\dfrac{70}{111}$

So, $6.\overline{630} = 6\dfrac{70}{111}$.

40. Let $N = 0.\overline{48}$. Then $100N = 48.\overline{48}$.
$100N = 48.\overline{48}$
$\underline{-\ \ N = \ 0.\overline{48}}$
$99N = 48$
$N = \dfrac{48}{99} = \dfrac{16}{33}$
So, $0.\overline{48} = \dfrac{16}{33}$.

41. Let $N = -0.\overline{03}$. Then $100N = -3.\overline{03}$.
$100N = -3.\overline{03}$
$\underline{-\ \ N = -0.\overline{03}}$
$99N = -3$
$N = -\dfrac{3}{99} = -\dfrac{1}{33}$

So, $-0.\overline{03} = -\dfrac{1}{33}$.

42. $\dfrac{8}{20} = \dfrac{2}{5}$ 43. $\dfrac{15}{20} = \dfrac{3}{4}$ 44. $\dfrac{5+7}{20} = \dfrac{12}{20} = \dfrac{3}{5}$

45. $15 = 3 \cdot 5$ 46. $18 = 2 \cdot 3 \cdot 3$
$20 = 2 \cdot 2 \cdot 5$ $24 = 2 \cdot 2 \cdot 2 \cdot 3$
$LCM = 2^2 \cdot 3 \cdot 5 = 60$ $LCM = 2^3 \cdot 3^2 = 72$

47. $54 = 2 \cdot 3 \cdot 3 \cdot 3$
$72 = 2 \cdot 2 \cdot 2 \cdot 3 \cdot 3$
$LCM = 2^3 \cdot 3^3 = 216$

48. $8 = 2 \cdot 2 \cdot 2$
$20 = 2 \cdot 2 \cdot 5$
$24 = 2 \cdot 2 \cdot 2 \cdot 3$
$LCM = 2^3 \cdot 3 \cdot 5 = 120$

49. $5 = 5$ 50. $-10.29 > -10.30$
$174 = 2 \cdot 3 \cdot 29$
$30 = 2 \cdot 3 \cdot 5$
$LCM = 2 \cdot 3 \cdot 5 \cdot 29 = 870$

51. $\dfrac{4}{5} = \dfrac{12}{15}$ 52. $\dfrac{3}{8} = 0.375$

$\dfrac{11}{15} < \dfrac{4}{5}$

53. $0.\overline{4} > 0.4$ 54. $5,830,000$
$5,830,000 = 5.83 \times 10^6$

55. 0.0000735 56. $12,500$
$0.0000735 = 7.35 \times 10^{-5}$ $12,500 = 1.25 \times 10^4$

57. 0.00068
$0.00068 = 6.8 \times 10^{-4}$

58. $95,700,000$
$95,700,000 = 9.57 \times 10^7$

59.

Week	Eva's Savings	Karl's Savings	Combined Savings
1	$11.75	$10.05	$21.80
2	$13.35	$11.80	$25.15
3	$14.95	$13.55	$28.50
4	$16.55	$15.30	$31.85

4th week

60. $3.0 \times 10^8 = 3.0 \times 100,000,000$

$= 300,000,000$

$3.4 \times 10^2 = 3.4 \times 100$

$= 340$

$300,000,000 - 340 = 299,999,660$

Chapter 6 Test

PAGE 251

1. no; The number formed by the last two digits, 18, is not divisible by four.

2. $40 = 2 \cdot 2 \cdot 2 \cdot 5$
$24 = 2 \cdot 2 \cdot 2 \cdot 3$
$GCF = 2 \cdot 2 \cdot 2 = 8$

3. $56 = 2 \cdot 2 \cdot 2 \cdot 7$
$98 = 2 \cdot 7 \cdot 7$
$GCF = 2 \cdot 7 = 14$

4. $108 = 2 \cdot 2 \cdot 3 \cdot 3 \cdot 3$
$234 = 2 \cdot 3 \cdot 3 \cdot 13$
$30 = 2 \cdot 3 \cdot 5$
$GCF = 2 \cdot 3 = 6$

5. $320 = 2 \cdot 2 \cdot 2 \cdot 2 \cdot 2 \cdot 2 \cdot 5$
$16 = 2 \cdot 2 \cdot 2 \cdot 2$
$176 = 2 \cdot 2 \cdot 2 \cdot 2 \cdot 11$
$GCF = 2 \cdot 2 \cdot 2 \cdot 2 = 16$

6. $-\dfrac{10}{16} = -\dfrac{\cancel{2} \cdot 5}{\cancel{2} \cdot 2 \cdot 2 \cdot 2} = -\dfrac{5}{8}$

7. $\dfrac{42}{72} = \dfrac{\cancel{2} \cdot \cancel{3} \cdot 7}{\cancel{2} \cdot 2 \cdot 2 \cdot \cancel{3} \cdot 3} = \dfrac{7}{12}$

8. $-\dfrac{18}{81} = -\dfrac{2 \cdot \cancel{3} \cdot \cancel{3}}{\cancel{3} \cdot \cancel{3} \cdot 3 \cdot 3} = -\dfrac{2}{9}$

9. $\dfrac{90}{21} = \dfrac{2 \cdot \cancel{3} \cdot 3 \cdot 5}{\cancel{3} \cdot 7} = \dfrac{30}{7} = 4\dfrac{2}{7}$

10. $360 = 5 \cdot 72$
$360 = 5 \cdot 3 \cdot 24$
$360 = 5 \cdot 3 \cdot 3 \cdot 8$
$360 = 5 \cdot 3 \cdot 3 \cdot 2 \cdot 4$
$360 = 5 \cdot 3 \cdot 3 \cdot 2 \cdot 2 \cdot 2$
$360 = 2^3 \cdot 3^2 \cdot 5$

11. $-3.45 = -3\dfrac{45}{100}$
$= -3\dfrac{9}{20}$

12. $\dfrac{5}{16} = 0.3125$

13. $0.4 = \dfrac{4}{10}$
$= \dfrac{2}{5}$

14. $-\dfrac{3}{8} = -0.375$

15. $20.8125 = 20\dfrac{8,125}{10,000}$
$= 20\dfrac{13}{16}$

16. Let $N = -3.\overline{2}$. Then $10N = -32.\overline{2}$.
$10N = -32.\overline{2}$
$\underline{-\ N = -3.\overline{2}}$
$9N = -29$
$N = -\dfrac{29}{9} = -3\dfrac{2}{9}$
So, $-3.\overline{2} = -3\dfrac{2}{9}$.

17. Let $N = 0.\overline{621}$. Then $1,000N = 621.\overline{621}$.
$1,000N = 621.\overline{621}$
$\underline{-\ \ \ N = \ \ \ 0.\overline{621}}$
$999N = 621$
$N = \dfrac{621}{999} = \dfrac{23}{37}$
So, $0.\overline{621} = \dfrac{23}{37}$.

18. Let $N = 5.\overline{28}$. Then $100N = 528.\overline{28}$.
$100N = 528.\overline{28}$
$\underline{-\ \ N = \ \ 5.\overline{28}}$
$99N = 523$
$N = \dfrac{523}{99} = 5\dfrac{28}{99}$
So, $5.\overline{28} = 5\dfrac{28}{99}$.

19. $P(c) = \dfrac{1}{9}$

20. $P(o \text{ or } p) = \dfrac{2+1}{9} = \dfrac{3}{9} = \dfrac{1}{3}$

21. $P(\text{vowel}) = \dfrac{4}{9}$

22. $P(\text{not } o \text{ or } t) = \dfrac{3}{9} = \dfrac{1}{3}$

23. $18.4\overline{27}$

24. $24 = 2 \cdot 2 \cdot 2 \cdot 3$
$28 = 2 \cdot 2 \cdot 7$
$LCM = 2^3 \cdot 3 \cdot 7 = 168$

25. $9 = 3 \cdot 3$
$21 = 3 \cdot 7$
$LCM = 3^2 \cdot 7 = 63$

26. $12 = 2 \cdot 2 \cdot 3$
$15 = 3 \cdot 5$
$18 = 2 \cdot 3 \cdot 3$
$LCM = 2^2 \cdot 3^2 \cdot 5 = 180$

27. $81 = 3 \cdot 3 \cdot 3 \cdot 3$
$34 = 2 \cdot 17$
$54 = 2 \cdot 3 \cdot 3 \cdot 3$
$LCM = 2 \cdot 3^4 \cdot 17 = 2,754$

28. $\dfrac{4}{9} = \dfrac{12}{27}$
$\dfrac{4}{9} > \dfrac{11}{27}$

29. $5\dfrac{31}{100} = 5.31$

30. $-4.68 > -4.7$

31. $3.7 \times 10^{-4} = 3.7 \times 0.0001$
$= 0.00037$

32. $58,930,000$
$58,930,000 = 5.893 \times 10^7$

33. CD's: $426 + 509 - 453 = 482$
LP's: $152 + 209 - 183 = 178$
V's: $102 + 205 - 198 = 109$

PAGE 251   BONUS

yes; sample answer: 3, 4, 5

Academic Skills Test

PAGES 252–253

1. B; $3.4 \rightarrow 3.6$
   $\underline{-1.8} \rightarrow \underline{-2.0}$

2. C; Each will pay about $10

3. D; $96 \div 3 = 32 \rightarrow 96$ yd $= 32$ ft

4. A; $b(10 - c) = 5(10 - 8)$
   $ = 5(2)$
   $ = 10$

5. D; $4.2 = \dfrac{x}{3}$
   $3 \cdot 4.2 = \left(\dfrac{x}{3}\right) 3$
   $12.6 = x$

6. B; $2x - 10 = 96$
   $2x - 10 + 10 = 96 + 10$
   $2x = 106$
   $\dfrac{2x}{2} = \dfrac{106}{2}$
   $x = 53$

7. B; $-3 + 8 + (-3) + 1 = [-3 + 8] + [(-3) + 1]$
   $ = 5 + (-2)$
   $ = 3$

8. D; $-145 - 86 = -145 + (-86)$
   $ = -231$

9. A

10. D

11. C; 36, 38, 42, 44, 45, 46, 46, 48, 48, 48, 49, 50, 50, 52
    Median: $\dfrac{46 + 48}{2} = \dfrac{94}{2} = 47$

12. B; LQ: 44
    UQ: 49
    Interquartile Range: $49 - 44 = 5$

13. B

14. D;

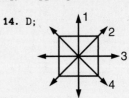

15. D;

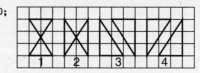

16. A; $2x = 40$
    $\dfrac{2x}{2} = \dfrac{40}{2}$
    $x = 20$

17. B

18. A; $-13.6 = -13\dfrac{3}{5}$

19. B; $\dfrac{2}{4} = \dfrac{1}{2} = 0.5$

20. B; 0.00075
    $0.00075 = 7.5 \times 10^{-4}$

Chapter 7   Rational Numbers

 Adding and Subtracting Like Fractions

PAGE 257   CHECKING FOR UNDERSTANDING

1. $\frac{5}{6} + \frac{5}{6} = \frac{5+5}{6} = \frac{10}{6} = 1\frac{4}{6} = 1\frac{2}{3}$

2.

$\frac{5}{8} + \frac{5}{8} = 1\frac{1}{4}$

3. Answers may vary. Sample answer: Add the numerators and leave denominators the same.

4. $\frac{3}{8} + \frac{1}{8} = d$

$\frac{3+1}{8} = d$

$\frac{4}{8} = d$

$\frac{1}{2} = d$

5. $\frac{3}{5} + \left(-\frac{2}{5}\right) = x$

$\frac{3 + (-2)}{5} = x$

$\frac{1}{5} = x$

6. $\frac{36}{21} - \frac{8}{21} = y$

$\frac{36 - 8}{21} = y$

$\frac{28}{21} = y$

$1\frac{7}{21} = y$

$1\frac{1}{3} = y$

7. $\frac{3}{16} + \frac{15}{16} = m$

$\frac{3 + 15}{16} = m$

$\frac{18}{16} = m$

$1\frac{2}{16} = m$

$1\frac{1}{8} = m$

8. $s = -\frac{4}{5} - \left(-\frac{3}{5}\right)$

$s = \frac{-4 - (-3)}{5}$

$s = \frac{-4 + 3}{5}$

$s = -\frac{1}{5}$

9. $r = \frac{9}{7} - \frac{5}{7}$

$r = \frac{9 - 5}{7}$

$r = \frac{4}{7}$

PAGE 258   EXERCISES

10. $\frac{5}{8} + \frac{1}{8} = n$

$\frac{5+1}{8} = n$

$\frac{6}{8} = n$

$\frac{3}{4} = n$

11. $\frac{17}{9} + \left(-\frac{1}{9}\right) = y$

$\frac{17 + (-1)}{9} = y$

$\frac{16}{9} = y$

$1\frac{7}{9} = y$

12. $b = -\frac{7}{12} - \frac{5}{12}$

$b = \frac{-7 - 5}{12}$

$b = \frac{-12}{12}$

$b = -1$

13. $z = \frac{1}{18} - \frac{7}{18}$

$z = \frac{1 - 7}{18}$

$z = \frac{-6}{18}$

$z = -\frac{1}{3}$

14. $5\frac{3}{4} + 2\frac{3}{4} = g$

$7 + \frac{3+3}{4} = g$

$7 + \frac{6}{4} = g$

$7 + 1\frac{2}{4} = g$

$8\frac{1}{2} = g$

15. $c = \frac{21}{8} - \frac{49}{8}$

$c = \frac{21 - 49}{8}$

$c = \frac{-28}{8}$

$c = -3\frac{4}{8}$

$c = -3\frac{1}{2}$

16. $m = -\frac{3}{5} - \left(-\frac{4}{5}\right)$

$m = \frac{-3 - (-4)}{5}$

$m = \frac{-3 + 4}{5}$

$m = \frac{1}{5}$

17. $-2\frac{5}{9} - \frac{5}{9} = r$

$-2 + \frac{-5 - 5}{9} = r$

$-2 + \frac{-10}{9} = r$

$-2 + \left(-1\frac{1}{9}\right) = r$

$-3\frac{1}{9} = r$

18. $k = -\frac{2}{3} - \frac{1}{3}$

$k = \frac{-2 - 1}{3}$

$k = \frac{-3}{3}$

$k = -1$

19. $\frac{5}{6} + \left(-\frac{1}{6}\right) = \frac{5 + (-1)}{6}$

$= \frac{4}{6}$

$= \frac{2}{3}$

20. $-\frac{5}{12} + \left(-\frac{1}{12}\right) = \frac{-5 + (-1)}{12}$

$= \frac{-6}{12}$

$= -\frac{1}{2}$

21. $-\frac{1}{8} - \left(-\frac{5}{8}\right) = \frac{-1 - (-5)}{8}$

$= \frac{-1 + 5}{8}$

$= \frac{4}{8}$

$= \frac{1}{2}$

22. $5\frac{1}{2} - \left(-2\frac{1}{2}\right) = 5 - (-2) + \frac{1}{2} - \left(-\frac{1}{2}\right)$

$= 5 - (-2) + \frac{1 - (-1)}{2}$

$= 5 + 2 + \frac{1 + 1}{2}$

$= 7 + \frac{2}{2}$

$= 7 + 1$

$= 8$

23. $-\frac{25}{6} + \frac{7}{6} = \frac{-25 + 7}{6}$

$= \frac{-18}{6}$

$= -3$

24. $\frac{4}{9} - \left(-\frac{7}{9}\right) = \frac{4 - (-7)}{9}$

$= \frac{4 + 7}{9}$

$= \frac{11}{9}$

$= 1\frac{2}{9}$

25. $d - c = \dfrac{12}{5} - \left(-\dfrac{3}{5}\right)$ 26. $c + d = -\dfrac{3}{5} + \dfrac{12}{5}$

$ = \dfrac{12 - (-3)}{5}$ $= \dfrac{-3 + 12}{5}$

$ = \dfrac{12 + 3}{5}$ $= \dfrac{9}{5}$

$ = \dfrac{15}{5}$ $= 1\dfrac{4}{5}$

$ = 3$

27. $c - d = -\dfrac{3}{5} - \dfrac{12}{5}$

$ = \dfrac{-3 - 12}{5}$

$ = \dfrac{-15}{5}$

$ = -3$

28. $4\dfrac{1}{2}y + \dfrac{1}{2}y - 2\dfrac{1}{2}y = \left(4\dfrac{1}{2} + \dfrac{1}{2} - 2\dfrac{1}{2}\right)y$

$\phantom{4\dfrac{1}{2}y + \dfrac{1}{2}y - 2\dfrac{1}{2}y} = \left(4\dfrac{1+1}{2} - 2\dfrac{1}{2}\right)y$

$\phantom{4\dfrac{1}{2}y + \dfrac{1}{2}y - 2\dfrac{1}{2}y} = \left(4\dfrac{2}{2} - 2\dfrac{1}{2}\right)y$

$\phantom{4\dfrac{1}{2}y + \dfrac{1}{2}y - 2\dfrac{1}{2}y} = \left(2\dfrac{2-1}{2}\right)y$

$\phantom{4\dfrac{1}{2}y + \dfrac{1}{2}y - 2\dfrac{1}{2}y} = 2\dfrac{1}{2}y$

29. $-2\dfrac{1}{3}n + \left(-\dfrac{2}{3}n\right) + 4n = \left(-2\dfrac{1}{3} + \left(-\dfrac{2}{3}\right) + 4\right)n$

$\phantom{-2\dfrac{1}{3}n + \left(-\dfrac{2}{3}n\right) + 4n} = \left(-2 + \dfrac{-1 + (-2)}{3} + 4\right)n$

$\phantom{-2\dfrac{1}{3}n + \left(-\dfrac{2}{3}n\right) + 4n} = \left(-2 + \dfrac{-3}{3} + 4\right)n$

$\phantom{-2\dfrac{1}{3}n + \left(-\dfrac{2}{3}n\right) + 4n} = (-2 - 1 + 4)n$

$\phantom{-2\dfrac{1}{3}n + \left(-\dfrac{2}{3}n\right) + 4n} = (-3 + 4)n$

$\phantom{-2\dfrac{1}{3}n + \left(-\dfrac{2}{3}n\right) + 4n} = 1n$

$\phantom{-2\dfrac{1}{3}n + \left(-\dfrac{2}{3}n\right) + 4n} = n$

30. $\dfrac{9}{5}r + \left(-\dfrac{1}{5}r\right) - \dfrac{3}{5}r = \left(\dfrac{9}{5} + \left(-\dfrac{1}{5}\right) - \dfrac{3}{5}\right)r$

$\phantom{\dfrac{9}{5}r + \left(-\dfrac{1}{5}r\right) - \dfrac{3}{5}r} = \left(\dfrac{9 + (-1)}{5} - \dfrac{3}{5}\right)r$

$\phantom{\dfrac{9}{5}r + \left(-\dfrac{1}{5}r\right) - \dfrac{3}{5}r} = \left(\dfrac{8}{5} - \dfrac{3}{5}\right)r$

$\phantom{\dfrac{9}{5}r + \left(-\dfrac{1}{5}r\right) - \dfrac{3}{5}r} = \left(\dfrac{8 - 3}{5}\right)r$

$\phantom{\dfrac{9}{5}r + \left(-\dfrac{1}{5}r\right) - \dfrac{3}{5}r} = \dfrac{5}{5}r$

$\phantom{\dfrac{9}{5}r + \left(-\dfrac{1}{5}r\right) - \dfrac{3}{5}r} = 1r$

$\phantom{\dfrac{9}{5}r + \left(-\dfrac{1}{5}r\right) - \dfrac{3}{5}r} = r$

31. 7,000 lbs = ? tons   32. $-42 \div (-14) = p$

    $7{,}000 \div 2{,}000 = 3\dfrac{1}{2}$ tons $\dfrac{-42}{-14} = p$

                                         $3 = p$

33. Since you can turn the figure less than $360°$ and it looks like the original, the figure has rotational symmetry.

34. $52{,}380{,}000 = 5.238 \times 10^{7}$

35. $15 - 3\dfrac{1}{4} - 5\dfrac{3}{4} = 14\dfrac{4}{4} - 3\dfrac{1}{4} - 5\dfrac{3}{4}$

$\phantom{15 - 3\dfrac{1}{4} - 5\dfrac{3}{4}} = 14 - 3 + \dfrac{4 - 1}{4} - 5\dfrac{3}{4}$

$\phantom{15 - 3\dfrac{1}{4} - 5\dfrac{3}{4}} = 11 + \dfrac{3}{4} - 5\dfrac{3}{4}$

$\phantom{15 - 3\dfrac{1}{4} - 5\dfrac{3}{4}} = 11\dfrac{3}{4} - 5\dfrac{3}{4}$

$\phantom{15 - 3\dfrac{1}{4} - 5\dfrac{3}{4}} = 6\dfrac{0}{4}$ or 6 minutes left

36. If $x = -2$, $\dfrac{x}{1} = \dfrac{-2}{1} = -2$

$\phantom{\text{If } x = -2,} \dfrac{1}{x} = \dfrac{1}{-2} = -\dfrac{1}{2}$

    If $x = 1$, $\dfrac{x}{1} = \dfrac{1}{1} = 1$

$\phantom{\text{If } x = 1,} \dfrac{1}{x} = \dfrac{1}{1} = 1$

    If $x = \dfrac{1}{2}$, $\dfrac{x}{1} = \dfrac{\frac{1}{2}}{1} = \dfrac{1}{2}$

$\phantom{\text{If } x = \dfrac{1}{2},} \dfrac{1}{x} = \dfrac{1}{\frac{1}{2}} = 2$

    If $x = 3$, $\dfrac{x}{1} = \dfrac{3}{1} = 3$

$\phantom{\text{If } x = 3,} \dfrac{1}{x} = \dfrac{1}{3} = \dfrac{1}{3}$

    If $x > 1$, then $\dfrac{x}{1} > \dfrac{1}{x}$. If $x < 1$, then $\dfrac{x}{1} < \dfrac{1}{x}$.

37. a. $P(\text{rolling a 3 or a 6}) = \dfrac{2}{6} = \dfrac{1}{3}$

    b. $P(\text{not rolling a 3 or a 6}) = \dfrac{4}{6} = \dfrac{2}{3}$

    c. $\dfrac{1}{3} + \dfrac{2}{3} = \dfrac{1 + 2}{3} = \dfrac{3}{3} = 1$

38. See students' work.

7-2   Adding and Subtracting Unlike Fractions

1. Rename one or both fractions so they have common denominators.

2. Answers may vary. Sample answer: The number being subtracted contains $\dfrac{6}{8}$ or $\dfrac{7}{8}$.

3. $7\dfrac{2}{5} = 6\dfrac{2 + 5}{5}$ 4. $3\dfrac{1}{4} = 2\dfrac{1 + 4}{4}$

$\phantom{7\dfrac{2}{5}} = 6\dfrac{7}{5}$ $= 2\dfrac{5}{4}$

5. $4\dfrac{5}{12} = 3\dfrac{5 + 12}{12}$ 6. $9\dfrac{3}{8} = 8\dfrac{3 + 8}{8}$

$\phantom{4\dfrac{5}{12}} = 3\dfrac{17}{12}$ $= 8\dfrac{11}{8}$

7. $\dfrac{2}{3} - \dfrac{3}{4} = a$ 8. $x = \dfrac{1}{2} + \dfrac{2}{3}$

   $\dfrac{8}{12} - \dfrac{9}{12} = a$ $x = \dfrac{3}{6} + \dfrac{4}{6}$

   $\dfrac{8 - 9}{12} = a$ $x = \dfrac{3 + 4}{6}$

   $-\dfrac{1}{12} = a$ $x = \dfrac{7}{6} = 1\dfrac{1}{6}$

9. $\frac{1}{2} + \left(-\frac{7}{8}\right) = y$

$\frac{4}{8} - \frac{7}{8} = y$

$\frac{4-7}{8} = y$

$-\frac{3}{8} = y$

10. $h = 3\frac{1}{2} - 2\frac{2}{9}$

$h = 3\frac{9}{18} - 2\frac{4}{18}$

$h = 1\frac{9-4}{18}$

$h = 1\frac{5}{18}$

11. $5 - 3\frac{1}{3} = k$

$4\frac{3}{3} - 3\frac{1}{3} = k$

$1\frac{3-1}{3} = k$

$1\frac{2}{3} = k$

12. $g = 9\frac{1}{3} - 2\frac{1}{2}$

$g = 9\frac{2}{6} - 2\frac{3}{6}$

$g = 8\frac{8}{6} - 2\frac{3}{6}$

$g = 6\frac{8-3}{6}$

$g = 6\frac{5}{6}$

PAGE 261   EXERCISES

13. $h = \frac{1}{2} + \frac{4}{5}$

$h = \frac{5}{10} + \frac{8}{10}$

$h = \frac{13}{10}$

$h = 1\frac{3}{10}$

14. $-\frac{7}{10} + \frac{1}{5} = f$

$-\frac{7}{10} + \frac{2}{10} = f$

$\frac{-5}{10} = f$

$-\frac{1}{2} = f$

15. $j = -\frac{3}{4} + \left(-\frac{1}{3}\right)$

$j = -\frac{9}{12} + \left(-\frac{4}{12}\right)$

$j = -\frac{13}{12}$

$j = -1\frac{1}{12}$

16. $5\frac{1}{5} - \left(-2\frac{7}{10}\right) = z$

$5\frac{2}{10} + 2\frac{7}{10} = z$

$7\frac{9}{10} = z$

17. $w = -4\frac{1}{8} - 5\frac{1}{4}$

$w = -4\frac{1}{8} - 5\frac{2}{8}$

$w = -9\frac{3}{8}$

18. $9 - 6\frac{1}{4} = x$

$8\frac{4}{4} - 6\frac{1}{4} = x$

$2\frac{3}{4} = x$

19. $7\frac{3}{4} - \left(-1\frac{1}{8}\right) = y$

$7\frac{6}{8} + 1\frac{1}{8} = y$

$8\frac{7}{8} = y$

20. $t = 3\frac{2}{3} + \left(-5\frac{3}{4}\right)$

$t = 3\frac{8}{12} + \left(-5\frac{9}{12}\right)$

$t = -5\frac{9}{12} + 3\frac{8}{12}$

$t = -2\frac{1}{12}$

21. $-8\frac{5}{9} - 2\frac{1}{6} = m$

$-8\frac{10}{18} - 2\frac{3}{18} = m$

$-10\frac{13}{18} = m$

22. $\frac{7}{6} + \frac{5}{18} = \frac{21}{18} + \frac{5}{18}$

$= \frac{26}{18}$

$= 1\frac{8}{18}$

$= 1\frac{4}{9}$

23. $-8\frac{1}{5} - 2\frac{1}{2} = -8\frac{2}{10} - 2\frac{5}{10}$

$= -10\frac{7}{10}$

24. $c - b = -\frac{5}{9} - 3\frac{11}{12}$

$= -\frac{20}{36} - 3\frac{33}{36}$

$= -3\frac{53}{36}$

$= -4\frac{17}{36}$

25. $a + b + c = \frac{5}{8} + 3\frac{11}{12} + \left(-\frac{5}{9}\right)$

$= \frac{45}{72} + 3\frac{66}{72} + \left(-\frac{40}{72}\right)$

$= 3\frac{111}{72} - \frac{40}{72}$

$= 3\frac{71}{72}$

26. $a - c = \frac{5}{8} - \left(-\frac{5}{9}\right)$

$= \frac{5}{8} + \frac{5}{9}$

$= \frac{45}{72} + \frac{40}{72}$

$= \frac{85}{72}$

$= 1\frac{13}{72}$

27. $b - (-c) = b + c$

$= 3\frac{11}{12} + \left(-\frac{5}{9}\right)$

$= 3\frac{33}{36} + \left(-\frac{20}{36}\right)$

$= 3\frac{13}{36}$

28. $16 + n = 43$

$16 - 16 + n = 43 - 16$

$n = 27$

29. 120, 128, 132, 140, 146

Median: 132

$UQ: \frac{140 + 146}{2} = \frac{286}{2} = 143$

$LQ: \frac{120 + 128}{2} = \frac{248}{2} = 124$

30. $\frac{24}{32} = \frac{24 \div 8}{32 \div 8} = \frac{3}{4}$

31. $-5\frac{1}{6} + 2\frac{5}{6} = -4\frac{7}{6} + 2\frac{5}{6}$

$= -2\frac{2}{6}$

$= -2\frac{1}{3}$

32. $\frac{1}{16} + \frac{3}{4} = \frac{1}{16} + \frac{12}{16}$

$= \frac{13}{16}$ in.

33. $1 - \frac{1}{5} = \frac{5}{5} - \frac{1}{5} = \frac{4}{5}$

So $\frac{4}{5}$ of half of the pipe is 12 feet long and $\frac{1}{5}$ of the piece must be 3 feet long. This means that $\frac{1}{2}$ of the original pipe is 12 + 3 or 15 feet long. The original pipe must then be 15 + 15 or 30 feet long.

34. $13\frac{3}{4} - \frac{7}{16} - \frac{1}{2} = 13\frac{12}{16} - \frac{7}{16} - \frac{8}{16}$

$= 13\frac{5}{16} - \frac{8}{16}$

$= 12\frac{21}{16} - \frac{8}{16}$

$= 12\frac{13}{16}$

35. See students' work.

69

7-3 Multiplying Fractions

PAGES 263-264   CHECKING FOR UNDERSTANDING

1. $\frac{1}{3} \cdot \frac{3}{4} = \frac{3}{12} = \frac{1}{4}$

2. One of 3 rows is shaded blue to represent $\frac{1}{3}$. Three of 4 columns is shaded yellow to represent $\frac{3}{4}$. Three of the sections overlap and appear green. This represents 3 out of 12 or $\frac{1}{4}$.

3.

4. $\frac{3}{5} \cdot \frac{5}{8} = a$

$\frac{15}{40} = a$

$\frac{3}{8} = a$

5. $\frac{5}{9} \cdot \frac{8}{15} = r$

$\frac{40}{135} = r$

$\frac{8}{27} = r$

6. $y = \frac{4}{9} \cdot \frac{2}{1}$

$y = \frac{8}{9}$

7. $-4\frac{1}{2}\left(-\frac{2}{3}\right) = j$

$\left(-\frac{9}{2}\right)\left(-\frac{2}{3}\right) = j$

$\frac{18}{6} = j$

$3 = j$

8. $5\frac{1}{3} \cdot \frac{5}{12} = g$

$\frac{16}{3} \cdot \frac{5}{12} = g$

$\frac{80}{36} = g$

$2\frac{8}{36} = g$

$2\frac{2}{9} = g$

9. $d = -2\left(\frac{3}{8}\right)$

$d = \left(-\frac{2}{1}\right)\left(\frac{3}{8}\right)$

$d = -\frac{6}{8}$

$d = -\frac{3}{4}$

10. $\frac{15}{16} \cdot 3\frac{3}{5} = k$

$\frac{15}{16} \cdot \frac{18}{5} = k$

$\frac{270}{80} = k$

$3\frac{30}{80} = k$

$3\frac{3}{8} = k$

11. $-2\frac{1}{4} \cdot \frac{2}{3} = h$

$\left(-\frac{9}{4}\right)\left(\frac{2}{3}\right) = h$

$-\frac{18}{12} = h$

$-1\frac{6}{12} = h$

$-1\frac{1}{2} = h$

12. $-2\frac{2}{5}\left(-1\frac{3}{4}\right) = x$

$\left(-\frac{12}{5}\right)\left(-\frac{7}{4}\right) = x$

$\frac{84}{20} = x$

$4\frac{4}{20} = x$

$4\frac{1}{5} = x$

13. $\left(-\frac{1}{3}\right)\left(2\frac{1}{4}\right) = \left(-\frac{1}{3}\right)\left(\frac{9}{4}\right)$

$= -\frac{9}{12}$

$= -\frac{3}{4}$

14. $\frac{2}{7} \cdot \frac{3}{4} = p$

$\frac{6}{28} = p$

$\frac{3}{14} = p$

15. $-\frac{5}{12} \cdot \frac{8}{9} = n$

$-\frac{40}{108} = n$

$-\frac{10}{27} = n$

16. $\frac{1}{19}\left(-\frac{15}{16}\right) = x$

$-\frac{15}{304} = x$

17. $-3\frac{3}{8}\left(-\frac{5}{6}\right) = y$

$-\frac{27}{8}\left(-\frac{5}{6}\right) = y$

$\frac{135}{48} = y$

$2\frac{39}{48} = y$

$2\frac{13}{16} = y$

18. $z = \frac{1}{6} \cdot 1\frac{3}{5}$

$z = \frac{1}{6} \cdot \frac{8}{5}$

$z = \frac{8}{30}$

$z = \frac{4}{15}$

19. $k = (-6)\left(2\frac{1}{4}\right)$

$k = \left(-\frac{6}{1}\right)\left(\frac{9}{4}\right)$

$k = -\frac{54}{4}$

$k = -13\frac{2}{4}$

$k = -13\frac{1}{2}$

20. $-3\frac{1}{3}\left(-1\frac{1}{5}\right) = d$

$\left(-\frac{10}{3}\right)\left(-\frac{6}{5}\right) = d$

$\frac{60}{15} = d$

$4 = d$

21. $h = 8\frac{1}{4} \cdot 3\frac{1}{3}$

$h = \frac{33}{4} \cdot \frac{10}{3}$

$h = \frac{330}{12}$

$h = 27\frac{6}{12}$

$h = 27\frac{1}{2}$

22. $6\left(-7\frac{1}{2}\right) = m$

$\left(\frac{6}{1}\right)\left(-\frac{15}{2}\right) = m$

$-\frac{90}{2} = m$

$-45 = m$

23. $x = \left(\frac{2}{3}\right)^2$

$x = \frac{2}{3} \cdot \frac{2}{3}$

$x = \frac{4}{9}$

24. $b = \left(-\frac{8}{13}\right)^2$

$b = \left(-\frac{8}{13}\right)\left(-\frac{8}{13}\right)$

$b = \frac{64}{169}$

25. $5 \cdot \left(\frac{4}{5}\right)^2 = t$

$\frac{5}{1}\left(\frac{4}{5}\right)\left(\frac{4}{5}\right) = t$

$\frac{80}{25} = t$

$3\frac{5}{25} = t$

$3\frac{1}{5} = t$

26. $ar = \left(\frac{4}{5}\right)\left(\frac{1}{2}\right)$

$= \frac{4}{10}$

$= \frac{2}{5}$

27. $2d = 2\left(-3\frac{3}{4}\right)$

$= \left(\frac{2}{1}\right)\left(-\frac{15}{4}\right)$

$= -\frac{30}{4}$

$= -\frac{15}{2}$

$= -7\frac{1}{2}$

28. $p^2 = \left(-1\frac{1}{3}\right)^2$

$= \left(-\frac{4}{3}\right)^2$

$= \left(-\frac{4}{3}\right)\left(-\frac{4}{3}\right)$

$= \frac{16}{9}$

$= 1\frac{7}{9}$

29. $r^2\left(-d\right) = \left(\frac{1}{2}\right)^2\left(-\left(-3\frac{3}{4}\right)\right)$

$= \left(\frac{1}{2}\right)\left(\frac{1}{2}\right)\left(3\frac{3}{4}\right)$

$= \left(\frac{1}{4}\right)\left(\frac{15}{4}\right)$

$= \frac{15}{16}$

30. $P = 4s$

$P = 4(5)$

$P = 20\ cm$

$A = s^2$

$A = (5)^2$

$A = (5)(5)$

$A = 25\ cm^2$

31. $d = 56 + (-18)$

$d = 38$

32. $-\frac{1}{5}, -\frac{1}{10}, \frac{1}{8}, \frac{1}{3}, \frac{1}{2}$

33. $-1\frac{3}{8} + \left(-3\frac{5}{12}\right) = -1\frac{9}{24} - 3\frac{10}{24}$

$= -4\frac{19}{24}$

34. a. $1\frac{9}{10} \cdot 18 = \frac{19}{10} \cdot \frac{18}{1}$ $A = lw$ or fly $\times$ hoist

$= \frac{342}{10}$ $= \left(34\frac{1}{5}\right)(18)$

$= 34\frac{2}{10}$ $= \left(\frac{171}{5}\right)\left(\frac{18}{1}\right)$

$= 34\frac{1}{5}$ $= \frac{3,078}{5}$

$= 615\frac{3}{5}\ m^2$

b. $1\frac{9}{10}\left(9\frac{1}{2}\right) = \left(\frac{19}{10}\right)\left(\frac{19}{2}\right)$ $A = lw$

$= \frac{361}{20}$ $A = \frac{722}{100} \cdot \frac{133}{26}$

length $= \frac{361}{20} \cdot \frac{2}{5}$ $A = \frac{96,026}{2,600}$

$= \frac{722}{100}$ $A = 36\frac{2,426}{2,600}$

width $= \frac{19}{2} \cdot \frac{7}{13}$ $A = 36\frac{1,213}{1,300}$

$= \frac{133}{26}$

35. $\left(-\frac{3}{4}\right)^2 = \left(-\frac{3}{4}\right)\left(-\frac{3}{4}\right)$

$= \frac{9}{16}$

$-\left(\frac{3}{4}\right)^2 = -\left(\frac{3}{4}\right)\left(\frac{3}{4}\right)$

$= -\frac{9}{16}$

36. The product will be greater than the original number. For example,

$\frac{2}{3} \cdot (-6) = \frac{2}{3} \cdot \left(-\frac{6}{1}\right)$

$= -\frac{12}{3}$

$= -4$

$-4 > -6$

7-4   Properties of Rational Numbers

1. $\frac{7}{5}$

2. Write $-4\frac{2}{5}$ as $-\frac{22}{5}$. Then find the reciprocal which is $-\frac{5}{22}$.

3. Answers may vary. Sample answer: $\frac{3}{4} \cdot \frac{4}{5} = \frac{4}{5} \cdot \frac{3}{4}$

4. associative property of multiplication

5. yes   **6.** No, it would be $-\frac{5}{6}$.

7. No, it would be $\frac{4}{3}$.   **8.** Yes, because $1\frac{1}{5} = \frac{6}{5}$.

9. $5 = \frac{5}{1}$ **10.** $-\frac{3}{2}$ **11.** $0.2 = \frac{2}{10}$ or $\frac{1}{5}$

Mult. Inv. $= \frac{1}{5}$ Mult. Inv. $= \frac{5}{1}$ or 5

12. $2\frac{4}{5} = \frac{14}{5}$ **13.** $m = -\frac{1}{12}$

Mult. Inv. $= \frac{5}{14}$

14. $n = \frac{1}{2}\left(12 + \frac{4}{5}\right)$

$n = \left(\frac{1}{2} \cdot 12\right) + \left(\frac{1}{2} \cdot \frac{4}{5}\right)$

$n = 6 + \frac{2}{5}$

$n = 6\frac{2}{5}$

15. $4\left(5 + \frac{1}{2}\right) = k$

$\left(4 \cdot 5\right) + \left(4 \cdot \frac{1}{2}\right) = k$

$20 + 2 = k$

$22 = k$

16. $10 = \frac{10}{1}$ **17.** $-\frac{5}{3}$ **18.** $0.4 = \frac{4}{10}$ or $\frac{2}{5}$

Mult. Inv. $= \frac{1}{10}$ Mult. Inv. $= \frac{5}{2}$

19. $2\frac{8}{9} = \frac{26}{9}$ **20.** $\frac{8}{7}$

Mult. Inv. $= \frac{9}{26}$

21. $-1 = -\frac{1}{1}$ **22.** $\frac{d}{c}$

Mult. Inv. $= -\frac{1}{1}$ or -1

71

23. $-x = -\dfrac{x}{1}$

Mult. Inv. $= -\dfrac{1}{x}$

24. $\dfrac{9}{8} = 1\dfrac{1}{8}$; No, reciprocal is $1\dfrac{1}{8}$.

25. $0.3 = \dfrac{3}{10}$

Mult. Inv. $= \dfrac{10}{3}$ or $3\dfrac{1}{3}$

yes

26. $by = \left(\dfrac{2}{3}\right)\left(1\dfrac{5}{6}\right)$

$= \left(\dfrac{2}{3}\right)\left(1 + \dfrac{5}{6}\right)$

$= \left(\dfrac{2}{3} \cdot 1\right) + \left(\dfrac{2}{3} \cdot \dfrac{5}{6}\right)$

$= \dfrac{2}{3} + \dfrac{10}{18}$

$= \dfrac{6}{9} + \dfrac{5}{9}$

$= \dfrac{11}{9}$

$= 2\dfrac{2}{9}$

27. $2x = 2\left(-2\dfrac{1}{4}\right)$

$= 2\left(-2 + -\dfrac{1}{4}\right)$

$= (2 \cdot (-2)) + \left(2 \cdot \left(-\dfrac{1}{4}\right)\right)$

$= -4 + \left(-\dfrac{1}{2}\right)$

$= -4\dfrac{1}{2}$

28. $a^2 = \left(-\dfrac{1}{2}\right)^2$

$= \left(-\dfrac{1}{2}\right)\left(-\dfrac{1}{2}\right)$

$= \dfrac{1}{4}$

29. $ax + \dfrac{1}{2} = \left(-\dfrac{1}{2}\right)\left(-2\dfrac{1}{4}\right) + \dfrac{1}{2}$

$= -\dfrac{1}{2}\left(-2 + \left(\dfrac{1}{4}\right)\right) + \dfrac{1}{2}$

$= \left(-\dfrac{1}{2} \cdot (-2)\right) + \left(-\dfrac{1}{2} \cdot \left(-\dfrac{1}{4}\right)\right) + \dfrac{1}{2}$

$= 1 + \dfrac{1}{8} + \dfrac{1}{2}$

$= 1 + \dfrac{1}{8} + \dfrac{4}{8}$

$= 1\dfrac{5}{8}$

30. $3b - 4a = 3\left(\dfrac{2}{3}\right) - 4\left(-\dfrac{1}{2}\right)$

$= 2 + 2$

$= 4$

31. $\dfrac{1}{2} + a = \dfrac{1}{2} + \left(-\dfrac{1}{2}\right)$

$= 0$

32. $b^2\left(y + 5\right) = \left(\dfrac{2}{3}\right)^2\left(1\dfrac{5}{6} + 5\right)$

$= \left(\dfrac{2}{3}\right)\left(\dfrac{2}{3}\right)\left(6\dfrac{5}{6}\right)$

$= \dfrac{4}{9}\left(6 + \dfrac{5}{6}\right)$

$= \left(\dfrac{4}{9} \cdot 6\right) + \left(\dfrac{4}{9} \cdot \dfrac{5}{6}\right)$

$= \dfrac{24}{9} + \dfrac{20}{54}$

$= \dfrac{144}{54} + \dfrac{20}{54}$

$= \dfrac{164}{54}$

$= \dfrac{82}{27}$

$= 3\dfrac{1}{27}$

33. $a + b + x = \left(-\dfrac{1}{2}\right) + \dfrac{2}{3} + \left(-2\dfrac{1}{4}\right)$

$= -\dfrac{1}{2} + \dfrac{2}{3} + \left(-\dfrac{9}{4}\right)$

$= -\dfrac{6}{12} + \dfrac{8}{12} + \left(-\dfrac{27}{12}\right)$

$= -\dfrac{25}{12}$

$= -2\dfrac{1}{12}$

34. $2.75 \times 1{,}000 = 2{,}750$ millimeters

35. $35 - 5 = 30$

36. $24 = 2 \cdot 2 \cdot 2 \cdot 3$

$64 = 2 \cdot 2 \cdot 2 \cdot 2 \cdot 2 \cdot 2$

$GCF = 2 \cdot 2 \cdot 2 = 8$

37. $-\dfrac{7}{16} \cdot \dfrac{4}{9} = j$

$-\dfrac{28}{144} = j$

$-\dfrac{7}{36} = j$

38. $16 + 4 = 4$

$4\left(1\dfrac{3}{4}\right) = 4\left(1 + \dfrac{3}{4}\right)$

$= \left(4 \cdot 1\right) + \left(4 \cdot \dfrac{3}{4}\right)$

$= 4 + 3$

$= 7$

39. a. Row 1 increases by 1. Row 2 increases by consecutive odd integers. Row 3 decreases by consecutive odd integers divided by LCD of those two fractions.

b. They are multiplicative inverses of each other.

Decision Making

1. The profit on each medium adult shirt depends on the number of shirts ordered.

No. of Shirts Ordered	Cost Each	Printing Cost Each	Total Cost to Manufacture	3 × Wholesale Price	Profit per Shirt
1	$5	$2.50	$7.50	$15.00	$7.50
2-5	$5	$1.00	$6.00	$15.00	$9.00
6-15	$4	$1.00	$5.00	$12.00	$7.00
16-25	$3	$1.00	$4.00	$9.00	$5.00
over 25	$3	$0.50	$3.50	$9.00	$5.50

2. Cost of manufacture: 15 tapes @ $4 = $60.00
   Cost of shipping: = $ 8.75
   Total cost of 15 tapes: = $68.75
   Cost of each tape: $68.75 ÷ 15 ≈ $4.58

   Cost of manufacture: 25 tapes @ $4 = $100.00
   Cost of shipping: = $ 8.75
   Total cost of 25 tapes: = $108.75

   Cost of each tape: $108.75 ÷ 25 = $4.35

3. 5 youth shirts size L   = 5($4) or $20
   5 adult shirts size M   = 5($5) or $25
   5 adult shirts size L   = 5($5) or $25
   cost of printing 15 shirts = 15($1) or $15
            TOTAL COST = $20 + $25 + $25 + $15 or $85

4. See students' work.

5. See students' work.

6. See students' work.

7. See students' work.

7-5 Find a Pattern

1. Answers may vary. Sample answer: Two comes from the fact that the goose flies $\frac{1}{2}$ the remaining distance each time; n is the number of flights the goose has made.

$$\frac{1}{2^1} + \frac{1}{2^2} + \frac{1}{2^3} + \frac{1}{2^4} + \ldots + \frac{1}{2^n}$$

2. $\frac{1}{2^8} = \frac{1}{256}$ is how far the goose has left.

   So $1 - \frac{1}{256} = \frac{256}{256} - \frac{1}{256} = \frac{255}{256}$ miles is how far the goose has traveled.

3. 6 rectangles with area $A = l \times w$
   5 rectangles with area $A = l \times 2w$
   4 rectangles with area $A = l \times 3w$
   3 rectangles with area $A = l \times 4w$
   2 rectangles with area $A = l \times 5w$
   1 rectangle with area $A = l \times 6w$
   Total number of rectangles
   = 1 + 2 + 3 + 4 + 5 + 6 = 21

4.

   0   2   5   9

   3 sides → 0 diagonals
   4 sides → 2 diagonals (+2)
   5 sides → 5 diagonals (+3)
   6 sides → 9 diagonals (+4)
   So a 7-sided polygon has 9 + 5 = 14 diagonals.

5. 100 - 5 = 95
   95 - 10 = 85
   85 - 15 = 70
   The next number is 70 - 20 = 50.

6. 34 - 1 = 33 points
   33 - 3 = 30 → 1 field goal
   30 ÷ 6 = 5 → 5 touchdowns
                6 scores

   33 - 6 = 27 → 2 field goals
   27 ÷ 6 = 4.5 → can't do

   33 - 9 = 24 → 3 field goals
   24 ÷ 6 = 4 → 4 touchdowns
                7 scores

   The team made 4 touchdowns.

7. 11 + 7 = 18
   18 × 2 = 36 exercises assigned

8. Apts. 1-9 use 1 each of numbers 1-9.

Apts. 10-19 use 1 each of numbers 0-9 plus
  10 number 1's.

Apts. 20-29 use 1 each of numbers 0-9 plus
  10 number 2's.

Apts. 30-39 use 1 each of numbers 0-9 plus
  10 number 3's.

Apts. 40-48 use 1 each of numbers 0-8 plus
  9 number 4's.

$1 + 1 + 1 + 1 = 4 - 0$'s

$1 + 1 + 10 + 1 + 1 + 1 = 15 - 1$'s

$1 + 1 + 1 + 10 + 1 + 1 = 15 - 2$'s

$1 + 1 + 1 + 1 + 10 + 1 = 15 - 3$'s

$1 + 1 + 1 + 1 + 1 + 9 = 14 - 4$'s

$1 + 1 + 1 + 1 + 1 = 5 - 5$'s

$1 + 1 + 1 + 1 + 1 = 5 - 6$'s

$1 + 1 + 1 + 1 + 1 = 5 - 7$'s

$1 + 1 + 1 + 1 + 1 = 5 - 8$'s

$1 + 1 + 1 + 1 = 4 - 9$'s

9. Since the sum of the digits is 9, look at the numbers that sum to 9. Namely, 0 and 9, 1 and 8, 2 and 7, 3 and 6, 4 and 5. Then look at the product for each pair. $0 \times 9 = 0$, $1 \times 8 = 8$, $2 \times 7 = 14$, $3 \times 6 = 18$, and $4 \times 5 = 20$. So the digits must be 4 and 5. Since the number is even and the tens digit is one more than the ones digit, the number must be 54.

10. a. $B4 \times B2 = B1 * 0.40$

$= 25 * 0.40$

$= 10$

b. Change cell $B2$ to 0.50.

7-6   Sequences

PAGE 274   CHECKING FOR UNDERSTANDING

1. Answers may vary. Sample answer: 1, 5, 9, 13, ...

2. Multiply the known term by the common ratio.

3. $9 + 3 = 12$; $12 + 3 = 15$, The sixth term is 15.

4. $20 \cdot 0.5 = 10$

$10 \cdot 0.5 = 5$

$5 \cdot 0.5 = 2.5$

$2.5 \cdot 0.5 = 1.25$

The first five terms are 20, 10, 5, 2.5, 1.25.

5. $1 + 3 = 4$

$4 + 5 = 9$

$9 + 7 = 16$

$16 + 9 = 25$

$25 + 11 = 36$

$36 + 13 = 49$

neither; Next three terms are 25, 36, 49.

---

6. $-5 \cdot \left(-\dfrac{1}{5}\right) = 1$

$1 \cdot \left(-\dfrac{1}{5}\right) = -\dfrac{1}{5}$

$-\dfrac{1}{5} \cdot \left(-\dfrac{1}{5}\right) = \dfrac{1}{25}$

$\dfrac{1}{25} \cdot \left(-\dfrac{1}{5}\right) = -\dfrac{1}{125}$

$-\dfrac{1}{125} \cdot \left(-\dfrac{1}{5}\right) = \dfrac{1}{625}$

$\dfrac{1}{625} \cdot \left(-\dfrac{1}{5}\right) = -\dfrac{1}{3,125}$

geometric; Next three terms are $-\dfrac{1}{125}$, $\dfrac{1}{625}$, $-\dfrac{1}{3,125}$.

7. $2 \cdot 2 = 4$

$4 \cdot 2 = 8$

$8 \cdot 2 = 16$

$16 \cdot 2 = 32$

$32 \cdot 2 = 64$

$64 \cdot 2 = 128$

geometric; Next three terms are 32, 64, 128.

8. $98.6 - 0.4 = 98.2$

$98.2 - 0.4 = 97.8$

$97.8 - 0.4 = 97.4$

$97.4 - 0.4 = 97.0$

$97.4 - 0.4 = 96.6$

arithmetic; Next three terms are 97.4, 97.0, 96.6.

9. $9 - 6 = 3$

$3 - 6 = -3$

$-3 - 6 = -9$

$-9 - 6 = -15$

$-15 - 6 = -21$

$-21 - 6 = -27$

arithmetic; Next three terms are -15, -21, -27.

10. $20 + 4 = 24$

$24 + 4 = 28$

$28 + 4 = 32$

$32 + 4 = 36$

$36 + 4 = 40$

$40 + 4 = 44$

arithmetic; Next three terms are 36, 40, 44.

11. $99 - 11 = 88$

$88 - 11 = 77$

$77 - 11 = 66$

$66 - 11 = 55$

$55 - 11 = 44$

$44 - 11 = 33$

arithmetic; Next three terms are 55, 44, 33.

12. $1 \cdot (-3) = -3$
$-3 \cdot (-3) = 9$
$9 \cdot (-3) = -27$
$-27 \cdot (-3) = 81$
$81 \cdot (-3) = -243$
$-243 \cdot (-3) = 729$
geometric; Next three terms are 81, -243, 729.

13. $1.5 + 1.5 = 3$
$3 + 1.5 = 4.5$
$4.5 + 1.5 = 6$
$6 + 1.5 = 7.5$
$7.5 + 1.5 = 9$
$9 + 1.5 = 10.5$
arithmetic; Next three terms are 7.5, 9, 10.5.

14. $89 + 0 = 89$ $89 \cdot 1 = 89$
$89 + 0 = 89$ $89 \cdot 1 = 89$
$89 + 0 = 89$ $89 \cdot 1 = 89$
$89 + 0 = 89$ $89 \cdot 1 = 89$
$89 + 0 = 89$ $89 \cdot 1 = 89$
$89 + 0 = 89$ $89 \cdot 1 = 89$
arithmetic and geometric; Next three terms are 89, 89, 89.

15. $-6 + 2 = -4$
$-4 + 2 = -2$
$-2 + 2 = 0$
$0 + 2 = 2$
$2 + 2 = 4$
$4 + 2 = 6$
arithmetic; Next three terms are 2, 4, 6.

16. $-256 \cdot (-0.5) = 128$
$128 \cdot (-0.5) = -64$
$-64 \cdot (-0.5) = 32$
$32 \cdot (-0.5) = -16$
$-16 \cdot (-0.5) = 8$
geometric; Next three terms are 32, -16, 8.

PAGES 274-275   EXERCISES

17. $100 - 9 = 91$
$91 - 9 = 82$
$82 - 9 = 73$
$73 - 9 = 64$
$64 - 9 = 55$
$55 - 9 = 46$
Next three terms are 64, 55, 46.

18. $25 \cdot \frac{1}{5} = 5$
$5 \cdot \frac{1}{5} = 1$
$1 \cdot \frac{1}{5} = \frac{1}{5}$
$\frac{1}{5} \cdot \frac{1}{5} = \frac{1}{25}$
$\frac{1}{25} \cdot \frac{1}{5} = \frac{1}{125}$
$\frac{1}{125} \cdot \frac{1}{5} = \frac{1}{625}$
Next three terms are $\frac{1}{25}$, $\frac{1}{125}$, $\frac{1}{625}$.

19. $9 - 3 = 6$
$6 - 3 = 3$
$3 - 3 = 0$
$0 - 3 = -3$
$-3 - 3 = -6$
$-6 - 3 = -9$
Next three terms are -3, -6, -9.

20. $0.3 \cdot (-3) = -0.9$
$-0.9 \cdot (-3) = 2.7$
$2.7 \cdot (-3) = -8.1$
$-8.1 \cdot (-3) = 24.3$
$24.3 \cdot (-3) = -72.9$
$-72.9 \cdot (-3) = 218.7$
Next three terms are 24.3, -72.9, and 218.7.

21. $1256 \cdot \left(-\frac{1}{2}\right) = -628$
$-628 \cdot \left(-\frac{1}{2}\right) = 314$
$314 \cdot \left(-\frac{1}{2}\right) = -157$
$-157 \cdot \left(-\frac{1}{2}\right) = 78\frac{1}{2}$
$78\frac{1}{2} \cdot \left(-\frac{1}{2}\right) = -39\frac{1}{4}$
Next three terms are
-157, $78\frac{1}{2}$, $-39\frac{1}{4}$.

22. $97 - 12 = 85$
$85 + 25 = 110$
$110 - 12 = 98$
$98 + 25 = 123$
$123 - 12 = 111$
$111 + 25 = 136$
$136 - 12 = 124$
$124 + 25 = 149$
$149 - 12 = 137$
Next three terms are 124, 149, 137.

23. $5 + 1.5 = 6.5$
$6.5 + 1.5 = 8$
$8 + 1.5 = 9.5$
$9.5 + 1.5 = 11$
$11 + 1.5 = 12.5$
$12.5 + 1.5 = 14$
Next three terms are 11, 12.5, 14.

24. $54 + 6 = 60$
$60 + 6 = 66$
$66 + 6 = 72$
$72 + 6 = 78$
$78 + 6 = 84$
$84 + 6 = 90$
Next three terms are 78, 84, 90.

25. $1 + 1 = 2$
$2 + 3 = 5$
$5 + 5 = 10$
$10 + 7 = 17$
$17 + 9 = 26$
$26 + 11 = 37$
$37 + 13 = 50$
Next three numbers are 26, 37, 50.

26. $-3 \cdot (-4) = 12$
$12 \cdot (-4) = -48$
$-48 \cdot (-4) = 192$
$192 \cdot (-4) = -768$
$-768 \cdot (-4) = 3{,}072$
$3{,}072 \cdot (-4) = -12{,}288$
Next three terms are
-768, $3{,}072$, $-12{,}288$.

27. $\frac{1}{4} \cdot \frac{1}{3} = \frac{1}{12}$
$\frac{1}{12} \cdot \frac{1}{3} = \frac{1}{36}$
$\frac{1}{36} \cdot \frac{1}{3} = \frac{1}{108}$
$\frac{1}{108} \cdot \frac{1}{3} = \frac{1}{324}$
$\frac{1}{324} \cdot \frac{1}{3} = \frac{1}{972}$
Next three terms are
$\frac{1}{108}$, $\frac{1}{324}$, $\frac{1}{972}$.

28. $4\frac{3}{6} - \frac{2}{6} = 4\frac{1}{6}$

$4\frac{1}{6} - \frac{2}{6} = 3\frac{7}{6} - \frac{2}{6} = 3\frac{5}{6}$

$3\frac{5}{6} - \frac{2}{6} = 3\frac{3}{6} = 3\frac{1}{2}$

$3\frac{3}{6} - \frac{2}{6} = 3\frac{1}{6}$

$3\frac{1}{6} - \frac{2}{6} = 2\frac{7}{6} - \frac{2}{6} = 2\frac{5}{6}$

$2\frac{5}{6} - \frac{2}{6} = 2\frac{3}{6} = 2\frac{1}{2}$

Next three terms are

$3\frac{1}{6}$, $2\frac{5}{6}$, $2\frac{1}{2}$.

29. $100 - 5 = 95$

$95 - 5 = 90$

$90 - 5 = 85$

Common difference $d = -5$ since $95 - (-5) = 100$.

Use the formula $a_n = a + (n - 1)d$ with $n = 10$.

$a_{10} = 100 + (10 - 1)(-5)$

$a_{10} = 100 + (9)(-5)$

$a_{10} = 100 + (-45)$

$a_{10} = 55$

30. $16 \cdot \frac{3}{4} = \frac{48}{4} = 12$

$12 \cdot \frac{3}{4} = \frac{36}{4} = 9$

$9 \cdot \frac{3}{4} = \frac{27}{4} = 6\frac{3}{4}$

The first four terms are 16, 12, 9, $6\frac{3}{4}$.

31. $14 - (-2) = 14 + 2 = 16$

$16 - (-2) = 16 + 2 = 18$

$18 - (-2) = 18 + 2 = 20$

$20 - (-2) = 20 + 2 = 22$

The first four terms are 22, 20, 18, 16.

32. $16 \cdot \frac{1}{2} = 8$

$8 \cdot \frac{1}{2} = 4$

$4 \cdot \frac{1}{2} = 2$

$2 \cdot \frac{1}{2} = 1$

$1 \cdot \frac{1}{2} = \frac{1}{2}$

$\frac{1}{2} \cdot \frac{1}{2} = \frac{1}{4}$

$\frac{1}{4} \cdot \frac{1}{2} = \frac{1}{8}$

The eighth term is $\frac{1}{8}$.

33. $700 - 365 = 335$

34. $x = -43 - (-89)$

$x = -43 + 89$

$x = 46$

35.

```
                     X
          X    X
 X   X    X    X         X              X    X
 X   X    X    X    X    X    X    X    X    X
 |___|____|____|____|____|____|____|____|____|__→
 16  17   18   19   20   21   22   23   24   25
```

36.
```
      0.625
  8)5.000
   -4 8
      20
     -16
      40
     -40
       0
```
$-\frac{5}{8} = -0.625$

37. $\frac{5}{6} \cdot 3\frac{3}{7} = \frac{5}{6}\left(3 + \frac{3}{7}\right)$

$= \left(\frac{5}{6} \cdot 3\right) + \left(\frac{5}{6} \cdot \frac{3}{7}\right)$

$= \frac{15}{6} + \frac{15}{42}$

$= \frac{105}{42} + \frac{15}{42}$

$= \frac{120}{42}$

$= 2\frac{36}{42}$

$= 2\frac{6}{7}$

38. $29 + 23 = 52$

$52 + 23 = 75$

$75 + 23 = 98$

It would cost 98¢ to mail a 4-ounce letter.

39.

$1 - \frac{1}{5} = \frac{5}{5} - \frac{1}{5} = \frac{4}{5}$

$12,200 \cdot \frac{4}{5} = \frac{48,800}{5} = 9,760$

$9,760 \cdot \frac{4}{5} = \frac{39,040}{5} = 7,808$

$7,808 \cdot \frac{4}{5} = \frac{31,232}{5} = 6,246.4$

The car is worth $6,246.40 after 3 years.

40. Only if the sequence contains only zeros.

41. a. $38 - 6 = 32$ and $6 - 2 = 4$.

So $32 \div 4 = 8$ which is the common difference.

Simplified, it is $\frac{38 - 6}{6 - 2} = \frac{32}{4} = 8$.

b. $\dfrac{a_n - a_m}{n - m}$ where $n > m$

42. a.

b. 2, 4, 6, 8, 10, ...

c. Arithmetic, because you add two pieces every time.

d. 1, 2, 3, 4, 5, ...

e. The number of cuts is one-half the number of pieces.

Mid-Chapter Review

PAGE 275

1. $n = -\frac{3}{4} + \frac{1}{4}$

$n = \frac{-3 + 1}{4}$

$n = \frac{-2}{4}$

$n = -\frac{1}{2}$

2. $\frac{7}{8} - \frac{3}{8} = m$

$\frac{7 - 3}{8} = m$

$\frac{4}{8} = m$

$\frac{1}{2} = m$

3. $2\frac{8}{11} + 3\frac{6}{11} = d$

$5\frac{14}{11} = d$

$6\frac{3}{11} = d$

4. $x = \frac{3}{4} + \frac{4}{5}$

$x = \frac{15}{20} + \frac{16}{20}$

$x = \frac{15 + 16}{20}$

$x = \frac{31}{20}$

$x = 1\frac{11}{20}$

5. $y = -1\frac{5}{6} + \left(-8\frac{3}{8}\right)$

$y = -1\frac{20}{24} + \left(-8\frac{9}{24}\right)$

$y = -9\frac{29}{24}$

$y = -10\frac{5}{24}$

6. $g = 12 - 5\frac{3}{7}$

$g = 11\frac{7}{7} - 5\frac{3}{7}$

$g = 6\frac{4}{7}$

7. $a = 2\frac{4}{5}(-10)$

$a = \frac{14}{5}\left(-\frac{10}{1}\right)$

$a = \frac{-140}{5}$

$a = -28$

8. $\left(-\frac{4}{9}\right)^2 = h$

$\left(-\frac{4}{9}\right)\left(-\frac{4}{9}\right) = h$

$\frac{16}{81} = h$

9. $12\left(3\frac{3}{4}\right) = 12\left(3 + \frac{3}{4}\right)$

$= (12 \cdot 3) + \left(12 \cdot \frac{3}{4}\right)$

10. $2 + 2 = 4$

$4 + 2 = 6$

$6 + 2 = 8$

$8 + 2 = 10$

$10 + 2 = 12$

$12 + 2 = 14$

Marianne will reach her goal on the seventh day.

11. $20 + 3 = 23$

$23 + 3 = 26$

$26 + 3 = 29$

$29 + 3 = 32$

$32 + 3 = 35$

$35 + 3 = 38$

arithmetic; The next three terms are 32, 35, 38.

12. $768 \cdot \frac{1}{4} = 192$

$192 \cdot \frac{1}{4} = 48$

$48 \cdot \frac{1}{4} = 12$

$12 \cdot \frac{1}{4} = 3$

$3 \cdot \frac{1}{4} = \frac{3}{4}$

geometric; The next three terms are 12, 3, $\frac{3}{4}$.

7-6B Mathematics Lab: The Fibonacci Sequence

PAGE 277 WHAT DO YOU THINK?

1. Each number is the sum of the previous two numbers.

2. $8 + 13 = 21$; Add cell E which has 8 paths with cell F which has 13 paths.

3. $8 + 13 = 21$

$13 + 21 = 34$

$21 + 34 = 55$

$34 + 55 = 89$

$55 + 89 = 144$

The next five numbers and 21, 34, 55, 89, 144.

4. Neither, because there is no common difference or common ratio.

PAGE 277 APPLICATIONS

5. a. $1 \to Q$

$2 \to QQ, H$

$3 \to QQQ, HQ, QH$

$4 \to QQQQ, HQQ, QHQ, HQQ, HH$

$5 \to QQQQQ, HQQQ, QHQQ, QQHQ, QQQH, HHQ, HQH, QHH$

$6 \to QQQQQQ, HQQQQ, QHQQQ, QQHQQ, QQQHQ, QQQQH, HHQQ, HQHQ, HQQH, QHQH, QQHH, QHHQ, HHH$

$7 \to QQQQQQQ, HQQQQQ, QHQQQQ, QQHQQQ, QQQHQQ, QQQQHQ, QQQQQH, HHQQQ, HQHQQ, HQQHQ, HQQQH, QHHQQ, QHQHQ, QHQQH, QQHHQ, QQHQH, QQQHH, HHHQ, HHQH, HQHH, QHHH.$

Number of Tokens	1	2	3	4	5	6	7
Ways to Buy	1	2	3	5	8	13	21

b. They are the same as the Fibonacci Sequence.

6. a. 13 clockwise spirals

b. 8 counterclockwise spirals.

c. 8 and 13 are numbers in the Fibonacci Sequence.

7-7 Area of Triangles and Trapezoids

PAGE 280 CHECKING FOR UNDERSTANDING

1. The two parallel sides are the bases.

77

2.

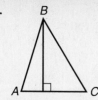

3. $A = \frac{1}{2}bh$ where the height, h, is the length of the altitude to the base, b.

4. Answers may vary. Sample answer:

$$A = \frac{1}{2}(5)(7 + 5)$$

$$A = \left(\frac{5}{2}\right)(12)$$

$$A = 30 \text{ units}^2$$

5. $b = 2\frac{2}{3}$ ft; $h = 3\frac{3}{4}$ ft;

$$A = \frac{1}{2}bh$$

$$A = \left(\frac{1}{2}\right)\left(2\frac{2}{3}\right)\left(3\frac{3}{4}\right)$$

$$A = \left(\frac{1}{2}\right)\left(\frac{8}{3}\right)\left(\frac{15}{4}\right)$$

$$A = \frac{120}{24}$$

$$A = 5 \text{ft}^2$$

6. $a = 2.2$ cm; $b = 5.8$cm; $h = 3.6$ cm

$$A = \frac{1}{2}h(a + b)$$

$$A = (0.5)(3.6)(2.2 + 5.8)$$

$$A = (1.8)(8)$$

$$A = 14.4 \text{ cm}^2$$

7. $a = 4\frac{1}{2}$ in.; $b = 5\frac{1}{3}$ in.; $h = 6$ in.

$$A = \frac{1}{2}h(a + b)$$

$$A = \left(\frac{1}{2}\right)(6)\left(4\frac{1}{2} + 5\frac{1}{3}\right)$$

$$A = (3)\left(\frac{9}{2} + \frac{16}{3}\right)$$

$$A = (3)\left(\frac{27}{6} + \frac{32}{6}\right)$$

$$A = (3)\left(\frac{59}{6}\right)$$

$$A = \frac{177}{6}$$

$$A = 29\frac{3}{6}$$

$$A = 29\frac{1}{2} \text{ in.}^2$$

8. $A = \frac{1}{2}bh$

$$A = \left(\frac{1}{2}\right)\left(3\frac{3}{4}\right)\left(4\frac{1}{2}\right)$$

$$A = \left(\frac{1}{2}\right)\left(\frac{15}{4}\right)\left(\frac{9}{2}\right)$$

$$A = \frac{135}{16}$$

$$A = 8\frac{7}{16} \text{ ft}^2$$

9. $A = \frac{1}{2}bh$

$$A = (0.5)(9)(2.6)$$

$$A = 11.7 \text{cm}^2$$

10. $A = \frac{1}{2}bh$

$$A = (0.5)(10)(7)$$

$$A = 35 \text{ in.}^2$$

11. $A = \frac{1}{2}h(a + b)$

$$A = (0.5)(9)(12 + 8)$$

$$A = (4.5)(20)$$

$$A = 90 \text{ m}^2$$

12. $A = \frac{1}{2}h(a + b)$

$$A = (0.5)(0.2)(0.3 + 0.5)$$

$$A = (0.1)(0.8)$$

$$A = 0.08 \text{ km}^2$$

13. $A = \frac{1}{2}h(a + b)$

$$A = \left(\frac{1}{2}\right)(3)\left(2\frac{1}{3} + 4\frac{1}{6}\right)$$

$$A = \left(\frac{3}{2}\right)\left(\frac{7}{3} + \frac{25}{6}\right)$$

$$A = \left(\frac{3}{2}\right)\left(\frac{14}{6} + \frac{25}{6}\right)$$

$$A = \left(\frac{3}{2}\right)\left(\frac{39}{6}\right)$$

$$A = \frac{117}{12}$$

$$A = 9\frac{3}{4}$$

PAGES 280-281   EXERCISES

14. $b = 12$ cm; $h = 5$ cm

$$A = \frac{1}{2}bh$$

$$A = \left(\frac{1}{2}\right)(12)(5)$$

$$A = 30 \text{ cm}^2$$

15. $a = 3\frac{1}{2}$ ft; $b = 5\frac{1}{2}$ ft; $h = 2\frac{2}{3}$ ft

$$A = \frac{1}{2}h(a + b)$$

$$A = \left(\frac{1}{2}\right)\left(2\frac{2}{3}\right)\left(3\frac{1}{2} + 5\frac{1}{2}\right)$$

$$A = \left(\frac{1}{2}\right)\left(\frac{8}{3}\right)\left(\frac{7}{2} + \frac{11}{2}\right)$$

$$A = \left(\frac{8}{6}\right)\left(\frac{18}{2}\right)$$

$$A = \frac{144}{12}$$

$$A = 12 \text{ ft}^2$$

16. $a = 12\frac{2}{3}$in.; $b = 7\frac{1}{2}$ in.; $h = 5\frac{1}{4}$ in.

$$A = \frac{1}{2}h(a + b)$$

$$A = \frac{1}{2}\left(5\frac{1}{4}\right)\left(12\frac{2}{3} + 7\frac{1}{2}\right)$$

$$A = \left(\frac{1}{2}\right)\left(\frac{21}{4}\right)\left(\frac{38}{3} + \frac{15}{2}\right)$$

$$A = \left(\frac{21}{8}\right)\left(\frac{76}{6} + \frac{45}{6}\right)$$

$$A = \left(\frac{21}{8}\right)\left(\frac{121}{6}\right)$$

$$A = \frac{2,541}{48}$$

$$A = 52\frac{45}{48} \qquad A = 52\frac{15}{16} \text{ in.}^2$$

78

17. $b = 30$ cm; $h = 12$ cm

$A = \frac{1}{2}bh$

$A = \left(\frac{1}{2}\right)\left(30\right)\left(12\right)$

$A = 180$ cm^2

18. $a = 12$ yd; $b = 18$ yd; $h = 10$ yd

$A = \frac{1}{2}h(a + b)$

$A = \left(\frac{1}{2}\right)\left(10\right)\left(12 + 18\right)$

$A = (5)(30)$

$A = 150$ yd^2

19. $b = 3$ ft; $h = 4$ ft

$A = \frac{1}{2}bh$

$A = \left(\frac{1}{2}\right)\left(3\right)\left(4\right)$

$A = 6$ ft^2

20. $A = \frac{1}{2}bh$

$A = (0.5)(8)(3.8)$

$A = 15.2$ cm^2

21. $A = \frac{1}{2}bh$

$A = \left(\frac{1}{2}\right)\left(22\right)\left(27\right)$

$A = 297$ yd^2

22. $A = \frac{1}{2}bh$

$A = \left(\frac{1}{2}\right)\left(2\frac{2}{3}\right)\left(3\frac{1}{12}\right)$

$A = \left(\frac{1}{2}\right)\left(\frac{8}{3}\right)\left(\frac{37}{12}\right)$

$A = \frac{296}{72}$

$A = 4\frac{8}{72}$

$A = 4\frac{1}{9}$ ft^2

23. $A = \frac{1}{2}bh$

$A = \left(\frac{1}{2}\right)\left(1\frac{3}{4}\right)\left(5\frac{1}{8}\right)$

$A = \left(\frac{1}{2}\right)\left(\frac{7}{4}\right)\left(\frac{41}{8}\right)$

$A = \frac{287}{64}$

$A = 4\frac{31}{64}$ in.^{2}

24. $A = \frac{1}{2}bh$

$A = \left(\frac{1}{2}\right)(20)(17)$

$A = 170$ m^2

25. $A = \frac{1}{2}bh$

$A = \left(\frac{1}{2}\right)(16)(14)$

$A = 112$ mm^2

26. $A = \frac{1}{2}h(a + b)$

$A = \left(\frac{1}{2}\right)(12)(19 + 24)$

$A = (6)(43)$

$A = 258$ cm^2

27. $A = \frac{1}{2}h(a + b)$

$A = \left(\frac{1}{2}\right)\left(17\right)\left(12 + 18\right)$

$A = \left(\frac{17}{2}\right)\left(30\right)$

$A = 255$ ft^2

28. $A = \frac{1}{2}h(a + b)$

$A = \left(\frac{1}{2}\right)\left(15\right)\left(26 + 24\right)$

$A = \left(\frac{15}{2}\right)\left(50\right)$

$A = 375$ in.^{2}

29. $A = \frac{1}{2}h(a + b)$

$A = (0.5)(8.2)(8.3 + 8.5)$

$A = (4.1)(16.8)$

$A = 68.88$ km^2

30. $A = \frac{1}{2}h(a + b)$

$A = (0.5)(2.2)(4.7 + 5.9)$

$A = (1.1)(10.6)$

$A = 11.66$ cm^2

31. $A = \frac{1}{2}h(a + b)$

$A = (0.5)(0.4)(0.3 + 0.72)$

$A = (0.2)(1.02)$

$A = 0.204$ m^2

32. $3 + 2c = 15$

33. $\frac{w}{4} = -125$

$4\left(\frac{w}{4}\right) = 4(-125)$

$w = -500$

34. 19, 23, 27, 31, 35, 39, 40, 40

Mean: $\dfrac{19 + 23 + 27 + 31 + 35 + 39 + 40 + 40}{8}$

$= \dfrac{254}{8} = 31.75$

Median: $\dfrac{31 + 35}{2} = \dfrac{66}{2} = 33$

Mode: 40

35. Similar because they have the same shape but differ in size.

36. $80 - 4 = 76$

$76 - 4 = 72$

$72 - 4 = 68$

$68 - 4 = 64$

$64 - 4 = 60$

$60 - 4 = 56$

The next three terms are 64, 60, 56.

37. $A_1 = \left(\frac{1}{2}\right)(5)(12 + 19)$ $A_2 = \left(\frac{1}{2}\right)(5)(19 + 22)$

$A_1 = \left(\frac{5}{2}\right)(31)$ $A_2 = \left(\frac{5}{2}\right)(41)$

$A_1 = \frac{155}{2}$ $A_2 = \frac{205}{2}$

$A_1 = 77.5$ ft^2 $A_2 = 102.5$ ft^2

$A_3 = \left(\frac{1}{2}\right)(5)(22 + 23)$ $A_4 = \left(\frac{1}{2}\right)(5)(23 + 21)$

$A_3 = \left(\frac{5}{2}\right)(45)$ $A_4 = \left(\frac{5}{2}\right)(44)$

$A_3 = \frac{225}{2}$ $A_4 = \frac{220}{2}$

$A_3 = 112.5$ ft^2 $A_4 = 110$ ft^2

$A_5 = \left(\frac{1}{2}\right)(5)(21 + 17)$ $A_6 = \left(\frac{1}{2}\right)(5)(17 + 12)$

$A_5 = \left(\frac{5}{2}\right)(38)$ $A_6 = \left(\frac{5}{2}\right)(29)$

$A_5 = \frac{190}{2}$ $A_6 = \frac{145}{2}$

$A_5 = 95$ ft^2 $A_6 = 72.5$ ft^2

Area $= A_1 + A_2 + A_3 + A_4 + A_5 + A_6$

Area $= 77.5 + 102.5 + 112.5 + 110 + 95 + 72.5$

Area $= 570$ ft^2

38. Since area of a trapezoid is represented in square units, or units^2, if you double the length of the base and double the height, then the area is double · double, or 2 · 2 = 4. Thus the area is quadrupled.

39. a. $A = \frac{1}{2}bh$

$A \approx \left(\frac{1}{2}\right)(273)(219)$

b. $A \approx \left(\frac{1}{2}\right)(273)(219)$

$A \approx 29{,}893.5 \text{ mi}^2 \text{ or } 29{,}894 \text{ mi}^2$

40. See students' work.

| **7-7B** | **Mathematics Lab:** **Area and Pick's Theorem** |

1. Triangle 1: scalene, acute
Triangle 2: scalene, obtuse
Triangle 3: scalene, acute

2. They are the same.

3. Area = $\dfrac{\text{dots on figure}}{2}$ + (dots inside figure) - 1

$A = \frac{x}{2} + y - 1$

4. Yes, because it works for a right triangle and a rectangle is two right triangles put together. See students' work.

5. Yes, because if you draw one diagonal of a trapezoid it forms two triangles. See students' work.

6. a. Count the square units.
b. Pick's Theorem works for all of the figures.

| **7-8** | **Circles and Circumference** |

1. Diameter is 2 times the radius, or $d = 2r$.

2. $C = 2\pi r$

3. Circumference is approximately 3 times the diameter, or $C \approx 3d$.

4. $C = \pi d$
$C = \pi(18)$
$C \approx 56.55$ in.

5. $C = \pi d$
$C = \pi(2.6)$
$C \approx 8.17$ m

6. $C = 2\pi r$
$C = 2\pi(2.5)$
$C \approx 15.7$ cm

7. $C = 2\pi r$
$C = 2\pi(7)$
$C \approx 43.98$ in.

8. $C = \pi d$
$C = \pi(13.6)$
$C = 42.73$ m

9. $C = \pi d$
$C = \pi\left(5\frac{1}{4}\right)$
$C = \pi\left(\frac{21}{4}\right)$
$C \approx 16.49$ in.

10. $C = 2\pi r$
$C = 2\pi(3.5)$
$C \approx 21.99$ km

11. $C = 2\pi r$
$C = 2\pi\left(\frac{1}{2}\right)$
$C \approx 3.14$ ft

12. $C = \pi d$
$C = \pi(21)$
$C \approx 65.97$ ft

13. $C = 2\pi r$
$C = 2\pi\left(4\frac{3}{8}\right)$
$C = 2\pi\left(\frac{35}{8}\right)$
$C \approx 27.49$ in.

14. $C = \pi d$
$C = \pi(49)$
$C \approx 153.94$ cm

15. $C = 2\pi r$
$C = 2\pi(6.78)$
$C \approx 42.6$ m

16. $C = \pi d$
$C = \pi(36)$
$C \approx 113.1$ in.

17. $C = 2\pi r$
$C = 2\pi(8)$
$C \approx 50.27$ ft

18. $C = 2\pi r$
$C = 2\pi(3.4)$
$C \approx 21.36$ cm

19. $C = \pi d$
$C = \pi(8.8)$
$C \approx 27.65$ m

20. $C = \pi d$
$C = \pi\left(2\frac{1}{3}\right)$
$C = \pi\left(\frac{7}{3}\right)$
$C \approx 7.33$ ft

21. $C = 2\pi r$
$C = 2\pi\left(4\frac{1}{2}\right)$
$C = 2\pi\left(\frac{9}{2}\right)$
$C \approx 28.27$ yd

22. $2^6 = 2 \cdot 2 \cdot 2 \cdot 2 \cdot 2 \cdot 2$
$= 64$

23. a.

5	8
6	257
7	1123569
8	23458
9	1347

8|3 means 83

b. Most scores lie in the 70-79 interval.

24. $a = 15$ yd; $b = 20$ yd; $h = 10$ yd

$A = \frac{1}{2}h(a + b)$

$A = \left(\frac{1}{2}\right)(10)(15 + 20)$

$A = (5)(35)$

$A = 175 \text{ yd}^2$

25. Since the label goes around the can, it must be rectangular. The circumference of the can corresponds to the length of the label and the height of the can corresponds to the width of the label.

$$C = \pi d \qquad \text{height} = 7.5 \text{ cm}$$
$$C = \pi(9.1)$$
$$C \approx 28.6 \text{ cm}$$

So the size of the label must be 28.6 cm × 7.5 cm (or 214.5 cm^2) to fit the can exactly.

26. The height of the can is the same as the height of the three tennis balls, or 3d, where d is the diameter of one ball. The circumference of the can is πd where d is again the diameter of one ball. Using 3.14 for π, you can say that 3d < 3.14d, so the circumference is greater.

27. $C = \pi d$
$$C = \pi(75,100)$$
$$C \approx 235,933.6 \text{ miles}$$

28. Answers may vary. Sample answer: A metal pipe is to be put in the ground, but it must have insulation put around it. The diameter of the pipe is 36 inches. How wide must the insulation be that is needed?

29. a. $C = \pi d$
$$C = \pi(18)$$
$$C \approx 56.55 \text{ in.}$$

   b. First, find the radius of the ball and rim.
$$C = 2\pi r \qquad d = 2r$$
$$\frac{30}{2\pi} = \frac{2\pi r}{2\pi} \qquad \frac{18}{2} = \frac{2r}{2}$$
$$4.8 \approx r \qquad 9 = r$$

   Looking at both radii while the ball is in the center of the rim, we see that the space between the rim and the ball is 9 − 4.8 = 4.2 inches.

30. $\frac{19}{60}$

7-9 Dividing Fractions

PAGES 289-290   CHECKING FOR UNDERSTANDING

1. Zero cannot be the denominator of a fraction because you cannot divide by zero.

2. $3 \div \frac{3}{4} = \frac{3}{1} \cdot \frac{4}{3}$
$$= \frac{12}{3}$$
$$= 4$$

3. There are 4 sets of $\frac{3}{4}$, which equals 3.

4.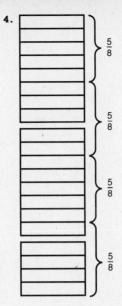

5. $10 \div \frac{1}{2} = 10 \cdot \frac{2}{1}$
$$= 10 \cdot 2$$
$$= 20$$

So $10 \div \frac{1}{2} > 10$ since 20 > 10, or since dividing by $\frac{1}{2}$ is the same as multiplying by 2.

6. $\frac{2}{3} \div \frac{5}{6} = \frac{2}{3} \cdot \frac{6}{5}$
$$= \frac{12}{15}$$
$$= \frac{4}{5}$$

7. $\frac{3}{8} \div \frac{9}{10} = \frac{3}{8} \cdot \frac{10}{9}$
$$= \frac{30}{72}$$
$$= \frac{5}{12}$$

8. $-\frac{5}{6} \div \frac{2}{9} = -\frac{5}{6} \cdot \frac{9}{2}$
$$= -\frac{45}{12}$$
$$= -3\frac{9}{12}$$
$$= -3\frac{3}{4}$$

9. $\frac{4}{9} \div \frac{6}{1} = \frac{4}{9} \cdot \frac{1}{6}$
$$= \frac{4}{54}$$
$$= \frac{2}{27}$$

10. $-12 \div \left(-3\frac{3}{8}\right) = -\frac{12}{1} \div \left(-\frac{27}{8}\right)$
$$= -\frac{12}{1} \cdot \left(-\frac{8}{27}\right)$$
$$= \frac{96}{27}$$
$$= 3\frac{15}{27}$$
$$= 3\frac{5}{9}$$

11. $1\frac{1}{3} \div 2\frac{2}{9} = \frac{4}{3} \div \frac{20}{9}$
$$= \frac{4}{3} \cdot \frac{9}{20}$$
$$= \frac{36}{60}$$
$$= \frac{3}{5}$$

12. $15 \div 2\frac{8}{11} = \frac{15}{1} \div \frac{30}{11}$
$$= \frac{15}{1} \cdot \frac{11}{30}$$
$$= \frac{165}{30}$$
$$= \frac{11}{2}$$
$$= 5\frac{1}{2}$$

13. $7\frac{5}{9} \div (-8) = \frac{68}{9} \div \left(-\frac{8}{1}\right)$

$\qquad = \frac{68}{9} \cdot \left(-\frac{1}{8}\right)$

$\qquad = -\frac{68}{72}$

$\qquad = -\frac{17}{18}$

14. $3\frac{3}{5} \div 10 = \frac{18}{5} \div \frac{10}{1}$

$\qquad = \frac{18}{5} \cdot \frac{1}{10}$

$\qquad = \frac{18}{50}$

$\qquad = \frac{9}{25}$

15. $-6 \div \left(-1\frac{1}{2}\right) = -\frac{6}{1} \div \left(-\frac{3}{2}\right)$

$\qquad = -\frac{6}{1} \cdot \left(-\frac{2}{3}\right)$

$\qquad = \frac{12}{3}$

$\qquad = 4$

PAGE 290   EXERCISES

16. $a = \frac{3}{4} \div \frac{5}{6}$

$a = \frac{3}{4} \cdot \frac{6}{5}$

$a = \frac{18}{20}$

$a = \frac{9}{10}$

17. $10 \div (-2) = t$

$\frac{10}{-2} = t$

$-5 = t$

18. $b = \frac{8}{9} \div \frac{6}{7}$

$b = \frac{8}{9} \cdot \frac{7}{6}$

$b = \frac{56}{54}$

$b = 1\frac{2}{54}$

$b = 1\frac{1}{27}$

19. $7\frac{1}{3} \div 1\frac{2}{9} = d$

$\frac{22}{3} \div \frac{11}{9} = d$

$\frac{22}{3} \cdot \frac{9}{11} = d$

$\frac{198}{33} = d$

$\frac{6}{1} = d$

$6 = d$

20. $n = \frac{3}{8} \div (-6)$

$n = \frac{3}{8} \div \left(-\frac{6}{1}\right)$

$n = \frac{3}{8} \cdot \left(-\frac{1}{6}\right)$

$n = -\frac{3}{48}$

$n = -\frac{1}{16}$

21. $4\frac{1}{2} \div \frac{3}{4} = h$

$\frac{9}{2} \div \frac{3}{4} = h$

$\frac{9}{2} \cdot \frac{4}{3} = h$

$\frac{36}{6} = h$

$6 = h$

22. $j = \frac{9}{10} \div \frac{6}{1}$

$\qquad = \frac{9}{10} \cdot \frac{1}{6}$

$\qquad = \frac{9}{60}$

$\qquad = \frac{3}{20}$

23. $2\frac{2}{3} \div \frac{4}{1} = y$

$\frac{8}{3} \cdot \frac{1}{4} = y$

$\frac{8}{12} = y$

$\frac{2}{3} = y$

24. $g = -3\frac{3}{4} \div \left(-2\frac{1}{2}\right)$

$g = -\frac{15}{4} \div \left(-\frac{5}{2}\right)$

$g = -\frac{15}{4} \cdot \left(-\frac{2}{5}\right)$

$g = \frac{30}{20}$

$g = 1\frac{10}{20}$

$g = 1\frac{1}{2}$

25. $c \div d = \frac{1}{2} \div 2\frac{1}{3}$

$\qquad = \frac{1}{2} \div \frac{7}{3}$

$\qquad = \frac{1}{2} \cdot \frac{3}{7}$

$\qquad = \frac{3}{14}$

26. $a^2 \div b^2 = \left(-\frac{2}{3}\right)^2 \div \left(\frac{4}{5}\right)^2$

$\qquad = \left(-\frac{2}{3}\right)\left(-\frac{2}{3}\right) \div \left(\frac{4}{5}\right)\left(\frac{4}{5}\right)$

$\qquad = \frac{4}{9} \div \frac{16}{25}$

$\qquad = \frac{4}{9} \cdot \frac{25}{16}$

$\qquad = \frac{100}{144}$

$\qquad = \frac{25}{36}$

27. $x + y \div z = \frac{3}{4} + 0.5 \div \frac{1}{4}$

$\qquad = \frac{3}{4} + \frac{1}{2} \div \frac{1}{4}$

$\qquad = \frac{3}{4} + \frac{1}{2} \cdot \frac{4}{1}$

$\qquad = \frac{3}{4} + \frac{4}{2}$

$\qquad = \frac{3}{4} + \frac{8}{4}$

$\qquad = \frac{11}{4}$

$\qquad = 2\frac{3}{4}$

28. $\frac{b}{2} + 7 > 3$

$\frac{b}{2} + 7 - 7 > 3 - 7$

$\frac{b}{2} > -4$

$2\left(\frac{b}{2}\right) > 2(-4)$

$b > -8$

-12 -10 -8 -6 -4

29. $r = (-8) + 12 + 3 + 9$ or $r = (-8) + 12 + 3 + 9$

$r = -8 + 24 \qquad\qquad r = 4 + 3 + 9$

$r = 16 \qquad\qquad\qquad r = 7 + 9$

$\qquad\qquad\qquad\qquad\qquad r = 16$

30. $15.363636\ldots = 15.\overline{36}$

31. $C = 2\pi r$

$C = 2\pi(5)$

$C \approx 31.4$ mm

32. $11 \div 3 = \frac{11}{1} \div \frac{3}{1}$

$\qquad = \frac{11}{1} \cdot \frac{1}{3}$

$\qquad = \frac{11}{3}$

$\qquad = 3\frac{2}{3}$ in.

33. $8 \div \frac{1}{16} = 8 \cdot \frac{16}{1}$

$\qquad\quad = 8 \cdot 16$

$\qquad\quad = 128$ slices

82

34. The quotient is greater. This is because dividing by a proper fraction is actually multiplying by an improper fraction.

7-10 Solving Equations

1. Add 4 to both sides then multiply both sides by $\frac{3}{2}$.

2. Answers may vary. Sample answer: $-1\frac{5}{8}x - 3 = 10$.

3.
$$1.1 + y = -4.4$$
$$1.1 - 1.1 + y = -4.4 - 1.1$$
$$y = -5.5$$
Check:
$$1.1 + y = -4.4$$
$$1.1 + (-5.5) \stackrel{?}{=} -4.4$$
$$-4.4 = -4.4 \checkmark$$

4.
$$-\frac{5}{8}x + \frac{1}{6} = \frac{3}{5}$$
$$-\frac{5}{8}x + \frac{1}{6} - \frac{1}{6} = \frac{3}{5} - \frac{1}{6}$$
$$-\frac{5}{8}x = \frac{18}{30} - \frac{5}{30}$$
$$-\frac{5}{8}x = \frac{13}{30}$$
$$\left(-\frac{8}{5}\right)\left(-\frac{5}{8}\right)x = \frac{13}{30}\left(-\frac{8}{5}\right)$$
$$x = -\frac{104}{150}$$
$$x = -\frac{52}{45}$$
Check:
$$-\frac{5}{8}x + \frac{1}{6} = \frac{3}{5}$$
$$-\frac{5}{8}\left(-\frac{52}{75}\right) + \frac{1}{6} \stackrel{?}{=} \frac{3}{5}$$
$$\frac{260}{600} + \frac{1}{6} \stackrel{?}{=} \frac{3}{5}$$
$$\frac{260}{600} + \frac{100}{600} \stackrel{?}{=} \frac{3}{5}$$
$$\frac{360}{600} \stackrel{?}{=} \frac{3}{5}$$
$$\frac{3}{5} = \frac{3}{5} \checkmark$$

5.
$$3.6 = \frac{c}{0.9}$$
$$0.9 \cdot 3.6 = \frac{c}{0.9} \cdot 0.9$$
$$3.24 = c$$
Check:
$$3.6 = \frac{c}{0.9}$$
$$3.6 \stackrel{?}{=} \frac{3.24}{0.9}$$
$$3.6 = 3 6 \checkmark$$

6.
$$\frac{2}{3}h - (-3) = 6$$
$$\frac{2}{3}h + 3 = 6$$
$$\frac{2}{3}h + 3 - 3 = 6 - 3$$
$$\frac{2}{3}h = 3$$
$$\frac{3}{2} \cdot \frac{2}{3}h = 3 \cdot \frac{3}{2}$$
$$h = \frac{9}{2}$$
$$h = 4\frac{1}{2}$$
Check:
$$\frac{2}{3}h + 3 = 6$$
$$\frac{2}{3}\left(\frac{9}{2}\right) + 3 \stackrel{?}{=} 6$$
$$\frac{18}{6} + 3 \stackrel{?}{=} 6$$
$$3 + 3 \stackrel{?}{=} 6$$
$$6 = 6 \checkmark$$

7.
$$2\frac{1}{2}d = 5\frac{3}{4}$$
$$\frac{5}{2}d = \frac{23}{4}$$
$$\frac{2}{5} \cdot \frac{5}{2}d = \frac{23}{4} \cdot \frac{2}{5}$$
$$d = \frac{46}{20}$$
$$d = 2\frac{6}{20}$$
$$d = 2\frac{3}{10}$$
Check:
$$\frac{5}{2}d = \frac{23}{4}$$
$$\frac{5}{2}\left(\frac{23}{10}\right) \stackrel{?}{=} \frac{23}{4}$$
$$\frac{115}{20} \stackrel{?}{=} \frac{23}{4}$$
$$\frac{23}{4} = \frac{23}{4} \checkmark$$

8.
$$-\frac{8t}{5} = 4$$
$$\left(-\frac{5}{8}\right)\left(-\frac{8t}{5}\right) = 4\left(-\frac{5}{8}\right)$$
$$t = -\frac{20}{8}$$
$$t = -2\frac{4}{8}$$
$$t = -2\frac{1}{2}$$
Check:
$$-\frac{8t}{5} = 4$$
$$-\frac{8\left(-\frac{20}{8}\right)}{5} \stackrel{?}{=} 4$$
$$\frac{20}{5} \stackrel{?}{=} 4$$
$$4 = 4 \checkmark$$

9.
$$\frac{b}{1.5} - 13 = 2.2$$
$$\frac{b}{1.5} - 13 + 13 = 2.2 + 13$$
$$\frac{b}{1.5} = 15.2$$
$$1.5 \cdot \frac{b}{1.5} = 15.2 \cdot 1.5$$
$$b = 22.8$$
Check:
$$\frac{b}{1.5} - 13 = 2.2$$
$$\frac{22.8}{1.5} - 13 \stackrel{?}{=} 2.2$$
$$15.2 - 13 \stackrel{?}{=} 2.2$$
$$2.2 = 2.2 \checkmark$$

10.
$$-12 = -\frac{z}{7}$$
$$(-7)(-12) = \left(-\frac{z}{7}\right)(-7)$$
$$84 = z$$
Check:
$$-12 = -\frac{z}{7}$$
$$-12 \stackrel{?}{=} -\frac{84}{7}$$
$$-12 = -12 \checkmark$$

11.
$$-11g + 15 = 12.5$$
$$-11g + 15 - 15 = 12.5 - 15$$
$$-11g = -2.5$$
$$\left(-\frac{1}{11}\right)(-11g) = (-2.5)\left(-\frac{1}{11}\right)$$
$$g = \frac{2.5}{11}$$
$$g = 0.2\overline{27}$$
Check: $-11g + 15 = 12.5$
$$-11\left(\frac{2.5}{11}\right) + 15 \stackrel{?}{=} 12.5$$
$$-2.5 + 15 \stackrel{?}{=} 12.5$$
$$12.5 = 12.5 \checkmark$$

PAGE 293 EXERCISES

12.
$$2x = -12$$
$$\frac{1}{2} \cdot 2x = -12 \cdot \frac{1}{2}$$
$$x = -6$$
Check: $2x = -12$
$$2(-6) \stackrel{?}{=} -12$$
$$-12 = -12 \checkmark$$

13.
$$\frac{t}{3} = -6$$
$$3 \cdot \frac{t}{3} = -6 \cdot 3$$
$$t = -18$$
Check: $\frac{t}{3} = -6$
$$\frac{-18}{3} \stackrel{?}{=} -6$$
$$-6 = -6 \checkmark$$

14.
$$a - (-0.03) = 3.2$$
$$a + 0.03 = 3.2$$
$$a + 0.03 - 0.03 = 3.2 - 0.03$$
$$a = 3.17$$
Check: $a + 0.03 = 3.2$
$$3.17 + 0.03 \stackrel{?}{=} 3.2$$
$$3.2 = 3.2 \checkmark$$

15.
$$-\frac{1}{4}c = 3.8$$
$$\left(-\frac{4}{1}\right)\left(-\frac{1}{4}c\right) = (3.8)\left(-\frac{4}{1}\right)$$
$$c = -15.2$$
Check: $-\frac{1}{4}c = 3.8$
$$-\frac{1}{4}(-15.2) \stackrel{?}{=} 3.8$$
$$\frac{15.2}{4} \stackrel{?}{=} 3.8$$
$$3.8 = 3.8 \checkmark$$

16.
$$\frac{y}{3.2} = -4.5$$
$$3.2 \cdot \frac{y}{3.2} = -4.5 \cdot 3.2$$
$$y = -14.4$$
Check: $\frac{y}{3.2} = -4.5$
$$\frac{-14.4}{3.2} \stackrel{?}{=} -4.5$$
$$-4.5 = -4.5 \checkmark$$

17.
$$-1.6w + 3.5 = 0.48$$
$$-1.6w + 3.5 - 3.5 = 0.48 - 3.5$$
$$-1.6w = -3.02$$
$$\left(-\frac{1}{1.6}\right)(-1.6w) = (-3.02)\left(-\frac{1}{1.6}\right)$$
$$w = \frac{3.02}{1.6}$$
$$w = 1.8875$$
Check: $-1.6w + 3.5 = 0.48$
$$-1.6(1.8875) + 3.5 \stackrel{?}{=} 0.48$$
$$-3.02 + 3.5 \stackrel{?}{=} 0.48$$
$$0.48 = 0.48 \checkmark$$

18.
$$\frac{n}{2} = -1.6$$
$$2 \cdot \frac{n}{2} = -1.6 \cdot 2$$
$$n = -3.2$$
Check: $\frac{n}{2} = -1.6$
$$\frac{-3.2}{2} \stackrel{?}{=} -1.6$$
$$-1.6 = -1.6 \checkmark$$

19.
$$\frac{6d}{2} = -0.36$$
$$3d = -0.36$$
$$\frac{1}{3} \cdot 3d = -0.36 \cdot \frac{1}{3}$$
$$d = \frac{-0.36}{3}$$
$$d = -0.12$$
Check: $3d = -0.36$
$$3(-0.12) \stackrel{?}{=} -0.36$$
$$-0.36 = -0.36 \checkmark$$

20.
$$\frac{m}{2.3} - 1.3 = -5.2$$
$$\frac{m}{2.3} - 1.3 + 1.3 = -5.2 + 1.3$$
$$\frac{m}{2.3} = -3.9$$
$$2.3 \cdot \frac{m}{2.3} = -3.9 \cdot 2.3$$
$$m = -8.97$$
Check: $\frac{m}{2.3} - 1.3 = -5.2$
$$\frac{-8.97}{2.3} - 1.3 \stackrel{?}{=} -5.2$$
$$-3.9 - 1.3 \stackrel{?}{=} -5.2$$
$$-5.2 = -5.2 \checkmark$$

21.
$$k + \frac{2}{3} = -\frac{4}{9}$$
$$k + \frac{2}{3} - \frac{2}{3} = -\frac{4}{9} - \frac{2}{3}$$
$$k = -\frac{4}{9} - \frac{6}{9}$$
$$k = -\frac{10}{9}$$
$$k = -1\frac{1}{9}$$
Check: $k + \frac{2}{3} = -\frac{4}{9}$
$$-\frac{10}{9} + \frac{2}{3} \stackrel{?}{=} -\frac{4}{9}$$
$$-\frac{10}{9} + \frac{6}{9} \stackrel{?}{=} -\frac{4}{9}$$
$$-\frac{4}{9} = -\frac{4}{9} \checkmark$$

22.
$$-\frac{3}{5}h = \frac{2}{3}$$
$$\left(-\frac{5}{3}\right)\left(-\frac{3}{5}h\right) = \left(\frac{2}{3}\right)\left(-\frac{5}{3}\right)$$
$$h = -\frac{10}{9}$$
$$h = -1\frac{1}{9}$$
Check: $-\frac{3}{5}h = \frac{2}{3}$
$$-\frac{3}{5}\left(-\frac{10}{9}\right) \stackrel{?}{=} \frac{2}{3}$$
$$\frac{30}{45} \stackrel{?}{=} \frac{2}{3}$$
$$\frac{2}{3} = \frac{2}{3} \checkmark$$

23. $4p - \frac{1}{5} = -7\frac{2}{5}$ Check: $4p - \frac{1}{5} = -\frac{37}{5}$

$4p - \frac{1}{5} + \frac{1}{5} = -\frac{37}{5} + \frac{1}{5}$ $4\left(-\frac{36}{20}\right) - \frac{1}{5} \overset{?}{=} -\frac{37}{5}$

$4p = -\frac{36}{5}$ $-\frac{36}{5} - \frac{1}{5} \overset{?}{=} -\frac{37}{5}$

$\frac{1}{4} \cdot 4p = -\frac{36}{5} \cdot \frac{1}{4}$ $-\frac{37}{5} = -\frac{37}{5} \;\checkmark$

$p = -\frac{36}{20}$

$p = -1\frac{16}{20}$

$p = -1\frac{4}{5}$

24. $x - \frac{2}{5} = -2$ Check: $x - \frac{2}{5} = -2$

$x - \frac{2}{5} + \frac{2}{5} = -2 + \frac{2}{5}$ $-\frac{8}{5} - \frac{2}{5} \overset{?}{=} -2$

$x = -\frac{10}{5} + \frac{2}{5}$ $-\frac{10}{5} \overset{?}{=} -2$

$x = -\frac{8}{5}$ $-2 = -2 \;\checkmark$

$x = -1\frac{3}{5}$

25. $600 + 200 + 400 = 1,200$

26. positive relationship

27. $46 = 8k - 2$

$46 + 2 = 8k - 2 + 2$

$48 = 8k$

$\frac{48}{8} = \frac{8k}{8}$

$6 = k$

Check: $46 = 8k - 2$

$46 \overset{?}{=} 8(6) - 2$

$46 \overset{?}{=} 48 - 2$

$46 = 46 \;\checkmark$

28. multiples of 9: 0, 9, 18, 27, 36, 45, 54, 63, 72, 81, 90, 99

multiples of 30: 0, 30, 60, 90, 120

The LCM is 90.

29. $g = \frac{5}{6} \div \frac{4}{3}$

$g = \frac{5}{6} \cdot \frac{3}{4}$

$g = \frac{15}{24}$

$g = \frac{5}{8}$

30. Replace C with 0. Multiply each side by $\frac{9}{5}$. Add 32 to each side.

$0 = \frac{5}{9}(F - 32)$

$\frac{9}{5} \cdot 0 = \frac{9}{5} \cdot \frac{5}{9}(F - 32)$

$0 = F - 32$

$32 + 0 = F - 32 + 32$

$32 = F$

31. a. because $35 \times 3 = 105$

b. 55

32. a. 35 mph because $35 \times 3 = 105$

b. 55 mph because $55 \times 4 = 220$

c. 25 mph because $25 \times 2\frac{1}{2} = \frac{25}{1} \times \frac{5}{2} = \frac{125}{2} = 62\frac{1}{2}$

d. With every 10 mph increase, the difference in stopping distance increases about 10 ft.

Chapter 7 Study Guide and Review

PAGE 294   COMMUNICATING MATHEMATICS

1. g; mixed number   **2.** c; 6

3. h; geometric sequence

4. i; arithmetic sequence

5. j; trapezoid   **6.** e; diameter

7. f; circumference   **8.** b; $\frac{4}{3}$

9. Answers may vary. Sample answer: Rewrite the mixed numbers as fractions. Multiply the numerators and multiply the denominators. Then simplify.

PAGES 294–296   SKILLS AND CONCEPTS

10. $\frac{2}{7} + \frac{3}{7} = n$ **11.** $w = -\frac{1}{8} - \frac{5}{8}$ **12.** $x = \frac{5}{12} + \frac{7}{12}$

$\frac{5}{7} = n$ $w = -\frac{6}{8}$ $x = \frac{12}{12}$

        $w = -\frac{3}{4}$ $x = 1$

13. $m = -\frac{3}{5} + \frac{1}{3}$ **14.** $z = 4 - 2\frac{3}{5}$

$m = -\frac{9}{15} + \frac{5}{15}$ $z = \frac{20}{5} - \frac{13}{5}$

$m = -\frac{4}{15}$ $z = \frac{7}{5}$

        $z = 1\frac{2}{5}$

15. $t = -4\frac{2}{3} + \left(-6\frac{3}{4}\right)$ **16.** $p = \left(-\frac{1}{6}\right)\left(-\frac{3}{5}\right)$

$t = -\frac{14}{3} + \left(-\frac{27}{4}\right)$ $p = \frac{3}{30}$

$t = -\frac{56}{12} + \left(-\frac{81}{12}\right)$ $p = \frac{1}{10}$

$t = -\frac{137}{12}$

$t = -11\frac{5}{12}$

17. $2\frac{2}{5}\left(-4\frac{3}{8}\right) = s$ **18.** $-\frac{7}{10} \cdot \frac{4}{7} = k$

$\frac{12}{5}\left(-\frac{35}{8}\right) = s$ $-\frac{28}{70} = k$

$\frac{420}{40} = s$ $-\frac{2}{5} = k$

$10\frac{20}{40} = s$

$10\frac{1}{2} = s$

19. $g = \frac{4}{9} \cdot 5\frac{1}{4}$ **20.** $\frac{7}{5}$ **21.** $-6\frac{1}{3} = -\frac{19}{3}$

$g = \frac{4}{9} \cdot \frac{21}{4}$ Mult. Inv. $= -\frac{3}{19}$

$g = \frac{84}{36}$

$g = 2\frac{12}{36}$

$g = 2\frac{1}{3}$

22. $5 \cdot 7\frac{2}{5} = \frac{5}{1} \cdot \frac{37}{5}$

$= \frac{185}{5}$

$= 37$

23. $\left(-\frac{4}{5}\right)\left(-3\frac{1}{2}\right) = \left(-\frac{4}{5}\right)\left(-\frac{7}{2}\right)$

$= \frac{28}{10}$

$= 2\frac{8}{10}$

$= 2\frac{4}{5}$

24. $-10 + 3 = -7$
$-7 + 3 = -4$
$-4 + 3 = -1$
$-1 + 3 = 2$
$2 + 3 = 5$
$5 + 3 = 8$

arithmetic; Next three terms are 2, 5, 8.

25. $27 \cdot \frac{1}{3} = 9$

$9 \cdot \frac{1}{3} = 3$

$3 \cdot \frac{1}{3} = 1$

$1 \cdot \frac{1}{3} = \frac{1}{3}$

$\frac{1}{3} \cdot \frac{1}{3} = \frac{1}{9}$

$\frac{1}{9} \cdot \frac{1}{3} = \frac{1}{27}$

geometric; Next three terms are $\frac{1}{3}$, $\frac{1}{9}$, $\frac{1}{27}$.

26. $6 + 7 = 13$
$13 + 6 = 19$
$19 + 5 = 24$
$24 + 4 = 28$
$28 + 3 = 31$
$31 + 2 = 33$

neither; Next three terms are 28, 31, 33.

27. $60 - 4 = 56$
$56 - 4 = 52$
$52 - 4 = 48$
$48 - 4 = 44$
$44 - 4 = 40$
$40 - 4 = 36$

arithmetic; Next three terms are 44, 40, 36.

28. $A = \frac{1}{2}bh$

$A = \left(\frac{1}{2}\right)\left(2\frac{1}{2}\right)\left(3\frac{1}{4}\right)$

$A = \left(\frac{1}{2}\right)\left(\frac{5}{2}\right)\left(\frac{13}{4}\right)$

$A = \frac{65}{16}$

$A = 4\frac{1}{16}$ cm^2

29. $A = \frac{1}{2}h(a + b)$

$A = \left(\frac{1}{2}\right)(6)(10 + 7)$

$A = (3)(17)$

$A = 51$ m^2

30. $C = \pi d$

$C = \pi\left(3\frac{1}{3}\right)$

$C = \pi\left(\frac{10}{3}\right)$

$C \approx 10.47$ ft

31. $C = 2\pi r$

$C = 2\pi(2.4)$

$C \approx 15.08$ m

32. $C = 2\pi r$

$C = 2\pi(19)$

$C \approx 119.38$ yd

33. $C = \pi d$

$C = \pi(5.5)$

$C = 17.28$ in.

34. $i = -\frac{7}{9} \div \left(-\frac{2}{3}\right)$

$i = -\frac{7}{9} \cdot \left(-\frac{3}{2}\right)$

$i = \frac{21}{18}$

$i = 1\frac{3}{18}$

$i = 1\frac{1}{6}$

35. $2\frac{2}{5} \div 4 = f$

$\frac{12}{5} \div \frac{4}{1} = f$

$\frac{12}{5} \cdot \frac{1}{4} = f$

$\frac{12}{20} = f$

$\frac{3}{5} = f$

36. $3\frac{1}{7} \div \left(-2\frac{1}{5}\right) = d$

$\frac{22}{7} \div \left(-\frac{11}{5}\right) = d$

$\frac{22}{7} \cdot \left(-\frac{5}{11}\right) = d$

$-\frac{110}{77} = d$

$-1\frac{33}{77} = d$

$-1\frac{3}{7} = d$

37. $q = \frac{3}{4} \div 3\frac{3}{5}$

$q = \frac{3}{4} \div \frac{18}{5}$

$q = \frac{3}{4} \cdot \frac{5}{18}$

$q = \frac{15}{72}$

$q = \frac{5}{24}$

38. $\frac{x}{6} = -4.3$

$6 \cdot \frac{x}{6} = -4.3 \cdot 6$

$x = -25.8$

39.

$-6.2 = \frac{e}{1.7} + 4$

$-6.2 - 4 = \frac{e}{1.7} + 4 - 4$

$-10.2 = \frac{e}{1.7}$

$1.7 \cdot (-10.2) = \frac{e}{1.7} \cdot 1.7$

$-17.34 = e$

40. $2b - \frac{4}{7} = 6\frac{1}{7}$

$2b - \frac{4}{7} + \frac{4}{7} = \frac{43}{7} + \frac{4}{7}$

$2b = \frac{47}{7}$

$\frac{1}{2} \cdot 2b = \frac{47}{7} \cdot \frac{1}{2}$

$b = \frac{47}{14} = 3\frac{5}{14}$

41. $t - (-0.9) = 5$

$t + 0.9 = 5$

$t + 0.9 - 0.9 = 5 - 0.9$

$t = 4.1$

PAGE 296   APPLICATIONS AND PROBLEM SOLVING

42. $12 \cdot \frac{3}{2} = 18$

$18 \cdot \frac{3}{2} = 27$

$27 \cdot \frac{3}{2} = 40.5$

Total miles ridden after four days is
$12 + 18 + 27 + 40.5 = 97.5$ miles.

43. The minute hand represents the radius of the face of the clock. Also, $\frac{4}{12} = \frac{1}{3}$, so going from 12 to 4 is $\frac{1}{3}$ of the circumference of the face of the clock.

$C = 2\pi r$

$C = 2\pi(9)$

$C \approx 56.55$ cm

And $\frac{1}{3} \cdot 56.55 = 18.85$ cm. So the end of the minute hand moves 18.85 cm.

Chapter 7 Test

1. $1\frac{1}{9} = \frac{10}{9}$

Mult. Inv. $= \frac{9}{10}$

2. $5\frac{1}{3} \cdot \left(-2\frac{1}{4}\right) = \frac{16}{3} \cdot \left(-\frac{9}{4}\right)$

$= -\frac{144}{12}$

$= -12$

3. $-6\frac{3}{7} + 4\frac{6}{7} = m$

$-\frac{45}{7} + \frac{34}{7} = m$

$-\frac{11}{7} = m$

$-1\frac{4}{7} = m$

4. $\frac{8}{15} + \frac{8}{15} = a$

$\frac{16}{15} = a$

$1\frac{1}{15} = a$

5. $\frac{5}{8} - \frac{4}{5} = g$

$\frac{25}{40} - \frac{32}{40} = g$

$-\frac{7}{40} = g$

6. $\frac{33}{40} \cdot \frac{8}{9} = t$

$\frac{264}{360} = t$

$\frac{11}{15} = t$

7. $c = -\frac{7}{8} \div 2\frac{4}{5}$

$c = -\frac{7}{8} \div \frac{14}{5}$

$c = -\frac{7}{8} \cdot \frac{5}{14}$

$c = -\frac{35}{112}$

$c = -\frac{5}{16}$

8. $5\frac{5}{6} \div \left(-1\frac{2}{3}\right) = x$

$\frac{35}{6} \div \left(-\frac{5}{3}\right) = x$

$\frac{35}{6} \cdot \left(-\frac{3}{5}\right) = x$

$-\frac{105}{30} = x$

$-3\frac{15}{30} = x$

$-3\frac{1}{2} = x$

9. $20 + 2 = 22$

$22 + 2 = 24$

$24 + 2 = 26$

The first four terms are 20, 22, 24, 26.

10. $6 \cdot 2 = 12$

$12 \cdot 2 = 24$

$24 \cdot 2 = 48$

$48 \cdot 2 = 96$

The first four terms are 96, 48, 24, 12.

11. $A = \frac{1}{2}bh$

$A = \left(\frac{1}{2}\right)(12)(19)$

$A = 114 \text{ m}^2$

12. $A = \frac{1}{2}bh$

$A = \left(\frac{1}{2}\right)\left(4\frac{1}{2}\right)\left(6\frac{3}{4}\right)$

$A = \left(\frac{1}{2}\right)\left(\frac{9}{2}\right)\left(\frac{27}{4}\right)$

$A = \frac{243}{16}$

$A = 15\frac{3}{16} \text{ ft}^2$

13. $A = \frac{1}{2}h(a + b)$

$A = \left(\frac{1}{2}\right)\left(9\frac{1}{2}\right)(15 + 26)$

$A = \left(\frac{1}{2}\right)\left(\frac{19}{2}\right)(41)$

$A = \frac{779}{4}$

$A = 194\frac{3}{4} \text{ in.}^2$

14. $A = \frac{1}{2}h(a + b)$

$A = \left(\frac{1}{2}\right)(8.2)(3.7 + 5.4)$

$A = (4.1)(9.1)$

$A = 37.31 \text{ mm}^2$

15. $C = \pi d$

$C = \pi(6.3)$

$c \approx 19.79 \text{ yd}$

16. $C = 2\pi r$

$C = 2\pi\left(2\frac{5}{8}\right)$

$C = 2\pi\left(\frac{21}{8}\right)$

$C \approx 16.49 \text{ m}$

17. $2\frac{1}{2}w = 4\frac{3}{8}$

$\frac{5}{2}w = \frac{35}{8}$

$\frac{2}{5} \cdot \frac{5}{2}w = \frac{35}{8} \cdot \frac{2}{5}$

$w = \frac{70}{40}$

$w = 1\frac{30}{40}$

$w = 1\frac{3}{4}$

18. $\frac{a}{2.8} - 6.8 = 12$

$\frac{a}{2.8} - 6.8 + 6.8 = 12 + 6.8$

$\frac{a}{2.8} = 18.8$

$2.8 \cdot \frac{a}{2.8} = 28.8 \cdot 2.8$

$a = 52.64$

19. $\frac{1}{4} = -\frac{5}{6}x + \frac{9}{16}$

$\frac{4}{16} - \frac{9}{16} = -\frac{5}{6}x + \frac{9}{16} - \frac{9}{16}$

$-\frac{5}{16} = -\frac{5}{6}x$

$\left(-\frac{6}{5}\right)\left(-\frac{5}{16}\right) = \left(-\frac{5}{6}x\right)\left(-\frac{6}{5}\right)$

$\frac{30}{80} = x$

$\frac{3}{8} = x$

20. $12 - 2 = 10$

$10 + 3 = 13$

$13 - 2 = 11$

$11 + 3 = 14$

$14 - 2 - 12$

$12 + 3 = 15$

$15 - 2 = 13$

Pattern: subtract 2, then add 3. There were 8 rows in the showcase.

PAGE 297   BONUS

$0 = \frac{0}{1}$

The reciprocal is $\frac{1}{0}$ which is impossible because zero cannot be a denominator. So zero has no multiplicative inverse.

Chapter 8   Real Numbers

8-1   Square Roots

PAGE 301   CHECKING FOR UNDERSTANDING

1. It is the square of 6.   2. $\sqrt{100}$

3.

4 cm

4 cm

4. Since $7^2 = 49$, $\sqrt{49} = 7$.

5. Since $9^2 = 81$, $\sqrt{81} = 9$.
6. Since $11^2 = 121$, $\sqrt{121} = 11$.
7. Since $8^2 = 64$, $-\sqrt{64} = -8$.

PAGES 301-302   EXERCISES

8. Since $5^2 = 25$, $\sqrt{25} = 5$.
9. Since $20^2 = 400$, $\sqrt{400} = 20$.
10. Since $15^2 = 225$, $\sqrt{225} = 15$.
11. Since $3^2 = 9$, $-\sqrt{9} = -3$.
12. Since $14^2 = 196$, $\sqrt{196} = 14$.
13. Since $25^2 = 625$, $\sqrt{625} = 25$.
14. Since $17^2 = 289$, $-\sqrt{289} = -17$.
15. Since $10^2 = 100$, $-\sqrt{100} = -10$.
16. Since $\left(\frac{2}{3}\right)^2 = \frac{4}{9}$, $\sqrt{\frac{4}{9}} = \frac{2}{3}$.
17. Since $(0.4)^2 = 0.16$, $\sqrt{0.16} = 0.4$.
18. Since $(1.7)^2 = 2.89$, $-\sqrt{2.89} = -1.7$.
19. Since $\left(\frac{8}{10}\right)^2 = \frac{64}{100}$, $\sqrt{\frac{64}{100}} = \frac{8}{10}$.
20. 15 and -15; 15 is the principal square root because it is nonnegative.
21. $\sqrt{1.69} = 1.3$ meters
22. $270 \div 36 = 7.5 \rightarrow 270$ in. $= 7.5$ yd
23.

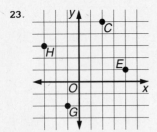

24. $12 = 2 \cdot 2 \cdot 3$
    $63 = 3 \cdot 3 \cdot 7$
    GCF = 3

25. $3x - 5 = -6$
    $3x - 5 + 5 = -6 + 5$
    $3x = -1$
    $\frac{3x}{3} = \frac{-1}{3}$
    $x = -\frac{1}{3}$

26. yes; The product of the square roots of each perfect square is the square root of the new perfect square.

27. The length of one side of the garden is $\sqrt{289}$ or 17 feet. The perimeter of the garden is $4 \cdot 17$ or 68 feet. The cost to fence the garden will be $0.35 \cdot 68$ or \$23.80.

28. See students' work.

8-2A   Mathematics Lab: Estimating Square Roots

PAGE 303   WHAT DO YOU THINK?

1. 7   2. 8   3. 7 and 8
4. 7; 50 is closer to 49 than 64.

PAGE 303   APPLICATIONS

5. 4   6. 9   7. 12
8. 12   9. 14   10. 1

8-2   Estimating Square Roots

PAGE 305   CHECKING FOR UNDERSTANDING

1. Since 12 is between 9 and 16, $\sqrt{12}$ is between 3 and 4.

2.

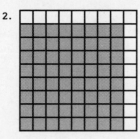

3. $49 < 50 < 64$
   $7^2 < 50 < 8^2$
   $7 < \sqrt{50} < 8$
   Since 50 is closer to 49 than to 64, the best whole integer estimate for $\sqrt{50}$ is 7.

4. $121 < 135 < 144$
   $11^2 < 135 < 12^2$
   $11 < \sqrt{135} < 12$
   Since 135 is closer to 144 than to 121, the best whole integer estimate for $\sqrt{135}$ is 12.

5. $25 < 29 < 36$
   $5^2 < 29 < 6^2$
   $5 < \sqrt{29} < 6$
   Since 29 is closer to 25 than to 36, the best whole integer estimate for $\sqrt{29}$ is 5.

6. $9 < 11 < 16$

$3^2 < 11 < 4^2$

$3^2 < \sqrt{11} < 4$

Since 11 is closer to 9 than to 16, the best whole integer estimate for $\sqrt{11}$ is 3.

PAGE 305 EXERCISES

7. $16 < 23 < 25$

$4^2 < 23 < 5^2$

$4 < \sqrt{23} < 5$

Since 23 is closer to 25 than to 16, the best whole integer estimate for $\sqrt{23}$ is 5.

8. $36 < 44 < 49$

$6^2 < 44 < 7^2$

$6 < \sqrt{44} < 7$

Since 44 is closer to 49 than to 36, the best whole integer estimate for $\sqrt{44}$ is 7.

9. $49 < 56 < 64$

$7^2 < 56 < 8^2$

$7 < \sqrt{56} < 8$

Since 56 is closer to 49 than to 64, the best whole integer estimate for $\sqrt{56}$ is 7.

10. $16 < 17.5 < 25$

$4^2 < 17.5 < 5^2$

$4 < \sqrt{17.5} < 5$

Since 17.5 is closer to 16 than to 25, the best whole integer estimate for $\sqrt{17.5}$ is 4.

11. $36 < 47 < 49$

$6^2 < 47 < 7^2$

$6 < \sqrt{47} < 7$

Since 47 is closer to 49 than to 36, the best whole integer estimate for $\sqrt{47}$ is 7.

12. $100 < 113 < 121$

$10^2 < 113 < 11^2$

$10 < \sqrt{113} < 11$

Since 113 is closer to 121 than to 100, the best whole integer estimate for $\sqrt{113}$ is 11.

13. $169 < 175 < 196$

$13^2 < 175 < 14^2$

$13 < \sqrt{175} < 14$

Since 175 is closer to 169 than to 196, the best whole integer estimate for $\sqrt{175}$ is 13.

14. $196 < 200 < 225$

$14^2 < 200 < 15^2$

$14 < \sqrt{200} < 15$

Since 200 is closer to 196 than to 225, the best whole integer estimate for $\sqrt{200}$ is 14.

15. $400 < 408 < 441$

$20^2 < 408 < 21^2$

$20 < \sqrt{408} < 21$

Since 408 is closer to 400 than to 441, the best whole integer estimate for $\sqrt{408}$ is 20.

16. $16 < 17.25 < 25$

$4^2 < 17.25 < 5^2$

$4 < \sqrt{17.25} < 5$

Since 17.25 is closer to 16 than to 25, the best whole integer estimate for $\sqrt{17.25}$ is 4.

17. $900 < 957 < 961$

$30^2 < 957 < 31^2$

$30 < \sqrt{957} < 31$

Since 957 is closer to 961 to 900, the best whole integer estimate for $\sqrt{957}$ is 31.

18. $25 < 30.8 < 36$

$5^2 < 30.8 < 6^2$

$5 < \sqrt{30.8} < 6$

Since 30.8 is closer to 36 than to 25, the best whole integer estimate for $\sqrt{30.8}$ is 6.

19. $s = 3.6 \div 0.6$

$s = 6$

20. $4\frac{2}{3} - 6\frac{1}{4} = m$

$4\frac{2}{3} - 5\frac{5}{4} = m$

$4\frac{8}{12} - 5\frac{15}{12} = m$

$-1\frac{7}{12} = m$

21. Since $30^2 = 900$, $\sqrt{900} = 30$.

22. $s = \sqrt{24d}$

$s = \sqrt{24 \cdot 20}$

$s = \sqrt{480}$

$441 < 480 < 484$

$21^2 < 480 < 22^2$

$21 < \sqrt{480} < 22$

approximately 22 mph

23. $d = 1.22 \times \sqrt{h}$

$d = 1.22 \times \sqrt{900}$

$d = 1.22 \times 30$

$d = 36.6$

about 36.6 mi

24. $(4.4)^2 = 19.36$ and $(4.5)^2 = 20.25$; $19.36 < 20 < 20.25$; so $4.4 < \sqrt{20} < 4.5$.

8-3 The Real Number System

PAGE 308 CHECKING FOR UNDERSTANDING

1. The set of real numbers is the set of rational numbers combined with the set of irrational numbers.
2. It is an irrational number since it is not a repeating decimal.

3.

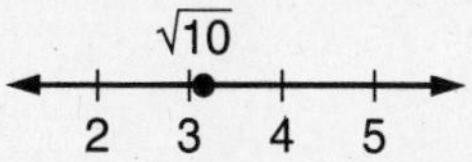

4. $x^2 = 25$

$x = \sqrt{25}$ or $x = -\sqrt{25}$

$x = 5$ or $x = -5$

5. $\sqrt{5} = 2.2360679...$

not a repeating decimal; irrational

6. repeating decimal; rational

7. $-\sqrt{9} = -3$

integer, rational

8. terminating decimal; rational

9. $\sqrt{7} \approx 2.6$

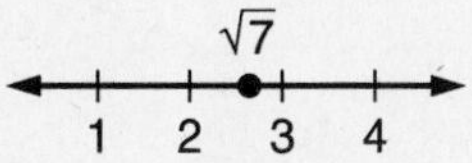

10. $\sqrt{8} \approx 2.6$

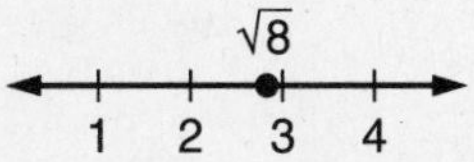

11. $\sqrt{20} \approx 4.5$

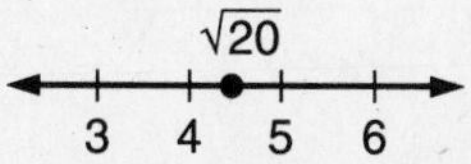

12. $-\sqrt{2} \approx -1.4$

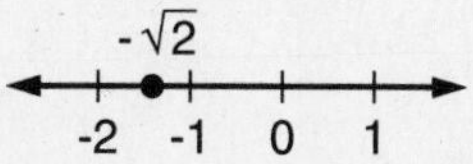

13. $x^2 = 144$

$x = \sqrt{144}$ or x $-\sqrt{144}$

$x = 12$ or $x = -12$

14. $x^2 = 900$

$x = \sqrt{900}$ or $x = -\sqrt{900}$

$x = 30$ or $x = -30$

15. $y^2 = 50$

$y = \sqrt{50}$ or $y = -\sqrt{50}$

$y \approx 7.1$ or $y \approx -7.1$

PAGE 309   EXERCISES

16. natural, whole, integer, rational

17. $\sqrt{11} = 3.3166247\ldots$

not a repeating decimal; irrational

18. $-\sqrt{36} = -6$

integer, rational

19. repeating decimal; rational

20. rational   21. repeating decimal; rational

22. not a repeating decimal; irrational

23. $\sqrt{6} \approx 2.4$ 24. $\sqrt{50} \approx 7.1$

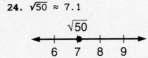

25. $\sqrt{27} \approx 5.2$ 26. $\sqrt{108} \approx 10.4$

27. $x^2 = 64$ 28. $m^2 = 12$

$x = \sqrt{64}$ or $x = -\sqrt{64}$ $m = \sqrt{12}$ or $m = -\sqrt{12}$

$x = 8$ or $x = -8$ $m \approx 3.5$ or $m \approx -3.5$

29. $y^2 = 360$ 30. $n^2 = 17$

$y = \sqrt{360}$ or y $-\sqrt{360}$ $n = \sqrt{17}$ or $n = -\sqrt{17}$

$y \approx 19.0$ or $y \approx -19.0$ $n \approx 4.1$ or $n \approx -4.1$

31. $p^2 = 1.44$

$p = \sqrt{1.44}$ or $p = -\sqrt{1.44}$

$p = 1.2$ or $p = -1.2$

32. $t^2 = 1$

$t = \sqrt{1}$ or $t = -\sqrt{1}$

$t = 1$ or $t = -1$

33. $33 = 4x - 15$ 34. $d = 28(-12)$

$33 + 15 = 4x - 15 + 15$ $d = -336$

$48 = 4x$

$\dfrac{48}{4} = \dfrac{4x}{4}$

$12 = x$

35. 50, 52, 55, 57, 59, 61, 64, 65, 68

Mean: $\dfrac{50 + 52 + 55 + 57 + 59 + 61 + 64 + 65 + 68}{9}$

$= \dfrac{531}{9} = 59$

Median: 59

Mode: none

36. $x = -\dfrac{5}{8}\left(-3\dfrac{2}{5}\right)$

$x = -\dfrac{5}{8}\left(-\dfrac{17}{5}\right)$

$x = \dfrac{85}{40}$

$x = \dfrac{17}{8}$ or $2\dfrac{1}{8}$

37. $289 < 300 < 324$

$17^2 < 300 < 18^2$

$17 < \sqrt{300} < 18$

Since 300 is closer to 289 than to 324, the best whole integer estimate for $\sqrt{300}$ is 17.

38. $d = 16t^2$

$25 = 16t^2$

$\dfrac{25}{16} = \dfrac{16t^2}{16}$

$\dfrac{25}{16} = t^2$

$\sqrt{\dfrac{25}{16}} = t$

$\dfrac{5}{4} = t$

$1.25 = t$

1.25 sec

39. $\sqrt{ab} = \sqrt{12 \cdot 108}$

$= \sqrt{1,296}$

$= 36$

40. 10, 11, 12, 13, 14, 15

41.

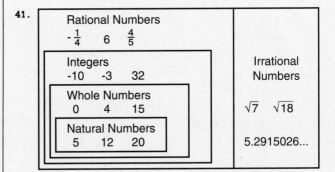

8-4   **Use a Formula**

PAGE 311   CHECKING FOR UNDERSTANDING

1. distance = rate · time   2. $A = \ell \cdot w$

3. $d = 45 \cdot 3$ 4. $P = I - E$

$d = 135$ miles $P = \$12,995 - \$15,000$

$P = -\$2,005$

5. Subtract to find the time between the starting and arriving times.

$8:08 - 6:20 = 7:68 - 6:20 = 1:48$

Subtract the time when the train was not moving.

$1:48 - 0:12 = 1:36$

Since 36 minutes is $\dfrac{36}{60}$ or 0.6 hour, another way to express the time is 1.6 hours.

$d = rt$

$104 = r(1.6)$

$\dfrac{104}{1.6} = \dfrac{r(1.6)}{1.6}$ The average running speed of the train is

$65 = r$ 65 miles per hour.

6. List all pairs of whole numbers whose product is 360: 1, 360; 2, 180; 3, 120; 4, 90; 5, 72; 6, 60; 8, 45; 9, 40; 10, 36; 12, 30; 15, 24; 18, 20. Find the pair whose difference is 9: 15, 24.

7. $A = \ell \cdot w$
$A = 60 \cdot 12$
$A = 720$ square feet

8.

The length of the base stays the same and the height increases.

9. a. $d = 0.2t$
$d = 0.2(20)$
$d = 4$ miles

   b. $d = 0.2t$
$4 = 0.2t$
$\dfrac{4}{0.2} = \dfrac{0.2t}{0.2}$
$20 = t$
about 20 sec

Mid-Chapter Review

PAGE 312

1. $\sqrt{36} = 6$ 2. $\sqrt{225} = 15$ 3. $-\sqrt{25} = -5$

4. $-\sqrt{0.16} = -0.4$

5. $81 < 90 < 100$
$9^2 < 90 < 10^2$
$9 < \sqrt{90} < 10$
Since 90 is closer to 81 than to 100, the best whole integer estimate for $\sqrt{90}$ is 9.

6. $1 < 2 < 4$
$1^2 < 2 < 2^2$
$1 < \sqrt{2} < 2$
Since 2 is closer to 1 than 4, the best whole integer estimate for $\sqrt{2}$ is 1.

7. $25 < 28 < 36$
$5^2 < 28 < 6^2$
$5 < \sqrt{28} < 6$
Since 28 is closer to 25 than to 36, the best whole integer estimate for $\sqrt{28}$ is 5.

8. $196 < 200 < 225$
$14^2 < 200 < 15^2$
$14 < \sqrt{200} < 15$
Since 200 is closer to 196 than to 225, the best whole integer estimate for $\sqrt{200}$ is 14.

9. natural, whole, integer, rational

10. $\sqrt{4} = 2$
natural, whole, integer, rational

11. repeating decimal; rational

12. $\sqrt{3} = 1.7320508\ldots$
not a repeating decimal; irrational

13. $x^2 = 49$
$x = \sqrt{49}$ or $x -\sqrt{49}$
$x = 7$ or $x = -7$

14. $y^2 = 50$
$y = \sqrt{50}$ or $y = -\sqrt{50}$
$y \approx 7.1$ or $y \approx -7.1$

15. $d = rt$
$60 = r(0.5)$
$\dfrac{60}{0.5} = \dfrac{r(0.5)}{0.5}$
$120 = r$
120 ft per sec

8-5A Mathematics Lab: The Pythagorean Theorem

PAGE 314   WHAT DO YOU THINK?

1.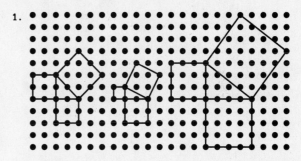

4 square units, 1 square unit, 9 square units, 4 square units, 4 square units, 16 square and 8 square and 5 square units, and 25 units units square units

2. The sum of the areas of the two smaller squares is equal to the area of the larger square.

3. See students' work; $a^2 + b^2 = c^2$, where c is the length of the hypotenuse.

PAGE 314   APPLICATIONS

4. $2^2 + 3^2 = c^2$
$4 + 9 = c^2$
$13 = c^2$
13 square units

5. $a^2 + 2^2 = 6^2$
$a^2 + 4 = 36$
$a^2 + 4 - 4 = 36 - 4$
$a^2 = 32$ square units

PAGE 314   EXTENSION

6. See students' work.

8-5   The Pythagorean Theorem

1. 100 square units

2.
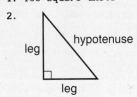

3. $c^2 = a^2 + b^2$
$6^2 \stackrel{?}{=} 4^2 + 5^2$
$36 \stackrel{?}{=} 16 + 25$
$36 \neq 41$; no

4. $c^2 = 9^2 + 12^2$
$c^2 = 81 + 144$
$c^2 = 225$
$c = 15$

5. $c^2 = 5^2 + 12^2$
$c^2 = 25 + 144$
$c^2 = 169$
$c = 13$

6. $41^2 = 9^2 + b^2$
$1{,}681 = 81 + b^2$
$1{,}681 - 81 = 81 - 81 + b^2$
$1{,}600 = b^2$
$40 = b$

7. $c^2 = a^2 + b^2$
$15^2 \stackrel{?}{=} 10^2 + 12^2$
$225 \stackrel{?}{=} 100 + 144$
$225 \neq 244$; no

8. $c^2 = a^2 + b^2$
$30^2 \stackrel{?}{=} 18^2 + 24^2$
$900 \stackrel{?}{=} 324 + 576$
$900 = 900$; yes

9. $12^2 = 9^2 + b^2$
$144 = 81 + b^2$
$144 - 81 = 81 - 81 + b^2$
$63 = b^2$
$b \approx 7.9$ ft

10. $c^2 = 5^2 + 5^2$
$c^2 = 25 + 25$
$c^2 = 50$
$c \approx 7.1$ in.

11. $8^2 = 3^2 + b^2$
$64 = 9 + b^2$
$64 - 9 = 9 - 9 + b^2$
$55 = b^2$
$b \approx 7.4$ m

12. $101^2 = a^2 + 99^2$
$10{,}201 = a^2 + 9{,}801$
$10{,}201 - 9{,}801 = a^2 + 9{,}801 - 9{,}801$
$400 = a^2$
$a = 20$ mm

13. $22^2 = a^2 + 12^2$
$484 = a^2 + 144$
$484 - 144 = a^2 + 144 - 144$
$340 = a^2$
$a \approx 18.4$ cm

14. $c^2 = 48^2 + 55^2$
$c^2 = 2{,}304 + 3{,}025$
$c^2 = 5{,}329$
$c = 73$ yd

15. $41^2 = 40^2 + b^2$
$1{,}681 = 1{,}600 + b^2$
$1{,}681 - 1{,}600 = 1{,}600 - 1{,}600 + b^2$
$81 = b^2$
$b = 9$ in.

16. $c^2 = (3.5)^2 + (12.5)^2$
$c^2 = 12.25 + 156.25$
$c^2 = 168.5$
$c \approx 13.0$ m

17. $x^2 = 10^2 + 10^2$
$x^2 = 100 + 100$
$x^2 = 200$
$x = 14.1$ in.

18. $8^2 = x^2 + 4^2$
$64 = x^2 + 16$
$64 - 16 = x^2 + 16 - 16$
$48 = x^2$
$6.9 \approx x$

19. $x^2 = 1^2 + (\sqrt{2})^2$
$x^2 = 1 + 2$
$x^2 = 3$
$x \approx 1.7$

20. $c^2 = a^2 + b^2$
$12^2 \stackrel{?}{=} 5^2 + 10^2$
$144 \stackrel{?}{=} 25 + 100$
$144 \neq 125$; no

21. $c^2 = a^2 + b^2$
$(\sqrt{2})^2 \stackrel{?}{=} 1^2 + 1^2$
$2 \stackrel{?}{=} 1 + 1$
$2 = 2$; yes

22. $c^2 = a^2 + b^2$
$7^2 \stackrel{?}{=} 4^2 + 5^2$
$49 \stackrel{?}{=} 16 + 25$
$49 \neq 41$; no

23. $c^2 = a^2 + b^2$
$197^2 \stackrel{?}{=} 195^2 + 28^2$
$38{,}809 \stackrel{?}{=} 38{,}025 + 784$
$38{,}809 = 38{,}809$; yes

24. $c^2 = a^2 + b^2$
$41^2 \stackrel{?}{=} 9^2 + 40^2$
$1{,}681 \stackrel{?}{=} 81 + 1{,}600$
$1{,}681 = 1{,}681$; yes

25. $c^2 = a^2 + b^2$
$145^2 \stackrel{?}{=} 143^2 + 24^2$
$21{,}025 \stackrel{?}{=} 20{,}449 + 576$
$21{,}025 = 21{,}025$; yes

26. $1.25 \times 1{,}000 = 1{,}250 \rightarrow 1.25$ kg $= 1{,}250$ g

27. 32, 33, 34, 35

28. $-3.47 \times 10^{-5} = -3.47 \times 0.00001$
$= -0.0000347$

29. $t^2 = 144$
$t = \sqrt{144}$ or $t = -\sqrt{144}$
$t = 12$ or $t = -12$

30. $x^2 = 8^2 + 5^2$
$x^2 = 64 + 25$
$x^2 = 89$
$x \approx 9.4$ units

31. $x^2 = 25^2 + 8^2$
$x^2 = 225 + 64$
$x^2 = 289$
$x = 17$ yd

32. $8^2 = x^2 + x^2$
$64 = 2x^2$
$\dfrac{64}{2} = \dfrac{2x^2}{2}$
$32 = x^2$
$x \approx 5.7$ units
$P = a + b + c$
$P = 16 + 12 + 20$
$P = 48$ cm
$A = \dfrac{1}{2}bh$
$A = \dfrac{1}{2}(12)(16)$
$A = 96$ cm^2

33. $20^2 = x^2 + 12^2$
$400 = x^2 + 144$
$400 - 144 = x^2 + 144 - 144$
$256 = x^2$
$16 = x$

8-6   Using the Pythagorean Theorem

1. $c^2 = a^2 + b^2$
$c^2 = 1^2 + 2^2$
$c^2 = 1 + 4$
$c^2 = 5$ units^2

2. Sample answer:
10-24-26; 20-48-52

92

3. $r^2 = 9^2 + 18^2$ $r^2 = 9^2 + 12^2$
   $r^2 = 81 + 324$ $r^2 = 81 + 144$
   $r^2 = 405$ $r^2 = 225$
   $r \approx 20.1$ ft $r = 15$ ft

4. $30^2 = \ell^2 + 21^2$
            $900 = \ell^2 + 441$
   $900 - 441 = \ell^2 + 441 - 441$
            $459 = \ell^2$
            $\ell \approx 21.4$ m

PAGES 321-322   EXERCISES

5. $15^2 = 3^2 + h^2$
          $225 = 9 + h^2$
   $225 - 9 = 9 - 9 + h^2$
          $216 = h^2$
          $h = 14.7$ ft

6. $x^2 = 5^2 + 8^2$
    $x^2 = 25 + 64$
    $x^2 = 89$
    $x \approx 9.4$ mi

7. 16-30-34; 40-75-85   8. 14-48-50; 35-120-125

9. 18-80-82; 45-200-205   10. 3-4-5

11. $4^2 - 2^3 = 16 - 8$
          $= 8$

12. $c^2 = a^2 + b^2$
    $20^2 \overset{?}{=} 12^2 + 13^2$
    $400 \overset{?}{=} 144 + 169$
    $400 \neq 313$; no
    $20^2 = 15^2 + h^2$
    $400 = 225 + h^2$
    $400 - 225 = 225 + h^2 - h^2$
    $175 = h^2$
    $h \approx 13.2$ m

13.
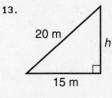

14.
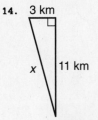

$x^2 = 3^2 + 11^2$
$x^2 = 9 + 121$
$x^2 = 130$
$x \approx 11.4$ km

15.
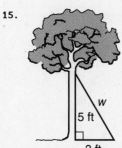

$w^2 = 5^2 + 3^2$
$w^2 = 25 + 9$
$w^2 = 34$
$w = \sqrt{34}$
The length of 12 wires
is $12\sqrt{34}$ or about 70
feet.

16.
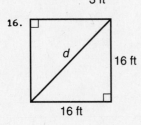

$d^2 = 16^2 + 16^2$
$d^2 = 256 + 256$
$d^2 = 512$
$d \approx 22.6$ ft
No, the diagonal of a
16 feet by 16 feet
square is about
22.6 feet

17. **a.** 9 + 2 = 11, 40 + 20 = 60, 41 + 20 = 61
    The Pythagorean triple is 11-60-61.
    b. 11 + 2 = 13, 60 + 24 = 84, 61 + 24 = 85
    The Pythagorean triple is 13-84-85.

18. **a.** $a = x^2 - y^2$; $b = xy$; $c = x^2 + y^2$
    b. See students' work.

8-6B   **Mathematics Lab:**
          Graphing Irrational Numbers

PAGE 324   WHAT DO YOU THINK?

1. Draw a number line. At 1, construct a
   perpendicular line segment 1 unit in length.
   Draw a line from 0 to the top of the
   perpendicular line segment. Label it c. Open
   the compass to the length of c. With the tip
   of the compass at 0, draw an arc that intersects
   the number line to the right of 0 at A. The
   distance from 0 to A is $\sqrt{2}$ units.

2. First method: Draw a number line. At 2,
   construct a perpendicular line segment 2
   units in length. Draw a line from 0 to the
   top of the perpendicular line segment. Label
   it b. Open the compass to the length of b.
   With the tip of the compass at 0, draw an
   arc that intersects the number line to the
   right of 0 at B. The distance from 0 to B
   is $\sqrt{8}$ units.
   Second method: Draw a number line. At 1,
   construct a perpendicular line segment. Put the
   tip of the compass at 0. With the compass set at
   3 units, construct an arc that intersects the
   perpendicular line segment. Label the
   perpendicular leg a. Open the compass to the
   length of a. With the tip of the compass at 0,
   draw an arc that intersects the number line to
   the right of 0 at D. The distance from 0 to D
   is $\sqrt{8}$ units.

3. Draw a number line. At 1, construct a
   perpendicular line segment $\sqrt{2}$ units in length.
   Draw a line segment from 0 to the top of the
   perpendicular line segment. Label it d. Open
   the compass to the length of d. With the tip
   of the compass at 0, draw an arc that intersects
   the number line to the right of 0 at C. The
   distance from 0 to C is $\sqrt{3}$ units.

93

4. Draw a number line. At 1, construct a perpendicular line segment 2 units in length. Draw a line segment from 0 to the top of the perpendicular line segment. Label it c. Open the compass to the length of c. With the tip of the compass at 0, draw an arc that intersects the number line to the left of 0 at B. The distance from 0 to B is $\sqrt{5}$ units.

5.

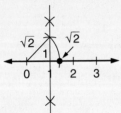

6.

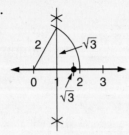

7.

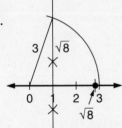

8.

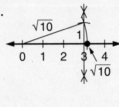

8-7 Distance on the Coordinate Plane

PAGE 326   CHECKING FOR UNDERSTANDING

1. 5 units, 3 units

2. 1) Graph the points (5,5) and (2,2) on a coordinate plane and connect them with a line segment.
   2) Draw a horizontal line through (2,2) and a vertical line through (5,5).
   3) Use the Pythagorean Theorem.

3.

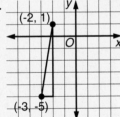

4. $c^2 = a^2 + b^2$
   $c^2 = 3^2 + 4^2$
   $c^2 = 9 + 16$
   $c^2 = 25$
   $c = 5$ units

5. $c^2 = a^2 + b^2$
   $c^2 = 6^2 + 8^2$
   $c^2 = 36 + 64$
   $c^2 = 100$
   $c = 10$ units

6. $c^2 = a^2 + b^2$
   $c^2 = 4^2 + 3^2$
   $c^2 = 16 + 9$
   $c^2 = 25$
   $c = 5$ units

PAGE 327   EXERCISES

7. $c^2 = a^2 + b^2$
   $c^2 = 4^2 + 1^2$
   $c^2 = 16 + 1$
   $c^2 = 17$
   $c \approx 4.1$ units

8. $c^2 = a^2 + b^2$
   $c^2 = 3^2 + 5^2$
   $c^2 = 9 + 25$
   $c^2 = 34$
   $c \approx 5.8$ units

9. $c^2 = a^2 + b^2$
   $c^2 = 5^2 + 1^2$
   $c^2 = 25 + 1$
   $c^2 = 26$
   $c \approx 5.1$ units

10.

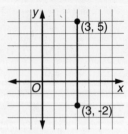

7 units

$c^2 = a^2 + b^2$
$c^2 = 3^2 + 7^2$
$c = 9 + 49$
$c^2 = 58$
$c \approx 7.6$ units

11.

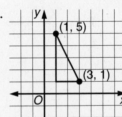

12.

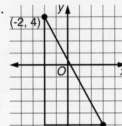

$c^2 = a^2 + b^2$
$c^2 = 2^2 + 4^2$
$c^2 = 4 + 16$
$c^2 = 20$
$c \approx 4.5$ units

13.

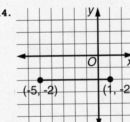

$c^2 = a^2 + b^2$
$c^2 = 5^2 + 9^2$
$c^2 = 25 + 81$
$c^2 = 106$
$c \approx 10.3$ units

14.

6 units

94

15.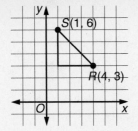

$$c^2 = a^2 + b^2$$
$$c^2 = 3^2 + 3^2$$
$$c^2 = 9 + 9$$
$$c^2 = 18$$
$$c \approx 4.2 \text{ units}$$

16.
$$h - 15 = 27$$
$$h - 15 + 15 = 27 + 15$$
$$h = 42$$

17.
$$\frac{n}{10} = -8$$
$$10\left(\frac{n}{10}\right) = -8 \cdot 10$$
$$n = -80$$

18.
$$c^2 = a^2 + b^2$$
$$66^2 = 58^2 + b^2$$
$$4{,}356 = 3{,}364 + b^2$$
$$4{,}356 - 3{,}364 = 3{,}364 - 3{,}364 + b^2$$
$$992 = b^2$$
$$b \approx 31.5 \text{ ft}$$

19. a.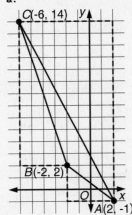

b. The distance between A and B is:
$$c^2 = a^2 + b^2$$
$$c^2 = 4^2 + 3^2$$
$$c^2 = 16 + 9$$
$$c^2 = 25$$
$$c = 5 \text{ units.}$$

The distance between A and C is:
$$c^2 = a^2 + b^2$$
$$c^2 = 8^2 + 15^2$$
$$c^2 = 64 + 225$$
$$c^2 = 289$$
$$c = 17 \text{ units.}$$

The distance between B and C is:
$$c^2 = a^2 + b^2$$
$$c^2 = 4^2 + 12^2$$
$$c^2 = 16 + 144$$
$$c^2 = 160$$
$$c \approx 12.6 \text{ units.}$$

The perimeter of triangle ABC is about
5 + 17 + 12.6 or 34.6 units.

20.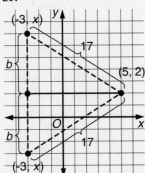

$$c^2 = a^2 + b^2$$
$$17^2 = 8^2 + b^2$$
$$289 = 64 + b^2$$
$$289 - 64 = 64 - 64 + b^2$$
$$225 = b^2$$
$$15 = b$$
$$x = 2 + 15 = 17$$
or
$$x = 2 - 15 = -13$$

21.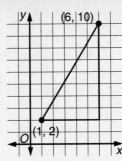

$$c^2 = a^2 + b^2$$
$$c^2 = 5^2 + 8^2$$
$$c^2 = 25 + 64$$
$$c^2 = 89$$
$$c \approx 9.4 \text{ mi}$$

22.
$$d = rt$$
$$5 = 50t$$
$$\frac{5}{50} = \frac{50t}{50}$$
$$\frac{1}{10} = t$$
$$\frac{1}{10} \text{ hr} = 6 \text{ min}$$
$$6 \text{ min} = 360 \text{ sec}$$

8-8 **Special Right Triangles**

PAGE 330   CHECKING FOR UNDERSTANDING

1.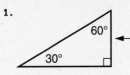

2. The two legs have equal length.

3. The length of the hypotenuse is twice the length of the leg opposite the 30° angle.

4.
$$c = 2a$$
$$c = 2(5)$$
$$c = 10 \text{ cm}$$

$$c^2 = a^2 + b^2$$
$$10^2 = 5^2 + b^2$$
$$100 = 25 + b^2$$
$$100 - 25 = 25 - 25 + b^2$$
$$75 = b^2$$
$$b \approx 8.7 \text{ cm}$$

5.
$$a = b$$
$$a = 8 \text{ ft}$$

$$c^2 = a^2 + b^2$$
$$c^2 = 8^2 + 8^2$$
$$c^2 = 64 + 64$$
$$c^2 = 128$$
$$c \approx 11.3 \text{ ft}$$

6.
$$a = \frac{1}{2}c$$
$$a = \frac{1}{2}(12)$$
$$a = 6 \text{ in.}$$

$$c^2 = a^2 + b^2$$
$$12^2 = 6^2 + b^2$$
$$144 = 36 + b^2$$
$$144 - 36 = 36 - 36 + b^2$$
$$108 = b^2$$
$$b \approx 10.4 \text{ in.}$$

7.
$$a = b$$
$$a = 15 \text{ cm}$$

8.
$$c = 2a$$
$$c = 2(3)$$
$$c = 6 \text{ in.}$$

9. $c = 2a$

$c = 2(20)$

$c = 40$ ft

$c^2 = a^2 + b^2$

$40^2 = 20^2 + b^2$

$1{,}600 = 400 + b^2$

$1{,}600 - 400 = 400 - 400 + b^2$

$1{,}200 = b^2$

$b \approx 34.6$ ft

10. $b = a$

$b = 3.2$ m

$c^2 = a^2 + b^2$

$c^2 = (3.2)^2 + (3.2)^2$

$c^2 = 10.24 + 10.24$

$c^2 = 20.48$

$c \approx 4.5$ m

11. $a = \frac{1}{2}c$

$a = \frac{1}{2}(19)$

$a = 9.5$ in.

$c^2 = a^2 + b^2$

$19^2 = (19.5)^2 + b^2$

$361 = 90.25 + b^2$

$361 - 90.25 = 90.25 - 90.25 + b^2$

$270.75 = b^2$

$b \approx 16.5$ in.

12. $a = b$

$a = 21.5$ in.

$c^2 = a^2 + b^2$

$c^2 = (21.5)^2 + (21.5)^2$

$c^2 = 462.25 + 462.25$

$c^2 = 924.5$

$c \approx 30.4$ in.

13. $a = \frac{1}{2}c$

$a = \frac{1}{2}(7.5)$

$a = 3.75$ in.

14. 48, 50, 56, 60, 62, 64, 71

Median: 60

LQ: 50

UQ: 64

15. $\dfrac{54}{81} = \dfrac{2 \cdot \cancel{3}^{1} \cdot \cancel{3}^{1} \cdot \cancel{3}^{1}}{3 \cdot \underset{1}{\cancel{3}} \cdot \underset{1}{\cancel{3}} \cdot \underset{1}{\cancel{3}}} = \dfrac{2}{3}$

16.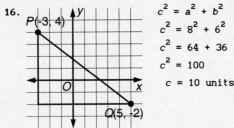

$c^2 = a^2 + b^2$

$c^2 = 8^2 + 6^2$

$c^2 = 64 + 36$

$c^2 = 100$

$c = 10$ units

17. $c = 2a$

$c = 2(6)$

$c = 12$ ft

18. $c^2 = a^2 + b^2$

$c^2 = 17^2 + 17^2$

$c^2 = 289 + 289$

$c^2 = 578$

$c \approx 24$ in.

19. Each side is 20 meters long.

$c^2 = a^2 + b^2$

$c^2 = 20^2 + 20^2$

$c^2 = 400 + 400$

$c^2 = 800$

$c \approx 28.3$ m

20. Solve for a: $a = \frac{1}{2}c$

$a = \frac{1}{2}(18)$

$a = 9$

Solve for b:

$c^2 = a^2 + b^2$

$18^2 = 9^2 + b^2$

$324 = 81 + b^2$

$324 - 81 = 81 - 81 + b^2$

$243 = b^2$

$b \approx 15.6$

Find the area of the triangle: $A = \frac{1}{2}bh$

$A \approx \frac{1}{2}(9)(15.6)$

$A \approx 70.2$ m^2

About 70.2 square meters of material will be needed.

Chapter 8 Study Guide and Review

1. b   **2.** g   **3.** c   **4.** d   **5.** i

6. h   **7.** i

8. If $c^2 = a^2 + b^2$, then the triangle is a right triangle.

9. A rational number can be expressed as $\frac{a}{b}$, where a and b are integers, $b \neq 0$. An irrational number cannot be expressed as $\frac{a}{b}$, where a and b are integers, $b \neq 0$. Rational number: 10; irrational number: $\sqrt{2}$

10. $\sqrt{36} = 6$

11. $-\sqrt{2.25} = -1.5$

12. $-\sqrt{\dfrac{9}{16}} = -\dfrac{3}{4}$

13. $\sqrt{\dfrac{49}{100}} = \dfrac{7}{10}$

14. $-\sqrt{169} = -13$

15. $\sqrt{5.29} = 2.3$

16. $121 < 136 < 144$

$11^2 < 136 < 12^2$

$11 < \sqrt{136} < 12$

Since 136 is closer to 144 than to 121, the best whole integer estimate for $\sqrt{136}$ is 12.

17. $49 < 50.2 < 64$

$7^2 < 50.2 < 8^2$

$7 < \sqrt{50.2} < 8$

Since 50.2 is closer to 49 than to 64, the best whole integer estimate for $\sqrt{50.2}$ is 7.

18. $676 < 725 < 729$
$28^2 < 725 < 29^2$
$28 < \sqrt{725} < 29$
Since 725 is closer to 729 than to 676, the best whole integer estimate for $\sqrt{725}$ is 29.

19. $361 < 372 < 400$
$19^2 < 372 < 20^2$
$19 < \sqrt{372} < 20$
Since 372 is closer to 361 than to 400, the best whole integer estimate for $\sqrt{372}$ is 19.

20. $16 < 19.33 < 25$
$4^2 < 19.33 < 5^2$
$4 < \sqrt{19.33} < 5$
Since 19.33 is closer to 16 than to 25, the best whole integer estimate for $\sqrt{19.33}$ is 4.

21. $225 < 250 < 256$
$15^2 < 250 < 16^2$
$15 < \sqrt{250} < 16$
Since 250 is closer to 256 than to 225, the best whole integer estimate for $\sqrt{250}$ is 16.

22. $\sqrt{33} = 5.7445626...$
not a repeating decimal; irrational

23. integer, rational

24. not a repeating decimal; irrational

25. repeating decimal; rational

26.
$c^2 = a^2 + b^2$
$20^2 = 16^2 + b^2$
$400 = 256 + b^2$
$400 - 256 = 256 - 256 + b^2$
$144 = b^2$
$b = 12$ ft

27. $c^2 = a^2 + b^2$
$c^2 = 5^2 + 7^2$
$c^2 = 25 + 49$
$c^2 = 74$
$c \approx 8.6$ cm

28.
$c^2 = a^2 + b^2$
$55^2 = a^2 + 28^2$
$3,025 = a^2 + 784$
$3,025 - 784 = a^2 + 784 - 784$
$2,241 = a^2$
$a \approx 47.3$ mm

29.
$c^2 = a^2 + b^2$
$8.5^2 = 7.5^2 + b^2$
$72.25 = 56.25 + b^2$
$72.25 - 56.25 = 56.25 - 56.25 + b^2$
$16 = b^2$
$b = 4$ in.

30. $c^2 = a^2 + b^2$
$c^2 = 18^2 + 30^2$
$c^2 = 324 + 900$
$c^2 = 1,224$
$c \approx 35.0$ m

31.
$c^2 = a^2 + b^2$
$(86.8)^2 = a^2 + 79^2$
$7,534.24 = a^2 + 6,241$
$7,534.24 - 6,241 = a^2 + 6,241 - 6,241$
$1,293.24 = a^2$
$a \approx 36.0$ in.

32. $c^2 = a^2 + b^2$
$c^2 = 15^2 + (9.1)^2$
$c^2 = 225 + 82.81$
$c^2 = 307.81$
$c \approx 17.5$ km

33.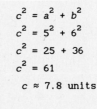
$c^2 = a^2 + b^2$
$c^2 = 2^2 + 3^2$
$c^2 = 4 + 9$
$c^2 = 13$
$c \approx 3.6$ units

34.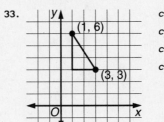
$c^2 = a^2 + b^2$
$c^2 = 5^2 + 6^2$
$c^2 = 25 + 36$
$c^2 = 61$
$c \approx 7.8$ units

35.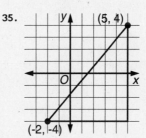
$c^2 = a^2 + b^2$
$c^2 = 7^2 + 8^2$
$c^2 = 49 + 64$
$c^2 = 113$
$c \approx 10.6$ units

36.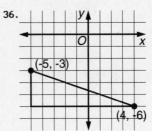
$c^2 = a^2 + b^2$
$c^2 = 9^2 + 3^2$
$c^2 = 81 + 9$
$c^2 = 90$
$c \approx 9.5$ units

37. $a = \frac{1}{2}c$
$a = \frac{1}{2}(28)$
$a = 14$ in.

$c^2 = a^2 + b^2$
$28^2 = 14^2 + b^2$
$784 = 196 + b^2$
$784 - 196 = 196 - 196 + b^2$
$588 = b^2$
$b \approx 24.2$ in.

38. $c = 2a$
$c = 2(5)$
$c = 10$ km

$c^2 = a^2 + b^2$
$10^2 = 5^2 + b^2$
$100 = 25 + b^2$
$100 - 25 = 25 - 25 + b^2$
$75 = b^2$
$b \approx 8.7$ km

39. $a = b$

$a = 15$ mm

$c^2 = a^2 + b^2$

$c^2 = 15^2 + 15^2$

$c^2 = 225 + 225$

$c^2 = 450$

$c \approx 21.2$ mm

40. $b = a$

$b = 6$ m

$c^2 = a^2 + b^2$

$c^2 = 6^2 + 6^2$

$c^2 = 36 + 36$

$c^2 = 72$

$c \approx 8.5$ m

PAGE 334   APPLICATIONS AND PROBLEM SOLVING

41. $d = rt$

$20 = r(16)$

$\dfrac{20}{16} = \dfrac{r(16)}{16}$

$r = 1.25$ m per sec

42. $P = I - E$

$P = \$599.99 - (\$390.29 + \$49.72)$

$P = \$599.99 - \$440.01$

$P = \$159.98$

Chapter 8 Test

PAGE 335

1.

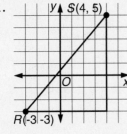

$c^2 = a^2 + b^2$

$c^2 = 7^2 + 8^2$

$c^2 = 49 + 64$

$c^2 = 113$

$c \approx 10.6$ units

2. $-\sqrt{144} = -12$

3. $\sqrt{\dfrac{49}{64}} = \dfrac{7}{8}$

4. $-\sqrt{0.25} = -0.5$

5. $64 < 66 < 81$

$8^2 < 66 < 9^2$

$8 < \sqrt{66} < 9$

Since 66 is closer to 64 than to 81, the best whole integer estimate for $\sqrt{66}$ is 8.

6. $576 < 605 < 625$

$24^2 < 605 < 25^2$

$24 < \sqrt{605} < 25$

Since 605 is closer to 625 than to 576, the best whole integer estimate for $\sqrt{605}$ is 25.

7. $121 < 137.8 < 144$

$11^2 < 137.8 < 12^2$

$11 < \sqrt{137.8} < 12$

Since 137.8 is closer to 144 than to 121, the best whole integer estimate for $\sqrt{137.8}$ is 12.

8. In a right triangle, the square of the length of the hypotenuse is equal to the sum of the squares of the legs.

9. $\sqrt{13} = 3.6055512\ldots$

not a repeating decimal; irrational

10. $-\sqrt{25} = -5$

integer, rational

11. repeating decimal; rational

12. $\sqrt{28.347} = 5.34190\ldots$

not a repeating decimal; irrational

13. $y^2 = 80$

$y = \sqrt{80}$ or $y = -\sqrt{80}$

$y \approx 8.9$ or $y \approx -8.9$

14. $x^2 = 225$

$x = \sqrt{225}$ or $x = -\sqrt{225}$

$x = 15$ or $x = -15$

15. $c^2 = a^2 + b^2$

$c^2 = (1.5)^2 + 2^2$

$c^2 = 2.25 + 4$

$c^2 = 6.25$

$c = 2.5$ km

16. $c^2 = a^2 + b^2$

$33^2 = a^2 + 20^2$

$1{,}089 = a^2 + 400$

$1{,}089 - 400 = a^2 + 400 - 400$

$689 = a^2$

$a \approx 26.2$ in.

17. $c^2 = a^2 + b^2$

$34^2 \overset{?}{=} 16^2 + 30^2$

$1{,}156 \overset{?}{=} 256 + 900$

$1{,}156 = 1{,}156$

The triangle is a right triangle.

18. $c^2 = a^2 + b^2$

$23^2 \overset{?}{=} 12^2 + 18^2$

$529 \overset{?}{=} 144 + 324$

$529 \neq 468$

The triangle is not a right triangle.

19. $c^2 = a^2 + b^2$

$c^2 = 15^2 + 20^2$

$c^2 = 225 + 400$

$c^2 = 625$

$c = 25$ ft

20. $c^2 = a^2 + b^2$

$c^2 = 9^2 + 8^2$

$c^2 = 81 + 64$

$c^2 = 145$

$c \approx 12.0$ in.

$P = a + b + c$

$P \approx 9 + 8 + 12$

$P \approx 29$ in.

$c^2 = a^2 + b^2$

$34^2 = 17^2 + b^2$

$1{,}156 = 289 + b^2$

$1{,}156 - 289 = 289 - 289 + b^2$

$867 = b^2$

$b \approx 29.4$ in.

21. $a = \dfrac{1}{2}c$

$a = \dfrac{1}{2}(34)$

$a = 17$ in.

22. $a = \frac{1}{2}c$

$a = \frac{1}{2}(57)$

$a = 28.5$ m

$c^2 = a^2 + b^2$

$57^2 = (28.5)^2 + b^2$

$3{,}249 = 812.25 + b^2$

$3{,}249 - 812.25 = 812.25 - 812.25 + b^2$

$2{,}436.75 = b^2$

$b \approx 49.4$ mm

23. $b = a$

$b = 12$ yd

$c^2 = a^2 + b^2$

$c^2 = 12^2 + 12^2$

$c^2 = 144 + 144$

$c^2 = 288$

$c \approx 17.0$ yd

24. $a = b$

$a = 20$ cm

$c^2 = a^2 + b^2$

$c^2 = 20^2 + 20^2$

$c^2 = 400 + 400$

$c^2 = 800$

$c \approx 28.3$ cm

25. No; you can only go $28 \cdot 13$ or 364 miles.

PAGE 335   BONUS

$c^2 = a^2 + b^2$

$c^2 = 4^2 + 5^2$

$c^2 = 16 + 25$

$c^2 = 41$

$c \approx 6.4$ m

$x^2 = c^2 + y^2$

$x^2 \approx (6.4)^2 + 3^2$

$x^2 \approx 40.96 + 9$

$x^2 \approx 49.96$

$x \approx 7.1$ m

Chapter 9 Applications with Proportion

1. A ratio is the comparison of two numbers by division with the same units of measurement while a rate is a comparison of two numbers with different units of measurement.

2. A unit rate is frequently used when comparing statistics.

3. a. See students' work. b. Answers may vary.

4. $\frac{5}{7}$

5. $\frac{2}{16} = \frac{1}{8}$

6. $\frac{20}{25} = \frac{4}{5}$

7. $\frac{35}{55} = \frac{7}{11}$

8. $\frac{18 \text{ brown-eyed}}{12 \text{ blue-eyed}} = \frac{3 \text{ brown-eyed}}{2 \text{ blue-eyed}}$

9. $\frac{1}{3}$

10. $\frac{100 \text{ miles}}{4 \text{ hours}} = \frac{25 \text{ miles}}{1 \text{ hour}}$; unit rate

11. $\frac{24 \text{ pounds}}{8 \text{ weeks}} = \frac{3 \text{ pounds}}{1 \text{ week}}$; unit rate

12. $\frac{4 \text{ inches}}{30 \text{ days}} = \frac{2 \text{ inches}}{15 \text{ days}}$; not a unit rate

13. $\frac{102 \text{ passengers}}{9 \text{ minivans}} = \frac{34 \text{ passengers}}{3 \text{ minivans}}$; not a unit rate

14. $\frac{11}{12}$

15. $\frac{49}{77} = \frac{7}{11}$

16. $\frac{27}{15} = \frac{9}{5}$

17. $\frac{99 \text{ wins}}{99 \text{ losses}} = \frac{1 \text{ win}}{1 \text{ loss}}$

18. $\frac{18 \text{ boys}}{27 \text{ students}} = \frac{2 \text{ boys}}{3 \text{ students}}$

19. $\frac{65}{105} = \frac{13}{21}$

20. $\frac{17}{51} = \frac{1}{3}$

21. $\frac{64}{16} = \frac{4}{1}$

22. $\frac{165}{200} = \frac{33}{40}$

23. $\frac{144}{96} = \frac{3}{2}$

24. $\frac{188 \text{ students}}{\$354} = \frac{94 \text{ students}}{\$177}$

25. $\frac{3}{12} = \frac{1}{4}$

26. $\frac{6 \text{ absences}}{180 \text{ days}} = \frac{1 \text{ absence}}{30 \text{ days}}$

27. $\frac{20}{60} = \frac{1}{3}$

28. $\frac{\$1.75}{5 \text{ minutes}} = \frac{\$0.35}{1 \text{ minute}}$

29. $\frac{\$25}{10 \text{ disks}} = \frac{\$2.50}{1 \text{ disk}}$

30. $\frac{300 \text{ students}}{20 \text{ teachers}} = \frac{15 \text{ students}}{1 \text{ teacher}}$

31. $\frac{\$420}{15 \text{ tickets}} = \frac{\$28}{1 \text{ ticket}}$

32. $\frac{\$8.80}{11 \text{ pounds}} = \frac{\$0.80}{1 \text{ pound}}$

33. $\frac{96¢}{12 \text{ eggs}} = \frac{8¢}{1 \text{ egg}}$

34. $\frac{\$25,000}{100 \text{ winners}} = \frac{\$250}{1 \text{ winner}}$

35.
$$2x - 8 = 12$$
$$2x - 8 + 8 = 12 + 8$$
$$2x = 20$$
$$\frac{2x}{2} = \frac{20}{2}$$
$$x = 10$$

36. The mean is the sum of the data divided by the number of pieces of data. The median is the number in the middle when the data are arranged in order. The mode is the number in a set of data that appears most often.

37. $\frac{5}{50} = \frac{1}{10}$

38. $7\frac{2}{7} \approx 7.29, \frac{37}{5} = 7.4$

$7\frac{2}{7}, 7.35, \frac{37}{5}$

39. $11 + 4 = 15$

40. natural numbers, whole numbers, integers, rational numbers, real numbers

41. $\frac{\$7.50}{18 \text{ minutes}} = \frac{\$28}{1 \text{ hour}}$

42. $\frac{6}{10} = \frac{3}{5}$

43. Eisenhower Middle School:

$\frac{432 \text{ students}}{24 \text{ computers}} = \frac{18 \text{ students}}{1 \text{ computer}}$

Central Middle School:

$\frac{567 \text{ students}}{27 \text{ computers}} = \frac{21 \text{ students}}{1 \text{ computer}}$

Since Eisenhower Middle School has less students per computer, you would have a better chance of getting computer time there.

44. a. $\frac{354 \text{ miles}}{6 \text{ hours}} = \frac{59 \text{ miles}}{1 \text{ hour}}$ b. yes

45. $\frac{98}{306} \approx 0.320$

1. All are near 1.6. 2. no; See students' work.

3. about 1.6

4. See students' work.

5. See students' work.

6. See students' work.

7. See students' work.

8. See students' work. Exercise 8 is the least like a golden rectangle.

9. See students' work.

10. a. See students' work. b. See students' work.

9-2 Proportions

1. Write each ratio in simplest form. The two ratios form a proportion if their simplest forms are equal. Another method is to find the cross products of the two ratios. The ratios form a proportion if their cross products are equal.

2. Answers may vary. The cross products are not equal.

3. $16 \cdot 9 \overset{?}{=} 12 \cdot 12$
   $144 = 144$; yes

4. $7 \cdot 7 \overset{?}{=} 6 \cdot 6$
   $49 \neq 36$; no

5. $75 \cdot 4 \overset{?}{=} 3 \cdot 100$
   $300 = 300$; yes

6. $3 \cdot 200 \overset{?}{=} 55 \cdot 11$
   $600 \neq 605$; no

7. $5c = 10 \cdot 3$
   $5c = 30$
   $\dfrac{5c}{5} = \dfrac{30}{5}$
   $c = 6$

8. $2.7a = 0.9 \cdot 0.6$
   $2.7a = 0.54$
   $\dfrac{2.7a}{2.7} = \dfrac{0.54}{2.7}$
   $a = 0.2$

9. $24b = 120 \cdot 60$
   $24b = 7{,}200$
   $\dfrac{24b}{24} = \dfrac{7{,}200}{24}$
   $b = 300$

10. $3 \cdot d = 7 \cdot 2.1$
    $3d = 14.7$
    $\dfrac{3d}{3} = \dfrac{14.7}{3}$
    $d = 4.9$

PAGE 346   EXERCISES

11. $8 \cdot 15 \overset{?}{=} 10 \cdot 12$
    $120 = 120$; yes

12. $3 \cdot 6 \overset{?}{=} 4 \cdot 2$
    $18 \neq 8$; no

13. $10 \cdot 6 \overset{?}{=} 5 \cdot 12$
    $60 = 60$; yes

14. $2 \cdot 21 \overset{?}{=} 6 \cdot 7$
    $42 = 42$; yes

15. $6 \cdot 12 \overset{?}{=} 8 \cdot 9$
    $72 = 72$; yes

16. $10 \cdot 45 \overset{?}{=} 25 \cdot 16$
    $450 \neq 400$; no

17. $75 \cdot 3 \overset{?}{=} 4 \cdot 100$
    $225 \neq 400$; no

18. $18 \cdot 42 \overset{?}{=} 54 \cdot 14$
    $756 = 756$; yes

19. $4y = 12 \cdot 5$
    $4y = 60$
    $\dfrac{4y}{4} = \dfrac{60}{4}$
    $y = 15$

20. $4n = 12 \cdot 100$
    $4n = 1{,}200$
    $\dfrac{4n}{4} = \dfrac{1{,}200}{4}$
    $n = 300$

21. $2x = 5 \cdot 34$
    $2x = 170$
    $\dfrac{2x}{2} = \dfrac{170}{2}$
    $x = 85$

22. $1n = 14 \cdot 9$
    $n = 126$

23. $2y = 7 \cdot 3$
    $2y = 21$
    $\dfrac{2y}{2} = \dfrac{21}{2}$
    $y = 10.5$

24. $3c = 18 \cdot 0.35$
    $3c = 6.3$
    $\dfrac{3c}{3} = \dfrac{6.3}{3}$
    $c = 2.1$

25. $4n = 2 \cdot 7$
    $4n = 14$
    $\dfrac{4n}{4} = \dfrac{14}{4}$
    $n = 3.5$

26. $6y = 26 \cdot 10$
    $6y = 260$
    $\dfrac{6y}{6} = \dfrac{260}{6}$
    $y = 43\frac{1}{3}$

27. $480 \div (-40) = t$
    $-12 = t$

28. $3x + 30 = 150$
    $3x + 30 - 30 = 150 - 30$
    $3x = 120$
    $\dfrac{3x}{3} = \dfrac{120}{3}$
    $x = 40$

29. $\left(-2\frac{6}{7}\right)\left(-5\frac{3}{5}\right) = y$
    $\left(-\frac{20}{7}\right)\left(-\frac{28}{5}\right) = y$
    $\dfrac{560}{35} = y$
    $16 = y$

30. $\dfrac{240 \text{ shrimp}}{6 \text{ pounds}} = \dfrac{40 \text{ shrimp}}{1 \text{ pound}}$

31. $x \cdot x = 9 \cdot 16$
    $x^2 = 144$
    $x = \sqrt{144}$ or $x = -\sqrt{144}$
    $x = 12$ or $x = -12$

32. $\dfrac{1{,}860{,}000}{10} = \dfrac{93{,}000{,}000}{x}$
    $1{,}860{,}000x = 93{,}000{,}000 \cdot 10$
    $1{,}860{,}000x = 930{,}000{,}000$
    $\dfrac{1{,}860{,}000x}{1{,}860{,}000} = \dfrac{930{,}000{,}000}{1{,}860{,}000}$
    $x = 500$ sec or $8\frac{1}{3}$ min

33. Answers will vary.

34. $\dfrac{124.80}{1} = \dfrac{2{,}500}{x}$
    $124.80x = 2{,}500$
    $\dfrac{124.80x}{124.80} = \dfrac{2{,}500}{124.80}$
    $x \approx 20$

9-3 Using Proportions

1. 25 ⎡×⎤ 9 ⎡÷⎤ $15 = 15$

2. a, b, c, f

3. $\dfrac{40}{43} = \dfrac{25}{x}$
   $40x = 25 \cdot 43$
   $40x = 1{,}075$
   $\dfrac{40x}{40} = \dfrac{1{,}075}{40}$
   $x \approx \$26.88$

4. $\dfrac{10}{4} = \dfrac{y}{5.6}$
   $4y = 5.6 \cdot 10$
   $4y = 56$
   $\dfrac{4y}{4} = \dfrac{56}{4}$
   $y = 14$ lbs

5. $\dfrac{1\frac{1}{4}}{25} = \dfrac{c}{60}$
   $25c = 60 \cdot 1\frac{1}{4}$
   $25c = 75$
   $\dfrac{25c}{25} = \dfrac{75}{25}$
   $c = 3$ cups

6. $\dfrac{60}{10} = \dfrac{k}{15}$

$10k = 15 \cdot 60$

$10k = 900$

$\dfrac{10k}{10} = \dfrac{900}{10}$

$k = 90$ lines

7. $\dfrac{2}{15} = \dfrac{35}{x}$

$2x = 15 \cdot 35$

$2x = 525$

$\dfrac{2x}{2} = \dfrac{525}{2}$

$x = 262\frac{1}{2}$ min

8. $\dfrac{72}{60} = \dfrac{x}{15}$

$60x = 15 \cdot 72$

$60x = 1,080$

$\dfrac{60x}{60} = \dfrac{1,080}{60}$

$x = 18$ times

9. $\dfrac{24}{6.24} = \dfrac{x}{4.68}$

$6.24x = 24 \cdot 4.68$

$6.24x = 112.32$

$\dfrac{6.24x}{6.24} = \dfrac{112.32}{6.24}$

$x = 18$ cans

10. $9\dfrac{3}{5} = 9.6$

11. $-\sqrt{64} = -8$

12. $\dfrac{3}{7} = \dfrac{n}{28}$

$7n = 28 \cdot 3$

$7n = 84$

$\dfrac{7n}{7} = \dfrac{84}{7}$

$n = 12$

13. $\dfrac{1}{6} = \dfrac{x}{126}$

$6x = 126 \cdot 1$

$6x = 126$

$\dfrac{6x}{6} = \dfrac{126}{6}$

$x = 21$ lbs

14. $\$2.59 \div 8$ cans $\approx \$0.32$ per can

$\$1.79 \div 6$ cans $\approx \$0.30$ per can

The better buy is 6 cans for $1.79.

15. Alvarez: $\dfrac{45}{150} = \dfrac{x}{250,000}$

$150x = 250,000 \cdot 45$

$150x = 11,250,000$

$\dfrac{150x}{150} = \dfrac{11,250,000}{150}$

$x = 75,000$ votes

Cruz: $\dfrac{54}{150} = \dfrac{x}{250,000}$

$150x = 250,000 \cdot 54$

$150x = 13,500,000$

$\dfrac{150x}{150} = \dfrac{13,500,000}{150}$

$x = 90,000$ votes

Hoffman: $\dfrac{33}{150} = \dfrac{x}{250,000}$

$150x = 250,000 \cdot 33$

$150x = 8,250,000$

$\dfrac{150x}{150} = \dfrac{8,250,000}{150}$

$x = 55,000$ votes

Newton: $\dfrac{18}{150} = \dfrac{x}{250,000}$

$150x = 250,000 \cdot 18$

$150x = 4,500,000$

$\dfrac{150x}{150} = \dfrac{4,500,000}{150}$

$x = 30,000$ votes

16. Arturo: $\dfrac{200}{1,000} = \dfrac{x}{1,500}$

$1,000x = 1,500 \cdot 200$

$1,000x = 300,000$

$\dfrac{1,000x}{1,000} = \dfrac{300,000}{1,000}$

$x = \$300$

Beth: $\dfrac{300}{1,000} = \dfrac{x}{1,500}$

$1,000x = 1,500 \cdot 300$

$1,000x = 450,000$

$\dfrac{1,000x}{1,000} = \dfrac{450,000}{1,000}$

$x = \$450$

Carmen: $\dfrac{500}{1,000} = \dfrac{x}{1,500}$

$1,000x = 1,500 \cdot 500$

$1,000x = 750,000$

$\dfrac{1,000x}{1,000} = \dfrac{750,000}{1,000}$

$x = \$750$

9-4 Draw a Diagram

1. Diagrams help organize information and help you decide how to solve the problem.

2. $233 + 377 = 610$ pairs

3.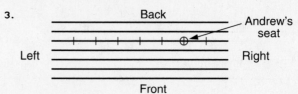

There are seven seats in each of seven rows, so there are a total of 49 seats.

4.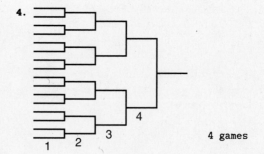

4 games

5. $x - 4 = -23$

$x - 4 + 4 = -23 + 4$

$x = -19$

6. 1, 2, 3; 1, 2, 4; 1, 2, 5;
1, 2, 6; 1, 3, 4; 1, 3, 5;
1, 3, 6; 1, 4, 5; 1, 4, 6;
1, 5, 6; 2, 3, 4; 2, 3, 5;
2, 3, 6; 2, 4, 5; 2, 4, 6;
2, 5, 6; 3, 4, 5; 3, 4, 6;
3, 5, 6; 4, 5, 6

20 teams

7.

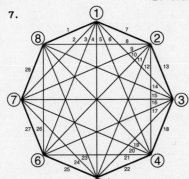

28 handshakes

8.

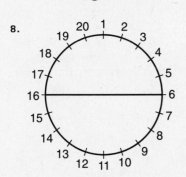

20 people

9. $x + x + 2 = 20$

$2x + 2 = 20$

$2x + 2 - 2 = 20 - 2$

$2x = 18$

$\frac{2x}{2} = \frac{18}{2}$

$x = 9m$

10. a. 0.618033989

b. Both ratios lie between 0.6 and 0.625.

Mid-Chapter Review

1. $\frac{15}{20} = \frac{3}{4}$

2. $\frac{\$500}{320 \text{ students}} = \frac{\$25}{16 \text{ students}}$

3. $\frac{\$0.80}{1 \text{ dozen}}$ or $\frac{\$0.20}{3}$

4. $\frac{2}{5} = \frac{x}{250}$

$5x = 250 \cdot 2$

$5x = 500$

$\frac{5x}{5} = \frac{500}{5}$

$x = 100$

---

5. $\frac{7.5}{a} = \frac{3}{4}$

$3a = 7.5 \cdot 4$

$3a = 30$

$\frac{3a}{3} = \frac{30}{3}$

$a = 10$

6. $\frac{6.5}{19.5} = \frac{13}{y}$

$6.5y = 13 \cdot 19.5$

$6.5y = 253.5$

$\frac{6.5y}{6.5} = \frac{253.5}{6.5}$

$y = 39$

7. $\frac{10}{750} = \frac{14}{n}$

$10n = 14 \cdot 750$

$10n = 10,500$

$\frac{10n}{10} = \frac{10,500}{10}$

$n = 1,050$ bushels

8.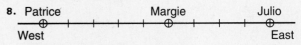

Patrice   Margie   Julio

West   East

5 blocks east of Patrice

9-5   Similar Polygons

1. Similar polygons have congruent corresponding angles and their corresponding sides are in proportion.

2. See students' work.

3. Congruent polygons have corresponding angles and corresponding sides that are congruent, while similar polygons have corresponding angles that are congruent and corresponding sides that are in proportion.

4. no; The sides are not in proportion.

5. yes

6. $\frac{BC}{GF} = \frac{CD}{GH}$

$\frac{4}{6} = \frac{8}{x}$

$4x = 8 \cdot 6$

$4x = 48$

$\frac{4x}{4} = \frac{48}{4}$

$x = 12$

The length of $\overline{GH}$ is 12 feet.

7. $\frac{BC}{GF} = \frac{AD}{EH}$

$\frac{4}{6} = \frac{12}{x}$

$4x = 12 \cdot 6$

$4x = 72$

$\frac{4x}{4} = \frac{72}{4}$

$x = 18$

The length of $\overline{EH}$ is 18 feet.

8. They would be half of the original lengths.

9. yes

10. yes

11. $\angle EAD \cong \angle CAB$,
$\angle AED \cong \angle ACB$,
$\angle ADE \cong \angle ABC$

12. $\frac{AE}{AC}, \frac{ED}{CB}, \frac{DA}{BA}$

13. $\dfrac{18}{9} = \dfrac{24}{x}$

$18x = 24 \cdot 9$

$18x = 216$

$\dfrac{18x}{18} = \dfrac{216}{18}$

$x = 12$

14. $\dfrac{18}{9} = \dfrac{y}{15}$

$9y = 15 \cdot 18$

$9y = 270$

$\dfrac{9y}{9} = \dfrac{270}{9}$

$y = 30$

15. $4 \cdot 4 \cdot 8 \cdot 8 \cdot 4 = 4 \cdot 4 \cdot 4 \cdot 8 \cdot 8$
$= 4^3 \cdot 8^2$

16. 51, 23, 0, -8, -16, -30, -51

17. $a = \dfrac{7}{12} \div \dfrac{3}{4}$

$a = \dfrac{7}{12} \cdot \dfrac{4}{3}$

$a = \dfrac{28}{36}$

$a = \dfrac{7}{9}$

18. $\dfrac{6}{3} = \dfrac{n}{5}$

$3n = 5 \cdot 6$

$3n = 30$

$\dfrac{3n}{3} = \dfrac{30}{3}$

$n = 10$ tablespoons

19. All congruent figures are similar (~) and more specifically, equal to each other (≅).

20. $\dfrac{8}{5} = \dfrac{4}{x}$

$8x = 4 \cdot 5$

$8x = 20$

$\dfrac{8x}{8} = \dfrac{20}{8}$

$x = 2\dfrac{1}{2}$

$\dfrac{8}{5} = \dfrac{5}{y}$

$8y = 5 \cdot 5$

$8y = 25$

$\dfrac{8y}{8} = \dfrac{25}{8}$

$y = 3\dfrac{1}{8}$

The new dimensions are $2\dfrac{1}{2}$ in. $\times 3\dfrac{1}{8}$ in.

21. $\dfrac{174}{66} = \dfrac{6}{h}$

$174h = 6 \cdot 66$

$174h = 396$

$\dfrac{174h}{174} = \dfrac{396}{174}$

$h \approx 2.3$ in.

9-6 Indirect Measurement

PAGE 357   **CHECKING FOR UNDERSTANDING**

1. Indirect measurement is finding a measure by using proportions.

2. Answers may vary.

3.

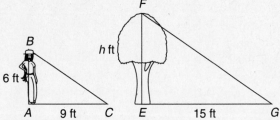

4. Sample answer: finding the height of a building

5.

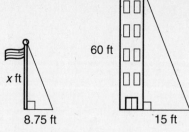

$\dfrac{x}{60} = \dfrac{8.75}{15}$

$15x = 60 \cdot 8.75$

$15x = 525$

$\dfrac{15}{x} = \dfrac{525}{15}$

$x = 35$

The flagpole is 35 feet tall.

6.

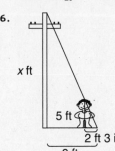

$\dfrac{2.25}{9} = \dfrac{5}{x}$

$2.25x = 5 \cdot 9$

$2.25x = 45$

$\dfrac{2.25x}{2.25} = \dfrac{45}{2.25}$

$x = 20$

The telephone pole is 20 feet tall.

PAGE 358   **EXERCISES**

7. $\dfrac{8}{20} = \dfrac{5}{x}$

$8x = 5 \cdot 20$

$8x = 100$

$\dfrac{8x}{8} = \dfrac{100}{8}$

$x = 12.5$ km

8. Tampa Bay to Houston:

$\dfrac{5.4}{12.6} = \dfrac{4.2}{x}$

$5.4x = 4.2 \cdot 21.6$

$5.4x = 90.72$

$\dfrac{5.4x}{5.4} = \dfrac{90.72}{5.4}$

$x = 16.8$ cm

Buffalo to Houston:

$\dfrac{5.4}{21.6} = \dfrac{6.7}{y}$

$5.4y = 6.7 \cdot 21.6$

$5.4y = 144.72$

$\dfrac{5.4y}{5.4} = \dfrac{144.72}{5.4}$

$y = 26.8$ cm

9. $\dfrac{30}{60} = \dfrac{x}{90}$

$60x = 90 \cdot 30$

$60x = 2,700$

$\dfrac{60x}{60} = \dfrac{2,700}{60}$

$x = 45$ mi

10. $n = -28 + 73$

$n = 45$

11. $48 = 2 \cdot 2 \cdot 2 \cdot 2 \cdot 3$

$60 = 2 \cdot 2 \cdot 3 \cdot 5$

The LCM of 48 and 60 is $2^4 \cdot 3 \cdot 5$ or 240.

12. $\dfrac{AC}{DF}, \dfrac{AB}{DE}, \dfrac{BC}{EF}$

13. $\dfrac{5}{25} = \dfrac{33.85}{n}$

$5n = 33.85 \cdot 25$

$5n = 846.25$

$\dfrac{5n}{5} = \dfrac{846.25}{5}$

$n = 169.25$ ft

14. $\dfrac{y}{1.83} = \dfrac{13.3}{0.4}$

$0.4y = 1.83 \cdot 13.3$

$0.4y = 24.339$

$\dfrac{0.4y}{0.4} = \dfrac{24.339}{0.4}$

$y = 60.8475$ m

15. $\dfrac{123.24}{181.75} = \dfrac{a}{1,454}$

$181.75a = 1,454 \cdot 123.24$

$181.75a = 179,190.96$

$\dfrac{181.75a}{181.75} = \dfrac{179,190.96}{181.75}$

$a = 985.92$ ft

16. Sample answers: An incorrect measurement might be obtained if the figures used in the proportion are not similar triangles or if the wrong sides are compared in the proportion.

17. See students' work.

9-7 Scale Drawings

PAGE 360   CHECKING FOR UNDERSTANDING

1. A scale drawing is either an enlarged or reduced drawing of an original-sized object.

2. Scale drawings are drawn in a ratio of a given length on the drawing to its corresponding length in reality. Proportions are used to find lengths of corresponding sides.

3. Sample answers: road maps, house plans

4. wingspan: $\dfrac{\frac{1}{8}\text{ in.}}{1\text{ ft}} = \dfrac{15\text{ in.}}{x\text{ ft}}$

$\dfrac{1}{8}x = 15$

$8\left(\dfrac{1}{8}x\right) = 15 \cdot 8$

$x = 120$

The wingspan is 120 feet.

tail: $\dfrac{\frac{1}{8}\text{ in.}}{1\text{ ft}} = \dfrac{2\text{ in.}}{x\text{ ft}}$

$\dfrac{1}{8}x = 2$

$8\left(\dfrac{1}{8}x\right) = 2 \cdot 8$

$x = 16$

The tail is 16 feet.

5. $\dfrac{1\text{ in.}}{60\text{ mi}} = \dfrac{3\text{ in.}}{x\text{ mi}}$

$x = 3 \cdot 60$

$x = 180$ mi

6. $\dfrac{1\text{ in.}}{60\text{ mi}} = \dfrac{2\frac{1}{4}\text{ in.}}{x\text{ mi}}$

$x = 2\frac{1}{4} \cdot 60$

$x = 135$ mi

7. $\dfrac{1\text{ in.}}{60\text{ mi}} = \dfrac{4\frac{1}{8}\text{ in.}}{y\text{ mi}}$

$y = 4\frac{1}{8} \cdot 60$

$y = 247\frac{1}{2}$ mi

8. $\dfrac{1\text{ in.}}{60\text{ mi}} = \dfrac{\frac{5}{8}\text{ in.}}{y\text{ mi}}$

$y = \dfrac{5}{8} \cdot 60$

$y = 37.5$ mi

PAGE 360   EXERCISES

9. $\dfrac{1\text{ square}}{2\text{ feet}} = \dfrac{12\text{ squares}}{x\text{ feet}}$

$x = 2 \cdot 12$

$x = 24$

The width of the house is 24 feet.

10. $\dfrac{1\text{ square}}{2\text{ feet}} = \dfrac{2\text{ squares}}{x\text{ feet}}$

$x = 2 \cdot 2$

$x = 4$

The width of the door is 4 feet.

11. $\dfrac{1\text{ square}}{2\text{ feet}} = \dfrac{5\text{ square}}{x\text{ feet}}$

$x = 5 \cdot 2$

$x = 10$

The height of the wall is 10 feet.

12. $\dfrac{1\text{ square}}{2\text{ feet}} = \dfrac{4\frac{1}{2}\text{ squares}}{x\text{ feet}}$

$x = 4\frac{1}{2} \cdot 2$

$x = 9$

The height of the roof is 9 feet.

13. 73, 75, 78, 79, 80, 81, 84, 84

Mean: $\dfrac{79 + 80}{2} = \dfrac{159}{2} = 79.5$

LQ: $\dfrac{75 + 78}{2} = \dfrac{153}{2} = 76.5$

UQ: $\dfrac{81 + 84}{2} = \dfrac{165}{2} = 82.5$

Interquartile Range: $82.5 - 76.5 = 6$

14. $\dfrac{156.25}{10.5} = \dfrac{x}{84}$

$10.5x = 84 \cdot 156.25$

$10.5x = 13,125$

$\dfrac{10.5x}{10.5} = \dfrac{13,125}{10.5}$

$x = 1,250$ ft

15. $\dfrac{1}{12} = \dfrac{32}{x}$

$x = 32 \cdot 12$

$x = 384$ cm

16. 12 units^2; 192 ft^2; The area of the real figure equals the area of the scale drawing times the scale factor squared.

17. See students' work.

1. the enlarging or reducing of an image in mathematics

2. Multiply each member of the ordered pair (x, y) by the scale factor k.

3. See students' work.

4. $A(3, 4) \rightarrow (3 \cdot 2, 4 \cdot 2) \rightarrow A'(6, 8)$

5. $A(3, 4) \rightarrow (3 \cdot 5, 4 \cdot 5) \rightarrow A'(15, 20)$

6. $OA' \div OA = 48 \div 16$
   $= 3$

7. $A'B' = AB \cdot \frac{5}{4}$
   $= 20 \cdot \frac{5}{4}$
   $= 25$

PAGES 362-363   EXERCISES

8. $G(-2, -2) \rightarrow (-2 \cdot 6, -2 \cdot 6) \rightarrow G'(-12, -12)$
   $H(3, -3) \rightarrow (3 \cdot 6, -3 \cdot 6) \rightarrow H'(18, -18)$

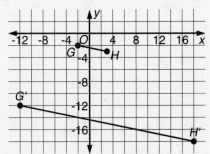

9. $Q(-6, -6) \rightarrow \left(-6 \cdot \frac{3}{4}, -6 \cdot \frac{3}{4}\right) \rightarrow Q'\left(-4\frac{1}{2}, -4\frac{1}{2}\right)$
   $R(12, -12) \rightarrow \left(12 \cdot \frac{3}{4}, -12 \cdot \frac{3}{4}\right) \rightarrow R'(9, -9)$

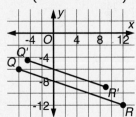

10. $P(-4, 12) \rightarrow (-4 \cdot 2, 12 \cdot 2) \rightarrow P'(-8, 24)$
    $Q(8, 6) \rightarrow (8 \cdot 2, 6 \cdot 2) \rightarrow Q'(16, 12)$
    $R(-2, -4) \rightarrow (-2 \cdot 2, -4 \cdot 2) \rightarrow R'(-4, -8)$

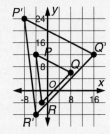

11. $P(-4, 12) \rightarrow \left(-4 \cdot \frac{1}{4}, 12 \cdot \frac{1}{4}\right) \rightarrow P'(-1, 3)$
    $Q(8, 6) \rightarrow \left(8 \cdot \frac{1}{4}, 6 \cdot \frac{1}{4}\right) \rightarrow Q'\left(2, 1\frac{1}{2}\right)$
    $R(-2, -4) \rightarrow \left(-2 \cdot \frac{1}{4}, -4 \cdot \frac{1}{4}\right) \rightarrow R'\left(-\frac{1}{2}, -1\right)$

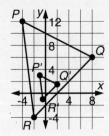

12. $P(-4, 12) \rightarrow (-4 \cdot 1, 12 \cdot 1) \rightarrow P'(-4, 12)$
    $Q(8, 6) \rightarrow (8 \cdot 1, 6 \cdot 1) \rightarrow Q'(8, 6)$
    $R(-2, -4) \rightarrow (-2 \cdot 1, -4 \cdot 1) \rightarrow R'(-2, -4)$

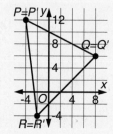

13. $1.29b = 5.16$
    $\frac{1.29b}{1.29} = \frac{5.16}{1.29}$
    $b = 4$

14. no; 284 is divisible by 2 but not divisible by 3.

15. $\frac{1 \text{ in.}}{300 \text{ mi}} = \frac{2\frac{3}{8} \text{ in.}}{x \text{ mi}}$
    $x = 2\frac{3}{8} \cdot 300$
    $x = 712\frac{1}{2} \text{ mi}$

16. $P(1, 1) \rightarrow (1 \cdot -1, 1 \cdot -1) \rightarrow P'(-1, -1)$
    $Q(1, 4) \rightarrow (1 \cdot -1, 4 \cdot -1) \rightarrow Q'(-1, -4)$
    $R(5, 1) \rightarrow (5 \cdot -1, 1 \cdot -1) \rightarrow R'(-5, -1)$

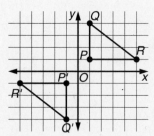

Negative scale factors invert the original graph.

17.

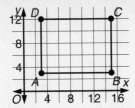

a. rectangle

b. $P = 2\ell + 2w$ $\qquad$ $A = \ell w$

$\quad P = 2 \cdot 12 + 2 \cdot 9$ $\quad$ $A = 12 \cdot 9$

$\quad P = 24 + 18$ $\qquad\qquad$ $A = 108 \text{ units}^2$

$\quad P = 42 \text{ units}$

c. $A(3, 3) \rightarrow (3 \cdot 3, 3 \cdot 3) \rightarrow A'(9, 9)$

$\quad B(15, 3) \rightarrow (15 \cdot 3, 3 \cdot 3) \rightarrow B'(45, 9)$

$\quad C(15, 12) \rightarrow (15 \cdot 3, 12 \cdot 3) \rightarrow C'(45, 36)$

$\quad D(3, 12) \rightarrow (3 \cdot 3, 12 \cdot 3) \rightarrow D'(9, 36)$

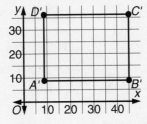

d. $P = 2\ell + 2w$ $\qquad$ $A = \ell w$

$\quad P = 2 \cdot 36 + 2 \cdot 27$ $\quad$ $A = 36 \cdot 27$

$\quad P = 72 + 54$ $\qquad\qquad$ $A = 972 \text{ units}^2$

$\quad P = 126 \text{ units}$

e. $\dfrac{126}{42} = \dfrac{3}{1}$

f. $\dfrac{972}{108} = \dfrac{9}{1}$

g. The perimeter of the dilation of a polygon is equal to the perimeter of the original polygon times the scale factor. The area of the dilation of a polygon is equal to the area of the original polygon times the scale factor squared.

9-9A Mathematics Lab: Right Triangles

PAGE 364 WHAT DO YOU THINK?

1. Ratios are the same. 2. Ratio equals 1:2.

3. Ratio equals 1:1.

PAGE 364 EXTENSION

4. It equals 1.

9-9 The Tangent Ratio

PAGE 366 CHECKING FOR UNDERSTANDING

1. The tangent ratio equals the measure of the side opposite a specified angle divided by the measure of the side adjacent to that specified angle.

2. Write the tangent ratio using x to represent the missing leg measure. Solve for x.

3. Find the ratio of the leg opposite the angle to the one adjacent to the angle. Then use the inverse of the tangent function on a calculator.

4. $\tan J = \dfrac{12}{20} = \dfrac{3}{5}$ $\qquad$ 5. $\tan S = \dfrac{20}{12} = \dfrac{5}{3}$

6. $\tan K = \dfrac{9}{5}$ $\qquad$ 7. $\tan T = \dfrac{5}{9}$

8. $m\angle J \approx 31°$ $\qquad$ 9. $m\angle S \approx 59°$

10. $m\angle K \approx 61°$ $\qquad$ 11. $m\angle T \approx 29°$

12. $\quad \tan 53° = \dfrac{4}{x}$

$\quad (\tan 53°)(x) = \left(\dfrac{4}{x}\right)x$

$\quad (\tan 53°)(x) = 4$

$\quad \dfrac{(\tan 53°)(x)}{\tan 53°} = \dfrac{4}{\tan 53°}$

$\qquad x = \dfrac{4}{\tan 53°}$

$\qquad x \approx 3.0 \text{ in.}$

13. $\quad \tan 29° = \dfrac{x}{9}$

$\quad 9(\tan° 29) = \left(\dfrac{x}{9}\right)9$

$\quad 9(\tan 29°) = x$

$\qquad 5 \text{ ft} \approx x$

PAGE 367 EXERCISES

14. $\tan A = \dfrac{9}{12} = \dfrac{3}{4}$ $\qquad$ 15. $\tan Z = \dfrac{24}{10} = \dfrac{12}{5}$

$\quad \tan B = \dfrac{12}{9} = \dfrac{4}{3}$ $\qquad$ $\tan E = \dfrac{10}{24} = \dfrac{5}{12}$

$\quad m\angle A \approx 37°$ $\qquad\qquad$ $m\angle Z \approx 67°$

$\quad m\angle B \approx 53°$ $\qquad\qquad$ $m\angle E \approx 23°$

16. $\tan F = \dfrac{20}{21}$ $\qquad$ 17. $\quad \tan 30° = \dfrac{4}{x}$

$\quad \tan Y = \dfrac{21}{20}$ $\qquad$ $x(\tan 30°) = \left(\dfrac{4}{x}\right)x$

$\quad m\angle F \approx 44°$ $\qquad\qquad$ $x(\tan 30°) = 4$

$\quad m\angle Y \approx 46°$ $\qquad\qquad$ $\dfrac{x(\tan 30°)}{\tan 30°} = \dfrac{4}{\tan 30°}$

$\qquad\qquad\qquad\qquad\qquad x = \dfrac{4}{\tan 30°}$

$\qquad\qquad\qquad\qquad\qquad x \approx 6.9 \text{ in.}$

18. $\quad \tan 40° = \dfrac{x}{8}$

$\quad 8(\tan 40°) = \left(\dfrac{x}{8}\right)8$

$\quad 8(\tan 40°) = x$

$\qquad 6.7 \text{ m} \approx x$

19. $\quad \tan 20° = \dfrac{x}{10}$

$\quad 10(\tan 20°) = \left(\dfrac{x}{10}\right)10$

$\quad 10(\tan 20°) = x$

$\qquad 3.6 \text{ km} \approx x$

20. $\tan 65° = \dfrac{x}{2}$ **21.** See students' work.

$2(\tan 65°) = \left(\dfrac{x}{2}\right)2$

$2(\tan 65°) = x$

$4.3\ m \approx x$

22.

$7\dfrac{3}{8} = 2\dfrac{9}{16} + j$

$7\dfrac{3}{8} - 2\dfrac{9}{16} = 2\dfrac{9}{16} - 2\dfrac{9}{16} + j$

$(6 - 2) + \left(\dfrac{22}{16} - \dfrac{9}{16}\right) = j$

$4 + \dfrac{13}{16} = j$

$4\dfrac{13}{16} = j$

23. $E(2, 6) \rightarrow \left(2 \cdot \dfrac{1}{2},\ 6 \cdot \dfrac{1}{2}\right) \rightarrow E'(1, 3)$

$F(4, -4) \rightarrow \left(4 \cdot \dfrac{1}{2},\ -4 \cdot \dfrac{1}{2}\right) \rightarrow F'(2, -2)$

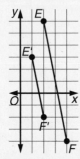

24. The following tangents are equal:

$\tan 90° = \tan 270°$

$\tan 120° = \tan 300°$

$\tan 150° = \tan 330°$

$\tan 180° = \tan 360°$

Tangents of angles 180° apart are equal.

25. $\tan 50° = \dfrac{x}{40}$

$40(\tan 50°) = \left(\dfrac{x}{40}\right)40$

$40(\tan 50°) = x$

$48\ ft \approx x$

9-10   The Sine and Cosine Ratios

PAGE 370   CHECKING FOR UNDERSTANDING

1. The sine ratio of an acute angle equals the measure of the leg opposite that angle divided by the measure of the hypotenuse. The cosine ratio of an acute angle equals the measure of the leg adjacent to that angle divided by the measure of the hypotenuse.

2. trigonometry

3. Sample answers:

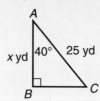

$\cos 40° = \dfrac{x}{25}$

$25(\cos 40°) = \left(\dfrac{x}{25}\right)25$

$25(\cos 40°) = x$

$19.2 \approx x$

$\sin 32° = \dfrac{x}{70}$

$70(\sin 32°) = \left(\dfrac{x}{70}\right)70$

$70(\sin 32°) = x$

$37.1 \approx x$

4. $\cos A = \dfrac{6}{10} = \dfrac{3}{5}$ **5.** $\sin A = \dfrac{8}{10} = \dfrac{4}{5}$

6. $m\angle A \approx 53°$ **7.** $\sin B = \dfrac{6}{10} = \dfrac{3}{5}$

8. $\cos B = \dfrac{8}{10} = \dfrac{4}{5}$ **9.** $m\angle B \approx 37°$

10. $\cos Y = \dfrac{10}{26} = \dfrac{5}{13}$ **11.** $\sin X = \dfrac{10}{26} = \dfrac{5}{13}$

12. $m\angle X \approx 23°$ **13.** $m\angle Y \approx 67°$

PAGES 370-371   EXERCISES

14. $\sin A = \dfrac{16}{34} = \dfrac{8}{17}$ **15.** $\sin R = \dfrac{8}{10} = \dfrac{4}{5}$

$\sin B = \dfrac{30}{34} = \dfrac{15}{17}$ $\cos R = \dfrac{6}{10} = \dfrac{3}{5}$

$\cos A = \dfrac{30}{34} = \dfrac{15}{17}$ $\sin S = \dfrac{6}{10} = \dfrac{3}{5}$

$\cos B = \dfrac{16}{34} = \dfrac{8}{17}$ $\cos S = \dfrac{8}{10} = \dfrac{4}{5}$

$m\angle A \approx 28°$ $m\angle R \approx 53°$

$m\angle B \approx 62°$ $m\angle S \approx 37°$

16. $\sin E = \dfrac{20}{29}$ **17.** $\sin 67° = \dfrac{x}{13}$

$\cos F = \dfrac{20}{29}$ $13(\sin 67°) = \left(\dfrac{x}{13}\right)13$

$m\angle E \approx 44°$ $13(\sin 67°) = x$

$\cos E = \dfrac{21}{29}$ $12.0\ yd \approx x$

$\tan F = \dfrac{21}{20}$

$m\angle F \approx 46°$

18. $\cos x = \dfrac{10}{26}$ **19.** $\sin x = \dfrac{15}{21.2}$

$x \approx 67°$ $x \approx 45°$

20. $\tan x = \dfrac{5}{8.66}$ **21.** $g = -5(12)(3)$

$x \approx 30°$ $g = -5(36)$

$g = -180$

22. $9.2 \times 10^{-4} = 9.2 \times 0.0001$ **23.** $\tan A = \dfrac{6}{8} = \dfrac{3}{4}$

$= 0.00092$

24. They are the same.

25. $\sin 50° = \dfrac{30}{x}$

$x(\sin 50°) = \left(\dfrac{30}{x}\right)x$

$x(\sin 50°) = 30$

$\dfrac{x(\sin 50°)}{\sin 50°} = \dfrac{30}{\sin 50°}$

$x = \dfrac{30}{\sin 50°}$

$x \approx 39.2 \text{ ft}$

26. *e, f*

27. $\sin 72° = \dfrac{63.2}{x}$

$x(\sin 72°) = \left(\dfrac{63.2}{x}\right)x$

$x(\sin 72°) = 63.2$

$\dfrac{x(\sin 72°)}{\sin 72°} = \dfrac{63.2}{\sin 72°}$

$x = \dfrac{63.2}{\sin 72°}$

$x \approx 66 \text{ ft}$

28. See students' work.

Chapter 9 Study Guide and Review

PAGE 372   COMMUNICATING MATHEMATICS

1. h   **2.** i   **3.** f   **4.** c   **5.** b   **6.** e

7. g   **8.** The scale is determined by the ratio of a given length on the drawing to its corresponding length in reality.

PAGES 372-374   SKILLS AND CONCEPTS

9. $\dfrac{10}{20} = \dfrac{1}{2}$

10. $\dfrac{20}{100} = \dfrac{1}{5}$

11. $\dfrac{36}{5}$

12. $\dfrac{4}{20} = \dfrac{1}{5}$

13. $\dfrac{3}{8} = \dfrac{n}{40}$

$8n = 3 \cdot 40$

$8n = 120$

$\dfrac{8n}{8} = \dfrac{120}{8}$

$n = 15$

14. $\dfrac{6}{r} = \dfrac{15}{20}$

$15r = 6 \cdot 20$

$15r = 120$

$\dfrac{15r}{15} = \dfrac{120}{15}$

$r = 8$

15. $\dfrac{d}{18} = \dfrac{9}{4}$

$4d = 9 \cdot 18$

$4d = 162$

$\dfrac{4d}{4} = \dfrac{162}{4}$

$d = 40.5$

16. $\dfrac{0.5}{30} = \dfrac{0.25}{b}$

$0.5b = 0.25 \cdot 30$

$0.5b = 7.5$

$\dfrac{0.5b}{0.5} = \dfrac{7.5}{0.5}$

$b = 15$

17. $\dfrac{70}{8} = \dfrac{n}{20}$

$8n = 70 \cdot 20$

$8n = 1,400$

$\dfrac{8n}{8} = \dfrac{1,400}{8}$

$n = 175$

18. $\dfrac{6}{3} = \dfrac{x}{5}$

$3x = 6 \cdot 5$

$3x = 30$

$\dfrac{3x}{3} = \dfrac{30}{3}$

$x = 10 \text{ in.}$

19. $\dfrac{1.20}{10} = \dfrac{3.00}{a}$

$1.20a = 3.00 \cdot 10$

$1.20a = 30.0$

$\dfrac{1.20a}{1.20} = \dfrac{30.0}{12.0}$

$a = 25 \text{ pages}$

20. not similar; The sides are not in proportion.

21. similar

22. $\dfrac{6\frac{2}{3}}{26\frac{2}{3}} = \dfrac{5}{x}$

$6\frac{2}{3}x = 5 \cdot 26\frac{2}{3}$

$\dfrac{20}{3}x = \dfrac{400}{3}$

$\dfrac{3}{20}\left(\dfrac{20}{3}x\right) = \left(\dfrac{400}{3}\right)\dfrac{3}{20}$

$x = 20 \text{ ft}$

23. $\dfrac{2 \text{ cm}}{35 \text{ km}} = \dfrac{6 \text{ cm}}{x \text{ km}}$

$2x = 6 \cdot 35$

$2x = 210$

$\dfrac{2x}{2} = \dfrac{210}{2}$

$x = 105 \text{ km}$

24. $\dfrac{2 \text{ cm}}{35 \text{ km}} = \dfrac{9 \text{ cm}}{x \text{ km}}$

$2x = 9 \cdot 35$

$2x = 315$

$\dfrac{2x}{2} = \dfrac{315}{2}$

$x = 157.5 \text{ km}$

25. $\dfrac{2 \text{ cm}}{35 \text{ km}} = \dfrac{3.2 \text{ cm}}{x \text{ km}}$

$2x = 3.2 \cdot 35$

$2x = 112$

$\dfrac{2x}{2} = \dfrac{112}{2}$

$x = 56 \text{ km}$

26. $\dfrac{2 \text{ cm}}{35 \text{ km}} = \dfrac{4.6 \text{ cm}}{x \text{ km}}$

$2x = 4.6 \cdot 35$

$2x = 161$

$\dfrac{2x}{2} = \dfrac{161}{2}$

$x = 80.5 \text{ km}$

27. $\dfrac{2 \text{ cm}}{35 \text{ km}} = \dfrac{8.4 \text{ cm}}{x \text{ km}}$

$2x = 8.4 \cdot 35$

$2x = 294$

$\dfrac{2x}{2} = \dfrac{294}{2}$

$x = 147 \text{ km}$

28. $H(2, 4) \rightarrow \left(2 \cdot \dfrac{1}{2}, \ 4 \cdot \dfrac{1}{2}\right) \rightarrow H'(1, 2)$

$I(-6, -4) \rightarrow \left(-6 \cdot \dfrac{1}{2}, \ -4 \cdot \dfrac{1}{2}\right) \rightarrow I'(-3, -2)$

$J(6, -8) \rightarrow \left(6 \cdot \dfrac{1}{2}, \ -8 \cdot \dfrac{1}{2}\right) \rightarrow J'(3, -4)$

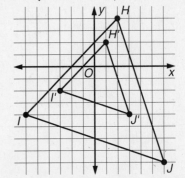

29. $H(2, 4) \rightarrow (2 \cdot 2, 4 \cdot 2) \rightarrow H'(4, 8)$
$I(-6, -4) \rightarrow (-6 \cdot 2, -4 \cdot 2) \rightarrow I'(-12, -8)$
$J(6, -8) \rightarrow (6 \cdot 2, -8 \cdot 2) \rightarrow J'(12, -16)$

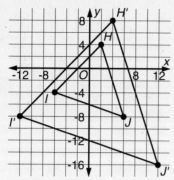

30. $H(2, 4)\ \left(2 \cdot \frac{1}{4}, 4 \cdot \frac{1}{4}\right) \rightarrow H'\left(\frac{1}{2}, 1\right)$

$I(-6, -4) \rightarrow \left(-6 \cdot \frac{1}{4}, -4 \cdot \frac{1}{4}\right) \rightarrow I'\left(-1\frac{1}{2}, -1\right)$

$J(6, -8) \rightarrow \left(6 \cdot \frac{1}{4}, -8 \cdot \frac{1}{4}\right) \rightarrow J'\left(1\frac{1}{2}, -2\right)$

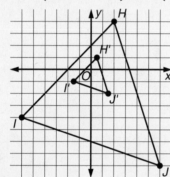

31. $\tan A = \frac{5}{12} \approx 0.4167$ **32.** $\tan B = \frac{12}{5} = 2.4$

33. $\sin Q = \frac{15}{17} \approx 0.8824$ **34.** $\sin R = \frac{8}{17} \approx 0.4706$

35. $\cos Q = \frac{8}{17} \approx 0.4706$ **36.** $\cos R = \frac{15}{17} \approx 0.8824$

PAGE 374   APPLICATIONS AND PROBLEM SOLVING

37. $\frac{56}{128} = \frac{7}{16}$

38. Let x denote a game.

	1	2	3	4	5	6	7	8
1		x	x	x	x	x	x	x
2			x	x	x	x	x	x
3				x	x	x	x	x
4					x	x	x	x
5						x	x	x
6							x	x
7								x
8								

There are 28 games.

Chapter 9 Test

PAGE 375

1. $\frac{8}{20} = \frac{2}{5}$ **2.** $\frac{9}{14}$ **3.** $\frac{12}{4} = \frac{3}{1}$

4. $\frac{38}{24} = \frac{19}{12}$ **5.** $\frac{290 \text{ miles}}{5 \text{ hours}} = \frac{58 \text{ miles}}{1 \text{ hour}}$

6. $\frac{5}{6} = \frac{11}{x}$ **7.** $\frac{n}{30} = \frac{5}{10}$ **8.** $\frac{9}{33} = \frac{b}{11}$
$5x = 11 \cdot 6$ $10n = 5 \cdot 30$ $33b = 9 \cdot 11$
$5x = 66$ $10n = 150$ $33b = 99$
$\frac{5x}{5} = \frac{66}{5}$ $\frac{10n}{10} = \frac{150}{10}$ $\frac{33b}{33} = \frac{99}{33}$
$x = 13.2$ $n = 15$ $b = 3$

9. $\frac{2}{y} = \frac{8}{5}$ **10.** $\frac{32}{88} \overset{?}{=} \frac{12}{36}$
$8y = 2 \cdot 5$ $32 \cdot 36 \overset{?}{=} 12 \cdot 88$
$8y = 10$ $1,152 \neq 1,056; \text{ no}$
$\frac{8y}{8} = \frac{10}{8}$
$y = 1.25$

11. $\frac{4}{96} = \frac{n}{60}$ **12.** yes
$96n = 4 \cdot 60$
$96n = 240$
$\frac{96n}{96} = \frac{240}{96}$
$n = 2.5 \text{ gal}$

13. no; The sides are not in proportion.

14. $\frac{1 \text{ in.}}{100 \text{ mi}} = \frac{4 \text{ in.}}{x \text{ mi}}$ **15.** $\frac{1 \text{ in.}}{100 \text{ mi}} = \frac{\frac{1}{4} \text{ in.}}{x \text{ mi}}$
$x = 4 \cdot 100$ $x = \frac{1}{4} \cdot 100$
$x = 400 \text{ mi}$ $x = 25 \text{ mi}$

16. $\frac{1 \text{ in.}}{100 \text{ mi}} = \frac{3\frac{1}{8} \text{ in.}}{x \text{ mi}}$
$x = 3\frac{1}{8} \cdot 100$
$x = 312.5 \text{ mi}$

17. $A(4, 3) \rightarrow (4 \cdot 3, 3 \cdot 3) \rightarrow A'(12, 9)$
$B(-3, 2) \rightarrow (-3 \cdot 3, 2 \cdot 3) \rightarrow B'(-9, 6)$
$C(-1, -4) \rightarrow (-1 \cdot 3, -4 \cdot 3) \rightarrow C'(-3, -12)$
$D(5, -5) \rightarrow (5 \cdot 3, -5 \cdot 3) \rightarrow D'(15, -15)$

18. $\tan A = \frac{36}{48} = 0.75$ **19.** $m\angle A \approx 37°$

20. $\cos B = \frac{36}{60} = 0.6$ **21.** $m\angle B \approx 53°$

22. $\sin B = \frac{48}{60} = 0.8$ **23.** $m\angle C = 90°$

24. $\frac{20}{30} = \frac{24}{x}$
$20x = 24 \cdot 30$
$20x = 720$
$\frac{20x}{20} = \frac{720}{20}$
$x = 36 \text{ ft}$

25.

Clothespins

```
 1   2   3   4   5   6   7   8   9  10
```

```
 1   2   3   4   5   6   7   8   9
```
Photographs

9 photographs

PAGE 375   BONUS

$\sin A = \dfrac{\text{opposite}}{\text{hypotenuse}}, \cos A = \dfrac{\text{adjacent}}{\text{hypotenuse}}$

$\dfrac{\sin A}{\cos A} = \dfrac{\text{opposite}}{\text{hypotenuse}} \div \dfrac{\text{adjacent}}{\text{hypotenuse}}$

$\qquad = \dfrac{\text{opposite}}{\text{hypotenuse}} \cdot \dfrac{\text{hypotenuse}}{\text{adjacent}}$

$\qquad = \dfrac{\text{opposite}}{\text{adjacent}}$

$\qquad = \tan A$

Academic Skills Test

PAGES 376-377

1. C; estimate by rounding: \$1 + \$3 + \$1 + \$1 = \$6;

2. C

3. D; $\quad \dfrac{x}{5} + 4 = 32$

$\qquad \dfrac{x}{5} + 4 - 4 = 32 - 4$

$\qquad\qquad\qquad \dfrac{x}{5} = 28$

$\qquad\qquad 5\left(\dfrac{x}{5}\right) = 28 \cdot 5$

$\qquad\qquad\qquad\quad x = 140$

4. A; $(-8)^3 = (-8)(-8)(-8)$

$\qquad\qquad\quad = 64(-8)$

$\qquad\qquad\quad = -512$

5. B; $3 + 4 = 7$

6. A; $\dfrac{1}{2} \cdot 30 = 15$

7. D

8. B; $e° = 180° - 72° = 108°$

9. D

10. B; $14 = 2 \cdot 7$
$\qquad 50 = 2 \cdot 5 \cdot 5$
$\qquad \text{GCF} = 2$

11. C; $2\dfrac{1}{8} = 2.125$

12. D; $\quad x + 2\dfrac{2}{3} = -4\dfrac{1}{3}$

$x + 2\dfrac{2}{3} - 2\dfrac{2}{3} = -4\dfrac{1}{3} - 2\dfrac{2}{3}$

$\qquad\qquad x = [-4 + (-2)] + \left[-\dfrac{1}{3} + \left(-\dfrac{2}{3}\right)\right]$

$\qquad\qquad x = -6 + (-1)$

$\qquad\qquad x = -7$

13. D; $17 + 9 = 26$, $26 + 11 = 37$

14. C; $A = 8 \cdot 8 + \dfrac{1}{2} \cdot 6 \cdot 8$

$\qquad A = 64 + \dfrac{1}{2} \cdot 48$

$\qquad A = 64 + 24$

$\qquad A = 88 \text{ ft}^2$

15. B; $-\sqrt{0.81} = -0.9$

16. $c^2 = a^2 + b^2$
$\quad c^2 = 20^2 + 50^2$
$\quad c^2 = 400 + 2{,}500$
$\quad c^2 = 2{,}900$
$\quad c \approx 54 \text{ in.}$

17. C; $\sin 30° = \dfrac{50}{c}$

$\qquad c(\sin 30°) = \left(\dfrac{50}{c}\right)c$

$\qquad c(\sin 30°) = 50$

$\qquad \dfrac{c(\sin 30°)}{\sin 30°} = \dfrac{50}{\sin 30°}$

$\qquad\qquad\quad c = \dfrac{50}{\sin 30°}$

$\qquad\qquad\quad c = 100$

18. B

19. C

20. B; $\dfrac{x}{6} = \dfrac{12}{8}$

$\qquad 8x = 12 \cdot 6$

$\qquad 8x = 72$

$\qquad \dfrac{8x}{8} = \dfrac{72}{8}$

$\qquad\quad x = 9 \text{ cm}$

Chapter 10   Applications with Percent

1. A percent is a ratio that compares a number to 100.

2. $\frac{53}{100} = \frac{x}{215}$

3. $\frac{3}{8} = \frac{37.5}{100} = 37.5\%$

4. $\frac{17}{25} = \frac{r}{100}$

$17 \cdot 100 = 25r$

$1,700 = 25r$

$\frac{1,700}{25} = \frac{25r}{25}$

$68 = r$

$\frac{17}{25} = 68\%$

5. $\frac{35}{100} = 35\%$

6. $\frac{7}{8} = \frac{r}{100}$

$7 \cdot 100 = 8r$

$700 = 8r$

$\frac{700}{8} = \frac{8r}{8}$

$87.5 = r$

$\frac{7}{8} = 87.5\%$

7. $\frac{9}{10} = \frac{r}{100}$

$9 \cdot 100 = 10r$

$900 = 10r$

$\frac{900}{10} = \frac{10r}{10}$

$90 = r$

$\frac{9}{10} = 90\%$

8. $\frac{1}{20} = \frac{r}{100}$

$100 = 20r$

$\frac{100}{20} = \frac{20r}{20}$

$5 = r$

$\frac{1}{20} = 5\%$

9. $b; \frac{24}{B} = \frac{25}{100}$

10. $a; \frac{24}{25} = \frac{r}{100}$

11. $c; \frac{P}{24} = \frac{25}{100}$

12. $\frac{P}{532} = \frac{19}{100}$

$100P = 19 \cdot 532$

$100P = 10,108$

$\frac{100P}{100} = \frac{10,108}{100}$

$P \approx 101.1$

13. $\frac{P}{88} = \frac{12.5}{100}$

$100P = 12.5 \cdot 88$

$100P = 1,100$

$\frac{100P}{100} = \frac{1,100}{100}$

$P = 11$

14. $\frac{111}{185} = \frac{r}{100}$

$111 \cdot 100 = 185r$

$11,100 = 185r$

$\frac{11,100}{185} = \frac{185r}{185}$

$60 = r$

$\frac{111}{185} = 60\%$

15. $\frac{9}{100} = 9\%$

16. $\frac{1}{8} = \frac{r}{100}$

$100 = 8r$

$\frac{100}{8} = \frac{8r}{8}$

$12.5 = r$

$\frac{1}{8} = 12.5\%$

17. $\frac{7}{10} = \frac{r}{100}$

$7 \cdot 100 = 10r$

$700 = 10r$

$\frac{700}{10} = \frac{10r}{10}$

$70 = r$

$\frac{7}{10} = 70\%$

18. $\frac{3}{4} = \frac{r}{100}$

$3 \cdot 100 = 4r$

$300 = 4r$

$\frac{300}{4} = \frac{4r}{4}$

$75 = r$

$\frac{3}{4} = 75\%$

19. $\frac{23}{50} = \frac{r}{100}$

$23 \cdot 100 = 50r$

$2,300 = 50r$

$\frac{2,300}{50} = \frac{50r}{50}$

$46 = r$

$\frac{23}{50} = 46\%$

20. $\frac{5}{8} = \frac{r}{100}$

$5 \cdot 100 = 8r$

$500 = 8r$

$\frac{500}{8} = \frac{8r}{8}$

$62.5 = r$

$\frac{5}{8} = 62.5\%$

21. $\frac{2}{3} = \frac{r}{100}$

$2 \cdot 100 = 3r$

$200 = 3r$

$\frac{200}{3} = \frac{3r}{3}$

$66.7 \approx r$

$\frac{2}{3} \approx 66.7\%$ or $66\frac{2}{3}\%$

22. $\frac{27}{30} = \frac{r}{100}$

$27 \cdot 100 = 30r$

$2,700 = 30r$

$\frac{2,700}{30} = \frac{30r}{30}$

$90 = r$

$\frac{27}{30} = 90\%$

23. $\frac{4}{5} = \frac{r}{100}$

$4 \cdot 100 = 5r$

$400 = 5r$

$\frac{400}{5} = \frac{5r}{5}$

$80 = r$

$\frac{4}{5} = 80\%$

24. $\frac{15}{40} = \frac{r}{100}$

$15 \cdot 100 = 40r$

$1,500 = 40r$

$\frac{1,500}{40} = \frac{40r}{40}$

$37.5 = r$

$\frac{15}{40} = 37.5\%$ or $37\frac{1}{2}\%$

25. $\frac{35}{100} = \frac{P}{230}$

$35 \cdot 230 = 100P$

$8,050 = 100P$

$\frac{8,050}{100} = \frac{100P}{100}$

$80.5 = P$

26.
$$\frac{37.5}{100} = \frac{P}{104}$$
$$37.5 \cdot 104 = 100P$$
$$3,900 = 100P$$
$$\frac{3,900}{100} = \frac{100P}{100}$$
$$39 = P$$

27.
$$\frac{50}{400} = \frac{r}{100}$$
$$50 \cdot 100 = 400r$$
$$5,000 = 400r$$
$$\frac{5,000}{400} = \frac{400r}{400}$$
$$12.5 = r$$
$$\frac{50}{400} = 12.5\%$$

28.
$$\frac{17.8}{178} = \frac{r}{100}$$
$$17.8 \cdot 100 = 178r$$
$$1,780 = 178r$$
$$\frac{1,780}{178} = \frac{178r}{178}$$
$$10 = r$$
$$\frac{17.8}{178} = 10\%$$

29.
$$\frac{57}{B} = \frac{30}{100}$$
$$57 \cdot 100 = 30B$$
$$5,700 = 30B$$
$$\frac{5,700}{30} = \frac{30B}{30}$$
$$190 = B$$

30.
$$\frac{80}{B} = \frac{45}{100}$$
$$80 \cdot 100 = 45B$$
$$8,000 = 45B$$
$$\frac{8,000}{45} = \frac{45B}{45}$$
$$177.8 \approx B$$

31.
$$\frac{28}{B} = \frac{25}{100}$$
$$28 \cdot 100 = 25B$$
$$2,800 = 25B$$
$$\frac{2,800}{25} = \frac{25B}{25}$$
$$112 = B$$

32.
$$\frac{15}{B} = \frac{40}{100}$$
$$15 \cdot 100 = 40B$$
$$1,500 = 40B$$
$$\frac{1,500}{40} = \frac{40B}{40}$$
$$37.5 = B$$

33.
$$\frac{16}{25} = \frac{r}{100}$$
$$16 \cdot 100 = 25r$$
$$1,600 = 25r$$
$$\frac{1,600}{25} = \frac{25r}{25}$$
$$64 = r$$
$$\frac{16}{25} = 64\%$$

34. $14 \times 20 = 280$ ft^2
24¢ = \$0.24
$280 \times 0.24 = \$67.20$
It will cost \$67.20
to paint the ceiling.

35. 10, 12, 12, 13, 14,
17, 17, 18, 19, 20,
20, 20, 21, 21, 21,
21, 21, 21, 22, 23,
23, 24, 24, 25, 25,
28
Median: 21
UQ: 23
LQ: 17

36. ∠7 and ∠8 are supplementary angles.
$$m\angle 7 + m\angle 8 = 180°$$
$$100° + m\angle 8 = 180°$$
$$100° - 100° + m\angle 8 = 180° - 100°$$
$$m\angle 8 = 80°$$

37. $40 = 2 \cdot 2 \cdot 2 \cdot 5$
$72 = 2 \cdot 2 \cdot 2 \cdot 3 \cdot 3$
GCF $= 2 \cdot 2 \cdot 2 = 8$
$$\frac{40 \div 8}{72 \div 8} = \frac{5}{9}$$

38. $\sqrt{220} \approx 14.8$

39. $\sin x = \frac{5}{13}$
$x \approx 23°$

40.
$$\frac{11}{48} = \frac{r}{100}$$
$$11 \cdot 100 = 48r$$
$$1,100 = 48r$$
$$\frac{1,100}{48} = \frac{48r}{48}$$
$$22.9 \approx r$$
$$\frac{11}{48} \approx 22.9\%$$

41.
$$\frac{7}{13} = \frac{r}{100}$$
$$7 \cdot 100 = 13r$$
$$700 = 13r$$
$$\frac{700}{13} = \frac{13r}{13}$$
$$53.8 \approx r$$
It will hurt her average,
because $\frac{7}{13} = 53.8\% < 56\%$.

42. a.
$$\frac{55 \times 10^9}{B} = \frac{63.6}{100}$$
$$100(55 \times 10^9) = 63.6B$$
$$5,500 \times 10^9 = 63.6B$$
$$\frac{5,500 \times 10^9}{63.6} = \frac{63.6B}{63.6}$$
$$86.5 \times 10^9 \approx B$$
About 86.5 billion cans were produced.

b.
$$\frac{2,500}{6,250} = \frac{r}{100}$$
$$2,500 \cdot 100 = 6,250r$$
$$250,000 = 6,250r$$
$$\frac{250,000}{6,250} = \frac{6,250r}{6,250}$$
$$40 = r$$
$$\frac{2,500}{6,250} = 40\%$$
This is twice the national average.

10-2 Fractions, Decimals, and Percent

PAGES 386-387   CHECKING FOR UNDERSTANDING

1. Write the decimal as a fraction with a denominator of 100, then express the fraction as a percent.
2. Express the percent in the form $\frac{r}{100}$ and simplify.
3. Multiply the decimal by 100, then add a percent sign.
4. $0.7 = 0.70$
$$= \frac{70}{100}$$
$$= 70\%$$

5. $0.605 = \frac{605}{1000}$
$$= \frac{60.5}{100}$$
$$= 60.5\%$$

6. $0.26 = \frac{26}{100}$
$$= 26\%$$

7. $0.02 = \dfrac{2}{100}$

$= 2\%$

8. $65\% = \dfrac{65}{100}$

$= \dfrac{13}{20}$

9. $6.5\% = \dfrac{6.5}{100}$

$= \dfrac{65}{1000}$

$= \dfrac{13}{200}$

10. $12.5\% = \dfrac{12.5}{100}$

$= \dfrac{125}{1000}$

$= \dfrac{1}{8}$

11. $96\% = \dfrac{96}{100}$

$= \dfrac{24}{25}$

12. $78\% = \dfrac{78}{100}$

$= 0.78$

13. $9\% = \dfrac{9}{100}$

$= 0.09$

14. $12.3\% = \dfrac{12.3}{100}$

$= \dfrac{123}{1000}$

$= 0.123$

15. $8.4\% = \dfrac{8.4}{100}$

$= \dfrac{84}{1000}$

$= 0.084$

PAGE 387   EXERCISES

16. $15\% = \dfrac{15}{100}$

$= 0.15$

$\dfrac{1}{8} = 1 \div 8$

$= 0.125$

$15\% > \dfrac{1}{8}$

17. $3.2\% = \dfrac{3.2}{100}$

$= \dfrac{32}{1000}$

$= 0.032$

$0.3 > 3.2\%$

18. $\dfrac{1}{4} = 1 \div 4$

$= 0.25$

$28\% = \dfrac{28}{100}$

$= 0.28$

$28\% > \dfrac{1}{4}$

19. $0.18 = \dfrac{18}{100}$

$= 18\%$

20. $0.08 = \dfrac{8}{100}$

$= 8\%$

21. $0.704 = \dfrac{704}{1000}$

$= \dfrac{70.4}{100}$

$= 70.4\%$

22. $0.039 = \dfrac{39}{1000}$

$= \dfrac{3.9}{100}$

$= 3.9\%$

23. $0.553 = \dfrac{553}{1000}$

$= \dfrac{55.3}{100}$

$= 55.3\%$

24. $0.6306 = \dfrac{6306}{10000}$

$= \dfrac{63.06}{100}$

$= 63.06\%$

25. $58\% = \dfrac{58}{100}$

$= \dfrac{29}{50}$

26. $37\% = \dfrac{37}{100}$

27. $44.5\% = \dfrac{44.5}{100}$

$= \dfrac{445}{1000}$

$= \dfrac{89}{200}$

28. $83\tfrac{1}{3}\% = \dfrac{250}{3}\%$

$\dfrac{250}{3}\% = \dfrac{\frac{250}{3}}{100}$

$= \dfrac{250}{3} \div 100$

$= \dfrac{250}{3} \cdot \dfrac{1}{100}$

$= \dfrac{250}{300}$

$= \dfrac{5}{6}$

29. $18.25\% = \dfrac{18.25}{100}$

$= \dfrac{1825}{10000}$

$= \dfrac{73}{400}$

30. $12\tfrac{3}{4}\% = 12.75\%$

$12.75\% = \dfrac{12.75}{100}$

$= \dfrac{1275}{10000}$

$= \dfrac{51}{400}$

31. $28\% = \dfrac{28}{100}$

$= 0.28$

32. $74\% = \dfrac{74}{100}$

$= 0.74$

33. $84.25\% = \dfrac{84.25}{100}$

$= \dfrac{8425}{10000}$

$= 0.8425$

34. $81.5\% = \dfrac{81.5}{100}$

$= \dfrac{815}{1000}$

$= 0.815$

35. $38.4\% = \dfrac{38.4}{100}$

$= \dfrac{384}{1000}$

$= 0.384$

36. $9.01\% = \dfrac{9.01}{100}$

$= \dfrac{901}{10000}$

$= 0.0901$

37. $\dfrac{11}{55} = \dfrac{1}{5} = \dfrac{2}{10} = 0.2;$

$\dfrac{11}{55} = \dfrac{r}{100}$

$1100 = 55r$

$\dfrac{1100}{55} = \dfrac{55r}{55}$

$20 = r$

$\dfrac{11}{55} = 20\%;$

$\dfrac{11}{55} = \dfrac{1}{5}$

38. $r = 9 + (-14) + 5 + (-21)$

$r = -5 + (-16)$

$r = -21$

Check:

$-21 \overset{?}{=} 9 + (-14) + 5 + (-21)$

$-21 \overset{?}{=} 0 + (-21)$

$-21 = -21 \quad \checkmark$

39. $-162 = -2 \cdot 81$

$= -2 \cdot 3 \cdot 27$

$= -2 \cdot 3 \cdot 3 \cdot 9$

$= -2 \cdot 3 \cdot 3 \cdot 3 \cdot 3$

$= -2 \cdot 3^4$

40. $\dfrac{x}{3} = -2.4$

$3\left(\dfrac{x}{3}\right) = (-2.4)3$

$x = -7.2$

41. The polygons have the same shape but differ in size.

42. $\dfrac{28}{100} = \dfrac{P}{250}$

$28 \cdot 250 = 100\,P$

$7{,}000 = 100P$

$\dfrac{7{,}000}{100} = \dfrac{100P}{100}$

$70 = P$

43. a. $r = \frac{1}{2}d$ $\qquad$ $r = \frac{1}{2}d$

$\qquad$ $r = \frac{1}{2}(8)$ $\qquad$ $r = \frac{1}{2} \cdot 16$

$\qquad$ $r = 4$ $\qquad\qquad$ $r = 8$

$\qquad$ $A = \pi r^2$ $\qquad\quad$ $A = \pi r^2$

$\qquad$ $A = \pi(4)^2$ $\qquad$ $A = \pi(8)^2$

$\qquad$ $A = 16\pi \text{ in}^2$ $\quad$ $A = 64\pi \text{ in}^2$

$\qquad$ $\frac{16\pi}{64\pi} = \frac{16}{64} = \frac{1}{4} = 25\%$

b. $\frac{\$6}{16\pi \text{ in}^2} \approx \$0.12$ per in^2

$\qquad$ $\frac{\$12}{64\pi \text{ in}^2} \approx \$0.06$ per in^2

The 16 inch pizza is the better buy.

10-3 Large and Small Percents

PAGES 389-390 $\qquad$ CHECKING FOR UNDERSTANDING

1. Move the decimal point two places to the left and drop the percent sign.

2.

3. Draw a 10 × 10 square on a piece of graph paper. Shade $\frac{1}{4}$ of a region that represents 1%.

4. $50\% = 0.50$ and $\frac{1}{2}\% = 0.005$.

5. $0.02\% = \frac{0.02}{100}$ $\qquad\qquad$ 6. $0.1\% = \frac{0.1}{100}$

$\qquad$ $= \frac{2}{10000}$ $\qquad\qquad\qquad$ $= \frac{1}{1000}$

$\qquad$ $= \frac{1}{5000}$

7. $175\% = \frac{175}{100}$ $\qquad\qquad$ 8. $\frac{1}{5}\% = 0.2\% = \frac{0.2}{100}$

$\qquad$ $= 1\frac{75}{100}$ $\qquad\qquad\qquad\qquad$ $= \frac{2}{1000}$

$\qquad$ $= 1\frac{3}{4}$ $\qquad\qquad\qquad\qquad\quad$ $= \frac{1}{500}$

9. $178\% = \frac{178}{100}$ $\qquad$ 10. $201.2\% = \frac{201.2}{100}$

$\qquad$ $= 1.78$ $\qquad\qquad\qquad\qquad$ $= \frac{2012}{1000}$

$\qquad\qquad\qquad\qquad\qquad\qquad\qquad$ $= 2.012$

11. $0.6\% = \frac{0.6}{100}$ $\qquad$ 12. $0.05\% = \frac{0.05}{100}$

$\qquad$ $= \frac{6}{1000}$ $\qquad\qquad\qquad\qquad$ $= \frac{5}{10000}$

$\qquad$ $= 0.006$ $\qquad\qquad\qquad\qquad$ $= 0.0005$

13. Example: $112\% = \frac{112}{100}$

$\qquad\qquad\qquad$ $= 1.12$

So a percent greater than 100 is a number greater than 1.

14. Example: $\frac{1}{2}\% = 0.5\% = \frac{0.5}{100}$

$\qquad\qquad\qquad\qquad$ $= \frac{5}{1000}$

$\qquad\qquad\qquad\qquad$ $= \frac{1}{200}$

$\qquad\qquad\qquad\qquad$ $= 0.005$

Since $\frac{1}{100} = 0.01$, a percent less than 1 is a number less than $\frac{1}{100}$.

PAGE 390 $\qquad$ EXERCISES

15. $0.3\% = \frac{0.3}{100}$ $\qquad$ 16. $0.04\% = \frac{0.04}{100}$

$\qquad$ $= \frac{3}{1000}$ $\qquad\qquad\qquad\qquad$ $= \frac{4}{10000}$

$\qquad\qquad\qquad\qquad\qquad\qquad\qquad$ $= \frac{1}{2500}$

17. $760\% = \frac{760}{100}$ $\qquad$ 18. $123.092\% = \frac{12309.2}{100}$

$\qquad$ $= 7\frac{60}{100}$ $\qquad\qquad\qquad\qquad$ $= \frac{123092}{1000}$

$\qquad$ $= 7\frac{3}{5}$ $\qquad\qquad\qquad\qquad\quad$ $= 123\frac{92}{1000}$

$\qquad\qquad\qquad\qquad\qquad\qquad\qquad$ $= 123\frac{23}{250}$

19. $243\% = \frac{243}{100}$ $\qquad$ 20. $\frac{3}{4}\% = 0.75\% = \frac{0.75}{100}$

$\qquad$ $= 2\frac{43}{100}$ $\qquad\qquad\qquad\qquad$ $= \frac{75}{10000}$

$\qquad\qquad\qquad\qquad\qquad\qquad\qquad$ $= \frac{3}{400}$

21. $\frac{4}{25}\% = 0.16\% = \frac{0.16}{100}$ $\quad$ 22. $33\frac{1}{3}\% = \frac{\frac{100}{3}}{100}$

$\qquad\qquad$ $= \frac{16}{10000}$ $\qquad\qquad\qquad$ $= \frac{100}{3} \div 100$

$\qquad\qquad$ $= \frac{1}{625}$ $\qquad\qquad\qquad\quad$ $= \frac{100}{3} \cdot \frac{1}{100}$

$\qquad\qquad\qquad\qquad\qquad\qquad\quad$ $= \frac{100}{300}$

$\qquad\qquad\qquad\qquad\qquad\qquad\quad$ $= \frac{1}{3}$

23. $212\% = \frac{212}{100}$ $\qquad$ 24. $1819\% = \frac{1819}{100}$

$\qquad$ $= 2.12$ $\qquad\qquad\qquad\qquad$ $= 18.19$

25. $0.03\% = \frac{0.03}{100}$ $\qquad$ 26. $10.088\% = \frac{10.088}{100}$

$\qquad$ $= \frac{3}{10000}$ $\qquad\qquad\qquad\qquad$ $= \frac{10088}{100000}$

$\qquad$ $= 0.0003$ $\qquad\qquad\qquad\qquad$ $= 0.10088$

27. $\frac{7}{10}\% = 0.7\% = \frac{0.7}{100}$ $\quad$ 28. $\frac{13}{20}\% = 0.65\% = \frac{0.65}{100}$

$\qquad\qquad$ $= \frac{7}{1000}$ $\qquad\qquad\qquad\qquad$ $= \frac{65}{10000}$

$\qquad\qquad$ $= 0.007$ $\qquad\qquad\qquad\qquad$ $= 0.0065$

29. $0.008\% = \frac{0.008}{100}$ $\qquad$ 30. $16\frac{2}{5}\% = 16.4\% = \frac{16.4}{100}$

$\qquad$ $= \frac{8}{100000}$ $\qquad\qquad\qquad\qquad$ $= \frac{164}{1000}$

$\qquad$ $= 0.00008$ $\qquad\qquad\qquad\qquad$ $= 0.164$

31. $67\% = \dfrac{67}{100} = 0.67$

$\dfrac{3}{8}\% = 0.375\% = \dfrac{0.375}{100} = \dfrac{375}{100000} = 0.00375$

From least to greatest: $\dfrac{3}{8}\%$, 67%, 0.8, 7

32. $2.4m = 14.4$

$\dfrac{2.4m}{2.4} = \dfrac{14.4}{2.4}$

$m = 6$

33. $0.000084 = 8.4 \times 0.00001$

$= 8.4 \times 10^{-5}$

34. $a^2 + b^2 = c^2$

$4^2 + b^2 = 15^2$

$16 + b^2 = 225$

$16 - 16 + b^2 = 225 - 16$

$b^2 = 209$

$b = \sqrt{209}$

$b \approx 14.5 \text{ ft}$

35. $81 \cdot \dfrac{1}{3} = 27$

$27 \cdot \dfrac{1}{3} = 9$

$9 \cdot \dfrac{1}{3} = 3$

$3 \cdot \dfrac{1}{3} = 1$

$1 \cdot \dfrac{1}{3} = \dfrac{1}{3}$

$\dfrac{1}{3} \cdot \dfrac{1}{3} = \dfrac{1}{9}$

$\dfrac{1}{9} \cdot \dfrac{1}{3} = \dfrac{1}{27}$

The eighth term is $\dfrac{1}{27}$.

36. $38.5\% = \dfrac{38.5}{100}$

$= \dfrac{385}{1000}$

$= 0.385$

$38.5\% = \dfrac{38.5}{100}$

$= \dfrac{385}{1000}$

$= \dfrac{77}{200}$

37. $9.85\% = \dfrac{9.85}{100}$

$= \dfrac{985}{10000}$

$= 0.0985$

38. No, the price has increased by 100% because percent increase = $\dfrac{\text{amount of increase}}{\text{price before increase}}$.

39. The price of the camera is 100% + 5.5% sales tax or 105.5%. Yes, the total cost is 105.5% of the purchase price.

40. Answers may vary. Sample answer: A decimal representing more than 100% would be larger than 1, while a decimal less than 1% would be less than 0.01.

10-4   Solve a Simpler Problem

1. Answers may vary. Sample answer: Use fraction-decimal-percent equivalencies and mental math to solve a problem using a simpler method.

2. Answers may vary. Sample answer: Solve one or more simpler problems using mental math.

3. $20\% = \dfrac{1}{5}$ so divide 525 by 5 to get 105.

4. $1 + 200 = 201$

$2 + 199 = 201$

$3 + 198 = 201$

$4 + 197 = 201$

$\vdots$

$100 + 101 = 201$

There are 100 sums of 201. So the sum of the whole numbers from 1 to 200 is 100(201) or 20,100.

5. $30\% = \dfrac{30}{100} = 0.30$

Multiply 210 by 0.3 to get 63 visitors.

6. 1st cut $\rightarrow$ 2 parts

2nd cut $\rightarrow$ 3 parts

3rd cut $\rightarrow$ 4 parts

To get 19 parts you will need 19 - 1 or 18 cuts.

7. $\dfrac{14.30}{220} = 0.065$

$0.065 = \dfrac{65}{1000}$

$= \dfrac{6.5}{100}$

The sales tax is 6.5%.

8. $3x + (-16) = 2$

$3x + (-16) + 16 = 2 + 16$

$3x = 18$

$\dfrac{3x}{3} = \dfrac{18}{3}$

$x = 6$

9. $25\% = \dfrac{1}{4}$, so divide 200 by 4. About $200 \div 4 = 50$ calories are from fat.

10. Guess 1 can of peaches:

$12.51 - 1.29 = 11.22$

$11.22 \div 2.16 = 5.19\overline{4}$

Guess 2 cans of peaches:

$12.51 - 2(1.29) = 12.51 - 2.58 = 9.93$

$9.93 \div 2.16 = 4.597\overline{2}$

Guess 3 cans of peaches:

$12.51 - 3(1.29) = 12.51 - 3.87 = 8.64$

$8.64 \div 2.16 = 4$

Benjamin bought 3 cans of peaches and 4 cartons of cream.

11. $\dfrac{4}{5} \cdot 160{,}000 = \dfrac{4(160{,}000)}{5}$

$= 128{,}000 \text{ people}$

12. Two clothespins are needed for the first towel. If you overlap corners and use one clothespin to hold one corner from the first towel and one corner from the second towel, you will need one additional clothespin for the second towel. Repeat this process for 8 towels and you will use $2 + 1 + 1 + 1 + 1 + 1 + 1 + 1$ or 9 clothespins.

13. $(0.15)(12{,}000) = \$1{,}800$

116

14.

Shirt	Pants
red	black
red	navy
red	white
gray	black
gray	navy
gray	white
white	black
white	navy
white	white

There are 9 combinations of uniforms.

10-5 Percent and Estimation

1. Round 23% to 25%. Round $98.95 to $100. Then $\frac{1}{4}$ of $100 is $25.

2. See students' work.

3. Round $24.90 to $25. Since 15% = 10% + 5%, take 10% of $25 or $2.50. Also, 5% is $\frac{1}{2}$ of 10%, so take $\frac{1}{2}$ of $2.50 or $1.25. Add $2.50 + $1.25 to get $3.75.

4. a; Since 40 is $\frac{1}{2}$ or 50% of 80 and 46% < 50%, an estimate less than 40 is the better estimate.

5. b; Since 60 is $\frac{1}{5}$ or 20% of 300 and 22% > 20%, an estimate greater than 300 is the better estimate.

6. b; Since $42 is 100% of $42 and 107 > 100, an estimate greater than $42 is the better estimate.

7. a; Since 40 is 1% of 4,000 and $\frac{1}{4}$% < 1%, an estimate less than 40 is the better estimate.

8. 32% is about $33\frac{1}{3}$% and 89 is about 90. Then $33\frac{1}{3}$% of 90 is $\frac{1}{3} \cdot 90$ or 30. So 32% of 89 is about 30.

9. 14% is about 12.5% or $\frac{1}{8}$ and 78 is about 80. Then $\frac{1}{8}$ of 80 is $\frac{1}{8} \cdot 80$ or 10. So 14% of 78 is about 10.

10. 88% is about 90% or $\frac{9}{10}$ and 61 is about 60. Then $\frac{9}{10}$ of 60 is 54. So 88% of 61 is about 54.

11. 7 is about 8 and $\frac{8}{16} = \frac{1}{2}$ or 50%.

12. 13 is about 12 and $\frac{8}{12} = \frac{2}{3}$ or $66\frac{2}{3}$%.

13. 11 is about 10 and $\frac{15}{10} = \frac{3}{2} = 1\frac{1}{2}$ or 150%.

14. There are 21 squares that are completely shaded or almost completely shaded. There are 14 squares that contain some shading, so estimate $\frac{14}{2}$ or 7 squares with some shading. The estimate for percent of shaded area is then 21 + 7 = 28 out of 100 or about 28%.

15. There are 14 squares that are completely shaded or almost completely shaded. There are 12 squares that contain some shading, so estimate $\frac{12}{2}$ or 6 squares with some shading. The estimate for percent of shaded area is then 14 + 6 = 20 out of 100 or about 20%.

16. 73% is about 75% or $\frac{3}{4}$ and 65 is about 64. Then $\frac{3}{4}$ of 64 is $\frac{3}{4} \cdot 64$ or 48. So 73% of 65 is about 48.

17. 16% is about 15% and 55 is about 60. Then 10% of 60 is 6 and 5% of 60 is $\frac{1}{2}$ of 6 or 3. The estimate is 6 + 3 or 9. So 16% of 55 is about 9.

18. 19% is about 20% or $\frac{1}{5}$ and 72 is about 70. Then 70 ÷ 5 = 14. So 19% of 72 is about 14.

19. 68% is about $66\frac{2}{3}$% or $\frac{2}{3}$. Then $\frac{2}{3}$ of 33 is $\frac{2}{3} \cdot 33$ or 22. So 68% of 33 is about 22.

20. 29% is about $33\frac{1}{3}$% or $\frac{1}{3}$ and 50 is about 45. Then $\frac{1}{3}$ of 45 is 15. So 29% of 50 is about 15.

21. 12.4% is about 12.5% or $\frac{1}{8}$ and 39 is about 40. Then $\frac{1}{8}$ of 40 is 5. So 12.4% of 39 is about 5.

22. 10% of 400 is 40 and 5% of 200 is 10. So 8% of 400 is greater than 5% of 200.

23. 32% is about 30% and 154 is about 150.

24. There are about 30 squares completely shaded or almost completely shaded. There are about 12 squares that are partly shaded, so estimate $\frac{12}{2}$ or 6 squares with some shading. The estimate for percent of shaded area is then 30 + 6 = 36 out of 100 or 36%.

25. There are about 56 squares completely shaded or almost completely shaded. There are also about 16 squares that are partly shaded, so estimate $\frac{16}{2}$ or 8 squares with some shading. The estimate for percent of shaded area is then 56 + 8 = 64 out of 100 or 64%.

26. 4 is about 5 and $\frac{5}{25} = \frac{1}{5}$ or about 20%.

27. 62 is about 60 and $\frac{24}{60} = \frac{2}{5}$ or about 40%.

28. 61 is about 60 and 88 is about 90, so
$\frac{60}{90} = \frac{2}{3}$ or about $66\frac{2}{3}\%$.

29. $\frac{12}{60} = \frac{1}{5}$ or 20%

30. $\frac{7}{56} = \frac{1}{8}$ or 12.5%

31. 38 is about 40 and 159 is about 160, so
$\frac{40}{160} = \frac{1}{4}$ or about 25%.

32. 13 is about 15 and 22 is about 20. Then
$\frac{15}{20} = \frac{3}{4}$ or about 75%.

33. $A = \ell w$
$= 9 \cdot 6.5$
$= 58.5 \text{ ft}^2$

34. P (sum is seven) =
$\frac{\text{number of ways to add to seven}}{\text{total possible combinations}}$

Die #1		Die #2		
1	+	6	=	7
2	+	5	=	7
3	+	4	=	7
4	+	3	=	7
5	+	2	=	7
6	+	1	=	7

$P(\text{sum is seven}) = \frac{6}{36} = \frac{1}{6}$

35. $\frac{\$2.88}{9 \text{ ounces}} = \frac{\$0.32}{1 \text{ ounce}}$

36. $\frac{2}{5}\% = 0.4\% = \frac{0.4}{100}$
$= \frac{4}{1000}$
$= \frac{1}{250}$

37. Example: If x is $\frac{1}{2}$ of y, then y is 2 times x; or if x is 50% of y, then y is 200% of x.

Example: If x is $\frac{1}{4}$ of y, then y is 4 times x; or if x is 25% of y, then y is 400% of x.

Since $50\% = \frac{50}{100} = 0.5$ and $200\% = \frac{200}{100} = 2$, we see that $(0.5)(2) = 1$. Also, since $25\% = \frac{25}{100} = 0.25$ and $400\% = \frac{400}{100} = 4$, we see that $(0.25)(4) = 1$. Using these examples and the inverse property of multiplication, $285\% = \frac{285}{100} = 2.85$ and $(2.85)\left(\frac{1}{2.85}\right) = 1$. Then y is about $\frac{1}{2.85} \approx 0.35$
$= \frac{35}{100} = 35\%$ of x.

38. 6% is about 5% or $\frac{1}{20}$. Round 1,413 to 1,400.
$\frac{1}{20}$ of 1,400 is 70. Approximately 70 shoppers would be willing to pay more.

39.

Beverages	Estimate
Soft Drinks	17,600
Coffee	8,000
Tea	7,200
Other	8,800
Milk	880
Bottled Water	440

40. See students' work.

Mid-Chapter Review

PAGE 396

1. $\frac{P}{60} = \frac{40}{100}$
$100P = 40 \cdot 60$
$100P = 2,400$
$\frac{100P}{100} = \frac{2,400}{100}$
$P = 24$

2. $\frac{75}{B} = \frac{30}{100}$
$75 \cdot 100 = 30B$
$7,500 = 30B$
$\frac{7,500}{30} = \frac{30B}{30}$
$250 = B$

3. $\frac{44}{100} = 44\%$

4. $\frac{2}{3} = \frac{r}{100}$
$2 \cdot 100 = 3r$
$200 = 3r$
$\frac{200}{3} = \frac{3r}{3}$
$66\frac{2}{3} = r$
$\frac{2}{3} = 66\frac{2}{3}\%$

5. $\frac{5}{8} = \frac{r}{100}$
$5 \cdot 100 = 8r$
$500 = 8r$
$\frac{500}{8} = \frac{8r}{8}$
$62.5 = r$
$\frac{5}{8} = 62.5\%$

6. $\frac{2}{5} = \frac{r}{100}$
$2 \cdot 100 = 5r$
$200 = 5r$
$\frac{200}{5} = \frac{5r}{5}$
$40 = r$
$\frac{2}{5} = 40\%$

7. $80\% = \frac{80}{100}$
$= 0.80$

$80\% = \frac{80}{100}$
$= \frac{4}{5}$

8. $9\% = \frac{9}{100}$
$= 0.09$

$9\% = \frac{9}{100}$

9. $37\frac{1}{2}\% = 37.5\% = \frac{37.5}{100}$
$= \frac{375}{1000}$
$= 0.375$

$37.5\% = \frac{37.5}{100}$
$= \frac{375}{1000}$
$= \frac{3}{8}$

118

10. $7.09\% = \dfrac{7.09}{100}$
    $= \dfrac{709}{10000}$
    $= 0.0709$

$7.09\% = \dfrac{7.09}{100}$
$= \dfrac{709}{10000}$

11. $0.4\% = \dfrac{0.4}{100}$
    $= \dfrac{4}{1000}$
    $= 0.004$

$0.4\% = \dfrac{0.4}{100}$
$= \dfrac{4}{1000}$
$= \dfrac{1}{250}$

12. $118\% = \dfrac{118}{100}$
    $= 1.18$

$118\% = \dfrac{118}{100}$
$= 1\dfrac{18}{100}$
$= 1\dfrac{9}{50}$

13. $\dfrac{7}{8}\% = 0.875\%$
    $= \dfrac{0.875}{100}$
    $= \dfrac{875}{100000}$
    $= 0.00875$

$\dfrac{7}{8}\% = \dfrac{\frac{7}{8}}{100}$
$= \dfrac{7}{8} \div 100$
$= \dfrac{7}{8} \cdot \dfrac{1}{100}$
$= \dfrac{7}{800}$

14. $1\dfrac{3}{50}\% = \dfrac{53}{50}\%$
    $= 1.06\%$
    $= \dfrac{1.06}{100}$
    $= \dfrac{106}{10000}$
    $= 0.0106$

$1\dfrac{3}{50}\% = \dfrac{53}{50}\%$
$= \dfrac{\frac{53}{50}}{100}$
$= \dfrac{53}{50} \div 100$
$= \dfrac{53}{50} \cdot \dfrac{1}{100}$
$= \dfrac{53}{5000}$

15. 25% is $\dfrac{1}{4}$ and $24 \div 4 = 6$. Therefore 6 cheerleaders are freshmen.

16. c; Since 47.5% is about 50% and 50% of 600 is 300, the best estimate is 300.

17. b; Since 17% is about 20% or $\dfrac{1}{5}$ and 42 is about 40, $\dfrac{1}{5} \times 40$ or 8 is the best estimate.

18. b; Since 41 is about 42 and $\dfrac{7}{42} \approx 0.17 = \dfrac{17}{100} = 17\%$, the best estimate is 17%.

19. c; $\dfrac{9}{16}\%$ is about $\dfrac{8}{16}\%$ or $\dfrac{1}{2}\%$ and 415 is about 400. Also 1% of 400 is 4 and $\dfrac{1}{2}$ of 4 is 2. The best estimate is 2.

20. c; Since 108% is about 100% and 1,988 is about 2,200, the best estimate is 100% of 2,200 or 2,200.

PAGE 397   WHAT DO YOU THINK?

1. See students' work.
2. See students' work.

Decision Making

PAGES 398–399

1. $\dfrac{\$2.96}{8} = \$0.37$
   $\dfrac{\$1.20}{10} = \$0.12$
   $\$0.37 + 0.12 = \$0.49$
   One hot dog with bun costs about 49¢.

2. $\dfrac{\$2.78}{15} \approx \$0.19$
   One slice of cheese costs about 19¢.

3. There are $8\dfrac{1}{4}$-cups in 2 cups. So the cost of the chili in hot dog #1 is $\dfrac{\$3.09}{8}$ or $\$0.39$. The onions are $\dfrac{\$0.30}{5}$ or $\$0.06$ per onion and an medium-sized onion is about 6 tablespoons. The cost of the onion is then about $\dfrac{\$0.06}{6} = \$0.01$ per tablespoon or $(2)(\$0.01) = 2$¢ per hot dog for #1. To prepare hot dot #1, it will cost 49¢ for the hot dog and bun, 19¢ for the cheese, 39¢ for the chili, and 2¢ for the onion. In total, $49 + 19 + 39 + 2 = 109$¢ or $\$1.09$.

4. Answers may vary. Sample answer: About 50¢ on each sale.

5. Answers may vary. Sample answer: No, not if you plan to make the same amount of profit on each hot dog sold.

6. Answers may vary. Sample answer: Calculate the cost for each hot dog plus the amount of profit you want to make. If these values are close to the actual prices of the hot dogs, then the prices are reasonable.

7. See students' work.
8. See students' work.

10-6   The Percent Equation

PAGE 401   CHECKING FOR UNDERSTANDING

1. In words, 28 is what percent of 34.
   In symbols, $28 = P \cdot 34$.

119

2. $R = 35\% = \dfrac{35}{100} = 0.35$

3. When the rate is less than 100, the percentage is less than the base.

4. $P = R \cdot B$
$P = 0.47 \cdot 52$
$P = 24.44$

5. $P = R \cdot B$
$P = 0.56 \cdot 80$
$P = 44.8$

6. $P = R \cdot B$
$25 = R \cdot 52$
$\dfrac{25}{52} = \dfrac{R \cdot 52}{52}$
$0.481 \approx R$
$48.1\% \approx R$

7. $P = R \cdot B$
$2 = R \cdot 3{,}600$
$\dfrac{2}{3{,}600} = \dfrac{R \cdot 3{,}600}{3{,}600}$
$0.0006 \approx R$
$0.06\% \approx R$

8. $P = R \cdot B$
$48 = 0.30 \cdot B$
$\dfrac{48}{0.30} = \dfrac{0.03 \cdot B}{0.03}$
$\$160 = B$

9. $P = R \cdot B$
$64 = R \cdot 78$
$\dfrac{64}{78} = \dfrac{R \cdot 78}{78}$
$0.821 \approx R$
$82.1\% \approx R$

10. $P = R \cdot B$
$1.12 = R \cdot 4.8$
$\dfrac{1.12}{4.8} = \dfrac{R \cdot 4.8}{4.8}$
$0.2\overline{3} = R$
$23\frac{1}{3}\% = R$

11. $P = R \cdot B$
$P = 0.165 \cdot 60$
$P = 9.9$

12. $P = R \cdot B$
$5{,}000 = 0.30 \cdot B$
$\dfrac{5{,}000}{0.30} = \dfrac{0.30 \cdot B}{0.30}$
$\$16{,}666.67 \approx B$

PAGE 402   EXERCISES

13. $P = R \cdot B$
$P = 0.81 \cdot 11.2$
$P = 9.072$

14. $P = R \cdot B$
$36 = R \cdot 90$
$\dfrac{36}{90} = \dfrac{R \cdot 90}{90}$
$0.4 = R$
$40\% = R$

15. $P = R \cdot B$
$50 = 0.10 \cdot B$
$\dfrac{50}{0.1} = \dfrac{0.1 \cdot B}{0.1}$
$500 = B$

16. $P = R \cdot B$
$P = 0.005 \cdot 3200$
$P = 16$

17. $P = R \cdot B$
$P = 0.074 \cdot 40$
$P = 2.96$

18. $P = R \cdot B$
$96 = R \cdot 21$
$\dfrac{96}{21} = \dfrac{R \cdot 21}{21}$
$4.571 \approx R$
$457.1\% \approx R$

19. $P = R \cdot B$
$65 = 0.2 \cdot B$
$\dfrac{65}{0.2} = \dfrac{0.2 \cdot B}{0.2}$
$325 = B$

20. $P = R \cdot B$
$P = 0.28 \cdot 231.90$
$P \approx \$64.93$

21. $P = R \cdot B$
$66 = R \cdot 55$
$\dfrac{66}{55} = \dfrac{R \cdot 55}{55}$
$1.2 = R$
$120\% = R$

22. $P = R \cdot B$
$17 = R \cdot 51$
$\dfrac{17}{51} = \dfrac{R \cdot 51}{51}$
$0.\overline{3} = R$
$33\frac{1}{3}\% = R$

23. $P = R \cdot B$
$54 = 1.08 \cdot B$
$\dfrac{54}{1.08} = \dfrac{1.08 \cdot B}{1.08}$
$\$50 = B$

24. $P = R \cdot B$
$P = 1.24 \cdot 72$
$P = 89.28$

25. $P = R \cdot B$
$16 = 0.\overline{6} \cdot B$
$\dfrac{16}{0.\overline{6}} = \dfrac{0.\overline{6} \cdot B}{0.\overline{6}}$
$24 = B$

26. $P = R \cdot B$
$6 = R \cdot 50$
$\dfrac{6}{50} = \dfrac{R \cdot 50}{50}$
$0.12 = R$
$12\% = R$

27. $P = R \cdot B$
$6{,}899.70 = 1.055 \cdot B$
$\dfrac{6{,}899.70}{1.055} = \dfrac{1.055 \cdot B}{1.055}$
$\$6{,}540 = B$

28. $P = R \cdot B$
$8 = R \cdot 35$
$\dfrac{8}{35} = \dfrac{R \cdot 35}{35}$
$0.229 \approx R$
$22.9\% \approx R$

29. $m\angle S + m\angle T + m\angle U + m\angle V = 360°$
$90° + 3x° + 60° + 90° = 360°$
$3x° + 240° = 360°$
$3x° + 240° - 240° = 360° - 240°$
$3x° = 120°$
$\dfrac{3x°}{3} = \dfrac{120°}{3}$
$x° = 40°$
$x = 40$

30. Mult. Inv. $= -\dfrac{a}{1} = -a$

31. $x^2 = 121$
$x = \sqrt{121}$ or $x = -\sqrt{121}$
$x = 11$ or -11

32. 20.5% is about 20% or $\dfrac{1}{5}$ and 89 is about 90.
Then $90 \div 5 = 18$. So 20.5% of 89 is about 18.

33. $P = R \cdot B$
$3{,}896 = 0.08 \cdot B$
$\dfrac{3{,}896}{0.08} = \dfrac{0.08 \cdot B}{0.08}$
$48{,}700 = B$

34. $P = R \cdot B$
$10.92 = R \cdot 84$
$\dfrac{10.92}{84} = \dfrac{R \cdot 84}{84}$
$0.13 = R$
$13\% = R$

35. $P = R \cdot B$
$P = 0.07 \cdot 2(60{,}100)$
$P = 0.07 \cdot 120{,}200$
$P = \$8{,}414$

120

36. no; Answers may vary. Sample answer:

$100 + 0.1($100) = $100 + 10
$= 110
$110 - 0.1($110) = $110 - 11
$= 99

The result is $99 \neq 100. They are not the same.

37. $P = R \cdot B$

$P = 0.055 \cdot 229.99$

$P = 12.65

Then $229.99 + 12.65 = 24.64.

Jeremiah paid $24.64.

38. $P = R \cdot B$

$21 = 0.84 \cdot B$

$\dfrac{21}{0.84} = \dfrac{0.84 \cdot B}{0.84}$

$25 = B$

39. $P = R \cdot B$

$1.47 = R \cdot 21$

$\dfrac{1.47}{21} = \dfrac{R \cdot 21}{21}$

$0.07 = R$

$7\% = R$

40. See students' work.

10-7 Circle Graphs

1. They compare parts of a whole.

2. See students' work.

3. The sum of the percents in a circle graph should total 100%.

4. See students' work.

5. 100% since all partial percents add up to 100%

6. 360° since there are 360° in a circle

7.

Monthly Budget			
Category	Amount	Percent of Total	Degrees in Graph
Housing	$775	31%	112°
Food	$375	15%	54°
Insurance	$225	9%	32°
Transportation	$475	19%	68°
Other	$650	26%	94%
Total	$2,500	100%	360°

$775 + 375 + 225 + 475 + 650 = $2,000$

$\dfrac{775}{2,500} = 0.31 = 31\%; \ 0.31 \times 360 \approx 112°$

$\dfrac{375}{2,500} = 0.15 = 15\%; \ 0.15 \times 360 = 54°$

$\dfrac{225}{2,500} = 0.09 = 9\%; \ 0.09 \times 360 \approx 32°$

$\dfrac{475}{2,500} = 0.19 = 19\% = 0.19 \times 360 \approx 68°$

$\dfrac{650}{2,500} = 0.26 = 26\%; \ 0.26 \times 360 \approx 94°$

$31 + 15 + 9 + 19 + 26 = 100\%$

$112 + 54 + 32 + 68 + 94 = 360°$

8.

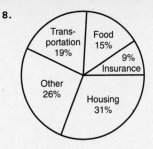

9. $5 + 8 + 8 + 22 + 47 = 90$

Canada: $\dfrac{5}{90} = 0.0\overline{5} \approx 6\%; \ 0.0\overline{5} \times 360 = 20°$

Gr. Brit: $\dfrac{8}{90} = 0.0\overline{8} \approx 9\%; \ 0.0\overline{8} \times 360 = 32°$

France: $\dfrac{8}{90} = 0.0\overline{8} \approx 9\%; \ 0.0\overline{8} \times 360 = 32°$

W. Germany: $\dfrac{22}{90} = 0.2\overline{4} \approx 24\%; \ 0.2\overline{4} \times 360 = 88°$

Japan: $\dfrac{47}{90} = 0.5\overline{2} \approx 52\%; \ 0.5\overline{2} \times 360 = 188°$

$6 + 9 + 9 + 24 + 52 = 100\%$

$20 + 32 + 32 + 88 + 188 = 360°$

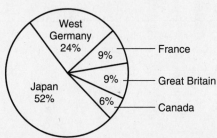

Daily Patents Issued to Foreign Inventors

10. $2 + 7 = 9$

$P(\text{winning}) = \dfrac{2}{9} = 0.\overline{2} \approx 22\%; \ 0.\overline{2} \times 360 = 80°$

$P(\text{losing}) = \dfrac{7}{9} = 0.\overline{7} \approx 78\%; \ 0.\overline{7} \times 360 = 280°$

$22 + 78 = 100\%$

$80 + 280 = 360°$

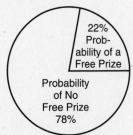

Probabilities of a Free Prize

11. $|-28| = 28$

121

12. 18 = 2 · 3 · 3
34 = 2 · 17
6 = 2 · 3
LCM = 2 · 3 · 3 · 17 = 306

13. $P = R \cdot B$
12 = R · 32
$\dfrac{12}{32} = \dfrac{R \cdot 32}{32}$
0.375 = R
37.5% = R

14. The total is more than 360° due to the way she rounded her answers. Review all answers and make sure that for each answer rounded up, one is rounded down.

15. 46 + 64 + 93 + 754 + 1,127 = 2,084
2,749 - 2,084 = 665. This represents enrollment in other languages.

Chinese: $\dfrac{46}{2,749} \approx 0.017 \approx 1.7\%$; 0.017 × 360 ≈ 6°

Japanese: $\dfrac{64}{2,749} \approx 0.023 \approx 2.3\%$; 0.023 × 360 ≈ 8°

Russian: $\dfrac{93}{2,749} \approx 0.034 \approx 3.4\%$; 0.034 × 360 ≈ 12°

French: $\dfrac{754}{2,749} \approx 0.274 \approx 27.4\%$; 0.274 × 360 ≈ 99°

Spanish: $\dfrac{1,127}{2,749} \approx 0.41 \approx 41\%$; 0.41 × 360 ≈ 148°

Other: $\dfrac{665}{2,749} \approx 0.242 \approx 24.2\%$; 0.242 × 360 ≈ 87°

1.7 + 2.3 + 3.4 + 27.4 + 41 + 24.2 = 100%
6 + 8 + 12 + 99 + 148 + 87 = 360°

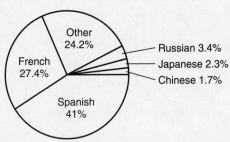

Daily Enrollment in a Foreign Language

16. See students' work.

17. 100 + 270 + 60 + 50 + 20 = 500

1-2 Times a Day: $\dfrac{100}{500}$ = 0.2 = 20%; 0.2 × 360 = 72°

Several Times a Week: $\dfrac{270}{500}$ = 0.54 = 54%;
0.54 × 360 ≈ 195°

Once a Week: $\dfrac{60}{500}$ = 0.12 = 12%; 0.12 × 360 ≈ 43°

1-3 Times a Month: $\dfrac{50}{500}$ = 0.1 = 10%;
0.1 × 360 = 36°

Less Than Once a Month: $\dfrac{20}{500}$ = 0.04 = 4%;
0.04 × 360 ≈ 14°

20 + 54 + 12 + 10 + 4 = 100%
72 + 195 + 43 + 36 + 14 = 360°

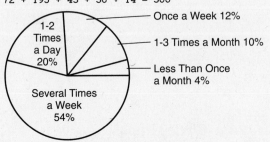

Frequency of Eating Salad

18. a. 0.18 + 0.82 + 1.67 = 2.67

Recycled: $\dfrac{0.18}{2.67}$ ≈ 0.068 = 6.8%;
0.068 × 360 ≈ 24°

Combustion: $\dfrac{0.82}{2.67}$ ≈ 0.307 = 30.7%;
0.307 × 360 ≈ 111°

Landfill: $\dfrac{1.67}{2.67}$ ≈ 0.625 = 62.5%;
0.625 × 360 ≈ 225°

6.8 + 30.7 + 62.5 = 100%
24 + 111 + 225 = 360°

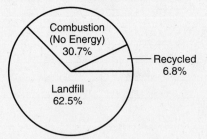

1960 Waste Distribution

b. $0.52 + 0.59 + 0.02 + 2.87 = 4.00$

Recycled: $\frac{0.52}{4.00} = 0.13 = 13\%$; $0.13 \times 360 \approx 47°$

Combustion (E): $\frac{0.59}{4.00} \approx 0.147 = 14.7\%$;

$0.147 \times 360 \approx 53°$

Combustion (No E): $\frac{0.02}{4.00} = 0.005 = 0.5\%$;

$0.005 \times 360 \approx 2°$

Landfill: $\frac{2.87}{4.00} \approx 0.718 = 71.8\%$;

$0.718 \times 360 \approx 258°$

$13 + 14.7 + 0.5 + 71.8 = 100\%$

$47 + 53 + 2 + 258 = 360°$

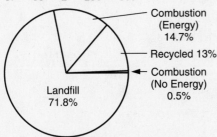

Combustion (Energy) 14.7%
Recycled 13%
Combustion (No Energy) 0.5%
Landfill 71.8%

1988 Waste Distribution

c. Answers may vary. Sample answer: The percent of waste recycled in 1988 was about double the percent recycled in 1960. No waste was burned for energy in 1960 and about 15% of the waste was burned for energy in 1988. The percent of waste deposited in landfills rose about 10% from 1960 to 1988.

10-8 Percent of Change

PAGES 407-408   CHECKING FOR UNDERSTANDING

1. Subtract to find the amount of change.

2. Use the original amount because the percent of change relates to the original amount.

3.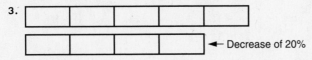

← Decrease of 20%

4. Sample answer: $6 - 4 = 2$

$\frac{2}{4} = \frac{1}{2}$ or 50%

5. Sample answer: $60 - 55 = 5$

$\frac{5}{50} = \frac{1}{10}$ or 10%

6. $90 - 75 = 15$

$\frac{15}{90} = 0.1\overline{6}$ or $16\frac{2}{3}\%$

7. $3 - 2 = 1$

$\frac{1}{3} = 0.\overline{3} \approx 33\%$

8. $80 - 72 = 8$

$\frac{8}{72} = 0.\overline{1} \approx 11\%$

9. $600 - 533 = 67$

$\frac{67}{533} \approx 0.13 = 13\%$

PAGE 408   EXERCISES

10. $7 - 5 = 2$

$\frac{2}{5} = 0.4 = 40\%$

11. $49 - 37 = 12$

$\frac{12}{49} \approx \frac{12}{48} = \frac{1}{4} = 0.25 = 25\%$

12. $45 - 40 = 5$

$\frac{5}{45} = \frac{1}{9} = 0.\overline{1} \approx 10\%$

13. $6 - 5 = 1$

$\frac{1}{6} = 0.1\overline{6} \approx 17\%$

14. $64 - 48 = 16$

$\frac{16}{48} = 0.\overline{3} \approx 33\%$

15. $300 - 221 = 79$

$\frac{79}{221} \approx 0.36 = 36\%$

16. $30 - 21 = 9$

$\frac{9}{21} \approx 0.43 = 43\%$

17. $90 - 80 = 10$

$\frac{10}{90} = 0.\overline{1} \approx 11\%$

18. $400 - 315 = 85$

$\frac{85}{315} \approx 0.27 = 27\%$

19. $57.78 - 54 = 3.78$

$\frac{3.78}{54} = 0.07 = 7\%$

20. 2 cups are in each pint, so $\frac{9}{2} = 4.5$ pints.

21. $a = b = 6.5$ feet

$a^2 + b^2 = c^2$

$(6.5)^2 + (6.5)^2 = c^2$

$42.25 + 42.25 = c^2$

$84.5 = c^2$

$9.2 \approx c$

The hypotenuse is about 9.2 feet.

22. $9 + 4 + 1.5 + 5 + 4.5 = 24$

Sleep: $\frac{9}{24} = 0.375 = 37.5\%$; $0.375 \times 360 = 135°$

TV: $\frac{4}{24} = 0.1\overline{6} \approx 16.6\%$; $0.1\overline{6} \times 360 = 60°$

Eating: $\frac{1.5}{24} = 0.0625 \approx 6.3\%$; $0.0625 \times 360 = 23°$

Friends: $\frac{5}{24} = 0.208\overline{3} \approx 20.8\%$; $0.208\overline{3} \times 360 = 75°$

Family: $\frac{4.5}{24} = 0.1875 \approx 18.8\%$; $0.1875 \times 360 = 67°$

$37.5 + 16.6 + 6.3 + 20.8 + 18.8 = 100\%$

$135 + 60 + 23 + 75 + 67 = 360°$

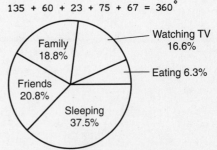

Family 18.8%
Watching TV 16.6%
Friends 20.8%
Eating 6.3%
Sleeping 37.5%

Kelly's Average Saturday

23. Example: Say the sweaters were bought at $20 and sold at $30. Then 50% of $30 is $15. The store lost money.

   Using variables: Let x be the cost to the store. Each sweater is sold at $x + 0.50x = 1.5x$. Then each sweater is put on sale for 50% and sold at a cost of $\frac{1}{2}(1.5x) = 0.75x$. So the final sale price is $\frac{3}{4}$ of the cost to the store, so the store lost money.

24. a. $50 - 11 = 39$

   $\frac{39}{11} \approx 3.55 = 355\%$

   b. 1985

25. See students' work.

10-9 Discount

1. Answers may vary. Sample answer: Subtract to find the amount of change. Use the percent equation to compare the amount of change to the original amount.

2. $3.74 = R \cdot 19.98$

   $\frac{3.74}{19.98} = \frac{R \cdot 19.98}{19.98}$

   $\frac{3.74}{19.98} = R$

3. $P = 0.2 \cdot 49$

   $P = \$9.80$

4. $P = \frac{1}{3} \cdot 300$

   $P = \$100$

5. $P = 0.4 \cdot 8.60$

   $P = \$3.44$

6. $P = 0.15 \cdot 38.50$

   $P = \$5.78$

7. $P = 0.1 \cdot 899$

   $P = \$89.90$

   $899 - 89.90 = \$809.10$

8. $P = 0.05 \cdot 210$

   $P = \$10.50$

   $210 - 10.50 = \$199.50$

9. $P = 0.25 \cdot 37.95$

   $P = \$9.49$

   $37.95 - 9.49 = \$28.46$

10. $P = 0.3 \cdot 40$

    $P = \$12$

    $40 - 12 = \$28$

11. $25 = R \cdot 65$

    $\frac{25}{65} = \frac{R \cdot 65}{65}$

    $0.385 \approx R$

    $38.5\% \approx R$

12. $40 - 35 = 5$

    $5 = R \cdot 40$

    $\frac{5}{40} = \frac{R \cdot 40}{40}$

    $0.125 = R$

    $12.5\% = R$

13. $P = 0.25 \cdot 29.95$

    $P = \$7.49$

    $29.95 - 7.49 = \$22.46$

    Discount: $7.46

    Sale Price: $22.46

14. $P = 0.3 \cdot 3$

    $P = \$0.90$

    $3.00 - 0.90 = \$2.10$

    Discount: $0.90

    Sale Price: $2.10

15. $P = 0.15 \cdot 14.50$

    $P = \$2.18$

    $14.50 - 2.18 = \$12.32$

    Discount: $2.18

    Sale Price: $12.32

16. $P = 0.2 \cdot 13$

    $P = \$2.60$

    $13 - 2.60 = \$10.40$

    Discount: $2.60

    Sale Price: $10.40

17. $P = 0.\overline{3} \cdot 119.50$

    $P = \$39.83$

    $119.50 - 39.83 = \$79.67$

    Discount: $39.83

    Sale Price: $79.67

18. $P = 0.25 \cdot 3.59$

    $P = \$0.90$

    $3.59 - 0.90 = \$2.69$

    Discount: $0.90

    Sale Price: $2.69

19. $22.25 = R \cdot 89$

    $\frac{22.25}{89} = \frac{R \cdot 89}{89}$

    $0.25 = R$

    $25\% = R$

20. $30 = R \cdot 75$

    $\frac{30}{75} = \frac{R \cdot 75}{75}$

    $0.4 = R$

    $40\% = R$

21. $72 - 36 = 36$

    $36 = R \cdot 72$

    $\frac{36}{72} = \frac{R \cdot 72}{72}$

    $0.5 = R$

    $50\% = R$

22. $108 - 72 = 36$

    $36 = R \cdot 108$

    $\frac{36}{108} = \frac{R \cdot 108}{108}$

    $0.\overline{3} = R$

    $33\frac{1}{3}\% = R$

23. $P = 0.15 \cdot 22.75$

    $P = \$3.41$

    Discount: $3.41

24. $P = 0.1 \cdot 169.95$

    $P \approx \$17.00$

    $169.95 - 17 = \$152.95$

    Sale price: $152.95

25. $25 - 20 = 5$

    $5 = R \cdot 25$

    $\frac{5}{25} = \frac{R \cdot 25}{25}$

    $0.2 = R$

    $20\% = R$

26. $100 - 30 = 70$

    $\frac{25.95}{B} = \frac{70}{100}$

    $25.95 \cdot 100 = 70B$

    $2,595 = 70B$

    $\frac{2,595}{70} = \frac{70B}{70}$

    $\$37.07 = B$

27. $n - 12 = 8$

    $n - 12 + 12 = 8 + 12$

    $n = 20$

28. $\left(-3\frac{5}{8}\right)\left(-5\frac{1}{4}\right) = S$

    $\left(-\frac{29}{8}\right)\left(-\frac{21}{4}\right) = S$

    $\frac{609}{32} = S$

    $19\frac{1}{32} = S$

29. $\tan 40° = \frac{6}{x}$

    $(\tan 40°)(x) = 6$

    $\frac{(\tan 40°)(x)}{\tan 40°} = \frac{6}{\tan 40°}$

    $x = \frac{6}{\tan 40°}$

    $x \approx 7.2$

30. $1.19 - 1.15 = 0.04$

    $0.04 = R \cdot 1.15$

    $\frac{0.04}{1.15} = \frac{R \cdot 1.15}{1.15}$

    $0.035 \approx R$

    $3.5\% \approx R$

31. a. $P = 0.6 \cdot 7.60$
$P = \$4.56$

b. $P = 0.3 \cdot 4.2$
$P = \$1.26$
$4.20 - 1.26 = \$2.94$
The call costs $2.94.

c. $26.75 - 10.70 = 16.05$
$16.05 = R \cdot 26.75$
$\dfrac{16.05}{26.75} = \dfrac{R \cdot 26.75}{26.75}$
$0.6 = R$
$60\% = R$

32. The first sale is a 25% off sale, so the jewelry will sell for 75% of its original cost. Then, 10% off an item selling for 75% of its original cost is $(0.10)(0.75) = 0.075$ or an additional 7.5% off. So 25% + 7.5% is a total of 32.5% off on Saturday.

33. a. $100 - 25 = 75$
$\dfrac{51}{B} = \dfrac{75}{100}$
$51 \cdot 100 = 75B$
$5,100 = 75B$
$\dfrac{5,100}{75} = \dfrac{75B}{75}$
$\$68 = B$

b. $68 - 51 = 17$
$17 = R \cdot 51$
$\dfrac{17}{51} = \dfrac{R \cdot 51}{51}$
$0.\overline{3} = R$
$33\frac{1}{3}\% = R$

34. In cell E3: $C3/B3 * 100 = 90.00/450.00 * 100$
$= \dfrac{90}{450} \cdot 100$
$= \dfrac{9000}{450}$
$= 20$

In cell E4: $C4/B4 * 100 = 54.53/389.50 * 100$
$= \dfrac{54.53}{389.50} \cdot 100$
$= \dfrac{5453}{389.50}$
$= 14$

10-10　Simple Interest

PAGES 413-414　CHECKING FOR UNDERSTANDING

1. $\dfrac{9}{12} = \dfrac{3}{4}$ year

2. Principal on a loan is the amount of money borrowed. Principal on a savings account is the amount of money in the account.

3. Answers may vary. Sample answer: to avoid paying interest and to have a good credit rating

4. $I = prt$
$I = (345)(0.0625)\left(\dfrac{6}{12}\right)$
$I = (21.5625)(0.5)$
$I = 10.78125$
$I = \$10.78$

5. $I = prt$
$I = (400)(0.15)\left(\dfrac{18}{12}\right)$
$I = (60)(1.5)$
$I = \$90$

6. $I = prt$
$I = (1,088)(0.18)(1)$
$I = \$195.84$

7. $I = prt$
$I = (62.25)(0.055)\left(\dfrac{9}{12}\right)$
$I = (3.42375)(0.75)$
$I = 2.5678125$
$I = \$2.57$

8. $I = prt$
$I = (615)(0.07)\left(\dfrac{8}{12}\right)$
$I = (43.05)(0.\overline{6})$
$I = \$28.70$
Total in account is 615 + 28.70 or $643.70.

9. $I = prt$
$I = (120)(0.1275)(1.5)$
$I = \$22.95$
Total in account is 120 + 22.95 or $142.95.

10. $I = prt$
$I = (118)(0.055)\left(\dfrac{19}{12}\right)$
$I = (6.49)(1.58\overline{3})$
$I = 10.2758\overline{3}$
$I = \$10.28$
Total in account is 118 + 10.28 or $128.28.

11. $I = prt$
$I = (217.75)(0.06)\left(\dfrac{36}{12}\right)$
$I = (13.065)(3)$
$I = 39.195$
$I = \$39.20$
Total in account is 217.75 + 39.20 or $256.95.

12. $I = prt$
$31.50 = (700)(r)\left(\dfrac{9}{12}\right)$
$31.50 = (700)(r)(0.75)$
$31.50 = 525r$
$\dfrac{31.50}{525} = \dfrac{525r}{525}$
$0.06 = r$
Rate is 6%.

13. $I = prt$
$142.80 = (560)(r)(2)$
$142.80 = 1120r$
$\dfrac{142.80}{1120} = \dfrac{1120r}{1120}$
$0.1275 = r$
Rate is 12.75% or $12\frac{3}{4}\%$.

PAGES 414-415　EXERCISES

14. $I = prt$
$I = (205)(0.0625)\left(\dfrac{9}{12}\right)$
$I = (12.8125)(0.75)$
$I = 9.609375$
$I = \$9.61$

15. $I = prt$
$I = (500)(0.12)\left(\dfrac{15}{12}\right)$
$I = (60)(1.25)$
$I = \$75$

16. $I = prt$
$I = (78.75)(0.065)\left(\dfrac{8}{12}\right)$
$I = (5.11875)(0.\overline{6})$
$I = 3.4125$
$I = \$3.41$

17. $I = prt$
$I = (2,108)(0.16)(2)$
$I = \$674.56$

18. $I = prt$

$I = (100)(0.05)\left(\dfrac{18}{12}\right)$

$I = (5)(1.5)$

$I = 7.5$

$I = \$7.50$

19. $I = prt$

$I = (4{,}000)(0.135)\left(\dfrac{21}{12}\right)$

$I = (540)(1.75)$

$I = \$945$

20. $I = prt$

$I = (708)(0.08)\left(\dfrac{6}{12}\right)$

$I = (56.64)(0.5)$

$I = \$28.32$

Total in account is
708 + 28.32 or \$736.32.

21. $I = prt$

$I = (200)(0.0675)\left(\dfrac{9}{12}\right)$

$I = (13.5)(0.75)$

$I = 10.125$

$I = \$10.13$

Total in account is
200 + 10.13 or
\$210.13.

22. $I = prt$

$I = (235)(0.0525)\left(\dfrac{14}{12}\right)$

$I = (12.3375)(1.1\overline{6})$

$I = 14.39375$

$I = \$14.39$

Total in account is
235 + 14.39 or
\$249.39.

23. $I = prt$

$I = (176.77)(0.06)(6)$

$I = 63.6372$

$I = \$63.64$

Total in account is
176.77 + 63.64 or
\$240.41.

24. $I = prt$

$I = (1{,}860)(0.075)(5)$

$I = 697.5$

$I = \$697.50$

Total in account is
1,860 + 697.50 or
\$2,557.50

25. $I = prt$

$I = (10{,}000)(0.13)\left(\dfrac{6}{12}\right)$

$I = (1300)(0.5)$

$I = 650$

$I = \$650$

Total in the account
is 10,000 + 650 or
\$10,650.

26. $5{,}920 - 4{,}000 = 1{,}920$

$I = prt$

$1{,}920 = (4{,}000)(r)(3)$

$1{,}920 = 12{,}000r$

$\dfrac{1{,}920}{12{,}000} = \dfrac{12{,}000r}{12{,}000}$

$0.16 = r$

Annual rate is 16%.

27. $3{,}632 - 3{,}200 = 432$

$I = prt$

$32 = (3{,}200)(r)\left(\dfrac{18}{12}\right)$

$432 = (3{,}200)(r)(1.5)$

$432 = 4{,}800r$

$\dfrac{432}{4{,}800} = \dfrac{4{,}800r}{4{,}800}$

$0.09 = r$

Annual rate is 9%.

28. $(\$257.25)(5)(12) = \$15{,}435.00$

$15{,}435 - 9{,}800 = 5{,}635$

$I = prt$

$5{,}635 = (9{,}800)(r)(5)$

$5{,}635 = 49{,}000r$

$\dfrac{5{,}635}{49{,}000} = \dfrac{49{,}000r}{49{,}000}$

$0.115 = r$

Annual rate was 11.5%.

29. $4 + 8 = 12$ and $4 \times 3 = 12$

The number of people who watch 0–5 hours is
three times the number of people who watch
15–17 hours.

30. $6p = \dfrac{5}{9}$

$\dfrac{1}{6} \cdot 6p = \dfrac{1}{6} \cdot \dfrac{5}{9}$

$p = \dfrac{5}{54}$

31. $\dfrac{1 \text{ inch}}{20 \text{ miles}} = \dfrac{2\frac{3}{4} \text{ inches}}{x \text{ miles}}$

$x = (20)\left(2\dfrac{3}{4}\right)$

$x = (20)\left(\dfrac{11}{4}\right)$

$x = \dfrac{220}{4}$

$x = 55$

The actual distance
is 55 miles.

32. $P = R \cdot B$

$P = 0.30 \cdot 89$

$P = \$26.70$

$89 - 26.70 = \$62.30$

Discount: \$26.70

Sale price: \$62.30

33. $I = prt$

$27.93 = (p)(0.0525)\left(\dfrac{6}{12}\right)$

$27.93 = (p)(0.0525)(0.5)$

$27.93 = 0.02625p$

$\dfrac{27.93}{0.02625} = \dfrac{0.02625p}{0.02625}$

$1{,}064 = p$

\$1,064 was in his account.

34. $\dfrac{16\%}{12} = 1\frac{1}{3}\%$ per month, or $1.5\% \cdot 12 = 18\%$
annually. The credit union has the better
loan.

35. $50 \cdot 2 = 100$

$100 - 50 = 50$

$I = prt$

$50 = (50)(r)(8)$

$50 = 400r$

$\dfrac{50}{400} = \dfrac{400r}{400}$

$0.125 = r$

Annual rate is 12.5%.

36. $191 - 100 = 91$

$I = prt$

$91 = (100)(0.07)(t)$

$91 = 7t$

$\dfrac{91}{7} = \dfrac{7t}{7}$

$13 = t$

Tim opened his
account 13 years ago.

37. a. in order to change the percent to a decimal

b. $A6 = 2000$

$B6 = 5.5/100 = 0.055$

$C6 = 3$

$D6 = (2000)(0.055)(3) = 330$

$E6 = 2000 + 330 = \$2330$

c. $A10 = 4000$

$B10 = B2/100$

$C10 = C2$

$D10 = A10 * B10 * C10$

$E10 = A10 + D10$

d. Change cell $A3$ to 900. Enter 6 in cell $B2$.

Enter $\dfrac{15}{12}$ or 1.25 in cell $C2$.

Chapter 10 Study Guide and Review

1. false; 100
2. false; 25%
3. true
4. true
5. false; balance
6. true
7. true
8. Answers may vary. Sample answer: Solve the percent proportion $\frac{P}{B} = \frac{r}{100}$.
9. $160\% = \frac{160}{100} = 1\frac{60}{100} = 1\frac{3}{5}$
10. $I = prt$

    $I = (400)(0.055)(1)$

    $I = \$22$

    Simple interest is $22.

11. $\frac{P}{400} = \frac{28}{100}$

    $100P = 28 \cdot 400$

    $100P = 11{,}200$

    $\frac{100P}{100} = \frac{11{,}200}{100}$

    $P = 112$

    112 is 28% of 400.

12. $\frac{54}{180} = \frac{r}{100}$

    $54 \cdot 100 = 180r$

    $5{,}400 = 180r$

    $\frac{5{,}400}{180} = \frac{180r}{180}$

    $300 = r$

    54 is 30% of 180.

13. $\frac{61.5}{B} = \frac{75}{100}$

    $61.5 \cdot 100 = 75B$

    $6{,}150 = 75B$

    $\frac{6{,}150}{75} = \frac{75B}{75}$

    $82 = B$

    So 61.5 is 75% of 82.

14. $\frac{220}{800} = \frac{r}{100}$

    $220 \cdot 100 = 800r$

    $22{,}000 = 800r$

    $\frac{22{,}000}{800} = \frac{800r}{800}$

    $27.5 = r$

    So 220 is 27.5% of 800.

15. $\frac{P}{128} = \frac{62.5}{100}$

    $100P = 62.5 \cdot 128$

    $100P = 8{,}000$

    $\frac{100P}{100} = \frac{8{,}000}{100}$

    $P = 80$

    So 80 is 62.5% of 128.

16. $65\% = \frac{65}{100}$

    $= \frac{13}{20}$

17. $8\% = \frac{8}{100}$

    $= \frac{2}{25}$

18. $30\% = \frac{30}{100}$

    $= \frac{3}{10}$

19. $17.5\% = \frac{17.5}{100}$

    $= \frac{175}{1000}$

    $= \frac{7}{40}$

20. $145\% = \frac{145}{100}$

    $= 1\frac{45}{100}$

    $= 1\frac{9}{20}$

21. $\frac{4}{5}\% = \frac{\frac{4}{5}}{100}$

    $= \frac{4}{5} \div 100$

    $= \frac{4}{5} \cdot \frac{1}{100}$

    $= \frac{4}{500} = \frac{1}{125}$

22. $428\% = \frac{428}{100}$

    $= 4\frac{28}{100}$

    $= 4\frac{7}{25}$

23. $\frac{3}{7}\% = \frac{\frac{3}{7}}{100}$

    $= \frac{3}{7} \div 100$

    $= \frac{3}{7} \cdot \frac{1}{100}$

    $= \frac{3}{700}$

24. Round 8% to $8\frac{1}{3}\%$ and round 64 to 60. $8\frac{1}{3}\% = \frac{1}{12}$ and $\frac{1}{12}$ of 60 is 5. So 8% of 64 is about 5.

25. Round 66% to $66\frac{2}{3}\%$. Round 31 to 30. $66\frac{2}{3}\% = \frac{2}{3}$ and $\frac{2}{3}$ of 30 is 20. So 66% of 31 is about 20.

26. Round 59% to 60%. $60\% = \frac{3}{5}$ and $\frac{3}{5}$ of 80 is 48. So 59% of 80 is about 48.

27. Round 26% to 25% or $\frac{1}{4}$. Round 37 to 36. Then $\frac{1}{4}$ of 36 is 9. So 26% of 37 is about 9.

28. Round 98% to 100%. Then 100% of 20 is 20. So 98% of 20 is about 20.

29. Round 49% to 50% or $\frac{1}{2}$. Then $\frac{1}{2}$ of 56 is 28. So 49% of 56 is about 28.

30. $P = R \cdot B$

    $P = 0.36 \cdot 75$

    $P = 27$

31. $P = R \cdot B$

    $15 = R \cdot 80$

    $\frac{15}{80} = \frac{R \cdot 80}{80}$

    $0.1875 = R$

    $18.75\% = R$ or

    $18\frac{3}{4}\% = R$

32. $P = R \cdot B$

    $P = 0.30 \cdot 128.50$

    $P = 38.55$

    $P = \$38.55$

33. $P = R \cdot B$

    $42 = 0.28 \cdot B$

    $\frac{42}{0.28} = \frac{0.28 \cdot B}{0.28}$

    $150 = B$

34. See students' work.

35. $36 - 30 = 6$

    $\frac{6}{30} = \frac{r}{100}$

    $6 \cdot 100 = 30r$

    $600 = 30r$

    $\frac{600}{30} = \frac{30r}{30}$

    $20 = r$

    The percent of increase is 20%.

36. $250 - 210 = 40$

    $\frac{40}{250} = \frac{r}{100}$

    $40 \cdot 100 = 250r$

    $4{,}000 = 250r$

    $\frac{4{,}000}{250} = \frac{250r}{250}$

    $16 = r$

    The percent of decrease is 16%.

37. $60 - 48 = 12$

    $\frac{12}{48} = \frac{r}{100}$

    $12 \cdot 100 = 48\,r$

    $1{,}200 = 48r$

    $\frac{1{,}200}{48} = \frac{48r}{48}$

    $25 = r$

    The percent of increase is 25%.

38. $P = 0.20 \cdot 54.95$

    $P = \$10.99$

    $54.95 - 10.99 = \$43.96$

    Discount: $10.99

    Sale Price: $43.96

127

39. $P = 0.15 \cdot 60$
$P = \$9$
$60 - 9 = \$51$
Discount: \$9
Sale Price: \$51

40. $P = 0.30 \cdot 120$
$P = \$36$
$120 - 36 = \$84$
Discount: \$36
Sale Price: \$84

41. $P = 0.25 \cdot 84$
$P = \$21$
$84 - 21 = \$63$
Discount: \$21
Sale Price: \$63

42. $I = prt$
$I = (820)(0.075)(1)$
$I = \$61.50$

43. $I = prt$
$I = (1,728)(0.0575)\left(\frac{9}{12}\right)$
$I = (99.36)(0.75)$
$I = \$74.52$

44. $I = prt$
$I = (96)(0.06)\left(\frac{15}{12}\right)$
$I = (5.76)(1.25)$
$I = \$7.20$

45. $I = prt$
$I = (240)(0.0625)\left(\frac{18}{12}\right)$
$I = (15)(1.5)$
$I = \$22.50$

PAGE 418   APPLICATIONS AND PROBLEM SOLVING

46. $P = R \cdot B$
$P = 0.15 \cdot 2,000$
$P = 300$
Randy needed a
\$300 deposit.

47. $P = R \cdot B$
$P = 0.20 \cdot 149.95$
$P = \$29.99$
Emilio will save
\$29.99.

48. $55\% = \frac{55}{100}$
$= \frac{11}{20}$
$\frac{11}{20}$ of Mrs. Kackley's
class are boys.

49. $5.5 - 5.0 = 0.5$
$\frac{0.5}{5.0} = \frac{r}{100}$
$0.5 \cdot 100 = 5r$
$50 = 5r$
$\frac{50}{5} = \frac{5r}{5}$
$10 = r$
There was a 10%
increase.

Chapter 10 Test

PAGE 419

1. $P = R \cdot B$
$17 = 0.\overline{3} \cdot B$
$\frac{17}{0.\overline{3}} = \frac{0.\overline{3} \cdot B}{0.\overline{3}}$
$51 = B$

2. $P = R \cdot B$
$P = 0.0075 \cdot 2,400$
$P = 18$

3. $P = R \cdot B$
$58 = 0.8 \cdot B$
$\frac{58}{0.8} = \frac{0.8 \cdot B}{0.8}$
$72.5 = B$

4. $\frac{P}{B} = \frac{r}{100}$
$\frac{18}{45} = \frac{r}{100}$
$8 \cdot 100 = 45r$
$1,800 = 45r$
$\frac{1,800}{45} = \frac{45r}{45}$
$40 = r$
18 is 40% of 45.

5. $\frac{42}{28} = \frac{r}{100}$
$42 \cdot 100 = 28r$
$4,200 = 28r$
$\frac{4,200}{28} = \frac{28r}{28}$
$150 = r$
42 is 150% of 28.

6. $\frac{8}{5} = \frac{r}{100}$
$8 \cdot 100 = 5r$
$800 = 5r$
$\frac{800}{5} = \frac{5r}{5}$
$160 = r$
$\frac{8}{5}$ is 160%.

7. $12.8\% = \frac{12.8}{100}$
$= \frac{128}{1000}$
$= 0.128$

$12.8\% = \frac{12.8}{100}$
$= \frac{128}{1000}$
$= \frac{16}{125}$

8. $285\% = \frac{285}{100}$
$= 2.85$

$285\% = \frac{285}{100}$
$= 2\frac{85}{100}$
$= 2\frac{17}{20}$

9. $35\% = \frac{35}{100}$
$= 0.35$

$35\% = \frac{35}{100}$
$= \frac{7}{20}$

10. $\frac{1}{4}\% = \frac{\frac{1}{4}}{100}$
$= \frac{0.25}{100}$
$= \frac{25}{10000}$
$= 0.0025$

$\frac{1}{4}\% = \frac{\frac{1}{4}}{100}$
$= \frac{1}{4} \div 100$
$= \frac{1}{4} \cdot \frac{1}{100}$
$= \frac{1}{400}$

11. $6 + 4 + 10 = 20$
$\frac{4}{20} = \frac{1}{5} = 20\%$

12. Red: $\frac{6}{20} = 0.3 = 30\%$; $0.3 \times 360 = 108°$
Blue: $\frac{4}{20} = 0.2 = 20\%$; $0.2 \times 360 = 72°$
Green: $\frac{10}{20} = 0.5 = 50\%$; $0.5 \times 360 = 180°$

13. $84 - 70 = 14$
$\frac{14}{70} = \frac{r}{100}$
$14 \cdot 100 = 70r$
$1,400 = 70r$
$\frac{1,400}{70} = \frac{70r}{70}$
$20 = r$
It was a 20% increase.

14. $P = 0.15 \cdot 28$
$P = \$4.20$
$28 - 4.20 = \$23.80$
Discount: \$4.20
Sale Price: \$23.80

15. $P = 0.2 \cdot 299$

    $P = \$59.80$

    $299 - 59.80 = \$239.20$

    Discount: $59.80

    Sale Price: $239.20

16. $P = 0.25 \cdot 16$

    $P = \$4$

    $16 - 4 = \$12$

    Discount: $4

    Sale Price: $12

17. $P = 0.1 \cdot 59.90$

    $P = \$5.99$

    $59.90 - 5.99 = \$53.91$

    Discount: $5.99

    Sale Price: $53.91

18. $60 - 42 = 18$

    $\dfrac{18}{60} = \dfrac{r}{100}$

    $1{,}800 = 60r$

    $\dfrac{1{,}800}{60} = \dfrac{60r}{60}$

    $30 = r$

    The discount rate
    is 30%.

19. a; Round $\frac{7}{16}$% to $\frac{8}{16}$% or $\frac{1}{2}$%. Round 595 to 600.

    Then 1% of 600 is 6 and $\frac{1}{2}$ of 6 is 3.

    So 3 is the best estimate.

20. b; Round 24% to 25% or $\frac{1}{4}$. Then $\frac{1}{4}$ of 60 is 15.

    So 15 is the best estimate.

21. b; Round 12.3% to 12.5% or $\frac{1}{8}$. Round 74 to 72.

    Then $\frac{1}{8}$ of 72 is 9. So 9 is the best estimate

22. c; Round 204% to 200%. Round 1,309 to 1,300.

    Then 100% of 1,300 is 1,300 and $2 \cdot 1{,}300 =$
    2,600. So the best estimate is 2,600.

23. $I = prt$

    $540 = (3{,}000)(r)\left(\dfrac{18}{12}\right)$

    $540 = (3{,}000)(r)(1.5)$

    $540 = 4{,}500r$

    $\dfrac{540}{4{,}500} = \dfrac{4{,}500r}{4{,}500}$

    $0.12 = r$

    The interest rate
    is 12%.

24. $I = prt$

    $I = (600)(0.055)\left(\dfrac{9}{12}\right)$

    $I = (33)(0.75)$

    $I = \$24.75$

    $600 + 24.75 = \$624.75$

    Total in account is
    $624.75.

25. $357 - 265 = 92$

    Since you include both lockers 357 and 265,
    there are $92 + 1$ or 93 lockers in the hall.

PAGE 419   BONUS

$100\% = \dfrac{100}{100}$

$ = \dfrac{1}{1}$

$ = 1$

Chapter 11　Algebra: Functions and Graphs

11-1　Functions

PAGE 423　CHECKING FOR UNDERSTANDING

1. domain　　　　　　　　　　2. range

3. See students' work.

4. Substitute 6 for n in the equation. So
$f(6) = 2(6)^2 - 18 = 72 - 18 = 54.$

5. $f(n) = -5n$

n	$-5n$	$f(n)$
-4	-5(-4)	20
-2	-5(-2)	10
0	-5(0)	0
2.5	-5(2.5)	-12.5

6. $f(n) = 2n + (-6)$

n	$2n + (-6)$	$f(n)$
-2	2(-2) + (-6)	-10
-1	2(-1) + (-6)	-8
0	2(0) + (-6)	-6
$\frac{1}{2}$	$2\left(\frac{1}{2}\right) + (-6)$	-5

7. $f(n) = -2n - 4$
$f(-3) = -2(-3) - 4$
$= 6 - 4$
$= 2$

8. $f(n) = 15 - 3n$
$f\left(\frac{1}{3}\right) = 15 - 3\left(\frac{1}{3}\right)$
$= 15 - 1$
$= 14$

9. 　$f(n) = 100n$
$f(0.25) = 100(0.25)$
$= 25$

PAGE 424　EXERCISES

10. $f(n) = n + 5$

n	$n + 5$	$f(n)$
-2	-2 + 5	3
-1	-1 + 5	4
0	0 + 5	5
1	1 + 5	6
2	2 + 5	7

11. $f(n) = 3n$

n	$3n$	$f(n)$
-1	3(-1)	-3
0	3(0)	0
$\frac{2}{3}$	$3\left(\frac{2}{3}\right)$	2
1	3(1)	3

12. $f(n) = 2n + 3$

n	$2n + 3$	$f(n)$
-2.5	2(-2.5) + 3	-2
-1.5	2(-1.5) + 3	0
0.5	2(0.5) + 3	4
1	2(1) + 3	5
2	2(2) + 3	7

13. $f(n) = -0.5n + 1$

n	$-0.5n + 1$	$f(n)$
-4	-0.5(-4) + 1	3
-2	-0.5(-2) + 1	2
0	-0.5(0) + 1	1
2.5	-0.5(2.5) + 1	-0.25
8	-0.5(8) + 1	-3

14. $f(n) = 3n + 24$
$f(-8) = 3(-8) + 24$
$= -24 + 24$
$= 0$

15. $f(n) = -5n - 4$
$f\left(\frac{4}{5}\right) = -5\left(\frac{4}{5}\right) - 4$
$= -4 - 4$
$= -8$

16. $f(n) = n^2 + 1$
$f(1.5) = (1.5)^2 + 1$
$= 2.25 + 1$
$= 3.25$

17. 　$f(n) = 2n^2 - 5$
$f(-3.4) = 2(-3.4)^2 - 5$
$= 23.12 - 5$
$= 18.12$

18. Answers may vary. Sample answer:

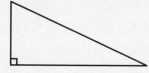

19. 　$c = 2a$
$12 = 2a$
$\frac{12}{2} = \frac{2a}{2}$
$6 = a$

The length of the side
opposite the 30°-angle
is 6 cm.

20. 292 · 12 = 3,504
3,504 - 3,200 = $304
Mrs. Sanchez paid
$304 in interest.

21. Look at each pair of numbers

-3 and 2 $\Longrightarrow$ -3 + 5 = 2, $-3\left(-\frac{2}{3}\right) = 2$

-1 and 4 $\Longrightarrow$ -1 + 5 = 4, -1(-4) = 4

1 and 6 $\Longrightarrow$ 1 + 5 = 6

3 and 8 $\Longrightarrow$ 3 + 5 = 8

So the function can be written as $f(n) = n + 5$.

22. DN = AN * BN - CN

D1 = A1 * B1 - C1	D2 = A2 * B2 - C2
= (40)(4.30) - 5	= (32)(5.75) - 4
= 172 - 5	= 184 - 4
= $167	= $180

D3 = A3 * B3 - C3	D4 = A4 * B4 - C4
= (30)(6.00) - 6	= (27)(4.80) - 3
= 180 - 6	= 129.60 - 3
= $174	= $126.60

11-2 Graphing Functions

PAGE 426   CHECKING FOR UNDERSTANDING

1. Use the n values for x and the $f(n)$ values for y and graph the coordinates (x, y).

2. $f(0)$ is the height when the river crested.

3. $4n = 84$

   $\dfrac{4n}{4} = \dfrac{84}{4}$

   $n = 21$

   It will take 21 hours for the river to recede. More rain will affect this.

4. Input numbers are on the x-axis and output numbers are on the y-axis.

5. $f(n) = n + 4$

n	$n + 4$	$f(n)$	$(n, f(n))$
-1	-1 + 4	3	(-1, 3)
1	1 + 4	5	(1, 5)
2	2 + 4	6	(2, 6)
4	4 + 4	8	(4, 8)
5	5 + 4	9	(5, 9)

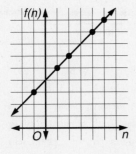

6. $f(n) = \dfrac{8}{n}$

n	$\dfrac{8}{n}$	$f(n)$	$(n, f(n))$
$\dfrac{1}{2}$	$\dfrac{8}{1/2}$	16	$\left(\dfrac{1}{2}, 16\right)$
2	$\dfrac{8}{2}$	4	(2, 4)
4	$\dfrac{8}{4}$	2	(4, 2)
8	$\dfrac{8}{8}$	1	(8, 1)
16	$\dfrac{8}{16}$	$\dfrac{1}{2}$	$\left(16, \dfrac{1}{2}\right)$

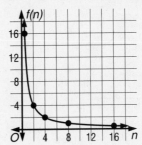

PAGE 427   EXERCISES

7. $f(n) = 3n + 1$

n	$3n + 1$	$f(n)$	$(n, f(n))$
0	3(0) + 1	1	(0, 1)
1	3(1) + 1	4	(1, 4)
2	3(2) + 1	7	(2, 7)
3	3(3) + 1	10	(3, 10)

8. $f(n) = 6n$

n	$6n$	$f(n)$	$(n, f(n))$
-1	6(-1)	-6	(-1, -6)
1	6(1)	6	(1, 6)
2.5	6(2.5)	15	(2.5, 15)
3.5	6(3.5)	21	(3.5, 21)
4	6(4)	24	(4, 24)

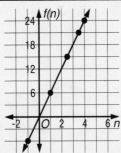

9. $f(n) = \dfrac{16}{n}$

n	$\dfrac{16}{n}$	$f(n)$	$(n,\ f(n))$
8	$\dfrac{16}{8}$	2	$(8,\ 2)$
2	$\dfrac{16}{2}$	8	$(2,\ 8)$
4	$\dfrac{16}{4}$	4	$(4,\ 4)$
$\dfrac{8}{3}$	$\dfrac{16}{8/3}$	6	$\left(\dfrac{8}{3},\ 6\right)$

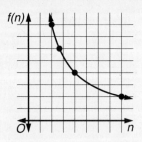

10. $f(n) = 0.25n + 3$

n	$0.25n + 3$	$f(n)$	$(n,\ f(n))$
-2	$0.25(-2) + 3$	2.5	$(-2,\ 2.5)$
-1	$0.25(-1) + 3$	2.75	$(-1,\ 2.75)$
0	$0.25(0) + 3$	3	$(0,\ 3)$
1	$0.25(1) + 3$	3.25	$(1,\ 3.25)$
2	$0.25(2) + 3$	3.5	$(2,\ 3.5)$

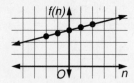

11. $f(n) = n^2 + (-2)$

n	$n^2 + (-2)$	$f(n)$	$(n,\ (f)n))$
-3	$(-3)^2 + (-2)$	7	$(-3,\ 7)$
-2	$(-2)^2 + (-2)$	2	$(-2,\ 2)$
0	$(0)^2 + (-2)$	-2	$(0,\ -2)$
2	$(2)^2 + (-2)$	2	$(2,\ 2)$
3	$(3)^2 + (-2)$	7	$(3,\ 7)$

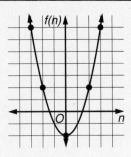

12. $C = 2\pi r$

$C = 2\pi(2.7)$

$C \approx 16.96$ mm

13. $f(n) = 8n - 1$

$f\left(-\dfrac{3}{4}\right) = 8\left(-\dfrac{3}{4}\right) - 1$

$\qquad\qquad = -6 - 1$

$\qquad\qquad = -7$

14. $f(n) = |n + 2|$

n	$|n + 2|$	$f(n)$	$(n,\ f(n))$
-4	$|-4 + 2|$	2	$(-4,\ 2)$
-3	$|-3 + 2|$	1	$(-3,\ 1)$
-2	$|-2 + 2|$	0	$(-2,\ 0)$
0	$|0 + 2|$	2	$(0,\ 2)$
1	$|1 + 2|$	3	$(1,\ 3)$

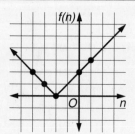

The shape of the graph is a "v". The range is $y \geq 0$.

15. a. $f(n) = 8n + 20$

n	$8n + 20$	$f(n)$	$(n,\ f(n))$
-3	$8(-3) + 20$	-4	$(-3,\ -4)$
-2	$8(-2) + 20$	4	$(-2,\ 4)$
-1	$8(-1) + 20$	12	$(-1,\ 12)$
0	$8(0) + 20$	20	$(0,\ 20)$
1	$8(1) + 20$	28	$(1,\ 28)$

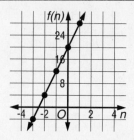

b. No, once the water reaches the boiling point, its temperature does not increase. This does not affect the domain because it represents minutes or time, but once the water boils, the function does not represent the temperature of the water.

16. a. Since you round each weight up, there are four choices for the cost of a package, namely 29¢, 52¢, 75¢, and 98¢. Rounding weights up to the nearest whole ounce, the values for *n* become:

0.1 → 1.0   1.1 → 2.0   2.1 → 3.0   3.1 → 4.0
0.3 → 1.0   1.5 → 2.0   2.4 → 3.0   3.2 → 4.0
0.6 → 1.0   1.9 → 2.0   2.8 → 3.0   3.7 → 4.0
1.0 → 1.0   2.0 → 2.0   3.0 → 3.0   4.0 → 4.0

n oz	$f(n)$ cents
0.1	29
0.3	29
0.6	29
1.0	29

n oz	$f(n)$ cents
1.1	52
1.5	52
1.9	52
2.0	52

n oz	$f(n)$ cents
2.1	75
2.4	75
2.8	75
3.0	75

n oz	$f(n)$ cents
3.1	98
3.2	98
3.7	98
4.0	98

b.

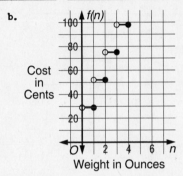

Each part of the graph looks like a step.

c. The graph looks like stair steps.

17. See students' work. Answers should include statements such as the line or curve contains *all* solutions to the function.

11-3   Equations With Two Variables

PAGE 429 CHECKING FOR UNDERSTANDING

1. (x, y) is the solution to an equation with two variables. This is also an ordered pair of a function.

2. $3x - 6 = y$. Test $(-2, -12)$, $(0, -6)$, $(1, -3)$, and $(5, 9)$.

$3(-2) - 6 \overset{?}{=} -12$ $3(0) - 6 \overset{?}{=} -6$
   $-6 - 6 \overset{?}{=} -12$ $0 - 6 \overset{?}{=} -6$
       $-12 = -12$ ✓ $-6 = -6$ ✓

$3(1) - 6 \overset{?}{=} -3$ $3(5) - 6 \overset{?}{=} 9$
   $3 - 6 \overset{?}{=} -3$ $15 - 6 \overset{?}{=} 9$
     $-3 = -3$ ✓ $9 = 9$ ✓

3. $y = -2x + 3$

$-1 \overset{?}{=} -2(-2) + 3$ $2 \overset{?}{=} -2\left(\frac{1}{2}\right) + 3$
$-1 \overset{?}{=} 4 + 3$ $2 \overset{?}{=} -1 + 3$
$-1 \ne 7$ $2 = 2$ ✓
no solution   solution

$1 \overset{?}{=} -2(0) + 3$ $-3 \overset{?}{=} -2(3) + 3$
$1 \overset{?}{=} 0 + 3$ $-3 \overset{?}{=} -6 + 3$
$1 \ne 3$ $-3 = -3$ ✓
no solution   solution

$\left(\frac{1}{2}, 2\right)$ and $(3, -3)$ are solutions.

4. $y = x + 1$

$y = (-3) + 1$ $y = -1 + 1$ $y = 1 + 1$
  $= -2$ $= 0$ $= 2$
$(-3, -2)$ $(-1, 0)$ $(1, 2)$

$y = 2 + 1$
  $= 3$
$(2, 3)$

x	y
-3	-2
-1	0
1	2
2	3

5. $y = -0.5x$

$y = -0.5(-4)$ $y = -0.5(2)$ $y = -0.5(0)$
  $= 2$ $= -1$ $= 0$
$(-4, 2)$ $(2, -1)$ $(0, 0)$

$y = -0.5(6)$
  $= -3$
$(6, -3)$

x	y
-4	2
2	-1
0	0
6	-3

6. $y = 5x - 2$

$y = 5\left(-\frac{4}{5}\right) - 2$ $y = 5(2) - 2$ $y = 5\left(\frac{7}{15}\right) - 2$
  $= -4 - 2$ $= 10 - 2$ $= \frac{7}{3} - \frac{6}{3}$
  $= -6$ $= 8$ $= \frac{1}{3}$
$\left(-\frac{4}{5}, -6\right)$ $(2, 8)$ $\left(\frac{7}{15}, \frac{1}{3}\right)$

x	y
$-\frac{4}{5}$	-6
2	8
$\frac{7}{15}$	$\frac{1}{3}$

7. Answers may vary. Sample answers: Select four values for x, say 0, -1, 5, -4.

$y = x + 3$

x	$x + 3$	y	(x, y)
0	0 + 3	3	(0, 3)
-1	-1 + 3	2	(-1, 2)
5	5 + 3	8	(5, 8)
-4	-4 + 3	-1	(-4, -1)

Four solutions are (0, 3), (-1, 2), (5, 8) and (-4, -1).

8. $y = 0.2x + 7$

$y = 0.2(-5) + 7$ $y = 0.2(0) + 7$ $y = 0.2(5) + 7$

$= -1 + 7$ $= 0 + 7$ $= 1 + 7$

$= 6$ $= 7$ $= 8$

$y = 0.2(10) + 7$

$= 2 + 7$

$= 9$

x	y
-5	6
0	7
5	8
10	9

9. $y = \dfrac{x}{3} + 4$

$y = \dfrac{-3}{3} + 4$ $y = \dfrac{3}{3} + 4$ $y = \dfrac{6}{3} + 4$

$= -1 + 4$ $= 1 + 4$ $= 2 + 4$

$= 3$ $= 5$ $= 6$

$y = \dfrac{8}{3} + 4$

$= \dfrac{8}{3} + \dfrac{12}{3}$

$= \dfrac{20}{3}$

$= 6\dfrac{2}{3}$

x	y
-3	3
3	5
6	6
8	$6\dfrac{2}{3}$

10. $y = -5x - 1$

$y = -5(-2) - 1$ $y = -5(-1) - 1$ $y = -5(0) - 1$

$= 10 - 1$ $= 5 - 1$ $= 0 - 1$

$= 9$ $= 4$ $= -1$

$y = -5(2) - 1$ $y = -5(4) - 1$

$= -10 - 1$ $= -20 - 1$

$= -11$ $= -21$

x	y
-2	9
-1	4
0	-1
2	-11
4	-21

11. Answers may vary. Sample answers:

$y = 2x + 1$

x	$2x + 1$	y	(x, y)
0	$2(0) + 1$	1	$(0, 1)$
2	$2(2) + 1$	5	$(2, 5)$
-3	$2(-3) + 1$	-5	$(-3, -5)$
-1	$2(-1) + 1$	-1	$(-1, -1)$

Four solutions are $(0, 1)$, $(2, 5)$, $(-3, -5)$, and $(-1, -1)$.

12. Answers may vary. Sample answer:

$y = -x + 1$

x	$-x + 1$	y	(x, y)
0	$0 + 1$	1	$(0, 1)$
2	$-2 + 1$	-1	$(2, -1)$
-3	$-(-3) + 1$	4	$(-3, 4)$
-1	$-(-1) + 1$	2	$(-1, 2)$

Four solutions are $(0, 1)$, $(2, -1)$, $(-3, 4)$ and $(-1, 2)$.

13. Answers may vary. Sample answer:

$y = \dfrac{x}{2} + 3$

x	$\dfrac{x}{2} + 3$	y	(x, y)
0	$\dfrac{0}{2} + 3$	3	$(0, 3)$
2	$\dfrac{2}{2} + 3$	4	$(2, 4)$
-4	$\dfrac{-4}{2} + 3$	1	$(-4, 1)$
-6	$\dfrac{-6}{2} + 3$	0	$(-6, 0)$

Four solutions are $(0, 3)$, $(2, 4)$, $(-4, 1)$, and $(-6, 0)$.

14. Answers may vary. Sample answer:

$y = 2.5x + 1$

x	$2.5x + 1$	y	(x, y)
0	$2.5(0) + 1$	1	$(0, 1)$
2	$2.5(2) + 1$	6	$(2, 6)$
-2	$2.5(-2) + 1$	-4	$(-2, -4)$
4	$2.5(4) + 1$	11	$(4, 11)$

Four solutions are $(0, 1)$, $(2, 6)$, $(-2, -4)$, and $(4, 11)$.

15. Answers may vary. Sample answer:

$y = -2x + 3$

x	$-2x + 3$	y	(x, y)
0	$-2(0) + 3$	3	$(0, 3)$
2	$-2(2) + 3$	-1	$(2, -1)$
-3	$-2(-3) + 3$	9	$(-3, 9)$
-1	$-2(-1) + 3$	5	$(-1, 5)$

Four solutions are $(0, 3)$, $(2, -1)$, $(-3, 9)$, and $(-1, 5)$.

16. Answers may vary. Sample answer:

$y = 15x - 57$

x	$15x - 57$	y	(x, y)
0	$15(0) - 57$	-57	$(0, -57)$
1	$15(1) - 57$	-42	$(1, -42)$
-1	$15(-1) - 57$	72	$(-1, -72)$
2	$15(2) - 57$	27	$(2, -27)$

Four solutions are $(0, -57)$, $(1, -42)$, $(-1, -72)$, and $(2, -27)$.

17. Let x = one number and y = other number. The sum of the two numbers is $x + y$, and twice the sum is $2(x + y)$. Then the equation is $2(x + y) = 16$. Solving for y we get

$$2(x + y) = 16$$
$$2x + 2y = 16$$
$$2x - 2x + 2y = 16 - 2x$$
$$2y = 16 - 2x$$
$$\frac{2y}{2} = \frac{16}{2} - \frac{2x}{2}$$
$$y = 8 - x$$

Now check the ordered pairs in the equation $y = 8 - x$.

$$4 \overset{?}{=} 8 - 12 \qquad\qquad 2 \overset{?}{=} 8 - 6$$
$$4 \neq -4 \qquad\qquad\qquad 2 = 2 \; \checkmark$$
no solution $\qquad\qquad$ solution

$$5 \overset{?}{=} 8 - 3 \qquad\qquad 53 \overset{?}{=} 8 - (-45)$$
$$5 = 5 \; \checkmark \qquad\qquad\quad 53 \overset{?}{=} 53 \; \checkmark$$
solution $\qquad\qquad\quad$ solution

The ordered pairs (6, 2), (3, 5), and (-45, 53) are solutions.

18. $8(35) = 4(70)$
$\qquad = 280$

19. $2.\overline{44} = 2.4444\ldots$

Let $N = 2.\overline{44}$. Then $10N = 24.\overline{44}$.

$$10N = 24.\overline{44}$$
$$-\quad N = 2.\overline{44}$$
$$\overline{9N = 22}$$
$$\frac{9N}{9} = \frac{22}{9}$$
$$N = \frac{22}{9} \text{ or } 2\frac{4}{9}$$

20. $f(n) = \dfrac{n}{2} - 1$

n	$\dfrac{n}{2} - 1$	$f(n)$	$(n, f(n))$
-4	$\dfrac{-4}{2} - 1$	-3	(-4, -3)
-2	$\dfrac{-2}{2} - 1$	-2	(-2, -2)
0	$\dfrac{0}{2} - 1$	-1	(0, -1)
2	$\dfrac{2}{2} - 1$	0	(2, 0)
4	$\dfrac{4}{2} - 1$	1	(4, 1)

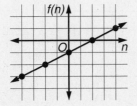

21. a. Let x = first number and y = second number. Then $x + 9 = y$ or $x = y - 9$.

x	$x + 9$	y	(x, y)
0	$0 + 9$	9	(0, 9)
-4	$-4 + 9$	5	(-4, 5)
1	$1 + 9$	10	(1, 10)

Three possible solutions are (0, 9), (-4, 5), and (1, 10).

b. Let x = first number and y = second number. Then $2x$ is twice the first, and $2x + 3 = y$ or $2x = y - 3$ is the equation.

x	$2x + 3$	y	(x, y)
0	$2(0) + 3$	3	(0, 3)
1	$2(1) + 3$	5	(1, 5)
-1	$2(-1) + 3$	1	(-1, 1)

Three possible solutions are (0, 3), (1, 5), and (-1, 1).

c. Let x = first number and y = second number. Then $x + y = 0$ or $y = -x$.

x	$-x$	y	(x, y)
-1	$-(-1)$	1	(-1, 1)
3	$-(3)$	-3	(3, -3)
-2	$-(-2)$	2	(-2, 2)

Three possible solutions are (-1, 1), (3, -3), and (-2, 2).

22. a. $y = 3x - 1$

x	$3x - 1$	y	(x, y)
0	$3(0) - 1$	-1	(0, -1)
1	$3(1) - 1$	2	(1, 2)
-1	$3(-1) - 1$	-4	(-1, -4)
2	$3(2) - 1$	5	(2, 5)

Now check the four solutions in the equation $6x - 2y = 2$.

$$6(0) - 2(-1) \overset{?}{=} 2 \qquad\qquad 6(1) - 2(2) \overset{?}{=} 2$$
$$0 + 2 \overset{?}{=} 2 \qquad\qquad\qquad 6 - 4 \overset{?}{=} 2$$
$$2 = 2 \; \checkmark \qquad\qquad\qquad\quad 2 = 2 \; \checkmark$$

$$6(-1) - 2(-4) \overset{?}{=} 2 \qquad\quad 6(2) - 2(5) \overset{?}{=} 2$$
$$-6 + 8 \overset{?}{=} 2 \qquad\qquad\quad 12 - 10 \overset{?}{=} 2$$
$$2 = 2 \; \checkmark \qquad\qquad\qquad 2 = 2 \; \checkmark$$

Four solutions are (0, -1), (1, 2), (-1, -4), and (2, 5).

b. Because the variable y is on one side of the equation by itself.

23. $t = c + 40$

c	$c + 40$	t	(c, t)
12	12 + 40	52	(12, 52)
23	23 + 40	63	(23, 63)
31	31 + 40	71	(31, 71)
47	47 + 40	87	(47, 87)
50	50 + 40	90	(50, 90)

chirps in seconds (c)	12	23	31	47	50
temperature in °F (t)	52	63	71	87	90

24. Let x = weekend profits and y = total

contribution. Then $\frac{2}{5}x + 1{,}000$ is the total

contribution, or $y = \frac{2}{5}x + 1{,}000$ is the equation.

The total profits are 800 + 1,560 + 1,020

or $3,380. The total contribution is then

$y = \frac{2}{5}(3{,}380) + 1{,}000$

$\quad = 1{,}352 + 1{,}000$

$\quad = \$2{,}352.$

Speedy Burger will contribute $2,352 to charity.

11-4A Mathematics Lab: Graphing Linear Functions

PAGE 431   WHAT DO YOU THINK?

1. See students' work.

2. See students' work.

3. The points should suggest a linear pattern or a straight line.

4. See students' work.

11-4 Graphing Linear Functions

PAGE 433   CHECKING FOR UNDERSTANDING

1. A linear function is one in which the graph of the equation is a line.

2. The third point is for a check.

3. Label the x-axis 0, 10, 20, 30, 40 and label the y-axis 0, 50, 100, 150, 200.

4. $y = 5x$

x	y	(x, y)
-4	-20	(-4, -20)
-1	-5	(-1, -5)
0	0	(0, 0)
2	10	(2, 10)

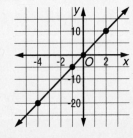

5. $y = 25 - x$

x	y	(x, y)
-5	30	(-5, 30)
0	25	(0, 25)
5	20	(5, 20)
10	15	(10, 15)

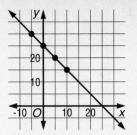

6. $y = 3x + 1$

x	y	(x, y)
-2	-5	(-2, -5)
-1	-2	(-1, -2)
0	1	(0, 1)
1	4	(1, 4)
2	7	(2, 7)

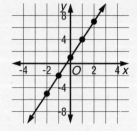

7. $y = 15 - 3x$

x	y	(x, y)
-2	21	(-2, 21)
-1	18	(-1, 18)
0	15	(0, 15)
1	12	(1, 12)
2	9	(2, 9)

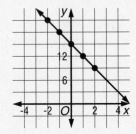

PAGE 434   EXERCISES

8. $y = 8x$

x	y	(x, y)
-2	-16	(-2, -16)
-1	-8	(-1, -8)
0	0	(0, 0)
1	8	(1, 8)
2	16	(2, 16)

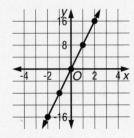

9. $y = -4x$

x	y	(x, y)
-1	4	(-1, 4)
-0.5	2	(-0.5, 2)
0	0	(0, 0)
0.5	-2	(0.5, -2)
1	-4	(1, -4)

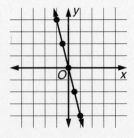

10. $y = 5x + 3$

x	y	(x, y)
-2	-7	(-2, -7)
-1	-2	(-1, -2)
0	3	(0, 3)
1	8	(1, 8)

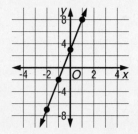

11. $y = 6x + 5$

x	y	(x, y)
-2	-7	(-2, -7)
-1.5	-4	(-1.5, -4)
-1	-1	(-1, -1)
0	5	(0, 5)
0.5	8	(0.5, 8)

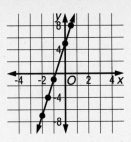

12. $y = 5x - 10$

x	y	(x, y)
-1	-15	(-1, -15)
0	-10	(0, -10)
1	-5	(1, -5)
1.5	-2.5	(1.5, -2.5)
2	0	(2, 0)

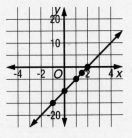

13. $y = 1.5x + 2.5$

x	y	(x, y)
-2	-0.5	(-2, -0.5)
-1	1	(-1, 1)
0	2.5	(0, 2.5)
1	4	(1, 4)
2	5.5	(2, 5.5)

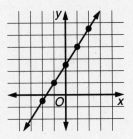

14. $y = \dfrac{x}{3} + 5$

x	y	(x, y)
-6	3	(-6, 3)
-3	4	(-3, 4)
0	5	(0, 5)
3	6	(3, 6)
6	7	(6, 7)

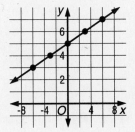

15. $y = 6 - \dfrac{x}{2}$

x	y	(x, y)
-4	8	(-4, 8)
-2	7	(-2, 7)
0	6	(0, 6)
2	5	(2, 5)
4	4	(4, 4)

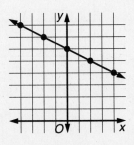

16. $y = 75 - 3x$

x	y	(x, y)
-5	90	(-5, 90)
0	75	(0, 75)
5	60	(5, 60)
10	45	(10, 45)
15	30	(15, 30)

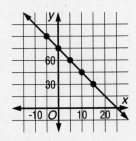

17. Let A = the amount Atepa has. Then $A + 6$ is six more dollars than Atepa.

18.

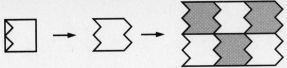

19. $A = \dfrac{1}{2}bh$

$A = (0.5)(2.5)(3.5)$

$A = 4.375 \text{ in}^2$

20. Answers may vary. Sample answers:

$y = \dfrac{x}{3} + 8$

x	y	(x, y)
0	8	(0, 8)
3	9	(3, 9)
-3	7	(-3, 7)
-6	6	(-6, 6)

Four solutions are (0, 8), (3, 9), (-3, 7) and (-6, 6).

21. a. Let the x-coordinate represent °C and the y-coordinate represent °F. Then two ordered pairs are (0, 32) and (100, 212).

b.

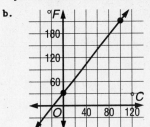

c. Find the coordinates of other points on the graph.

22. Let the x-axis represent distance in miles and the y-axis represent the time in seconds. Then find values for the graph.

$t = 5d$

d	t	(d, t)
0	0	(0, 0)
1	5	(1, 5)
2	10	(2, 10)
3	15	(3, 15)
4	20	(4, 20)

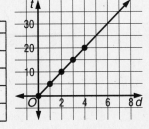

137

23. $y = 5x$ and $y = 5x + 5$

x	y	(x, y)
-2	-10	(-2, -10)
-1	-5	(-1, -5)
0	0	(0, 0)
1	5	(1, 5)
2	10	(2, 10)

x	y	(x, y)
-2	-5	(-2, -5)
-1	0	(-1, 0)
0	5	(0, 5)
1	10	(1, 10)
2	15	(2, 15)

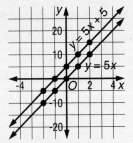

24. See students' work.

11-5   Graphing Systems of Equations

PAGE 437   CHECKING FOR UNDERSTANDING

1. two or more equations

2. coordinates of the point where the graphs of the equations meet, or no solution

3. $x + y = 4$ $2x - y = -1$
    $1 + 3 \overset{?}{=} 4$ $2(1) - 3 \overset{?}{=} -1$
        $4 = 4$ ✓ $2 - 3 \overset{?}{=} -1$
                        $-1 = -1$ ✓

4. any graph that contains parallel lines; Sample answer:

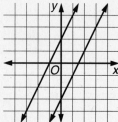

5. The two lines intersect at the point (-3, -1), so that point is the solution.

6. (6, 2)   7. (-4, -4)   8. (1, -1)

9. (0, 4)   10. (-3, 5)   11. (-1, 2)

---

12. $y = 3 + x$ $y = 2x + 5$

x	3 + x	y
-2	3 + (-2)	1
0	3 + 0	3
2	3 + 2	5

x	2x + 5y	y
-3	2(-3) + 5	-1
0	2(0) + 5	5
-1	2(-1) + 5	3

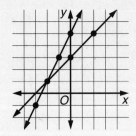

The solution is (-2, 1).

13. $y = 3x + 1$ $y = 3x - 1$

x	3x + 1	y
1	3(1) + 1	4
0	3(0) + 1	1
-1	3(-1) + 1	-2

x	3x - 1	y
2	3(2) - 1	5
0	3(0) - 1	-1
-1	3(-1) - 1	-4

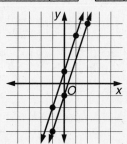

The lines do not intersect, so there is no solution.

PAGES 437-438   EXERCISES

14. $y = x - 4$ $y = -4x + 16$

x	x - 4	y
0	0 - 4	-4
1	1 - 4	-3
2	2 - 4	-2

x	-4x + 16	y
3	-4(3) + 16	4
4	-4(4) + 16	0
5	-4(5) + 16	-4

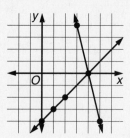

The solution is (4, 0).

15. $y = x$ $\qquad\qquad$ $y = -x + 4$

x	y
-2	-2
0	0
1	1

x	-x + 4	y
0	0 + 4	4
1	-1 + 4	3
2	-2 + 4	2

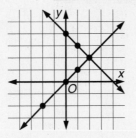

The solution is (2, 2).

16. $y = 2x$ $\qquad\qquad$ $y = -2x + 4$

x	2x	y
2	2(2)	4
0	2(0)	0
-1	2(-1)	-2

x	-2x + 4	y
4	-2(4) + 4	-4
2	-2(2) + 4	0
1	-2(1) + 4	2

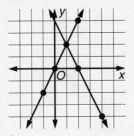

The solution is (1, 2).

17. $y = 4x - 15$ $\qquad\qquad$ $y = x + 3$

x	4x - 15	y
5	4(5) - 15	5
4	4(4) - 15	1
2	4(2) - 15	-7

x	x + 3	y
-3	-3 + 3	0
1	1 + 3	4
2	2 + 3	5

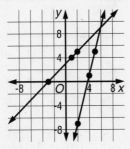

The solution is (6, 9).

18. $y = -2x - 6$ $\qquad\qquad$ $y = -2x - 3$

x	-2x - 6	y
-1	-2(-1) - 6	-4
-2	-2(-2) - 6	-2
-3	-2(-3) - 6	0

x	-2x - 3	y
-1	-2(-1) - 3	-1
-2	-2(-2) - 3	1
-3	-2(-3) - 3	3

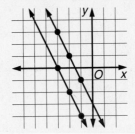

There is no solution.

19. $y = -x - 1$ $\qquad\qquad$ $y = -2x + 4$

x	-x - 1	y
3	-3 - 1	-4
1	-1 - 1	-2
-1	-(-1) - 1	0

x	-2x + 4	y
2	-2(2) + 4	0
-2	-2(-2) + 4	8
4	-2(4) + 4	-4

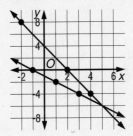

The solution is (5, -6)

20. $y = 4x - 13$ $\qquad\qquad$ $y = -\frac{1}{2}x + 5$

x	4x - 13	y
2	4(2) - 13	-5
3	4(3) - 13	-1
4	4(4) - 13	3

x	$-\frac{1}{2}x + 5$	y
-2	$-\frac{1}{2}(-2) + 5$	6
2	$-\frac{1}{2}(2) + 5$	4
4	$-\frac{1}{2}(4) + 5$	3

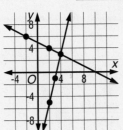

The solution is (4, 3).

21.

$$2x + y = 5$$
$$2x - 2x + y = 5 - 2x$$
$$y = 5 - 2x$$

x	5 - 2x	y
1	5 - 2(1)	3
2	5 - 2(2)	1
3	5 - 2(3)	-1

$$x - y = 1$$
$$x - x - y = 1 - x$$
$$-y = 1 - x$$
$$-1(-y) = (1 - x)(-1)$$
$$y = -1 + x$$

x	-1 + x	y
-2	-1 + (-2)	-3
0	-1 + 0	-1
2	-1 + 2	1

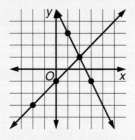

The solution is (2, 1).

22. positive relationship

23. $\frac{5}{6} = 0.8\overline{3}$

$\frac{7}{9} = 0.\overline{7}$

So $\frac{5}{6} > \frac{7}{9}$.

24. $49 < 60 < 64$
$7^2 < 60 < 8^2$
$7 < \sqrt{60} < 8$

Since 60 is closer to 64 than 49, the best whole number estimate is 8.

Check: $\sqrt{60} \approx 7.746$

25. $y = 3x + 1$

x	3x + 1	y
-1	3(-1) + 1	-2
0	3(0) + 1	1
1	3(1) + 1	4

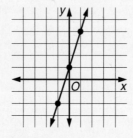

26. a. $c = 25t + 35$ $c = 30t + 20$

t	25t + 35	c	t	30t + 20	c
2	25(2) + 35	85	2	30(2) + 20	80
5	25(5) + 35	160	5	30(5) + 20	170
7	25(7) + 35	210	7	30(7) + 20	230

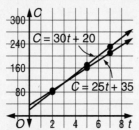

b. Their charges are equal at three hours.

c. Mr. Gill should hire the first electrician.

27. a. $y = 2x + 5$ $y = -\frac{1}{2}x + 10$

x	2x + 5	y
-2	2(-2) + 5	1
-1	2(-1) + 5	3
0	2(0) + 5	5

x	$-\frac{1}{2}x + 10$	y
6	$-\frac{1}{2}(6) + 10$	7
4	$-\frac{1}{2}(4) + 10$	8
2	$-\frac{1}{2}(2) + 10$	9

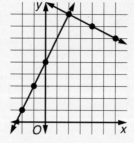

b. The solution is (2, 9).

c. They are perpendicular lines because the angles all measure 90°.

28. a.
$$2x + y = 6$$
$$2x - 2x + y = 6 - 2x$$
$$y = 6 - 2x$$

x	6 - 2x	y
1	6 - 2(1)	4
2	6 - 2(2)	2
3	6 - 2(3)	0

$$4x + 2y = 12$$
$$4x - 4x + 2y = 12 - 4x$$
$$2y = 12 - 4x$$

x	2y = 12 - 4x	y
1.5	2y = 12 - 4(1.5)	3
2	2y = 12 - 4(2)	2
3.5	2y = 12 - 4(3.5)	-1

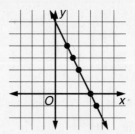

b. They are both the same line.

c. The solution is all points on the line (or an infinite number of solutions).

Mid-Chapter Review

1. Answers may vary. Sample answer:

    $f(n) = -2n + 5$

n	$-2n + 5$	$f(n)$	$(n, f(n))$
0	$-2(0) + 5$	5	$(0, 5)$
1	$-2(1) + 5$	3	$(1, 3)$
2	$-2(2) + 5$	1	$(2, 1)$
-1	$-2(-1) + 5$	7	$(-1, 7)$
-2	$-2(-2) + 5$	9	$(-2, 9)$

2.

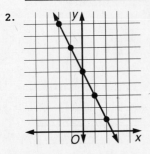

3. Answers may vary. Sample answers:

    $y = \frac{x}{3} + 4$

x	$\frac{x}{3} + 4$	y	(x, y)
0	$\frac{0}{3} + 4$	4	$(0, 4)$
3	$\frac{3}{3} + 4$	5	$(3, 5)$
-3	$\frac{-3}{3} + 4$	3	$(-3, 3)$
-6	$\frac{-6}{3} + 4$	2	$(-6, 2)$

Four solutions are $(0, 4)$, $(3, 5)$, $(-3, 3)$, and $(-6, 2)$.

4. $y = 10 - 2x$

x	$10 - 2x$	y	(x, y)
3	$10 - 2(3)$	4	$(3, 4)$
4	$10 - 2(4)$	2	$(4, 2)$
5	$10 - 2(5)$	0	$(5, 0)$

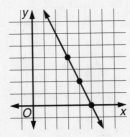

5. The solution is $(3, 2)$ because that is where the two lines intersect.

11-6 Use a Graph

1. Answers may vary. Sample answer: Increases do not occur at a regular rate.

2. Answers may vary. Sample answer: The horizontal scale is in years and most TV gadgets were not even invented until the mid-1900's.

3. about $660 billion

4. The biggest increase was from March to April.

5. The overall trend is a decrease in business loans and an increase in government securities.

6. Graph b, because graph a shows a decline in profits and graph c shows variable profit growth.

7. Let x = the number. Then $2x$ is the number doubled and $2x + (-19)$ adds -19 to the number doubled. The equation is then

$$2x + (-19) = 11$$
$$2x + (-19) - (-19) = 11 - (-19)$$
$$2x = 11 + 19$$
$$2x = 30$$
$$\frac{2x}{2} = \frac{30}{2}$$
$$x = 15$$

    The number is 15.

8. An onyx contains various colors, an amethyst is violet-purple and a sapphire is blue. So Corrine's stone must be a sapphire because her stone is blue. Risa wishes her stone was onyx so it cannot be onyx or sapphire. Therefore, it must be amethyst. James's stone is not amethyst and cannot be sapphire because that is Corrine's stone, so his stone must be onyx. So Risa has amethyst, James has onyx and Corine has sapphire.

9. during 1955-1960

10. about 1977

11. Answers may vary. Sample answer: Non-U.S. countries produce the majority of motor vehicles and U.S. production has dropped since 1950.

12.

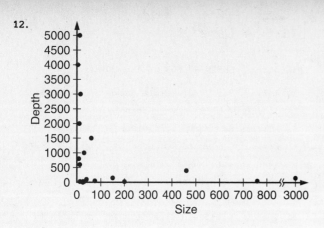

11-7   **Graphing Quadratic Functions**

PAGE 444   CHECKING FOR UNDERSTANDING

1. The greatest power of x in a quadratic function is 2.

2.

3. Answers may vary. Sample answer: There are no negative numbers in the domain or range. For Example 1, your eyes won't be negative feet high and the oil tanker won't be negative miles from shore. For Example 2, the length of the side of a square is not a negative distance and you can't have a negative area.

4. $f(x) = x^2$

x	x^2	$f(x)$	$(x, f(x))$
-2	$(-2)^2$	4	$(-2, 4)$
-1	$(-1)^2$	1	$(-1, 1)$
0	$(0)^2$	0	$(0, 0)$
1	$(1)^2$	1	$(1, 1)$
2	$(2)^2$	4	$(2, 4)$

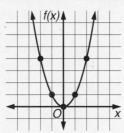

---

5. $y = x^2 - 1$

x	$x^2 - 1$	y	(x, y)
-2	$(-2)^2 - 1$	3	$(-2, 3)$
-1	$(-1)^2 - 1$	0	$(-1, 0)$
0	$(0)^2 - 1$	-1	$(0, -1)$
1	$(1)^2 - 1$	0	$(1, 0)$
2	$(2)^2 - 1$	3	$(2, 3)$

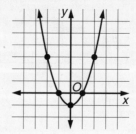

6. $y = 2x^2 + 1$

x	$2x^2 + 1$	y	(x, y)
-2	$2(-2)^2 + 1$	9	$(-2, 9)$
-1.5	$2(-1.5)^2 + 1$	5.5	$(-1.5, 5.5)$
0	$2(0)^2 + 1$	1	$(0, 1)$
3	$2(3)^2 + 1$	19	$(3, 19)$
4	$2(4)^2 + 1$	33	$(4, 33)$

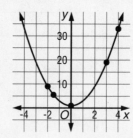

7. $f(x) = -x^2$

x	$-x^2$	$f(x)$	$(x, f(x))$
-3	$-(-3)^2$	-9	$(-3, -9)$
-1	$-(-1)^2$	-1	$(-1, -1)$
0	$-(0)^2$	0	$(0, 0)$
1.5	$-(1.5)^2$	-2.25	$(1.5, -2.25)$
2	$-(2)^2$	-4	$(2, -4)$

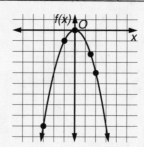

8. $f(n) = 3n^2$

n	$3n^2$	$f(n)$	$(n, f(n))$
-2	$3(-2)^2$	12	(-2, 12)
-1	$3(-1)^2$	3	(-1, 3)
0	$3(0)^2$	0	(0, 0)
1	$3(1)^2$	3	(1, 3)
2	$3(2)^2$	12	(2, 12)

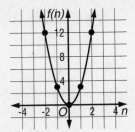

9. $f(n) = 5n^2 + 1$

n	$5n^2 + 1$	$f(n)$	$(n, f(n))$
-1	$5(-1)^2 + 1$	6	(-1, 6)
-0.5	$5(-0.5)^2 + 1$	2.25	(-0.5, 2.25)
0	$5(0)^2 + 1$	1	(0, 1)
0.5	$5(0.5)^2 + 1$	2.25	(0.5, 2.25)
1	$5(1)^2 + 1$	6	(1, 6)

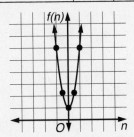

10. $f(n) = -n^2$

n	$-n^2$	$f(n)$	$(n, f(n))$
-2	$-(-2)^2$	-4	(-2, -4)
-1	$-(-1)^2$	-1	(-1, -1)
0	$-(0)^2$	0	(0, 0)
1	$-(1)^2$	-1	(1, -1)
2	$-(2)^2$	-4	(2, -4)

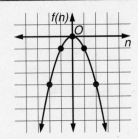

11. $y = -2x^2$

x	$-2x^2$	y	(x, y)
-2	$-2(-2)^2$	-8	(-2, -8)
-1	$-2(-1)^2$	-2	(-1, -2)
0	$-2(0)^2$	0	(0, 0)
1	$-2(1)^2$	-2	(1, -2)
2	$-2(2)^2$	-8	(2, -8)

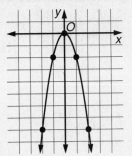

12. $y = \frac{1}{2}x^2 + 2$

x	$\frac{1}{2}x^2 + 2$	y	(x, y)
-2	$\frac{1}{2}(-2)^2 + 2$	4	(-2, 4)
-1	$\frac{1}{2}(-1)^2 + 2$	2.5	(-1, 2.5)
0	$\frac{1}{2}(0)^2 + 2$	2	(0, 2)
1	$\frac{1}{2}(1)^2 + 2$	2.5	(1, 2.5)
2	$\frac{1}{2}(2)^2 + 2$	4	(2, 4)

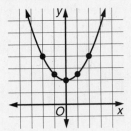

13. $y = 1.5x^2 - 1$

x	$1.5x^2 - 1$	y	(x, y)
-2	$1.5(-2)^2 - 1$	5	(-2, 5)
-1	$1.5(-1)^2 - 1$	0.5	(-1, 0.5)
0	$1.5(0)^2 - 1$	-1	(0, -1)
1	$1.5(1)^2 - 1$	0.5	(1, 0.5)
2	$1.5(2)^2 - 1$	5	(2, 5)

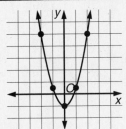

143

14. $y = -1.5x^2 - 1$

x	$-1.5x^2 - 1$	y	(x, y)
-2	$-1.5(-2)^2 - 1$	-7	(-2, -7)
-1	$-1.5(-1)^2 - 1$	-2.5	(-1, -2.5)
0	$-1.5(0)^2 - 1$	-1	(0, -1)
1	$-1.5(1)^2 - 1$	-2.5	(1, -2.5)
2	$-1.5(2)^2 - 1$	-7	(2, -7)

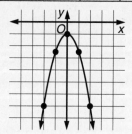

15. $f(n) = 10 - n^2$

n	$10 - n^2$	$f(n)$	$(n, f(n))$
-2	$10 - (-2)^2$	6	(-2, 6)
-1	$10 - (-1)^2$	9	(-1, 9)
0	$10 - (0)^2$	10	(0, 10)
1	$10 - (1)^2$	9	(1, 9)
2	$10 - (2)^2$	6	(2, 6)

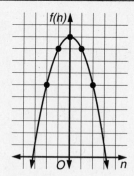

16. $y = x^2 + x$

x	$x^2 + x$	y	(x, y)
-2	$(-2)^2 + (-2)$	2	(-2, 2)
-1	$(-1)^2 + (-1)$	0	(-1, 0)
-0.5	$(-0.5)^2 + (-0.5)$	-0.25	(-0.5, -0.25)
0	$(0)^2 + (0)$	0	(0, 0)
1	$(1)^2 + (1)$	2	(1, 2)

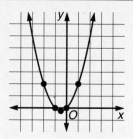

17. $y = 3x^2 - 4$

$8 \overset{?}{=} 3(-2)^2 - 4$ $-7 \overset{?}{=} 3(-1)^2 - 4$ $-4 \overset{?}{=} 3(0) - 4$
$8 \overset{?}{=} 12 - 4$ $-7 \overset{?}{=} 3 - 4$ $-4 \overset{?}{=} 0 - 4$
$8 = 8$ ✓ $-7 \neq -1$ $-4 = -4$ ✓

$-1 \overset{?}{=} 3(1)^2 - 4$ $-8 \overset{?}{=} 3(2)^2 - 4$
$-1 \overset{?}{=} 3 - 4$ $-8 \overset{?}{=} 12 - 4$
$-1 = -1$ ✓ $-8 \neq 8$

The set of ordered pairs {(-2, 8), (0, -4), (1, -1)} are solutions.

18. $f(x) = -x^2 + x$

$2 \overset{?}{=} -(-2)^2 + (-2)$ $-3.75 \overset{?}{=} -(-1.5)^2 + (-1.5)$
$2 \overset{?}{=} -4 - 2$ $-3.75 \overset{?}{=} -2.25 - 1.5$
$2 \neq -6$ $-3.75 = -3.75$ ✓

$0 \overset{?}{=} -(2)^2 + 2$ $-8.75 \overset{?}{=} -(3.5)^2 + 3.5$
$0 \overset{?}{=} -4 + 2$ $-8.75 \overset{?}{=} -12.25 + 3.5$
$0 \neq -2$ $-8.75 = -8.75$ ✓

$0 \overset{?}{=} -(0)^2 + 0$
$0 = 0$ ✓

The set of ordered pairs {(-1.5, -3.75), (3.5, -8.75), (0, 0)} are solutions.

19. $6a^2 + b = 6(4)^2 + 1$
$= 6(16) + 1$
$= 96 + 1$
$= 97$

20. $j = -496 \div 16$
$= -31$

21. $a + b - c = \frac{1}{2} + 4\frac{3}{5} - 1\frac{3}{4}$
$= \frac{1}{2} + \frac{23}{5} - \frac{7}{4}$
$= \frac{10}{20} + \frac{92}{20} - \frac{35}{20}$
$= \frac{67}{20}$
$= 3\frac{7}{20}$

22. $y = -x + 5$ $y = 2x - 4$

x	$-x + 5$	y
0	0 + 5	5
1	-1 + 5	4
2	-2 + 5	3

x	$2x - 4$	y
0	2(0) - 4	-4
1	2(1) - 4	-2
2	2(2) - 4	0

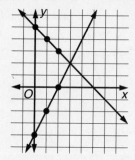

The solution is (3, 2).

23. a. upward - #8, 9, 12, 13, 16

downward - #10, 11, 14, 15

b. If the squared term is positive then it turns upward. If the squared term is negative then it turns downward.

24. $h(t) = 96t - 16t^2$

t	$96t - 16t^2$	$h(t)$	$(t, h(t))$
0	$96(0) - 16(0)^2$	0	$(0, 0)$
1	$96(1) - 16(1)^2$	80	$(1, 80)$
2	$96(2) - 16(2)^2$	128	$(2, 128)$
3	$96(3) - 16(3)^2$	144	$(3, 144)$
4	$96(4) - 16(4)^2$	128	$(4, 128)$
5	$96(5) - 16(5)^2$	80	$(5, 80)$
6	$96(6) - 16(6)^2$	0	$(6, 0)$

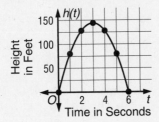

25. $f(r) = \pi(r + 0.5)^2$

r	$\pi(r + 0.5)^2$	$f(r)$
-2	$\pi(-2 + 0.5)^2$	7.1
-1	$\pi(-1 + 0.5)^2$	0.8
-0.5	$\pi(-0.5 + 0.5)^2$	0
0	$\pi(0 + 0.5)^2$	0.8
1	$\pi(1 + 0.5)^2$	7.1

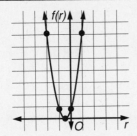

26. a. $f(s) = s^2$

s	s^2	$f(s)$
0	$(0)^2$	0
1	$(1)^2$	1
2	$(2)^2$	4
3	$(3)^2$	9

$f(s) = 4s$

s	$4s$	$f(s)$
0	$4(0)$	0
1	$4(1)$	4
2	$4(2)$	8
3	$4(3)$	12

b. The area and perimeter have the same measure when $s = 4$.

27. a.

x	x^2	$\frac{1}{2}x^2$	$2x^2$
-2	$(-2)^2 = 4$	$\frac{1}{2}(-2)^2 = 2$	$2(-2)^2 = 8$
-1	$(-1)^2 = 1$	$\frac{1}{2}(-1)^2 = \frac{1}{2}$	$2(-1)^2 = 2$
0	$(0)^2 = 0$	$\frac{1}{2}(0)^2 = 0$	$2(0)^2 = 0$
1	$(1)^2 = 1$	$\frac{1}{2}(1)^2 = \frac{1}{2}$	$2(1)^2 = 2$
2	$(2)^2 = 4$	$\frac{1}{2}(2)^2 = 2$	$2(2)^2 = 8$

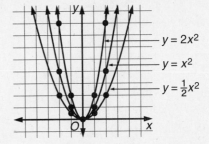

b. The graph of $y = \frac{1}{2}x^2$ is wider than the graph of $y = x^2$, and the graph of $y = 2x^2$ is narrower than the graph of $y = x^2$.

c.

x	x^2	$x^2 + 2$
-2	$(-2)^2 = 4$	$(-2)^2 + 2 = 6$
-1	$(-1)^2 = 1$	$(-1)^2 + 2 = 3$
0	$0^2 = 0$	$0^2 + 2 = 2$
1	$1^2 = 1$	$1^2 + 2 = 3$
2	$2^2 = 4$	$2^2 + 2 = 6$

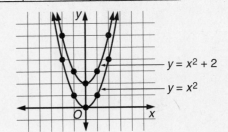

The graph of $y = x^2 + 2$ is the same as the graph of $y = x^2$ except it is moved up 2 units.

d. Graphs of positive numbers less than 1 multiplied by x^2 have a wider graph than $y = x^2$. Graphs of numbers greater than 1 multiplied by x^2 have a narrower graph than x^2. If the number is negative, the graph opens downward. Graphs of numbers added to x^2 shifts the graph of $y = x^2$ up for positive numbers or down for negative numbers.

28. a. $600 billion - $200 billion = $400 billion

b. Bank card spending began to steadily increase around 1983-1984.

1. a slide

2. Two units left because the x-coordinate is negative and three units up because the y-coordinate is positive.

3. See students' work.

4. $(1, 0) \rightarrow (5, 5)$

$5 - 1 = 4 \rightarrow a$

$5 - 0 = 5 \rightarrow b$

The ordered pair is (a, b) or $(4, 5)$.

5. $(-2, 0) \rightarrow (8, -5)$

$8 - (-2) = 10 \rightarrow a$

$-5 - 0 = -5 \rightarrow b$

The ordered pair is (a, b) or $(10, -5)$.

6. 6 units left $= -6$; 3 units up $= 3 \Rightarrow (-6, 3)$

$P(0, 0) + (-6, 3) \rightarrow P'(-6, 3)$

$Q(-3, -4) + (-6, 3) \rightarrow Q'(-9, -1)$

$R(1, 3) + (-6, 3) \rightarrow R'(-5, 6)$

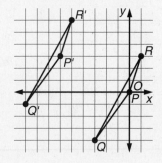

7. $W(2, 1) + (-1, 3) = W'(1, 4)$

$X(4, 3) + (-1, 3) = X'(3, 6)$

$Y(2, 5) + (-1, 3) = Y'(1, 8)$

$Z(0, 3) + (-1, 3) = Z'(-1, 6)$

8. $A(-5, -2) + (6, 3) = A'(1, 1)$

$B(-2, 3) + (6, 3) = B'(4, 6)$

$C(2, -3) + (6, 3) = C'(8, 0)$

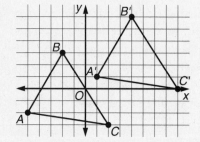

9. $P(-4, 1) + (-1, 4) = P'(-5, 5)$

$Q(2, 4) + (-1, 4) = Q'(1, 8)$

$R(3, 2) + (-1, 4) = R'(2, 6)$

$S(-3, -1) + (-1, 4) = S'(-4, 3)$

10. a. 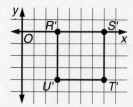   The fourth vertex is $(-5, 1)$.

b. $R(-5, 5) + (8, -5) = R'(3, 0)$

$S(-1, 5) + (8, -5) = S'(7, 0)$

$T(-1, 1) + (8, -5) = T'(7, -4)$

$U(-5, 1) + (8, -5) = U'(3, -4)$

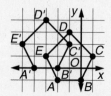

11. $R(-2, 3) + (a, b) = R'(3, 5)$

$-2 + a = 3$	$3 + b = 5$
$-2 + 2 + a = 3 + 2$	$3 - 3 + b = 5 - 3$
$a = 5$	$b = 2$

The translation using an ordered pair is $(5, 2)$.

12. a. $C(1, 1) + (a, b) = C'(-1, 2)$

$1 + a = -1$	$1 + b = 2$
$1 - 1 + a = -1 - 1$	$1 - 1 + b = 2 - 1$
$a = -2$	$b = 1$

The translation using an ordered pair is $(-2, 1)$.

b. $A(-2, -1) + (-2, 1) = A'(-4, 0)$

$B(0, -1) + (-2, 1) = B'(-2, 0)$

$C(1, 1) + (-2, 1) = C'(-1, 2)$

$D(-1, 3) + (-2, 1) = D'(-3, 4)$

$E(-3, 1) + (-2, 1) = E'(-5, 2)$

13. $(10)^2 + (24)^2 \overset{?}{=} (26)^2$

$100 + 576 \overset{?}{=} 676$

$676 = 676$ ✓

The triangle is a right triangle.

14. $y = 2x^2 - 8$

x	$2x^2 - 8$	y	(x, y)
-2	$2(-2)^2 - 8$	0	(-2, 0)
-1	$2(-1)^2 - 8$	-6	(-1, -6)
0	$2(0)^2 - 8$	-8	(0, -8)
1	$2(1)^2 - 8$	-6	(1, -6)
2	$2(2)^2 - 8$	0	(2, 0)

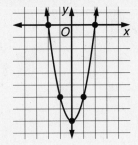

15. a.

ABCDEFGH

b. Marc must move over 4 seats and back 10 seats.

16. a. (1, 5), (1, 6), (1, 9), (1, 8), (1, 5)

b. about 33 million households

c. Answers may vary. Sample answer: They grew rapidly from 1986-1989 but have slowed in growth since then.

17. The triangle will end up in the same position because $(x, y) + (-3, 5) \rightarrow (x - 3, y + 5)$. Then $(x - 3, y + 5) + (3, -5) \rightarrow (x, y)$; or $(-3, 5) + (3, -5) \rightarrow (0, 0)$.

11-8B **Mathematics Lab: Slope**

PAGE 450 **WHAT DO YOU THINK?**

1. They are all on the same line.

2. y move from B to $A \rightarrow -2$

x move from B to $A \rightarrow -4$

The ordered pair is (-2, -4).

a. $\dfrac{y \text{ move from } B \text{ to } A}{x \text{ move from } B \text{ to } A} = \dfrac{-4}{-2} = 2$

b. It is the same slope as the slope from A to B.

---

3. a. Answers may vary. Sample answer:

x	$2x - 5$	y	(x, y)
4	$2(4) - 5$	3	(4, 3)
0	$2(0) - 5$	-5	(0, -5)

b. Sample answer: $(0, -5) + (a, b) = (4, 3)$

$0 + a = 4 \qquad -5 + b = 3$

$a = 4 \qquad -5 + 5 + b = 3 + 5$

$b = 8$

A translation that relates one ordered pair to the other is (4, 8).

c. $\dfrac{y \text{ move}}{x \text{ move}} = \dfrac{8}{4} = 2$

The is the same as the slope from A to B.

PAGE 450 **EXTENSION**

4. a. $\dfrac{1}{2} \rightarrow$ move 1 up, 2 right for each point

$(3, 2) + (2, 1) \rightarrow (5, 3)$

$(5, 3) + (2, 1) \rightarrow (7, 4)$

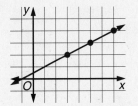

b. Answers may vary. Sample answers:

Two other solutions are (5, 3) and (7, 4).

5. a. $\dfrac{-4}{3} \rightarrow$ move 4 units down, 3 units right

$(-2, -4) + (3, -4) \rightarrow (1, -8)$

$(1, -8) + (3, -4) \rightarrow (4, -12)$

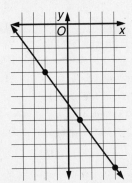

b. Answers may vary. Sample answer: Two other solutions are (-5, 0) and (1, -8).

6. a. $\frac{2}{1} \rightarrow$ 2 units up, 1 unit right

$(0, 0) + (1, 2) \rightarrow (1, 2)$

$(1, 2) + (1, 2) \rightarrow (2, 4)$

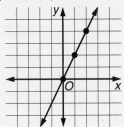

b. Answers may vary. Sample answer: Two other
solutions are $(-1, -2)$ and $(1, 2)$.

11-9 Reflections

PAGES 452-453   CHECKING FOR UNDERSTANDING

1. Answers may vary. Sample answer: In a mirror,
   the object seen is the flip of the real object.
   In a geometric reflection, what is on one side
   of a line is flipped from what is on the other
   side of the line.

2. Reflection over x: same x, opposite y.
   Reflection over y: same y, opposite x.

3.

4. If you fold the graph along the y-axis the
   two triangles would overlap. The line of
   symmetry is then the y-axis.

5. If you fold the graph along the x-axis the
   two hexagons would overlap. The line of
   symmetry is then the x-axis.

6. If you fold the graph along the x-axis the
   two rectangles would overlap. The line of
   symmetry is then the x-axis.

---

7. a. $C(3, 3), \rightarrow C'(3, -3)$

$O(0, 0) \rightarrow O'(0, 0)$

$W(6, -1) \rightarrow W'(6, 1)$

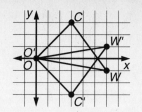

b. $C(3, 3) \rightarrow C'(-3, 3)$

$O(0, 0) \rightarrow O'(0, 0)$

$W(6, -1) \rightarrow W'(-6, -1)$

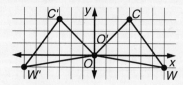

PAGE 453   EXERCISES

8.

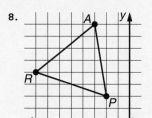

a. $R(-8, 4) \rightarrow R'(8, 4)$

$A(-3, 8) \rightarrow A'(3, 8)$

$P(-2, 2) \rightarrow P'(2, 2)$

b.

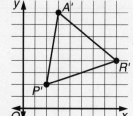

9.

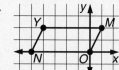

a. $M(1, 2) \rightarrow M'(1, -2)$

$O(0, 0) \rightarrow O'(0, 0)$

$N(-5, 0) \rightarrow N'(-5, 0)$

$Y(-4, 2) \rightarrow Y'(-4, -2)$

b.

148

10.

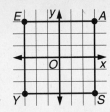

a. $E(-3, 3) \rightarrow E'(-3, -3)$
$A(3, 3) \rightarrow A'(3, -3)$
$S(3, -3) \rightarrow S'(3, 3)$
$Y(-3, -3) \rightarrow Y'(-3, 3)$

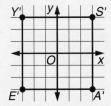

b. $E(-3, 3) \rightarrow E'(3, 3)$
$A(3, 3) \rightarrow A'(-3, 3)$
$S(3, -3) \rightarrow S'(-3, -3)$
$Y(-3, -3) \rightarrow Y'(3, -3)$

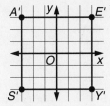

c. All three graphs coincide.

11.
$$\frac{2}{n} = \frac{7}{98}$$
$$2 \cdot 98 = 7n$$
$$196 = 7n$$
$$\frac{196}{7} = \frac{7n}{7}$$
$$28 = n$$

12. 2 units right $\rightarrow$ 2; 3 units up $\rightarrow$ 3.
$A(-3, -2) + (2, 3) \rightarrow A'(-1, 1)$
$B(-1, 1) + (2, 3) \rightarrow B'(1, 4)$
$C(2, -1) + (2, 3) \rightarrow C'(4, 2)$

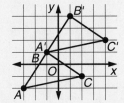

13. Graph the points (-3, 0) and (0, 6) and connect
the two points. Then use this segment and
reflections to create another segment that
is congruent. First, reflect the segment over
the y-axis. Then (-3, 0) $\rightarrow$ (3, 0) and (0, 6)
stays (0, 6). The three vertices for the
first isosceles triangle are then (-3, 0),
(0, 6), and (3, 0). Second, reflect the
segment over the x-axis. Then (-3, 0) stays
(-3, 0) and (0, 6) $\rightarrow$ (0, -6). The three
vertices for the second isosceles triangle
are then (-3, 0), (0, 6), and (0, -6).

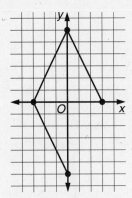

14. a.

n	n^2	$f(n)$
0	$(0)^2$	0
1	1^2	1
2	2^2	4
3	3^2	9
4	4^2	16

b. Since quadratic functions have vertical lines
of symmetry, we use the y-axis as the line of
symmetry in this case. So
$(0, 0) \rightarrow (0, 0)$
$(1, 1) \rightarrow (-1, 1)$
$(2, 4) \rightarrow (-2, 4)$
$(3, 9) \rightarrow (-3, 9)$
$(4, 16) \rightarrow (-4, 16)$

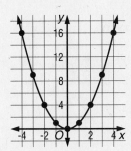

1. Answers may vary. Sample answers: the hands on a clock, the agitator on a washing machine, a rotary dial telephone

2. the fourth quadrant

3. Do the 90° rotation twice.

4. yes

5. yes

6. no

7.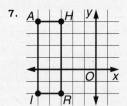

a. $H(-3, 4) \rightarrow (4, -3) \rightarrow H'(-4, -3)$
   $A(-5, 4) \rightarrow (4, -5) \rightarrow A'(-4, -5)$
   $I(-5, -2) \rightarrow (-2, -5) \rightarrow I'(2, -5)$
   $R(-3, -2) \rightarrow (-2, -3) \rightarrow R'(2, -3)$

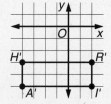

b. $H(-3, 4) \rightarrow H'(3, -4)$
   $A(-5, 4) \rightarrow A'(5, -4)$
   $I(-5, -2) \rightarrow I'(5, 2)$
   $R(-3, -2) \rightarrow R'(3, 2)$

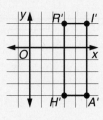

8. Answers may vary. Sample answers: square, hexagon, octagon

9. a.

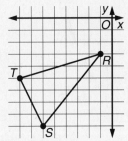

b. $R(-1, -3) \rightarrow (-3, -1) \rightarrow R'(3, -1)$
   $S(-6, -9) \rightarrow (-9, -6) \rightarrow S'(9, -6)$
   $T(-8, -5) \rightarrow (-5, -8) \rightarrow T'(5, -8)$

c.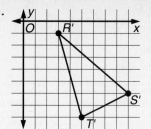

10. a. $A(3, -2) \rightarrow A'(-3, 2)$
    $B(7, -2) \rightarrow B'(-7, 2)$
    $C(9, -7) \rightarrow C'(-9, 7)$
    $D(-1, -7) \rightarrow D'(1, 7)$

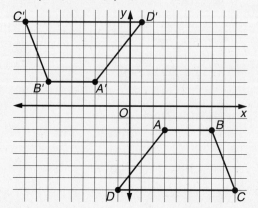

b. $A'(-3, 2) \rightarrow A''(3, -2)$ which is original point A
   $B'(-7, 2) \rightarrow B''(7, -2)$ which is original point B
   $C'(-9, 7) \rightarrow C''(9, -7)$ which is original point C
   $D'(1, 7) \rightarrow D''(-1, -7)$ which is original point D
   So the result of rotating trapezoid $A'B'C'D'$ 180° is trapezoid $ABCD$.

11. To find the original coordinates rotate the triangle 180° again.
    $(4, -1) \rightarrow (-4, 1)$
    $(1, -4) \rightarrow (-1, 4)$
    $(5, 8) \rightarrow (-5, -8)$
    The coordinates of the original triangle are $(-4, 1)$, $(-1, 4)$ and $(-5, -8)$.

12. a. Yes, because if you rotate it around the center of the pentagon, there are other positions in which the pentagon looks the same as it did originally.

    b. There are five positions of rotational symmetry and each degree turn is the same. Since there are 360° in a complete rotation, there are $360° \div 5 = 72°$ in the first rotation. The other four degree turns are $72°(2) = 144°$, $72°(3) = 216°$, $72°(4) = 288°$, and $72°(5) = 360°$.

13. $S - 34 = 71$ Check: $S - 34 = 71$
    $S - 34 + 34 = 71 + 34$ $105 - 34 \overset{?}{=} 71$
            $S = 105$ $71 = 71$ ✓

14. 36: $2 \cdot 2 \cdot 3 \cdot 3$
    84: $2 \cdot 2 \cdot 3 \cdot 7$
    The GCF is $2 \cdot 2 \cdot 3 = 12$.

15.

a. $T(1, -1) \rightarrow T'(1, 1)$
   $R(3, -1) \rightarrow R'(3, 1)$
   $A(3, -3) \rightarrow A'(3, 3)$
   $B(1, -3) \rightarrow B'(1, 3)$

b. $T(1, -1) \rightarrow T'(-1, -1)$
   $R(3, -1) \rightarrow R'(-3, -1)$
   $A(3, -3) \rightarrow A'(-3, -3)$
   $B(1, -3) \rightarrow B'(-1, -3)$

16.

a. $E(-6, 5) \rightarrow E'(-6, -5)$
   $I(-2, 5) \rightarrow I'(-2, -5)$
   $G(-2, 2) \rightarrow G'(-2, -2)$
   $H(-4, 1) \rightarrow H'(-4, -1)$
   $T(-6, 2) \rightarrow T'(-6, -2)$

   $E'(-6, -5) \rightarrow E''(6, -5)$
   $I'(-2, -5) \rightarrow I''(2, -5)$
   $G'(-2, -2) \rightarrow G''(2, -2)$
   $H'(-4, -1) \rightarrow H''(4, -1)$
   $T'(-6, -2) \rightarrow T''(6, -2)$

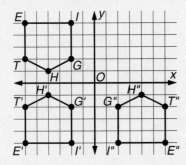

b. $E(-6, 5) \rightarrow E'(6, -5)$
   $I(-2, 5) \rightarrow I'(2, -5)$
   $G(-2, 2) \rightarrow G'(2, -2)$
   $H(-4, 1) \rightarrow H'(4, -1)$
   $T(-6, 2) \rightarrow T'(6, -2)$

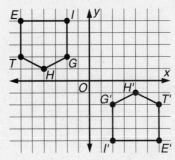

c. The result of a 180° rotation is the same as
the result of a reflection over the x-axis
and the y-axis.

17. Hearts: 2, 4, 10, J, Q, K

Clubs: 2, 4, 10, J, Q, K

Diamonds: 2, 3, 4, 5, 6, 8, 9, J, Q, K, A

Spades: 2, 4, 10, J, Q, K

18. A 90° rotation clockwise is the same as a 270°
rotation counterclockwise, or a 180° rotation
then a 90° rotation counterclockwise. So (x, y)
$\rightarrow (-x, -y)$ on the 180° rotation and then
$(-x, -y) \rightarrow (y, -x)$ on the 90° counterclockwise
rotation. Thus, a 90° clockwise rotation is
represented by $(x, y) \rightarrow (y, -x)$. A rule would
be switch the coordinates of each point and
multiply the second coordinate by −1.

19. See students' work.

Chapter 11 Study Guide and Review

PAGE 458   COMMUNICATING MATHEMATICS

1. domain
2. range
3. solution set
4. linear
5. quadratic
6. translation
7. reflection
8. Substitute the values into the original equation
   and check to see that a true sentence results.
9. Switch the coordinates of each point and
   multiply the first one by −1.

10. $f(n) = 2 - 4n$

n	2 - 4n	f(n)
-1	2 - 4(-1)	6
0	2 - 4(0)	2
2	2 - 4(2)	-6

11. $f(n) = 4n + 1$

n	4n + 1	f(n)	(n, f(n))
-1	4(-1) + 1	-3	(-1, -3)
0	4(0) + 1	1	(0, 1)
1	4(1) + 1	5	(1, 5)

12. $f(n) = \frac{1}{2}n - 2$

n	$\frac{1}{2}n - 2$	f(n)	(n, f(n))
-2	$\frac{1}{2}(-2) - 2$	-3	(-2, -3)
0	$\frac{1}{2}(0) - 2$	-2	(0, -2)
2	$\frac{1}{2}(2) - 2$	-1	(2, -1)

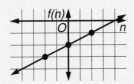

13. $f(n) = -3n$

n	-3n	f(n)	(n, f(n))
-1	-3(-1)	3	(-1, 3)
0	-3(0)	0	(0, 0)
1	-3(1)	-3	(1, -3)

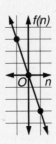

14. $y = -1.5x - 1$

x	-1.5x - 1	y	(x, y)
0	-1.5(0) - 1	-1	(0, -1)
2	-1.5(2) - 1	-4	(2, -4)
-2	-1.5(-2) - 1	2	(-2, 2)
-4	-1.5(-4) - 1	5	(-4, 5)

Answers may vary. Sample answer:

{(0, -1), (2, -4), (-2, 2), (-4, 5)}

15. $y = x + 4$

x	x + 4	y	(x, y)
0	0 + 4	4	(0, 4)
1	1 + 4	5	(1, 5)
-1	-1 + 4	3	(-1, 3)
2	2 + 4	6	(2, 6)

Answers may vary. Sample answer:

{(0, 4), (1, 5), (-1, 3), (2, 6)}

16. $y = -5x + 7$

x	-5x + 7	y	(x, y)
0	-5(0) + 7	7	(0, 7)
1	-5(1) + 7	2	(1, 2)
2	-5(2) + 7	-3	(2, -3)
-1	-5(-1) + 7	12	(-1, 12)

Answers may vary. Sample answer:

{(0, 7), (1, 2), (2, -3), (-1, 12)}

17. $y = -6x$

x	-6x	y	(x, y)
-1	-6(-1)	6	(-1, 6)
0	-6(0)	0	(0, 0)
1	-6(1)	-6	(1, -6)

18. $y = 2x + 7$

x	2x + 7	y	(x, y)
-4	2(-4) + 7	-1	(-4, -1)
-3	2(-3) + 7	1	(-3, 1)
-2	2(-2) + 7	3	(-2, 3)

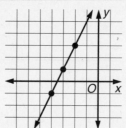

19. $y = -3.5x + 1.5$

x	-3.5x + 1.5	y	(x, y)
-1	-3.5(-1) + 1.5	5	(-1, 5)
1	-3.5(1) + 1.5	-2	(1, -2)
3	-3.5(3) + 1.5	-9	(3, -9)

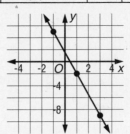

20. $y = \dfrac{x}{2} - 1$

x	$\dfrac{x}{2} - 1$	y	(x, y)
-2	$\dfrac{-2}{2} - 1$	-2	(-2, -2)
0	$\dfrac{0}{2} - 1$	-1	(0, -1)
2	$\dfrac{2}{2} - 1$	0	(2, 0)

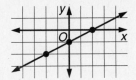

21. $y = 6x$ $y = x + 5$

x	$6x$	y
-0.5	6(-0.5)	-3
0	6(0)	0
0.5	6(0.5)	3

x	$x + 5$	y
-3	-3 + 5	2
-1	-1 + 5	4
0	0 + 5	5

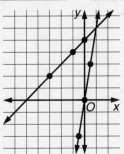

The solution is (1, 6).

22. $y = 4x - 6$ $y = x + 3$

x	$4x - 6$	y
2	4(2) - 6	2
1	4(1) - 6	-2
0	4(0) - 6	-6

x	$x + 3$	y
-1	-1 + 3	2
0	0 + 3	3
1	1 + 3	4

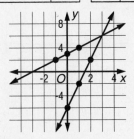

The solution is (3, 6).

23. $y = \dfrac{1}{2}x^2 + 3$

x	$\dfrac{1}{2}x^2 + 3$	y
-2	$\dfrac{1}{2}(-2)^2 + 3$	5
-1	$\dfrac{1}{2}(-1)^2 + 3$	3.5
0	$\dfrac{1}{2}(0)^2 + 3$	3
1	$\dfrac{1}{2}(1)^2 + 3$	3.5
2	$\dfrac{1}{2}(2)^2 + 3$	5

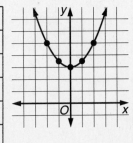

24. $y = x^2 - 1$

x	$x^2 - 1$	y
-2	$(-2)^2 - 1$	3
-1	$(-1)^2 - 1$	0
0	$0^2 - 1$	-1
1	$1^2 - 1$	0
2	$2^2 - 1$	3

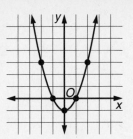

25. $f(n) = 4 - n^2$

n	$4 - n^2$	$f(n)$
-2	$4 - (-2)^2$	0
-1	$4 - (-1)^2$	3
0	$4 - 0^2$	4
1	$4 - 1^2$	3
2	$4 - 2^2$	0

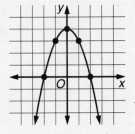

26. $y = -1.25x^2 - 1.5$

x	$-1.25x^2 - 1.5$	y
-2	$-1.25(-2)^2 - 1.5$	-6.5
-1	$-1.25(-1)^2 - 1.5$	-2.75
0	$-1.25(0)^2 - 1.5$	-1.5
1	$-1.25(1)^2 - 1.5$	-2.75
2	$-1.25(2)^2 - 1.5$	-6.5

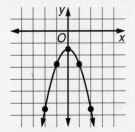

27. $R(-4, 1) + (3, 4) \rightarrow R'(-1, 5)$
    $S(-2, 1) + (3, 4) \rightarrow S'(1, 5)$
    $T(-2, -1) + (3, 4) \rightarrow T'(1, 3)$
    $U(-4, -1) + (3, 4) \rightarrow U'(-1, 3)$

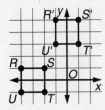

28. $D(1, 1) + (-5, -3) \rightarrow D'(-4, -2)$
    $E(2, 4) + (-5, -3) \rightarrow E'(-3, 1)$
    $F(4, 2) + (-5, -3) \rightarrow F'(-1, -1)$

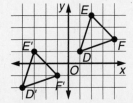

29. $A(2, 5) \rightarrow A'(2, -5)$
$B(6, 5) \rightarrow B'(6, -5)$
$C(6, 3) \rightarrow C'(6, -3)$
$D(2, 3) \rightarrow D'(2, -3)$

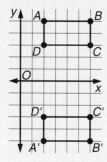

30. $C(-4, -5) \rightarrow C'(4, -5)$
$A(-3, -2) \rightarrow A'(3, -2)$
$R(-5, -3) \rightarrow R'(5, -3)$

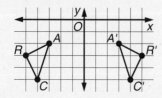

31. $L(1, 4) \rightarrow (4, 1) \rightarrow L'(-4, 1)$
$A(4, 7) \rightarrow (7, 4) \rightarrow A'(-7, 4)$
$T(7, 4) \rightarrow (4, 7) \rightarrow T'(-4, 7)$
$E(4, 1) \rightarrow (1, 4) \rightarrow E'(-1, 4)$

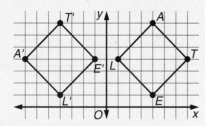

32. $X(3, 1) \rightarrow X'(-3, -1)$
$Y(5, -2) \rightarrow Y'(-5, 2)$
$Z(2, -4) \rightarrow Z'(-2, 4)$

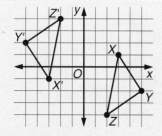

33. $y = 300x - 400$ $\qquad$ $y = 300x + 100$

x	300x - 400	y
0	300(0) - 400	-400
1	300(1) - 400	-100
2	300(2) - 400	200

x	300x + 100	y
0	300(0) + 100	100
1	300(1) + 100	400
2	300(2) + 100	700

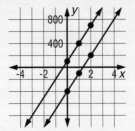

It will never occur since the graphs of their profit equations never meet.

34. $A = \frac{1}{2}bh$

$12 = \frac{1}{2}bh$

$12 \cdot 2 = 2 \cdot \frac{1}{2}bh$

$24 = bh$

b	24 = bh	h
2	24 = 2(h)	12
3	24 = 3(h)	8
4	24 = 4(h)	6

Answers may vary. Sample answers:

$(2, 12)$, $(3, 8)$, and $(4, 6)$

Chapter 11 Test

1. $f(n) = -4n$

n	-4n	f(n)	(n, f(n))
-1	-4(-1)	4	(-1, 4)
0	-4(0)	0	(0, 0)
1	-4(1)	-4	(1, -4)

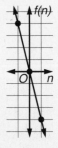

2. $f(n) = 2n - 2$

n	2n - 2	f(n)	(n, f(n))
-1	2(-1) - 2	-4	(-1, -4)
0	2(0) - 2	-2	(0, -2)
1	2(1) - 2	0	(1, 0)

3. $f(n) = \dfrac{16}{n}$

$f\left(-\dfrac{1}{4}\right) = \dfrac{16}{-\dfrac{1}{4}}$

$\qquad\qquad = 16 \div \left(-\dfrac{1}{4}\right)$

$\qquad\qquad = 16 \cdot \left(-\dfrac{4}{1}\right)$

$\qquad\qquad = -64$

4. $y = \dfrac{x}{4} + 1$

x	$\dfrac{x}{4} + 1$	y	(x, y)
0	$\dfrac{0}{4} + 1$	1	(0, 1)
4	$\dfrac{4}{4} + 1$	2	(4, 2)
-4	$\dfrac{-4}{4} + 1$	0	(-4, 0)
-8	$\dfrac{-8}{4} + 1$	-1	(-8, -1)

Answers may vary. Sample answer:

{(0, 1), (4, 2), (-4, 0), (-8, -1)}

5. $y = -2.5x - 5$

x	$-2.5x - 5$	y	(x, y)
0	-2.5(0) - 5	-5	(0, -5)
2	-2.5(2) - 5	-10	(2, -10)
-2	-2.5(-2) - 5	0	(2, 0)
-4	-2.5(-4) - 5	5	(-4, 5)

Answers may vary. Sample answer:

{(0, -5), (2, -10), (2, 0), (-4, 5)}

6. $y = 3 - x$

x	$3 - x$	y	(x, y)
0	3 - 0	3	(0, 3)
1	3 - 1	2	(1, 2)
-1	3 - (-1)	4	(-1, 4)
2	3 - 2	1	(2, 1)

Answers may vary. Sample answer:

{(0, 3), (1, 2), (-1, 4), (2, 1)}

7. $y = 9x - 15$

x	$9x - 15$	y	(x, y)
0	9(0) - 15	-15	(0, -15)
1	9(1) - 15	-6	(1, -6)
2	9(2) - 15	3	(2, 3)
3	9(3) - 15	12	(3, 12)

Answers may vary. Sample answer:

{(0, -15), (1, -6), (2, 3), (3, 12)}

8. $y = \dfrac{x}{3} - 2$

x	$\dfrac{x}{3} - 2$	y	(x, y)
-3	$\dfrac{-3}{3} - 2$	-3	(-3, -3)
0	$\dfrac{0}{3} - 2$	-2	(0, -2)
3	$\dfrac{3}{3} - 2$	-1	(3, -1)

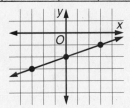

9. $y = -\dfrac{1}{2}x^2 + 6$

x	$-\dfrac{1}{2}x^2 + 6$	y	(x, y)
-4	$-\dfrac{1}{2}(-4)^2 + 6$	-2	(-4, -2)
-2	$-\dfrac{1}{2}(-2)^2 + 6$	4	(-2, 4)
0	$-\dfrac{1}{2}(0)^2 + 6$	6	(0, 6)
2	$-\dfrac{1}{2}(2)^2 + 6$	4	(2, 4)
4	$-\dfrac{1}{2}(4)^2 + 6$	-2	(4, -2)

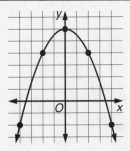

10. $f(n) = 3n^2 - 1$

n	$3n^2 - 1$	$f(n)$	$(n, f(n))$
-2	$3(-2)^2 - 1$	11	(-2, 11)
-1	$3(-1)^2 - 1$	2	(-1, 2)
0	$3(0)^2 - 1$	-1	(0, -1)
1	$3(1)^2 - 1$	2	(1, 2)
2	$3(2)^2 - 1$	11	(2, 11)

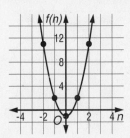

155

11. $y = 35 - 4x$

x	$35 - 4x$	y	(x, y)
2	35 - 4(2)	27	(2, 27)
3	35 - 4(3)	23	(3, 23)
4	35 - 4(4)	19	(4, 19)

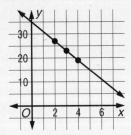

12. $y = 5x + 2$ $y = 2x - 1$

x	$5x + 2$	y
-1	5(-1) + 2	-3
0	5(0) + 2	2
1	5(1) + 2	7

x	$2x - 1$	y
-1	2(-1) - 1	-3
0	2(0) - 1	-1
2	2(2) - 1	3

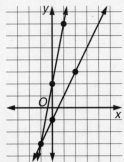

The solution is (-1, -3).

13. $10 \overset{?}{=} \frac{1}{3}(3) + 7$ $10 \overset{?}{=} 4(3) - 5$

$10 \overset{?}{=} \frac{3}{3} + 7$ $10 \overset{?}{=} 12 - 5$

$10 \overset{?}{=} 1 + 7$ $10 \neq 7$

$10 \neq 8$

No, it does not satisfy either equation.

14. $P(-5, -2) + (a, b) \rightarrow P'(2, 7)$

$-5 + a = 2$ $-2 + b = 7$

$-5 + 5 + a = 2 + 5$ $-2 + 2 + b = 7 + 2$

$a = 7$ $b = 9$

The translation can be described by (7, 9).

15. $Q(-3, -2) + (7, 9) \rightarrow Q'(4, 7)$
$R(-3, -5) + (7, 9) \rightarrow R'(4, 4)$
$S(-5, -5) + (7, 9) \rightarrow S'(2, 4)$

16. $C(-5, 2) \rightarrow C'(5, 2)$
$A(-2, 3) \rightarrow A'(2, 3)$
$T(-3, 6) \rightarrow T'(3, 6)$

17. $C(-5, 2) \rightarrow C'(-5, -2)$
$A(-2, 3) \rightarrow A'(-2, -3)$
$T(-3, 6) \rightarrow T'(-3, -6)$

18. Since two 180° rotations result in the original figure, rotate $\Delta A'B'C'$ 180° to find the vertices of ΔABC.
$A'(4, 4) \rightarrow A(-4, -4)$
$B'(1, 2) \rightarrow B(-1, -2)$
$C'(3, 1) \rightarrow C(-3, -1)$

19. $A'(4, 4) \rightarrow (4, 4) \rightarrow A''(-4, 4)$
$B'(1, 2) \rightarrow (2, 1) \rightarrow B''(-2, 1)$
$C'(3, 1) \rightarrow (1, 3) \rightarrow C''(-1, 3)$

20. $253,000 - 239,000 = 14,000$

The circulation was about 14,000 newspapers higher in 1991 than in 1989.

PAGE 461   BONUS

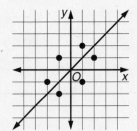

From the graph, a reflection through the line $y = x$ results in the following points:

$(2, 1) \rightarrow (1, 2)$
$(1, -1) \rightarrow (-1, 1)$
$(-1, -2) \rightarrow (-2, -1)$

So a rule would be to switch the coordinates of the point.

Chapter 12   Area and Volume

PAGE 466   CHECKING FOR UNDERSTANDING

1. Since r is given in units, r^2 would result in square units.

2. Let $\pi \approx 3$. So $A = \pi r^2$ becomes $A = 3(5^2) = 75$ m^2.

3. Divide the diameter by 2 to get the radius. Then use the formula.

4. $A = \frac{1}{2}\pi r^2 = \frac{1}{2}\pi(10)^2 \approx 157$ m^2

5. $A = \pi r^2 = \pi(7)^2 \approx 153.9$ ft^2

6. $A = \pi r^2 = \pi(3.2)^2 \approx 32.2$ km^2

7. $r = \frac{d}{2} = \frac{11}{2} = 5.5$ yd

   $A = \pi r^2 = \pi(5.5)^2 \approx 95.0$ yd^2

8. area of entire well $= \pi(5)^2 = 25\pi$ ft

   area of bucket $= \pi(0.5)^2 = 0.25\pi$ ft

   $P(\text{landing in bucket}) = \dfrac{\text{area of bucket}}{\text{area of entire well}}$

   $= \dfrac{0.25\pi}{25\pi} = \dfrac{1}{100}$

PAGE 467   EXERCISES

9. $A = \pi(2.5)^2 \approx 19.6$ cm^2

10. $A = \pi(6)^2 \approx 113.1$ in^2

11. $A = \pi(4.5)^2 \approx 63.6$ cm^2

12. $A = \pi(13)^2 \approx 530.9$ ft^2

13. $A = \pi(5)^2 \approx 78.5$ m^2

14. $49\pi = \pi r^2$

    $\dfrac{49\pi}{\pi} = \dfrac{\pi r^2}{\pi}$

    $49 = r^2$

    $7 = r$

15. area of square $= 6 \cdot 6 = 36$ m^2

    area of circle $= \pi(3)^2 \approx 28.3$ m^2

    shaded area $\approx 36 - 28.3 = 7.7$ m^2

16. area of square $= 4 \cdot 4 = 16$ ft^2

    area of circle $= \pi(2)^2 \approx 12.6$ ft^2

    shaded area $\approx 16 + 12.6 = 28.6$ ft^2

17. area of large circle $= \pi(4)^2 \approx 50.2$ in^2

    area of both small circles $= 2\pi(2)^2 \approx 25.1$ in^2

    shaded area $\approx 50.2 - 25.1 = 25.1$ in^2

18. $m\angle R + m\angle S + m\angle T = 180°$

    $54 + 90 + 3x = 180$

    $144 + 3x = 180$

    $144 - 144 + 3x = 180 - 144$

    $3x = 36$

    $\dfrac{3x}{3} = \dfrac{36}{3}$

    $x = 12$

19. $d = \sqrt{(-5 - 3)^2 + (-4 - (-2))^2}$

    $d = \sqrt{(-8)^2 + (-2)^2}$

    $d = \sqrt{64 + 4}$

    $d = \sqrt{68}$

    $d \approx 8.2$ units

20.

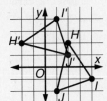

21. a. area of center $= \pi(3)^2 \approx 28.3$ in^2

    area of middle ring $= \pi(6)^2 - \pi(3)^2$

    $= (6^2 - 3^2)\pi$

    $= (36 - 9)\pi$

    $= 27\pi$

    ≈ 84.8 in^2

    area of outer ring $= \pi(9)^2 - \pi(6)^2$

    $= (9^2 - 6^2)\pi$

    $= (81 - 36)\pi$

    $= 45\pi$

    ≈ 141.4 in^2

    b. area of entire board $= \pi(9)^2 = 81\pi$

    $P(\text{hitting white ring}) = \dfrac{27\pi}{81\pi} = \dfrac{1}{3}$

22. The circumference doubles and the area quadruples.

23. a. area of $L = \pi(8)^2 \approx 201.06$ in^2

    area of $2M = 2\pi(6)^2 \approx 226.19$ in^2

    b. $L = \$0.0447126$

    $M = \$0.0441655$

    Medium costs less per square inch.

    c. $L = \$0.04$, $M = \$0.04$; They have the same price per square inch.

PAGE 469   CHECKING FOR UNDERSTANDING

1. Count the cubes in the model or multiply length times width of the layer.

2. Build the side view. The front says the figure is 5 cubes wide. Add cubes to make the base. Then add cubes for the second layer to match the side view. Then complete the top layer.

3. 12 cubes

4. 6 + 6 + 6(5) = 6 + 6 + 30   **5.** 0.6x = 45

$\qquad$ = 42 tiles $\dfrac{0.6x}{0.6} = \dfrac{45}{0.6}$

$\qquad\qquad\qquad\qquad\qquad x = \$75$

6. Toni: anchovy; Matsue: plain; Juana: mushroom.

7. c; Volume of cubes = 30 · 2 · 2 · 2 = 30 · 8

$\qquad$ = 240 in^2 6 × 4 × 10 = 240 in^2

12-3   Three-Dimensional Figures

1. any prism, a pyramid

2. Draw a triangle for the base. Draw a segment from each vertex so that all the segments are congruent and parallel. Finish drawing a triangle for the other base.

3. The edges you can see from your perspective are solid. The dashed lines are for edges you can't see from your perspective.

4. 2 × 3 × 5 units

5.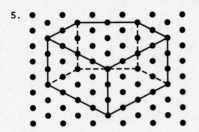

6. a. 4 units   **b.** cube

7. 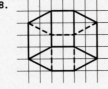   **8.**

9. Draw a parallelogram for the base. Choose a point above the parallelogram. Connect this point to each vertex of the base.

10. Draw an oval for the base. Draw two edges. Draw an oval for the top. For drawing see students' work.

11.

12. 64, 68, 70, 71, 71, 73, 74, 78, 79

Median: 71

LQ: $\dfrac{68 + 70}{2} = \dfrac{138}{2} = 69$

UQ: $\dfrac{74 + 78}{2} = \dfrac{152}{2} = 76$

Interquartile Range: 76 − 69 = 7

13. 17n = 3 · 68   **14.** $A = \pi(6.2)^2 \approx 120.8$ m^2

17n = 204

$\dfrac{17n}{17} = \dfrac{204}{17}$

n = 12

15.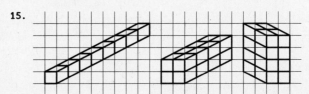

16.

17. See students' work.

12-3B   Mathematics Lab: Nets

1. pyramid   **2.** See students' work.

3. yes;

Sample answer: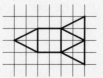

4. a. a staircase   **b.** triangular prism

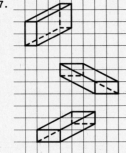

5.

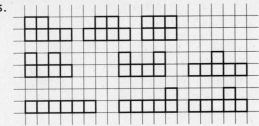

12-4   **Surface Area of Prisms**

PAGE 476   CHECKING FOR UNDERSTANDING

1. triangle, rectangle, parallelogram

2. cube

3. Sample answer:

$$2(\ell h + \ell w + wh)$$

4. rectangular prism

$$2(6 \cdot 3 + 6 \cdot 4 + 4 \cdot 3) = 2(18 + 24 + 12)$$
$$= 2 \cdot 54$$
$$= 108 \text{ ft}^2$$

5. triangular prism

$$3 \cdot 4 \cdot 7 + 2 \cdot \frac{1}{2} \cdot 4 \cdot 3.46 = 84 + 13.84$$
$$= 97.84 \text{ m}^2$$

6. rectangular prism

$$2(15 \cdot 2 + 15 \cdot 12 + 12 \cdot 2) = 2(30 + 180 + 24)$$
$$= 2 \cdot 234$$
$$= 468 \text{ in}^2$$

PAGE 477   EXERCISES

7. S.A. $= 2 \cdot \frac{1}{2} \cdot 6 \cdot 8 + 8 \cdot 20 + 10 \cdot 20 + 6 \cdot 20$

   S.A. $= 48 + 160 + 200 + 120$

   S.A. $= 528 \text{ yd}^2$

8. S.A. $= 2 \cdot 3 \cdot 3 + 4 \cdot 3 \cdot 12$

   S.A. $= 18 + 144$

   S.A. $= 162 \text{ m}^2$

9. S.A. $= 2 \cdot \frac{1}{2} \cdot 6 \cdot 6 + (7.2)(25.2) + (6.3)(25.2)$

   $+ 6 (25.2)$

   S.A. $= 36 + 181.44 + 158.76 + 151.2$

   S.A. $= 527.4 \text{ cm}^2$

10. S.A. $= 6 \cdot 2\frac{1}{2} \cdot 2\frac{1}{2}$

    S.A. $= 37\frac{1}{2} \text{ ft}^2$ or 37.5 ft^2

11. S.A. $= 2(1.5)(1.5) + 4(10)(1.5)$

    S.A. $= 4.5 + 60$

    S.A. $= 64.5 \text{ m}^2$

---

12. S.A. $= 2 \cdot 10 \cdot 3 + 2 \cdot 12 \cdot 3 + 2 \cdot 10 \cdot 12$

    S.A. $= 60 + 72 + 240$

    S.A. $= 372 \text{ in}^2$

13. S.A. $= 2 \cdot 4 \cdot 7 + 2 \cdot 7 \cdot 3 + 2 \cdot 3 \cdot 4$

    S.A. $= 56 + 42 + 24$

    S.A. $= 122 \text{ cm}^2$

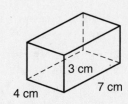
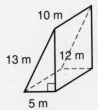

14. S.A. $= 2 \cdot \frac{1}{2} \cdot 5 \cdot 12 + 5 \cdot 10 + 12 \cdot 10$

    $+ 13 \cdot 10$

    S.A. $= 60 + 50 + 120 + 130$

    S.A. $= 360 \text{ m}^2$

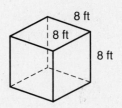

15. S.A. $= 6 \cdot 8 \cdot 8$

    S.A. $= 384 \text{ ft}^2$

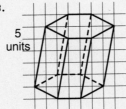

16. $2^4 \cdot 4^3 = 16 \cdot 64 = 1,024$

17. no; The last two digits are not divisible by 4.

18.

19. S.A. of Monica's $= 2 \cdot 3 \cdot 2 + 2 \cdot 6 \cdot 2$

    $+ 2 \cdot 3 \cdot 6$

    $= 12 + 24 + 36$

    $= 72 \text{ cm}^2$

    S.A. of Larry's $= 4 \cdot 3 \cdot 4 + 2 \cdot 3 \cdot 3$

    $= 48 + 18$

    $= 66 \text{ cm}^2$

    Monica's cube; It has the greatest surface area.

20. cube

21. S.A. $= 25 \cdot 35 + 25 \cdot 45 + 25 \cdot 30 + 25 \cdot 92 +$

    $2 \cdot 25 \cdot \left(\dfrac{92 + 30}{2}\right)$

    S.A. $= 875 + 1,125 + 750 + 2,300 + 3,050$

    S.A. $= 8,100 \text{ in}^2$

22. See students' work.

12-5 Surface Area of Cylinders

1. Find 2 times the area of the base plus height times circumference of the base.

2. See students' work.

3. The value of π is approximate.

4.

5. S.A. $= 2\pi(4)^2 + 6 \cdot 2\pi \cdot 4$
   S.A. $= 32\pi + 48\pi$
   S.A. $= 80\pi$
   S.A. ≈ 251.3 m^2

6. S.A. $= 2\pi(8)^2 + 20 \cdot 2\pi \cdot 8$
   S.A. $= 128\pi + 320\pi$
   S.A. $= 448\pi$
   S.A. $\approx 1,407.4$ cm^2

7. S.A. $= 2\pi(1.5)^2 + 2 \cdot 2\pi \cdot (1.5)$
   S.A. $= 4.5\pi + 6\pi$
   S.A. $= 10.5\pi$
   S.A. ≈ 32.99 in^2

8. S.A. $= 2\pi(5)^2 + 11 \cdot 2\pi \cdot 5$
   S.A. $= 50\pi + 110\pi$
   S.A. $= 160\pi$
   S.A. ≈ 502.7 yd^2

9. S.A. $= 2\pi(3.25)^2 + (10.5)(2\pi)(3.25)$
   S.A. $= 21.125\pi + 68.25\pi$
   S.A. $= 89.375\pi$
   S.A. ≈ 280.8 cm^2

10. S.A. $= 2\pi(9)^2 + 3 \cdot 2\pi \cdot 9$
    S.A. $= 162\pi + 54\pi$
    S.A. $= 216\pi$
    S.A. ≈ 678.6 m^2

11. S.A. $= 2\pi(3)^2 + 5 \cdot 2\pi \cdot 3$
    S.A. $= 18\pi + 30\pi$
    S.A. $= 48\pi$
    S.A. ≈ 150.8 in^2

12. S.A. $= 2\pi(15)^2 + 12 \cdot 2\pi \cdot 15$
    S.A. $= 450\pi + 360\pi$
    S.A. $= 810\pi$
    S.A. $\approx 2,544.7$ cm^2

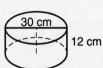

13. $24.2 = \pi r^2$; $r \approx 2.78$
    S.A. $= 2(24.2) + 20(2\pi)(2.78)$
    S.A. $\approx 48.4 + 349.3$
    S.A. ≈ 397.7 m^2

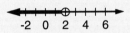

14. $6b - 5 < 7$
     $6b - 5 + 5 < 7 + 5$
     $6b < 12$
     $\dfrac{6b}{6} < \dfrac{12}{6}$
     $b < 2$

15. $h = \dfrac{35}{4} \div \dfrac{1}{2}$

    $h = \dfrac{35}{4} \cdot \dfrac{2}{1}$

    $h = \dfrac{70}{4}$

    $h = 17\dfrac{2}{4}$

    $h = 17\dfrac{1}{2}$

16. 0.352

17. S.A. $= 2 \cdot 5 \cdot 3 + 2 \cdot 3 \cdot 2 + 2 \cdot 2 \cdot 5$
    S.A. $= 30 + 12 + 20$
    S.A. $= 62$ in^2

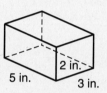

18. S.A. $= 2\pi(4)^2 + 4 \cdot \pi \cdot 8$
    S.A. $= 32\pi + 32\pi$
    S.A. $= 64\pi$
    S.A. ≈ 201.1 in^2

19. Double the radius; See students' work.

20. **a.** S.A. $= 2(1.5) + 2(3)(1.5) + 2(3)(2) +$
       $\dfrac{1}{2}(2)(2\pi)(0.75) + \pi(0.75)^2$
    S.A. $\approx 3 + 9 + 12 + 4.71 + 1.77$
    S.A. ≈ 30.4 ft^2

    b. $\dfrac{200 \text{ ft}^2}{30.4 \text{ ft}^2} \approx 6.6$

21. S.A. $= \left[5\dfrac{1}{2} - \left(2 \cdot \dfrac{1}{4}\right)\right] \cdot 2\pi \cdot 1.75$
    S.A. $= 5 \cdot 3.5\pi$
    S.A. ≈ 55 in^2

22. basketball: $30 = 2\pi r$ $A \approx \pi(4.775)^2$

$$\frac{30}{2\pi} = \frac{2\pi r}{2\pi} \qquad A \approx 71.62 \text{ in}^2$$

$$\frac{30}{2\pi} = r$$

$$r \approx 4.775 \text{ in.}$$

baseball: $9.25 = 2\pi r$ $A \approx \pi(1.472)^2$

$$\frac{9.25}{2\pi} = \frac{2\pi r}{2\pi} \qquad A \approx 6.81 \text{ in}^2$$

$$\frac{9.25}{2\pi} = r$$

$$r \approx 1.472 \text{ in.}$$

soccer ball: $28 = 2\pi r$ $A \approx \pi(4.456)$

$$\frac{28}{2\pi} = \frac{2\pi r}{2\pi} \qquad A \approx 62.39 \text{ in}^2$$

$$\frac{28}{2\pi} = r$$

$$r \approx 4.456$$

Mid-Chapter Review

PAGE 481

1. $A = \pi(6)^2 \approx 113.1 \text{ cm}^2$

2. entire area $= \pi(16)^2 \approx 804.25 \text{ in}^2$

area of 50 point range $= \pi(4)^2 \approx 50.27 \text{ in}^2$

P(hitting 50 point range) $= \dfrac{\text{area of 50 pt. range}}{\text{entire area}}$

$$= \frac{50.27}{804.25}$$

$$= 0.06 \text{ or about } \frac{1}{16}$$

3.

4.

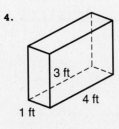 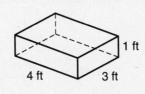

3 ft   4 ft   1 ft

4 ft   3 ft

1 ft

5. S.A. $= 2 \cdot \pi \cdot (10)^2 + 20 \cdot 2\pi \cdot 10$

S.A. $= 200\pi + 400\pi$

S.A. $= 600\pi$

S.A. $\approx 1,885 \text{ m}^2$

6. S.A. $= 2 \cdot 2 \cdot 3 + 2 \cdot 10 \cdot 3 + 2 \cdot 10 \cdot 2$

S.A. $= 12 + 60 + 40$

S.A. $= 112 \text{ ft}^2$

---

7. S.A. $= 2 \cdot \frac{1}{2} \cdot 12 \cdot 9 + 30 \cdot 9 + 30 \cdot 15$

    $+ 30 \cdot 12$

S.A. $= 108 + 270 + 450 + 360$

S.A. $= 1,188 \text{ in}^2$

12-6   **Volume of Prisms and Cylinders**

PAGE 484   CHECKING FOR UNDERSTANDING

1. All volumes can be found using the formula $V = Bh$.

2. In a prism, $B = \ell w$ and in a clinder, $B = \pi r^2$.

3. A square has only two dimensions. Volume requires three dimensions.

4. $V = \ell \cdot w \cdot h$ or $V = s^3$

5. The value of π is approximate.

6. $V = 4 \cdot 5 \cdot 6$ **7.** $V = \pi(5)^2(4)$

$V = 120 \text{ m}^3$ $V = 100\pi$

                          $V \approx 314.2 \text{ ft}^2$

8. $V = \frac{1}{2} \cdot 3 \cdot 4 \cdot 10$ **9.** $V = \pi(3)^2(5)$

$V = 60 \text{ yd}^3$ $V = 45\pi$

                          $V \approx 141.4 \text{ cm}^3$

10. $V = 3(1.5)(4)$ **11.** $V = \pi(5.25)^2(13)$

$V = 18 \text{ in}^3$ $V = 358.3125\pi$

                          $V \approx 1,125.7 \text{ cm}^3$

PAGES 484-485   EXERCISES

12. $V = 7 \cdot 7 \cdot 8$ **13.** $V = \pi(3.7)^2(24)$

$V = 392 \text{ yd}^2$ $V = 328.56\pi$

                          $V \approx 1,032.2 \text{ cm}^3$

14. $V = \frac{1}{2} \cdot 10 \cdot 2 \cdot 10$ **15.** $V = (1.2)^3$

$V = 100 \text{ ft}^3$ $V = 1.728 \text{ cm}^3$

16. $V = \frac{1}{2} \cdot 5 \cdot 4 \cdot 7$ **17.** $V = \pi(3)^2(195)$

$V = 70 \text{ ft}^3$ $V = 1,755\pi$

                          $V \approx 5,513.5 \text{ mm}$

18. $V = \pi(6)^2(14)$

$V = 504\pi$

$V \approx 1,583.4 \text{ m}^3$

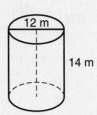

12 m

14 m

19. $V = \frac{1}{2} \cdot 5 \cdot 12 \cdot 10$

   $V = 300 \text{ ft}^3$

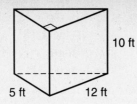

10 ft

5 ft   12 ft

20. $V = 25.4 \cdot 5$

   $V = 127 \text{ cm}^3$

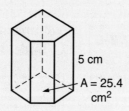

5 cm

$A = 25.4 \text{ cm}^2$

21.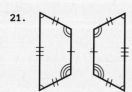

22. $64 < 76 < 81$

   $8^2 < 76 < 9^2$

   $8 < \sqrt{76} < 9$

   Since 76 is closer to 81 than to 64, the best whole integer estimate for $\sqrt{76}$ is 9.

23. S.A. $= 2\pi(4)^2 + 9 \cdot 2 \cdot \pi \cdot 4$

   S.A. $= 32\pi + 72\pi$

   S.A. $= 104\pi$

   S.A. $\approx 326.73 \text{ cm}^2$

24. a. LP's

   b. CD's

   c. Sample answer: CD's became more affordable, have better sound quality and have more songs. The quality and convenience of the LP's was less than that of the CD's and cassettes.

   d. CD 1986 : $V = \pi(2.5)^2\, 53 \approx 104{,}065.3 \text{ mm}^3$

   CD 1990 : $V = \pi(25)^2\, 287 \approx 563{,}523.2 \text{ mm}^3$

   LP 1986 : $V = \pi(25)^2\, 125 \approx 245{,}436.9 \text{ mm}^2$

   LP 1990 : $V = \pi(25)^2\, 12 \approx 23{,}561.9 \text{ mm}^2$

   Cassette 1986 : $V = \pi(25)^2\, 345 \approx 677{,}405.9 \text{ mm}^3$

   Cassette 1990: $V = \pi(25)^2\, 442 \approx 867{,}865 \text{ mm}^3$

25. volume of rectangular ditch $= 5 \cdot 4 \cdot 20$

   $\qquad\qquad\qquad\qquad = 400 \text{ ft}^2$

   volume of pipe $= \pi(1.5)^2(20) \approx 141 \text{ ft}^2$

   volume of dirt $\approx 400 - 141 = 259 \text{ ft}^3$

26. Sample answer: the cube, because

   $10^3 \text{ m}^3 > \pi(5^2)(10) \text{ m}^3$

12-6B Mathematics Lab: Surface Area and Volume

PAGE 486   WHAT DO YOU THINK?

1. See students' work.   2. See students' work.

3. It is less than the original height.

4. a. Answers may vary. Sample answer: The circumference of a can is about the same as the circumference of the glass bottles previously used.

   b. Answers may vary.

12-7 Volume of Pyramids and Cones

PAGES 488-489   CHECKING FOR UNDERSTANDING

1. triangles   2. Each can be defined as $V = \frac{1}{3}Bh$.

3. V(pyramid) $= \frac{1}{3} \cdot 10^2 \cdot 10 = 333.\overline{3} \text{ cm}^3$

   V(cone) $= \frac{1}{3} \cdot \pi \cdot (5)^2 \cdot 10 \approx 261.8 \text{ cm}^3$

   The pyramid has a greater volume than the cone.

4. $V = \frac{1}{3} \cdot 8 \cdot 5 \cdot 3$

   $V = 40 \text{ in}^3$

5. $V = \frac{1}{3} \cdot \pi \cdot (2)^2 \cdot 5$

   $V \approx 20.9 \text{ m}^3$

6. $V = \frac{1}{3} \cdot \frac{1}{2} \cdot 6 \cdot 8 \cdot 7$

   $V = 56 \text{ yd}^3$

PAGE 489   EXERCISES

7. $V = \frac{1}{3} \cdot \pi \cdot (6)^2 \cdot 9$

   $V \approx 339.3 \text{ m}^3$

8. $V = \frac{1}{3} \cdot 6 \cdot 8 \cdot 7$

   $V = 112 \text{ in}^3$

9. $V = \frac{1}{3} \cdot (11.2)^2(2.4)$

   $V \approx 100.4 \text{ m}^3$

10. $V = \frac{1}{3} \cdot \pi \cdot (5.5)^2 \cdot 16$

   $V \approx 506.8 \text{ ft}^3$

11. $V = \frac{1}{3} \cdot \frac{1}{2} \cdot 5 \cdot 12 \cdot 8$

   $V = 80 \text{ yd}^3$

12. $V = \frac{1}{3} \cdot \left(\frac{10 + 18}{2} \right) \cdot 7 \cdot 12$

   $V = \frac{1}{3} \cdot 14 \cdot 7 \cdot 12$

   $V = 392 \text{ cm}^2$

13. $V = \frac{1}{3} \cdot 15 \cdot 9$

   $V = 45 \text{ cm}^3$

14. $V = \frac{1}{3}(235.2)(12)$

   $V = 940.8 \text{ ft}^2$

15. 27, 33, 39, 45

16. $D(3, 6) \rightarrow (3 \cdot 2, 6 \cdot 2) \rightarrow D'(6, 12)$

    $E(10, 8) \rightarrow (10 \cdot 2, 8 \cdot 2) \rightarrow E'(20, 16)$

    $F(9, 3) \rightarrow (9 \cdot 2, 3 \cdot 2) \rightarrow F'(18, 6)$

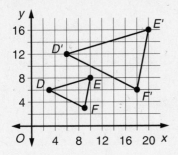

17. $V = \pi \cdot (4)^2 \cdot 10$

    $V \approx 502.65 \text{ ft}^3$

18. The dimensions of the pyramid would also need to be doubled.

19. $V(\text{cylinder}) = \pi \cdot (0.5)^2 \cdot 4 \approx 3 \text{ cm}^3$

    $V(\text{pyramid}) = \frac{1}{3} \cdot \pi \cdot (6)^2 \cdot 6 \approx 226 \text{ cm}^3$

    Total volume $\approx 3 + 226 = 229 \text{ cm}^3$

12-7B   ## Mathematics Lab: Exploring Spheres

PAGE 490   WHAT DO YOU THINK?

1. $\frac{1}{4}$ 2. 4 patterns   3. πr^2 4. $4\pi r^2$

PAGE 490   EXTENSION

5. a. pyramid

    b. h = radius of sphere

       base = part of surface area

    c. Volume of sphere equals the sum of volumes of all the wedges.

       The height of each wedge is the radius of the sphere.

       Use the distributive property to find common factor.

       All the bases together equal the surface area of the sphere.

       Surface area = $4\pi r^2$.

       Simplify the expression.

12-8   ## Precision and Significant Digits

PAGES 492-493   CHECKING FOR UNDERSTANDING

1. no, because of the density of numbers

2. Answers may vary.   3. sixteenth of an inch

4. a. 3

    b. closer to 5.5 than to 5.51.

5. 20.3 - accurate to meter, 3 tenths is estimate

    4,200 - accurate to thousands, 200 is estimate

    0.00251 - accurate to ten-thousandths, 1 hundred-thousandths is estimate

    0.0580 - accurate to thousandths, 0 ten-thousandths is estimate

6. 34.3 oz; Tenths of an ounce is a more precise unit than an ounce or a pound.

7. accurate to $212 billion; $900 million is estimate; It is closer to $212.9 billion than to $212.8 or $213.0 billion.

PAGE 493   EXERCISES

8. accurate to the foot; tenths of a foot is an estimate

9. accurate to tenths of an inch; hundredths of an inch is an estimate

10. accurate to hundredths of a millimeter; thousandths of a millimeter is an estimate

11. accurate to hundredths of a mile; thousandths of a mile is an estimate

12. accurate to ten thousandths of a centimeter; hundred thousandths is an estimate

13. accurate to ten kilometers; 0 kilometers is an estimate

14. 18.0 cm; accurate to nearest centimeter

15. 305 ft

16. a. 1

    b. 2

    c. 0.02 meters is an estimate of 2 centimeters. 2.2 centimeters is accurate to 2 centimeters with an estimate of 0.2 centimeters.

17.

6	5	
84	6	
99850	7	
99765430	8	278899
520	9	00333455679
	10	00

    $5|6 = 56$

18. $9.4 \times 10^{-5} = 9.4 \times 0.00001$

              $= 0.000094$

19. $V = \frac{1}{3} \cdot \pi \cdot (3.5)^2 \cdot 12$ 20. $A = \pi(4.2)^2$

    $V \approx 153.94 \text{ m}^3$ $A \approx 55.4 \text{ cm}^2$

21. They are all exact to 10 million.

22. Sizes are accurate to the nearest inch. The half inch is an estimate.

23. accurate to next to last digit of input

Chapter 12 Study Guide and Review

PAGE 494   COMMUNICATING MATHEMATICS

1. f   2. i   3. g   4. d   5. e   6. b

7. a   8. Sample answer: Find the sum of the surface areas of the 6 faces.

9. rectangle   10. $V = \pi\left(\frac{d}{2}\right)^2 h$

PAGES 494-496   SKILLS AND CONCEPTS

11. $A = \pi(4)^2 \approx 50.3 \text{ m}^2$ 12. $A = \pi(7.5)^2 \approx 176.7 \text{ in}^2$

13.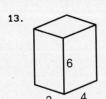

14.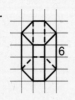

15.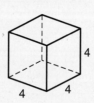

16. S.A. $= 2 \cdot 2 \cdot 3 + 2 \cdot 3 \cdot 5 + 2 \cdot 2 \cdot 5$
    S.A. $= 12 + 30 + 20$
    S.A. $= 62 \text{ ft}^2$

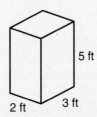

17. S.A. $= 6 \cdot 3 \cdot 3$
    S.A. $= 54 \text{ cm}^2$

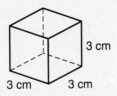

18. S.A. $= 2\pi(5)^2 + 2\pi(5)(8)$
    S.A. $= 50\pi + 80\pi$
    S.A. $= 130\pi$
    S.A. $\approx 408.41 \text{ m}^2$

19. S.A. $= 2\pi(20)^2 + 2\pi(20)(16)$
    S.A. $= 800\pi + 640\pi$
    S.A. $= 1,440\pi$
    S.A. $\approx 4,523.89 \text{ yd}^2$

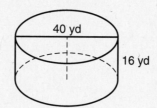

20. $V = \pi(8)^2(12)$
    $V = 768\pi$
    $V \approx 2,412.74 \text{ in}^3$

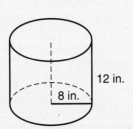

21. $V = 6 \cdot 9 \cdot 7$
    $V = 378 \text{ m}^3$

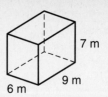

22. $V = \frac{1}{3} \cdot \pi \cdot 8^2 \cdot 10$
    $V = 670.2 \text{ in}^3$

23. $V = \frac{1}{3} \cdot \frac{1}{2} \cdot 4 \cdot 3 \cdot 3$
    $V = 6 \text{ mm}^3$

24. 1   25. 3   26. 2   27. 4   28. 4

29. accurate to 5.0 miles; two hundredths is an estimate

PAGE 496   APPLICATIONS AND PROBLEM SOLVING

30. $A = \pi(6)^2 \approx 113.10 \text{ cm}^2$
    $A = \pi(0.75)^2 \approx 1.77 \text{ cm}^2$
    A(disc) $\approx 113.10 - 1.77 = 111.33 \text{ cm}^2$

31. 55 cubes

32. $V = \pi \cdot (4.2)^2 \cdot 13 \cdot 8$
    $V \approx 764.76 \text{ cm}^3$

Chapter 12 Test

PAGE 497

1. A(entire circle) $= \pi(4)^2 \approx 50.3 \text{ m}^2$
   A(center) $= \pi(2)^2 \approx 12.6 \text{ m}^2$
   A(outer ring) $\approx 50.3 - 12.6 = 37.7 \text{ m}^2$

2. $A = \frac{1}{2}\pi(10)^2 \approx 157.1 \text{ yd}^2$

3. A (entire circle) $= \pi(8)^2 \approx 201.1 \text{ in}^2$
   A(small circle) $= \pi(4)^2 \approx 50.3 \text{ in}^2$
   A(shaded) $\approx 201.1 - 50.3 = 150.8 \text{ in}^2$

4.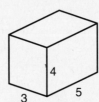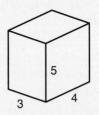

5. S.A. $= 2 \cdot \frac{1}{2} \cdot 12 \cdot 5 + 5 \cdot 18 + 13 \cdot 18 + 12 \cdot 18$
   S.A. $= 60 + 90 + 234 + 216$
   S.A. $= 600 \text{ ft}^2$

6. S.A. $= 2 \cdot 2 \cdot 3 + 2 \cdot 3 \cdot 6 + 2 \cdot 2 \cdot 6$
   S.A. $= 12 + 36 + 24$
   S.A. $= 72 \text{ cm}^2$

7. S.A. $= 6(10.5)^2$
   S.A. $= 661.5 \text{ yd}^2$

8. S.A. $= 2\pi(3.5)^2 + 2\pi(3.5)(4.5)$
    S.A. $= 24.5\pi + 31.5\pi$
    S.A. $= 56\pi$
    S.A. ≈ 175.9 m^2

9.

10. V $= (9.5)(14)(4)$
    V $= 532$ mm^3

11. V $= \frac{1}{2} \cdot 9 \cdot 12 \cdot 20$
    V $= 1{,}080$ in^3

12. V $= 6^3$
    V $= 216$ ft^3

13. V $= \pi(4.5)^2(22)$
    V $\approx 1{,}399.6$ m^3

14. V $= \frac{1}{3} \cdot 10 \cdot 8 \cdot 9$
    V $= 240$ mm^3

15. V $= \frac{1}{3} \cdot \pi \cdot 3^2 \cdot 9$
    V ≈ 84.8 m^3

16. V $= \frac{1}{3} \cdot \frac{1}{2} \cdot 12 \cdot 16 \cdot 14$
    V $= 448$ in^3

17. 1

18. accurate to 8.2 feet; 0 hundredths is an estimate.

19. V(silo #1) $= \pi(10)^2(52) \approx 16{,}336.3$ ft^3
    V(silo #2) $= \pi(15)^2(38) \approx 26{,}860.6$ ft^3
    The silo measuring 30 ft × 38 ft has a larger volume.

20. 5 tricycles × 3 wheels = 15 wheels
    1 bicycle × 2 wheels = 2 wheels
    6 cyclists   17 wheels
    1 bicycle and 5 tricycles

PAGE 497   BONUS
Find the sum of the areas of the base and each triangular face.

Academic Skills Test

PAGES 498-499

1. *D*; 186 ÷ 3 = 62 pages
2. C
3. A
4. *D*; $c^2 = a^2 + b^2$
    $c^2 = 4^2 + 2^2$
    $c^2 = 16 + 4$
    $c^2 = 20$
    $c \approx 4.5$
5. D

6. A

7. A; $A = \pi r^2$

8. D; Area of each base: $\frac{1}{2} \cdot 3 \cdot 4 = 6$
    Area of sides: $5 \cdot 10 = 50$
                   $4 \cdot 10 = 40$
                   $3 \cdot 10 = 30$
    Surface area: $6 + 6 + 50 + 40 + 30 = 132$ cm^2

9. A: $A = 2\pi(5)(12)$
    $A \approx 380$ cm^2

10. C; $5 + |-4| = 5 + 4 = 9$
    $|5| + |-4| = 5 + 4 = 9$

11. A; 11, 12, 14, 14, 15, 15, 16, 18, 19, 20
    Mean: $\dfrac{11 + 12 + 14 + 14 + 15 + 15 + 16 + 18 +}{10}$
    $\dfrac{19 + 20}{10} = \dfrac{154}{10} = 15.4$
    Median: 15

12. B; $V = 4 \cdot 5 \cdot 10 = 200$ ft^3
    $V = \pi(5)^2(12) \approx 942.5$ ft^2

13. B; $\frac{1}{5} \cdot \frac{1}{5} = \frac{1}{25}$
    $\frac{1}{4} \cdot \frac{1}{6} = \frac{1}{24}$

14. C; $C = 2\pi r$ $C = \pi d$
    $4\pi = 2\pi r$ $2\pi = \pi d$
    $\dfrac{4\pi}{2\pi} = \dfrac{2\pi r}{2\pi}$ $\dfrac{2\pi}{\pi} = \dfrac{\pi d}{\pi}$
    $2 = r$ $2 = d$

15. B; $\sqrt{100} = 10$
    $\sqrt{50} + \sqrt{50} \approx 7.1 + 7.1 = 14.2$

16. C; $\frac{3}{8} = \frac{c}{12}$ $8c = 8 \cdot \frac{9}{2} = 36$
    $8c = 3 \cdot 12$ $3(12) = 36$
    $8c = 36$
    $\dfrac{8c}{8} = \dfrac{36}{8}$
    $c = \dfrac{9}{2}$

17. D

18. B; $\tan A = \frac{4}{7}$, $\tan B = \frac{7}{4}$

19. C; $\$50 \cdot 80\% = \$40$
    $\$50 - \$10 = \$40$

20. B; $\$550 \cdot 8\% \cdot 1 = \$44$
    $\$550 \cdot 4.5\% \cdot 2 = \$45$

21. A, $f(5) = 2 \cdot 5 + 3$
    $f(5) = 10 + 3$
    $f(50) = 13$

22. A; $100 = 2 \cdot 2 \cdot 5 \cdot 5$
    $36 = 2 \cdot 2 \cdot 3 \cdot 3$
    LCM $= 2 \cdot 2 \cdot 3 \cdot 3 \cdot 5 \cdot 5 = 900$
    $50 = 2 \cdot 5 \cdot 5$
    $90 = 2 \cdot 3 \cdot 3 \cdot 5$
    LCM $= 2 \cdot 3 \cdot 3 \cdot 5 \cdot 5 = 450$

23. B; $\frac{3}{25} = 0.12$

Chapter 13   Discrete Math and Probability

<table>
<tr><td>

13-1A

</td><td>

**Mathematics Lab:
Fair and Unfair Games**

</td></tr>
</table>

PAGE 503   WHAT DO YOU THINK?

1. There are 9 different outcomes: scissors, paper; scissors, stone; scissors, scissors; paper, scissors; paper, stone; paper, paper; stone, scissors; stone, paper; stone, stone.

2. Player A can win 3 ways: scissors, paper; paper, stone; stone, scissors.

3. Player B can win 3 ways: scissors, stone; paper, scissors; stone, paper.

4. Three outcomes are a draw: scissors, scissors; paper, paper; stone, stone.

5. yes

6. yes; Each player's chance of winning is $33\frac{1}{3}$%.

PAGE 503   WHAT DO YOU THINK?

7. There are 8 different outcome: AAB, AAC, ACB, ACC, BAB, BAC, BCB, BCC.

8. Player 1 can win 6 ways: AAB, AAC, ACC, BAB, BCB, BCC.

9. Player 2 can win 2 ways: ACB, BAC.

10. no; No draw is possible.

11. no

12. This is an unfair game. Player 1's chances of winning are $\frac{6}{8}$ or 75%, and Player 2's chances of winning are $\frac{2}{8}$ or 25%.

PAGE 503   APPLICATION

13. The game is fair. There are four possible outcomes: RR, RB, BR, BB. Player X has 2 ways to win, namely RR and BB. This is a $\frac{2}{4}$ or 50% chance of winning. Player Y has 2 ways to win also, namely RB and BR. This is a $\frac{2}{4}$ or 50% chance of winning. There are no draws. Since both players have the same chance of winning, the game is fair.

PAGE 503   EXTENSION

14. See students' work.

<table>
<tr><td>

13-1

</td><td>

Counting Outcomes

</td></tr>
</table>

PAGES 505-506   CHECKING FOR UNDERSTANDING

1.

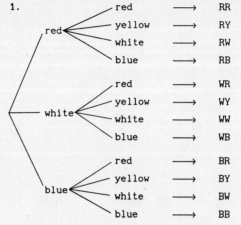

2. See students' work.

3. Answers may vary. Sample answer: When there are many outcomes, a tree diagram takes a lot of time and space.

4. Yes they are, since the cane dice fall freely.

5. a.

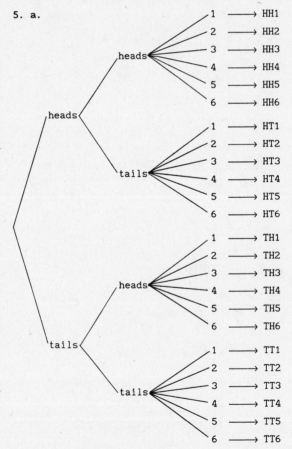

b. 24 outcomes are possible.

c. 6 outcomes show two heads: HH1, HH2, HH3, HH4, HH5, HH6.

d. 4 outcomes show 6 on the die: HH6, HT6, TH6, TT6.

e. 1 outcome shows two tails and a 3: TT3.

f. HT2, HT4, HT6, TH2, TH4, TH6

P(one head and an even number) $= \frac{6}{24} = \frac{1}{4}$

6. There are two choices for each question, and there are five questions. Then there are $2 \cdot 2 \cdot 2 \cdot 2 \cdot 2$ or 32 outcomes.

PAGES 506   EXERCISES

7.

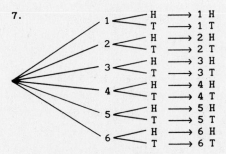

There are 12 outcomes.

8. To save space, this diagram is divided into 5 sections

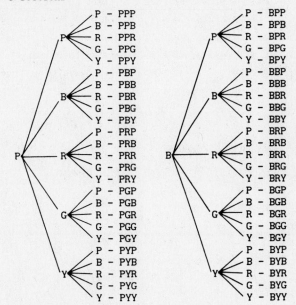

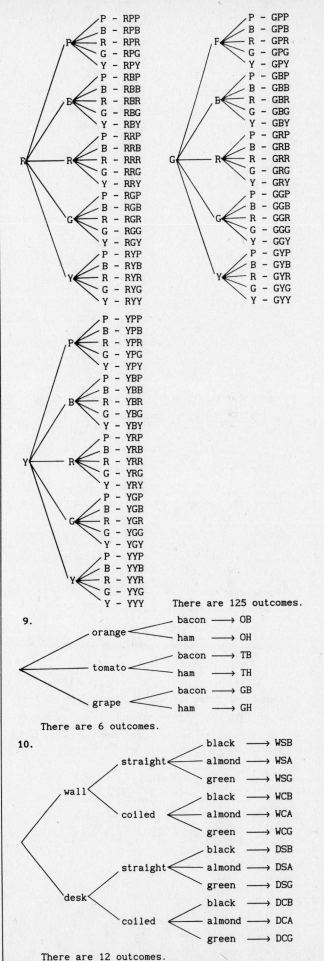

There are 125 outcomes.

9.

orange ⟨ bacon → OB, ham → OH
tomato ⟨ bacon → TB, ham → TH
grape ⟨ bacon → GB, ham → GH

There are 6 outcomes.

10.

wall
  straight ⟨ black → WSB, almond → WSA, green → WSG
  coiled ⟨ black → WCB, almond → WCA, green → WCG
desk
  straight ⟨ black → DSB, almond → DSA, green → DSG
  coiled ⟨ black → DCB, almond → DCA, green → DCG

There are 12 outcomes.

167

11. Each coin has two possible outcomes. Since there are 4 coins there are 2 · 2 · 2 · 2 or 16 outcomes.

12. Each die has six possible outcomes. Since there are two dice, there are 6 · 6 or 36 outcomes.

13. (3 shorts) · (4 shirts) · (2 shoes) = 24 outfits

14. (3 sizes) · (2 colors) = 6 outcomes

15. (3 pasta) · (3 sauce) · (3 meat) = 27 combinations

16. $\frac{f}{2} + 10 = 14$

$\frac{f}{2} + 10 - 10 = 14 - 10$

$\frac{f}{2} = 4$

$2 \cdot \frac{f}{2} = 4 \cdot 2$

$f = 8$

17. $b = -3\frac{1}{3}\left(-6\frac{3}{5}\right)$

$b = \left(-\frac{10}{3}\right)\left(-\frac{33}{5}\right)$

$b = \frac{330}{15}$

$b = 22$

18. In 14.4, all the digits are significant, so there are 3 significant digits.

19.

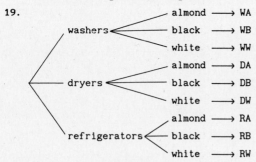

There are 9 outcomes.

20. There are 2 possible outcomes for each coin. Since there are x coins, you multiply 2 · 2 · 2... x times which is 2^x.

21. no; The possible outcomes are found by multiplying the number of ways the first event can occur times the number of ways the second event can occur. Multiplication is commutative so it does not matter which event occurs first.

22. See students' work.

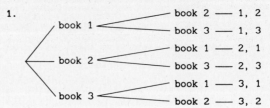

Permutations

1.

```
                              ┌─── book 2 ── 1, 2
              ┌─ book 1 ──────┤
              │               └─── book 3 ── 1, 3
              │               ┌─── book 1 ── 2, 1
         ─────┼─ book 2 ──────┤
              │               └─── book 3 ── 2, 3
              │               ┌─── book 1 ── 3, 1
              └─ book 3 ──────┤
                              └─── book 2 ── 3, 2
```

There are 6 ways.

2. 6! = 6 · 5 · 4 · 3 · 2 · 1

3. $P(4, 3) = 4 \cdot 3 \cdot 2 = 24$

4. $P(12, 4) = 12 \cdot 11 \cdot 10 \cdot 9 = 11,880$

5. 3! = 3 · 2 · 1 = 6

6. 7! = 7 · 6 · 5 · 4 · 3 · 2 · 1 = 5,040

7. STUDY ⟹ There are 5 letters so there are 5! = 5 · 4 · 3 · 2 · 1 = 120 different ways to arrange them.

8. MATH ⟹ There are 4 letters so there are 4! = 4 · 3 · 2 · 1 = 24 different ways to arrange them.

9. EQUALS ⟹ There are 6 letters so there are 6! = 6 · 5 · 4 · 3 · 2 · 1 = 720 different ways to arrange them.

10. FUN ⟹ There are 3 letters so there are 3! = 3 · 2 · 1 = 6 different ways to arrange them.

11. $P(6, 3) = 6 \cdot 5 \cdot 4$
= 120

12. 0! = 1

13. $P(8, 4) = 8 \cdot 7 \cdot 6 \cdot 5$
= 1,680

14. 9! = 9 · 8 · 7 · 6 · 5 · 4 · 3 · 2 · 1
= 362,880

15. 6! = 6 · 5 · 4 · 3 · 2 · 1
= 720

16. $P(10, 5) = 10 \cdot 9 \cdot 8 \cdot 7 \cdot 6$
= 30,240

17. 5! = 5 · 4 · 3 · 2 · 1
= 120

18. $P(8, 8) = 8!$
= 8 · 7 · 6 · 5 · 4 · 3 · 2 · 1
= 40,320

19. CARDS has 5 letters so there are $P(5, 4) = 5 \cdot 4 \cdot 3 \cdot 2 = 120$ different ways to arrange the letters.

20. There are $P(4, 4) = 4! = 4 \cdot 3 \cdot 2 \cdot 1 = 24$ different numbers.

21. Since the father is seated in the aisle, you are actually seating 4 people in 4 seats, or $P(4, 4) = 4! = 4 \cdot 3 \cdot 2 \cdot 1 = 24$ different ways the family can be seated.

22. $r = \dfrac{352}{-11}$

$r = -32$

23. $28 = 2 \cdot 2 \cdot 7$
$56 = 2 \cdot 2 \cdot 2 \cdot 7$
$126 = 2 \cdot 3 \cdot 3 \cdot 7$
$GCF = 2 \cdot 7 = 14$

24. $\dfrac{42}{70} = \dfrac{r}{100}$

$42 \cdot 100 = 70r$

$4{,}200 = 70r$

$\dfrac{4{,}200}{70} = \dfrac{70r}{70}$

$60 = r$

42 is 60% of 70.

25. There are 3 choices for the 5 questions, so there are $3 \cdot 3 \cdot 3 \cdot 3 \cdot 3$ or 243 possible outcomes.

26. $P(6, 3) = 6 \cdot 5 \cdot 4$
$= 120$
There are 120 ways to award the medals.

27. $P(5, 3) = 5 \cdot 4 \cdot 3$
$= 60$
There are 60 ways to seat the players.

28. There are 8 letters in the word PURCHASE. There are 5 ways to choose the first letter and 3 ways to choose the last letter. There are then 6! or $6 \cdot 5 \cdot 4 \cdot 3 \cdot 2 \cdot 1$ ways to arrange the letters in between. In total, there are $5 \cdot (6 \cdot 5 \cdot 4 \cdot 3 \cdot 2 \cdot 1) \cdot 3$ or 10,800 different arrangments.

29. Answers may vary. Sample answer: Jane has ten posters she wants to put on a wall in her bedroom. Only three posters will fit on the wall. How many possible ways can she arrange the posters?

30. $9! = 9 \cdot 8 \cdot 7 \cdot 6 \cdot 5 \cdot 4 \cdot 3 \cdot 2 \cdot 1$
$= 362{,}880$
The photographer can arrange the cheerleaders in 362,880 different ways.

Decision Making

PAGES 510-511

1. The bumper stickers are $10.59 per lot and are sold in lots of 20. Each bumper sticker then costs $10.59 ÷ 20 or about $0.53 each. To make 100% profit you will need to charge ($0.53) $\cdot$ 2 or $1.06 for each bumper sticker.

2. Since you are planning to sell 10% more head bands this year than last, you are actually planning to sell 110% of 125. So

$\dfrac{x}{125} = \dfrac{110}{100}$

$100x = 13{,}750$

$\dfrac{100x}{100} = \dfrac{13{,}750}{100}$

$x = 137.50$

So you are planning to sell about 138 head bands. Since they are sold in lots of 12, you will need to order $\dfrac{138}{12}$ or 11.5 lots. Since half-lots are not available, order 12 lots of head bands.

3. You should choose your school colors for items with logos.

4. no; It is a flea market and many of the items are not very expensive.

5. No, since it is a community-wide flea market, surveying students would not be a representative sample.

6. See students' work.

7. See students' work.

13-3 Combinations

PAGES 513-514 **CHECKING FOR UNDERSTANDING**

1. Find $P(52, 5)$ and divide by 5!.

2. Answers may vary. Sample answer:
For a class of 25 students,
$C(25, 5) = \dfrac{25 \cdot 24 \cdot 23 \cdot 22 \cdot 21}{5!}$.

3. $P(3, 2) > C(3, 2)$. To get $C(3, 2)$ you take $P(3, 2)$ and divide by 2!.

4. Answers may vary. Sample answer:
Shapes: □ △ ○
$C(3, 2) =$ □△, □○, △○

5. $C(5, 2) = \dfrac{5 \cdot 4}{2!}$

$= \dfrac{20}{2}$

$= 10$

6. $C(4, 4) = \dfrac{4 \cdot 3 \cdot 2 \cdot 1}{4!}$

$= \dfrac{24}{24}$

$= 1$

7. $C(3, 2) = \dfrac{3 \cdot 2}{2!}$

$= \dfrac{6}{2}$

$= 3$

8. $C(12, 5) = \dfrac{12 \cdot 11 \cdot 10 \cdot 9 \cdot 8}{5!}$

$= \dfrac{95,040}{120}$

$= 792$

9. permutation; The books must be in a row so order is important.

10. combination; Order is not important because it does not matter if a person was selected first or last.

11. combination; Order is not important because the CD's are not in a row or in any order.

12. permutation; The cars must be in a line so order is important.

13. CARD has 4 letters so we are looking for $C(4, 3)$.

$C(4, 3) = \dfrac{4 \cdot 3 \cdot 2}{3!}$

$= \dfrac{24}{6}$

$= 4$

There are 4 three-letter combinations.

PAGE 514   EXERCISES

14. $C(7, 2) = \dfrac{7 \cdot 6}{2!}$

$= \dfrac{42}{2}$

$= 21$

15. $C(6, 5) = \dfrac{6 \cdot 5 \cdot 4 \cdot 3 \cdot 2}{5!}$

$= \dfrac{720}{120}$

$= 6$

16. $C(9, 4) = \dfrac{9 \cdot 8 \cdot 7 \cdot 6}{4!}$

$= \dfrac{3,024}{24}$

$= 126$

17. $C(25, 9) = \dfrac{25 \cdot 24 \cdot 23 \cdot 22 \cdot 21 \cdot 20 \cdot 19 \cdot 18 \cdot 17}{9!}$

$= \dfrac{25 \cdot \overset{}{24} \cdot 23 \cdot \overset{11}{22} \cdot 21 \cdot 20 \cdot 19 \cdot 18 \cdot 17}{9 \cdot 8 \cdot 7 \cdot 6 \cdot 5 \cdot 4 \cdot 3 \cdot 2 \cdot 1}$

$= 25 \cdot 23 \cdot 11 \cdot 19 \cdot 17$

$= 2,042,975$

18. $C(12, 3) = \dfrac{12 \cdot 11 \cdot 10}{3!}$

$= \dfrac{1,320}{6}$

$= 220$ combinations

19. $C(52, 5) = \dfrac{52 \cdot 51 \cdot 50 \cdot 49 \cdot 48}{5!}$

$= \dfrac{52 \cdot 51 \cdot \overset{5}{50} \cdot 49 \cdot \overset{4}{48}}{5 \cdot 4 \cdot 3 \cdot 2 \cdot 1}$

$= 52 \cdot 51 \cdot 5 \cdot 49 \cdot 4$

$= 2,598,960$ hands

20. $P(5, 3) = 5 \cdot 4 \cdot 3$

$= 60$ numbers

21. $C(8, 3) = \dfrac{8 \cdot 7 \cdot 6}{3!}$

$= \dfrac{336}{6}$

$= 56$ ways

22. $C(12, 6) = \dfrac{12 \cdot 11 \cdot 10 \cdot 9 \cdot 8 \cdot 7}{6!}$

$= \dfrac{665,280}{720}$

$= 924$ different teams

23. 78 ml $= \dfrac{78}{1,000}$ liters

$= 0.078$ liters

24. $m \angle 7 = 100°$

$m \angle 7 = m \angle 3$ since they are corresponding angles.

$100° = m \angle 3$

$m \angle 3 + m \angle 4 = 180°$ since the angles are supplementary.

$100° + m \angle 4 = 180°$

$100° - 100° + m \angle 4 = 180° - 100°$

$m \angle 4 = 80°$

25. $\dfrac{1}{100} = \dfrac{2.25}{x}$

$x = 2.25 \cdot 100$

$= 225$ mi

26. $P(8, 3) = 8 \cdot 7 \cdot 6$

$= 336$

27. First find the number of combinations of males and females independently. Then use the Fundamental Principle of Counting to find the number of ways to select the group.

$C(18, 2) = \dfrac{18 \cdot 17}{2!}$

$= \dfrac{306}{2}$

$= 153$

$C(12, 3) = \dfrac{12 \cdot 11 \cdot 10}{3!}$

$= \dfrac{1,320}{6}$

$= 220$

There are $(153)(220) = 33,660$ ways to form the study group.

28. There are 4 toppings on the pizza if you order the special. So find $C(12, 4)$.

$C(12, 4) = \dfrac{12 \cdot 11 \cdot 10 \cdot 9}{4!}$

$= \dfrac{11,880}{24}$

$= 495$

There are 495 ways to order the pizza.

29. Each segment contains 2 points, so we are looking for the number of ways to connect 8 points using 2 at a time. Find $C(8, 2)$.

$$C(8, 2) = \frac{8 \cdot 7}{2!}$$

$$= \frac{56}{2}$$

$$= 28$$

There are 28 different line segments.

30. Answers may vary. Sample answer: Jane wants to dye one dozen eggs. The dye comes in a package of 5 different colors. How many different ways can Jane dye the eggs?

31. Answers may vary. Sample answer: An arrangement or listing in which order is important is a permutation. An arrangement or listing where order is not important is a combination.

13-4 Pascal's Triangle

PAGES 516-517   CHECKING FOR UNDERSTANDING

1. Row 4: $1 + 4 + 6 + 4 + 1 = 16$

   Outcomes for 4 coins: $2 \cdot 2 \cdot 2 \cdot 2 = 16$

   The sum of row 4 of Pascal's Triangle is 16 and the number of outcomes possible for tossing 4 coins is 16.

2. Row 6 of Pascal's Triangle: 1 6 15 20 15 6 1

   Row 7   1 7 21

   The third number in the seventh row is 21.

3. Row 7: 1st number: 1

   2nd number: $1 + 6 = 7$

   3rd number: $6 + 15 = 21$

   4th number: $15 + 20 = 35$

   5th number: $20 + 15 = 35$

   6th number: $15 + 6 = 21$

   7th number: $6 + 1 = 7$

   8th number: 1

   Row 7 is then 1, 7, 21, 35, 35, 21, 7, 1.

   Row 8: 1st number: 1

   2nd number: $1 + 7 = 8$

   3rd number: $7 + 21 = 28$

   4th number: $21 + 35 = 56$

   5th number: $35 + 35 = 70$

   6th number: $35 + 21 = 56$

   7th number: $21 + 7 = 28$

   8th number: $7 + 1 = 8$

   9th number: 1

   Row 8 is then 1, 8, 28, 56, 70, 56, 28, 8, 1.

4. $C(5, 2)$ = third number of row 5

   $= 10$

5. $C(7, 6)$ = seventh number of row 7

   $= 7$

6. $C(8, 3)$ = fourth number of row 8

   $= 56$

7. $C(4, 4)$ = fifth number of row 4

   $= 1$

8. Find $C(8, 5)$ = sixth number of row 8

   $= 56$ teams

9. Find $C(7, 4)$ = fifth number of row 7

   $= 35$ quizzes

10. 8

11. Since the second number in each row is 1 plus the previous row number, the second number in row 28 is 28.

PAGES 517-518   EXERCISES

12. $C(5, 3)$ = fourth number in row 5

    $= 10$

13. $C(4, 1)$ = second number in row 4

    $= 4$

14. $C(9, 5)$ = sixth number in row 9

    $= 56 + 70$

    $= 126$

15. $C(10, 4)$ = the fifth number in row 10

    $= 84 + 126$

    $= 210$

16. $1 + 4 + 6 + 4 + 1 = 16$ varieties of pizza

17. $1 + 3 + 3 + 1 = 8$ branches

18. There is only 1 way to toss 6 heads. There are $1 + 6 + 15 + 20 + 15 + 6 + 1$ or 64 possibilities.

    The probability is then $\frac{1}{64}$.

19. $C(6, 5)$ = sixth number of row 6.

    $= 6$ ways

20. in the sixth row

21. the number of combinations of 4 things taken 2 at a time.

22. 152, 154, 155, 158, 160, 161, 164

    Mean: $\dfrac{152 + 154 + 155 + 158 + 160 + 161 + 164}{7}$

    $= \dfrac{1104}{7} \approx 157.7$

    Median: 158

23. $t = 5\frac{1}{6} + 4\frac{2}{9}$

    $t = \dfrac{31}{6} + \dfrac{38}{9}$

    $t = \dfrac{93}{18} + \dfrac{76}{18}$

    $t = \dfrac{169}{18}$

    $t = 9\frac{7}{18}$

24. $y = 3x + 10$

x	$3x + 10$	y	(x, y)
1	3(1) + 10	13	(1, 13)
2	3(2) + 10	16	(2, 16)
3	3(3) + 10	19	(3, 19)
4	3(4) + 10	22	(4, 22)

Answers may vary. Sample answer:

$\{(1, 13), (2, 16), (3, 19), (4, 22)\}$

25. $C(10, 3) = \dfrac{10 \cdot 9 \cdot 8}{3!}$

$\qquad = \dfrac{720}{6}$

$\qquad = 120$

26. Row 1: sums to $2 = 2$

Row 2: sums to $4 = 2 \cdot 2 = 2^2$

Row 3: sums to $8 = 2 \cdot 2 \cdot 2 = 2^3$

Row 4: sums to $16 = 2 \cdot 2 \cdot 2 \cdot 2 = 2^4$

Row 5: sums to $32 = 2 \cdot 2 \cdot 2 \cdot 2 \cdot 2 = 2^5$

Row 6: sums to $64 = 2 \cdot 2 \cdot 2 \cdot 2 \cdot 2 \cdot 2 = 2^6$

So Row n can be represented by 2^n.

27. a. The tray has 4 levels at which the ball bearing can go right or left at each peg. This resembles Pascal's Triangle. The numbers in row 4 of Pascal's Triangle are 1, 4, 6, 4, 1, whose total is 16. Therefore, there will be 1 in the first tray, 4 in the second, 6 in the third, 4 in the fourth, and 1 in the fifth.

b. If 64 ball bearings are used, the probability for each tray section is in the same ratio. Just multiply by 4 to get 4(1), 4(4), 4(6), 4(4), 4(1) or 4, 16, 24, 16, 4.

28. There are a total of $5 \cdot 2$ or 10 bells that can ring. If you want 4 bells to ring at a time, find $C(10, 4)$.

$C(10, 4) = \dfrac{10 \cdot 9 \cdot 8 \cdot 7}{4!}$

$\qquad = \dfrac{5040}{24}$

$\qquad = 210$

There are 210 combinations.

29. We need to find $C(10, 5)$.

$C(10, 5) = \dfrac{10 \cdot 9 \cdot 8 \cdot 7 \cdot 6}{5!}$

$\qquad = \dfrac{30,240}{120}$

$\qquad = 252$

There are 252 different groupings.

30. We are looking for $C(8, 2)$.

$C(8, 2) = \dfrac{8 \cdot 7}{2!}$

$\qquad = \dfrac{56}{2}$

$\qquad = 28$

There are 28 combinations.

31. There are 7 choices for juice. So we are looking for $C(7, 3)$.

$C(7, 3) = \dfrac{7 \cdot 6 \cdot 5}{3!}$

$\qquad = \dfrac{210}{6}$

$\qquad = 35$

There are 35 combinations of juices.

Mid-Chapter Review

PAGE 518

1.

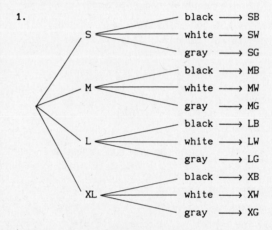

2. $2 \cdot 4 \cdot 3 = 24$ salads can be made

3. $6! = 720$ ways

4. $C(5, 2) = \dfrac{5 \cdot 4}{2!}$

$\qquad = \dfrac{20}{2}$

$\qquad = 10$ ways

5. Use row 6, position 4. Using Pascal's Triangle, there are 20 committees possible.

13-4B Mathematics Lab: Patterns in Pascal's Triangle

PAGE 519 WHAT DO YOU THINK?

1. 1, 2, 3, 5, 8, 13,...

Yes, the sums form the Fibonacci sequence.

2. The sum should be 13.

PAGE 519 WHAT DO YOU THINK?

3. See students' work.

4. The product of rings are perfect squares.

5. Inverted triangles is the pattern. Yes, because when two numbers next to each other have the same factor, the number below them will also have the same factor.

6. 3

13-5 Probability of Compound Events

1. Independent events are those in which the outcome of one event does not affect the outcome of the other event.

2. Answers may vary. Sample answer: Selecting one card from a deck of 52 cards and then selecting another card without replacing the first.

3. Multiply the probability of the first times the probability of the second.

4. $P(1) = \frac{1}{6}$

   $P(B) = \frac{1}{5}$

   $P(1 \text{ and } B) = \frac{1}{6} \cdot \frac{1}{5} = \frac{1}{30}$

5. $P(2) = \frac{1}{6}$

   $P(C) = \frac{1}{5}$

   $P(2 \text{ and } C) = \frac{1}{6} \cdot \frac{1}{5} = \frac{1}{30}$

6. $P(\text{prime}) = \frac{3}{6} = \frac{1}{2}$

   $P(D) = \frac{1}{5}$

   $P(\text{prime and } D) = \frac{1}{2} \cdot \frac{1}{5} = \frac{1}{10}$

7. $P(7) = 0$

   $P(E) = \frac{1}{5}$

   $P(7 \text{ and } E) = 0 \cdot \frac{1}{5} = 0$

8. $P(\text{an even number}) = \frac{3}{6} = \frac{1}{2}$

   $P(\text{a vowel}) = \frac{2}{5}$

   $P(\text{even number and vowel}) = \frac{1}{2} \cdot \frac{2}{5} = \frac{2}{10} = \frac{1}{5}$

9. Independent events because one outcome does not affect the other.

10. $P(\text{red}) = \frac{5}{8}$

    $P(\text{yellow after red}) = \frac{2}{7}$

    $P(\text{red then yellow}) = \frac{5}{8} \cdot \frac{2}{7} = \frac{10}{56} = \frac{5}{28}$

11. $P(\text{blue}) = \frac{1}{8}$

    $P(\text{yellow after blue}) = \frac{2}{7}$

    $P(\text{blue then yellow}) = \frac{1}{8} \cdot \frac{2}{7} = \frac{2}{56} = \frac{1}{28}$

12. $P(\text{red}) = \frac{5}{8}$

    $P(\text{blue after red}) = \frac{1}{7}$

    $P(\text{red then blue}) = \frac{5}{8} \cdot \frac{1}{7} = \frac{5}{56}$

13. $P(\text{any but yellow}) = \frac{6}{8} = \frac{3}{4}$

    $P(\text{yellow after any but yellow}) = \frac{2}{7}$

    $P(\text{any but yellow then yellow}) = \frac{3}{4} \cdot \frac{2}{7} = \frac{6}{28} = \frac{3}{14}$

14. $P(\text{red}) = \frac{5}{8}$

    $P(\text{red after red}) = \frac{4}{7}$

    $P(\text{red after 2 reds}) = \frac{3}{6} = \frac{1}{2}$

    $P(\text{three red}) = \frac{5}{8} \cdot \frac{4}{7} \cdot \frac{1}{2} = \frac{20}{112} = \frac{5}{28}$

15. dependent events because one outcome affects the other

16. $P(10) = \frac{1}{9}$

    $P(2 \text{ after } 10) = \frac{1}{8}$

    $P(10 \text{ then } 2) = \frac{1}{9} \cdot \frac{1}{8} = \frac{1}{72}$

17. $P(\text{odd}) = \frac{4}{9}$

    $P(\text{odd after odd}) = \frac{3}{8}$

    $P(\text{two odds}) = \frac{4}{9} \cdot \frac{3}{8} = \frac{12}{72} = \frac{1}{6}$

18. $P(\text{number greater than } 7) = \frac{3}{9} = \frac{1}{3}$

    $P(\text{2nd number greater than } 7) = \frac{2}{8} = \frac{1}{4}$

    $P(\text{two numbers greater than } 7) = \frac{1}{3} \cdot \frac{1}{4} = \frac{1}{12}$

19. $P(\text{even}) = \frac{5}{9}$

    $P(\text{even after even}) = \frac{4}{8} = \frac{1}{2}$

    $P(\text{even after 2 evens}) = \frac{3}{7}$

    $P(\text{three evens}) = \frac{5}{9} \cdot \frac{1}{2} \cdot \frac{3}{7} = \frac{15}{126} = \frac{5}{42}$

20. $P(\text{odd}) = \frac{4}{9}$

    $P(\text{even after odd}) = \frac{5}{8}$

    $P(\text{odd then even}) = \frac{4}{9} \cdot \frac{5}{8} = \frac{20}{72} = \frac{5}{18}$

21. $P(3) = \frac{1}{6}$

$P(D) = \frac{1}{5}$

$P(3 \text{ and } D) = \frac{1}{6} \cdot \frac{1}{5} = \frac{1}{30}$

22. $P(5) = \frac{1}{6}$

$P(B) = \frac{1}{5}$

$P(5 \text{ and } B) = \frac{1}{6} \cdot \frac{1}{5} = \frac{1}{30}$

23. $P(\text{composite}) = \frac{2}{6} = \frac{1}{3}$

$P(C) = \frac{1}{5}$

$P(\text{composite and } C) = \frac{1}{3} \cdot \frac{1}{5} = \frac{1}{15}$

24. $P(\text{odd}) = \frac{3}{6} = \frac{1}{2}$

$P(\text{consonant}) = \frac{3}{5}$

$P(\text{odd and consonant}) = \frac{1}{2} \cdot \frac{3}{5} = \frac{3}{10}$

25. $P(7) = 0$

$P(\text{letter not a vowel}) = \frac{3}{5}$

$P(7 \text{ and not a vowel}) = 0 \cdot \frac{3}{5} = 0$

26. $P(\text{car wash}) = \frac{1}{3 + 1} = \frac{1}{4}$

$P(\text{miniature golf}) = \frac{3}{3 + 2} = \frac{3}{5}$

$P(\text{car wash and miniature golf}) = \frac{1}{4} \cdot \frac{3}{5} = \frac{3}{20}$

27. $P(\text{CD}) = \frac{3}{3 + 1} = \frac{3}{4}$

$P(\text{miniature golf}) = \frac{3}{3 + 2} = \frac{3}{5}$

$P(\text{CD and miniature golf}) = \frac{3}{4} \cdot \frac{3}{5} = \frac{9}{20}$

28. $P(\text{CD}) = \frac{3}{3 + 1} = \frac{3}{4}$

$P(\text{CD}) = \frac{0}{3 + 2} = \frac{0}{5} = 0$

$P(\text{CD and CD}) = \frac{3}{4} \cdot 0 = 0$

29. $P(\text{car wash}) = \frac{1}{1 + 3} = \frac{1}{4}$

$P(\text{pizza}) = \frac{2}{2 + 3} = \frac{2}{5}$

$P(\text{car wash and pizza}) = \frac{1}{4} \cdot \frac{2}{5} = \frac{2}{20} = \frac{1}{10}$

30. $4y = 196$

$\frac{1}{4} \cdot 4y = 196 \cdot \frac{1}{4}$

$y = 49$

31. $\{-157, -28, -3, 2, 18, 226\}$

32. no; See students' work.

33. $C(6, 2)$ means row 6 number 3. So $C(6, 2) = 15$.

34. Since you are multiplying the probabilities, the combination least likely to occur is the one with the two smallest probabilities of occuring. So a bran muffin with nuts and a plain oat muffin would be least likely to occur.

35. $P(\text{woman}) = \frac{90}{100} = \frac{9}{10}$

$P(\text{woman having a credit card}) = \frac{75}{100} = \frac{3}{4}$

$P(\text{customer who is a woman with a credit card})$

$= \frac{9}{10} \cdot \frac{3}{4} = \frac{27}{40}$ or $67\frac{1}{2}\%$

36. a. $P(50\% \text{ off card}) = \frac{3}{9 + 8 + 5 + 3} = \frac{3}{25}$

b. $P(10\% \text{ off card}) = \frac{9}{25}$

$P(35\% \text{ off card second}) = \frac{5}{24}$

$P(10\% \text{ off then } 35\% \text{ off}) = \frac{9}{25} \cdot \frac{5}{24} = \frac{45}{600} = \frac{3}{40}$

37. Answers may vary. Sample answer: When events are dependent, one outcome depends on the other. If events are independent, one outcome does not depend on the other.

13-6 Act it Out

PAGE 526   CHECKING FOR UNDERSTANDING

1. Answers may vary. Sample answer: Acting out a situation is a simulation.

2. Use five identical slips of paper. Write "green" on two of them and "not green" on the other three. Fold the slips and put all of them in a box. Then draw a slip for each light making sure to replace the slip after each draw.

3. No, a simulation models what actually happens, while a theoretical result is what we think will happen.

4. Answers may vary. Sample answer:

Free Throw Attempt	Free Throw Made/Missed
1	Made
2	Made
3	Missed
4	Made
5	Missed
6	Missed

She will make 3 free throws.

5. Answers may vary. Sample answer:

Week #	Ties Worn
1	2, 2, 2, 3
2	1, 4, 2, 3
3	3, 4, 2, 5
4	6, 1, 3, 4
5	5, 1, 3, 5
6	3, 4, 5, 6
7	6, 2, 6, 3
8	6, 3, 6, 5
9	2, 3, 6, 1
10	2, 4, 5, 3

$P(\text{same tie more than once}) = \frac{4}{10}$ or $\frac{2}{5}$

6. Start with 50¢ pieces. David can have only 1 because two would make change for a dollar and three would total $1.50. If David has 1 – 50¢ piece, he can have only 1 quarter also because two would make change for a dollar and three would total $1.25. Now David can have only dimes left because five pennies make change for a nickel and two nickels make change for a dime. Since David has 6 coins total, he must have 6 – 2 or 4 dimes. Then 50¢ + 25¢ + 40¢ = $1.15 which is the total given.

PAGES 526-527   PROBLEM SOLVING

7. If Marlene needs to read twice as many pages as she has already read, then she has already read $\frac{1}{3}$ of the book. So Marlene has read $216 \cdot \frac{1}{3}$ or 72 pages.

8. 1st round: 8 matches
   2nd round: 4 matches
   3rd round: 2 matches
   4th round: 1 match
             15 matches

9. Answers may vary. Sample answer: $\frac{1}{45}$

10. Since the jacket costs four times as much as the shirt, the shirt is $\frac{1}{5}$ of the total cost. So $62.50 \cdot \frac{1}{5} = $12.50 for the shirt and $4 \cdot $12.50 = $50.00 for the jacket.

11. Mrs. Yamaguchi is not the math teacher because she taught more years than the math teacher, and she is not the music teacher because the music teacher has taught the least number of years. So Mrs. Yamaguchi must be the social studies teacher. Mrs. Gossell has a brother so she is not an only child and cannot be the music teacher. So Mrs. Gossell must be the math teacher. Then Mrs. Alvarez is the music teacher.

12. Antonio can use a minimum of 23 pennies. Place 10 pennies horizontally. Place 2 more pennies above and 2 more pennies below the sixth horizontal penny to make a vertical line of 5 pennies. Then place 3 more pennies above and 4 more pennies below the fifth horizontal penny to make a vertical line of 8 pennies. Then use the seventh horizontal penny and two pennies from the vertical lines as part of the diagonal. Add 2 more pennies to make a diagonal line of 5 pennies. Then Antonio will have used 10 + 4 + 7 + 2 or 23 pennies.

13. Work backwards and undo each process. First divide 100 by 20, so 100 ÷ 20 = 5. Then a number added to 8 must be 5. As an algebraic expression, this is
    $$x + 8 = 5$$
    $$x + 8 - 8 = 5 - 8$$
    $$x = -3$$
    The number is –3.

14.

Nickels	Dimes	Quarters
10	0	0
8	1	0
6	2	0
5	0	1
4	3	0
3	1	1
2	4	0
1	2	1
0	5	0
0	0	2

There are 10 ways to make 50¢.

15. 60 + 50 = 110 students that play at least one sport
    110 – 20 = 90 students that play only one sport
    120 – 90 = 30 students that play no sport
    So 30 students do not play baseball or soccer.

16. a. The output is 20 lines listing a 0 or a 1. A simulation could be tossing a coin 20 times; 0 is heads and 1 is tails.
    b. The output is 20 lines listing a 1, 2, 3, 4, 5, or 6. A simulation could be rolling a die 20 times.

13-7 Experimental Probability

1. Answers may vary. Sample answer: It is possible one of the outcomes doesn't turn up in an experiment.

2. See students' work.

3. a. $P(\text{1 head}) = \frac{15}{40} = \frac{3}{8}$

   b. $P(\text{2 heads}) = \frac{20}{40} = \frac{1}{2}$

   c. $P(\text{3 heads}) = \frac{3}{40}$

4. a. $P(\text{1 head}) = \frac{3}{8}$

   b. $P(\text{2 heads}) = \frac{3}{8}$

   c. $P(\text{3 heads}) = \frac{1}{8}$

5. a. Student 1: $P(\text{heads}) = \frac{21}{40}$ or 0.525

   Student 2: $P(\text{heads}) = \frac{22}{40} = \frac{11}{20}$ or 0.55

   Student 3: $P(\text{heads}) = \frac{18}{40} = \frac{9}{20}$ or 0.45

   Student 4: $P(\text{heads}) = \frac{26}{40} = \frac{13}{20}$ or 0.65

   Student 5: $P(\text{heads}) = \frac{21}{40} =$ or 0.525

   Student 6: $P(\text{heads}) = \frac{21}{40}$ or 0.525

   Student 7: $P(\text{heads}) = \frac{19}{40}$ or 0.475

   Student 8: $P(\text{heads}) = \frac{22}{40} = \frac{11}{20}$ or 0.55

   Student 9: $P(\text{heads}) = \frac{18}{40} = \frac{9}{20}$ or 0.45

   Student 10: $P(\text{heads}) = \frac{29}{40}$ or 0.725

   $P(\text{heads for all students}) =$

   $\frac{21 + 22 + 18 + 26 + 21 + 21 + 19 + 22 + 18 + 29}{400}$

   $= \frac{217}{400}$ or 0.5425

   b. yes

   c. A better estimate would come by doing more experiments.

6. a. See students' work.

   b. See students' work.

   c. See students' work.

   d. See students' work.

7. $p = -68 + 29$

   $p = -39$

8. $12 = 2 \cdot 2 \cdot 3$

   $63 = 3 \cdot 3 \cdot 7$

   GCF = 3

9. $P(\text{prime}) = \frac{3}{6} = \frac{1}{2}$

   $P(\text{odd}) = \frac{3}{6} = \frac{1}{2}$

   $P(\text{prime and odd}) = \frac{1}{2} \cdot \frac{1}{2} = \frac{1}{4}$

10. No, experimental probabilities vary.

11. No, experimental probabilities vary.

12. $P(\text{value higher than \$1000}) = \frac{3}{24} = \frac{1}{8}$

13. a. Answers may vary. Sample answer:

    $P(A) = 0.33$, $P(B) = 0.22$, $P(C) = 0.45$

    b. Replace 0.67 with 0.5 in lines 30 and 50.

13-8A Mathematics Lab: Punnett Squares

1.

	R	r
R	RR	Rr
r	Rr	rr

Pure dominant genes: $\frac{1}{4}$ of 40 = 10

Hybrid genes: $\frac{2}{4}$ of 40 = 20

Pure recessive genes: $\frac{1}{4}$ of 40 = 10

2. Expect Rr to occur most often.

3. $P(\text{pure dominant}) = \frac{1}{4}$

   $P(\text{hybrid}) = \frac{2}{4} = \frac{1}{2}$

   $P(\text{pure recessive}) = \frac{1}{4}$

4. See students' work.

5. The combination of genes that come together in the offspring determines how offspring will look.

6.

	F	F
F	FF	FF
f	Ff	Ff

$P(FF) = \frac{2}{4} = \frac{1}{2}$

$P(Ff) = \frac{2}{4} = \frac{1}{2}$

7.

	F	F
F	FF	FF
F	FF	FF

$P(FF) = \frac{4}{4} = 1$

8.

	f	f
f	ff	ff
f	ff	ff

$P(ff) = \frac{4}{4} = 1$

9.

	F	f
f	Ff	ff
f	Ff	ff

$P(Ff) = \frac{2}{4} = \frac{1}{2}$

$P(ff) = \frac{2}{4} = \frac{1}{2}$

10. Row 2 of Pascal's Triangle is 1, 2, 1.

13-8 Using Experiments to Predict

1. You can set up and solve a proportion to predict actions of a whole population.

2. Whether the people in the sample are chosen at random and are representative of the population.

3. $40 + 110 + 180 + 70 = 400$

4. $\frac{180}{400} = \frac{9}{20}$

5. $\frac{40}{400} = \frac{x}{158,800}$

$400x = 40 \cdot 158,800$

$400x = 6,352,000$

$\frac{400x}{400} = \frac{6,352,000}{400}$

$x = 15,880$

Expect 15,880 people to listen to WFRM.

6. $600 - 327 = 273$

$\frac{327}{273} = \frac{x}{1}$

$273x = 327$

$\frac{273x}{273} = \frac{327}{273}$

$x \approx 1.2$

false; $327:273 < 2:1$

7. true; $\frac{327}{600} = 0.545 = 54.5\%$

8. false; This cannot be determined from the survey.

9. $17 + 25 + 10 + 12 + 8 = 72$

10. cola, since it is selected most often

11. $\frac{12}{72} = \frac{1}{6}$

12. $\frac{25}{72} = \frac{x}{7,200}$

$72x = 25 \cdot 7,200$

$72x = 180,000$

$\frac{72x}{72} = \frac{180,000}{72}$

$x = 2,500$

The Band Boosters should order 2,500 colas.

13. Yes, each student is randomly selected.

14. $25 + 10 + 2 = 37$

$50 - 37 = 13$

So 13 students chose blue.

15.

$\frac{25}{50} = \frac{x}{450}$

$50x = 25 \cdot 450$

$50x = 11,250$

$\frac{50x}{50} = \frac{11,250}{50}$

$x = 225$

$\frac{10}{50} = \frac{x}{450}$

$50x = 10 \cdot 450$

$50x = 4,500$

$\frac{50x}{50} = \frac{4,500}{50}$

$x = 90$

$\frac{2}{50} = \frac{x}{450}$

$50x = 2 \cdot 450$

$50x = 900$

$\frac{50x}{50} = \frac{900}{50}$

$x = 18$

$\frac{13}{50} = \frac{x}{450}$

$50x = 13 \cdot 450$

$50x = 5,850$

$\frac{50x}{50} = \frac{5,850}{50}$

$x = 117$

Order 225 red, 90 green, 18 yellow, and 117 blue.

16. $8 + 80 + 82 + 10 = 180$

17. $82 + 10 = 92$ students

18. $80 + 82 + 10 = 172$

$\frac{172}{180} = \frac{x}{400}$

$180x = 172 \cdot 400$

$180x = 68,800$

$\frac{180x}{180} = \frac{68,800}{180}$

$382.\overline{2} = x$

About 382 students will buy a $26 jacket.

19. $8\frac{9}{25} = 8 + \frac{9}{25}$

$= 8 + 0.36$

$= 8.36$

20. $y = 2x - 7$

x	$2x - 7$	y
1	$2(1) - 7$	-5
2	$2(2) - 7$	-3
3	$2(3) - 7$	-1

$y = -2x - 9$

x	$-2x + 9$	y
2	$-2(2) + 9$	5
3	$-2(3) + 9$	3
4	$-2(4) + 9$	1

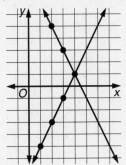

The solution is (4, 1).

21. $P(2 \text{ heads}) = \frac{20}{40} = \frac{1}{2}$

22. a. 45 soldiers

b.
$$\frac{5}{45} = \frac{x}{720} \qquad \frac{8}{45} = \frac{x}{720} \qquad \frac{20}{45} = \frac{x}{720}$$

$$45x = 5 \cdot 720 \qquad 45x = 8 \cdot 720 \qquad 45x = 20 \cdot 720$$

$$45x = 3{,}600 \qquad 45x = 5{,}760 \qquad 45x = 14{,}400$$

$$\frac{45x}{45} = \frac{3{,}600}{45} \qquad \frac{45x}{45} = \frac{5{,}760}{45} \qquad \frac{45x}{45} = \frac{14{,}400}{45}$$

$$x = 80 \qquad\quad x = 128 \qquad\quad x = 320$$

$$\frac{9}{45} = \frac{x}{720} \qquad \frac{3}{45} = \frac{x}{720}$$

$$45x = 9 \cdot 720 \qquad 45x = 3 \cdot 720$$

$$45x = 6{,}480 \qquad 45x = 2{,}160$$

$$\frac{45x}{45} = \frac{6{,}480}{45} \qquad \frac{45x}{45} = \frac{2{,}160}{45}$$

$$x = 144 \qquad\quad x = 48$$

Order 80 extra small, 128 small, 320 medium, 144 large, and 48 extra large.

23. You drew $6 + 14$ or 20 chips. Solve the proportion

$$\frac{\text{green chips drawn}}{\text{total chips drawn}} = \frac{\text{green chips in bag}}{\text{total chips in bag}} \text{ or}$$

$\frac{6}{20} = \frac{g}{100}$ to predict the number of green

chips. Solve the proportion

$$\frac{\text{red chips drawn}}{\text{total chips drawn}} = \frac{\text{red chips in bag}}{\text{total chips in bag}} \text{ or}$$

$\frac{14}{20} = \frac{r}{100}$ to predict the number of red chips.

Chapter 13 Study Guide and Review

1. f. permutation

2. e. combination

3. h. $n!$

4. g. tree diagram

5. d. sample

6. a. experimental probabilities

7. b. theoretical probabilities

8. See students' work.

9. Find $C(6, 0)$, $C(6, 1)$, $C(6, 2)$, $C(6, 3)$, $C(6, 4)$, $C(6, 5)$ and $C(6, 6)$.

10. $C(8, 2)$ means the number of combinations of 8 things taken 2 at a time.

11. 3 choices for soft drinks and 2 choices for ice is $3 \cdot 2$ or 6 outcomes.

12. 2 choices for models, 4 choices for color, and 2 choices for transmission is $2 \cdot 4 \cdot 2$ or 16 outcomes.

13. $6! = 720$

14. There are 7 letters in OBJECTS, so find $P(7, 3) = 7 \cdot 6 \cdot 5 = 210$ ways.

15. There are 6 kittens and we are selecting them 2 at a time, so find $C(6, 2) = \frac{6 \cdot 5}{2!} = \frac{30}{2} = 15$ pairs.

16. $C(20, 4) = \frac{20 \cdot 19 \cdot 18 \cdot 17}{4!} = \frac{116{,}280}{24} = 4{,}845$ groups

17. Use the number in row 7, position 5 of Pascal's Triangle to find 35 combinations.

18. Use the number in row 6, position 4 of Pascal's Triangle to find there are 20 pizzas that can be made.

19. $C(9, 3)$ is row 9, position 4 of Pascal's Triangle, which is 84.

20. $P(\text{even number}) = \frac{3}{6} = \frac{1}{2}$

$P(\text{odd number}) = \frac{3}{6} = \frac{1}{2}$

$P(\text{even number and odd number}) = \frac{1}{2} \cdot \frac{1}{2} = \frac{1}{4}$

21. $P(\text{prime number}) = \frac{3}{6} = \frac{1}{2}$

$P(\text{composite number}) = \frac{2}{6} = \frac{1}{3}$

$P(\text{prime and composite}) = \frac{1}{2} \cdot \frac{1}{3} = \frac{1}{6}$

22. $P(2) = \frac{1}{6}$

$P(\text{number divisible by 3}) = \frac{2}{6} = \frac{1}{3}$

$P(\text{2 and number divisible by 3}) = \frac{1}{6} \cdot \frac{1}{3} = \frac{1}{18}$

23. a. See students' work.

b. See students' work.

c. The possibilities are HH, HT, TH, and TT. So $P(\text{no heads}) = \frac{1}{4}$ and $P(\text{one head and one tail}) = \frac{2}{4} = \frac{1}{2}$.

24. $96 + 68 + 36 = 200$

25. $\frac{36}{200} = \frac{9}{50}$

26. $\frac{96}{200} = \frac{x}{8{,}000}$

$200x = 96 \cdot 8{,}000$

$200x = 768{,}000$

$\frac{200x}{200} = \frac{768{,}000}{200}$

$x = 3{,}840$

So 3,840 people would buy a Goody brand hot dog.

27. $9! = 362{,}880$ batting orders

178

28. $C(40, 3) = \dfrac{40 \cdot 39 \cdot 38}{3!} = \dfrac{59{,}280}{6} =$

9,880 combinations.

29.

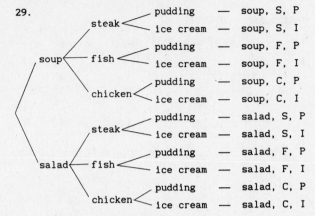

There are 12 outcomes.

30. Answers may vary. Sample answer:

$\left(\dfrac{3}{10}\right)\left(\dfrac{3}{10}\right)\left(\dfrac{3}{10}\right)\left(\dfrac{3}{10}\right) = \dfrac{81}{10{,}000} = 0.0081$

Chapter 13 Test

PAGE 539

1.

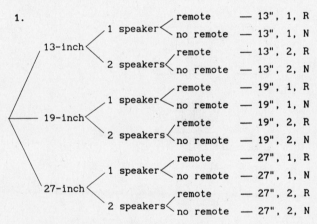

There are 12 outcomes.

2. $P(19'', \text{2 speakers, remote}) = \dfrac{1}{12}$

3. 6 outcomes show a one-speaker television.

4. $P(8, 3) = 8 \cdot 7 \cdot 6 = 336$

5. $C(15, 5) = \dfrac{15 \cdot 14 \cdot 13 \cdot 12 \cdot 11}{5!} = \dfrac{360{,}360}{120}$

   $= 3{,}003$

6. Order is important, so find $P(7, 4) =$
   $7 \cdot 6 \cdot 5 \cdot 4 = 840$ ways to arrange the trophies.

7. Order is not important, so find

   $C(18, 6) = \dfrac{18 \cdot 17 \cdot 16 \cdot 15 \cdot 14 \cdot 13}{6!} =$

   $\dfrac{13{,}366{,}080}{720} = 18{,}564$ teams.

8. $5! = 120$ ways

9. Use the number in row 5, position 4 for a total of 10 combinations.

10. The number of combinations of 6 things taken 3 at a time or $C(6, 3)$.

11. $P(\text{red marble}) = \dfrac{3}{10}$

    $P(\text{blue after red}) = \dfrac{5}{9}$

    $P(\text{red then blue}) = \dfrac{3}{10} \cdot \dfrac{5}{9} = \dfrac{15}{90} = \dfrac{1}{6}$

12. $P(\text{green}) = \dfrac{2}{10} = \dfrac{1}{5}$

    $P(\text{green after green}) = \dfrac{1}{9}$

    $P(\text{two green}) = \dfrac{1}{5} \cdot \dfrac{1}{9} = \dfrac{1}{45}$

13. Problem 11 represents dependent events because the first one affects the second.

14. $P(\text{2 heads}) = \dfrac{4}{20} = \dfrac{1}{5}$

15. There are 4 possibilities: HH, HT, TH, TT

    $P(\text{2 heads}) = \dfrac{1}{4}$

16. Because the experimental probability is based on the experiment and it varies as the experiment is repeated. Theoretical probability is an approximation of what will happen.

17. $13 + 18 + 11 + 8 = 50$

18. $\dfrac{18}{50} = \dfrac{9}{25} = 0.36$ or 36%

19. $\dfrac{18}{50} = \dfrac{x}{800}$

    $50x = 18 \cdot 800$

    $50x = 14{,}400$

    $\dfrac{50x}{50} = \dfrac{14{,}400}{50}$

    $x = 288$

    Order 288 chocolate bars with almonds.

20. Answers may vary. Sample answer:

    $\dfrac{2}{7} \cdot \dfrac{1}{6} = \dfrac{2}{42} = \dfrac{1}{21}$

PAGE 539   BONUS

The possibilities are $B_1 G_1 B_2 G_2$, $B_1 G_2 B_2 G_1$, $B_2 G_1 B_1 G_2$,

$B_2 G_2 B_1 G_1$, $G_1 B_1 G_2 B_2$, $G_1 B_2 G_2 B_1$, $G_2 B_1 G_1 B_2$, $G_2 B_2 G_1 B_1$.

So there are 8 ways to stand in a line.

Chapter 14   Algebra: Investigations with Polynomials

14-1A   Mathematics Lab:
Area Models

PAGE 542   WHAT DO YOU THINK?

1. 1, x, x^2 2. The area is the product of
                           the length and width.

PAGE 542   EXTENSION

3. See students' work.   4. See students' work.

14-1   Area Models of Polynomials

PAGES 544-545   CHECKING FOR UNDERSTANDING

1. Sample answers: a, $4y^3$; $a^2 + 2ab$, $6g^2 + 14g + 8$
2. Use two red x-tiles.   3. $2x^2 - x + 6$
4. $-3x^2 + 2x - 5$

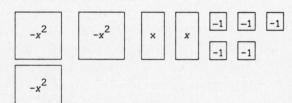

5. $-x^2 + 3x - 4$ 6. $-4x + 2$
7. $3x^2$

8. $2x - 1$

9. $-x^2 + 5x - 6$

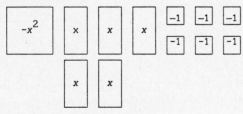

10. $x^2 - 3x - 4 = (5)^2 - 3(5) - 4$
                $= 25 - 15 - 4$
                $= 6$

PAGE 545   EXERCISES

11. $-4x$ 12. $x^2 + 4x$ 13. $-2x^2 + 9$ 14. $4x - 7$
15. $-2x^2$

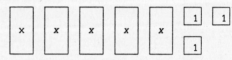

16. $5x + 3$

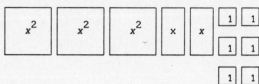

17. $3x^2 + 2x + 6$

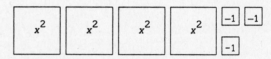

18. $4x^2 - 3$

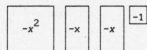

19. $-x^2 - 2x - 1$

20. $x^2 - 8$

21. $2x - 5 = 2(8) - 5$ 22. $x^2 + 3x = (-2)^2 + 3(-2)$
         $= 16 - 5$ $= 4 - 6$
         $= 11$ $= -2$
23. $x^2 - 10x + 25 = (5)^2 - 10(5) + 25$
                   $= 25 - 50 + 25$
                   $= 0$
24. $-x^2 + 4x = -(-1)^2 + 4(-1)$ 25. $C = 2\pi r$
         $= -1 - 4$ $C = 2\pi(8.2)$
         $= -5$ $C \approx 51.52$ mm
26. $0.6n = 30$ 27. $6,300\left(\frac{8}{72}\right) = \frac{6,300}{9}$
    $\frac{0.6n}{0.6} = \frac{30}{0.6}$ $= 700$ ginger ales
    $n = 50$
28. $13b + 7s + 10f$
    $= 13(\$1.99) + 7(\$1.49) + 10(\$0.99)$
    $= \$25.87 + \$10.43 + \$9.90$
    $= \$46.20$

29.

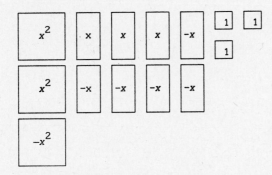

x (left side), y (bottom)

30. See students' work.

PAGE 548   CHECKING FOR UNDERSTANDING

1. by finding terms with the same variable to the same power

2. Sample answer: $x^2 - x + 3$

3. $2x^2 + 3x - x^2 - 5x + 3$

x^2	x	x	x	$-x$	$\boxed{1}$ $\boxed{1}$
x^2	$-x$	$-x$	$-x$	$-x$	$\boxed{1}$
$-x^2$					

4. No, the variables are not the same.

5. $3x^2$, $-2x^2$; $4x$, $10x$ **6.** $4y$, $-2y$, $-3y$; 8, 9

7. none   **8.** $-a^2$, $4a^2$

9. $x^2 + x - 1$ **10.** $a^2 + 3a$

PAGES 548-549   EXERCISES

11. $6y$, $-11y$ **12.** 4, -5

13. none   **14.** $7a$, $10a$; $6b$, $14b$

15. $6x$ **16.** $-2x + 2y$

17. $5x + 5$ **18.** $2y + 2$

19. $2x^2 + 4x - 4$ **20.** $-5y^2 - 4y + 3$

21. $-7a$ **22.** $2x + 8y$

23. $9a + 14b = 9(-2) + 14(7)$
$= -18 + 98$
$= 80$

24. $17a + 11b = 17(-2) + 11(7)$
$= -34 + 77$
$= 43$

25. $a + 9b = (-2) + 9(7)$
$= -2 + 63$
$= 61$

26. $3a + 3b = 3(-2) + 3(7)$
$= -6 + 21$
$= 15$

27. Subtract the lower quartile from the upper quartile.

---

28. $\dfrac{\$9.60}{8 \text{ feet}} = \dfrac{\$1.20}{1 \text{ foot}}$

29.

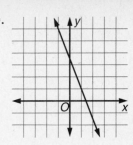

30. $2x^2 - 3x + 5 = 2(-2)^2 - 3(-2) + 5$
$= 8 + 6 + 5$
$= 19$

31. $3q + 5d + 2n + q + 3d + 3n = 4q + 8d + 5n$
$4q + 8d + 5n = 4(\$0.25) + 8(\$0.10) + 5(\$0.05)$
$= \$1.00 + \$0.80 + \$0.25$
$= \$2.05$

32. $3x^3 + 6x^2 - 5x + 3$

33. $3(\$26.90) + 4(\$23.89) = \$80.70 + \$95.56$
$= \$176.26$

PAGE 551   CHECKING FOR UNDERSTANDING

1. $-x^2 + 2x$, $3x - 4$
$\quad -x^2 + 2x$
$\underline{+ \qquad 3x - 4}$
$\quad -x^2 + 5x - 4$

2. $(3x^2 - 3x + 5) + (x^2 + 2x - 7)$

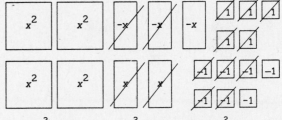

$(3x^2 - 3x + 5) + (x^2 + 2x - 7) = 4x^2 - x - 2$

3. $-x + 6$ **4.** $3a^2 - 10a$

5. $-7x^2 + x + 1$ **6.** $\quad -3y^2 + 4y$
$\underline{+ (-1y^2) - 3y}$
$\quad -4y^2 + \quad y$
$-4(1)^2 + (1) = -4 + 1$
$= -3$

PAGE 552   EXERCISES

7. $5x^2 - 2x + 5$
$\underline{+ \ x^2 + 4x - 3}$
$6x^2 + 2x + 2$

8. $-4r^2 + 3r - 2$
$\underline{+ \ 6r^2 - 5r - 7}$
$2r^2 - 2r - 9$

---

9. $2y^2 + y + 4$
    $\underline{+\ 3y^2 + 2y + 1}$
    $5y^2 + 3y + 5$

10. $4a - 7b - 6c$
    $\underline{+\ 3a + 5b + 2c}$
    $7a - 2b - 4c$

11. $3x + 7y$
    $\underline{+\ 9x + 5y}$
    $12x + 12y$

12. $5m + 3n$
    $\underline{+\ 4m + 2n}$
    $9m + 5n$

13. $8s - 3t$
    $\underline{+\ s + 5t}$
    $9s + 2t$

14. $5r - 7s$
    $\underline{+\ 3r + 8s}$
    $8r + s$

15. $3a^2 + 2a$
    $\underline{+\ 7a^2\qquad -\ 3}$
    $10a^2 + 2a - 3$

16. $-x^2 + 2x - 3$
    $\underline{+\ 3x^2 - 5x + 7}$
    $2x^2 - 3x + 4$

17. $\quad -3x + 4$
    $\underline{+\ 5x^2}$
    $5x^2 - 3x + 4$

18. $2c + 5d$
    $\underline{+\ 6c - 3d}$
    $8c + 2d$
    $8(8) + 2(5) = 64 + 10$
    $\qquad\qquad = 74$

19. $4c + 3d + 2$
    $\underline{+\ 3c - 4d - 1}$
    $7c - d + 1$
    $7(8) - (5) + 1 = 56 - 5 + 1$
    $\qquad\qquad\qquad = 52$

20. $-2c + 7d$
    $\underline{+\ 8c - 8d}$
    $6c - d$
    $6(8) - (5) = 48 - 5$
    $\qquad\qquad = 43$

21. $15c + 2d - 1$
    $\underline{+\quad c - 3d + 2}$
    $16c - d + 1$
    $16(8) - (5) + 1 = 128 - 5 + 1$
    $\qquad\qquad\qquad\quad = 124$

22. $[3(18 - 2)] - 4^2 = [3(16)] - 4^2$
    $\qquad\qquad\qquad = 48 - 4^2$
    $\qquad\qquad\qquad = 48 - 16$
    $\qquad\qquad\qquad = 32$

23. $b^2 = 1.69$
    $b = \sqrt{1.69}$ or $b = -\sqrt{1.69}$
    $b = 1.3$ or $b = -1.3$

24. $V = \frac{1}{3}\pi r^2 h$
    $V = \frac{1}{3} \cdot \pi \cdot (2)^2 \cdot 12$
    $V = 16\pi$
    $V \approx 50.27$ m^2

25. $4x^2 + 4x$

26. $x^2 + 2x - 3$
    $\underline{+\qquad x + 3}$
    $x^2 + 3x$

27. a. $(x + 5) + (3x + 7) + (x + 5) + (3x + 7) =$
    $8x + 24$
    b. $(x + 5) + (2x + 3) + (3x - 2) = 6x + 6$
    c. $(2x + 5) + (x + 7) + (x - 2) + (x + 5) +$
    $(x + 7) + (2x + 12) = 8x + 34$

28. $8x + 4y$

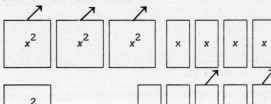

14-4 Subtracting Polynomials

PAGE 554   CHECKING FOR UNDERSTANDING

1. $-5x$

2. $(x^2 + 3x - 3) - (x^2 + 2x - 3)$

3. $(2x^2 + 5x) - (3x^2 - 2x)$

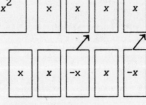

$(2x^2 + 5x) - (3x^2 - 2x) = -x^2 + 7x$

4. $-x$

5. $5x^2$

6. -4

7. $-10x^2;\ -3x$

8. $3x + 2$

9. $-x^2 + x$

10. $\quad 7x + 5$
    $\underline{+\ (-3x - 4)}$
    $\quad 4x + 1$

11. $\quad 5x^2 - 3x + 2$
    $\underline{+\ (-3x^2\qquad + 3)}$
    $\quad 2x^2 - 3x + 5$

12. $\quad 2x^2 - 5x - 1$
    $\underline{+\ (-x^2 + x + 1)}$
    $\quad x^2 - 4x$

13. $\quad -3x^2 + 2x + 1$
    $\underline{+\ (-x^2 - 3x + 1)}$
    $\quad -4x^2 - x + 2$

PAGE 555   EXERCISES

14. $\quad 3x + 7$
    $\underline{+\ (-2x - 5)}$
    $\quad x + 2$

15. $\quad 4a^2 - 3a - 2$
    $\underline{+\ (-2a^2 - 2a - 7)}$
    $\quad 2a^2 - 5a - 9$

16. $\quad 9s - 1$
    $\underline{+\ (-7s - 2)}$
    $\quad 2s - 3$

17. $\quad -4a + 5$
    $\underline{+\ (-a + 1)}$
    $\quad -5a + 6$

18. $\quad 5x^2 + 9$
    $\underline{+\ (-4x^2 - 9)}$
    $\quad x^2$

19. $\quad 10m - 2n$
    $\underline{+\ (-6m - 3n)}$
    $\quad 4m - 5n$

20. $\quad 6x^2 + 2x + 9$
    $\underline{+\ (-3x^2 - 5x - 9)}$
    $\quad 3x^2 - 3x$

21. $\quad 4p^2 - 3p + 1$
    $\underline{+\ (-2p^2 + 2p\qquad)}$
    $\quad 2p^2 - p + 1$

22. $\quad 3r^2 - 3rt + t^2$
    $\underline{+\ (-2r^2 - 5rt + 3t^2)}$
    $\quad r^2 - 8rt + 4t^2$

23. $\quad 7a^2 + ab - 2b^2$
    $\underline{+\ (a^2 + ab - b^2)}$
    $\quad 8a^2 + 2ab - 3b^2$

24. $j = -7(15)(-10)$
    $j = -7(-150)$
    $j = 1,050$

25. $48 = 2 \cdot 24$
    $48 = 2 \cdot 2 \cdot 12$
    $48 = 2 \cdot 2 \cdot 2 \cdot 6$
    $48 = 2 \cdot 2 \cdot 2 \cdot 2 \cdot 3$
    $48 = 2^4 \cdot 3$

26. $P(8, 3) = 8 \cdot 7 \cdot 6 = 336$

27. $\quad -3m^2 + 6m - 2$
    $\underline{+\ (-m^2 + 4m + 11)}$
    $\quad -4m^2 + 10m + 9$

28. $(7x + 2y) - (2x + y) - (3x - 5y) = 2x + 6y$

29. $2x^2 - 3x + 1$; $-x^2 + x - 4$

30. See students' work.

Mid-Chapter Review

PAGE 555

1. $3x^2 - 2x + 7$

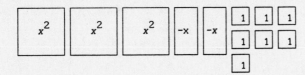

2. $-x^2 + 5x - 2$

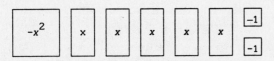

3. $8x^2 - 7$

4. $7a + 2b + 3c$

5. $\begin{array}{r} 4x^2 - 5x \\ + 3x^2 + x \\ \hline 7x^2 - 4x \end{array}$

6. $\begin{array}{r} a^2 - 6 \\ + (-3a^2 - 1) \\ \hline -2a^2 - 7 \end{array}$

7. $\begin{array}{r} 3n + 6 \\ + (-n + 1) \\ \hline 2n + 7 \end{array}$

8. $\begin{array}{r} 4x + 3y \\ + (-7x + 3y) \\ \hline -3x + 6y \end{array}$

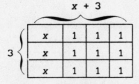

14-5A ### Mathematics Lab: Modeling Products

PAGE 556   APPLICATION

1. $3(x + 3) = 3x + 9$

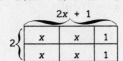

2. $x(x + 2) = x^2 + 2x$

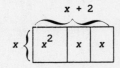

3. $2(2x + 1) = 4x + 2$

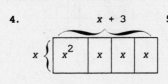

PAGE 556   EXTENSION

4. $x + 3$

5. $x + 2$

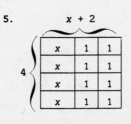

6.

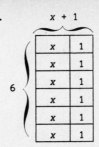

14-5 ### Multiplying a Polynomial by a Monomial

PAGES 558-559   CHECKING FOR UNDERSTANDING

1. distributive property

2. $6x^2 + 2x$

3.

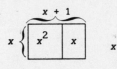 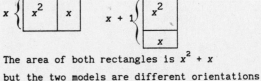

The area of both rectangles is $x^2 + x$ but the two models are different orientations of the same rectangle.

4. The factors are $x + 2$ and x.

5. $2x + 10$

6. $x^2 + 3x$

7. $5y - 45$

8. $y^2 - 2y$

9. $a^2 + 2a$

10. $4(z + 1)$

11. $y(y + 5)$

PAGE 559   EXERCISES

12. $6n + 60$

13. $4b - 12$

14. $6 + 3y$

15. $d^2 - 15d$

16. $6c - 12$

17. $4x^2 + 2x$

18. $5(x + 2)$

19. $3x(2x + 1)$

20. $1(2x + 5)$

21. $8(a^2 + 1)$

22. $6(2m + 1)$

23. $4(1 + 5x)$

24. $8y^2 + 2y$

25. $2(y + 4)$

26. $3x^2 + 6x$

27. $\begin{aligned} 156 &= y + 73 \\ 156 - 73 &= y + 73 - 73 \\ 83 &= y \end{aligned}$

28. $\$67.20 - \$52.50 = \$14.70$

$\dfrac{\$14.70}{\$52.50} = 0.28$

28% increase

29.

x	$-3x^2 + 1$	$f(x)$
2	$-3(2)^2 + 1$	-11
1	$-3(1)^2 + 1$	-2
0	$-3(0)^2 + 1$	1
-1	$-3(-1)^2 + 1$	-2
-2	$-3(-2)^2 + 1$	-11

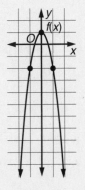

30.
$$8x - 1$$
$$+ (-5x - 3)$$
$$\overline{ 3x - 4}$$

31. a.

b. $2x(x + 3)$; $2x^2 + 6x$

c. $2(10)^2 + 6(10) = 200 + 60 = 260$ ft^2

32.
$$A = \frac{1}{2}h\left(b_1 + b_2\right)$$
$$19.5 = \frac{1}{2} \cdot 3 \cdot [x + (2x + 1)]$$
$$19.5 = 1.5[3x + 1]$$
$$19.5 = 4.5x + 1.5$$
$$19.5 - 1.5 = 4.5x + 1.5 - 1.5$$
$$18 = 4.5x$$
$$\frac{18}{4.5} = \frac{4.5x}{4.5}$$
$$x = 4 \text{ cm}$$

14-6 Multiplying Binomials

1. A binomial is a polynomial with two terms.

2.

3. $2x^2 + 5x + 2$

4. $x^2 + 3x + 2$ 5. $4x^2 + 10x + 6$

6. $(m + 4)(m + 3) = m(m + 3) + 4(m + 3)$
$$= m^2 + 3m + 4m + 12$$
$$= m^2 + 7m + 12$$

7. $(3a + 1)(2a + 3) = 3a(2a + 3) + 1(2a + 3)$
$$= 6a^2 + 9a + 2a + 3$$
$$= 6a^2 + 11a + 3$$

8. $(x + 1)(2x + 3) = x(2x + 3) + 1(2x + 3)$
$$= 2x^2 + 3x + 2x + 3$$
$$= 2x^2 + 5x + 3$$

9. $(3z + 1)(4z + 5) = 3z(4z + 5) + 1(4z + 5)$
$$= 12z^2 + 15z + 4z + 5$$
$$= 12z^2 + 19z + 5$$

10. c   11. d   12. b   13. a

14. $(x + 3)(x + 1) = x(x + 1) + 3(x + 1)$
$$= x^2 + x + 3x + 3$$
$$= x^2 + 4x + 3$$

15. $(x + 1)(x + 4) = x(x + 4) + 1(x + 4)$
$$= x^2 + 4x + x + 4$$
$$= x^2 + 5x + 4$$

16. $(2x + 1)(x + 5) = 2x(x + 5) + 1(x + 5)$
$$= 2x^2 + 10x + x + 5$$
$$= 2x^2 + 11x + 5$$

17. $(x + 2)(2x + 1) = x(2x + 1) + 2(2x + 1)$
$$= 2x^2 + x + 4x + 2$$
$$= 2x^2 + 5x + 2$$

18. $(2x + 2)(2x + 3) = 2x(2x + 3) + 2(2x + 3)$
$$= 4x^2 + 6x + 4x + 6$$
$$= 4x^2 + 10x + 6$$

19. $(x + 1)(x + 1) = x(x + 1) + 1(x + 1)$
$$= x^2 + x + x + 1$$
$$= x^2 + 2x + 1$$

20. $(2x + 5)(x + 1) = 2x(x + 1) + 5(x + 1)$
$$= 2x^2 + 2x + 5x + 5$$
$$= 2x^2 + 7x + 5$$

21. $\frac{3}{4}$

22. $116 \cdot 24 = 2{,}784$
$$2{,}784 - 2{,}400 = 384$$
$$I = prt$$
$$384 = 2{,}400 \cdot r \cdot 2$$
$$384 = 4{,}800r$$
$$\frac{384}{4{,}800} = \frac{4{,}800r}{4{,}800}$$
$$r = 0.08 \text{ or } 8\%$$

23. $2x^2 + 3x$

24. $(x + 3)(x + 4) = x(x + 4) + 3(x + 4)$
$$= x^2 + 4x + 3x + 12$$
$$= x^2 + 7x + 12$$

25. $(x + 2)(x - 1)$; $x^2 + x - 2$

26. a. $(a + b)(a + b)$

b. a^2, ab, b^2

c. $a^2 + 2ab + b^2$

27. See students' work.

14-6B Mathematics Lab: Factoring Polynomials

1. $(x + 3)$, $(x + 2)$

2. not factorable

PAGE 563   APPLICATION

3. $(x + 6)(x + 1)$

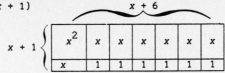

4. $(x + 3)(x + 3)$

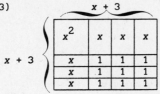

5. $(2x + 3)(x + 2)$

6. not factorable

14-7   Use Logical Reasoning

PAGE 565   CHECKING FOR UNDERSTANDING

1. Because only one of them plays each sport.
2. Answers will vary.
3. It will take three cuts to saw a log into four pieces. So it will take 3 · 3 or 9 minutes.
4. There are a total of 53 people. Three mini-buses will hold 48 people, so four mini-buses will be needed.

PAGE 565   PROBLEM SOLVING

5. 1,860,867; Three divides the cube of 123 since it divides 123. The sum of the digits of 1,860,867 is divisible by 3, whereas the sum of the digits of the other three numbers is not.
6. Since Tiger has orange markings, Tiger is calico.
   Since Snowball has spots, Snowball is white with brown markings.
   Since Beanie does not get along with the black cat, Beanie is all white.
   Thus Flower is all black.

	Beanie	Tiger	Flower	Snowball
White/Brown	×	×	×	✓
White	✓	×	×	×
Black	×	×	✓	×
Calico	×	✓	×	×

7. $(x + 2)(x + 4) = x(x + 4) + 2(x + 4)$
   $$= x^2 + 4x + 2x + 8$$
   $$= x^2 + 6x + 8$$

Chapter 14 Study Guide and Review

PAGE 566   COMMUNICATING MATHEMATICS

1. false; binomial   2. true
3. true   4. true
5. false; two
6.

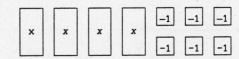

7. A monomial is a number, a variable, or a product of a number and one or more variables.
8. Model the polynomial. Then form a rectangle with the tiles. The factors are the dimensions of the rectangle.

PAGES 566-567   SKILLS AND CONCEPTS

9. $4x - 6$

10. $2x^2 - 3$

11. $-3x^2 + 4x - 8$

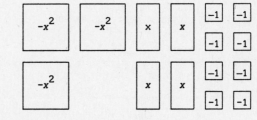

12. $x^2 - 5$

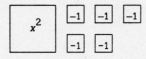

13. $15m^2 + 8m$ 14. $5p - 15$
15. $2x^2 + 6x$ 16. $2a + 3b$

185

17. $14m^2 + 2m$

18. $\begin{array}{r} 11m^2 - 2m \\ + \;\; 4m^2 + 5m \\ \hline 15m^2 + 3m \end{array}$

19. $\begin{array}{r} 5d + 1 \\ + \; 9d + 7 \\ \hline 14d + 8 \end{array}$

20. $\begin{array}{r} 2a^2 + 5a \\ + \; 2a^2 - 4a \\ \hline 4a^2 + a \end{array}$

21. $\begin{array}{r} b^2 - 4b + 2 \\ + \; 3b^2 + \;\; b - 6 \\ \hline 4b^2 - 3b - 4 \end{array}$

22. $\begin{array}{r} 3x^2 - 8x \\ + \;\; x^2 + 9x \\ \hline 4x^2 + \;\; x \end{array}$

23. $\begin{array}{r} 9g + 3 \\ + \; (-6g - 1) \\ \hline 3g + 2 \end{array}$

24. $\begin{array}{r} 2m - 8 \\ + \; (2m - \;\; 3) \\ \hline 4m - 11 \end{array}$

25. $\begin{array}{r} 4s^2 + 9 \\ + \; (-s^2 - 4) \\ \hline 3s^2 + 5 \end{array}$

26. $\begin{array}{r} 7k^2 \quad\;\; - 2 \\ + \; (-2k + 6k + 1) \\ \hline 5k^2 + 6k - 1 \end{array}$

27. $\begin{array}{r} 8p^2 + 4p - 7 \\ + \; (-6p^2 - 9p + 3) \\ \hline 2p^2 - 5p - 4 \end{array}$

28. $10y + 20$

29. $4z^2 + 12z$

30. $3c^2 + c$

31. $3t^2 + 18t$

32. $(x + 4)(x + 2) = x(x + 2) + 4(x + 2)$
$\qquad = x^2 + 2x + 4x + 8$
$\qquad = x^2 + 6x + 8$

33. $(x + 3)(2x + 2) = x(2x + 2) + 3(2x + 2)$
$\qquad = 2x^2 + 2x + 6x + 6$
$\qquad = 2x^2 + 8x + 6$

34. $(2x + 2)(2x + 5) = 2x(2x + 5) + 2(2x + 5)$
$\qquad = 4x^2 + 10x + 4x + 10$
$\qquad = 4x^2 + 14x + 10$

35. $(x + 5)(x + 2) = x(x + 2) + 5(x + 2)$
$\qquad = x^2 + 2x + 5x + 10$
$\qquad = x^2 + 7x + 10$

36. $(3x + 1)(x + 2) = 3x(x + 2) + 1(x + 2)$
$\qquad = 3x^2 + 6x + x + 2$
$\qquad = 3x^2 + 7x + 2$

PAGE 568   APPLICATIONS AND PROBLEM SOLVING

37.

$(2x - 3)$ meters by $(x + 2)$ meters

38. $(3x - 1) + (2x + 3) + (3x - 1) + (2x + 3) =$
$10x + 4$ meters

39. $4(3x + 8) = 12x + 32$ yards

40. $\begin{array}{r} -2x^2 - 3x + 9 \\ + \; (-3x^2 - \;\; x + \;\; 7) \\ \hline -5x^2 - 4x + 16 \end{array}$

$180 - (-5x^2 - 4x + 16) = 180 + 5x^2 + 4x - 16$
$\qquad\qquad\qquad = 5x^2 + 4x + 164$ degrees

41. c

Chapter 14 Test

PAGE 569

1. $6x^2 + 3x$

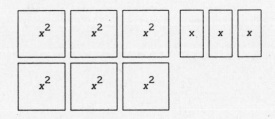

2. $-5x^2 - 2x + 8$

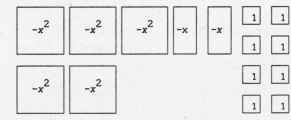

3. $4x^2 + 7x - 2$

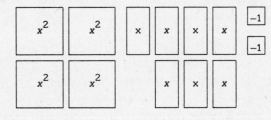

4. $x^2 - x$

5. $r^3t - s = (-1)^3(4) - 2$
$\qquad\quad = -4 - 2$
$\qquad\quad = -6$

6. $s^3 - 3s + t = 2^3 - 3(2) + 4$
$\qquad\qquad = 8 - 6 + 4$
$\qquad\qquad = 6$

7. $r^2st^2 - 3t = (-1)^2(2)(4)^2 - 3(4)$
$\qquad\qquad = 32 - 12$
$\qquad\qquad = 20$

8. $3x^2 + x + 4$

9. $7x^2 + 12x$

10. $3c^2 + 3c$

11. $-2x^2 + 2y$

12. $-a^2 + 12a - 1$

13.
$$
\begin{array}{r}
8z^2 - 2z \\
+ (-4z^2 - 9z) \\
\hline
4z^2 - 11z
\end{array}
$$

14.
$$
\begin{array}{r}
5c^2 + 3c \\
+ (-3c^2 + c) \\
\hline
2c^2 + 4c
\end{array}
$$

15.
$$
\begin{array}{r}
6n^2 - 5n + 1 \\
+ (\quad - 3n + 4) \\
\hline
6n^2 - 8n + 5
\end{array}
$$

16.
$$
\begin{array}{r}
-x^2 + 3x - 4 \\
+ x^2 - 7x \\
\hline
- 4x - 4
\end{array}
$$

17.
$$
\begin{array}{r}
6r^2 - 5r + 4 \\
+ r^2 - 4r - 8 \\
\hline
7r^2 - 9r - 4
\end{array}
$$

18.
$$
\begin{array}{r}
9y^2 + 5y - 8 \\
+ (-6y^2 - 8y + 9) \\
\hline
3y^2 - 3y + 1
\end{array}
$$

19. a; $x^2 + 7x + 12$

20. d; $x^2 + 2x + 1$

21. b; $2x^2 + 5x + 2$

22. c; $3x^2 + 5x + 2$

23. $8d^2 - 20d$

24. $-5x^2 + 3x$

25. Since Amarette has nothing to do with food, she either delivers fliers or babysits. But Jacob and the babysitter are brothers, so Amarette must deliver fliers and Lonny must be the babysitter.
Since Jacob does not know the stock person, he must work at the Chicken Flicken and Susan must be the stock person.

	Jacob	Amarette	Susan	Lonny
Chicken Flicken	✓	✗	✗	✗
Stock Person	✗	✗	✓	✗
Deliver Fliers	✗	✓	✗	✗
Babysit	✗	✗	✗	✓

PAGE 569   BONUS

$$
\begin{aligned}
(ax + b)(cx + d) &= ax(cx + d) + b(cx + d) \\
&= acx^2 + adx + bcx + bd \\
&= acx^2 + (ad + bc)x + bd
\end{aligned}
$$

Academic Skills Test

PAGES 570-571

1. C;
$$
\begin{aligned}
2c - 5 &= -3 \\
2c - 5 + 5 &= -3 + 5 \\
2c &= 2 \\
\frac{2c}{2} &= \frac{2}{2} \\
c &= 1
\end{aligned}
$$

2. C; Let $N = 0.\overline{39}$. Then $100 N = 39.\overline{39}$.
$$
\begin{array}{r}
100N = 39.\overline{39} \\
- \quad N = 0.\overline{39} \\
\hline
99N = 39 \\
N = \frac{39}{99} = \frac{13}{33}
\end{array}
$$

3. A; $0.3x = 5.28$
$$
\begin{aligned}
\frac{0.3x}{0.3} &= \frac{5.28}{0.3} \\
x &= 17.6
\end{aligned}
$$

4. A; $\frac{3}{6} \cdot \frac{2}{5} = \frac{6}{30} = \frac{1}{5}$

5. C; $x^2 + x^2 = (10\sqrt{2})^2$
$$
\begin{aligned}
2x^2 &= 200 \\
\frac{2x^2}{2} &= \frac{200}{2} \\
x^2 &= 100 \\
x &= 10
\end{aligned}
$$

6. B; $\dfrac{1 \text{ unit}}{6 \text{ in.}} = \dfrac{x \text{ units}}{40 \text{ in.}}$ $\qquad \dfrac{1 \text{ unit}}{6 \text{ in.}} = \dfrac{y \text{ units}}{60 \text{ in.}}$

$6x = 40 \qquad\qquad\qquad 6y = 60$

$\dfrac{6x}{6} = \dfrac{40}{6} \qquad\qquad\quad \dfrac{6y}{6} = \dfrac{60}{6}$

$x = 6\frac{2}{3}$ units $\qquad\qquad x = 10$ units

$$6\frac{2}{3} \times 10$$

7. C   **8.** A; $\frac{2.5}{30} = 0.08\overline{3}$ or $8\frac{1}{3}\%$

9. D

10. B; $M(-3, 1) \rightarrow (-3 + 2, 1 - 1) \rightarrow M'(-1, 0)$
$A(2, 6) \rightarrow (2 + 2, 6 - 1) \rightarrow A'(4, 5)$
$T(6, 2) \rightarrow (6 + 2, 2 - 1) \rightarrow T'(8, 1)$
$H(1, -3) \rightarrow (1 + 2, -3 - 1) \rightarrow H'(3, -4)$

11. A   **12.** C   **13.** D; $4 \cdot 3 \cdot 2 = 24$

14. C; $4 \cdot 3 \cdot 2 \cdot 1 = 24$

15. B; $C(12, 4) = \dfrac{P(12, 4)}{4!}$

$C(12, 4) = \dfrac{12 \cdot 11 \cdot 10 \cdot 9}{24}$

$C(12, 4) = \dfrac{11,880}{24} = 495$

16. B; $3x + 6x - 5x = 9x - 5x = 4x$

17. A; $\left(\dfrac{60}{150}\right) \cdot 800 = (0.4) \cdot 800 = 320$

18. B; $(3a + 1) + (2a + 5) = 5a + 6$

19. C   **20.** C; $\qquad\qquad A = \frac{1}{2}bh$

$6x^2 + x - 1 = \frac{1}{2}bh$

$2(6x^2 + x - 1) = 2\left(\frac{1}{2}bh\right)$

$12x^2 + 2x - 2 = bh$

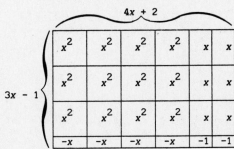

If $x = 2$, $bh = 12(2)^2 + 2(2) - 2$
$= 48 + 4 - 2$
$= 50$
$= 5 \cdot 10$

Extra Practice

Lesson 1-2

PAGE 584

1. $2 + (24 \div 6) = 2 + (4)$
$= 6$

2. $24 \div (10 + 2) = 24 \div 12$
$= 2$

3. $4 \cdot (25 \cdot 9) = (4 \cdot 25) \cdot 9$
$= 100 \cdot 9$
$= 900$

4. $500 \longrightarrow 499$
$\underline{-\ 468} \longrightarrow \underline{-\ 467}$
32

5. $(7 \cdot 20) \cdot 5 = 7 \cdot (20 \cdot 5)$
$= 7 \cdot 100$
$= 700$

6. $462 \longrightarrow 457$
$\underline{+\ 195} \longrightarrow \underline{+\ 200}$
657

7. $5 \times 25 = 5 \cdot 20 + 5 \cdot 5$
$= 100 + 25$
$= 125$

8. $26 + 41 + 14 = (26 + 14) + 41$
$= 40 + 41$
$= 81$

9. $\$1.99 \times 3 = 3 \cdot \$2.00 - 3 \cdot \$0.01$
$= \$6 - \$0.03$
$= \$5.97$

10. $5 \cdot (10 + 7) = 5 \cdot 10 + 5 \cdot 7$
$= 50 + 35$
$= 85$

11. $6 \times 35 = 6 \cdot 30 + 6 \cdot 5$
$= 180 + 30$
$= 210$

12. $2 \cdot 84 \cdot 50 = (2 \cdot 50) \cdot 84$
$= 100 \cdot 84$
$= 8{,}400$

13. $6 + 27 + 14 = (6 + 14) + 27$
$= 20 + 27$
$= 47$

14. $200 \longrightarrow 199$
$\underline{-\ \ 95} \longrightarrow \underline{-\ 94}$
105

15. $7 \cdot 19 = 7 \cdot 10 + 7 \cdot 9$
$= 70 + 63$
$= 133$

16. $1{,}762 \longrightarrow 1{,}760$
$\underline{+\ \ 124} \longrightarrow \underline{+\ \ 126}$
$1{,}886$

17. $5 \times 6 \times 2 = (5 \cdot 2) \cdot 6$
$= 10 \cdot 6$
$= 60$

18. $12 \times 25 = (12 \cdot 5) \cdot 5$
$= 60 \cdot 5$
$= 300$

Lesson 1-3

PAGE 584

For Exercises 1-17, sample answers are given.

1. $200 + 500 = 700$ **2.** $1{,}200 + 5{,}600 = 6{,}800$
3. $6{,}000 - 2{,}000 = 4{,}000$ **4.** $600 \div 6 = 100$
5. $300 + 100 = 400$ **6.** $9{,}000 - 1{,}000 = 8{,}000$
7. $360 \div 6 = 60$ **8.** $420 \div 7 = 60$
9. $0.2 + 0.3 = 0.5$ **10.** $18 - 9 = 9$
11. $12 \div 3 = 4$ **12.** $2{,}000 + 2{,}000 = 4{,}000$
13. $600 - 300 = 300$ **14.** $8.5 + 9.4 = 17.9$
15. $150 \div 5 = 30$ **16.** $40 \cdot 5 = 200$
17. $1 \cdot 5 = 5$

Lesson 1-6

PAGE 584

1. 1 kg · 1000 = 1,000 g
2. 632 mg ÷ 1000 = 0.632 g
3. 2.9 kL · 1000 = 2,900 L
4. 400 mm ÷ 10 = 40 cm
5. 30 g ÷ 1000 = 0.030 kg
6. 13.5 L ÷ 1000 = 0.0135 L
7. 0.3 km · 1000 = 300 m
8. 38.6 kg · 1000 = 38,600 g
9. 3.5 kL · 1000 = 3,500 L
10. 4.8 cm · 10 = 48 mm
11. 9.5 mg ÷ 1000 = 0.0095 g
12. 16 L · 1000 = 16,000 mL
13. 12.6 g · 1000 = 12,600 mg
14. 16.35 kL · 1000 = 16,350 L
15. 415 m · 100 = 41,500 cm
16. 21 g · 1000 = 21,000 mg
17. 63 L · 1000 = 63,000 mL
18. 1.7 m · 100 = 170 cm
19. 1.02 kg · 1000 = 1,020 g
20. 6.53 kL · 1000 = 6,530 L
21. 45 cm · 10 = 450 mm

Lesson 1-7

PAGE 585

1. 7 ft · 12 = 84 in. **2.** 5 T · 2000 = 10,000 lb
3. 2 lb · 16 = 32 oz **4.** 5 mi · 1760 = 8,800 yd

5. $\frac{1}{4}$ lb $\cdot$ 16 = 4 oz   6. 31,680 ft $\div$ 5,280 = 6 mi

7. $\frac{1}{4}$ mi $\cdot$ 5280 = 1,320 ft   8. 24 fl oz $\div$ 8 = 3 c

9. 8 pt $\cdot$ 2 = 16 c   10. 10 pt $\div$ 2 = 5 qt

11. 9 ft $\cdot$ 12 = 108 in.   12. 24 in. $\div$ 12 = 2 ft

13. 4 gal $\cdot$ 4 = 16 qt

14. (4 qt) $\cdot$ 2 $\cdot$ 2 $\cdot$ 8 = 128 fl oz

15. 12 pt $\cdot$ 2 = 24 c   16. 5 yd $\cdot$ 3 = 15 ft

17. 15 qt $\div$ 4 = $\frac{15}{4}$ gal   18. 4 pt $\cdot$ 2 = 8 c

$$= 3\frac{3}{4} \text{ gal}$$

19. 2 mi $\cdot$ 5,280 = 10,560 ft

20. 3T $\cdot$ 2,000 = 6,000 lb

21. 6 lb $\cdot$ 16 = 96 oz

Lesson 1-9

PAGE 585

1. $4 \cdot 4 \cdot 4 \cdot 4 = 4^4$ 2. $3 \cdot 3 = 3^2$

3. $7 \cdot 7 \cdot 7 \cdot 7 \cdot 7 \cdot 7 = 7^6$

4. $4^3 = 4 \cdot 4 \cdot 4$
   $= 16 \cdot 4$
   $= 64$

5. $6^2 = 6 \cdot 6$ 6. $2^6 = 2 \cdot 2 \cdot 2 \cdot 2 \cdot 2 \cdot 2$
   $= 36$ $= 8 \cdot 8$
                   $= 64$

7. $5^2 \times 6^2 = 5 \cdot 5 \times 6 \cdot 6$
   $= 25 \cdot 36$
   $= 900$

8. $3 \times 2^4 = 3 \times 2 \cdot 2 \cdot 2 \cdot 2$
   $= 6 \cdot 8$
   $= 48$

9. $10^4 \times 3^2 = 10 \cdot 10 \cdot 10 \cdot 10 \times 3 \cdot 3$
   $= 10,000 \cdot 9$
   $= 90,000$

10. $5^3 \times 1^9 = 5 \cdot 5 \cdot 5 \times 1$
    $= 25 \cdot 5$
    $= 125$

11. $2^2 \times 2^4 = 2 \cdot 2 \times 2 \cdot 2 \cdot 2 \cdot 2$
    $= 4 \cdot 16$
    $= 64$

12. $2 \times 3^2 \times 4^2 = 2 \times 3 \cdot 3 \times 4 \cdot 4$
    $= 2 \cdot 9 \cdot 16$
    $= 288$

13. $7^3 = 7 \cdot 7 \cdot 7$ 14. $9^2 + 3^2 = 9 \cdot 9 + 3 \cdot 3$
    $= 49 \cdot 7$ $= 81 + 9$
    $= 343$ $= 90$

15. $0.5^2 = 0.5 \cdot 0.5$
    $= 0.25$

Lesson 2-1

PAGE 585

1. $15 - 5 + 9 - 2 = 10 + 9 - 2$
   $= 19 - 2$
   $= 17$

2. $6 \times 6 + 3.6 = 36 + 3.6$
   $= 39.6$

3. $12 + 20 \div 4 - 5 = 12 + 5 - 5$
   $= 17 - 5$
   $= 12$

4. $6 \times 3 \div 9 - 1 = 18 \div 9 - 1$
   $= 2 - 1$
   $= 1$

5. $(4^2 + 2^3) \times 5 = (16 + 8) \times 5$
   $= 24 \times 5$
   $= 120$

6. $24 \div 8 - 2 = 3 - 2$
   $= 1$

7. $3 \times (4 + 5) - 7 = 3 \times (9) - 7$
   $= 27 - 7$
   $= 20$

8. $4.3 + 24 \div 6 = 4.3 + 4$
   $= 8.3$

9. $(5^2 + 2) \div 3 = (25 + 2) \div 3$
   $= 27 \div 3$
   $= 9$

10. $27 \div 3^2 \times 2 = 27 \div 9 \times 2$
    $= 3 \times 2$
    $= 6$

11. $4 \times 4^2 \times 2 - 8 = 4 \times 16 \times 2 - 8$
    $= 64 \times 2 - 8$
    $= 128 - 8$
    $= 120$

12. $12 \div 3 - 2^2 + 6 = 12 \div 3 - 4 + 6$
    $= 4 - 4 + 6$
    $= 0 + 6$
    $= 6$

13. $3^3 \times 2 - 5 \times 3 = 27 \times 2 - 5 \times 3$
    $= 54 - 15$
    $= 39$

14. $10 \times 2 + 7 \times 3 = 20 + 7 \times 3$
    $= 20 + 21$
    $= 41$

15. $7 - 2 \times 8 \div 4 = 7 - 16 \div 4$
    $= 7 - 4$
    $= 3$

16. $17 - 2^3 + 5 = 17 - 8 + 5$
    $= 9 + 5$
    $= 14$

17. $5 \times 6 + 10 + 1 = 30 \div 10 + 1$
    $= 3 + 1$
    $= 4$

18. $18 + 4 \div 2 = 18 + 2$
$= 20$

19. $(7 + 5 \times 4) \div 9 = (7 + 20) \div 9$
$= 27 \div 9$
$= 3$

20. $100 \div (28 + 9 \times 8) = 100 \div (28 + 72)$
$= 100 \div (100)$
$= 1$

21. $6 \times 4 - 8 \times 3 = 24 - 8 \times 3$
$= 24 - 24$
$= 0$

Lesson 2-2

PAGE 586

1. $19 + 4 = y$
$23 = y$

2. $5 \cdot 6 = n$
$30 = n$

3. $q - 7 = 7$
$14 - 7 \overset{?}{=} 7$
$7 = 7$

4. $7 + a = 10$
$7 + 3 \overset{?}{=} 10$
$10 = 10$

5. $x - 3 = 12$
$15 - 3 \overset{?}{=} 12$
$12 = 12$

6. $2m = 8$
$2 \cdot 4 \overset{?}{=} 8$
$8 = 8$

7. $4y = 24$
$4 \cdot 6 \overset{?}{=} 24$
$24 = 24$

8. $36 = 6x$
$36 \overset{?}{=} 6 \cdot 6$
$36 = 36$

9. $19 + j = 29$
$19 + 10 \overset{?}{=} 29$
$29 = 29$

10. $13 = 9 + c$
$13 \overset{?}{=} 9 + 4$
$13 = 13$

11. $p \div 4 = 4$
$16 \div 4 \overset{?}{=} 4$
$4 = 4$

12. $6 = t \div 5$
$6 \overset{?}{=} 30 \div 5$
$6 = 6$

13. $42 = 6n$
$42 \overset{?}{=} 6 \cdot 7$
$42 = 42$

14. $\frac{m}{7} = 5$
$\frac{35}{7} \overset{?}{=} 5$
$5 = 5$

15. $45 = 9d$
$45 \overset{?}{=} 9 \cdot 5$
$45 = 45$

16. $24 = 14 + k$
$24 \overset{?}{=} 14 + 10$
$24 = 24$

17. $2a = 18$
$2 \cdot 9 \overset{?}{=} 18$
$18 = 18$

18. $c \div 8 = 12$
$16 \div 8 \overset{?}{=} 2$
$2 = 2$

19. $12 + f = 15$
$12 + 3 \overset{?}{=} 15$
$15 = 15$

20. $17 = 37 - g$
$17 \overset{?}{=} 37 - 20$
$17 = 17$

21. $25 = 5x$
$25 \overset{?}{=} 5 \cdot 5$
$25 = 25$

Lesson 2-3

PAGE 586

1. $g - 3 = 10$
$g - 3 + 3 = 10 + 3$
$g = 13$
Check: $13 - 3 \overset{?}{=} 10$
$10 = 10$ √

2. $b + 7 = 12$
$b + 7 - 7 = 12 - 7$
$b = 5$
Check: $5 + 7 \overset{?}{=} 12$
$12 = 12$ √

3. $a + 3 = 15$
$a + 3 - 3 = 15 - 3$
$a = 12$
Check: $12 + 3 \overset{?}{=} 15$
$15 = 15$ √

4. $r - 3 = 4$
$r - 3 + 3 = 4 + 3$
$r = 7$
Check: $7 - 3 \overset{?}{=} 4$
$4 = 4$ √

5. $t + 3 = 21$
$t + 3 - 3 = 21 - 3$
$t = 18$
Check: $18 + 3 \overset{?}{=} 21$
$21 = 21$ √

6. $s + 10 = 23$
$s + 10 - 10 = 23 - 10$
$s = 13$
Check: $13 + 10 \overset{?}{=} 23$
$23 = 23$ √

7. $9 + n = 13$
$9 - 9 + n = 13 - 9$
$n = 4$
Check: $9 + 4 \overset{?}{=} 13$
$13 = 13$ √

8. $13 + v = 31$
$13 - 13 + v = 31 - 13$
$v = 18$
Check: $13 + 18 \overset{?}{=} 31$
$31 = 31$ √

9. $s - 0.4 = 6$
$s - 0.4 + 0.4 = 6 + 0.4$
$s = 6.4$
Check: $6.4 - 0.4 \overset{?}{=} 6$
$6 = 6$ √

10. $x - 1.3 = 12$
$x - 1.3 + 1.3 = 12 + 1.3$
$x = 13.3$
Check: $13.3 - 1.3 \overset{?}{=} 12$
$12 = 12$ √

11. $18 = y + 3.4$
$18 - 3.4 = y + 3.4 - 3.4$
$14.6 = y$
Check: $18 \overset{?}{=} 14.6 + 3.4$
$18 = 18$ √

12. $7 + g = 91$
$7 - 7 + g = 91 - 7$
$g = 84$
Check: $7 + 84 \overset{?}{=} 91$
$91 = 91$ √

13. $63 + f = 71$
$63 - 63 + f = 71 - 63$
$f = 8$
Check: $63 + 8 \overset{?}{=} 71$
$71 = 71$ √

14. $0.32 = w - 0.1$
$0.32 + 0.1 = w - 0.1 + 0.1$
$0.42 = w$
Check: $0.32 \overset{?}{=} 0.42 - 0.1$
$0.32 = 0.32$ √

15. $c - 18 = 13$
$c - 18 + 18 = 13 + 18$
$c = 31$
Check: $31 - 18 \overset{?}{=} 13$
$13 = 13$ √

16. $23 = n - 5$
$23 + 5 = n - 5 + 5$
$28 = n$
Check: $23 \overset{?}{=} 28 - 5$
$23 = 23$ √

17.
$$j - 3 = 7$$
$$j - 3 + 3 = 7 + 3$$
$$j = 10$$
Check: $10 - 3 \stackrel{?}{=} 7$
$$7 = 7 \ \checkmark$$

18.
$$18 = p + 3$$
$$18 - 3 = p + 3 - 3$$
$$15 = p$$
Check: $18 \stackrel{?}{=} 15 + 3$
$$18 = 18 \ \checkmark$$

19.
$$12 + p = 16$$
$$12 - 12 + p = 16 - 12$$
$$p = 4$$
Check: $12 + 4 \stackrel{?}{=} 16$
$$16 = 16 \ \checkmark$$

20.
$$25 = 50 - y$$
$$25 + y = 50 - y + y$$
$$25 + y = 50$$
$$25 - 25 + y = 50 - 25$$
$$y = 25$$
Check: $25 \stackrel{?}{=} 50 - 25$
$$25 = 25 \ \checkmark$$

21.
$$x + 2 = 4$$
$$x + 2 - 2 = 4 - 2$$
$$x = 2$$
Check: $2 + 2 \stackrel{?}{=} 4$
$$4 = 4 \ \checkmark$$

Lesson 2-4

PAGE 586

1. $4x = 36$
$$\frac{4x}{4} = \frac{36}{4}$$
$$x = 9$$
Check: $4(9) \stackrel{?}{=} 36$
$$36 = 36 \ \checkmark$$

2. $39 = 3y$
$$\frac{39}{3} = \frac{3y}{3}$$
$$13 = y$$
Check: $39 \stackrel{?}{=} 3(13)$
$$39 = 39 \ \checkmark$$

3. $4z = 16$
$$\frac{4z}{4} = \frac{16}{4}$$
$$z = 4$$
Check: $4(4) \stackrel{?}{=} 16$
$$16 = 16 \ \checkmark$$

4. $t \div 5 = 6$
$$t \div 5 \cdot 5 = 6 \cdot 5$$
$$t = 30$$
Check: $30 \div 5 \stackrel{?}{=} 6$
$$6 = 6 \ \checkmark$$

5. $100 = 20b$
$$\frac{100}{20} = \frac{20b}{20}$$
$$5 = b$$
Check: $100 \stackrel{?}{=} 20(5)$
$$100 = 100 \ \checkmark$$

6. $8 = w \div 8$
$$8 \cdot 8 = w \div 8 \cdot 8$$
$$64 = w$$
Check: $8 \stackrel{?}{=} 64 \div 8$
$$8 = 8 \ \checkmark$$

7. $10a = 40$
$$\frac{10a}{10} = \frac{40}{10}$$
$$a = 4$$
Check: $10(4) \stackrel{?}{=} 40$
$$40 = 40 \ \checkmark$$

8. $s \div 9 = 8$
$$s \div 9 \cdot 9 = 8 \cdot 9$$
$$s = 72$$
Check: $72 \div 9 \stackrel{?}{=} 8$
$$8 = 8 \ \checkmark$$

9. $420 = 5s$
$$\frac{420}{5} = \frac{5s}{5}$$
$$84 = s$$
Check: $420 \stackrel{?}{=} 5(84)$
$$420 = 420 \ \checkmark$$

10. $8k = 72$
$$\frac{8k}{8} = \frac{72}{8}$$
$$k = 9$$
Check: $8(9) \stackrel{?}{=} 72$
$$72 = 72 \ \checkmark$$

11. $2m = 18$
$$\frac{2m}{2} = \frac{18}{2}$$
$$m = 9$$
Check: $2(9) \stackrel{?}{=} 18$
$$18 = 18 \ \checkmark$$

12. $\frac{m}{8} = 5$
$$\frac{m}{8} \cdot 8 = 5 \cdot 8$$
$$m = 40$$
Check: $\frac{40}{8} \stackrel{?}{=} 5$
$$5 = 5 \ \checkmark$$

13. $0.12 = 3h$
$$\frac{0.12}{3} = \frac{3h}{3}$$
$$0.04 = h$$
Check: $0.12 \stackrel{?}{=} 3(0.04)$
$$0.12 = 0.12 \ \checkmark$$

14. $\frac{w}{7} = 8$
$$\frac{w}{7} \cdot 7 = 8 \cdot 7$$
$$w = 56$$
Check: $\frac{56}{7} \stackrel{?}{=} 8$
$$8 = 8 \ \checkmark$$

15. $18q = 36$
$$\frac{18q}{18} = \frac{36}{18}$$
$$q = 2$$
Check: $18(2) \stackrel{?}{=} 36$
$$36 = 36 \ \checkmark$$

16. $9w = 54$
$$\frac{9w}{9} = \frac{54}{9}$$
$$w = 6$$
Check: $9(6) \stackrel{?}{=} 54$
$$54 = 54 \ \checkmark$$

17. $4 = p \div 4$
$$4 \cdot 4 = p \div 4 \cdot 4$$
$$16 = p$$
Check: $4 \stackrel{?}{=} 16 \div 4$
$$4 = 4 \ \checkmark$$

18. $14 = 2p$
$$\frac{14}{2} = \frac{2p}{2}$$
$$7 = p$$
Check: $14 \stackrel{?}{=} 2(7)$
$$14 = 14 \ \checkmark$$

19. $12 = 3t$
$$\frac{12}{3} = \frac{3t}{3}$$
$$4 = t$$
Check: $12 \stackrel{?}{=} 3(4)$
$$12 = 12 \ \checkmark$$

20. $\frac{m}{4} = 12$
$$\frac{m}{4} \cdot 4 = 12 \cdot 4$$
$$m = 48$$
Check: $\frac{48}{4} \stackrel{?}{=} 12$
$$12 = 12 \ \checkmark$$

21. $6h = 12$
$$\frac{6h}{6} = \frac{12}{6}$$
$$h = 2$$
Check: $6(2) \stackrel{?}{=} 12$
$$12 = 12 \ \checkmark$$

Lesson 2-6

PAGE 587

1. $12 + n$

2. $n - 3$

3. $\frac{n}{4}$ or $n \div 4$

4. $n + 7$

5. $n - 12$

6. $8n$ or $8 \cdot n$ or $8(n)$

7. $28m$ or $28 \cdot m$ or $28(m)$

8. $\frac{15}{n}$ or $15 \div n$

9. $\frac{54}{n}$ or $54 \div n$

10. $18 + y$

11. $q - 20$

12. $41n$ or $41 \cdot n$ or $41(n)$

PAGE 587

1. $2x + 4 = 14$
$2x + 4 - 4 = 14 - 4$
$2x = 10$
$\dfrac{2x}{2} = \dfrac{10}{2}$
$x = 5$
Check: $2(5) + 4 \stackrel{?}{=} 14$
$10 + 4 \stackrel{?}{=} 14$
$14 = 14 \checkmark$

2. $5p - 10 = 0$
$5p - 10 + 10 = 0 + 10$
$5p = 10$
$\dfrac{5p}{5} = \dfrac{10}{5}$
$p = 2$
Check: $5(2) - 10 \stackrel{?}{=} 0$
$10 - 10 \stackrel{?}{=} 0$
$0 = 0 \checkmark$

3. $5 + 6a = 41$
$5 - 5 + 6a = 41 - 5$
$6a = 36$
$\dfrac{6a}{6} = \dfrac{36}{6}$
$a = 6$
Check: $5 + 6(6) \stackrel{?}{=} 41$
$5 + 36 \stackrel{?}{=} 41$
$41 = 41 \checkmark$

4. $\dfrac{x}{3} - 7 = 2$
$\dfrac{x}{3} - 7 + 7 = 2 + 7$
$\dfrac{x}{3} = 9$
$\dfrac{x}{3} \cdot 3 = 9 \cdot 3$
$x = 27$
Check: $\dfrac{27}{3} - 7 \stackrel{?}{=} 2$
$9 - 7 \stackrel{?}{=} 2$
$2 = 2 \checkmark$

5. $18 = 6(q - 4)$
$\dfrac{18}{6} = \dfrac{6(q - 4)}{6}$
$3 = q - 4$
$3 + 4 = q - 4 + 4$
$7 = q$
Check: $18 \stackrel{?}{=} 6(7 - 4)$
$18 \stackrel{?}{=} 6(3)$
$18 = 18 \checkmark$

6. $18 = 4m - 6$
$18 + 6 = 4m - 6 + 6$
$24 = 4m$
$\dfrac{24}{4} = \dfrac{4m}{4}$
$6 = m$
Check: $18 \stackrel{?}{=} 4(6) - 6$
$18 \stackrel{?}{=} 24 - 6$
$18 = 18 \checkmark$

7. $3(r - 1) = 9$
$\dfrac{3(r - 1)}{3} = \dfrac{9}{3}$
$r - 1 = 3$
$r - 1 + 1 = 3 + 1$
$r = 4$
Check: $3(4 - 1) \stackrel{?}{=} 9$
$3(3) \stackrel{?}{=} 9$
$9 = 9 \checkmark$

8. $2x + 3 = 5$
$2x + 3 - 3 = 5 - 3$
$2x = 2$
$\dfrac{2x}{2} = \dfrac{2}{2}$
$x = 1$
Check: $2(1) + 3 \stackrel{?}{=} 5$
$2 + 3 \stackrel{?}{=} 5$
$5 = 5 \checkmark$

9. $0 = 4x - 28$
$0 + 28 = 4x - 28 + 28$
$28 = 4x$
$\dfrac{28}{4} = \dfrac{4x}{4}$
$7 = x$
Check: $0 \stackrel{?}{=} 4(7) - 28$
$0 \stackrel{?}{=} 28 - 28$
$0 = 0 \checkmark$

10. $3x - 1 = 5$
$3x - 1 + 1 = 5 + 1$
$3x = 6$
$\dfrac{3x}{3} = \dfrac{6}{3}$
$x = 2$
Check: $3(2) - 1 \stackrel{?}{=} 5$
$6 - 1 \stackrel{?}{=} 5$
$5 = 5 \checkmark$

11. $3x + 5 = 14$
$3x + 5 - 5 = 14 - 5$
$3x = 9$
$\dfrac{3x}{9} = \dfrac{9}{3}$
$x = 3$
Check: $3(3) + 5 \stackrel{?}{=} 14$
$9 + 5 \stackrel{?}{=} 14$
$14 = 14 \checkmark$

12. $3(x - 5) = 12$
$\dfrac{3(x - 5)}{3} = \dfrac{12}{3}$
$x - 5 = 4$
$x - 5 + 5 = 4 + 5$
$x = 9$
Check: $3(9 - 5) \stackrel{?}{=} 12$
$3(4) \stackrel{?}{=} 12$
$12 = 12 \checkmark$

13. $9a - 8 = 73$
$9a - 8 + 8 = 73 + 8$
$9a = 81$
$\dfrac{9a}{9} = \dfrac{81}{9}$
$a = 9$
Check: $9(9) - 8 \stackrel{?}{=} 73$
$81 - 8 \stackrel{?}{=} 73$
$73 = 73 \checkmark$

14. $2x - 3 = 7$
$2x - 3 + 3 = 7 + 3$
$2x = 10$
$\dfrac{2x}{2} = \dfrac{10}{2}$
$x = 5$
Check: $2(5) - 3 \stackrel{?}{=} 7$
$10 - 3 \stackrel{?}{=} 7$
$7 = 7 \checkmark$

15. $3t + 6 = 9$
$3t + 6 - 6 = 9 - 6$
$3t = 3$
$\dfrac{3t}{3} = \dfrac{3}{3}$
$t = 1$
Check: $3(1) + 6 \stackrel{?}{=} 9$
$3 + 6 \stackrel{?}{=} 9$
$9 = 9 \checkmark$

16. $2y + 10 = 22$
$2y + 10 - 10 = 22 - 10$
$2y = 12$
$\dfrac{2y}{2} = \dfrac{12}{2}$
$y = 6$
Check: $2(6) + 10 \stackrel{?}{=} 22$
$12 + 10 \stackrel{?}{=} 22$
$22 = 22 \checkmark$

17. $15 = 2y - 5$
$15 + 5 = 2y - 5 + 5$
$20 = 2y$
$\dfrac{20}{2} = \dfrac{2y}{2}$
$10 = y$
Check: $15 \stackrel{?}{=} 2(10) - 5$
$15 \stackrel{?}{=} 20 - 5$
$15 = 15 \checkmark$

18. $3c - 4 = 2$
$3c - 4 + 4 = 2 + 4$
$3c = 6$
$\dfrac{3c}{3} = \dfrac{6}{3}$
$c = 2$
Check: $3(2) - 4 \stackrel{?}{=} 2$
$6 - 4 \stackrel{?}{=} 2$
$2 = 2 \checkmark$

19. $6 + 2p = 16$
$6 - 6 + 2p = 16 - 6$
$2p = 10$
$\dfrac{2p}{2} = \dfrac{10}{2}$
$p = 5$
Check: $6 + 2(5) \stackrel{?}{=} 16$
$6 + 10 \stackrel{?}{=} 16$
$16 = 16 \checkmark$

20. $8 = 2 + 3x$
$8 - 2 = 2 - 2 + 3x$
$6 = 3x$
$\dfrac{6}{3} = \dfrac{3x}{3}$
$2 = x$
Check: $8 \stackrel{?}{=} 2 + 3(2)$
$8 \stackrel{?}{=} 2 + 6$
$8 = 8 \checkmark$

21. $4(b + 6) = 24$
$\dfrac{4(b + 6)}{4} = \dfrac{24}{4}$
$b + 6 = 6$
$b + 6 - 6 = 6 - 6$
$b = 0$
Check: $4(0 + 6) \stackrel{?}{=} 24$
$4(6) \stackrel{?}{=} 24$
$24 = 24 \checkmark$

Lesson 2-9

PAGE 587

1. $P = 2a + 2b$ $A = bh$
$P = 2(20) + 2(25)$ $A = (25)(15)$
$P = 40 + 50$ $A = 375 \text{ m}^2$
$P = 90 \text{ m}$

2. $P = 4s$ $A = s^2$
$P = 4(2)$ $A = (2)^2$
$P = 8 \text{ yd}$ $A = 4 \text{ yd}^2$

3. $P = 2\ell + 2w$ $A = \ell w$
$P = 2(5) + 2(3)$ $A = (5)(3)$
$P = 10 + 6$ $A = 15 \text{ in}^2$
$P = 16 \text{ in.}$

4. $P = 6 + 3 + 2 + 2 + 2 + 4 + 3 + 3 + 3 + 6$
$P = 34 \text{ units}$
$A = (6)^2 + (3)^2 + (2)^2$
$A = 36 + 9 + 4$
$A = 49 \text{ units}^2$

5. $P = 2a + 2b$ $A = bh$
$P = 2(4) + 2(7)$ $A = (7)(3)$
$P = 8 + 14$ $A = 21 \text{ cm}^2$
$P = 22 \text{ cm}$

6. $P = 2\ell + 2w$ $A = \ell w$
$P = 2(4) + 2(3)$ $A = (4)(3)$
$P = 8 + 6$ $A = 12 \text{ mm}^2$
$P = 14 \text{ mm}$

Lesson 2-10

PAGE 588

1. $y + 3 > 7$
$y + 3 - 3 > 7 - 3$
$y > 4$

2. $c - 9 < 5$
$c - 9 + 9 < 5 + 9$
$c < 14$

3. $x + 4 > 9$
$x + 4 - 4 > 9 - 4$
$x > 5$

4. $y - 3 < 15$
$y - 3 + 3 < 15 + 3$
$y < 18$

5. $t - 13 > 5$
$t - 13 + 13 > 5 + 13$
$t > 18$

6. $5p < 25$
$\dfrac{5p}{5} < \dfrac{25}{5}$
$p < 5$

7. $4x < 12$
$\dfrac{4x}{4} < \dfrac{12}{4}$
$x < 3$

8. $15 < 3m$
$\dfrac{15}{3} < \dfrac{3m}{3}$
$5 < m$

9. $\dfrac{d}{3} > 15$
$\dfrac{d}{3} \cdot 3 > 15 \cdot 3$
$d > 45$

10. $8 < r \div 7$
$8 \cdot 7 < r \div 7 \cdot 7$
$56 < r$

11. $2y + 5 > 15$
$2y + 5 - 5 > 15 - 5$
$2y > 10$
$\dfrac{2y}{2} > \dfrac{10}{2}$
$y > 5$

12. $16 < 5d + 6$
$16 - 6 < 5d + 6 - 6$
$10 < 5d$
$\dfrac{10}{5} < \dfrac{5d}{5}$
$2 < d$

13. $3x + 2 > 11$
$3x + 2 - 2 > 11 - 2$
$3x > 9$
$\dfrac{3x}{3} > 9$
$x > 3$

14. $\dfrac{a}{3} - 2 > 1$
$\dfrac{a}{3} - 2 + 2 > 1 + 2$
$\dfrac{a}{3} > 3$
$\dfrac{a}{3} \cdot 3 > 3 \cdot 3$
$a > 9$

15. $9g < 27$
$\dfrac{9g}{9} < \dfrac{27}{9}$
$g < 3$

16. $14 < 2x + 4$
$14 - 4 < 2x + 4 - 4$
$10 < 2x$
$\dfrac{10}{2} < \dfrac{2x}{2}$
$5 < x$

17. $\dfrac{x}{2} - 6 > 0$
$\dfrac{x}{2} - 6 + 6 > 0 + 6$
$\dfrac{x}{2} > 6$
$\dfrac{x}{2} \cdot 2 > 6 \cdot 2$
$x > 12$

18. $k + 5 < 6$
$k + 5 - 5 < 6 - 5$
$k < 1$

19. $15 > c - 2$
$15 + 2 > c - 2 + 2$
$17 > c$

20. $4p > 24$

$$\frac{4p}{4} > \frac{24}{4}$$

$$p > 6$$

$$0 \quad 2 \quad 4 \quad 6 \quad 8$$

21. $24 < 14 + k$

$$24 - 14 < 14 - 14 + k$$

$$10 < k$$

$$k > 10$$

$$6 \quad 8 \quad 10 \quad 12 \quad 14$$

Lesson 3-1

PAGE 588

1. $\{-8, -9, -6, -10\}$

$$-12 \; -10 \; -8 \; -6 \; -4$$

2. $\{-3, 2, 0, -1\}$

$$-4 \; -2 \quad 0 \quad 2 \quad 4$$

3. $\{5, 6, 7, 8, 9\}$

$$2 \quad 4 \quad 6 \quad 8 \quad 10$$

4. $|-1| = 1$

5. $|-92| = 92$

6. $|3| = 3$

7. $|160 + 32| = |192|$
$$= 192$$

8. $|80 - 100| = |-20|$
$$= 20$$

9. $|0| = 0$

10. $|7 - 3| = |4|$
$$= 4$$

11. $|3 - 7| = |-4|$
$$= 4$$

12. $|-161| = 161$

13. $|150| = 150$

14. $|2 - 102| = |-100|$
$$= 100$$

15. $|-116| = 116$

Lesson 3-2

PAGE 588

1. $-3 < 0$

2. $-1 > -2$

3. $-5 < -4$

4. $6 > -7$

5. $8 < 10$

6. $-6 < 6$

7. $-11 > -20$

8. $-8 < 2$

9. $-13 < -12$

10. $5 > 2$

11. $9 > -8$

12. $19 > -19$

13. $|-2| = 2$
$|5| = 5$
$|-2| < |5|$

14. $|13| = 13$
$|-19| = 19$
$|13| < |-19|$

15. $|-6| = 6$
$|2| = 2$
$|-6| > |2|$

16. $|14| = 14$
$|-14| = 14$
$|14| = |-14|$

17. $|0| = 0$
$|-4| = 4$
$|0| < |-4|$

18. $|23| = 23$
$|-20| = 20$
$|23| > |-20|$

19. $|-75| = 75$
$|75| = 75$
$|-75| = |75|$

20. $-71 < 72$

21. $-15 > -35$

Lesson 3-3

PAGE 589

1. $-7 + (-7) = h$
$$-14 = h$$

2. $h = -36 + 40$
$|-36| = 36$
$|40| = 40$
$40 > 36$
$40 - 36 = 4$
$h = 4$

3. $m = 18 + (-32)$
$|18| = 18$
$|-32| = 32$
$32 > 18$
$32 - 18 = 14$
$m = -14$

4. $47 + 12 = y$
$$59 = y$$

5. $y = -69 + (-32)$
$y = -101$

6. $-120 + (-2) = c$
$$-122 = c$$

7. $x = -56 + (-4)$
$x = -60$

8. $14 + 16 = k$
$$30 = k$$

9. $-18 + 11 = d$
$|-18| = 18$
$|11| = 11$
$18 > 11$
$18 - 11 = 7$
$d = -7$

10. $-42 + 29 = r$
$|-42| = 42$
$|29| = 29$
$42 > 29$
$42 - 29 = 13$
$r = -13$

11. $h = -13 + (-11)$
$h = -24$

12. $x = 95 + (-5)$
$|95| = 95$
$|-5| = 5$
$95 > 5$
$95 - 5 = 90$
$x = 90$

13. $-120 + 2 = b$
$|-120| = 120$
$|2| = 2$
$120 > 2$
$120 - 2 = 118$
$b = -118$

14. $w = 25 + (-25)$
$|25| = 25$
$|-25| = 25$
$25 = 25$
$25 - 25 = 0$
$w = 0$

15. $a = -4 + 8$
$|-4| = 4$
$|8| = 8$
$8 > 4$
$8 - 4 = 4$
$a = 4$

16. $g = -9 + (-6)$
$g = -15$

17. $42 + (-18) = f$
$|42| = 42$
$|-18| = 18$
$42 > 18$
$42 - 18 = 24$
$f = 24$

18. $-33 + (-12) = w$
$$-45 = w$$

19. $-96 + (-18) = g$
$-114 = g$

20. $-100 + 98 = a$
$|-100| = 100$
$|98| = 98$
$100 > 98$
$100 - 98 = 2$
$a = -2$

21. $5 + (-7) = y$
$|5| = 5$
$|-7| = 7$
$7 > 5$
$7 - 5 = 2$
$y = -2$

Lesson 3-4

PAGE 589

1. $a = 7 + (-13) + 6 + (-7)$
$a = 7 + 6 + (-13) + (-7)$
$a = 13 + (-20)$
$a = -7$
Check: $7 + (-13) + 6 + (-7) = -6 + (-1) = -7$ √

2. $x = -6 + 12 + (-20)$ Check: $-6 + 12 + (-20)$
$x = -6 + (-20) + 12$ $= 6 + (-20)$
$x = -26 + 12$ $= -14$ √
$x = -14$

3. $4 + 9 + (-14) = k$ **4.** $c = -20 + 0 + (-9) + 25$
$13 + (-14) = k$ $c = -29 + 25$
$-1 = k$ $c = -4$
Check: $4 + (-14) + 9$ Check: $-20 + 25 + (-9)$
       $= -10 + 9$ $= 5 + (-9)$
       $= -1$ √ $= -4$ √

5. $b = 5 + 9 + 3 + (-17)$ **6.** $-36 + 40 + (-10) = y$
$b = 14 + (-14)$ $4 + (-10) = y$
$b = 0$ $-6 = y$
Check: $5 + 9 + 3 + (-17)$ Check: $-36 + 40 + (-10)$
       $= 17 + (-17)$ $= -36 + 30$
       $= 0$ √ $= -6$ √

7. $(-2) + 2 + (-2) + 2 = m$
$0 + 0 = m$
$0 = m$
Check: $(-2) + (-2) + 2 + 2 = -4 + 4 = 0$ √

8. $6 + (-4) + 9 + (-2) = d$
$2 + 7 = d$
$9 = d$
Check: $6 + (-4) + 9 + (-2)$
       $= 6 + 9 + (-4) + (-2)$
       $= 15 + -6$
       $= 9$ √

9. $9 + (-7) + 2 = n$
$2 + 2 = n$
$4 = n$
Check: $9 + 2 + (-7) = 11 + (-7) = 4$ √

10. $b = 100 + (-75) + (-20)$
$b = 100 + (-95)$
$b = 5$
Check: $100 + (-75) + (-20) = 25 + (-20) = 5$ √

11. $x = -12 + 24 + (-12) + 2$
$x = 12 + (-10)$
$x = 2$
Check: $-12 + (-12) + 24 + 2 = -24 + 26 = 2$ √

12. $9 + (-18) + 6 + (-3) = c$
$-9 + 3 = c$
$-6 = c$
Check: $9 + 6 + (-18) + (-3) = 15 + -21 = -6$ √

13. $(-10) + 4 + 6 = k$ **14.** $c = 4 + (-8) + 12$
$(-10) + 10 = k$ $c = -4 + 12$
$0 = k$ $c = 8$
Check: $(-10) + 4 + 6$ Check: $4 + 12 + (-8)$
     $= -6 + 6$ $= 16 + (-8)$
     $= 0$ √ $= 8$ √

Lesson 3-5

PAGE 589

1. $3 - 7 = y$ **2.** $-5 - 4 = w$
$3 + (-7) = y$ $-5 + (-4) = w$
$-4 = y$ $-9 = w$

3. $a = -6 - 2$ **4.** $12 - 9 = x$
$a = -6 + (-2)$ $3 = x$
$a = -8$

5. $a = 0 - (-14)$ **6.** $a = 58 - (-10)$
$a = 0 + 14$ $a = 58 + 10$
$a = 14$ $a = 68$

7. $n = -41 - 15$ **8.** $c = -81 - 21$
$n = -41 + (-15)$ $c = -81 + (-21)$
$n = -56$ $c = -102$

9. $26 - (-14) = y$ **10.** $6 - (-4) = b$
$26 + 14 = y$ $6 + 4 = b$
$40 = y$ $10 = b$

11. $z = 63 - 78$ **12.** $-5 - (-9) = h$
$z = 63 + (-78)$ $-5 + 9 = h$
$z = -15$ $4 = h$

13. $m = 72 - (-19)$ **14.** $-51 - 47 = x$
$m = 72 + 19$ $-51 + (-47) = x$
$m = 91$ $-98 = x$

15. $-99 - 1 = p$ **16.** $r = 8 - 13$
$-99 + (-1) = p$ $r = 8 + (-13)$
$-100 = p$ $r = -5$

17. $-2 - 23 = c$
$-2 + (-23) = c$
$-25 = c$

18. $-20 - 0 = d$
$-20 = d$

19. $55 - 33 = k$
$22 = k$

20. $84 - (-61) = a$
$84 + 61 = a$
$145 = a$

21. $z = -4 - (-4)$
$z = -4 + 4$
$z = 0$

13. $81 \div (-9) = w$
$-9 = w$

14. $18 \div (-2) = a$
$-9 = a$

15. $x = -21 \div 3$
$x = -7$

16. $d = 32 \div 8$
$d = 4$

17. $8 \div (-8) = y$
$-1 = y$

18. $c = -14 + (-7)$
$c = 2$

19. $-81 \div 9 = y$
$-9 = y$

20. $q = -81 + (-9)$
$q = 9$

21. $-49 \div (-7) = y$
$7 = y$

Lesson 3-6

PAGE 590

1. $5(-2) = d$
$-10 = d$

2. $-11(-5) = c$
$55 = c$

3. $-5(-5) = z$
$25 = z$

4. $x = -12(6)$
$x = -72$

5. $b = 2(-2)$
$b = -4$

6. $-3(2)(-4) = j$
$-6(-4) = j$
$24 = j$

7. $a = (-4)(-4)$
$a = 16$

8. $4(21) = y$
$84 = y$

9. $a = -50(0)$
$a = 0$

10. $b = 3(-13)$
$b = -39$

11. $a = 2(2)$
$a = 4$

12. $d = -2(-2)$
$d = 4$

13. $x = 5(-12)$
$x = -60$

14. $2(2)(-2) = b$
$4(-2) = b$
$-8 = b$

15. $a = 6(-4)$
$a = -24$

16. $x = -6(5)$
$x = -30$

17. $-4(8) = a$
$-32 = a$

18. $3(-16) = y$
$-48 = y$

19. $c = -2(2)$
$c = -4$

20. $6(3)(-2) = k$
$18(-2) = k$
$-36 = k$

21. $y = -3(12)$
$y = -36$

Lesson 3-7

PAGE 590

1. $a = 4 + (-2)$
$a = -2$

2. $16 + (-8) = x$
$-2 = x$

3. $-14 \div (-2) = c$
$7 = c$

4. $h = -18 \div 3$
$h = -6$

5. $-25 \div 5 = k$
$-5 = k$

6. $n = -56 \div (-8)$
$n = 7$

7. $x = 81 \div 9$
$x = 9$

8. $-55 \div 11 = c$
$-5 = c$

9. $-42 \div (-7) = y$
$6 = y$

10. $g = 18 \div (-3)$
$g = -6$

11. $t = 0 \div (-1)$
$t = 0$

12. $-32 \div 8 = m$
$-4 = m$

Lesson 3-9

PAGE 590

1. $-4 + b = 12$
$-4 + 4 + b = 12 + 4$
$b = 16$
Check: $-4 + 16 \stackrel{?}{=} 12$
$12 = 12$ ✓

2. $z - 10 = -8$
$z - 10 + 10 = -8 + 10$
$z = 2$
Check: $2 - 10 \stackrel{?}{=} -8$
$-8 = -8$ ✓

3. $-7 = x + 12$
$-7 - 12 = x + 12 - 12$
$-19 = x$
Check: $-7 \stackrel{?}{=} -19 + 12$
$-7 = -7$ ✓

4. $a + 6 = -9$
$a + 6 - 6 = -9 - 6$
$a = -15$
Check: $-15 + 6 \stackrel{?}{=} -9$
$-9 = -9$ ✓

5. $r \div 7 = -8$
$r \div 7 \cdot 7 = -8 \cdot 7$
$r = -56$
Check: $-56 \div 7 \stackrel{?}{=} -8$
$-8 = -8$ ✓

6. $-2a = -8$
$\dfrac{-2a}{-2} = \dfrac{-8}{-2}$
$a = 4$
Check: $-2(4) \stackrel{?}{=} -8$
$-8 = -8$ ✓

7. $r - (-8) = 14$
$r + 8 = 14$
$r + 8 - 8 = 14 - 8$
$r = 6$
Checking: $6 + 8 \stackrel{?}{=} 14$
$14 = 14$ ✓

8. $0 = 6r$
$\dfrac{0}{6} = \dfrac{6r}{6}$
$0 = r$
Check: $0 \stackrel{?}{=} 6(0)$
$0 = 0$ ✓

9. $\dfrac{y}{12} = -6$
$\dfrac{y}{12} \cdot 12 = -6 \cdot 12$
$y = -72$
Check: $\dfrac{-72}{12} \stackrel{?}{=} -6$
$-6 = -6$ ✓

10. $m + (-2) = 6$
$m + (-2) - (-2) = 6 - (-2)$
$m = 6 + 2$
$m = 8$
Check: $8 + (-2) \stackrel{?}{=} 6$
$6 = 6$ ✓

11. $3m = -15$

$\dfrac{3m}{3} = \dfrac{-15}{3}$

$m = -5$

Check: $3(-5) \overset{?}{=} -15$

$-15 = -15$ ✓

12. $c + (-4) = 10$

$c + (-4) \cdot (-4) = 10(-4)$

$c = -40$

Check: $(-40) + (-4) \overset{?}{=} 10$

$10 = 10$ ✓

13. $5 + q = 12$

$5 - 5 + q = 12 - 5$

$q = 7$

Check: $5 + (7) \overset{?}{=} 12$

$12 = 12$ ✓

14. $\dfrac{16}{x} = -4$

$\dfrac{16}{x} \cdot x = -4 \cdot x$

$16 = -4x$

$\dfrac{16}{-4} = \dfrac{-4x}{-4}$

$-4 = x$

Check: $\dfrac{16}{-4} \overset{?}{=} -4$

$-4 = -4$ ✓

15. $-6f = -36$

$\dfrac{-6f}{-6} = \dfrac{-36}{-6}$

$f = 6$

Check: $-6(6) \overset{?}{=} -36$

$-36 = -36$ ✓

16. $81 = -9w$

$\dfrac{81}{-9} = \dfrac{-9w}{-9}$

$-9 = w$

Check: $81 \overset{?}{=} -9(-9)$

$81 = 81$ ✓

17. $t + 12 = 6$

$t + 12 - 12 = 6 - 12$

$t = -6$

Check: $(-6) + 12 \overset{?}{=} 6$

$6 = 6$ ✓

18. $8 + p = 0$

$8 - 8 + p = 0 - 8$

$p = -8$

Check: $8 + (-8) \overset{?}{=} 0$

$0 = 0$ ✓

19. $0.12 = -3h$

$\dfrac{0.12}{-3} = \dfrac{-3h}{-3}$

$-0.04 = h$

Check: $0.12 \overset{?}{=} -3(-0.04)$

$0.12 = 0.12$ ✓

20. $12 - x = 8$

$12 - 12 - x = 8 - 12$

$-x = -4$

$\dfrac{-x}{-1} = \dfrac{-4}{-1}$

$x = 4$

Check: $12 - (4) \overset{?}{=} 8$

$8 = 8$ ✓

21. $14 + t = 10$

$14 - 14 + t = 10 - 14$

$t = -4$

Check: $14 + (-4) \overset{?}{=} 10$

$10 = 10$ ✓

Lesson 3-10

PAGE 591

1. (3, 1)   2. (-2, -1)   3. (2, -2)

4. (0, -1)   5. (-3, 2)   6. (4, -1)

7. (-5, 0)   8. (-2, 1)   9. (-4, -2)

10-19.

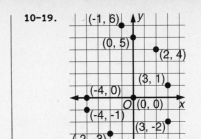

Lesson 4-2

PAGE 591

1. Each interval is 10 feet.

2. interval 31-40 because it has 11 buildings

3. interval 81-90 because it has 3 buildings

4. Look at the intervals with heights greater than 70. These are intervals 71-80 and 81-90. Interval 71-80 has 7 buildings and interval 81-90 has 3 buildings. So 7 + 3 or 10 buildings are above 70 feet tall. There are 45 buildings so $\dfrac{10}{45}$ or about $\dfrac{1}{4}$ are over 70 feet tall.

5. The number of buildings between 61 and 80 feet tall are 10 + 7 or 17. The number of buildings between 31 and 50 feet tall are 11 + 8 or 19. So there are 19 - 17 or 2 more buildings between 31 and 50 feet tall.

Lesson 4-3

PAGE 591

1.
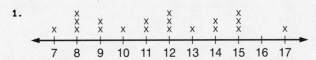

2.
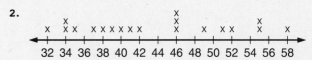

3.
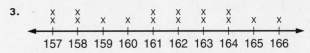

4.
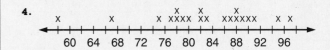

5.
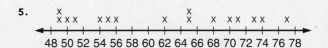

6.

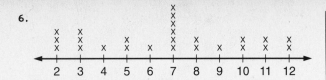

7.

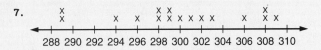

8.

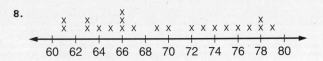

Lesson 4-4

PAGE 592

1.
5	45799
6	1238
7	135
8	2488

8|4 means 8.4

2.
11	259
12	1359
13	367
14	025
15	3456

15|4 means 154

3.
4	5779
5	235568
6	0135

5|3 means 53

4.
71	389
72	234
73	5679
74	28

72|4 means 72.4

5.
39	1358
40	157
41	22359
42	2477

40|7 means 407

6.
1	1579
2	12367
3	223566
4	169

3|2 means 32

7. Quiz 2   Quiz 3

9	2	
98776432	3	79
65543221	4	0124556788999
	5	00

4|3 means 43

Lesson 4-5

PAGE 592

1. 2, 3, 4, 5, 7, 8, 9, 10, 12, 14

Mean: $\dfrac{2 + 3 + 4 + 5 + 7 + 8 + 9 + 10 + 12 + 14}{10}$

$= \dfrac{74}{10} = 7.4$

Median: $\dfrac{7 + 8}{2} = \dfrac{15}{2} = 7.5$

Mode: none

2. 49, 50, 52, 56, 58, 60, 61, 61

Mean: $\dfrac{49 + 50 + 52 + 56 + 58 + 60 + 61 + 61}{8}$

$= \dfrac{447}{8} = 55.875 \approx 55.9$

Median: $\dfrac{56 + 58}{2} = \dfrac{114}{2} = 57$

Mode: 61

3. 122, 125, 129, 134, 134, 137, 140

Mean: $\dfrac{122 + 125 + 129 + 134 + 134 + 137 + 140}{7}$

$= \dfrac{921}{7} \approx 131.6$

Median: 134

Mode: 134

4. 20.9, 23.4, 24.0, 25.5, 25.7, 26.7, 26.8

Mean: $\dfrac{20.9 + 23.4 + 24.0 + 25.5 + 25.7 + 26.7 + }{7}$

$\dfrac{26.8}{7} = \dfrac{173}{7} \approx 24.7$

Median: 25.5

Mode: none

5. Mean: $\dfrac{36 + 41 + 43 + 45 + 48 + 52 + 54 + 56 + }{13}$

$\dfrac{56 + 57 + 60 + 64 + 65}{13} = \dfrac{677}{13} \approx 52.1$

Median: 54

Mode: 56

6. Mean: $\dfrac{30 + 32 + 32 + 33 + 33 + 33 + 33 + 34 + }{15}$

$\dfrac{34 + 34 + 35 + 36 + 36 + 38 + 39}{15}$

$= \dfrac{512}{15} \approx 34.1$

Lesson 4-6

PAGE 592

1. 25 − 11 = 14   **2.** 13 − 2 = 11

3. 190 − 141 = 49   **4.** 510 − 388 = 122

5. 6, 9, 14, 15, 18, 19, 22, 26, 28

Median: 18

UQ: $\dfrac{22 + 26}{2} = \dfrac{48}{2} = 24$

LQ: $\dfrac{9 + 14}{2} = \dfrac{23}{2} = 11.5$

6. 238, 241, 245, 248, 250, 251, 255

Median: 248

UQ: 251

LQ: 241

7. 40, 42, 45, 46, 49, 50, 52

Median: 46

UQ: 50

LQ: 42

8. 120, 128, 130, 142, 148, 152, 164, 168

Median: $\frac{142 + 148}{2} = \frac{290}{2} = 145$

UQ: $\frac{152 + 164}{2} = \frac{316}{2} = 158$

LQ: $\frac{128 + 130}{2} = \frac{258}{2} = 129$

9. 2, 2, 3, 4, 6, 6, 8, 10, 11, 12

Median: 6

UQ: 10

LQ: 3

10. 84, 87, 88, 90, 92, 93, 96, 97

Median: $\frac{90 + 92}{2} = \frac{182}{2} = 91$

UQ: $\frac{93 + 96}{2} = \frac{189}{2} = 94.5$

LQ: $\frac{87 + 88}{2} = \frac{175}{2} = 87.5$

11. 328, 336, 339, 345, 361, 370, 378, 388, 394, 410

Median: $\frac{361 + 370}{2} = \frac{731}{2} = 365.5$

UQ: 388

LQ: 339

Lesson 4-7

PAGE 593

1. 64, 66, 70, 72, 75, 79, 82, 84

Median: $\frac{72 + 75}{2} = \frac{147}{2} = 73.5$

UQ: $\frac{79 + 82}{2} = \frac{161}{2} = 80.5$

LQ: $\frac{66 + 70}{2} = \frac{136}{2} = 68$

IQ Range: 80.5 - 68 = 12.5

12.5 × 1.5 = 18.75

80.5 + 18.75 = 99.25

68 - 18.75 = 49.25

No outliers

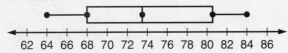

2. 301, 304, 306, 307, 310, 312, 313

Median: 307   8 · 1.5 = 12

UQ: 312   312 + 12 = 324

LQ: 304   304 - 12 = 292

IQ Range: 312 - 304 = 8   No outliers

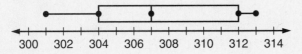

3. 2, 3, 3, 4, 6, 7, 7, 9, 10

Median: 6   5 · 1.5 = 7.5

UQ: $\frac{7 + 9}{2} = \frac{16}{2} = 8$ 8 + 7.5 = 15.5

LQ: 3   3 - 7.5 = -4.5

IQ Range: 8 - 3 = 5   No outliers

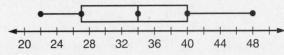

4. 22, 24, 27, 30, 32, 36, 39, 40, 45, 48

Median: $\frac{32 + 36}{2} = \frac{68}{2} = 34$ 13 · 1.5 = 19.5

UQ: 40   40 + 19.5 = 59.5

LQ: 27   27 - 19.5 = 7.5

IQ Range: 40 - 27 = 13   No outliers

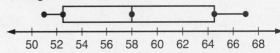

5. 51, 52, 53, 56, 58, 61, 63, 66, 67

Median: 58   12 · 1.5 = 18

UQ: $\frac{63 + 66}{2} = \frac{129}{2} = 64.5$ 64.5 + 18 = 82.5

                    52.5 - 18 = 34.5

LQ: $\frac{52 + 53}{2} = \frac{105}{2} = 52.5$ No outliers

IQ Range: 64.5 - 52.5 = 12

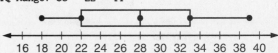

6. 18, 21, 23, 26, 30, 32, 34, 39

Median: $\frac{26 + 30}{2} = \frac{56}{2} = 28$ 11 · 1.5 = 16.5

                    33 + 16.5 = 49.5

UQ: $\frac{32 + 34}{2} = \frac{66}{2} = 33$ 22 - 16.5 = 5.5

                    No outliers

LQ: $\frac{21 + 23}{2} = \frac{44}{2} = 22$

IQ Range: 33 - 22 = 11

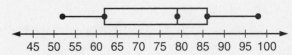

7. Median: $\frac{78 + 80}{2} = \frac{158}{2} = 79$ 24 · 1.5 = 36

                    86 + 36 = 122

UQ: $\frac{85 + 87}{2} = \frac{172}{2} = 86$ 62 - 36 = 26

                    No outliers

LQ: $\frac{61 + 63}{2} = \frac{124}{2} = 62$

IQ Range: 86 - 62 = 24

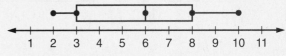

8. Median: 6.6
UQ: 6.7
LQ: 6.5
IQ Range: 6.7 - 6.5 = 0.2

$0.2 \times 1.5 = 0.3$
$6.7 + 0.3 = 7$
$6.5 - 0.3 = 6.2$
Outlier: 7.1

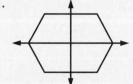

Lesson 4-8

PAGE 593

1. no relationship   **2.** positive
3. no relationship   **4.** negative
5. positive   **6.** negative
7. no relationship   **8.** negative
9. positive

Lesson 5-1

PAGE 593

1. no parallel segments   **2.** $\overline{MT} || \overline{KH}$; $\overline{MK} || \overline{TH}$
3. $\overline{WX} || \overline{ZY}$; $\overline{WZ} || \overline{XY}$
4. $m\angle 2 = m\angle 6$, because they are alternate exterior angles. So $m\angle 6 = 42°$.
5. $m\angle 4 = m\angle 8$, because they are corresponding angles. So $m\angle 8 = 71°$. Then $m\angle 7 + m\angle 8 = 180°$ because they are supplementary angles.
$$m\angle 7 + 71° = 180°$$
$$m\angle 7 + 71° - 71° = 180° - 71°$$
$$m\angle 7 = 109°$$
6. $m\angle 1 = m\angle 8$, because they are alternate exterior angles. So $m\angle 1 = 128°$.
7. $m\angle 7 = m\angle 2$, because they are alternate interior angles. So $m\angle 7 = 83°$.

Lesson 5-3

PAGE 594

1. scalene, acute   **2.** equilateral, acute
3. scalene, right   **4.** isosceles, obtuse
5. isosceles, acute   **6.** scalene, obtuse
7. isosceles, right   **8.** equilateral, acute

Lesson 5-4

PAGE 594

1. Q   **2.** Q,T   **3.** Q, P, RH   **4.** Q, P, R
5. Q, T **6.** Q, P, RH **7.** Q, T **8.** Q, P, R, S, RH

Lesson 5-5

PAGE 594

1.

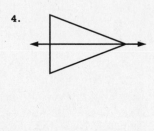

2. no symmetry

3.

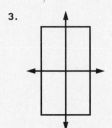

4.

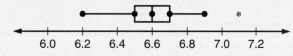

5. Yes, rotate the figure 120° or 240°.
6. Yes, rotate the figure 180°.
7. no
8. Yes, rotate the figure 60°, 120°, 180°, 240°, or 300°.

Lesson 5-6

PAGE 595

1. neither; One figure has two pairs of congruent sides and the other has four congruent sides.
2. congruent; All corresponding sides and angles are congruent.
3. similar; The angles have the same measure and the figures have the same shape, but the sides are not congruent.
4. Since $\triangle ABC \cong \triangle JKI$, $AC = JI$.
$$2x - 5 = 15$$
$$2x - 5 + 5 = 15 + 5$$
$$2x = 20$$
$$\frac{2x}{2} = \frac{20}{2}$$
$$x = 10$$

5. Since $\Delta LFR \sim \Delta GPC$, $m\angle FLR = m\angle PGC$.

$$3x + 1 = 40$$
$$3x + 1 - 1 = 40 - 1$$
$$3x = 39$$
$$\frac{3x}{3} = \frac{39}{3}$$
$$x = 13$$

6. Since $\square XTDH \cong \square PEBL$, $DH = BL$.

$$4x + 8 = 32$$
$$4x + 8 - 8 = 32 - 8$$
$$4x = 24$$
$$\frac{4x}{4} = \frac{24}{4}$$
$$x = 6$$

Lesson 6-1

PAGE 595

1. 2: Yes, 0 is divisible by 2.
   3: Yes, 2 + 1 + 0 = 3 which is divisible by 3.
   4: No, 10 is not divisible by 4.
   5: Yes, the ones digit is 0.
   6: Yes, 210 is divisible by 2 and 3.
   8: No, 210 is not divisible by 8.
   9: No, 2 + 1 + 0 = 3 which is not divisible by 9.
   10: Yes, the ones digit is 0.
   So 210 is divisible by 2, 3, 5, 6, and 10.

2. 2: Yes, 4 is divisible by 2.
   3: No, 6 + 1 + 4 = 11 which is not divisible by 3.
   4: No, 14 is not divisible by 4.
   5: No, the ones digit is 4, not 0 or 5.
   6: No, 614 is divisible by 2 but not by 3.
   8: No, 614 is not divisible by 8.
   9: No, 6 + 1 + 4 = 11 which is not divisible by 9.
   10: No, the ones digit is 4, not 0.
   So 614 is divisible by 2.

3. 2: No, 5 is not divisible by 2.
   3: No, 9 + 8 + 5 = 22 which is not divisible by 3.
   4: No, 85 is not divisible by 4.
   5: Yes, the ones digit is 5.
   6: No, 985 is not divisible by 2 or 3.
   8: No, 985 is not divisible by 8.
   9: No, 9 + 8 + 5 = 22 which is not divisible by 9.
   10: No, the ones digit is 5, not 0.
   So 985 is divisible by 5.

4. 2: Yes, 6 is divisible by 2.
   3: Yes, 7 + 5 + 6 = 18 which is divisible by 3.
   4: Yes, 56 is divisible by 4.
   5: No, the ones digit is 6, not 0 or 5.
   6: Yes, 756 is divisible by both 2 and 3.
   8: No, 756 is not divisible by 8.
   9: Yes, 7 + 5 + 6 = 18 which is divisible by 9.
   10: No, the ones digit is 6, not 0.
   So 756 is divisible by 2, 3, 4, 6, and 9.

5. 2: Yes, 2 is divisible by 2.
   3: Yes, 4 + 3 + 2 = 9 which is divisible by 3.
   4: Yes, 32 is divisible by 4.
   5: No, the ones digit is 2, not 0 or 5.
   6: Yes, 432 is divisible by both 2 and 3.
   8: Yes, 432 is divisible by 8.
   9: Yes, 4 + 3 + 2 = 9 which is divisible by 9.
   10: No, the ones digit is 2, not 0.
   So 432 is divisible by 2, 3, 4, 6, 8, and 9.

6. 2: Yes, 6 is divisible by 2.
   3: Yes, 9 + 6 = 15 which is divisible by 3.
   4: Yes, 96 is divisible by 4.
   5: No, the ones digit is 6, not 0 or 5.
   6: Yes, 96 is divisible by both 2 and 3.
   8: Yes, 96 is divisible by 8.
   9: No, 9 + 6 = 15 which is not divisible by 9.
   10: No, the ones digit is 6, not 0.
   So 96 is divisible by 2, 3, 4, 6, and 8.

7. 2: No, 7 is not divisible by 2.
   3: Yes, 8 + 7 = 15 which is divisible by 3.
   4: No, 87 is not divisible by 4.
   5: No, the ones digit is 7, not 0 or 5.
   6: No, 87 is divisible by 3 but not by 2.
   8: No, 87 is not divisible by 8.
   9: No, 8 + 7 = 15 which is not divisible by 9.
   10: No, the ones digit is 7, not 0.
   So 87 is divisible by 3.

8. 2: No, 3 is not divisible by 2.
   3: No, 1 + 1 + 3 = 5 which is not divisible by 3.
   4: No, 13 is not divisible by 4.
   5: No, the ones digit is 3, not 0 or 5.
   6: No, 113 is not divisible by 2 or 3.
   8: No, 113 is not divisible by 8.
   9: No, 1 + 1 + 3 = 5 which is not divisible by 9.
   10: No, the ones digit is 3, not 0.
   So 113 is not divisible by any of the numbers.

9. 2: Yes, 6 is divisible by 2.
   3: Yes, 9 + 3 + 6 = 18 which is divisible by 3.
   So 936 is divisible by 6 because it is divisible by both 2 and 3.

10. 2: Yes, 2 is divisible by 2.
    3: No, 7 + 5 + 2 = 14 which is not divisible by 3.
    So 752 is not divisible by 6 because it is not divisible by 3.

11. 1,249 is not divisible by 8 because 249 is not divisible by 8.

12. 208 is divisible by 4 because 08 or 8 is divisible by 4.

13. 216 is divisible by 9 because 2 + 1 + 6 = 9 which is divisible by 9.

14. 1,346 is divisible by 2 because 6 is divisible by 2.

15. 1,687 is not divisible by 3 because 1 + 6 + 8 + 7 = 22 which is not divisible by 3.

16. 448 is divisible by 8 because 448 is divisible by 8.

Lesson 6-2

PAGE 595

1. 17 has no factors other than 1 and 17, so it is prime.

2. 1,258 has a factor of 2, so it is composite.

3. 37 has no factors other than 1 and 37, so it is prime.

4. 483 has a factor of 3, so it is composite.

5. 97 has no factors other than 1 and 97, so it is prime.

6. 0 is neither prime nor composite.

7. 25 has a factor of 5, so it is composite.

8. 61 has no factors other than 1 and 61, so it is prime.

9. −45 has a factor of 3, so it is composite.

10. 419 has no factors other than 1 and 419, so it is prime.

11. $20 = 2 \times 10$
$20 = 2 \times 2 \times 5$
$20 = 2^2 \times 5$

12. $65 = 5 \times 13$

13. $52 = 2 \times 26$
$52 = 2 \times 2 \times 13$
$52 = 2^2 \times 13$

14. $30 = 2 \times 15$
$30 = 2 \times 3 \times 5$

15. $28 = 2 \times 14$
$28 = 2 \times 2 \times 7$
$28 = 2^2 \times 7$

16. $72 = 2 \times 36$
$72 = 2 \times 2 \times 18$
$72 = 2 \cdot 2 \cdot 2 \cdot 9$
$72 = 2 \cdot 2 \cdot 2 \cdot 3 \cdot 3$
$72 = 2^3 \times 3^2$

17. $155 = 5 \times 31$

18. $50 = 2 \times 25$
$50 = 2 \times 5 \times 5$
$50 = 2 \times 5^2$

19. $96 = 2 \times 48$
$96 = 2 \times 2 \times 24$
$96 = 2 \times 2 \times 2 \times 12$
$96 = 2 \times 2 \times 2 \times 2 \times 6$
$96 = 2 \times 2 \times 2 \times 2 \times 2 \times 3$
$96 = 2^5 \times 3$

20. $201 = 3 \times 67$

21. $1,250 = 2 \times 625$
$1,250 = 2 \times 5 \times 125$
$1,250 = 2 \times 5 \times 5 \times 25$
$1,250 = 2 \times 5 \times 5 \times 5 \times 5$
$1,250 = 2 \times 5^4$

22. $2,648 = 2 \times 1324$
$2,648 = 2 \times 2 \times 662$
$2,648 = 2 \times 2 \times 2 \times 331$
$2,648 = 2^3 \times 331$

Lesson 6-4

PAGE 596

1. $8 = 2 \cdot 2 \cdot 2$
$18 = 2 \cdot 3 \cdot 3$
GCF = 2

2. $6 = 2 \times 3$
$9 = 3 \times 3$
GCF = 3

3. $4 = 2 \cdot 2$
$12 = 2 \cdot 2 \cdot 3$
GCF = $2 \cdot 2 = 4$

4. $18 = 2 \cdot 3 \cdot 3$
$24 = 2 \cdot 2 \cdot 2 \cdot 3$
GCF = $2 \cdot 3 = 6$

5. $8 = 2 \cdot 2 \cdot 2$
$24 = 2 \cdot 2 \cdot 2 \cdot 3$
GCF = $2 \cdot 2 \cdot 2 = 8$

6. $17 = 17$
$51 = 3 \cdot 17$
GCF = 17

7. $65 = 5 \cdot 13$
$95 = 5 \cdot 19$
GCF = 5

8. $42 = 2 \cdot 3 \cdot 7$
$48 = 2 \cdot 2 \cdot 2 \cdot 2 \cdot 3$
GCF = $2 \cdot 3 = 6$

9. $64 = 2 \cdot 2 \cdot 2 \cdot 2 \cdot 2 \cdot 2$
$32 = 2 \cdot 2 \cdot 2 \cdot 2 \cdot 2$
GCF = $2 \cdot 2 \cdot 2 \cdot 2 \cdot 2 = 32$

10. $72 = 2 \cdot 2 \cdot 2 \cdot 3 \cdot 3$
$144 = 2 \cdot 2 \cdot 2 \cdot 2 \cdot 3 \cdot 3$
GCF = $2 \cdot 2 \cdot 2 \cdot 3 \cdot 3 = 72$

11. $54 = 2 \cdot 3 \cdot 3 \cdot 3$
$72 = 2 \cdot 2 \cdot 2 \cdot 3 \cdot 3$
GCF = $2 \cdot 3 \cdot 3 = 18$

12. $60 = 2 \cdot 2 \cdot 3 \cdot 5$
$75 = 3 \cdot 5 \cdot 5$
GCF = $3 \cdot 5 = 15$

13. $16 = 2 \cdot 2 \cdot 2 \cdot 2$
$24 = 2 \cdot 2 \cdot 2 \cdot 3$
GCF = $2 \cdot 2 \cdot 2 = 8$

14. $12 = 2 \cdot 2 \cdot 3$
$27 = 3 \cdot 3 \cdot 3$
GCF = 3

15. $25 = 5 \cdot 5$
$30 = 2 \cdot 3 \cdot 5$
GCF = 5

16. $48 = 2 \cdot 2 \cdot 2 \cdot 2 \cdot 3$
$60 = 2 \cdot 2 \cdot 3 \cdot 5$
GCF = $2 \cdot 2 \cdot 3 = 12$

17. $16 = 2 \cdot 2 \cdot 2 \cdot 2$
$20 = 2 \cdot 2 \cdot 5$
$36 = 2 \cdot 2 \cdot 3 \cdot 3$
GCF = $2 \cdot 2 = 4$

18. $12 = 2 \cdot 2 \cdot 3$
$18 = 2 \cdot 3 \cdot 3$
$42 = 2 \cdot 3 \cdot 7$
GCF = $2 \cdot 3 = 6$

19. $30 = 2 \cdot 3 \cdot 5$
$45 = 3 \cdot 3 \cdot 5$
$15 = 3 \cdot 5$
GCF = $3 \cdot 5 = 15$

20. $20 = 2 \cdot 2 \cdot 5$
$30 = 2 \cdot 3 \cdot 5$
$40 = 2 \cdot 2 \cdot 2 \cdot 5$
GCF = $2 \cdot 5 = 10$

21. $81 = 3 \cdot 3 \cdot 3 \cdot 3$ 22. $9 = 3 \cdot 3$
$27 = 3 \cdot 3 \cdot 3$ $18 = 2 \cdot 3 \cdot 3$
$108 = 2 \cdot 2 \cdot 3 \cdot 3 \cdot$ $12 = 2 \cdot 2 \cdot 3$
GCF $= 3 \cdot 3 \cdot 3 = 27$ GCF $= 3$

18. $6 = 2 \cdot 3$ 19. $15 = 3 \cdot 5$
$8 = 2 \cdot 2 \cdot 2$ $18 = 2 \cdot 3 \cdot 3$
GCF $= 2$ GCF $= 3$
$\dfrac{6}{8} = \dfrac{6 \div 2}{8 \div 2} = \dfrac{3}{4}$ $\dfrac{15}{18} = \dfrac{15 \div 3}{18 \div 3} = \dfrac{5}{6}$

20. $9 = 3 \cdot 3$ 21. $8 = 2 \cdot 2 \cdot 2$
$20 = 2 \cdot 2 \cdot 5$ $21 = 3 \cdot 7$
GCF $= 1$ GCF $= 1$
$\dfrac{9}{20}$ is in simplest form. $\dfrac{8}{21}$ is in simplest form.

Lesson 6-5

PAGE 596

1. $12 = 2 \cdot 2 \cdot 3$ 2. $28 = 2 \cdot 2 \cdot 7$
$16 = 2 \cdot 2 \cdot 2 \cdot 2$ $32 = 2 \cdot 2 \cdot 2 \cdot 2 \cdot 2$
GCF $= 2 \cdot 2 = 4$ GCF $= 2 \cdot 2 = 4$
$\dfrac{12}{16} = \dfrac{12 \div 4}{16 \div 4} = \dfrac{3}{4}$ $\dfrac{28}{32} = \dfrac{28 \div 4}{32 \div 4} = \dfrac{7}{8}$

3. $75 = 3 \cdot 5 \cdot 5$ 4. $8 = 2 \cdot 2 \cdot 2$
$100 = 2 \cdot 2 \cdot 5 \cdot 5$ $16 = 2 \cdot 2 \cdot 2 \cdot 2$
GCF $= 5 \cdot 5 = 25$ GCF $= 2 \cdot 2 \cdot 2 = 8$
$\dfrac{75}{100} = \dfrac{75 \div 25}{100 \div 25} = \dfrac{3}{4}$ $\dfrac{8}{16} = \dfrac{8 \div 8}{16 \div 8} = \dfrac{1}{2}$

5. $6 = 2 \cdot 3$ 6. $27 = 3 \cdot 3 \cdot 3$
$18 = 2 \cdot 3 \cdot 3$ $36 = 2 \cdot 2 \cdot 3 \cdot 3$
GCF $= 2 \cdot 3 = 6$ GCF $= 3 \cdot 3 = 9$
$\dfrac{6}{18} = \dfrac{6 \div 6}{18 \div 6} = \dfrac{1}{3}$ $\dfrac{27}{36} = \dfrac{27 \div 9}{36 \div 9} = \dfrac{3}{4}$

7. $16 = 2 \cdot 2 \cdot 2 \cdot 2$
$64 = 2 \cdot 2 \cdot 2 \cdot 2 \cdot 2 \cdot 2$
GCF $= 2 \cdot 2 \cdot 2 \cdot 2 = 16$
$\dfrac{16}{64} = \dfrac{16 \div 16}{64 \div 16} = \dfrac{1}{4}$

8. $8 = 2 \cdot 2 \cdot 2$ 9. $50 = 2 \cdot 5 \cdot 5$
$16 = 2 \cdot 2 \cdot 2 \cdot 2$ $100 = 2 \cdot 2 \cdot 5 \cdot 5$
GCF $= 2 \cdot 2 \cdot 2 = 8$ GCF $= 2 \cdot 5 \cdot 5 = 50$
$\dfrac{8}{16} = \dfrac{8 \div 8}{16 \div 8} = \dfrac{1}{2}$ $\dfrac{50}{100} = \dfrac{50 \div 50}{100 \div 50} = \dfrac{1}{2}$

10. $24 = 2 \cdot 2 \cdot 2 \cdot 3$ 11. $32 = 2 \cdot 2 \cdot 2 \cdot 2 \cdot 2$
$40 = 2 \cdot 2 \cdot 2 \cdot 5$ $80 = 2 \cdot 2 \cdot 2 \cdot 2 \cdot 5$
GCF $= 2 \cdot 2 \cdot 2 = 8$ GCF $= 2 \cdot 2 \cdot 2 \cdot 2 = 16$
$\dfrac{24}{40} = \dfrac{24 \div 8}{40 \div 8} = \dfrac{3}{5}$ $\dfrac{32}{80} = \dfrac{32 \div 16}{80 \div 16} = \dfrac{2}{5}$

12. $8 = 2 \cdot 2 \cdot 2$ 13. $20 = 2 \cdot 2 \cdot 5$
$24 = 2 \cdot 2 \cdot 2 \cdot 3$ $25 = 5 \cdot 5$
GCF $= 2 \cdot 2 \cdot 2 = 8$ GCF $= 5$
$\dfrac{8}{24} = \dfrac{8 \div 8}{24 \div 8} = \dfrac{1}{3}$ $\dfrac{20}{25} = \dfrac{20 \div 5}{25 \div 5} = \dfrac{4}{5}$

14. $4 = 2 \cdot 2$ 15. $3 = 3 \cdot 1$
$10 = 2 \cdot 5$ $5 = 5 \cdot 1$
GCF $= 2$ GCF $= 1$
$\dfrac{4}{10} = \dfrac{4 \div 2}{10 \div 2} = \dfrac{2}{5}$ $\dfrac{3}{5}$ is in simplest form.

16. $14 = 2 \cdot 7$ 17. $9 = 3 \cdot 3$
$19 = 19 \cdot 1$ $12 = 2 \cdot 2 \cdot 3$
GCF $= 1$ GCF $= 3$
$\dfrac{14}{19}$ is in simplest form. $\dfrac{9}{12} = \dfrac{9 \div 3}{12 \div 3} = \dfrac{3}{4}$

22. $10 = 2 \cdot 5$ 23. $9 = 3 \cdot 3$
$15 = 3 \cdot 5$ $24 = 2 \cdot 2 \cdot 2 \cdot 3$
GCF $= 5$ GCF $= 3$
$\dfrac{10}{15} = \dfrac{10 \div 5}{15 \div 5} = \dfrac{2}{3}$ $\dfrac{9}{24} = \dfrac{9 \div 3}{24 \div 3} = \dfrac{3}{8}$

24. $6 = 2 \cdot 3$ 25. $18 = 2 \cdot 3 \cdot 3$
$31 = 1 \cdot 31$ $32 = 2 \cdot 2 \cdot 2 \cdot 2 \cdot 2$
GCF $= 1$ GCF $= 2$
$\dfrac{6}{31}$ is in simplest form. $\dfrac{18}{32} = \dfrac{18 \div 2}{32 \div 2} = \dfrac{9}{16}$

Lesson 6-6

PAGE 596

1. $\dfrac{2}{5} = 0.4$ 2. $\dfrac{3}{8} = 0.375$ 3. $-\dfrac{3}{4} = -0.75$

4. $\dfrac{5}{16} = 0.3125$ 5. $\dfrac{3}{4} = 0.75$ 6. $-\dfrac{7}{8} = -0.875$

7. $\dfrac{17}{20} = 0.85$ 8. $\dfrac{14}{25} = 0.56$ 9. $\dfrac{7}{10} = 0.7$

10. $\dfrac{7}{20} = 0.35$ 11. $0.5 = \dfrac{5}{10}$ 12. $0.8 = \dfrac{8}{10}$
$= \dfrac{1}{2}$ $= \dfrac{4}{5}$

13. $0.32 = \dfrac{32}{100}$ 14. $-0.75 = -\dfrac{75}{100}$
$= \dfrac{8}{25}$ $= -\dfrac{3}{4}$

15. $1.54 = 1\dfrac{54}{100}$ 16. $0.38 = \dfrac{38}{100}$
$= 1\dfrac{27}{50}$ $= \dfrac{19}{50}$

17. $-0.486 = -\dfrac{486}{1000}$ 18. $20.08 = 20\dfrac{8}{100}$
$= -\dfrac{243}{500}$ $= 20\dfrac{2}{25}$

19. $-9.36 = -9\dfrac{36}{100}$ 20. $10.18 = 10\dfrac{18}{100}$
$= -9\dfrac{9}{25}$ $= 10\dfrac{9}{50}$

21. $0.06 = \dfrac{6}{100}$ 22. $1.75 = 1\dfrac{75}{100}$
$= \dfrac{3}{50}$ $= 1\dfrac{3}{4}$

23. $-0.375 = -\dfrac{375}{1000}$ **24.** $0.79 = \dfrac{79}{100}$

$ = -\dfrac{3}{8}$

25. $1.9 = 1\dfrac{9}{10}$

23. Let $N = 0.7\overline{3}$.

Then $10N = 7.\overline{3}$
$10N = 7.3\overline{3}$
$\underline{-\quad N = 0.7\overline{3}}$
$9N = 6.6$
$\dfrac{9N}{9} = \dfrac{6.6}{9}$
$N = \dfrac{6.6}{9} = \dfrac{66}{90} = \dfrac{11}{15}$

24. Let $N = 0.\overline{8}$.

Then $10N = 8.\overline{8}$
$10N = 8.\overline{8}$
$\underline{-\quad N = 0.\overline{8}}$
$9N = 8$
$\dfrac{9N}{9} = \dfrac{8}{9}$
$N = \dfrac{8}{9}$

Lesson 6-7

PAGE 597

1. $0.\overline{09} = 0.0909090909$
2. $0.\overline{076923} = 0.0769230769$
3. $0.84\overline{563} = 0.8456345634$
4. $0.987\overline{45} = 0.9874545454$
5. $0.\overline{254} = 0.2542542542$
6. $0.\overline{1470} = 0.1470147014$
7. $0.12\overline{7} = 0.1277777777$
8. $0.\overline{3} = 0.3333333333$
9. $0.161616\ldots = 0.\overline{16}$
10. $0.12351235\ldots = 0.\overline{1235}$
11. $0.6666\ldots = 0.\overline{6}$
12. $0.15151\ldots = 0.\overline{15}$
13. $0.125656\ldots = 0.12\overline{56}$
14. $0.1254777\ldots = 0.1254\overline{7}$
15. $85.0124124\ldots = 85.0\overline{124}$
16. $0.214111\ldots = 0.214\overline{1}$

17. Let $N = 0.\overline{3}$.

Then $10N = 3.\overline{3}$.
$10N = 3.\overline{3}$
$\underline{-\quad N = 0.\overline{3}}$
$9N = 3$
$\dfrac{9N}{9} = \dfrac{3}{9}$
$N = \dfrac{3}{9} = \dfrac{1}{3}$

18. Let $N = 0.\overline{4}$.

Then $10N = 4.\overline{4}$.
$10N = 4.\overline{4}$
$\underline{-\quad N = 0.\overline{4}}$
$9N = 4$
$\dfrac{9N}{9} = \dfrac{4}{9}$
$N = \dfrac{4}{9}$

19. Let $N = 0.\overline{27}$.

Then $100N = 27.\overline{27}$.
$100N = 27.\overline{27}$
$\underline{-\quad N = 0.\overline{27}}$
$99N = 27$
$\dfrac{99N}{99} = \dfrac{27}{99}$
$N = \dfrac{27}{99} = \dfrac{3}{11}$

20. Let $N = 0.8\overline{3}$.

Then $10N = 8.\overline{3}$.
$10N = 8.3\overline{3}$
$\underline{-\quad N = 0.8\overline{3}}$
$9N = 7.5$
$\dfrac{9N}{9} = \dfrac{7.5}{9}$
$N = \dfrac{7.5}{9} = \dfrac{75}{90} = \dfrac{5}{6}$

21. Let $N = 0.2\overline{4}$.

Then $100\,N = 24.\overline{24}$.
$100N = 24.\overline{24}$
$\underline{-\quad N = 0.2\overline{4}}$
$99N = 24$
$\dfrac{99N}{99} = \dfrac{24}{99}$
$N = \dfrac{24}{99} = \dfrac{8}{33}$

22. Let $N = 0.58\overline{3}$.

The $10N = 5.8\overline{3}$.
$10N = 5.83\overline{3}$
$\underline{-\quad N = 0.58\overline{3}}$
$9N = 5.25$
$\dfrac{9N}{9} = \dfrac{5.25}{9}$
$N = \dfrac{5.25}{9} = \dfrac{525}{900} = \dfrac{7}{12}$

Lesson 6-8

PAGE 597

1. $\dfrac{\text{number of 13}^{\text{th}}\text{'s}}{\text{number of days}} = \dfrac{1}{30}$

2. $\dfrac{\text{number of Fridays}}{\text{number of days}} = \dfrac{4}{30} = \dfrac{2}{15}$

3. $\dfrac{\text{number of days after 25}^{\text{th}}}{\text{number of days}} = \dfrac{5}{30} = \dfrac{1}{6}$

4. $\dfrac{\text{number of days before 7}^{\text{th}}}{\text{number of days}} = \dfrac{6}{30} = \dfrac{1}{5}$

5. $\dfrac{\text{number of odd-numbered days}}{\text{number of days}} = \dfrac{15}{30} = \dfrac{1}{2}$

6. $\dfrac{\text{number of days divisible by 3}}{\text{number of days}} = \dfrac{10}{30} = \dfrac{1}{3}$

Lesson 6-9

PAGE 597

1. $5 = 1 \cdot 5$
$6 = 2 \cdot 3$
$\text{LCM} = 5 \cdot 2 \cdot 3 = 30$

2. $9 = 3 \cdot 3$
$27 = 3 \cdot 3 \cdot 3$
$\text{LCM} = 3 \cdot 3 \cdot 3 = 27$

3. $12 = 2 \cdot 2 \cdot 3$
$15 = 3 \cdot 5$
$\text{LCM} = 2 \cdot 2 \cdot 3 \cdot 5 = 60$

4. $8 = 2 \cdot 2 \cdot 2$
$12 = 2 \cdot 2 \cdot 3$
$\text{LCM} = 2 \cdot 2 \cdot 2 \cdot 3 = 24$

5. $5 = 1 \cdot 5$
$15 = 3 \cdot 5$
$\text{LCM} = 5 \cdot 3 = 15$

6. $13 = 1 \cdot 13$
$39 = 3 \cdot 13$
$\text{LCM} = 13 \cdot 3 = 39$

7. $16 = 2 \cdot 2 \cdot 2 \cdot 2$
$24 = 2 \cdot 2 \cdot 2 \cdot 3$
$\text{LCM} = 2 \cdot 2 \cdot 2 \cdot 2 \cdot 3 = 48$

8. $18 = 2 \cdot 3 \cdot 3$
$20 = 2 \cdot 2 \cdot 5$
$\text{LCM} = 2 \cdot 2 \cdot 3 \cdot 3 \cdot 5 = 180$

9. $21 = 3 \cdot 7$
$14 = 2 \cdot 7$
$\text{LCM} = 2 \cdot 3 \cdot 7 = 42$

10. $25 = 5 \cdot 5$

    $30 = 2 \cdot 3 \cdot 5$

    LCM $= 5 \cdot 5 \cdot 2 \cdot 3 = 150$

11. $28 = 2 \cdot 2 \cdot 7$ 12. $7 = 1 \cdot 7$

    $42 = 2 \cdot 3 \cdot 7$ $13 = 1 \cdot 13$

    LCM $= 2 \cdot 2 \cdot 7 \cdot 3 = 84$ LCM $= 7 \cdot 13 = 91$

13. $6 = 2 \cdot 3$ 14. $12 = 2 \cdot 2 \cdot 3$

    $30 = 2 \cdot 3 \cdot 5$ $42 = 2 \cdot 3 \cdot 7$

    LCM $= 2 \cdot 3 \cdot 5 = 30$ LCM $= 2 \cdot 2 \cdot 3 \cdot 7 = 84$

15. $8 = 2 \cdot 2 \cdot 2$ 16. $30 = 2 \cdot 3 \cdot 5$

    $10 = 2 \cdot 5$ $10 = 2 \cdot 5$

    LCM $= 2 \cdot 2 \cdot 2 \cdot 5 = 40$ LCM $= 2 \cdot 3 \cdot 5 = 30$

17. $12 = 2 \cdot 2 \cdot 3$ 18. $15 = 3 \cdot 5$

    $18 = 2 \cdot 3 \cdot 3$ $75 = 3 \cdot 5 \cdot 5$

    $6 = 2 \cdot 3$ $25 = 5 \cdot 5$

    LCM $= 2 \cdot 2 \cdot 3 \cdot 3 = 36$ LCM $= 3 \cdot 5 \cdot 5 = 75$

19. $6 = 2 \cdot 3$ 20. $3 = 1 \cdot 3$

    $10 = 2 \cdot 5$ $6 = 2 \cdot 3$

    $15 = 3 \cdot 5$ $9 = 3 \cdot 3$

    LCM $= 2 \cdot 3 \cdot 5 = 30$ LCM $= 2 \cdot 3 \cdot 3 = 18$

21. $21 = 3 \cdot 7$

    $14 = 2 \cdot 7$

    $6 = 2 \cdot 3$

    LCM $= 3 \cdot 7 \cdot 2 = 42$

22. $12 = 2 \cdot 2 \cdot 3$

    $35 = 5 \cdot 7$

    $10 = 2 \cdot 5$

    LCM $= 2 \cdot 2 \cdot 3 \cdot 5 \cdot 7 = 420$

Lesson 6-10

PAGE 598

1. $-5.6 < 4.2$ 2. $4.256 > 4.25$ 3. $0.\overline{23} = 0.2323\ldots$

                                        $0.233 > 0.2323\ldots$

4. $\frac{5}{7} = 0.\overline{714285}$ 5. $\frac{6}{7} = 0.\overline{857142}$

    $\frac{2}{5} = 0.4$ $\frac{7}{9} = 0.\overline{7}$

    $0.\overline{714285} > 0.4$ $0.\overline{857142} > 0.\overline{7}$

    $\frac{5}{7} > \frac{2}{5}$ $\frac{6}{7} > \frac{7}{9}$

6. $\frac{2}{3} = 0.\overline{6}$ 7. $\frac{3}{8} = 0.375$

    $\frac{2}{5} = 0.4$ $0.375 = 0.375$

    $0.\overline{6} > 0.4$ $\frac{3}{8} = 0.375$

    $\frac{2}{3} > \frac{2}{5}$

8. $-\frac{1}{2} = -0.5$ 9. $12\frac{3}{8} = 12.375$

    $-0.5 < 0.5$ $12.56 > 12.375$

    $-\frac{1}{2} < 0.5$ $12.56 > 12\frac{3}{8}$

10. 02, 0.24, 0.245, 0.25, 2.24

11. $0.\overline{3} = 0.333\ldots$

    $0.3\overline{4} = 0.3444\ldots$

    $0.\overline{34} = 0.3434\ldots$

    So the order is 0.3, 0.33, $0.\overline{3}$, $0.\overline{34}$, $0.3\overline{4}$.

12. $\frac{2}{5} = 0.4$

    $\frac{2}{3} = 0.\overline{6}$ or $0.666\ldots$

    $\frac{2}{7} = 0.\overline{285714}$

    $\frac{2}{9} = 0.\overline{2}$ or 0.222

    $\frac{2}{1} = 2$

    So the order is $\frac{2}{9}$, $\frac{2}{7}$, $\frac{2}{5}$, $\frac{2}{3}$, $\frac{2}{1}$.

13. $\frac{1}{2} = 0.5$

    $\frac{5}{7} = 0.\overline{714285}$

    $\frac{2}{9} = 0.\overline{2}$ or $0.222\ldots$

    $\frac{8}{9} = 0.\overline{8}$ or $0.888\ldots$

    $\frac{6}{6} = 1$

    So the order is $\frac{2}{9}$, $\frac{1}{2}$, $\frac{5}{7}$, $\frac{8}{9}$, $\frac{6}{6}$.

Lesson 6-11

PAGE 598

1. $4.5 \times 10^3 = 4.5 \times 1000$ 2. $2 \times 10^4 = 2 \times 10,000$

            $= 4,500$ $= 20,000$

3. $1.725896 \times 10^6 = 1.725896 \times 1,000,000$

                    $= 1,725,896$

4. $9.61 \times 10^2 = 9.61 \times 100$

             $= 961$

5. $1 \times 10^7 = 1 \times 10,000,000$

           $= 10,000,000$

6. $8.256 \times 10^8 = 8.256 \times 100,000,000$

               $= 825,600,000$

7. $5.26 \times 10^4 = 5.26 \times 10,000$

              $= 52,600$

8. $3.25 \times 10^2 = 3.25 \times 100$

             $= 325$

9. $6.79 \times 10^5 = 6.79 \times 100,000$

             $= 679,000$

10. $720 = 7.2 \times 10^2$ 11. $7,560 = 7.56 \times 10^3$

12. $892 = 8.92 \times 10^2$ 13. $1,400 = 1.4 \times 10^3$

14. $91,256 = 9.1256 \times 10^4$ 15. $51,000 = 5.1 \times 10^4$

16. $145,600 = 1,456 \times 10^5$ 17. $90,100 = 9.01 \times 10^4$

18. $123,568,000,000 = 1.23568 \times 10^{11}$

Lesson 7-1

PAGE 598

1. $\frac{17}{21} + \left(-\frac{13}{21}\right) = m$

   $\frac{17 + (-13)}{21} = m$

   $\frac{4}{21} = m$

2. $t = \frac{5}{11} + \frac{6}{11}$

   $t = \frac{5 + 6}{11}$

   $t = \frac{11}{11}$

   $t = 1$

3. $k = -\frac{8}{13} + \left(-\frac{11}{13}\right)$

   $k = \frac{-8 + (-11)}{13}$

   $k = \frac{-19}{13}$

   $k = -1\frac{6}{13}$

4. $-\frac{7}{12} + \frac{5}{12} = a$

   $\frac{-7 + 5}{12} = a$

   $\frac{-2}{12} = a$

   $-\frac{1}{6} = a$

5. $\frac{13}{28} - \frac{9}{28} = g$

   $\frac{13 - 9}{28} = g$

   $\frac{4}{28} = g$

   $\frac{1}{7} = g$

6. $b = -1\frac{2}{9} - \frac{7}{9}$

   $b = -\frac{11}{9} - \frac{7}{9}$

   $b = \frac{-11 - 7}{9}$

   $b = \frac{-18}{9}$

   $b = -2$

7. $r = \frac{15}{16} + \frac{13}{16}$

   $r = \frac{15 + 13}{16}$

   $r = \frac{28}{16}$

   $r = 1\frac{12}{16}$

   $r = 1\frac{3}{4}$

8. $2\frac{1}{3} - \frac{2}{3} = n$

   $\frac{7}{3} - \frac{2}{3} = n$

   $\frac{7 - 2}{3} = n$

   $\frac{5}{3} = n$

   $1\frac{2}{3} = n$

9. $-\frac{4}{35} - \left(-\frac{17}{35}\right) = c$

   $\frac{-4 - (-17)}{35} = c$

   $\frac{-4 + 17}{35} = c$

   $\frac{13}{35} = c$

10. $\frac{3}{8} + \left(-\frac{5}{8}\right) = w$

    $\frac{3 + (-5)}{8} = w$

    $\frac{-2}{8} = w$

    $-\frac{1}{4} = w$

11. $s = \frac{8}{15} - \frac{2}{15}$

    $s = \frac{8 - 2}{15}$

    $s = \frac{6}{15}$

    $s = \frac{2}{5}$

12. $d = -2\frac{4}{7} - \frac{3}{7}$

    $d = -\frac{18}{7} - \frac{3}{7}$

    $d = \frac{-18 - 3}{7}$

    $d = \frac{-21}{7}$

    $d = -3$

13. $-\frac{29}{9} - \left(-\frac{26}{9}\right) = y$

    $\frac{-29 - (-26)}{9} = y$

    $\frac{-29 + 26}{9} = y$

    $-\frac{3}{9} = y$

    $-\frac{1}{3} = y$

14. $2\frac{3}{5} + 7\frac{3}{5} = i$

    $\frac{13}{5} + \frac{38}{5} = i$

    $\frac{13 + 38}{5} = i$

    $\frac{51}{5} = i$

    $10\frac{1}{5} = i$

15. $x = \frac{5}{18} - \frac{13}{18}$

    $x = \frac{5 - 13}{18}$

    $x = \frac{-8}{18}$

    $x = -\frac{4}{9}$

16. $j = -2\frac{2}{7} + \left(-1\frac{6}{7}\right)$

    $j = -\frac{16}{7} + \left(-\frac{13}{7}\right)$

    $j = \frac{-16 + (-13)}{7}$

    $j = \frac{-29}{7}$

    $j = -4\frac{1}{7}$

17. $p = -\frac{3}{10} + \frac{7}{10}$

    $p = \frac{-3 + 7}{10}$

    $p = \frac{4}{10}$

    $p = \frac{2}{5}$

18. $\frac{4}{11} + \frac{9}{11} = e$

    $\frac{4 + 9}{11} = e$

    $\frac{13}{11} = e$

    $1\frac{2}{11} = e$

Lesson 7-2

PAGE 599

1. $r = \frac{7}{12} + \frac{7}{24}$

   $r = \frac{14}{24} + \frac{7}{24}$

   $r = \frac{14 + 7}{24}$

   $r = \frac{21}{24}$

   $r = \frac{7}{8}$

2. $-\frac{3}{4} + \frac{7}{8} = z$

   $-\frac{6}{8} + \frac{7}{8} = z$

   $\frac{-6 + 7}{8} = z$

   $\frac{1}{8} = z$

3. $\frac{2}{5} + \left(-\frac{2}{7}\right) = q$

   $\frac{14}{35} + \left(-\frac{10}{35}\right) = q$

   $\frac{14 + (-10)}{35} = q$

   $\frac{4}{35} = q$

4. $d = -\frac{3}{5} - \left(-\frac{5}{6}\right)$

   $d = -\frac{18}{30} - \left(-\frac{25}{30}\right)$

   $d = \frac{-18 - (-25)}{30}$

   $d = \frac{-18 + 25}{30}$

   $d = \frac{7}{30}$

5. $\frac{5}{24} - \frac{3}{8} = j$

$\frac{5}{24} - \frac{9}{24} = j$

$\frac{5-9}{24} = j$

$\frac{-4}{24} = j$

$-\frac{1}{6} = j$

6. $g = -\frac{7}{12} + \frac{3}{4}$

$g = -\frac{7}{12} + \frac{9}{12}$

$g = \frac{-7+9}{12}$

$g = \frac{2}{12}$

$g = \frac{1}{6}$

7. $-\frac{3}{8} + \left(-\frac{4}{5}\right) = x$

$-\frac{15}{40} + \left(-\frac{32}{40}\right) = x$

$\frac{-15+(-32)}{40} = x$

$\frac{-47}{40} = x$

$-1\frac{7}{40} = x$

8. $t = \frac{2}{15} + \left(-\frac{3}{10}\right)$

$t = \frac{4}{30} + \left(-\frac{9}{30}\right)$

$t = \frac{4+(-9)}{30}$

$t = \frac{-5}{30}$

$t = -\frac{1}{6}$

9. $r = -\frac{2}{9} - \left(-\frac{2}{3}\right)$

$r = -\frac{2}{9} - \left(-\frac{6}{9}\right)$

$r = \frac{-2-(-6)}{9}$

$r = \frac{-2+6}{9}$

$r = \frac{4}{9}$

10. $a = -\frac{7}{15} - \frac{5}{12}$

$a = -\frac{28}{60} - \frac{25}{60}$

$a = \frac{-28-25}{60}$

$a = -\frac{53}{60}$

11. $\frac{3}{8} + \frac{7}{12} = s$

$\frac{9}{24} + \frac{14}{24} = s$

$\frac{9+14}{24} = s$

$\frac{23}{24} = s$

12. $-2\frac{1}{4} + \left(-1\frac{1}{3}\right) = m$

$-2\frac{3}{12} + \left(-1\frac{4}{12}\right) = m$

$-3 + \frac{-3-4}{12} = m$

$-3\frac{7}{12} = m$

13. $3\frac{2}{5} - 3\frac{1}{4} = v$

$3\frac{8}{20} - 3\frac{5}{20} = v$

$\frac{8-5}{20} = v$

$\frac{3}{20} = v$

14. $b = \frac{3}{4} + \left(-\frac{4}{15}\right)$

$b = \frac{45}{60} + \left(-\frac{16}{60}\right)$

$b = \frac{45-16}{60}$

$b = \frac{29}{60}$

15. $f = -1\frac{2}{3} + 4\frac{3}{4}$

$f = -1\frac{8}{12} + 4\frac{9}{12}$

$f = 3 + \frac{-8+9}{12}$

$f = 3\frac{1}{12}$

16. $-\frac{1}{8} - 2\frac{1}{2} = n$

$-\frac{1}{8} - 2\frac{4}{8} = n$

$-2 + \frac{-1-4}{8} = n$

$-2 + \frac{-5}{8} = n$

$-2\frac{5}{8} = n$

17. $p = 3\frac{2}{5} - 1\frac{1}{3}$

$p = 3\frac{6}{15} - 1\frac{5}{15}$

$p = 2 + \frac{6-5}{15}$

$p = 2\frac{1}{15}$

18. $y = 5\frac{1}{3} + \left(-8\frac{3}{7}\right)$

$y = 5\frac{7}{21} + \left(-8\frac{9}{21}\right)$

$y = -3 + \frac{7-9}{21}$

$y = -3 + \frac{-2}{21}$

$y = -3\frac{2}{21}$

Lesson 7-3

PAGE 599

1. $\frac{2}{11} \cdot \frac{3}{4} = m$

$\frac{6}{44} = m$

$\frac{3}{22} = m$

2. $4\left(-\frac{7}{8}\right) = r$

$\frac{4}{1} \cdot \left(-\frac{7}{8}\right) = r$

$-\frac{28}{8} = r$

$-3\frac{4}{8} = r$

$-3\frac{1}{2} = r$

3. $d = -\frac{4}{7} \cdot \frac{3}{5}$

$d = -\frac{12}{35}$

4. $g = \frac{6}{7}\left(-\frac{7}{12}\right)$

$g = -\frac{42}{84}$

$g = -\frac{1}{2}$

5. $b = \frac{7}{8} \cdot \frac{1}{3}$

$b = \frac{7}{24}$

6. $\frac{3}{4} \cdot \frac{4}{5} = t$

$\frac{12}{20} = t$

$\frac{3}{5} = t$

7. $-1\frac{1}{2} \cdot \frac{2}{3} = k$

$-\frac{3}{2} \cdot \frac{2}{3} = k$

$-\frac{6}{6} = k$

$-1 = k$

8. $x = \frac{5}{6} \cdot \frac{6}{7}$

$x = \frac{30}{42}$

$x = \frac{5}{7}$

9. $c = 8\left(-2\frac{1}{4}\right)$

$c = \frac{8}{1} \cdot \left(-\frac{9}{4}\right)$

$c = -\frac{72}{4}$

$c = -18$

10. $-3\frac{3}{4} \cdot \frac{8}{9} = q$

$-\frac{15}{4} \cdot \frac{8}{9} = q$

$-\frac{120}{36} = q$

$-\frac{10}{3} = q$

$-3\frac{1}{3} = q$

11. $\frac{10}{21} \cdot \left(-\frac{7}{8}\right) = n$

$-\frac{70}{168} = n$

$-\frac{5}{12} = n$

207

12. $w = -1\frac{4}{5}\left(-\frac{5}{6}\right)$ **13.** $a = 5\frac{1}{4} \cdot 6\frac{2}{3}$

$w = -\frac{9}{5}\left(-\frac{5}{6}\right)$ $a = \frac{21}{4} \cdot \frac{20}{3}$

$w = \frac{45}{30}$ $a = \frac{420}{12}$

$w = \frac{3}{2}$ $a = 35$

$w = 1\frac{1}{2}$

14. $-8\frac{3}{4} \cdot 4\frac{2}{5} = p$ **15.** $y = 6 \cdot 8\frac{2}{3}$

$-\frac{35}{4} \cdot \frac{22}{5} = p$ $y = \frac{6}{1} \cdot \frac{26}{3}$

$-\frac{770}{20} = p$ $y = \frac{156}{3}$

$-\frac{77}{2} = p$ $y = 52$

$-38\frac{1}{2} = p$

16. $i = \left(\frac{3}{5}\right)^2$ **17.** $-4\frac{1}{5}\left(-3\frac{1}{3}\right) = h$

$i = \left(\frac{3}{5}\right)\left(\frac{3}{5}\right)$ $-\frac{21}{5}\left(-\frac{10}{3}\right) = h$

$i = \frac{9}{25}$ $\frac{210}{15} = h$

$14 = h$

18. $-8 \cdot \left(\frac{3}{4}\right)^2 = v$

$-\frac{8}{1} \cdot \left(\frac{3}{4}\right)\left(\frac{3}{4}\right) = v$

$-\frac{72}{16} = v$

$-\frac{9}{2} = v$

$-4\frac{1}{2} = v$

Lesson 7-4

PAGE 599

1. $\frac{1}{3}$ **2.** $-\frac{1}{5}$ **3.** $\frac{3}{2}$ **4.** $2\frac{1}{8} = \frac{17}{8}$

$\frac{8}{17}$

5. $\frac{b}{a}$ **6.** $-\frac{1}{8}$ **7.** $\frac{15}{1} = 15$ **8.** $0.75 = \frac{3}{4}$

$\frac{4}{3}$

9. $\frac{1}{c}$ **10.** $-\frac{5}{3}$ **11.** $1\frac{1}{3} = \frac{4}{3}$ **12.** $0.5 = \frac{1}{2}$

$\frac{3}{4}$ $\frac{2}{1} = 2$

13. $-2\frac{3}{7} = -\frac{17}{7}$ **14.** $-\frac{11}{1} = -11$

$-\frac{7}{17}$

15. $\frac{1}{12}$ **16.** $\frac{9}{7}$ **17.** $\frac{y}{x}$ **18.** $-1\frac{3}{7} = -\frac{10}{7}$

$-\frac{7}{10}$

19. $\frac{4}{21}$ **20.** $\frac{5}{4}$ **21.** $0.8 = \frac{8}{10}$ or $\frac{4}{5}$

$\frac{5}{4}$

22. $-\frac{15}{8}$ **23.** $\frac{m}{1} = m$ **24.** $-6\frac{5}{11} = -\frac{71}{11}$

$-\frac{11}{71}$

25. $\frac{11}{3}$ **26.** $3\frac{1}{4} = \frac{13}{4}$ **27.** $-5\frac{3}{5} = -\frac{28}{5}$

$\frac{4}{13}$ $-\frac{5}{28}$

28. $\frac{9}{24}$ **29.** $-\frac{b}{1} = -b$ **30.** $4\frac{5}{8} = \frac{37}{8}$

$\frac{8}{37}$

Lesson 7-6

PAGE 600

1. $1 + 4 = 5$ **2.** $2 \cdot 3 = 6$
$5 + 4 = 9$ $6 \cdot 3 = 18$
$9 + 4 = 13$ $18 \cdot 3 = 54$
$13 + 4 = 17$ $54 \cdot 3 = 162$
$17 + 4 = 21$ $162 \cdot 3 = 486$
$21 + 4 = 25$ $486 \cdot 3 = 1,458$
arithmetic; Next geometric; Next three
three terms are 17, terms are 162, 486,
21, and 25. and 1,458.

3. $1 + 3 = 4$ **4.** $729 \cdot \frac{1}{3} = 243$
$4 + 5 = 9$
$9 + 7 = 16$ $243 \cdot \frac{1}{3} = 81$
$16 + 9 = 25$
$25 + 11 = 36$ $81 \cdot \frac{1}{3} = 27$
$36 + 13 = 49$
$49 + 15 = 64$ $27 \cdot \frac{1}{3} = 9$
neither; Next three
terms are 36, 49, $9 \cdot \frac{1}{3} = 3$
and 64.
  geometric; Next three
  terms are 27, 9, and
  3.

5. $2 + (-5) = -3$ **6.** $5 \cdot -1 = -5$
$-3 + (-5) = -8$ $-5 \cdot -1 = 5$
$-8 + (-5) = -13$ $5 \cdot -1 = -5$
$-13 + (-5) = -18$ $-5 \cdot -1 = 5$
$-18 + (-5) = -23$ $5 \cdot -1 = -5$
$-23 + (-5) = -28$ $-5 \cdot -1 = 5$
arithmetic; Next three geometric; Next three
terms are -18, -23, terms are 5, -5,
and -28. and 5.

7. $810 \cdot \left(-\frac{1}{3}\right) = -270$

$-270 \cdot \left(-\frac{1}{3}\right) = 90$

$90 \cdot \left(-\frac{1}{3}\right) = -30$

$-30 \cdot \left(-\frac{1}{3}\right) = 10$

$10 \cdot \left(-\frac{1}{3}\right) = -\frac{10}{3}$

$-\frac{10}{3} \cdot \left(-\frac{1}{3}\right) = \frac{10}{9}$

geometric; Next three terms are 10, $-\frac{10}{3}$, and $\frac{10}{9}$.

8. $11 + 3 = 14$
$14 + 3 = 17$
$17 + 3 = 20$
$20 + 3 = 23$
$23 + 3 = 26$
$26 + 3 = 29$
$29 + 3 = 32$
arithmetic; Next three terms are 26, 29, and 32.

9. $33 + (-6) = 27$
$27 + (-6) = 21$
$21 + (-6) = 15$
$15 + (-6) = 9$
$9 + (-6) = 3$
arithmetic; Next three terms are 15, 9, and 3.

10. $21 + (-6) = 15$
$15 + (-6) = 9$
$9 + (-6) = 3$
$3 + (-6) = -3$
$-3 + (-6) = -9$
$-9 + (-6) = -15$
arithmetic; next three terms are -3, -9, and -15.

11. $\frac{1}{8} \cdot (-2) = -\frac{1}{4}$

$-\frac{1}{4} \cdot (-2) = \frac{1}{2}$

$\frac{1}{2} \cdot (-2) = -1$

$-1 \cdot (-2) = 2$

$2 \cdot (-2) = -4$

$-4 \cdot (-2) = 8$

geometric; next three terms are 2, -4, and 8.

12. $\frac{1}{81} \cdot 3 = \frac{1}{27}$

$\frac{1}{27} \cdot 3 = \frac{1}{9}$

$\frac{1}{9} \cdot 3 = \frac{1}{3}$

$\frac{1}{3} \cdot 3 = 1$

$1 \cdot 3 = 3$

$3 \cdot 3 = 9$

geometric; Next three terms are 1, 3, and 9.

13. $\frac{3}{4} \cdot 2 = \frac{6}{4} = \frac{3}{2}$ or $1\frac{1}{2}$

$\frac{3}{2} \cdot 2 = \frac{3}{1}$ or 3

$3 \cdot 2 = 6$

$6 \cdot 2 = 12$

$12 \cdot 2 = 24$

geometric; Next three terms are 6, 12, and 24.

14. $2 + 3 = 5$
$5 + 4 = 9$
$9 + 5 = 14$
$14 + 6 = 20$
$20 + 7 = 27$
$27 + 8 = 35$
neither; Next three terms are 20, 27, and 35.

15. $-1\frac{1}{4} + \left(-\frac{2}{4}\right) = -1\frac{3}{4}$

$-1\frac{3}{4} + \left(-\frac{2}{4}\right) = -2\frac{1}{4}$

$-2\frac{1}{4} + \left(-\frac{2}{4}\right) = -2\frac{3}{4}$

$-2\frac{3}{4} + \left(-\frac{2}{4}\right) = -3\frac{1}{4}$

$-3\frac{1}{4} + \left(-\frac{2}{4}\right) = -3\frac{3}{4}$

$-3\frac{3}{4} + \left(-\frac{2}{4}\right) = -4\frac{1}{4}$

arithmetic; Next three terms are $-3\frac{1}{4}$, $-3\frac{3}{4}$, and $-4\frac{1}{4}$.

16. $9.9 + 3.8 = 13.7$
$13.7 + 3.8 = 17.5$
$17.5 + 3.8 = 21.3$
$21.3 + 3.8 = 25.1$
$25.1 + 3.8 = 28.9$
arithmetic; Next three terms are 21.3, 25.1, and 28.9.

17. $\frac{1}{2} + 1 = 1\frac{1}{2}$

$1\frac{1}{2} + 1 = 2\frac{1}{2}$

$2\frac{1}{2} + 1 = 3\frac{1}{2}$

$3\frac{1}{2} + 1 = 4\frac{1}{2}$

$4\frac{1}{2} + 1 = 5\frac{1}{2}$

$5\frac{1}{2} + 1 = 6\frac{1}{2}$

arithmetic; Next three terms are $4\frac{1}{2}$, $5\frac{1}{2}$, and $6\frac{1}{2}$.

18. $2 + 10 = 12$
$12 + 20 = 32$
$32 + 30 = 62$
$62 + 40 = 102$
$102 + 50 = 152$
$152 + 60 = 212$
neither; Next three terms are 102, 152, and 212.

19. $3 \cdot (-2) = -6$
$-6 \cdot (-2) = 12$
$12 \cdot (-2) = -24$
$-24 \cdot (-2) = 48$
$48 \cdot (-2) = -96$
$-96 \cdot (-2) = 192$
geometric; Next three terms are 48, -96, and 192.

20. $5 + 2 = 7$
$7 + 2 = 9$
$9 + 2 = 11$
$11 + 2 = 13$
$13 + 2 = 15$
$15 + 2 = 17$
$17 + 2 = 19$
arithmetic; Next three terms are 15, 17, and 19.

21. $-0.06 + 2.3 = 2.24$
$2.24 + 2.3 = 4.54$
$4.54 + 2.3 = 6.84$
$6.84 + 2.3 = 9.14$
$9.14 + 2.3 = 11.44$
arithmetic; Next three terms are 6.84, 9.14, and 11.44.

22. $7 \cdot 2 = 14$
$14 \cdot 2 = 28$
$28 \cdot 2 = 56$
$56 \cdot 2 = 112$
$112 \cdot 2 = 224$
geometric; Next three terms are 56, 112, and 224.

23. $-5.4 + 4 = -1.4$
    $-1.4 + 4 = 2.6$
    $2.6 + 4 = 6.4$
    $6.4 + 4 = 10.4$
    $10.4 + 4 = 14.4$
    arithmetic; Next
    three terms are
    6.4, 10.4, and 14.4.

24. $-96 \cdot \left(-\frac{1}{2}\right) = 48$
    $48 \cdot \left(-\frac{1}{2}\right) = -24$
    $-24 \cdot \left(-\frac{1}{2}\right) = 12$
    $12 \cdot \left(-\frac{1}{2}\right) = -6$
    $-6 \cdot \left(-\frac{1}{2}\right) = 3$
    $3 \cdot \left(-\frac{1}{2}\right) = -\frac{3}{2}$
    or $-1\frac{1}{2}$
    geometric; Next
    three terms are
    -6, 3, and $-1\frac{1}{2}$.

25. $4 \cdot 3 = 12$
      $12 \cdot 3 = 36$
      $36 \cdot 3 = 108$
      $108 \cdot 3 = 324$
      $324 \cdot 3 = 972$
      geometric; Next three
      terms are 108, 324,
      and 972.

26. $20 + (-1) = 19$
    $19 + (-1) = 18$
    $18 + (-1) = 17$
    $17 + (-1) = 16$
    $16 + (-1) = 15$
    $15 + (-1) = 14$
    arithmetic; Next
    three terms are
    16, 15, and 14.

27. $768 \cdot \frac{1}{4} = 192$
    $192 \cdot \frac{1}{4} = 48$
    $48 \cdot \frac{1}{4} = 12$
    $12 \cdot \frac{1}{4} = 3$
    $3 \cdot \frac{1}{4} = \frac{3}{4}$
    geometric; Next
    three terms are
    12, 3, and $\frac{3}{4}$.

Lesson 7-7

PAGE 600

1. $A = \frac{1}{2}bh$
   $A = \frac{1}{2}\left(2\frac{1}{2}\right)(7)$
   $A = \frac{1}{2}\left(\frac{5}{2}\right)\left(\frac{7}{1}\right)$
   $A = \frac{35}{4}$
   $A = 8\frac{3}{4}$ in^2

2. $A = \frac{1}{2}bh$
   $A = \frac{1}{2}(12)(3.2)$
   $A = 19.2$ cm^2

3. $A = \frac{1}{2}h(a + b)$
   $A = \frac{1}{2}(11)(5 + 7)$
   $A = \frac{1}{2}(11)(12)$
   $A = 66$ ft^2

4. $A = \frac{1}{2}h(a + b)$
   $A = \frac{1}{2}(5)\left(4\frac{1}{4} + 3\frac{1}{2}\right)$
   $A = \frac{1}{2}(5)\left(\frac{17}{4} + \frac{7}{2}\right)$
   $A = \frac{1}{2}(5)\left(\frac{17}{4} + \frac{14}{4}\right)$
   $A = \frac{1}{2}(5)\left(\frac{17 + 14}{4}\right)$
   $A = \frac{1}{2}(5)\left(\frac{31}{4}\right)$
   $A = \frac{155}{8}$
   $A = 19\frac{3}{8}$ yd^2

5. $b = 8$ m
   $h = 5$ m
   $A = \frac{1}{2}bh$
   $A = \frac{1}{2}(8)(5)$
   $A = 20$ m^2

6. $b = 5$ in.
   $h = 6$ in.
   $A = \frac{1}{2}bh$
   $A = \frac{1}{2}(5)(6)$
   $A = 15$ in^2

7. $a = 1.6$ cm
   $b = 2.3$ cm
   $h = 1.3$ cm
   $A = \frac{1}{2}h(a + b)$
   $A = \frac{1}{2}(1.3)(1.6 + 2.3)$
   $A = \frac{1}{2}(1.3)(3.9)$
   $A = 2.535$ cm^2

8. $a = 3$ km
   $b = 5$ km
   $h = 2$ km
   $A = \frac{1}{2}h(a + b)$
   $A = \frac{1}{2}(2)(3 + 5)$
   $A = \frac{1}{2}(2)(8)$
   $A = 8$ km^2

Lesson 7-8

PAGE 600

1. $C = \pi d$
   $C = \pi(14)$
   $C \approx 44.0$ mm

2. $C = \pi d$
   $C = \pi(18)$
   $C \approx 56.5$ cm

3. $C = 2\pi r$
   $C = 2\pi(24)$
   $C \approx 150.8$ in.

4. $C = \pi d$
   $C = \pi(42)$
   $C \approx 131.9$ m

5. $C = \pi d$
   $C = \pi(20)$
   $C \approx 62.8$ mm

6. $C = 2\pi r$
   $C = 2\pi(3.5)$
   $C \approx 22.0$ m

7. $C = 2\pi r$
   $C = 2\pi(6)$
   $C \approx 37.7$ yd

8. $C = 2\pi r$
   $C = 2\pi(4)$
   $C \approx 25.1$ in.

9. $C = \pi d$
   $C = \pi(16)$
   $C \approx 50.3$ ft

10. $C = 2\pi r$
    $C = 2\pi(2.4)$
    $C \approx 15.1$ cm

11. $C = \pi d$
    $C = \pi(56)$
    $C \approx 175.9$ mm

12. $C = \pi d$
    $C = \pi(35)$
    $C \approx 110.0$ in.

1. $x = \frac{2}{3} \div \frac{3}{4}$

$x = \frac{2}{3} \cdot \frac{4}{3}$

$x = \frac{8}{9}$

2. $-\frac{4}{9} \div \frac{5}{6} = c$

$-\frac{4}{9} \cdot \frac{6}{5} = c$

$-\frac{24}{45} = c$

$-\frac{8}{15} = c$

3. $\frac{7}{12} \div \frac{3}{8} = q$

$\frac{7}{12} \cdot \frac{8}{3} = q$

$\frac{56}{36} = q$

$\frac{14}{9} = q$

$1\frac{5}{9} = q$

4. $m = \frac{5}{18} \div \frac{2}{9}$

$m = \frac{5}{18} \cdot \frac{9}{2}$

$m = \frac{45}{36}$

$m = \frac{5}{4}$

$m = 1\frac{1}{4}$

5. $a = \frac{1}{3} \div 4$

$a = \frac{1}{3} \cdot \frac{1}{4}$

$a = \frac{1}{12}$

6. $5\frac{1}{4} \div \left(-2\frac{1}{2}\right) = g$

$\frac{21}{4} \div \left(-\frac{5}{2}\right) = g$

$\frac{21}{4} \cdot \left(-\frac{2}{5}\right) = g$

$-\frac{42}{20} = g$

$-\frac{21}{10} = g$

$-2\frac{1}{10} = g$

7. $-6 \div \left(-\frac{4}{7}\right) = d$

$-6 \cdot \left(-\frac{7}{4}\right) = d$

$\frac{42}{4} = d$

$\frac{21}{2} = d$

$10\frac{1}{2} = d$

8. $n = -6\frac{3}{8} \div \frac{1}{4}$

$n = -\frac{51}{8} \cdot \frac{4}{1}$

$n = -\frac{204}{8}$

$n = -\frac{51}{2}$

$n = -25\frac{1}{2}$

9. $p = \frac{6}{7} \div \frac{3}{5}$

$p = \frac{6}{7} \cdot \frac{5}{3}$

$p = \frac{30}{21}$

$p = \frac{10}{7}$

$p = 1\frac{3}{7}$

10. $e = 3\frac{1}{3} \div (-4)$

$e = \frac{10}{3} \cdot \left(-\frac{1}{4}\right)$

$e = -\frac{10}{12}$

$e = -\frac{5}{6}$

11. $2\frac{5}{12} \div 7\frac{1}{3} = r$

$\frac{29}{12} \div \frac{22}{3} = r$

$\frac{29}{12} \cdot \frac{3}{22} = r$

$\frac{87}{264} = r$

$\frac{29}{88} = r$

12. $v = \frac{5}{6} \div 1\frac{1}{9}$

$v = \frac{5}{6} \div \frac{10}{9}$

$v = \frac{5}{6} \cdot \frac{9}{10}$

$v = \frac{45}{60}$

$v = \frac{3}{4}$

13. $\frac{3}{8} \div (-6) = b$

$\frac{3}{8} \cdot \left(-\frac{1}{6}\right) = b$

$-\frac{3}{48} = b$

$-\frac{1}{16} = b$

14. $i = \frac{5}{8} \div \frac{1}{6}$

$i = \frac{5}{8} \cdot \frac{6}{1}$

$i = \frac{30}{8}$

$i = \frac{15}{4}$

$i = 3\frac{3}{4}$

15. $4\frac{1}{4} \div 6\frac{3}{4} = w$

$\frac{17}{4} \div \frac{27}{4} = w$

$\frac{17}{4} \cdot \frac{4}{27} = w$

$\frac{68}{108} = w$

$\frac{17}{27} = w$

16. $f = 4\frac{1}{6} \div 3\frac{1}{8}$

$f = \frac{25}{6} \div \frac{25}{8}$

$f = \frac{25}{6} \cdot \frac{8}{25}$

$f = \frac{200}{150}$

$f = \frac{4}{3}$

$f = 1\frac{1}{3}$

17. $t = 8 \div \left(-1\frac{4}{5}\right)$

$t = 8 \div \left(-\frac{9}{5}\right)$

$t = 8 \cdot \left(-\frac{5}{9}\right)$

$t = -\frac{40}{9}$

$t = -4\frac{4}{9}$

18. $j = -5 \div \frac{2}{7}$

$j = -5 \cdot \frac{7}{2}$

$j = -\frac{35}{2}$

$j = -17\frac{1}{2}$

19. $\frac{3}{5} \div \frac{6}{7} = y$

$\frac{3}{5} \cdot \frac{7}{6} = y$

$\frac{21}{30} = y$

$\frac{7}{10} = y$

20. $4\frac{8}{9} \div \left(-2\frac{2}{3}\right) = h$

$\frac{44}{9} \div \left(-\frac{8}{3}\right) = h$

$\frac{44}{9} \cdot \left(-\frac{3}{8}\right) = h$

$-\frac{132}{72} = h$

$-\frac{11}{6} = h$

$-1\frac{5}{6} = h$

21. $f = 8\frac{1}{6} \div 3$

$f = \frac{49}{6} \div \frac{3}{1}$

$f = \frac{49}{6} \cdot \frac{1}{3}$

$f = \frac{49}{18}$

$f = 2\frac{13}{18}$

22. $k = -\frac{3}{4} \div 9$

$k = -\frac{3}{4} \cdot \frac{1}{9}$

$k = -\frac{3}{36}$

$k = -\frac{1}{12}$

23. $s = 1\frac{11}{14} \div 2\frac{1}{2}$

$s = \frac{25}{14} \div \frac{5}{2}$

$s = \frac{25}{14} \cdot \frac{2}{5}$

$s = \frac{50}{70}$

$s = \frac{5}{7}$

24. $-2\frac{1}{4} \div \frac{4}{5} = z$

$-\frac{9}{4} \cdot \frac{5}{4} = z$

$-\frac{45}{16} = z$

$-2\frac{13}{16} = z$

PAGE 601

1. $434 = -31y$

$434\left(-\frac{1}{31}\right) = -31y\left(-\frac{1}{31}\right)$

$-14 = y$

Check: $434 \stackrel{?}{=} -31(-14)$

$434 = 434$ ✓

2. $6x = -4.2$

$6x \cdot \frac{1}{6} = -4.2 \cdot \frac{1}{6}$

$x = -0.7$

Check: $6(-0.7) \stackrel{?}{=} -4.2$

$-4.2 = -4.2$ ✓

3. $\frac{3}{4}a = -12$

$\frac{4}{3} \cdot \frac{3}{4}a = -12 \cdot \frac{4}{3}$

$a = \frac{-48}{3}$

$a = -16$

Check: $\frac{3}{4}(-16) \stackrel{?}{=} -12$

$-\frac{48}{4} \stackrel{?}{=} -12$

$-12 = -12$ ✓

4. $-10 = \frac{b}{-7}$

$-7 \cdot -10 = \frac{b}{-7} \cdot -7$

$70 = b$

Check: $-10 \stackrel{?}{=} \frac{70}{-7}$

$-10 = -10$ ✓

5. $7.2 = \frac{3}{4}c$

$7.2 \cdot \frac{4}{3} = \frac{3}{4}c \cdot \frac{4}{3}$

$\frac{28.8}{3} = c$

$9.6 = c$

Check: $7.2 \stackrel{?}{=} \frac{3}{4}(9.6)$

$7.2 \stackrel{?}{=} \frac{28.8}{4}$

$7.2 = 7.2$ ✓

6. $2r + 4 = 14$

$2r + 4 - 4 = 14 - 4$

$2r = 10$

$2r \cdot \frac{1}{2} = 10 \cdot \frac{1}{2}$

$r = 5$

Check: $2(5) + 4 \stackrel{?}{=} 14$

$10 + 4 \stackrel{?}{=} 14$

$14 = 14$ ✓

7. $-2.4i = 7.2$

$-\frac{1}{2.4}(-2.4i) = 7.2\left(-\frac{1}{2.4}\right)$

$i = -\frac{7.2}{2.4}$

$i = -3$

Check: $-2.4(-3) \stackrel{?}{=} 7.2$

$7.2 = 7.2$ ✓

8. $7 = \frac{1}{2}d - 3$

$7 + 3 = \frac{1}{2}d - 3 + 3$

$10 = \frac{1}{2}d$

$10 \cdot 2 = \frac{1}{2}d \cdot 2$

$20 = d$

Check: $7 \stackrel{?}{=} \frac{1}{2}(20) - 3$

$7 \stackrel{?}{=} 10 - 3$

$7 = 7$ ✓

9. $3.2n - 0.64 = -5.44$

$3.2n - 0.64 + 0.64 = -5.44 + 0.64$

$3.2n = -4.8$

$\frac{1}{3.2} \cdot 3.2n = -4.84 \cdot \frac{1}{3.2}$

$n = -\frac{4.8}{3.2}$

$n = -1.5$

Check: $3.2(-1.5) - 0.64 \stackrel{?}{=} -5.44$

$-4.8 - 0.64 \stackrel{?}{=} -5.44$

$-5.44 = -5.44$ ✓

10. $\frac{t}{3} - 7 = 2$

$\frac{t}{3} - 7 + 7 = 2 + 7$

$\frac{t}{3} = 9$

$3 \cdot \frac{t}{3} = 9 \cdot 3$

$t = 27$

Check: $\frac{27}{3} - 7 \stackrel{?}{=} 2$

$9 - 7 \stackrel{?}{=} 2$

$2 = 2$ ✓

11. $\frac{3}{8} = \frac{1}{2}x$

$\frac{3}{8} \cdot 2 = \frac{1}{2}x \cdot 2$

$\frac{6}{8} = x$

$\frac{3}{4} = x$

Check: $\frac{3}{8} \stackrel{?}{=} \frac{1}{2}\left(\frac{3}{4}\right)$

$\frac{3}{8} = \frac{3}{8}$ ✓

12. $\frac{1}{2}h - 3 = -14$

$\frac{1}{2}h - 3 + 3 = -14 + 3$

$\frac{1}{2}h = -11$

$\frac{1}{2}h \cdot 2 = -11 \cdot 2$

$h = -22$

Check: $\frac{1}{2}(-22) - 3 \stackrel{?}{=} -14$

$-11 - 3 \stackrel{?}{=} -14$

$-14 = -14$ ✓

13. $-0.46k - 1.18 = 1.58$

$-0.46k - 1.18 + 1.18 = 1.58 + 1.18$

$-0.46k = 2.76$

$-0.46k \cdot \left(-\frac{1}{0.46}\right) = 2.76\left(-\frac{1}{0.46}\right)$

$k = -6$

Check: $-0.46(-6) - 1.18 \stackrel{?}{=} 1.58$

$2.76 - 1.18 \stackrel{?}{=} 1.58$

$1.58 = 1.58$ ✓

14. $4\frac{1}{2}s = -30$

$\frac{9}{2}s = -30$

$\frac{9}{2}s \cdot \frac{2}{9} = -30 \cdot \frac{2}{9}$

$s = \frac{-60}{9}$

$s = \frac{-20}{3}$

$s = -6\frac{2}{3}$

Check: $\frac{9}{2}\left(-\frac{20}{3}\right) \overset{?}{=} -30$

$-\frac{180}{6} \overset{?}{=} -30$

$-30 = -30$ ✓

15. $\frac{2}{3}f = \frac{8}{15}$

$\frac{2}{3}f \cdot \frac{3}{2} = \frac{8}{15} \cdot \frac{3}{2}$

$f = \frac{24}{30}$

$f = \frac{4}{5}$

Check: $\frac{2}{3}\left(\frac{4}{5}\right) \overset{?}{=} \frac{8}{15}$

$\frac{8}{15} = \frac{8}{15}$ ✓

16. $\frac{2}{3}m + 10 = 22$

$\frac{2}{3}m + 10 - 10 = 22 - 10$

$\frac{2}{3}m = 12$

$\frac{2}{3}m \cdot \frac{3}{2} = 12 \cdot \frac{3}{2}$

$m = \frac{36}{2}$

$m = 18$

Check: $\frac{2}{3}(18) + 10 \overset{?}{=} 22$

$12 + 10 \overset{?}{=} 22$

$22 = 22$ ✓

17. $\frac{2}{3}g + 4 = 4\frac{5}{6}$

$\frac{2}{3}g + 4 - 4 = \frac{29}{6} - 4$

$\frac{2}{3}g = \frac{29}{6} - \frac{24}{6}$

$\frac{2}{3}g = \frac{5}{6}$

$\frac{2}{3}g \cdot \frac{3}{2} = \frac{5}{6} \cdot \frac{3}{2}$

$g = \frac{15}{12}$

$g = \frac{5}{4}$

$g = 1\frac{1}{4}$

Check: $\frac{2}{3}\left(\frac{5}{4}\right) + 4 \overset{?}{=} \frac{29}{6}$

$\frac{10}{12} + 4 \overset{?}{=} \frac{29}{6}$

$\frac{5}{6} + \frac{24}{6} \overset{?}{=} \frac{29}{6}$

$\frac{29}{6} = \frac{29}{6}$ ✓

18. $7 = \frac{1}{2}v + 3$

$7 - 3 = \frac{1}{2}v + 3 - 3$

$4 = \frac{1}{2}v$

$4 \cdot 2 = \frac{1}{2}v \cdot 2$

$8 = v$

Check: $7 \overset{?}{=} \frac{1}{2}(8) + 3$

$7 \overset{?}{=} 4 + 3$

$7 = 7$ ✓

19. $\frac{g}{1.2} = -6$

$1.2 \cdot \frac{g}{1.2} = -6 \cdot 1.2$

$g = -7.2$

Check: $\frac{-7.2}{1.2} \overset{?}{=} -6$

$-6 = -6$ ✓

20. $\frac{4}{7}x - 4\frac{5}{8} = 15\frac{3}{8}$

$\frac{4}{7}x - \frac{37}{8} = \frac{123}{8}$

$\frac{4}{7}x - \frac{37}{8} + \frac{37}{8} = \frac{123}{8} + \frac{37}{8}$

$\frac{4}{7}x = \frac{160}{8}$

$\frac{4}{7}x \cdot \frac{7}{4} = \frac{160}{8} \cdot \frac{7}{4}$

$x = \frac{1,120}{32}$

$x = 35$

Check: $\frac{4}{7}(35) - \frac{37}{8} \overset{?}{=} \frac{123}{8}$

$\frac{140}{7} - \frac{37}{8} \overset{?}{=} \frac{123}{8}$

$20 - \frac{37}{8} \overset{?}{=} \frac{123}{8}$

$\frac{160}{8} - \frac{37}{8} \overset{?}{=} \frac{123}{8}$

$\frac{123}{8} = \frac{123}{8}$ ✓

21. $-12 = \frac{1}{5}j$

$-12 \cdot 5 = \frac{1}{5}j \cdot 5$

$-60 = j$

Check: $-12 \overset{?}{=} \frac{1}{5}(-60)$

$-12 = -12$ ✓

Lesson 8-1

PAGE 601

1. $\sqrt{9} = 3$
2. $\sqrt{0.16} = 0.4$
3. $\sqrt{81} = 9$
4. $\sqrt{0.04} = 0.2$
5. $-\sqrt{625} = -25$
6. $\sqrt{36} = 6$
7. $-\sqrt{169} = -13$
8. $\sqrt{144} = 12$
9. $\sqrt{2.25} = 1.5$
10. $\sqrt{961} = 31$
11. $\sqrt{25} = 5$
12. $\sqrt{225} = 15$
13. $\sqrt{0.01} = 0.1$
14. $-\sqrt{4} = -2$
15. $-\sqrt{0.09} = -0.3$
16. $\sqrt{529} = 23$
17. $-\sqrt{484} = -22$
18. $\sqrt{196} = 14$
19. $\sqrt{0.49} = 0.7$
20. $\sqrt{1.69} = 1.3$
21. $\sqrt{729} = 27$
22. $\sqrt{0.36} = 0.6$
23. $\sqrt{289} = 17$
24. $-\sqrt{16} = -4$
25. $\sqrt{1024} = 32$
26. $\sqrt{\frac{289}{10,000}} = \frac{\sqrt{289}}{\sqrt{10,000}} = \frac{17}{100}$
27. $\sqrt{\frac{169}{121}} = \frac{\sqrt{169}}{\sqrt{121}} = \frac{13}{11}$
28. $-\sqrt{\frac{4}{9}} = -\frac{\sqrt{4}}{\sqrt{9}} = -\frac{2}{3}$
29. $-\sqrt{\frac{81}{64}} = -\frac{\sqrt{81}}{\sqrt{64}} = -\frac{9}{8}$
30. $\sqrt{\frac{25}{81}} = \frac{\sqrt{25}}{\sqrt{81}} = \frac{5}{9}$

Lesson 8-2

PAGE 602

1. $225 < 229 < 256$

   $15^2 < 229 < 16^2$

   $15 < \sqrt{229} < 16$

   15 is best estimate.

2. $49 < 63 < 64$

   $7^2 < 63 < 8^2$

   $7 < \sqrt{63} < 8$

   8 is best estimate.

3. $289 < 290 < 324$
$17^2 < 290 < 18^2$
$17 < \sqrt{290} < 18$
17 is best estimate.

4. $25 < 27 < 36$
$5^2 < 27 < 6^2$
$5 < \sqrt{27} < 6$
5 is best estimate.

5. $1 < 1.30 < 4$
$1^2 < 1.30 < 2^2$
$1 < \sqrt{1.30} < 2$
1 is best estimate.

6. $4 < 8.4 < 9$
$2^2 < 8.4 < 3^2$
$2 < \sqrt{8.4} < 3$
3 is best estimate.

7. $81 < 96 < 100$
$9^2 < 96 < 10^2$
$9 < \sqrt{96} < 10$
10 is best estimate.

8. $16 < 19 < 25$
$4^2 < 19 < 5^2$
$4 < \sqrt{19} < 5$
4 is best estimate.

9. $196 < 200 < 225$
$14^2 < 200 < 15^2$
$14 < \sqrt{200} < 15$
14 is best estimate.

10. $64 < 76 < 81$
$8^2 < 76 < 9^2$
$8 < \sqrt{76} < 9$
9 is best estimate.

11. $16 < 17 < 25$
$4^2 < 17 < 5^2$
$4 < \sqrt{17} < 5$
4 is best estimate.

12. $25 < 34 < 36$
$5^2 < 34 < 6^2$
$5 < \sqrt{34} < 6$
6 is best estimate.

13. $121 < 137 < 144$
$11^2 < 137 < 12^2$
$11 < \sqrt{137} < 12$
12 is best estimate.

14. $529 < 540 < 576$
$23^2 < 540 < 24^2$
$23 < \sqrt{540} < 24$
23 is best estimate.

15. $144 < 165 < 169$
$12^2 < 165 < 13^2$
$12 < \sqrt{165} < 13$
13 is best estimate.

16. $324 < 326 < 361$
$18^2 < 326 < 19^2$
$18 < \sqrt{326} < 19$
18 is best estimate.

17. $49 < 52 < 64$
$7^2 < 52 < 8^2$
$7 < \sqrt{52} < 8$
7 is best estimate.

18. $36 < 37 < 49$
$6^2 < 37 < 7^2$
$6 < \sqrt{37} < 7$
6 is best estimate.

19. $64 < 79 < 81$
$8^2 < 79 < 9^2$
$8 < \sqrt{79} < 9$
9 is best estimate.

20. $16 < 18.35 < 25$
$4^2 < 18.35 < 5^2$
$4 < \sqrt{18.35} < 5$
4 is best estimate.

21. $64 < 71 < 81$
$8^2 < 71 < 9^2$
$8 < \sqrt{71} < 9$
8 is best estimate.

22. $100 < 117 < 121$
$10^2 < 117 < 11^2$
$10 < \sqrt{117} < 11$
11 is best estimate.

23. $400 < 410 < 441$
$20^2 < 410 < 21^2$
$20 < \sqrt{410} < 21$
20 is best estimate.

24. $25 < 25.70 < 36$
$5^2 < 25.70 < 6^2$
$5 < \sqrt{25.70} < 6$
5 is best estimate.

25. $324 < 333 < 361$
$18^2 < 333 < 19^2$
$18 < \sqrt{333} < 19$
18 is best estimate.

26. $16 < 23 < 25$
$4^2 < 23 < 5^2$
$4 < \sqrt{23} < 5$
5 is best estimate.

27. $81 < 89 < 100$
$9^2 < 89 < 10^2$
$9 < \sqrt{89} < 10$
9 is best estimate.

28. $36 < 47 < 49$
$6^2 < 47 < 7^2$
$6 < \sqrt{47} < 7$
7 is best estimate.

29. $49 < 62 < 64$
$7^2 < 62 < 8^2$
$7 < \sqrt{62} < 8$
8 is best estimate.

30. $729 < 742 < 784$
$27^2 < 742 < 28^2$
$27 < \sqrt{742} < 28$
27 is best estimate.

Lesson 8-3

PAGE 602

1. 6.5; rational

2. $\sqrt{25} = 5$; natural, whole, integer, rational

3. $\sqrt{3}$; irrational

4. -7.2; rational

5. $-0.\overline{61}$; rational

6. $-\sqrt{12} \approx -3.5$

7. $\sqrt{23} \approx 4.8$

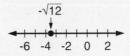

8. $\sqrt{2} \approx 1.4$

9. $\sqrt{10} \approx 3.2$

10. $-\sqrt{30} \approx -5.5$

11. $y^2 = 49$
$y = \sqrt{49}$ or $y = -\sqrt{49}$
$y = 7$ or $= -7$

12. $x^2 = 225$
$x = \sqrt{225}$ or $x = -\sqrt{225}$
$x = 15$ or $x = -15$

13. $x^2 = 64$
$x = \sqrt{64}$ or $x = -\sqrt{64}$
$x = 8$ or $x = -8$

14. $y^2 = 79$
$y = \sqrt{79}$ or $y = -\sqrt{79}$
$y \approx 8.9$ or $y \approx -8.9$

15. $x^2 = 16$
$x = \sqrt{16}$ or $x = -\sqrt{16}$
$x = 4$ or $x = -4$

16. $y^2 = 24$
$y = \sqrt{24}$ or $y = -\sqrt{24}$
$y \approx 4.9$ or $y \approx -4.9$

17. $y^2 = 625$
$y = \sqrt{625}$ or $y = -\sqrt{625}$
$y = 25$ or $y = -25$

18. $x^2 = 81$
$x = \sqrt{81}$ or $= -\sqrt{81}$
$x = 9$ or $x = -9$

Lesson 8-5

PAGE 602

1. $c^2 = a^2 + b^2$
$c^2 = (6)^2 + (5)^2$
$c^2 = 36 + 25$
$c^2 = 61$
$c = \sqrt{61}$
$c \approx 7.8$ cm

2. $c^2 = a^2 + b^2$
$c^2 = (12)^2 + (12)^2$
$c^2 = 144 + 144$
$c^2 = 288$
$c = \sqrt{288}$
$c \approx 17.0$ ft

3. $c^2 = a^2 + b^2$
$c^2 = (8)^2 + (6)^2$
$c^2 = 64 + 36$
$c^2 = 100$
$c = \sqrt{100}$
$c = 10$ in.

4. $c^2 = a^2 + b^2$
$(25)^2 = (20)^2 + b^2$
$625 = 400 + b^2$
$625 - 400 = 400 - 400 + b^2$
$225 = b^2$
$\sqrt{225} = b$
$15 = b$
$b = 15$ m

5. $c^2 = a^2 + b^2$
$(14)^2 = (9)^2 + b^2$
$196 = 81 + b^2$
$196 - 81 = 81 - 81 + b^2$
$115 = b^2$
$\sqrt{115} = b$
$10.7 \approx b$
$b \approx 10.7$ mm

6. $c^2 = a^2 + b^2$
$(20)^2 = a^2 + (15)^2$
$400 = a^2 + 225$
$400 - 225 = a^2 + 225 - 225$
$175 = a^2$
$\sqrt{175} = a$
$13.2 \approx a$
$a \approx 13.2$ m

7. $c^2 = a^2 + b^2$
$c^2 = (5)^2 + (50)^2$
$c^2 = 25 + 2,500$
$c^2 = 2,525$
$c = \sqrt{2,525}$
$c \approx 50.2$ ft

8. $c^2 = a^2 + b^2$
$(8.5)^2 = (4.5)^2 + b^2$
$72.25 = 20.25 + b^2$
$72.25 - 20.25 = 20.25 - 20.25 + b^2$
$52 = b^2$
$\sqrt{52} = b$
$7.2 \approx b$
$b \approx 7.2$ yd

9. $c^2 = a^2 + b^2$
$(5)^2 = (x)^2 + (4)^2$
$25 = x^2 + 16$
$25 - 16 = x^2 + 16 - 16$
$9 = x^2$
$\sqrt{9} = x$
$3 = x$

10. $c^2 = a^2 + b^2$
$(10)^2 = a^2 + (8)^2$
$100 = a^2 + 64$
$100 - 64 = a^2 + 64 - 64$
$36 = a^2$
$\sqrt{36} = a$
$6 = a$

$c^2 = a^2 + b^2$
$(x)^2 = 36 + (2)^2$
$x^2 = 36 + 4$
$x^2 = 40$
$x = \sqrt{40}$
$x \approx 6.3$

11. $c^2 = a^2 + b^2$
$(x)^2 = (8)^2 + (4)^2$
$x^2 = 64 + 16$
$x^2 = 80$
$x = \sqrt{80}$
$x \approx 8.9$

12. $c^2 = a^2 + b^2$
$(17)^2 \stackrel{?}{=} (8)^2 + (15)^2$
$289 \stackrel{?}{=} 64 + 225$
$289 = 289$
The triangle is a right triangle.

13. $c^2 = a^2 + b^2$
$(9)^2 \stackrel{?}{=} (5)^2 + (7)^2$
$81 \stackrel{?}{=} 25 + 49$
$81 \neq 74$
The triangle is not a right triangle.

14. $c^2 = a^2 + b^2$
$(13)^2 \stackrel{?}{=} (5)^2 + (12)^2$
$169 \stackrel{?}{=} 25 + 144$
$169 = 169$
The triangle is a right triangle.

Lesson 8-7

PAGE 603

1. $a = 1 - (-3) = 4$
$b = 2 - (-3) = 5$
$c^2 = a^2 + b^2$
$c^2 = (4)^2 + (5)^2$
$c^2 = 16 + 25$
$c^2 = 41$
$c = \sqrt{41}$
$c \approx 6.4$

2. $a = 4 - (-1) = 5$
$b = 4 - 1 = 3$
$c^2 = a^2 + b^2$
$c^2 = (5)^2 + (3)^2$
$c^2 = 25 + 9$
$c^2 = 34$
$c = \sqrt{34}$
$c \approx 5.8$

3. $a = 7 - 0 = 7$
$b = 4 - 1 = 3$
$c^2 = a^2 + b^2$
$c^2 = (7)^2 + (3)^2$
$c^2 = 49 + 9$
$c^2 = 58$
$c = \sqrt{58}$
$c \approx 7.6$

4.
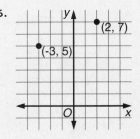

$a = 4 - (-4) = 8$
$b = 17 - 2 = 15$
$c^2 = a^2 + b^2$
$c^2 = (8)^2 + (15)^2$
$c^2 = 64 + 225$
$c^2 = 289$
$c = \sqrt{289}$
$c = 17$

5.

$a = 11 - 5 = 6$
$b = 7 - (-1) = 8$
$c^2 = a^2 + b^2$
$c^2 = (6)^2 + (8)^2$
$c^2 = 36 + 64$
$c^2 = 100$
$c = \sqrt{100}$
$c = 10$

6.

$a = 2 - (-3) = 5$
$b = 7 - 5 = 2$
$c^2 = a^2 + b^2$
$c^2 = (5)^2 + (2)^2$
$c^2 = 25 + 4$
$c^2 = 29$
$c = \sqrt{29}$
$c \approx 5.4$

7.

$a = 7 - 4 = 3$
$b = 3 - (-9) = 12$
$c^2 = a^2 + b^2$
$c^2 = (3)^2 + (12)^2$
$c^2 = 9 + 144$
$c = 153$
$c = \sqrt{153}$
$c \approx 12.4$

8.

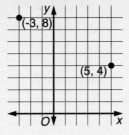

$a = 5 - (-3) = 8$
$b = 8 - 4 = 4$
$c^2 = a^2 + b^2$
$c^2 = (8)^2 + (4)^2$
$c^2 = 64 + 16$
$c^2 = 80$
$c = \sqrt{80}$
$c \approx 8.9$

9.

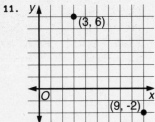

$a = -3 - (-8) = 5$
$b = 8 - (-4) = 12$
$c^2 = a^2 + b^2$
$c^2 = (5)^2 + (12)^2$
$c^2 = 25 + 144$
$c^2 = 169$
$c = \sqrt{169}$
$c = 13$

10.

$a = 10 - 2 = 8$
$b = 7 - (-4) = 11$
$c^2 = a^2 + b^2$
$c^2 = (8)^2 + (11)^2$
$c^2 = 64 + 121$
$c^2 = 185$
$c = \sqrt{185}$
$c \approx 13.6$

11.

$a = 9 - 3 = 6$
$b = 6 - (-2) = 8$
$c^2 = a^2 + b^2$
$c^2 = (6)^2 + (8)^2$
$c^2 = 36 + 64$
$c^2 = 100$
$c = \sqrt{100}$
$c = 10$

Lesson 8-8

PAGE 603

1. $c = 2a$ $c^2 = a^2 + b^2$
    $c = 2(4)$ $(8)^2 = (4)^2 + b^2$
    $c = 8$ $64 = 16 + b^2$
          $64 - 16 = 16 - 16 + b^2$
           $48 = b^2$
           $\sqrt{48} = b$
           $6.9 \approx b$

2. $b = a$ $c^2 = a^2 + b^2$
    $b = 6$ $c^2 = (6)^2 + (6)^2$
          $c^2 = 36 + 36$
          $c^2 = 72$
           $c = \sqrt{72}$
           $c \approx 8.5$

3. $a = \frac{1}{2}c$ $c^2 = a^2 + b^2$
    $a = \frac{1}{2}(14)$ $(14)^2 = (7)^2 + b^2$
    $a = 7$ $196 = 49 + b^2$
        $196 - 49 = 49 - 49 + b^2$
          $147 = b^2$
          $\sqrt{147} = b$
          $12.1 \approx b$

4. $a = b$ $c^2 = a^2 + b^2$
    $a = 10$ $c^2 = (10)^2 + (10)^2$
          $c^2 = 100 + 100$
          $c^2 = 200$
           $c = \sqrt{200}$
           $c \approx 14.1$

5. $c = 2a$ $c = 2a$
    $c^2 = a^2 + b^2$ $c \approx 2(2.9)$
    $(2a)^2 = a^2 + (5)^2$ $c \approx 5.8$
    $4a^2 = a^2 + 25$
   $4a^2 - a^2 = a^2 - a^2 + 25$
      $3a^2 = 25$
      $\frac{3a^2}{3} = \frac{25}{3}$
       $a^2 = \frac{25}{3}$
       $a^2 = \sqrt{\frac{25}{3}}$
       $a \approx 2.9$

6. $b = a$ $c^2 = a^2 + b^2$
    $b = 3$ $c^2 = (3)^2 + (3)^2$
          $c^2 = 9 + 9$
          $c^2 = 18$
           $c = \sqrt{18}$
           $c \approx 4.2$

7. $c = 2a$ $c^2 = a^2 + b^2$
    $c = 2(12)$ $(24)^2 = (12)^2 + b^2$
    $c = 24$ $576 = 144 + b^2$
        $576 - 144 = 144 - 144 + b^2$
          $432 = b^2$
          $\sqrt{432} = b$
          $20.8 \approx b$

8. $b = a$ $c^2 = a^2 + b^2$
    $b = 17$ $c^2 = (17)^2 + (17)^2$
               $c^2 = 289 + 289$
               $c^2 = 578$
               $c = \sqrt{578}$
               $c \approx 24.0$

Lesson 9-1

PAGE 603

1. $\dfrac{27}{9} = \dfrac{27 \div 9}{9 \div 9} = \dfrac{3}{1}$

2. $\dfrac{4 \text{ in.}}{1 \text{ ft}} = \dfrac{4 \text{ in.}}{12 \text{ in.}}$
    $\dfrac{4}{12} = \dfrac{4 + 4}{12 + 4} = \dfrac{1}{3}$

3. $\dfrac{16}{48} = \dfrac{16 \div 16}{48 \div 16} = \dfrac{1}{3}$

4. $\dfrac{10}{50} = \dfrac{10 \div 10}{50 \div 10} = \dfrac{1}{5}$

5. $\dfrac{40 \text{ min}}{1 \text{ hr}} = \dfrac{40 \text{ min}}{60 \text{ min}}$
    $\dfrac{40}{60} = \dfrac{40 \div 20}{60 \div 20} = \dfrac{2}{3}$

6. $\dfrac{35}{15} = \dfrac{35 \div 5}{15 \div 5} = \dfrac{7}{3}$

7. $\dfrac{16}{16} = \dfrac{16 \div 16}{16 \div 16} = \dfrac{1}{1}$

8. $\dfrac{7}{13}$

9. $\dfrac{5}{50} = \dfrac{5 \div 5}{50 \div 5} = \dfrac{1}{10}$

10. $\dfrac{\$24}{1 \text{ dozen}} = \dfrac{\$24}{12}$
    $\dfrac{24}{12} = \dfrac{24 \div 12}{12 \div 12} = \dfrac{2}{1}$
    \$2 each

11. $\dfrac{600}{30} = \dfrac{600 \div 30}{30 \div 30} = \dfrac{20}{1}$
    $\dfrac{20 \text{ students}}{1 \text{ teacher}}$

12. $\dfrac{6}{12} = \dfrac{6 \div 12}{12 \div 12} = \dfrac{0.5}{1}$
    $\dfrac{0.5 \text{ lb}}{1 \text{ week}}$

13. $\dfrac{800}{40} = \dfrac{800 \div 40}{40 \div 40} = \dfrac{20}{1}$
    $\dfrac{\$20}{1 \text{ ticket}}$

14. $\dfrac{6.5}{5} = \dfrac{6.5 \div 5}{5 \div 5} = \dfrac{1.3}{1}$
    $\dfrac{\$1.30}{1 \text{ lb}}$

15. $\dfrac{6}{3} = \dfrac{6 \div 3}{3 \div 3} = \dfrac{2}{1}$
    $\dfrac{2 \text{ in.}}{1 \text{ week}}$

Lesson 9-2

PAGE 604

1. $3 \cdot 10 \overset{?}{=} 5 \cdot 5$
      $30 \neq 25$
  no

2. $8 \cdot 3 \overset{?}{=} 6 \cdot 4$
      $24 = 24$
  yes

3. $10 \cdot 3 \overset{?}{=} 15 \cdot 5$
      $30 \neq 75$
  no

4. $\dfrac{2}{8} = \dfrac{2 + 2}{8 + 2} = \dfrac{1}{4}$
  yes

---

5. $\dfrac{6}{18} = \dfrac{6 + 2}{18 + 2} = \dfrac{3}{9}$
  yes

6. $14 \cdot 18 \overset{?}{=} 21 \cdot 12$
      $252 = 252$
      yes

7. $4 \cdot 25 \overset{?}{=} 20 \cdot 5$
    $100 = 100$
  yes

8. $\dfrac{9}{27} = \dfrac{9 + 9}{27 + 9} = \dfrac{1}{3}$
  yes

9. $\dfrac{2}{3} = \dfrac{a}{12}$
   $2 \cdot 12 = 3a$
      $24 = 3a$
     $\dfrac{24}{3} = \dfrac{3a}{3}$
       $8 = a$

10. $\dfrac{7}{8} = \dfrac{c}{16}$
   $7 \cdot 16 = 8c$
     $112 = 8c$
   $\dfrac{112}{8} = \dfrac{8c}{8}$
     $14 = c$

11. $\dfrac{3}{7} = \dfrac{21}{d}$
   $3d = 7 \cdot 21$
   $3d = 147$
   $\dfrac{3d}{3} = \dfrac{147}{3}$
     $d = 49$

12. $\dfrac{2}{5} = \dfrac{18}{x}$
   $2x = 5 \cdot 18$
   $2x = 90$
   $\dfrac{2x}{2} = \dfrac{90}{2}$
     $x = 45$

13. $\dfrac{3}{5} = \dfrac{n}{21}$
   $3 \cdot 21 = 5n$
     $63 = 5n$
   $\dfrac{63}{5} = \dfrac{5n}{5}$
   $12\dfrac{3}{5} = n$

14. $\dfrac{5}{12} = \dfrac{b}{5}$
   $5 \cdot 5 = 12b$
     $25 = 12b$
   $\dfrac{25}{12} = \dfrac{12b}{12}$
   $2\dfrac{1}{12} = b$

15. $\dfrac{4}{36} = \dfrac{2}{y}$
   $4y = 36 \cdot 2$
   $4y = 72$
   $\dfrac{4y}{4} = \dfrac{72}{4}$
     $y = 18$

16. $\dfrac{3}{10} = \dfrac{x}{36}$
   $3 \cdot 36 = 10x$
     $108 = 10x$
   $\dfrac{108}{10} = \dfrac{10x}{10}$
   $10\dfrac{8}{10} = x$
   $10\dfrac{4}{5} = x$

17. $\dfrac{2}{3} = \dfrac{t}{4}$
   $2 \cdot 4 = 3t$
     $8 = 3t$
   $\dfrac{8}{3} = \dfrac{3t}{3}$
   $2\dfrac{2}{3} = t$

18. $\dfrac{9}{10} = \dfrac{r}{25}$
   $9 \cdot 25 = 10r$
     $225 = 10r$
   $\dfrac{225}{10} = \dfrac{10r}{10}$
   $22\dfrac{5}{10} = r$
   $22\dfrac{1}{2} = r$

19. $\dfrac{16}{8} = \dfrac{y}{12}$
   $16 \cdot 12 = 8y$
     $192 = 8y$
   $\dfrac{192}{8} = \dfrac{8y}{8}$
     $24 = y$

20. $\dfrac{7}{8} = \dfrac{a}{12}$
   $7 \cdot 12 = 8a$
     $84 = 8a$
   $\dfrac{84}{8} = \dfrac{8a}{8}$
   $10\dfrac{4}{8} = a$
   $10\dfrac{1}{2} = a$

Lesson 9-3

PAGE 604

1. $\dfrac{3\frac{1}{2}}{m} = \dfrac{1}{2}$

   $\dfrac{3.5}{m} = \dfrac{1}{2}$

   $3.5 \cdot 2 = 1m$

   $7 = m$

   7 miles

2. $\dfrac{144}{4} = \dfrac{450}{g}$

   $144g = 4 \cdot 450$

   $144g = 1{,}800$

   $\dfrac{144g}{144} = \dfrac{1{,}800}{144}$

   $g = 12.5$

   12.5 gallons

3. $\dfrac{4}{3} = \dfrac{296}{p}$

   $4p = 3 \cdot 296$

   $4p = 888$

   $\dfrac{4p}{4} = \dfrac{888}{4}$

   $p = 222$

   222 perch

4. $\dfrac{8}{4{,}000} = \dfrac{1}{s}$

   $8s = 4{,}000 \cdot 1$

   $8s = 4{,}000$

   $\dfrac{8s}{8} = \dfrac{4{,}000}{8}$

   $s = 500$

   $500 per sofa

Lesson 9-5

PAGE 604

1. $\dfrac{2}{4} \overset{?}{=} \dfrac{5}{10}$

   $2 \cdot 10 \overset{?}{=} 4 \cdot 5$

   $20 = 20$

   yes

2. $\dfrac{2}{5} \overset{?}{=} \dfrac{3}{5}$

   $2 \cdot 5 \overset{?}{=} 3 \cdot 5$

   $10 \neq 15$

   no

3. $\dfrac{1\frac{1}{2}}{4\frac{1}{2}} \overset{?}{=} \dfrac{2}{6}$

   $\dfrac{1.5}{4.5} \overset{?}{=} \dfrac{2}{6}$

   $1.5 \cdot 6 \overset{?}{=} 4.5 \cdot 2$

   $9 = 9$

   yes

4. $\dfrac{1}{1} = 1$

   $\dfrac{0.5}{0.5} = 1$

   yes

Lesson 9-6

PAGE 605

1. $\dfrac{x}{3} = \dfrac{3}{1}$

   $1x = 3 \cdot 3$

   $x = 9$

2. $\dfrac{x}{3} = \dfrac{6}{4}$

   $4x = 3 \cdot 6$

   $4x = 18$

   $\dfrac{4x}{4} = \dfrac{18}{4}$

   $x = 4.5$

3. $\dfrac{x}{1} = \dfrac{3}{1.5}$

   $1.5x = 1 \cdot 3$

   $1.5x = 3$

   $\dfrac{1.5x}{1.5} = \dfrac{3}{1.5}$

   $x = 2$

4. $\dfrac{x}{1.2} = \dfrac{1}{0.8}$

   $0.8x = 1.2 \cdot 1$

   $0.8x = 1.2$

   $\dfrac{0.8x}{0.8} = \dfrac{1.2}{0.8}$

   $x = 1.5$

5. $\dfrac{x}{3} = \dfrac{1}{1}$

   $1x = 3 \cdot 1$

   $x = 3$

6. $\dfrac{x}{3} = \dfrac{6}{2}$

   $2x = 3 \cdot 6$

   $2x = 18$

   $\dfrac{2x}{2} = \dfrac{18}{2}$

   $x = 9$

Lesson 9-7

PAGE 605

1. $\dfrac{2}{x} = \dfrac{1}{50}$

   $2 \cdot 50 = 1x$

   $100 = x$

   100 miles

2. $\dfrac{0.5}{x} = \dfrac{1}{50}$

   $0.5 \cdot 50 = 1x$

   $25 = x$

   25 miles

3. $\dfrac{1}{x} = \dfrac{1}{50}$

   $1 \cdot 50 = 1x$

   $50 = x$

   50 miles

4. $\dfrac{5}{x} = \dfrac{1}{50}$

   $5 \cdot 50 = 1x$

   $250 = x$

   250 miles

5. $\dfrac{1.5}{x} = \dfrac{1}{50}$

   $1.5 \cdot 50 = 1x$

   $75 = x$

   75 miles

6. $\dfrac{2.8}{x} = \dfrac{1}{50}$

   $2.8 \cdot 50 = 1x$

   $140 = x$

   140 miles

7. $\dfrac{3.2}{x} = \dfrac{1}{50}$

   $3.2 \cdot 50 = 1x$

   $160 = x$

   160 miles

8. $\dfrac{10}{x} = \dfrac{1}{50}$

   $10 \cdot 50 = 1x$

   $500 = x$

   500 miles

9. $\dfrac{0.2}{x} = \dfrac{1}{50}$

   $0.2 \cdot 50 = 1x$

   $10 = x$

   10 miles

10. $\dfrac{4.5}{x} = \dfrac{1}{50}$

    $4.5 \cdot 50 = 1x$

    $225 = x$

    225 miles

11. $\dfrac{3}{x} = \dfrac{1}{50}$

    $3 \cdot 50 = 1x$

    $150 = x$

    150 miles

12. $\dfrac{6.4}{x} = \dfrac{1}{50}$

    $6.4 \cdot 50 = 1x$

    $320 = x$

    320 miles

13. $\dfrac{7}{x} = \dfrac{1}{50}$

    $7 \cdot 50 = 1x$

    $350 = x$

    350 miles

14. $\dfrac{0.6}{x} = \dfrac{1}{50}$

    $0.6 \cdot 50 = 1x$

    $30 = x$

    30 miles

15. $\dfrac{8}{x} = \dfrac{1}{50}$

    $8 \cdot 50 = 1x$

    $400 = x$

    400 miles

16. $\dfrac{45}{x} = \dfrac{1}{50}$

    $45 \cdot 50 = 1x$

    $2{,}250 = x$

    2,250 miles

Lesson 9-8

1. $P(4, 4) \rightarrow (4 \cdot 4, 4 \cdot 4) \rightarrow P'(16, 16)$

   $Q(2, 0) \rightarrow (2 \cdot 4, 0 \cdot 4) \rightarrow Q'(8, 0)$

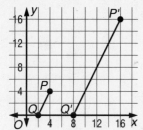

2. $A(3, 6) \rightarrow \left(3 \cdot \frac{1}{2}, 6 \cdot \frac{1}{2}\right) \rightarrow A'(1.5, 3)$

   $B(0, -1) \rightarrow \left(0 \cdot \frac{1}{2}, -1 \cdot \frac{1}{2}\right) \rightarrow B'(0, -0.5)$

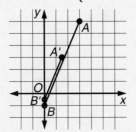

3. $X(-2, -4) \rightarrow (-2 \cdot 3, -4 \cdot 3) \rightarrow X'(-6, -12)$

   $Y(1, 3) \rightarrow (1 \cdot 3, 3 \cdot 3) \rightarrow Y'(3, 9)$

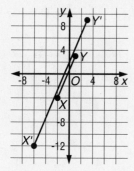

4. $A(2, 2) \rightarrow (2 \cdot 1, 2 \cdot 1) \rightarrow A'(2, 2)$

   $B(-1, 4) \rightarrow (-1 \cdot 1, 4 \cdot 1) \rightarrow B'(-1, 4)$

   $C(-3, -5) \rightarrow (-3 \cdot 1, -5 \cdot 1) \rightarrow C'(-3, -5)$

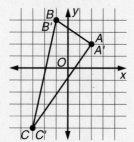

5. $A(2, 2) \rightarrow (2 \cdot 0.5, 2 \cdot 0.5) \rightarrow A'(1, 1)$

   $B(-1, 4) \rightarrow (-1 \cdot 0.5, 4 \cdot 0.5) \rightarrow B'(-0.5, 2)$

   $C(-3, -5) \rightarrow (-3 \cdot 0.5, -5 \cdot 0.5) \rightarrow C'(-1.5, -2.5)$

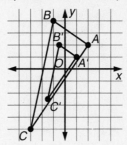

6. $A(2, 2) \rightarrow (2 \cdot 2, 2 \cdot 2) \rightarrow A'(4, 4)$

   $B(-1, 4) \rightarrow (-1 \cdot 2, 4 \cdot 2) \rightarrow B'(-2, 8)$

   $C(-3, -5) \rightarrow (-3 \cdot 2, -5 \cdot 2) \rightarrow C'(-6, -10)$

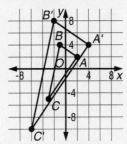

7. $A(2, 2) \rightarrow (2 \cdot 3, 2 \cdot 3) \rightarrow A'(6, 6)$

   $B(-1, 4) \rightarrow (-1 \cdot 3, 4 \cdot 3) \rightarrow B'(-3, 12)$

   $C(-3, -5) \rightarrow (-3 \cdot 3, -5 \cdot 3) \rightarrow C'(-9, -15)$

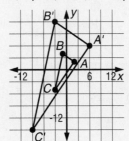

8. $A(2, 2) \rightarrow \left(2 \cdot \frac{1}{4}, 2 \cdot \frac{1}{4}\right) \rightarrow A'\left(\frac{1}{2}, \frac{1}{2}\right)$

   $B'(-1, 4) \rightarrow \left(-1 \cdot \frac{1}{4}, 4 \cdot \frac{1}{4}\right) \rightarrow B'\left(-\frac{1}{4}, 1\right)$

   $C(-3, -5) \rightarrow \left(-3 \cdot \frac{1}{4}, -5 \cdot \frac{1}{4}\right) \rightarrow C'\left(-\frac{3}{4}, -\frac{5}{4}\right)$

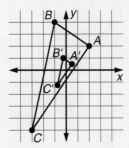

Lesson 9-9

1. $\tan X = \frac{YZ}{XZ}$ 2. $\tan Y = \frac{XZ}{YZ}$ 3. $\tan A = \frac{BC}{AC}$

$\tan X = \frac{4}{3}$ $\tan Y = \frac{3}{4}$ $\tan A = \frac{1}{1}$

$\tan A = 1$

4. $\tan B = \frac{AC}{BC}$ 5. $\tan X = \frac{4}{3}$ 6. $\tan Y = \frac{3}{4}$

$\tan B = \frac{1}{1}$ $m \angle X \approx 53°$ $m \angle Y \approx 37°$

$\tan B = 1$

7. $\tan A = 1$ 8. $\tan B = 1$

$m \angle A = 45°$ $m \angle B = 45°$

Lesson 9-10

PAGE 606

1. $\cos A = \frac{AC}{AB}$ 2. $\sin A = \frac{BC}{AB}$ 3. $\cos A = \frac{AC}{AB}$

$\cos A = \frac{1.4}{2}$ $\sin A = \frac{1.4}{2}$ $\cos A = \frac{1.4}{2}$

$\cos A = \frac{14}{20}$ $\sin A = \frac{14}{20}$ $\cos A = 0.7$

$\cos A = \frac{7}{10}$ $\sin A = \frac{7}{10}$ $m \angle A = 45°$

4. $\sin B = \frac{AC}{AB}$ 5. $\cos B = \frac{BC}{AB}$ 6. $\sin B = \frac{AC}{AB}$

$\sin B = \frac{1.4}{2}$ $\cos B = \frac{1.4}{2}$ $\sin B = \frac{1.4}{2}$

$\sin B = \frac{14}{20}$ $\cos B = \frac{14}{20}$ $\sin B = 0.7$

$\sin B = \frac{7}{10}$ $\cos B = \frac{7}{10}$ $m \angle B = 45°$

7. $\cos Y = \frac{ZY}{XY}$ 8. $\sin X = \frac{ZY}{XY}$

$\cos Y = \frac{7.68}{10}$ $\sin X = \frac{7.68}{10}$

$\cos Y = \frac{768}{1000}$ $\sin X = \frac{768}{1000}$

$\cos Y = \frac{96}{125}$ $\sin X = \frac{96}{125}$

9. $\sin X = \frac{ZY}{XY}$ 10. $\cos Y = \frac{ZY}{XY}$

$\sin X = \frac{7.68}{10}$ $\cos Y = \frac{7.68}{10}$

$\sin X = 0.768$ $\cos Y = 0.768$

$m \angle X \approx 50°$ $m \angle Y \approx 40°$

Lesson 10-1

PAGE 606

1. $\frac{2}{100} = 2\%$

2. $\frac{3}{25} = \frac{r}{100}$

$3 \cdot 100 = 25r$

$300 = 25r$

$\frac{300}{25} = \frac{25r}{25}$

$12 = r$

$\frac{3}{25} = 12\%$

3. $\frac{20}{25} = \frac{r}{100}$

$20 \cdot 100 = 25r$

$2,000 = 25r$

$\frac{2,000}{25} = \frac{25r}{25}$

$80 = r$

$\frac{20}{25} = 80\%$

4. $\frac{10}{16} = \frac{r}{100}$

$10 \cdot 100 = 16r$

$1,000 = 16r$

$\frac{1,000}{16} = \frac{16r}{16}$

$62.5 = r$

$\frac{10}{16} = 62.5\%$

5. $\frac{4}{6} = \frac{r}{100}$

$4 \cdot 100 = 6r$

$400 = 6r$

$\frac{400}{6} = \frac{6r}{6}$

$66\frac{2}{3} = r$

$\frac{4}{6} = 66\frac{2}{3}\%$

6. $\frac{1}{4} = \frac{r}{100}$

$1 \cdot 100 = 4r$

$100 = 4r$

$\frac{100}{4} = \frac{4r}{4}$

$25 = r$

$\frac{1}{4} = 25\%$

7. $\frac{26}{100} = 26\%$

8. $\frac{3}{10} = \frac{r}{100}$

$3 \cdot 100 = 10r$

$300 = 10r$

$\frac{300}{10} = \frac{10r}{10}$

$30 = r$

$\frac{3}{10} = 30\%$

9. $\frac{21}{50} = \frac{r}{100}$

$21 \cdot 100 = 50r$

$2,100 = 50r$

$\frac{2,100}{50} = \frac{50r}{50}$

$42 = r$

$\frac{21}{50} = 42\%$

10. $\frac{7}{8} = \frac{r}{100}$

$7 \cdot 100 = 8r$

$700 = 8r$

$\frac{700}{8} = \frac{8r}{8}$

$87.5 = r$

$\frac{7}{8} = 87.5\%$

11. $\frac{1}{3} = \frac{r}{100}$

$1 \cdot 100 = 3r$

$100 = 3r$

$\frac{100}{3} = \frac{3r}{3}$

$33\frac{1}{3} = r$

$\frac{1}{3} = 33\frac{1}{3}\%$

12. $\frac{2}{3} = \frac{r}{100}$

$2 \cdot 100 = 3r$

$200 = 3r$

$\frac{200}{3} = \frac{3r}{3}$

$66\frac{2}{3} = r$

$\frac{2}{3} = 66\frac{2}{3}\%$

13.
$$\frac{2}{5} = \frac{r}{100}$$
$$2 \cdot 100 = 5r$$
$$200 = 5r$$
$$\frac{200}{5} = \frac{5r}{5}$$
$$40 = r$$
$$\frac{2}{5} = 40\%$$

14.
$$\frac{2}{50} = \frac{r}{100}$$
$$2 \cdot 100 = 50r$$
$$200 = 50r$$
$$\frac{200}{50} = \frac{50r}{50}$$
$$4 = r$$
$$\frac{2}{50} = 4\%$$

25.
$$\frac{P}{B} = \frac{r}{100}$$
$$\frac{39}{B} = \frac{5}{100}$$
$$39 \cdot 100 = 5B$$
$$3,900 = 5B$$
$$\frac{3,900}{5} = \frac{5B}{5}$$
$$780 = B$$

26.
$$\frac{P}{B} = \frac{r}{100}$$
$$\frac{P}{200} = \frac{19}{100}$$
$$100P = 200 \cdot 19$$
$$100P = 3,800$$
$$\frac{100P}{100} = \frac{3,800}{100}$$
$$P = 38$$

15.
$$\frac{8}{10} = \frac{r}{100}$$
$$8 \cdot 100 = 10r$$
$$800 = 10r$$
$$\frac{800}{10} = \frac{10r}{10}$$
$$80 = r$$
$$\frac{8}{10} = 80\%$$

16.
$$\frac{5}{12} = \frac{r}{100}$$
$$5 \cdot 100 = 12r$$
$$500 = 12r$$
$$\frac{500}{12} = \frac{12r}{12}$$
$$41\frac{2}{3} = r$$
$$\frac{5}{12} = 41\frac{2}{3}\%$$

27.
$$\frac{P}{B} = \frac{r}{100}$$
$$\frac{28}{7} = \frac{r}{100}$$
$$28 \cdot 100 = 7r$$
$$2,800 = 7r$$
$$\frac{2,800}{7} = \frac{7r}{7}$$
$$400 = r$$
$$400\%$$

28.
$$\frac{P}{B} = \frac{r}{100}$$
$$\frac{24}{72} = \frac{r}{100}$$
$$24 \cdot 100 = 72r$$
$$2,400 = 72r$$
$$\frac{2,400}{72} = \frac{72r}{72}$$
$$33\frac{1}{3} = r$$
$$33\frac{1}{3}\%$$

17.
$$\frac{7}{10} = \frac{r}{100}$$
$$7 \cdot 100 = 10r$$
$$700 = 10r$$
$$\frac{700}{10} = \frac{10r}{10}$$
$$70 = r$$
$$\frac{7}{10} = 70\%$$

18.
$$\frac{9}{20} = \frac{r}{100}$$
$$9 \cdot 100 = 20r$$
$$900 = 20r$$
$$\frac{900}{20} = \frac{20r}{20}$$
$$45 = r$$
$$\frac{9}{20} = 45\%$$

29.
$$\frac{P}{B} = \frac{r}{100}$$
$$\frac{9}{B} = \frac{33\frac{1}{3}}{100}$$
$$9 \cdot 100 = 33\frac{1}{3}B$$
$$900 = \frac{100}{3}B$$
$$\frac{3}{100} \cdot 900 = \frac{100}{3}B \cdot \frac{3}{100}$$
$$27 = B$$

30.
$$\frac{P}{B} = \frac{r}{100}$$
$$\frac{P}{134} = \frac{55}{100}$$
$$100P = 134 \cdot 55$$
$$100P = 7,370$$
$$\frac{100P}{100} = \frac{7,370}{100}$$
$$P = 73.7$$

19.
$$\frac{1}{2} = \frac{r}{100}$$
$$1 \cdot 100 = 2r$$
$$100 = 2r$$
$$\frac{100}{2} = \frac{2r}{2}$$
$$50 = r$$
$$\frac{1}{2} = 50\%$$

20.
$$\frac{3}{20} = \frac{r}{100}$$
$$3 \cdot 100 = 20r$$
$$300 = 20r$$
$$\frac{300}{20} = \frac{20r}{20}$$
$$15 = r$$
$$\frac{3}{20} = 15\%$$

21.
$$\frac{10}{25} = \frac{r}{100}$$
$$10 \cdot 100 = 25r$$
$$1,000 = 25r$$
$$\frac{1,000}{25} = \frac{25r}{25}$$
$$40 = r$$
$$\frac{10}{25} = 40\%$$

22.
$$\frac{3}{8} = \frac{r}{100}$$
$$3 \cdot 100 = 8r$$
$$300 = 8r$$
$$\frac{300}{8} = \frac{8r}{8}$$
$$37.5 = r$$
$$\frac{3}{8} = 37.5\%$$

Lesson 10-2

PAGE 607

1. $0.35 = \frac{35}{100}$
$= 35\%$

2. $14.23 = \frac{1423}{100}$
$= 1,423\%$

3. $0.9 = 0.90$
$= \frac{90}{100}$
$= 90\%$

4. $0.13 = \frac{13}{100}$
$= 13\%$

23.
$$\frac{4}{20} = \frac{r}{100}$$
$$4 \cdot 100 = 20r$$
$$400 = 20r$$
$$\frac{400}{20} = \frac{20r}{20}$$
$$20 = r$$
$$\frac{4}{20} = 20\%$$

24.
$$\frac{19}{25} = \frac{r}{100}$$
$$19 \cdot 100 = 25r$$
$$1,900 = 25r$$
$$\frac{1,900}{25} = \frac{25r}{25}$$
$$76 = r$$
$$\frac{19}{25} = 76\%$$

5. $6.21 = \frac{621}{100}$
$= 621\%$

6. $0.23 = \frac{23}{100}$
$= 23\%$

7. $0.08 = \frac{8}{100}$
$= 8\%$

8. $0.036 = \frac{36}{1000}$
$= \frac{3.6}{100}$
$= 3.6\%$

9. $2.34 = \frac{234}{100}$
$= 234\%$

10. $0.39 = \frac{39}{100}$
$= 39\%$

11. $40\% = \dfrac{40}{100}$
$= \dfrac{2}{5}$

12. $24.5\% = \dfrac{24.5}{100}$
$= \dfrac{245}{1000}$
$= \dfrac{49}{200}$

3. $0.02\% = \dfrac{0.02}{100}$
$= \dfrac{2}{10,000}$
$= \dfrac{1}{5,000}$

4. $620\% = \dfrac{620}{100}$
$= \dfrac{31}{5}$
$= 6\dfrac{1}{5}$

13. $42\% = \dfrac{42}{100}$
$= \dfrac{21}{50}$

14. $33\frac{1}{3}\% = \dfrac{33\frac{1}{3}}{100}$
$= \dfrac{\frac{100}{3}}{100}$
$= \dfrac{100}{3} \div 100$
$= \dfrac{100}{3} \cdot \dfrac{1}{100}$
$= \dfrac{100}{300}$
$= \dfrac{1}{3}$

5. $0.7\% = \dfrac{0.7}{100}$
$= \dfrac{7}{1,000}$

6. $111.5\% = \dfrac{111.5}{100}$
$= \dfrac{1,115}{1,000}$
$= \dfrac{223}{200}$
$= 1\dfrac{23}{200}$

15. $81\% = \dfrac{81}{100}$

16. $8\% = \dfrac{8}{100}$
$= \dfrac{2}{25}$

17. $55\% = \dfrac{55}{100}$
$= \dfrac{11}{20}$

7. $\dfrac{7}{35}\% = \dfrac{\frac{7}{35}}{100}$
$= \dfrac{7}{35} \div 100$
$= \dfrac{1}{5} \cdot \dfrac{1}{100}$
$= \dfrac{1}{500}$

8. $0.72\% = \dfrac{0.72}{100}$
$= \dfrac{72}{10,000}$
$= \dfrac{9}{1,250}$

18. $4.5\% = \dfrac{4.5}{100}$
$= \dfrac{45}{1000}$
$= \dfrac{9}{200}$

19. $16.5\% = \dfrac{16.5}{100}$
$= \dfrac{165}{1000}$
$= \dfrac{33}{200}$

20. $2\% = \dfrac{2}{100}$
$= \dfrac{1}{50}$

9. $0.004\% = \dfrac{0.004}{100}$
$= \dfrac{4}{100,000}$
$= \dfrac{1}{25,000}$

10. $364\% = \dfrac{364}{100}$
$= \dfrac{91}{25}$
$= 3\dfrac{16}{25}$

21. $2\% = \dfrac{2}{100}$
$= 0.02$

22. $25\% = \dfrac{25}{100}$
$= 0.25$

23. $29\% = \dfrac{29}{100}$
$= 0.29$

11. $0.15\% = \dfrac{0.15}{100}$
$= \dfrac{15}{10,000}$
$= \dfrac{3}{2,000}$

12. $1,250\% = \dfrac{1,250}{100}$
$= \dfrac{25}{2}$
$= 12\dfrac{1}{2}$

24. $6.2\% = \dfrac{6.2}{100}$
$= \dfrac{62}{1000}$
$= 0.062$

25. $16.8\% = \dfrac{16.8}{100}$
$= \dfrac{168}{1000}$
$= 0.168$

26. $14\% = \dfrac{14}{100}$
$= 0.14$

13. $\dfrac{9}{10}\% = \dfrac{\frac{9}{10}}{100}$
$= \dfrac{9}{10} \div 100$
$= \dfrac{9}{10} \cdot \dfrac{1}{100}$
$= \dfrac{9}{1,000}$

14. $730\% = \dfrac{730}{100}$
$= \dfrac{73}{10}$
$= 7\dfrac{3}{10}$

27. $23.7\% = \dfrac{23.7}{100}$
$= \dfrac{237}{1000}$
$= 0.237$

28. $42\% = \dfrac{42}{100}$
$= 0.42$

29. $25.4\% = \dfrac{25.4}{100}$
$= \dfrac{254}{1000}$
$= 0.254$

30. $98\% = \dfrac{98}{100}$
$= 0.98$

15. $100.01\% = \dfrac{100.01}{100}$
$= \dfrac{10,001}{10,000}$
$= 1\dfrac{1}{10,000}$

16. $0.07\% = \dfrac{0.07}{100}$
$= \dfrac{7}{10,000}$
$= 0.0007$

Lesson 10-3

PAGE 607

1. $540\% = \dfrac{540}{100}$
$= \dfrac{27}{5}$
$= 5\dfrac{2}{5}$

2. $\dfrac{25}{50}\% = \dfrac{\frac{25}{50}}{100}$
$= \dfrac{25}{50} \div 100$
$= \dfrac{25}{50} \cdot \dfrac{1}{100}$
$= \dfrac{25}{5,000} = \dfrac{1}{200}$

17. $5\frac{2}{3}\% = \dfrac{\frac{17}{3}}{100}$
$= \dfrac{17}{3} \div 100$
$= \dfrac{17}{3} \cdot \dfrac{1}{100}$
$= \dfrac{17}{300}$
$= 0.05\overline{6}$

18. $310\% = \dfrac{310}{100}$
$= \dfrac{31}{10}$
$= 3.1$

19. $6.05\% = \dfrac{6.05}{100}$
$= \dfrac{605}{10,000}$
$= 0.0605$

20. $7,652\% = \dfrac{7652}{100}$
$= 76.52$

21. $\frac{12}{50}\% = \frac{\frac{12}{50}}{100}$

$= \frac{12}{50} \div 100$

$= \frac{6}{25} \cdot \frac{1}{100}$

$= \frac{6}{2,500}$

$= \frac{24}{10,000}$

$= 0.0024$

22. $0.93\% = \frac{0.93}{100}$

$= \frac{93}{10,000}$

$= 0.0093$

23. $200\% = \frac{200}{100}$

$= \frac{2}{1}$

$= 2$

24. $197.6\% = \frac{197.6}{100}$

$= \frac{1,976}{1,000}$

$= 1.976$

25. $10.75\% = \frac{10.75}{100}$

$= \frac{1,075}{10,000}$

$= 0.1075$

26. $0.66\% = \frac{0.66}{100}$

$= \frac{66}{10,000}$

$= 0.0066$

27. $417\% = \frac{417}{100}$

$= 4.17$

28. $7.76\% = \frac{7.76}{100}$

$= \frac{776}{10,000}$

$= 0.0776$

29. $390\% = \frac{390}{100}$

$= \frac{39}{10}$

$= 3.9$

30. $10\frac{7}{10}\% = \frac{10\frac{7}{10}}{100}$

$= \frac{107}{10} \div 100$

$= \frac{107}{10} \cdot \frac{1}{100}$

$= \frac{107}{1,000}$

$= 0.107$

Lesson 10-5

PAGE 607

1. 33% is about $\frac{1}{3}$.

$\frac{1}{3}$ of 12 is 4.

33% of 12 is about 4.

2. 24% is about 25% or $\frac{1}{4}$.

84 is about 80.

$\frac{1}{4}$ of 80 is 20.

24% of 84 is about 20.

3. 39% is about 40% or $\frac{2}{5}$.

$\frac{2}{5}$ of 50 is 20.

39% of 50 is about 20.

4. 1.5% is about 2%.

135 is about 100.

2% of 100 is 2.

1.5% of 135 is about 2.

5. About 18 out 49 squares are shaded, or about 20 out of 50 or about 40%.

6. About 22 out of 49 squares are shaded, or about 20 out of 50 or about 40%.

7. About 8 out of 49 squares are shaded, or about 8 out of 50 or about 16%.

8. 11 is about 10.

99 is about 100.

$\frac{10}{100} = 10\%$

9. 28 is about 30.

89 is about 90.

$\frac{30}{90} = \frac{1}{3} = 33\frac{1}{3}\%$

10. 9 is about 10.

$\frac{10}{20} = \frac{1}{2} = 50\%$

11. 270 is about 250.

$\frac{25}{250} = \frac{1}{10} = 10\%$

12. 25 is about 24.

$\frac{6}{24} = \frac{1}{4} = 25\%$

13. 17 is about 20.

65 is about 60.

$\frac{20}{60} = \frac{1}{3} = 33\frac{1}{3}\%$

14. 72 is about 70.

$\frac{70}{280} = \frac{1}{4} = 25\%$

15. 181 is about 180.

$\frac{120}{180} = \frac{2}{3} = 66\frac{2}{3}\%$

Lesson 10-6

PAGE 608

1. $P = R \cdot B$

$P = 0.05 \cdot 73$

$P = 3.65$

$3.65

2. $P = R \cdot B$

$P = 0.15 \cdot 15$

$P = 2.25$

3. $P = R \cdot B$

$P = 0.80 \cdot 12$

$P = 9.6$

$9.60

4. $P = R \cdot B$

$P = 0.073 \cdot 500$

$P = 36.5$

5. $P = R \cdot B$

$P = 0.21 \cdot 720$

$P = 151.2$

$151.20

6. $P = R \cdot B$

$P = 0.12 \cdot 62.5$

$P = 7.5$

$7.50

7. $P = R \cdot B$

$P = 0.003 \cdot 155$

$P = 0.465$

8. $P = R \cdot B$

$P = 0.75 \cdot 450$

$P = 337.5$

$337.50

9. $P = R \cdot B$

$P = 0.072 \cdot 10$

$P = 0.72$

10. $P = R \cdot B$

$P = 0.101 \cdot 60$

$P = 6.06$

$6.06

11. $P = R \cdot B$

$P = 0.23 \cdot 47$

$P = 10.81$

12. $P = R \cdot B$

$P = 0.89 \cdot 654$

$P = 582.06$

13. $P = R \cdot B$

$20 = R \cdot 64$

$\frac{20}{64} = \frac{R \cdot 64}{64}$

$0.3125 = R$

$R = 31.25\%$

14. $P = R \cdot B$

$69 = R \cdot 200$

$\frac{69}{200} = \frac{R \cdot 200}{200}$

$0.345 = R$

$R = 34.5\%$

15.
$$P = R \cdot B$$
$$70 = R \cdot 150$$
$$\frac{70}{150} = \frac{R \cdot 150}{150}$$
$$0.4\overline{6} = R$$
$$R = 46\tfrac{2}{3}\%$$

16.
$$P = R \cdot B$$
$$26 = 0.30 \cdot B$$
$$\frac{26}{0.3} = \frac{0.3 \cdot B}{0.3}$$
$$86.\overline{6} = B$$
$$B = 86\tfrac{2}{3}$$

17.
$$P = R \cdot B$$
$$7 = 0.14 \cdot B$$
$$\frac{7}{0.14} = \frac{0.14 \cdot B}{0.14}$$
$$50 = B$$

18.
$$P = R \cdot B$$
$$35.5 = R \cdot 150$$
$$\frac{35.5}{150} = \frac{R \cdot 150}{150}$$
$$0.23\overline{6} = R$$
$$R = 23\tfrac{2}{3}\%$$

19.
$$P = R \cdot B$$
$$17 = R \cdot 25$$
$$\frac{17}{25} = \frac{R \cdot 25}{25}$$
$$0.68 = R$$
$$R = 68\%$$

20.
$$P = R \cdot B$$
$$152 = 0.02 \cdot B$$
$$\frac{152}{0.02} = \frac{0.02 \cdot B}{0.02}$$
$$7{,}600 = B$$

Lesson 10-7

PAGE 608

1. Shoes: $0.44 \times 360 \approx 158°$

Apparel: $0.30 \times 360 = 108°$

Equipment: $0.26 \times 360 \approx 94°$

2. Heating/cooling: $0.51 \times 360° \approx 184°$

Appliances: $0.28 \times 360° \approx 101°$

Lights: $0.21 \times 360° \approx 75°$

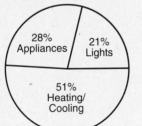

3. Primary job: $0.82 \times 360° \approx 295°$

Secondary Job: $0.09 \times 360° \approx 32°$

Investments: $0.05 \times 360° = 18°$

Other: $0.04 \times 360 \approx 15°$

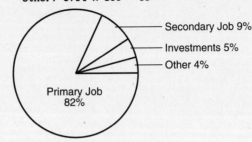

4. White: $0.30 \times 360° = 108°$

Black: $0.28 \times 360° \approx 101°$

Hispanic: $0.24 \times 360° \approx 86°$

Asian: $0.18 \times 360° \approx 65°$

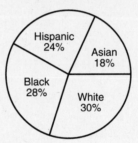

Lesson 10-8

PAGE 608

1. $150 - 100 = 50$
$$\frac{50}{100} = \frac{1}{2} = 0.5$$
50% increase

2. $60 - 50 = 10$
$$\frac{10}{50} = \frac{1}{5} = 0.2$$
20% increase

3. $1.20 - 0.40 = 0.80$
$$\frac{0.8}{0.4} = \frac{8}{4} = 2$$
200% increase

4. $450 - 315 = 135$
$$\frac{135}{450} = \frac{3}{10} = 0.3$$
30% decrease

5. $1.00 - 0.5 = 0.50$
$$\frac{0.50}{0.50} = 1$$
100% increase

6. $2.75 - 2.50 = 0.25$
$$\frac{0.25}{2.5} = 0.1$$
10% increase

7. $50 - 40 = 10$
$$\frac{10}{50} = \frac{1}{5} = 0.2$$
20% decrease

8. $1.00 - 0.50 = 0.50$
$$\frac{0.5}{0.5} = 1$$
100% increase

9. $35 - 29 = 6$
$$\frac{6}{35} = \frac{r}{100}$$
$$600 = 35r$$
$$\frac{600}{35} = \frac{35r}{35}$$
$$71 \approx r$$
17% decrease

10. $550 - 425 = 125$
$$\frac{125}{550} = \frac{r}{100}$$
$$12{,}500 = 550r$$
$$\frac{12{,}500}{550} = \frac{550r}{550}$$
$$23 \approx r$$
23% decrease

11. $88 - 72 = 16$

$$\frac{16}{72} = \frac{r}{100}$$

$$1{,}660 = 72r$$

$$\frac{1{,}600}{72} = \frac{72r}{72}$$

$$22 \approx r$$

22% increase

13. $28 - 19 = 9$

$$\frac{9}{28} = \frac{r}{100}$$

$$900 = 28r$$

$$\frac{900}{28} = \frac{28r}{28}$$

$$32 = r$$

32% decrease

15. $78 - 44 = 34$

$$\frac{34}{78} = \frac{r}{100}$$

$$3{,}400 = 78r$$

$$\frac{3{,}400}{78} = \frac{78r}{78}$$

$$44 \approx r$$

44% decrease

12. $35 - 25 = 10$

$$\frac{10}{25} = \frac{r}{100}$$

$$1{,}000 = 25r$$

$$\frac{1{,}000}{25} = \frac{25r}{25}$$

$$40 = r$$

40% increase

14. $55 - 46 = 9$

$$\frac{9}{46} = \frac{r}{100}$$

$$900 = 46r$$

$$\frac{900}{46} = \frac{46r}{46}$$

$$20 \approx r$$

20% increase

16. $120 - 75 = 45$

$$\frac{45}{120} = \frac{r}{100}$$

$$4{,}500 = 120r$$

$$\frac{4{,}500}{120} = \frac{120r}{120}$$

$$37.5 = r$$

38% decrease

Lesson 10-9

PAGE 609

1. $P = 0.35 \cdot 4{,}220$
$P = 1{,}477$
$4{,}220 - 1{,}477 = 2{,}743$
Discount: $1,477
Sale Price: $2,743

2. $P = 0.10 \cdot 14$
$P = 1.4$
$14 - 1.4 = 12.6$
Discount: $1.40
Sale Price: $12.60

3. $P = 0.40 \cdot 29$
$P = 11.6$
$29 - 11.6 = 17.4$
Discount: $11.60
Sale Price: $17.40

4. $P = 0.25 \cdot 38$
$P = 9.5$
$38 - 9.5 = 28.5$
Discount: $9.50
Sale Price: $28.50

5. $P = 0.5 \cdot 45$
$P = 22.5$
$45 - 22.5 = 22.5$
Discount: $22.50
Sale Price: $22.50

6. $P = 0.25 \cdot 280$
$P = 70$
$280 - 70 = 210$
Discount: $70
Sale Price: $210

7. $P = 0.30 \cdot 3{,}540$
$P = 1{,}062$
$3{,}540 - 1{,}062 = 2{,}478$
Discount: $1,062
Sale Price: $2,478

8. $P = 0.20 \cdot 15.95$
$P = 3.19$
$15.95 - 3.19 = 12.76$
Discount: $3.19
Sale Price: $12.76

9. $35 = R \cdot 250$

$$\frac{35}{250} = \frac{R \cdot 250}{250}$$

$$0.14 = R$$

Discount is 14%.

10. $2.48 = R \cdot 15.50$

$$\frac{2.48}{15.50} = \frac{R \cdot 15.50}{15.50}$$

$$0.16 = R$$

Discount is 16%.

11. $11 = R \cdot 27.50$

$$\frac{11}{27.50} = \frac{R \cdot 27.50}{27.50}$$

$$0.4 = R$$

Discount is 40%.

Lesson 10-10

PAGE 609

1. $I = prt$
$I = (500)(0.07)(2)$
$I = \$70$

2. $I = prt$
$I = (2{,}500)(0.065)(3)$
$I = \$487.50$

3. $I = prt$
$I = (8{,}000)(0.06)(1)$
$I = \$480$

4. $I = prt$
$I = (1{,}890)(0.09)(3.5)$
$I = \$595.35$

5. $I = prt$
$I = (300)(0.01)(3)$
$I = \$90$
$\$300 + 90 = \$390$

6. $I = prt$
$I = (3{,}200)(0.08)(0.5)$
$I = \$128$
$\$3{,}200 + 128 = \$3{,}328$

7. $I = prt$
$I = (20{,}000)(0.14)(20)$
$I = \$56{,}000$
$\$20{,}000 + 56{,}000 = \$76{,}000$

8. $I = prt$
$I = (4{,}000)(0.125)(4)$
$I = \$2{,}000$
$\$4{,}000 + 2{,}000 = \$6{,}000$

9. $I = prt$
$526.50 = 4{,}500 \cdot r \cdot 3$
$526.50 = 13{,}500r$

$$\frac{526.50}{13{,}500} = \frac{13{,}500r}{13{,}500}$$

$$0.039 = r$$

Interest rate is 3.9%.

10. $I = prt$
$878.75 = 7{,}400 \cdot r \cdot 2.5$
$878.75 = 18{,}500r$

$$\frac{878.75}{18{,}500} = \frac{18{,}500r}{18{,}500}$$

$$0.0475 = r$$

Interest rate is 4.75%.

Lesson 11-1

PAGE 609

1. $f(n) = -4n$

n	$-4n$	$f(n)$
-2	$-4(-2)$	8
-1	$-4(-1)$	4
0	$-4(0)$	0
1	$-4(1)$	-4
2	$-4(2)$	-8

2. $f(n) = n + 6$

n	$n + 6$	$f(n)$
-6	$-6 + 6$	0
-4	$-4 + 6$	2
-2	$-2 + 6$	4
0	$0 + 6$	6
2	$2 + 6$	8

3. $f(n) = 3n + 2$

n	3n + 2	f(n)
-3.5	3(-3.5) + 2	-8.5
-2.5	3(-2.5) + 2	-5.5
-1.5	3(-1.5) + 2	-2.5
0	3(0) + 2	2
1.5	3(1.5) + 2	6.5

4. $f(n) = 2n - 6$

n	2n - 6	f(n)
$-2\frac{1}{2}$	$2\left(-2\frac{1}{2}\right) - 6$	-11
-1	2(-1) - 6	-8
$-\frac{1}{4}$	$2\left(-\frac{1}{4}\right) - 6$	$-6\frac{1}{2}$
0	2(0) - 6	-6
$\frac{1}{2}$	$2\left(\frac{1}{2}\right) - 6$	-5

5. $f(n) = -\frac{1}{2}n + 4$

n	$-\frac{1}{2}n + 4$	f(n)
-4	$-\frac{1}{2}(-4) + 4$	6
-2	$-\frac{1}{2}(-2) + 4$	5
0	$-\frac{1}{2}(0) + 4$	4
2.5	$-\frac{1}{2}(2.5) + 4$	2.75
6	$-\frac{1}{2}(6) + 4$	1

6. $f(n) = -5n + 1$

n	-5n + 1	f(n)
-4	-5(-4) + 1	21
-2	-5(-2) + 1	11
0	-5(0) + 1	1
1	-5(1) + 1	-4
4	-5(4) + 1	-19

Lesson 11-2

PAGE 610

1. $f(n) = 6n + 2$

n	6n + 2	f(n)	(n, f(n))
-3	6(-3) + 2	-16	(-3, -16)
-1	6(-1) + 2	-4	(-1, -4)
1	6(1) + 2	8	(1, 8)
$\frac{7}{3}$	$6\left(\frac{7}{3}\right) + 2$	16	$\left(\frac{7}{3}, 16\right)$

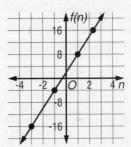

2. $f(n) = -2n + 3$

n	-2n + 3	f(n)	(n, f(n))
-2	-2(-2) + 3	7	(-2, 7)
-1	-2(-1) + 3	5	(-1, 5)
0	-2(0) + 3	3	(0, 3)
1	-2(1) + 3	1	(1, 1)
2	-2(2) + 3	-1	(2, -1)

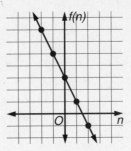

3. $f(n) = 4.5n$

n	4.5n	f(n)	(n, f(n))
-4	4.5(-4)	-18	(-4, -18)
-2	4.5(-2)	-9	(-2, -9)
0	4.5(0)	0	(0, 0)
1	4.5(1)	4.5	(1, 4.5)
6	4.5(6)	27	(6, 27)

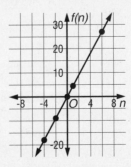

4. $f(n) = \dfrac{8}{n}$

n	$\dfrac{8}{n}$	$f(n)$	$(n, f(n))$
-8	$\dfrac{8}{-8}$	-1	(-8, -1)
-4	$\dfrac{8}{-4}$	-2	(-4, -2)
-1	$\dfrac{8}{-1}$	-8	(-1, -8)
1	$\dfrac{8}{1}$	8	(1, 8)
4	$\dfrac{8}{4}$	2	(4, 2)
8	$\dfrac{8}{8}$	1	(8, 1)

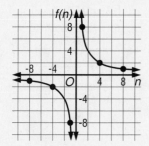

5. $f(n) = \dfrac{2}{3}n + 1$

n	$\dfrac{2}{3}n + 1$	$f(n)$	$(n, f(n))$
-3	$\dfrac{2}{3}(-3) + 1$	-1	(-3, -1)
0	$\dfrac{2}{3}(0) + 1$	1	(0, 1)
3	$\dfrac{2}{3}(3) + 1$	3	(3, 3)
6	$\dfrac{2}{3}(6) + 1$	5	(6, 5)

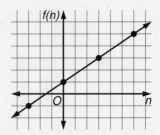

6. $f(n) = n^2 - 1$

n	$n^2 - 1$	$f(n)$	$(n, f(n))$
-2	$(-2)^2 - 1$	3	(-2, 3)
-1	$(-1)^2 - 1$	0	(-1, 0)
0	$(0)^2 - 1$	-1	(0, -1)
1	$(1)^2 - 1$	0	(1, 0)
2	$(2)^2 - 1$	3	(2, 3)

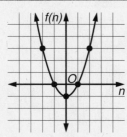

7. $f(n) = 3.5n$

n	$3.5n$	$f(n)$	$(n, f(n))$
-1	3.5(-1)	-3.5	(-1, -3.5)
0	3.5(0)	0	(0, 0)
1	3.5(1)	3.5	(1, 3.5)
2	3.5(2)	7	(2, 7)

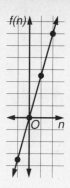

8. $f(n) = 4n - 1$

n	$4n - 1$	$f(n)$	$(n, f(n))$
$-\dfrac{1}{2}$	$4\left(-\dfrac{1}{2}\right) - 1$	-3	$\left(-\dfrac{1}{2}, -3\right)$
0	$4(0) - 1$	-1	(0, -1)
$\dfrac{1}{2}$	$4\left(\dfrac{1}{2}\right) - 1$	1	$\left(\dfrac{1}{2}, 1\right)$
1	$4(1) - 1$	3	(1, 3)

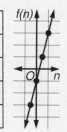

9. $f(n) = \dfrac{3}{5}n + \left(-\dfrac{1}{5}\right)$

n	$\dfrac{3}{5}n + \left(-\dfrac{1}{5}\right)$	$f(n)$	$(n, f(n))$
-5	$\dfrac{3}{5}(-5) + \left(-\dfrac{1}{5}\right)$	$-3\dfrac{1}{5}$	$\left(-5, -3\dfrac{1}{5}\right)$
0	$\dfrac{3}{5}(0) + \left(-\dfrac{1}{5}\right)$	$-\dfrac{1}{5}$	$\left(0, -\dfrac{1}{5}\right)$
5	$\dfrac{3}{5}(5) + \left(-\dfrac{1}{5}\right)$	$2\dfrac{4}{5}$	$\left(5, 2\dfrac{4}{5}\right)$

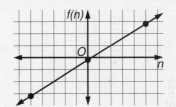

Lesson 11-3

PAGE 610

1. $y = 3x - 1$

x	y
-5	-16
-3	-10
-1	-4
0	-1
1	2

2. $y = \dfrac{x}{4} + 2$

x	y
-8	0
-4	1
0	2
4	3

3. $y = -1.5x - 3$

x	y
-4	3
-2	0
2	-6
6	-12
10	-18

4. $y = 4x - 3$

x	y
-2	-11
$\frac{1}{2}$	-1
0	-3
$2\frac{1}{4}$	6

5. Sample answer: $y = -3x + 5$

x	-3x + 5	y	(x, y)
-1	-3(-1) + 5	8	(-1, 8)
0	-3(0) + 5	5	(0, 5)
1	-3(1) + 5	2	(1, 2)
2	-3(2) + 5	-1	(2, -1)

{(-1, 8), (0, 5), (1, 2), (2, -1)}

6. Sample answer: $y = 2x - 1$

x	2x - 1	y	(x, y)
-1	2(-1) - 1	-3	(-1, -3)
0	2(0) - 1	-1	(0, -1)
1	2(1) - 1	1	(1, 1)
2	2(2) - 1	3	(2, 3)

{(-1, -3), (0, -1), (1, 1), (2, 3)}

7. Sample answer: $y = \frac{2}{3}x + 4$

x	$\frac{2}{3}x + 4$	y	(x, y)
-3	$\frac{2}{3}(-3) + 4$	2	(-3, 2)
0	$\frac{2}{3}(0) + 4$	4	(0, 4)
3	$\frac{2}{3}(3) + 4$	6	(3, 6)
6	$\frac{2}{3}(6) + 4$	8	(6, 8)

{(-3, 2), (0, 4), (3, 6), (6, 8)}

8. Sample answer: $y = -0.4x$

x	-0.4x	y	(x, y)
-5	-0.4(-5)	2	(-5, 2)
0	-0.4(0)	0	(0, 0)
5	-0.4(5)	-2	(5, -2)
10	-0.4(10)	-4	(10, -4)

{(-5, 2), (0, 0), (5, -2), (10, -4)}

9. Sample answer: $y = 12x - 8$

x	12x - 8	y	(x, y)
-1	12(-1) - 8	-20	(-1, -20)
0	12(0) - 8	-8	(0, -8)
1	12(1) - 8	4	(1, 4)
2	12(2) - 8	16	(2, 16)

{(-1, -20), (0, -8), (1, 4), (2, 16)}

10. Sample answer: $y = \frac{3}{4}x + 2$

x	$\frac{3}{4}x + 2$	y	(x, y)
-4	$\frac{3}{4}(-4) + 2$	-1	(-4, -1)
0	$\frac{3}{4}(0) + 2$	2	(0, 2)
4	$\frac{3}{4}(4) + 2$	5	(4, 5)
8	$\frac{3}{4}(8) + 2$	8	(8, 8)

{(-4, -1), (0, 2), (4, 5), (8, 8)}

11. Sample answer: $y = -2.4x - 3$

x	-2.4x - 3	y	(x, y)
-5	-2.4(-5) - 3	9	(-5, 9)
0	-2.4(0) - 3	-3	(0, -3)
5	-2.4(5) - 3	-15	(5, -15)
10	-2.4(10) - 3	-27	(10, -27)

{(-5, 9), (0, -3), (5, -15), (10, -27)}

12. Sample answer: $y = 5x + 7$

x	5x + 7	y	(x, y)
-2	5(-2) + 7	-3	(-2, -3)
-1	5(-1) + 7	2	(-1, 2)
0	5(0) + 7	7	(0, 7)
1	5(1) + 7	12	(1, 12)

{(-2, -3), (-1, 2), (0, 7), (1, 12)}

Lesson 11-4

PAGE 610

1. $y = -5x$

x	-5x	y	(x, y)
-1	-5(-1)	5	(-1, 5)
0	-5(0)	0	(0, 0)
1	-5(1)	-5	(1, -5)

2. $y = 10x - 2$

x	10x - 2	y	(x, y)
$-\frac{1}{2}$	$10\left(-\frac{1}{2}\right) - 2$	-7	$\left(-\frac{1}{2}, -7\right)$
0	10(0) - 2	-2	(0, -2)
$\frac{1}{2}$	$10\left(\frac{1}{2}\right) - 2$	3	$\left(\frac{1}{2}, 3\right)$

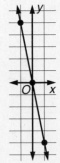

3. $y = -2.5x - 1.5$

x	-2.5x - 1.5	y	(x, y)
-3	-2.5(-3) - 1.5	6	(-3, 6)
-1	-2.5(-1) - 1.5	1	(-1, 1)
1	-2.5(1) - 1.5	-4	(1, -4)

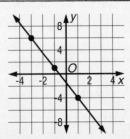

4. $y = 7x + 3$

x	$7(x) + 3$	y	(x, y)
-2	$7(-2) + 3$	-11	$(-2, -11)$
-1	$7(-1) + 3$	-4	$(-1, -4)$
0	$7(0) + 3$	3	$(0, 3)$

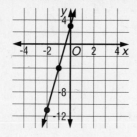

5. $y = \frac{x}{4} - 8$

x	$\frac{x}{4} - 8$	y	(x, y)
0	$\frac{0}{4} - 8$	-8	$(0, -8)$
4	$\frac{4}{4} - 8$	-7	$(4, -7)$
8	$\frac{8}{4} - 8$	-6	$(8, -6)$

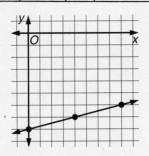

6. $y = 3x + 1$

x	$3x + 1$	y	(x, y)
-1	$3(-1) + 1$	-2	$(-1, -2)$
0	$3(0) + 1$	1	$(0, 1)$
1	$3(1) + 1$	4	$(1, 4)$

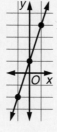

7. $y = 25 - 2x$

x	$25 - 2x$	y	(x, y)
10	$25 - 2(10)$	5	$(10, 5)$
9	$25 - 2(9)$	7	$(9, 7)$
8	$25 - 2(8)$	9	$(8, 9)$

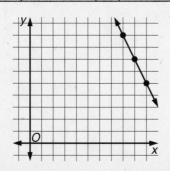

8. $y = \frac{x}{6}$

x	$\frac{x}{6}$	y	(x, y)
-6	$\frac{-6}{6}$	-1	$(-6, -1)$
0	$\frac{0}{6}$	0	$(0, 0)$
6	$\frac{6}{6}$	1	$(6, 1)$

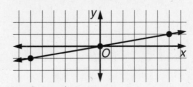

9. $y = -2x + 11$

x	$-2x + 11$	y	(x, y)
4	$-2(4) + 11$	3	$(4, 3)$
5	$-2(5) + 11$	1	$(5, 1)$
6	$-2(6) + 11$	-1	$(6, -1)$

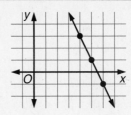

10. $y = 7x - 3$

x	$7x - 3$	y	(x, y)
-1	$7(-1) - 3$	-10	$(-1, -10)$
0	$7(0) - 3$	-3	$(0, -3)$
1	$7(1) - 3$	4	$(1, 4)$

11. $y = \frac{x}{2} + 5$

x	$\frac{x}{2} + 5$	y	(x, y)
-4	$\frac{-4}{2} + 5$	3	$(-4, 3)$
-2	$\frac{-2}{2} + 5$	4	$(-2, 4)$
0	$\frac{0}{2} + 5$	5	$(0, 5)$

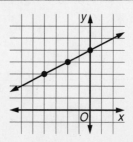

12. $y = 4 - 6x$

x	4 − 6x	y	(x, y)
0	4 − 6(0)	4	(0, 4)
1	4 − 6(1)	−2	(1, −2)
2	4 − 6(2)	−8	(2, −8)

13. $y = -3.5x - 1$

x	−3.5x − 1	y	(x, y)
−2	−3.5(−2) − 1	6	(−2, 6)
0	−3.5(0) − 1	−1	(0, −1)
2	−3.5(2) − 1	−8	(2, −8)

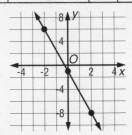

14. $y = 4x + 10$

x	4x + 10	y	(x, y)
−3	4(−3) + 10	−2	(−3, −2)
−2	4(−2) + 10	2	(−2, 2)
−1	4(−1) + 10 ·	6	(−1, 6)

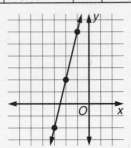

15. $y = 8x$

x	8x	y	(x, y)
$-\frac{1}{2}$	$8\left(-\frac{1}{2}\right)$	−4	$\left(-\frac{1}{2}, -4\right)$
0	8(0)	0	(0, 0)
$\frac{1}{2}$	$8\left(\frac{1}{2}\right)$	4	$\left(\frac{1}{2}, 4\right)$

16. $y = -5x + \frac{1}{2}$

x	$-5x + \frac{1}{2}$	y	(x, y)
$-\frac{1}{2}$	$-5\left(-\frac{1}{2}\right) + \frac{1}{2}$	3	$\left(-\frac{1}{2}, 3\right)$
$\frac{1}{2}$	$-5\left(\frac{1}{2}\right) + \frac{1}{2}$	−2	$\left(\frac{1}{2}, -2\right)$
$\frac{3}{2}$	$-5\left(\frac{3}{2}\right) + \frac{1}{2}$	−7	$\left(\frac{3}{2}, -7\right)$

17. $y = \frac{x}{3} + 9$

x	$\frac{x}{3} + 9$	y	(x, y)
−6	$\frac{-6}{3} + 9$	7	(−6, 7)
−3	$\frac{-3}{3} + 9$	8	(−3, 8)
0	$\frac{0}{3} + 9$	9	(0, 9)

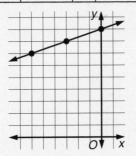

18. $y = -7x + 15$

x	−7x + 15	y	(x, y)
1	−7(1) + 15	8	(1, 8)
2	−7(2) + 15	1	(2, 1)
3	−7(3) + 15	−6	(3, −6)

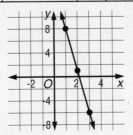

19. $y = 10x - 2$

x	10x − 2	y	(x, y)
$-\frac{1}{2}$	$10\left(-\frac{1}{2}\right) - 2$	−7	$\left(-\frac{1}{2}, -7\right)$
0	10(0) − 2	−2	(0, −2)
$\frac{1}{2}$	$10\left(\frac{1}{2}\right) - 2$	3	$\left(\frac{1}{2}, 3\right)$

20. $y = 1.5x - 7.5$

x	1.5x − 7.5	y	(x, y)
3	1.5(3) − 7.5	−3	(3, −3)
5	1.5(5) − 7.5	0	(5, 0)
7	1.5(7) − 7.5	3	(7, 3)

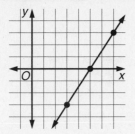

Lesson 11-5

PAGE 611

1. $y = x$ $y = -x + 4$

x	y
−1	−1
0	0
1	1

x	−x + 4	y
1	−1 + 4	3
2	−2 + 4	2
3	−3 + 4	1

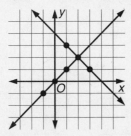

The solution is (2, 2).

2. $y = -x + 8$ $y = x - 2$

x	−x + 8	y
3	−3 + 8	5
4	−4 + 8	4
5	−5 + 8	3

x	x − 2	y
0	0 − 2	−2
1	1 − 2	−1
2	2 − 2	0

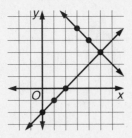

The solution is (5, 3).

3. $y = -3x$ $y = -4x + 2$

x	−3x	y
−1	−3(−1)	3
0	−3(0)	0
1	−3(1)	−3

x	−4x + 2	y
−1	−4(−1) + 2	6
0	−4(0) + 2	2
1	−4(1) + 2	−2

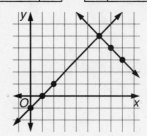

The solution is (2, −6).

4. $y = x - 1$ $y = -x + 11$

x	x − 1	y
0	0 − 1	−1
1	1 − 1	0
2	2 − 1	1

x	−x + 11	y
6	−6 + 11	5
7	−7 + 11	4
8	−8 + 11	3

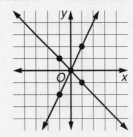

The solution is (6, 5).

5. $y = -x$ $y = 2x$

x	y
−1	1
0	0
1	−1

x	2x	y
−1	2(−1)	−2
0	2(0)	0
1	2(1)	2

The solution is (0, 0).

231

6. $y = -x + 3$ $y = x + 3$

x	-x + 3	y
2	-2 + 3	1
3	-3 + 3	0
4	-4 + 3	-1

x	x + 3	y
-3	-3 + 3	0
-2	-2 + 3	1
-1	-1 + 3	2

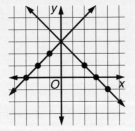

The solution is (0, 3).

7. $y = x - 3$ $y = 2x + 8$

x	x - 3	y
3	3 - 3	0
2	2 - 3	-1
1	1 - 3	-2

x	2x + 8	y
-4	2(-4) + 8	0
-3	2(-3) + 8	2
-2	2(-2) + 8	4

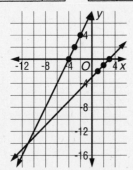

The solution is (-11, -14).

8. $y = -x + 6$ $y = x + 2$

x	-x + 6	y
4	-4 + 6	2
3	-3 + 6	3
2	-2 + 6	4

x	x + 2	y
-2	-2 + 2	0
-1	-1 + 2	1
0	0 + 2	2

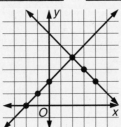

The solution is (2, 4).

9. $y = -x + 1$ $y = x - 4$

x	-x + 1	y
0	0 + 1	1
1	-1 + 1	0
2	-2 + 1	-1

x	x - 4	y
4	4 - 4	0
3	3 - 4	-1
2	2 - 4	-2

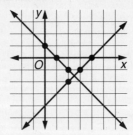

The solution is $\left(2\frac{1}{2}, -1\frac{1}{2}\right)$.

10. $y = -3x + 6$ $y = x - 2$

x	-3x + 6	y
3	-3(3) + 6	-3
2	-3(2) + 6	0
1	-3(1) + 6	3

x	x - 2	y
3	3 - 2	1
2	2 - 2	0
1	1 - 2	-1

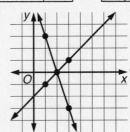

The solution is (2, 0).

11. $y = 3x - 4$ $y = -3x - 4$

x	3x - 4	y
0	3(0) - 4	-4
1	3(1) - 4	-1
2	3(2) - 4	2

x	-3x - 4	y
-2	-3(-2) - 4	2
-1	-3(-1) - 4	-1
0	-3(0) - 4	-4

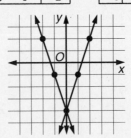

The solution is (0, -4).

232

12. $y = 2x + 4$ $y = 3x - 9$

x	2x + 4	y
-2	2(-2) + 4	0
1	2(1) + 4	6
4	2(4) + 4	12

x	3x - 9	y
2	3(2) - 9	-3
4	3(4) - 9	3
6	3(6) - 9	9

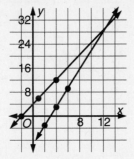

The solution is (13, 30).

13. $y = -x + 4$ $y = x - 10$

x	-x + 4	y
2	-2 + 4	2
3	-3 + 4	1
4	-4 + 4	0

x	x - 10	y
4	4 - 10	-6
6	6 - 10	-4
8	8 - 10	-2

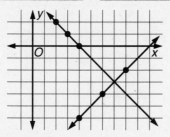

The solution is (7, -3).

14. $y = -x + 6$ $y = 2x$

x	-x + 6	y
4	-4 + 6	2
6	-6 + 6	0
8	-8 + 6	-2

x	2x	y
-2	2(-2)	-4
0	2(0)	0
2	2(2)	4

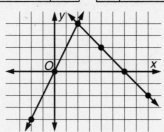

The solution is (2, 4).

15. $y = x - 4$ $y = -2x + 5$

x	x - 4	y
0	0 - 4	-4
2	2 - 4	-2
4	4 - 4	0

x	-2x + 5	y
0	-2(0) + 5	5
1	-2(1) + 5	3
2	-2(2) + 5	1

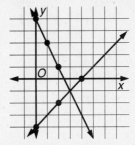

The solution is (3, -1).

16. $y = 2x$ $y = -x + 3$

x	2x	y
-1	2(-1)	-2
0	2(0)	0
1	2(1)	2

x	-x + 3	y
0	0 + 3	3
1	-1 + 3	2
2	-2 + 3	1

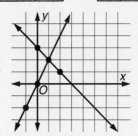

The solution is (1, 2).

Lesson 11-7

PAGE 611

1. $y = x^2 - 1$

x	$x^2 - 1$	y	(x, y)
-2	$(-2)^2 - 1$	3	(-2, 3)
-1	$(-1)^2 - 1$	0	(-1, 0)
0	$(0)^2 - 1$	-1	(0, -1)
1	$(1)^2 - 1$	0	(1, 0)
2	$(2)^2 - 1$	3	(2, 3)

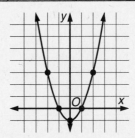

2. $y = 1.5x^2 + 3$

x	$1.5x^2 + 3$	y	(x, y)
-2	$1.5(-2)^2 + 3$	9	$(-2, 9)$
-1	$1.5(-1)^2 + 3$	4.5	$(-1, 4.5)$
0	$1.5(0)^2 + 3$	3	$(0, 3)$
1	$1.5(1)^2 + 3$	4.5	$(1, 4.5)$
2	$1.5(2)^2 + 3$	9	$(2, 9)$

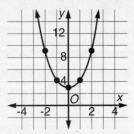

3. $f(n) = n^2 - n$

n	$n^2 - n$	$f(n)$	$(n, f(n))$
-2	$(-2)^2 - (-2)$	6	$(-2, 6)$
-1	$(-1)^2 - (-1)$	2	$(-1, 2)$
0	$(0)^2 - 0$	0	$(0, 0)$
1	$(1)^2 - 1$	0	$(1, 0)$
2	$(2)^2 - 2$	2	$(2, 2)$

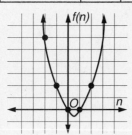

4. $y = 2x^2$

x	$2x^2$	y	(x, y)
-2	$2(-2)^2$	8	$(-2, 8)$
-1	$2(-1)^2$	2	$(-1, 2)$
0	$2(0)^2$	0	$(0, 0)$
1	$2(1)^2$	2	$(1, 2)$
2	$2(2)^2$	8	$(2, 8)$

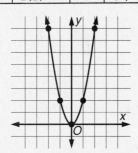

5. $y = x^2 + 3$

x	$x^2 + 3$	y	(x, y)
-2	$(-2)^2 + 3$	7	$(-2, 7)$
-1	$(-1)^2 + 3$	4	$(-1, 4)$
0	$(0)^2 + 3$	3	$(0, 3)$
1	$(1)^2 + 3$	4	$(1, 4)$
2	$(2)^2 + 3$	7	$(2, 7)$

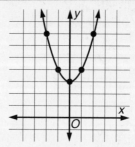

6. $y = -3x^2 + 4$

x	$-3x^2 + 4$	y	(x, y)
-2	$-3(-2)^2 + 4$	-8	$(-2, -8)$
-1	$-3(-1)^2 + 4$	1	$(-1, 1)$
0	$-3(0)^2 + 4$	4	$(0, 4)$
1	$-3(1)^2 + 4$	1	$(1, 1)$
2	$-3(2)^2 + 4$	-8	$(2, -8)$

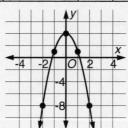

7. $y = -x^2 + 7$

x	$-x^2 + 7$	y	(x, y)
-2	$-(-2)^2 + 7$	3	$(-2, 3)$
-1	$-(-1)^2 + 7$	6	$(-1, 6)$
0	$-(0)^2 + 7$	7	$(0, 7)$
1	$-(1)^2 + 7$	6	$(1, 6)$
2	$-(2)^2 + 7$	3	$(2, 3)$

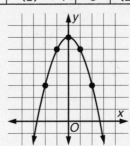

8. $f(n) = 3n^2$

n	$3n^2$	$f(n)$	$(n, f(n))$
-2	$3(-2)^2$	12	(-2, 12)
-1	$3(-1)^2$	3	(-1, 3)
0	$3(0)^2$	0	(0, 0)
1	$3(1)^2$	3	(1, 3)
2	$3(2)^2$	12	(2, 12)

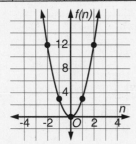

9. $f(n) = 3n^2 + 9n$

n	$3n^2 + 9$	$f(n)$	$(n, f(n))$
-3	$3(-3)^2 + 9(-3)$	0	(-3, 0)
-2	$3(-2)^2 + 9(-2)$	-6	(-2, -6)
-1.5	$3(-1.5) + 9(-1.5)$	-6.75	(-1.5, -6.75)
-1	$3(-1)^2 + 9(-1)$	-6	(-1, -6)
-0	$3(0)^2 + 9(0)$	0	(0, 0)

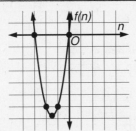

10. $y = -x^2$

x	$-x^2$	y	(x, y)
-2	$-(-2)^2$	-4	(-2, -4)
-1	$-(-1)^2$	-1	(-1, -1)
0	$-(0)^2$	0	(0, 0)
1	$-(1)^2$	-1	(1, -1)
2	$-(2)^2$	-4	(2, -4)

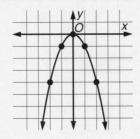

11. $y = \frac{1}{2}x^2 + 1$

x	$\frac{1}{2}x^2 + 1$	y	(x, y)
-2	$\frac{1}{2}(-2)^2 + 1$	3	(-2, 3)
-1	$\frac{1}{2}(-1)^2 + 1$	1.5	(-1, 1.5)
0	$\frac{1}{2}(0)^2 + 1$	1	(0, 1)
1	$\frac{1}{2}(1)^2 + 1$	1.5	(1, 1.5)
2	$\frac{1}{2}(2)^2 + 1$	3	(2, 3)

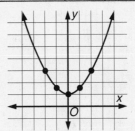

12. $y = 5x^2 - 4$

x	$5x^2 - 4$	y	(x, y)
-2	$5(-2)^2 - 4$	16	(-2, 16)
-1	$5(-1)^2 - 4$	1	(-1, 1)
0	$5(0)^2 - 4$	-4	(0, -4)
1	$5(1)^2 - 4$	1	(1, 1)
2	$5(2)^2 - 4$	16	(2, 16)

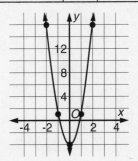

13. $y = -x^2 + 3x$

x	$-x^2 + 3x$	y	(x, y)
0	$-(0)^2 + 3(0)$	0	(0, 0)
1	$-(1)^2 + 3(1)$	2	(1, 2)
1.5	$-(1.5)^2 + 3(1.5)$	2.25	(1.5, 2.25)
2	$-(2)^2 + 3(2)$	2	(2, 2)
3	$-(3)^2 + 3(3)$	0	(3, 0)

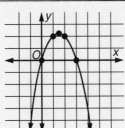

235

14. $f(n) = 2.5n^2$

n	$2.5n^2$	$f(n)$	$(n, f(n))$
-2	$2.5(-2)^2$	10	$(-2, 10)$
-1	$2.5(-1)^2$	2.5	$(-1, 2.5)$
0	$2.5(0)^2$	0	$(0, 0)$
1	$2.5(1)^2$	2.5	$(1, 2.5)$
2	$2.5(2)^2$	10	$(2, 10)$

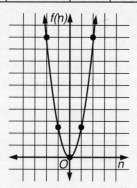

15. $y = -2x^2$

x	$-2x^2$	y	(x, y)
-2	$-2(-2)^2$	-8	$(-2, -8)$
-1	$-2(-1)^2$	-2	$(-1, -2)$
0	$-2(0)^2$	0	$(0, 0)$
1	$-2(1)^2$	-2	$(1, -2)$
2	$-2(2)^2$	-8	$(-2, -8)$

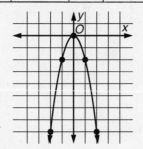

16. $y = 8x^2 + 3$

x	$8x^2 + 3$	y	(x, y)
-1	$8(-1)^2 + 3$	11	$(-1, 11)$
-0.5	$8(-0.5)^2 + 3$	5	$(-0.5, 5)$
0	$8(0)^2 + 3$	3	$(0, 3)$
0.5	$8(0.5)^2 + 3$	5	$(0.5, 5)$
1	$8(1)^2 + 3$	11	$(1, 11)$

17. $y = -x^2 + \frac{1}{2}x$

x	$-x^2 + \frac{1}{2}x$	y	(x, y)
-2	$-(-2)^2 + \frac{1}{2}(-2)$	-5	$(-2, -5)$
-1	$-(-1)^2 + \frac{1}{2}(-1)$	-1.5	$(-1, -1.5)$
0	$-(0)^2 + \frac{1}{2}(0)$	0	$(0, 0)$
1	$-(1)^2 + \frac{1}{2}(1)$	-0.5	$(1, -0.5)$
2	$-(2)^2 + \frac{1}{2}(2)$	-3	$(2, -3)$

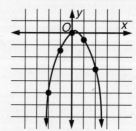

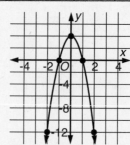

18. $y = -4x^2 + 4$

x	$-4x^2 + 4$	y	(x, y)
-2	$-4(-2)^2 + 4$	-12	$(-2, -12)$
-1	$-4(-1)^2 + 4$	0	$(-1, 0)$
0	$-4(0)^2 + 4$	4	$(0, 4)$
1	$-4(1)^2 + 4$	0	$(1, 0)$
2	$-4(2)^2 + 4$	-12	$(2, -12)$

19. $f(n) = 4n^2 + 3$

n	$4n^2 + 3$	$f(n)$	$(n, f(n))$
-2	$4(-2)^2 + 3$	19	$(-2, 19)$
-1	$4(-1)^2 + 3$	7	$(-1, 7)$
0	$4(0)^2 + 3$	3	$(0, 3)$
1	$4(1)^2 + 3$	7	$(1, 7)$
2	$4(2)^2 + 3$	19	$(2, 19)$

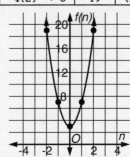

20. $y = -4x^2 + 1$

x	$-4x^2 + 1$	y	(x, y)
-2	$-4(-2)^2 + 1$	-15	(-2, -15)
-1	$-4(-1)^2 + 1$	-3	(-1, -3)
0	$-4(0)^2 + 1$	1	(0, 1)
1	$-4(1)^2 + 1$	-3	(1, -3)
2	$-4(2)^2 + 1$	-15	(2, -15)

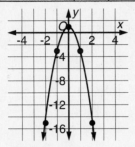

21. $y = 2x^2 + 1$

x	$2x^2 + 1$	y	(x, y)
-2	$2(-2)^2 + 1$	9	(-2, 9)
-1	$2(-1)^2 + 1$	3	(-1, 3)
0	$2(0)^2 + 1$	1	(0, 1)
1	$2(1)^2 + 1$	3	(1, 3)
2	$2(2)^2 + 1$	9	(2, 9)

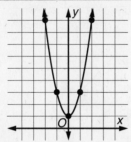

22. $y = x^2 - 4x$

x	$x^2 - 4x$	y	(x, y)
0	$0^2 - 4(0)$	0	(0, 0)
1	$1^2 - 4(1)$	-3	(1, -3)
2	$2^2 - 4(2)$	-4	(2, -4)
3	$3^2 - 4(3)$	-3	(3, -3)
4	$4^2 - 4(4)$	0	(4, 0)

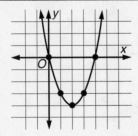

23. $y = 3x^2 + 5$

x	$3x^2 + 5$	y	(x, y)
-2	$3(-2)^2 + 5$	17	(-2, 17)
-1	$3(-1)^2 + 5$	8	(-1, 8)
0	$3(0)^2 + 5$	5	(0, 5)
1	$3(1)^2 + 5$	8	(1, 8)
2	$3(2)^2 + 5$	17	(2, 17)

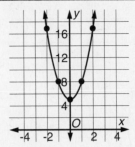

24. $f(n) = 0.5n^2$

n	$0.5n^2$	$f(n)$	$(n, f(n))$
-2	$0.5(-2)^2$	2	(-2, 2)
-1	$0.5(-1)^2$	0.5	(-1, 0.5)
0	$0.5(0)^2$	0	(0, 0)
1	$0.5(1)^2$	0.5	(1, 0.5)
2	$0.5(2)^2$	2	(2, 2)

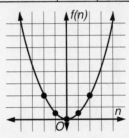

25. $f(n) = 2n^2 - 5n$

n	$2n^2 - 5n$	$f(n)$	$(n, f(n))$
0	$2(0)^2 - 5(0)$	0	(0, 0)
1	$2(1)^2 - 5(1)$	-3	(1, -3)
1.25	$2(1.25)^2 - 5(1.25)$	-3.125	(1.25, -3.125)
1.5	$2(1.5)^2 - 5(1.5)$	-3	(1.5, -3)
2.5	$2(2.5)^2 - 5(2.5)$	0	(2.5, 0)

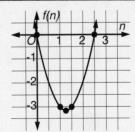

26. $y = \frac{3}{2}x^2 - 2$

x	$\frac{3}{2}x^2 - 2$	y	(x, y)
-2	$\frac{3}{2}(-2)^2 - 2$	4	(-2, 4)
-1	$\frac{3}{2}(-1)^2 - 2$	-0.5	(-1, -0.5)
0	$\frac{3}{2}(0)^2 - 2$	-2	(0, -2)
1	$\frac{3}{2}(1)^2 - 2$	-0.5	(1, -0.5)
2	$\frac{3}{2}(2)^2 - 2$	4	(2, 4)

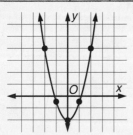

27. $y = 6x^2 + 2$

x	$6x^2 + 2$	y	(x, y)
-1	$6(-1)^2 + 2$	8	(-1, 8)
-0.5	$6(-0.5)^2 + 2$	3.5	(-0.5, 3.5)
0	$6(0)^2 + 2$	2	(0, 2)
0.5	$6(0.5)^2 + 2$	3.5	(0.5, 3.5)
1	$6(1)^2 + 2$	8	(1, 8)

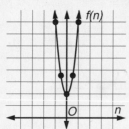

28. $f(n) = 5n^2 + 6n$

n	$5n^2 + 6n$	f(n)	(n, f(n))
-2	$5(-2)^2 + 6(-2)$	8	(-2, 8)
-1	$5(-1)^2 + 6(-1)$	-1	(-1, -1)
-0.5	$5(-0.5)^2 + 6(-0.5)$	-1.75	(-0.5, -1.75)
0	$5(0)^2 + 6(0)$	0	(0, 0)
1	$5(1)^2 + 6(1)$	11	(1, 11)

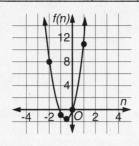

Lesson 11-8

PAGE 611

1. $A(-6, -2) + (4, 3) \rightarrow A'(-2, 1)$
$B(-1, 1) + (4, 3) \rightarrow B'(3, 4)$
$C(2, -2) + (4, 3) \rightarrow C'(6, 1)$

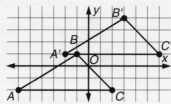

2. $X(-4, 3) + (5, -2) \rightarrow X'(1, 1)$
$Y(0, 3) + (5, -2) \rightarrow Y'(5, 1)$
$Z(-2, -1) + (5, -2) \rightarrow Z'(3, -3)$

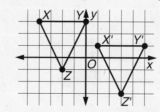

3. $H(1, 3) + (-4, -6) \rightarrow H'(-3, -3)$
$I(4, 0) + (-4, -6) \rightarrow I'(0, -6)$
$J(2, -2) + (-4, -6) \rightarrow J'(-2, -8)$
$K(-1, 1) + (-4, -6) \rightarrow K'(-5, -5)$

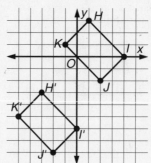

4. $P(-7, 6) + (9, -1) \rightarrow P'(2, 5)$
$Q(-5, 6) + (9, -1) \rightarrow Q'(4, 5)$
$R(-5, 2) + (9, -1) \rightarrow R'(4, 1)$
$S(-7, 2) + (9, -1) \rightarrow S'(2, 1)$

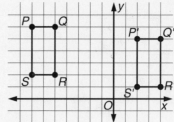

238

5. $D(1, 3) + (-5, -7) \rightarrow D'(-4, -4)$
   $G(2, 4) + (-5, -7) \rightarrow G'(-3, -3)$
   $L(4, 4) + (-5, -7) \rightarrow L'(-1, -3)$
   $M(5, 3) + (-5, -7) \rightarrow M'(0, -4)$
   $R(3, 1) + (-5, -7) \rightarrow R'(-2, -6)$

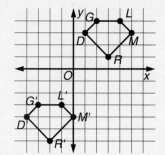

Lesson 11-9

PAGE 612

1. $C(2, 3) \rightarrow C'(-2, 3)$
   $A(8, 2) \rightarrow A'(-8, 2)$
   $T(4, -3) \rightarrow T'(-4, -3)$

2.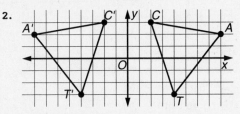

3. $T(-2, 5) \rightarrow T'(-2, -5)$
   $R(1, 5) \rightarrow R'(1, -5)$
   $A(4, 2) \rightarrow A'(4, -2)$
   $P(-5, 2) \rightarrow P'(-5, -2)$

4.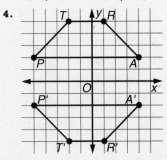

5. $A(4, -1) \rightarrow A'(-4, -1)$
   $B(7, -4) \rightarrow B'(-7, -4)$
   $C(4, -7) \rightarrow C'(-4, -7)$
   $D(1, -4) \rightarrow D'(-1, -4)$

6.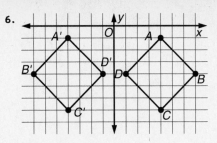

Lesson 11-10

PAGE 612

1.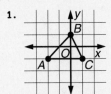

2. $A(-2, -1) \rightarrow (-1, -2) \rightarrow A'(1, -2)$
   $B(0, 1) \rightarrow (1, 0) \rightarrow B'(-1, 0)$
   $C(1, -1) \rightarrow (-1, 1) \rightarrow C'(1, 1)$

3.

4.    5. $W(1, 1) \rightarrow W'(-1, -1)$
   $X(1, 3) \rightarrow X'(-1, -3)$
   $Y(6, 3) \rightarrow Y'(-6, -3)$
   $Z(6, 1) \rightarrow Z'(-6, -1)$

6.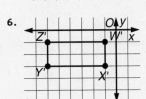

Lesson 12-1

PAGE 612

1. $A = \pi r^2$
   $A = \pi(4)^2$
   $A = \pi \cdot 16$
   $A \approx 50.3 \text{ m}^2$

2. $r = \frac{6}{2} = 3$
   $A = \pi r^2$
   $A = \pi(3)^2$
   $A = \pi \cdot 9$
   $A \approx 28.3 \text{ in}^2$

3. $A = \pi r^2$
   $A = \pi(12)^2$
   $A = \pi \cdot 144$
   $A \approx 452.4 \text{ in}^2$

4. $r = \frac{16}{2} = 8$ 5. $r = \frac{11}{2} = 5.5$ 6. $A = \pi r^2$

$A = \pi r^2$ $A = \pi r^2$ $A = \pi(5)^2$

$A = \pi(8)^2$ $A = \pi(5.5)^2$ $A = \pi \cdot 25$

$A = \pi \cdot 64$ $A = \pi \cdot 30.25$ $A \approx 78.5 \text{ in}^2$

$A \approx 201.1 \text{ yd}^2$ $A \approx 95.0 \text{ ft}^2$

7. $A = \pi r^2$ 8. $r = \frac{29}{2} = 14.5$ 9. $A = \pi r^2$

$A = \pi(19)^2$ $A = \pi r^2$ $A = \pi(8.5)^2$

$A = \pi \cdot 361$ $A = \pi(14.5)^2$ $A = \pi \cdot 72.25$

$A \approx 1{,}134.1 \text{ cm}^2$ $A = \pi \cdot 210.25$ $A \approx 227.0 \text{ mm}^2$

$A \approx 660.5 \text{ mm}^2$

10. $r = \frac{22.4}{2} = 11.2$ 11. $A = \pi r^2$

$A = \pi r^2$ $A = \pi(2)^2$

$A = \pi(11.2)^2$ $A = \pi \cdot 4$

$A = \pi \cdot 125.44$ $A \approx 12.6 \text{ in}^2$

$A \approx 394.1 \text{ m}^2$

12. $r = \frac{18}{2} = 9$ 13. $A = \pi r^2$

$A = \pi r^2$ $A = \pi(10)^2$

$A = \pi(9)^2$ $A = \pi \cdot 100$

$A = \pi \cdot 81$ $A \approx 314.2 \text{ yd}^2$

$A \approx 254.5 \text{ ft}^2$

14. $r = \frac{28}{2} = 14$ 15. $A = \pi r^2$

$A = \pi r^2$ $A = \pi(22)^2$

$A = \pi(14)^2$ $A = \pi \cdot 484$

$A = \pi \cdot 196$ $A \approx 1{,}520.5 \text{ cm}^2$

$A \approx 615.8 \text{ m}^2$

16. $r = \frac{7}{2} = 3.5$

$A = \pi r^2$

$A = \pi(3.5)^2$

$A = \pi \cdot 12.25$

$A \approx 38.5 \text{ in}^2$

Lesson 12-4

PAGE 613

1. side one: $2 \cdot 1 = 2$
   side two: $2 \cdot 1 = 2$
   side three: $2 \cdot 10 = 20$
   side four: $2 \cdot 10 = 20$
   side five: $1 \cdot 10 = 10$
   side six: $1 \cdot 10 = \underline{10}$
   surface area $= 64 \text{ in}^2$

2. side one: $18 \cdot 7 = 126$
   side two: $18 \cdot 7 = 126$
   side three: $18 \cdot 14 = 252$
   side four: $18 \cdot 14 = 252$
   side five: $7 \cdot 14 = 98$
   side six: $7 \cdot 14 = \underline{98}$
   surface area $= 952 \text{ m}^2$

3. side one: $2.5 \cdot 1 = 2.5$
   side two: $2.5 \cdot 1 = 2.5$
   side three: $2.5 \cdot 4.5 = 11.25$
   side four: $2.5 \cdot 4.5 = 11.25$
   side five: $1 \cdot 4.5 = 4.5$
   side six: $1 \cdot 4.5 = \underline{4.5}$
   surface area $= 36.5 \text{ cm}^2$

4. side one: $6 \cdot 4 = 24$
   side two: $6 \cdot 4 = 24$
   side three: $6 \cdot 10 = 60$
   side four: $6 \cdot 10 = 60$
   side five: $4 \cdot 10 = 40$
   side six: $4 \cdot 10 = \underline{40}$
   surface area $= 248 \text{ m}^2$

5. side one: $14 \cdot 7 = 98$
   side two: $14 \cdot 7 = 98$
   side three: $14 \cdot 14 = 196$
   side four: $14 \cdot 14 = 196$
   side five: $7 \cdot 14 = 98$
   side six: $7 \cdot 14 = \underline{98}$
   surface area $= 784 \text{ ft}^2$

6. side one: $10 \cdot 10 = 100$
   side two: $10 \cdot 10 = 100$
   side three: $10 \cdot 10 = 100$
   side four: $10 \cdot 10 = 100$
   side five: $10 \cdot 10 = 100$
   side six: $10 \cdot 10 = \underline{100}$
   surface area $= 600 \text{ cm}^2$

7. side one: $4.5 \cdot 3.6 = 16.2$
   side two: $4.5 \cdot 3.6 = 16.2$
   side three: $3.6 \cdot 10.6 = 38.16$
   side four: $3.6 \cdot 10.6 = 38.16$
   side five: $4.5 \cdot 10.6 = 47.7$
   side six: $4.5 \cdot 10.6 = \underline{47.7}$
   surface area $= 204.12 \text{ yd}^2$

8. side one: $18 \cdot 12 = 216$
   side two: $18 \cdot 12 = 216$
   side three: $18 \cdot 11 = 198$
   side four: $18 \cdot 11 = 198$
   side five: $11 \cdot 12 = 132$
   side six: $11 \cdot 12 = \underline{132}$
   surface area $= 1{,}092 \text{ in}^2$

9. side one: $12.6 \cdot 6.8 = 85.68$
   side two: $12.6 \cdot 6.8 = 85.68$
   side three: $12.6 \cdot 10.4 = 131.04$
   side four: $12.6 \cdot 10.4 = 131.04$
   side five: $6.8 \cdot 10.4 = 70.72$
   side six: $6.8 \cdot 10.4 = 70.72$
   surface area $= 574.88$ mm^2

Lesson 12-5

PAGE 613

1. base: $\pi(3)^2 \approx 28.27$
   base: $\pi(3)^2 \approx 28.27$
   rectangle: $14(2\pi(3)) \approx 263.89$
   surface area $\approx 28.27 + 28.27 + 263.89$
   ≈ 320.4 cm^2

2. base: $\pi\left(\frac{8}{2}\right)^2 = \pi \cdot 4^2$
   $= \pi \cdot 16$
   ≈ 50.26
   base: $\pi\left(\frac{8}{2}\right)^2 = \pi \cdot 4^2$
   $= \pi \cdot 16$
   ≈ 50.26
   rectangle: $6(\pi \cdot 8) \approx 150.80$
   surface area $\approx 50.26 + 50.26 + 150.80$
   ≈ 251.3 in^2

3. base: $\pi\left(\frac{14}{2}\right)^2 = \pi(7)^2$
   $= \pi \cdot 49$
   ≈ 153.94
   base: $\pi\left(\frac{14}{2}\right)^2 = \pi(7)^2$
   $= \pi \cdot 49$
   ≈ 153.94
   rectangle: $8(\pi \cdot 14) \approx 351.86$
   surface area $\approx 153.94 + 153.94 + 351.86$
   ≈ 659.7 mm^2

4. base: $\pi(3)^2 = \pi \cdot 9$
   ≈ 28.27
   base: $\pi(3)^2 = \pi \cdot 9$
   ≈ 28.27
   rectangle: $19(2\pi(3)) \approx 358.14$
   surface area $\approx 28.27 + 28.27 + 358.14$
   ≈ 414.7 m^2

5. base: $\pi(8.2)^2 = \pi \cdot 67.24$
   ≈ 211.24
   base: $\pi(8.2)^2 = \pi \cdot 67.24$
   ≈ 211.24
   rectangle: $22(2\pi(8.2)) \approx 1,133.49$
   surface area $\approx 211.24 + 211.24 + 1,133.5$
   $\approx 1,556.0$ in^2

6. base: $\pi(3.6)^2 = \pi \cdot 12.96$
   ≈ 40.72
   base: $\pi(3.6)^2 = \pi \cdot 12.96$
   ≈ 40.72
   rectangle: $14.2(2\pi(3.6)) \approx 321.20$
   surface area $\approx 40.72 + 40.72 + 331.20$
   ≈ 402.6 yd^2

7. base: $\pi(4.2)^2 = \pi(17.64)$
   ≈ 55.42
   base: $\pi(4.2)^2 = \pi(17.64)$
   ≈ 55.42
   rectangle: $12.4(2\pi(4.2)) \approx 327.23$
   surface area $\approx 55.42 + 55.42 + 327.23$
   ≈ 438.1 cm^2

8. base: $\pi(5)^2 = \pi \cdot 25$
   ≈ 78.54
   base: $\pi(5)^2 = \pi \cdot 25$
   ≈ 78.54
   rectangle: $10(2\pi(5)) \approx 314.16$
   surface area $\approx 78.54 + 78.54 + 314.16$
   $= 471.2$ in^2

9. base: $\pi(6.3)^2 = \pi \cdot 39.69$
   ≈ 124.69
   base: $\pi(6.3)^2 = \pi \cdot 39.69$
   ≈ 124.69
   rectangle: $4.6(2\pi(6.3)) \approx 182.09$
   surface area $\approx 124.69 + 124.69 + 182.09$
   ≈ 431.5 ft^2

Lesson 12-6

PAGE 613

1. $V = \ell wh$
   $V = (3)(3)(3)$
   $V = 27$ m^3

2. $V = \ell wh$
   $V = (10)(5)(5)$
   $V = 250$ in^3

3. $V = \pi r^2 h$
   $V = \pi(6)^2(11)$
   $V = \pi(36)(11)$
   $V \approx 1,244.1$ yd^2

4. $V = \pi r^2 h$
   $V = \pi\left(\frac{26}{2}\right)^2(8)$
   $V = \pi(13)^2(8)$
   $V = \pi(169)(8)$
   $V \approx 4,247.4$ cm^3

5. $V = \ell wh$
   $V = (8)(9)(7)$
   $V = 504$ mm^2

6. $V = \pi r^2 h$
   $V = \pi(7)^2(30)$
   $V = \pi(49)(30)$
   $V \approx 4,618.1$ ft^3

7. $V = \ell wh$
   $V = (18)(12)(4)$
   $V = 864$ in^3

8. $V = \pi r^2 h$
   $V = \pi(2)^2(10)$
   $V = \pi(4)(10)$
   $V \approx 125.7$ m^2

Lesson 12-7

PAGE 614

1. $V = \frac{1}{3}Bh$

   $V = \frac{1}{3}(3)(4)(5)$

   $V = 20 \text{ cm}^3$

2. $V = \frac{1}{3}Bh$

   $V = \frac{1}{3}(60)^2(60)$

   $V = \frac{1}{3}(3600)(60)$

   $V = 72{,}000 \text{ in}^3$

3. $V = \frac{1}{3}\pi r^2 h$

   $V = \frac{1}{3}\pi(7)^2(12)$

   $V = \frac{1}{3}\pi(49)(12)$

   $V \approx 615.8 \text{ yd}^3$

4. $V = \frac{1}{3}Bh$

   $V = \frac{1}{3}(2)(4)(3)$

   $V = 8 \text{ cm}^3$

5. $V = \frac{1}{3}\pi r^2 h$

   $V = \frac{1}{3}\pi(11)^2(15)$

   $V = \frac{1}{3}\pi(121)(15)$

   $V \approx 1{,}900.7 \text{ ft}^3$

6. $V = \frac{1}{3}Bh$

   $V = \frac{1}{3}(4)(18)(6)$

   $V = 144 \text{ mm}^3$

7. $V = \frac{1}{3}Bh$

   $V = \frac{1}{3}(7)^2(14)$

   $V = \frac{1}{3}(49)(14)$

   $V \approx 228.7 \text{ in}^3$

8. $V = \frac{1}{3}\pi r^2 h$

   $V = \frac{1}{3}\pi(9)^2(20)$

   $V = \frac{1}{3}\pi(81)(20)$

   $V \approx 1{,}696.5 \text{ m}^3$

Lesson 13-1

PAGE 614

1.

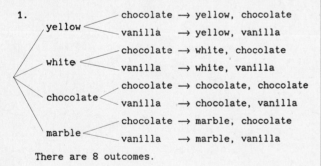

There are 8 outcomes.

2. ST = standard transmission

   AT = automatic transmission

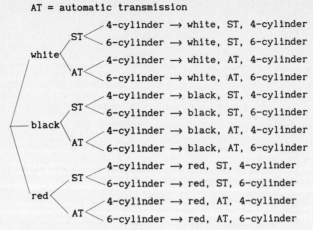

There are 12 outcomes.

3.

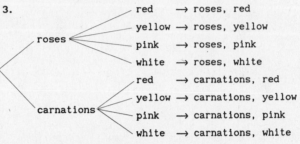

There are 8 outcomes.

4.

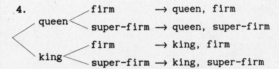

There are 4 outcomes.

5.

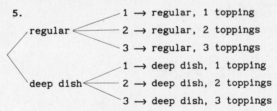

There are 6 outcomes.

6.

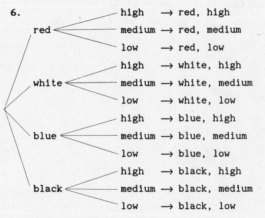

There are 12 outcomes.

Lesson 13-2

PAGE 614

1. $8! = 8 \cdot 7 \cdot 6 \cdot 5 \cdot 4 \cdot 3 \cdot 2 \cdot 1$
   $= 40,320$

2. $10! = 10 \cdot 9 \cdot 8 \cdot 7 \cdot 6 \cdot 5 \cdot 4 \cdot 3 \cdot 2 \cdot 1$
   $= 3,628,800$

3. $0! = 1$ 4. $7! = 7 \cdot 6 \cdot 5 \cdot 4 \cdot 3 \cdot 2 \cdot 1$
   $= 5,040$

5. $6! = 6 \cdot 5 \cdot 4 \cdot 3 \cdot 2 \cdot 1$
   $= 720$

6. $5! = 5 \cdot 4 \cdot 3 \cdot 2 \cdot 1$ 7. $2! = 2 \cdot 1$
   $= 120$ $= 2$

8. $11! = 11 \cdot 10 \cdot 9 \cdot 8 \cdot 7 \cdot 6 \cdot 5 \cdot 4 \cdot 3 \cdot 2 \cdot 1$
   $= 39,916,800$

9. $9! = 9 \cdot 8 \cdot 7 \cdot 6 \cdot 5 \cdot 4 \cdot 3 \cdot 2 \cdot 1$
   $= 362,880$

10. $4! = 4 \cdot 3 \cdot 2 \cdot 1$ 11. $P(5, 4) = 5 \cdot 4 \cdot 3 \cdot 2$
    $= 24$ $= 120$

12. $P(3, 3) = 3!$
    $= 3 \cdot 2 \cdot 1$
    $= 6$

13. $P(12, 5) = 12 \cdot 11 \cdot 10 \cdot 9 \cdot 8$
    $= 95,040$

14. $P(8, 6) = 8 \cdot 7 \cdot 6 \cdot 5 \cdot 4 \cdot 3$
    $= 20,160$

15. $P(10, 2) = 10 \cdot 9$
    $= 90$

16. $P(6, 4) = 6 \cdot 5 \cdot 4 \cdot 3$
    $= 360$

17. $P(7, 6) = 7 \cdot 6 \cdot 5 \cdot 4 \cdot 3 \cdot 2$
    $= 5,040$

18. $P(9, 9) = 9!$
    $= 362,880$

19. There are 3 people who can sit in different seats, so the number of ways is $3! = 6$ ways.

20. There are 6 letters taken 5 at a time, or $P(6, 5) = 6 \cdot 5 \cdot 4 \cdot 3 \cdot 2 = 720$ ways.

21. There are 4 marbles that can change position, so there are $4! = 4 \cdot 3 \cdot 2 \cdot 1 = 24$ ways to arrange the marbles.

22. There are 9 CDs that can change order, so there are $9! = 9 \cdot 8 \cdot 7 \cdot 6 \cdot 5 \cdot 4 \cdot 3 \cdot 2 \cdot 1 = 362,880$ ways to listen to his CDs.

Lesson 13-3

PAGE 615

1. $C(8, 4) = \dfrac{P(8, 4)}{4!}$
   $= \dfrac{8 \cdot 7 \cdot 6 \cdot 5}{4 \cdot 3 \cdot 2 \cdot 1}$
   $= \dfrac{1680}{24}$
   $= 70$

2. $C(30, 8) = \dfrac{P(30, 8)}{8!}$
   $= \dfrac{30 \cdot 29 \cdot 28 \cdot 27 \cdot 26 \cdot 25 \cdot 24 \cdot 23}{8 \cdot 7 \cdot 6 \cdot 5 \cdot 4 \cdot 3 \cdot 2 \cdot 1}$
   $= \dfrac{235,989,936,000}{40,320}$
   $= 5,852,925$

3. $C(10, 9) = \dfrac{P(10, 9)}{9!}$
   $= \dfrac{10 \cdot 9 \cdot 8 \cdot 7 \cdot 6 \cdot 5 \cdot 4 \cdot 3 \cdot 2}{9 \cdot 8 \cdot 7 \cdot 6 \cdot 5 \cdot 4 \cdot 3 \cdot 2 \cdot 1}$
   $= \dfrac{3,628,800}{362,880}$
   $= 10$

4. $C(7, 3) = \dfrac{P(7, 3)}{3!}$
   $= \dfrac{7 \cdot 6 \cdot 5}{3 \cdot 2 \cdot 1}$
   $= \dfrac{210}{6}$
   $= 35$

5. $C(12, 5) = \dfrac{P(12, 5)}{5!}$
   $= \dfrac{12 \cdot 11 \cdot 10 \cdot 9 \cdot 8}{5 \cdot 4 \cdot 3 \cdot 2 \cdot 1}$
   $= \dfrac{95,040}{120}$
   $= 792$

6. $C(17, 16) = \dfrac{P(17, 16)}{16!}$
   $= \dfrac{17 \cdot 16 \cdot 15 \cdot 14 \cdot 13 \cdot 12 \cdot 11 \cdot}{16 \cdot 15 \cdot 14 \cdot 13 \cdot 12 \cdot 11 \cdot 10 \cdot}$
   $\dfrac{10 \cdot 9 \cdot 8 \cdot 7 \cdot 6 \cdot 5 \cdot 4 \cdot 3 \cdot 2}{9 \cdot 8 \cdot 7 \cdot 6 \cdot 5 \cdot 4 \cdot 3 \cdot 2 \cdot 1}$
   $= \dfrac{17}{1}$
   $= 17$

7. $C(24, 17) = \dfrac{P(24, 17)}{17!}$
   $= \dfrac{24 \cdot 23 \cdot 22 \cdot 21 \cdot 20 \cdot 19 \cdot 18 \cdot 17 \cdot}{17 \cdot 16 \cdot 15 \cdot 14 \cdot 13 \cdot 12 \cdot 11 \cdot}$
   $\dfrac{16 \cdot 15 \cdot 14 \cdot 13 \cdot 12 \cdot 11 \cdot 10 \cdot 9 \cdot 8}{10 \cdot 9 \cdot 8 \cdot 7 \cdot 6 \cdot 5 \cdot 4 \cdot 3 \cdot 2 \cdot 1}$
   $= \dfrac{24 \cdot 23 \cdot 22 \cdot 21 \cdot 20 \cdot 19 \cdot 18}{7 \cdot 6 \cdot 5 \cdot 4 \cdot 3 \cdot 2 \cdot 1}$
   $= \dfrac{1,744,364,160}{5,040}$
   $= 346,104$

8. $C(9, 7) = \dfrac{P(9, 7)}{7!}$

$= \dfrac{9 \cdot 8 \cdot 7 \cdot 6 \cdot 5 \cdot 4 \cdot 3}{7 \cdot 6 \cdot 5 \cdot 4 \cdot 3 \cdot 2 \cdot 1}$

$= \dfrac{181,440}{5,040}$

$= 36$

9. $C(17, 5) = \dfrac{P(17, 5)}{5!}$

$= \dfrac{17 \cdot 16 \cdot 15 \cdot 14 \cdot 13}{5 \cdot 4 \cdot 3 \cdot 2 \cdot 1}$

$= \dfrac{742,560}{120}$

$= 6,188 \text{ ways}$

10. $C(25, 3) = \dfrac{P(25, 3)}{3!}$

$= \dfrac{25 \cdot 24 \cdot 23}{3 \cdot 2 \cdot 1}$

$= \dfrac{13,800}{6}$

$= 2,300 \text{ combinations}$

11. $C(10, 3) = \dfrac{P(10, 3)}{3!}$

$= \dfrac{10 \cdot 9 \cdot 8}{3 \cdot 2 \cdot 1}$

$= \dfrac{720}{6}$

$= 120 \text{ ways}$

12. $C(24, 7) = \dfrac{P(24, 7)}{7!}$

$= \dfrac{24 \cdot 23 \cdot 22 \cdot 21 \cdot 20 \cdot 19 \cdot 18}{7 \cdot 6 \cdot 5 \cdot 4 \cdot 3 \cdot 2 \cdot 1}$

$= \dfrac{1,744,364,160}{5,040}$

$= 346,104 \text{ ways}$

13. $C(10, 2) = \dfrac{P(10, 2)}{2!}$

$= \dfrac{10 \cdot 9}{2 \cdot 1}$

$= \dfrac{90}{2}$

$= 45 \text{ ways}$

Lesson 13-5

PAGE 615

1. $1 + 3 + 2 + 2 = 8$

$P(\text{black sock}) = \dfrac{2}{8} = \dfrac{1}{4}$

$P(\text{green after black}) = \dfrac{2}{7}$

$P(\text{black then green}) = \dfrac{1}{4} \cdot \dfrac{2}{7} = \dfrac{2}{28} = \dfrac{1}{14}$

2. $P(\text{red sock}) = \dfrac{1}{8}$

$P(\text{green after red}) = \dfrac{2}{7}$

$P(\text{red then green}) = \dfrac{1}{8} \cdot \dfrac{2}{7} = \dfrac{2}{56} = \dfrac{1}{28}$

3. $P(\text{blue sock}) = \dfrac{3}{8}$

$P(\text{blue after blue}) = \dfrac{2}{7}$

$P(\text{blue then blue}) = \dfrac{3}{8} \cdot \dfrac{2}{7} = \dfrac{6}{56} = \dfrac{3}{28}$

4. $P(\text{green sock}) = \dfrac{2}{8} = \dfrac{1}{4}$

$P(\text{green after green}) = \dfrac{1}{7}$

$P(\text{green then green}) = \dfrac{1}{4} \cdot \dfrac{1}{7} = \dfrac{1}{28}$

5. $3 + 5 + 12 = 20$

$P(\text{quarter}) = \dfrac{3}{20}$

$P(\text{penny after quarter}) = \dfrac{12}{19}$

$P(\text{quarter then penny}) = \dfrac{3}{20} \cdot \dfrac{12}{19} = \dfrac{36}{380} = \dfrac{9}{95}$

6. $P(\text{nickel}) = 0$

$P(\text{dime after nickel}) = \dfrac{5}{20} = \dfrac{1}{4}$

$P(\text{nickel then dime}) = 0 \cdot \dfrac{1}{4} = 0$

7. $P(\text{dime}) = \dfrac{5}{20} = \dfrac{1}{4}$

$P(\text{penny after dime}) = \dfrac{12}{19}$

$P(\text{dime then penny}) = \dfrac{1}{4} \cdot \dfrac{12}{19} = \dfrac{12}{76} = \dfrac{3}{19}$

8. $P(\text{dime}) = \dfrac{5}{20} = \dfrac{1}{4}$

$P(\text{dime after dime}) = \dfrac{4}{19}$

$P(\text{dime then dime}) = \dfrac{1}{4} \cdot \dfrac{4}{19} = \dfrac{4}{76} = \dfrac{1}{19}$

Lesson 13-8

PAGE 615

1. $72 + 41 + 45 + 92 = 250$

2. The mode is the most common selection, so it is light rock.

3. $\dfrac{72}{250} = \dfrac{36}{125}$ prefer country music.

4. $\dfrac{45}{250} = \dfrac{9}{50}$ prefer rap music.

5. $155 + 300 + 145 = 600$

6.

$$\frac{300}{600} = \frac{x}{7,950}$$

$$\frac{1}{2} = \frac{x}{7,950}$$

$$1 \cdot 7,950 = 2 \cdot x$$

$$7,950 = 2x$$

$$\frac{7,950}{2} = \frac{2x}{2}$$

$$3,975 = x$$

Expect 3,975 people to choose an orange.

Lesson 14-1

PAGE 616

1. 1 yellow x^2-title = x^2
   2 red x-tiles = $-2x$
   1 yellow 1-tile = 1
   Polynomial is $x^2 - 2x + 1$.

2. 1 red x-tile = $-x$
   5 red 1-tiles = -5
   Polynomial is $-x - 5$.

3. 2 red x^2-tiles = $-2x^2$
   1 yellow 1-tile = 1
   Polynomial is $-2x^2 + 1$.

4. 1 yellow x^2-tile = x^2
   3 red x-tiles = $-3x$
   Polynomial is $x^2 - 3x$.

5. $-x^2 + 7$

6. $3x + 3$

7. $3x^2 - 2x + 1$

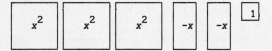

8. $-5x + 1$

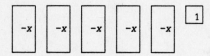

9. $x + 2$

10. $-2x^2 + 3x$

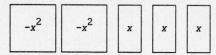

11. $-x - 4$

12. $x^2 + 2x + 3$

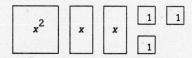

13. $2x^2 - 2$

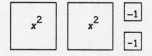

14. $2x - 5$

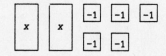

15. $-x^2 + 7x$

16. $2x^2 - 3x$

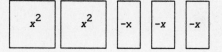

Lesson 14-2

PAGE 616

1. $10x$, $3x$ 2. $-a$, $-3a$; $2b^2$, b^2

3. $2m$, $-m$; n, n 4. 9, 2   5. 6, 5

6. $4x$, $2x$ 7. $2x - x^2 + x - 1 = -x^2 + 3x - 1$

8. $2x^2 + 1 + x^2 = 3x^2 + 1$

9. $-2y + 3 + x^2 + 5y = -2y + 5y + 3 + x^2$
   $$= 3y + 3 + x^2$$
   $$= x^2 + 3y + 3$$

10. $m + m^2 + n + 3m^2 = m^2 + 3m^2 + m + n$
    $$= 4m^2 + m + n$$

11. $a^2 + b^2 + 3 + 2b^2 = a^2 + b^2 + 2b^2 + 3$
    $$= a^2 + 3b^2 + 3$$

245

12. $1 + a + b + 6 = a + b + 1 + 6$
$$= a + b + 7$$

13. $x + x^2 + 5x - 3x^2 = x^2 - 3x^2 + x + 5x$
$$= -2x^2 + 6x$$

14. $-2y + 3 + y - 2 = -2y + y + 3 - 2$
$$= -y + 1$$

Lesson 14-3

PAGE 616

1.
$$2x^2 - 5x + 7$$
$$\underline{x^2 - x + 11}$$
$$3x^2 - 6x + 18$$

2.
$$2m^2 + m + 1$$
$$\underline{-m^2 + 2m + 3}$$
$$m^2 + 3m + 4$$

3.
$$2a - b + 6c$$
$$\underline{3a - 7b + 2c}$$
$$5a - 8b + 8c$$

4.
$$5a + 3a^2 - 2$$
$$\underline{2a + 8a^2 + 4}$$
$$7a + 11a^2 + 2$$

5.
$$3c + b + a$$
$$\underline{-\ c + b - a}$$
$$2c + 2b$$

6.
$$-z^2 + x^2 + 2y^2$$
$$\underline{3z^2 + x^2 + y^2}$$
$$2z^2 + 2x^2 + 3y^2$$

7.
$$5x + 6y$$
$$\underline{2x + 8y}$$
$$7x + 14y$$

8.
$$4a + 6b$$
$$\underline{2a + 3b}$$
$$6a + 9b$$

9.
$$7r + 11m$$
$$\underline{2r + 4m}$$
$$9r + 15m$$

10.
$$z^2 - z$$
$$\underline{z^2 - 2z}$$
$$2z^2 - 3z$$

11.
$$3x - 7y$$
$$\underline{4x + 3y + 1}$$
$$7x - 4y + 1$$

12.
$$5m + 3n - 3$$
$$\underline{8m \qquad + 6}$$
$$13m + 3n + 3$$

13.
$$a^2 + a$$
$$\underline{-2a^2 + 3a}$$
$$-a^2 + 4a$$

14.
$$3s - 5t$$
$$\underline{2s + 8t}$$
$$5s + 3t$$

Lesson 14-4

PAGE 617

1.
$$5a - 6m \qquad\qquad 5a - 6m$$
$$\underline{-\ (2a + 5m)} \rightarrow \underline{+\ (-2a - 5m)}$$
$$3a - 11m$$

2.
$$2a - 7 \qquad\qquad 2a - 7$$
$$\underline{-\ (8a - 11)} \rightarrow \underline{+\ (-8a + 11)}$$
$$-6a + 4$$

3.
$$a^2 + 2a + 3 \qquad\qquad a^2 + 2a + 3$$
$$\underline{-\ (\quad\ 8a + 5)} \rightarrow \underline{+\ (\quad - 8a - 5)}$$
$$a^2 - 6a - 2$$

4.
$$9r^2 - 3 \qquad\qquad 9r^2 - 3$$
$$\underline{-\ (11r^2 + 12)} \rightarrow \underline{+\ (-11r^2 - 12)}$$
$$-2r^2 - 15$$

5.
$$9x + 7y \qquad\qquad 9x + 7y$$
$$\underline{-\ (6x + 5y)} \rightarrow \underline{+\ (-6x - 5y)}$$
$$3x + 2y$$

6.
$$-2x + 5 \qquad\qquad -2x + 5$$
$$\underline{-\ (8x + 7)} \rightarrow \underline{+\ (-8x - 7)}$$
$$-10x - 2$$

7.
$$9x + 3y \qquad\qquad 9x + 3y$$
$$\underline{-\ (x + 9y)} \rightarrow \underline{+\ (-x - 9y)}$$
$$8x - 6y$$

8.
$$3x^2 + 2x - 1 \qquad\qquad 3x^2 + 2x - 1$$
$$\underline{-\ (\qquad 2x + 2)} \rightarrow \underline{+\ (\qquad - 2x - 2)}$$
$$3x^2 \qquad - 3$$

9.
$$a^2 + 6a + 3 \qquad\qquad a^2 + 6a + 3$$
$$\underline{-\ (5a^2 \qquad + 5)} \rightarrow \underline{+\ (-5a^2 \qquad - 5)}$$
$$-4a^2 + 6a - 2$$

10.
$$5a + 2 \qquad\qquad 5a + 2$$
$$\underline{-\ (3a^2 + a + 8)} \rightarrow \underline{+\ (-3a^2 - a - 8)}$$
$$-3a^2 + 4a - 6$$

11.
$$3x^2 - 7x \qquad\qquad 3x^2 - 7x$$
$$\underline{-\ (\qquad 8x - 6)} \rightarrow \underline{+\ (\qquad - 8x + 6)}$$
$$3x^2 - 15x + 6$$

12.
$$3m + 3n \qquad\qquad 3m + 3n$$
$$\underline{-\ (\ m + 2n)} \rightarrow \underline{+\ (-m - 2n)}$$
$$2m + n$$

13.
$$3m - 2 \qquad\qquad 3m - 2$$
$$\underline{-\ (2m + 1)} \rightarrow \underline{+\ (-2m - 1)}$$
$$m - 3$$

14.
$$x^2 - 2 \qquad\qquad x^2 - 2$$
$$\underline{-\ (\ x + 3)} \rightarrow \underline{+\ (\ - x - 3)}$$
$$x^2 - x - 5$$

15.
$$5x^2 - 4 \qquad\qquad 5x^2 - 4$$
$$\underline{-\ (3x^2 + 8x + 4)} \rightarrow \underline{+\ (-3x^2 - 8x - 4)}$$
$$2x^2 - 8x - 8$$

16.
$$7z^2 + 1 \qquad\qquad 7z^2 + 1$$
$$\underline{-\ (3z^2 + 2z - 6)} \rightarrow \underline{+\ (-3z^2 - 2z + 6)}$$
$$4z^2 - 2z + 7$$

Lesson 14-5

PAGE 617

1. $m(m + 2) = m \cdot m + m \cdot 2$
$$= m^2 + 2m$$

2. $x(x - 1) = x \cdot x - x \cdot 1$
$$= x^2 - x$$

3. $y(y - 2) = y \cdot y - y \cdot 2$
   $= y^2 - 2y$

4. $a(a - 3) = a \cdot a - a \cdot 3$
   $= a^2 - 3a$

5. $6(a + 3) = 6 \cdot a + 6 \cdot 3$
   $= 6a + 18$

6. $m(m - 7) = m \cdot m - m \cdot 7$
   $= m^2 - 7m$

7. $z(z + 3) = z \cdot z + z \cdot 3$
   $= z^2 + 3z$

8. $x(x + 10) = x \cdot x + x \cdot 10$
   $= x^2 + 10x$

9. $y(y - 5) = y \cdot y - y \cdot 5$
   $= y^2 - 5y$

10. $-2(x + 1) = -2 \cdot x + (-2)(1)$
    $= -2x - 2$

11. $m(m - 2) = m \cdot m - m \cdot 2$
    $= m^2 - 2m$

12. $3(y + 6) = 3 \cdot y + 3 \cdot 6$
    $= 3y + 18$

13. $3(m + 1) = 3 \cdot m + 3 \cdot 1$
    $= 3m + 3$

14. $z(z + 5) = z \cdot z + z \cdot 5$
    $= z^2 + 5z$

15. $b(b + 1) = b \cdot b + b \cdot 1$
    $= b^2 + b$

16. $-3(a + 2) = -3 \cdot a + (-3)(2)$
    $= -3a - 6$

17. $3m + 3 = 3 \cdot m + 3 \cdot 1$
    $= 3(m + 1)$

18. $-2x - 2 = -2 \cdot x + (-2)(1)$
    $= -2(x + 1)$

19. $-4b - 4 = -4 \cdot b + (-4)(1)$
    $= -4(b + 1)$

20. $2z + 2 = 2 \cdot z + 2 \cdot 1$
    $= 2(z + 1)$

21. $z^2 - 5z = z \cdot z - 5 \cdot z$
    $= z(z - 5)$

22. $c^2 + 2c = c \cdot c + 2 \cdot c$
    $= c(c + 2)$

23. $z^2 + 3z = z \cdot z + 3 \cdot z$
    $= z(z + 3)$

24. $-6a - 6 = -6 \cdot a + (-6)(1) = -6(a + 1)$

25. $a^2 + 3a = a \cdot a + 3 \cdot a = a(a + 3)$

26. $2m^2 + m = 2 \cdot m \cdot m + m \cdot 1 = m(2m + 1)$

27. $y^2 - 2y = y \cdot y - 2 \cdot y = y(y - 2)$

28. $n^2 + 4n = n \cdot n + 4 \cdot n = n(n + 4)$

29. $6b + 6 = 6 \cdot b + 6 \cdot 1 = 6(b + 1)$

30. $x^2 + 6x = x \cdot x + 6 \cdot x = x(x + 6)$

31. $5x + 5 = 5 \cdot x + 5 \cdot 1 = 5(x + 1)$

32. $7y - 7 = 7 \cdot y - 7 \cdot 1 = 7(y - 1)$

Lesson 14-6

PAGE 617

1. $(2x + 3)(x + 1) = 2x^2 + 5x + 3$

2. $(x + 4)(x + 2) = x^2 + 6x + 8$

3. $(r + 3)(r + 4) = r(r + 4) + 3(r + 4)$
   $= r^2 + 4r + 3r + 12$
   $= r^2 + 7r + 12$

4. $(z + 5)(z + 2) = z(z + 2) + 5(z + 2)$
   $= z^2 + 2z + 5z + 10$
   $= z^2 + 7z + 10$

5. $(3x + 7)(x + 1) = 3x(x + 1) + 7(x + 1)$
   $= 3x^2 + 3x + 7x + 7$
   $= 3x^2 + 10x + 7$

6. $(x + 5)(2x + 3) = x(2x + 3) + 5(2x + 3)$
   $= 2x^2 + 3x + 10x + 15$
   $= 2x^2 + 13x + 15$

7. $(c + 1)(c + 1) = c(c + 1) + 1(c + 1)$
   $= c^2 + 1c + 1c + 1$
   $= c^2 + 2c + 1$

8. $(a + 3)(a + 7) = a(a + 7) + 3(a + 7)$
   $= a^2 + 7a + 3a + 21$
   $= a^2 + 10a + 21$

9. $(b + 3)(b + 1) = b(b + 1) + 3(b + 1)$
   $= b^2 + 1b + 3b + 3$
   $= b^2 + 4b + 3$

10. $(2y + 1)(y + 3) = 2y(y + 3) + 1(y + 3)$
    $= 2y^2 + 6y + 1y + 3$
    $= 2y^2 + 7y + 3$

11. $(z + 8)(2z + 1) = z(2z + 1) + 8(2z + 1)$
    $= 2z^2 + z + 16z + 8$
    $= 2z^2 + 17z + 8$

12. $(2m + 4)(m + 5) = 2m(m + 5) + 4(m + 5)$
    $= 2m^2 + 10m + 4m + 20$
    $= 2m^2 + 14m + 20$

13. $(x + 3)(x + 2) = x(x + 2) + 3(x + 2)$
    $= x^2 + 2x + 3x + 6$
    $= x^2 + 5x + 6$

14. $(c + 2)(c + 8) = c(c + 8) + 2(c + 8)$
    $= c^2 + 8c + 2c + 16$
    $= c^2 + 10c + 16$

15. $(r + 4)(r + 4) = r(r + 4) + 4(r + 4)$
    $= r^2 + 4r + 4r + 16$
    $= r^2 + 8r + 16$

16. $(2x + 4)(x + 4) = 2x(x + 4) + 4(x + 4)$
    $= 2x^2 + 8x + 4x + 16$
    $= 2x^2 + 12x + 16$

17. $(6y + 1)(y + 3) = 6y(y + 3) + 1(y + 3)$
    $= 6y^2 + 18y + 1y + 3$
    $= 6y^2 + 19y + 3$